Collective Decision-Making:
Social Choice and Political Economy

RECENT ECONOMIC THOUGHT SERIES

Editors:

Warren J. Samuels
Michigan State University
East Lansing, Michigan, USA

William Darity, Jr.
University of North Carolina
Chapel Hill, North Carolina, USA

Other books in the series:

Tool, Marc R.: INSTITUTIONAL ECONOMICS:
THEORY, METHOD, POLICY
Babe, Robert E.: INFORMATION AND COMMUNICATION IN
ECONOMICS
Magnusson, Lars: MERCANTILIST ECONOMICS
Garston, Neil: BUREAUCRACY: THREE PARADIGMS
Friedman, James W.: PROBLEMS OF COORDINATION IN
ECONOMIC ACTIVITY
Magnusson, Lars: EVOLUTIONARY AND NEO-SCHUMPETERIAN
APPROACHES TO ECONOMICS
Reisman, D.: ECONOMIC THOUGHT AND POLITICAL THEORY
Burley, P. and Foster, J.: ECONOMICS AND THERMODYNAMICS:
NEW PERSPECTIVES ON ECONOMIC ANALYSIS
Brennan, H.G. and Waterman, A.C.: ECONOMICS AND RELIGION:
ARE THEY DISTINCT?
Klein, Philip A.: THE ROLE OF ECONOMIC THEORY
Semmler, Willi.: BUSINESS CYCLES: THEORY AND EMPIRICS
Little, Daniel: ON THE RELIABILITY OF ECOONOMIC MODELS:
ESSAYS IN THE PHILOSOPHY OF ECONOMICS
Weimer, David L.:
INSTITUTIONAL DESIGN
Davis, John B.:
THE STATE OF THE INTERPRETATION OF KEYNES
Wells, Paul:
POST-KEYNESIAN ECONOMIC THEORY
Hoover, Kevin D.:
  MACROECONOMETRICS: Developments, Tensions
  and Prospects
Kendrick, John W.:
  THE NEW SYSTEMS OF NATURAL ACCOUNTS
Groenewegen, John:
  TRANSACTION COST ECONOMICS AND BEYOND
King, J.E.:
  AN ALTERNATIVE MACROECONOMIC THEORY

Collective Decision-Making: Social Choice and Political Economy

Edited by
Norman Schofield
William Taussig Professor of Political Economy
Washington University in St. Louis

(with the assistance of **Annette Milford**)

Kluwer Academic Publishers
Boston / Dordrecht / London

Distributors for North America:
Kluwer Academic Publishers
101 Philip Drive
Assinippi Park
Norwell, Massachusetts 02061 USA

Distributors for all other countries:
Kluwer Academic Publishers Group
Distribution Centre
Post Office Box 322
3300 AH Dordrecht, THE NETHERLANDS

Library of Congress Cataloging-in-Publication Data

Collective decision-making : social choice and political economy /
  edited by Norman Schofield with the assistance of Annette Milford.
    p.   cm. -- (Recent economic thought series)
  Includes bibliographical references and index.
  ISBN 0-7923-9711-8
  1. Social choice.   2. Political science--Economic aspects.
3. Decision-making, Group.   I. Schofield, Norman, 1944-
II. Milford, Annette.   III. Series.
HB846.8.C654   1996
302'.13-dc20   96-28939
                                                                                              CIP

Copyright © 1996 by Kluwer Academic Publishers

All rights reserved. No part of this publication may be reproduced, stored in a retrieval system or transmitted in any form or by any means, mechanical, photo-copying, recording, or otherwise, without the prior written permission of the publisher, Kluwer Academic Publishers, 101 Philip Drive, Assinippi Park, Norwell, Massachusetts 02061.

Printed on acid-free paper.

Printed in the United States of America

Dedicated to the memory of

WILLIAM H. RIKER

TABLE OF CONTENTS

Chapter		page
	Editor's Preface	xi
	Foreword by *William Riker*	xv
	List of Contributors	xix
1	Introduction: Research Programs in Preference and Belief Aggregation *Norman Schofield*	1
Part I.	SOCIAL CHOICE	23
2	An Introduction to Arrovian Social Welfare Functions on Economic and Political Domains *Michel Le Breton and John Weymark*	25
3	Social Ranking of Allocations with and without Coalition Formation *Donald E. Campbell*	63
4	Non Binary Social Choice: A Brief Introduction *Yongsheng Xu*	79
5	Election Relations and a Partial Ordering for Positional Voting *Donald G. Saari*	93
Part II.	ELECTIONS AND COMMITTEES	111
6	Electing Legislatures *David Austen-Smith*	113
7	Preference-Based Stability: Experiments on Cooperative Solutions to Majority Rule Games *Cheryl L. Eavey*	149
8	The Heart of a Polity *Norman Schofield*	183
9	Refinements of the Heart *David Austen-Smith*	221

Part III. COALITION GOVERNMENTS   237

10   Bargaining in the Liberal Democratic Party of Japan
     Junichiro Wada and Norman Schofield   239

11   An Analysis of the Euskarian Parliament
     Francesc Carreras and Guillermo Owen   251

12   Extending a Dynamic Model of
     Protocoalition Formation
     Bernard Grofman   265

13   The Sequential Dynamics of Cabinet Formation,
     Stochastic Error, and a Test of Competing Models
     Bernard Grofman, Philip Straffin, and Nicholas Noviello 281

14   Subgame-Perfect Portfolio Allocations
     in Parliamentary Government Formation
     Michael Laver and Kenneth Shepsle   295

15   The Costs of Coalition: The Italian Anomaly
     Carol Mershon   315

Part IV. POLITICAL ECONOMY   335

16   Models of Interest Groups: Four Different Approaches
     Jan Potters and Frans van Winden   337

17   Partisan Electoral Cycles and Monetary Policy Games
     Rebecca B. Morton   363

18   Hypothesis Testing and Collective Decision-Making
     Krishna K. Ladha   385

19   Political Discourse, Factions, and the General Will:
     Correlated Voting and Condorcet's Jury Theorem
     Krishna K. Ladha and Gary Miller   393

     Name Index   411

     Subject Index   417

Editor's Preface

In the last decade the techniques of social choice theory, game theory and positive political theory have been combined in interesting ways so as to provide a common framework for analyzing the behavior of a developed political economy.

Social choice theory itself grew out of the innovative attempts by Kenneth Arrow (1951) and Duncan Black (1948, 1958) to extend the range of economic theory in order to deal with collective decision-making over public goods. Later work, by William Baumol (1952), and James Buchanan and Gordon Tullock (1962), focussed on providing an "economic" interpretation of democratic institutions. In the same period Anthony Downs (1957) sought to model representative democracy and elections while William Riker (1962) made use of work in cooperative game theory (by John von Neumann and Oscar Morgenstern, 1944) to study coalition behavior.

In my view, these "rational choice" analyses of collective decision-making have their antecedents in the arguments of Adam Smith (1759, 1776), James Madison (1787) and the Marquis de Condorcet (1785) about the "design" of political institutions. In the introductory chapter to this volume I briefly describe how some of the current normative and positive aspects of social choice date back to these earlier writers.

The main body of the volume presents recent research in the four main areas of the theory of collective decision-making. Part I can be viewed as continuing the Arrovian tradition of formal social choice theory. For example, Chapter 2 by Le Breton and Weymark and Chapter 3 by Campbell show that social choice theory is relevant not only to voting procedures but to the aggregation of "economic" preferences. Chapter 4, by Xu, continues the work of Amartya Sen (1970) by analyzing collective choice mechanisms, while Chapter 5 by Saari uses sophisticated mathematical techniques to return, in a sense, to the debate between Borda and Condorcet in the 1780's on the desirable properties of voting mechanisms.

Part II, on Elections and Committees, can be seen as a development of the insights of Anthony Downs and Duncan Black. The focus of Chapter 6 by Austen-Smith is on building a model of elections based on rational choice both by voters and candidates. In Chapter 7, Eavey surveys the experimental evidence on collective decision-making in committees. To some degree this work is based on the theoretical results obtained earlier in spatial voting theory by Charles Plott (1967), Gerald Kramer (1973), Richard McKelvey (1976) and Norman Schofield (1978, 1985). Chapters 8 and 9 by Schofield and Austen-Smith develop general solution or equilibrium concepts in spatial voting theory. Chapter 8 suggests how these can be used to study coalition formation in multiparty democracies.

One of the especially interesting aspects of current positive political theory is the attempt to construct a unified theory of democratic institutions. Such a theory could, in principle, be used to compare the behavior of democracies with very different institutional arrangements. The work of William Riker (1962), and later of Axelrod (1970), de Swaan (1973), Dodd (1976), and Browne and Dreijmanis (1982) provided the impetus for current work on one aspect of this, namely the analysis of multiparty coalition governments.

This tradition is continued in the chapters presented in Part III of the volume. Much of the recent work in this area (including the chapters in Part III) was triggered, to some degree at least, by a conference on Political Coalitions sponsored by the National Science Foundation (Grant No. SES-85-21151) and held at the European University Institute in Fiesole, Italy. Participants at this conference have made significant research contributions in coalition theory in the last few years (Austen-Smith and Banks 1988; Baron and Ferejohn 1989; Bennet and Zame 1988; Grofman and Withers 1993; Laver and Budge 1992; Laver and Schofield 1990; Laver and Shepsle 1990, 1996; Lupia and Strom 1995; McKelvey 1991; Mershon 1994; Sened 1995; Strom, 1990; Strom, *et al.* 1988; Strom, Budge and Laver 1994). William Riker also attended the conference and his enthusiasm for the research project contributed in no small degree to the success of the conference.

Finally, the work presented in Part IV of the volume can be interpreted, in part, as belonging to the Buchanan, Tullock tradition of political economy. In Chapter 16, Potters and van Winden integrate various theories of interest group behavior, while Morton, in Chapter 17, discusses the interaction of government and the electorate in the context of "rational partisan theory". The last two chapters of Part IV include a modern interpretation and generalization of Condorcet's work on "belief aggregation" as a basis for analyzing collective decision-making. In particular, Chapter 19, by Ladha and Miller, draws out the connections between Condorcet's "Jury Theorem" and Rousseau's notion of the general will.

A year spent as Fellow at the Center for Advanced Study in the Behavioral Sciences, Stanford, provided an opportunity for me to start thinking about representative democracy. Support from the National Science Foundation, under grant numbers SES-88-20845 and SBR-94-22548, and from the School of Arts and Sciences at Washington University is gratefully acknowledged. I thank Zachary Rolnik, the senior editor at Kluwer, for his forbearance over the delay between conception and completion of this collection of essays. Yana Lambert at Kluwer provided helpful advice on preparing the volume. I am most indebted to Annette Milford who copy-edited the manuscript and prepared the index as well as the camera-ready version.

William Riker passed away before the completion of this book. Throughout his life, Bill was an inspiration to everyone working in this field. Aside from his work on coalitions, he wrote on the relationship between social choice theory and democracy (Riker 1982), on "Heresthetic" (Riker 1986), on American Federalism (1987), and the ratification of the American constitution (Riker 1993). While this book was in preparation, he kindly responded to my request to write a brief foreword. The volume is dedicated to his memory.

Norman Schofield
St. Louis, June, 1996

References

Arrow, K. J. 1951. *Social Choice and Individual Values*. New York: Wiley.
Austen-Smith, D. and J. Banks. 1988. "Elections, Coalitions and Legislative Outcomes," *American Political Science Review* 82: 405-422.
Axelrod, R. 1970. *Conflict of Interest*. Chicago: Markham.
Baron, D. and J. Ferejohn. 1989. "Bargaining in Legislatures," *American Political Science Review* 83: 1181-1206.
Baumol, W. J. 1952. *Welfare Economics and the Theory of the State*. Cambridge: Harvard University Press.
Bennett, E. and W. Zame. 1988. "Bargaining in Cooperative Games," *International Journal of Game Theory* 17: 279-290.
Black, D. 1948. "On the Rationality of Group Decision Making," *Journal of Political Economy* 56: 23-34.
Black, D. 1958. *The Theory of Committees and Elections*. Cambridge: Cambridge University Press.
Browne, E. C. and J. Dreijmanis, eds. 1982. *Government Coalitions in Western Democracies*. New York: Longman.
Buchanan, J. M. and G. Tullock 1962. *The Calculus of Consent: Logical Foundations of Constitutional Democracy*. Ann Arbor: University of Michigan Press.
Condorcet, M. J. A. N. de C., Marquis de. [1785] 1972. *Essai sur l'application de l'analyse à la probabilité des voix*. New York: Chelsea (orig. Paris: Imprimerie Royale).
de Swaan, A. 1973. *Coalition Theories and Cabinet Formation*. Amsterdam: Elsevier.
Dodd, L. C. 1976. *Coalitions in Parliamentary Governments*. Princeton: Princeton University Press.
Downs, A. 1957. *An Economic Theory of Democracy*. New York: Harper and Row.
Grofman, B. and J. Withers. 1993. "Information-pooling Models and Electoral Politics," in *Information Participation and Choice*, B. Grofman, ed. Ann Arbor: Michigan University Press.
Kramer, G. 1973. "On a Class of Equilibrium Conditions for Majority Rule," *Econometrica* 41: 285-97.
Laver, M. and I. Budge, eds. 1992. *Party Policy and Government Coalitions*. New York: St. Martin's Press.
Laver, M. and N. Schofield. 1990. *Multiparty Government: The Politics of Coalition in Europe*. Oxford: Oxford University Press.
Laver, M. and K. Shepsle. 1990. "Coalitions and Cabinet Government," *American Political Science Review* 84: 873-890.
Laver, M. and K. Shepsle. 1996. *Making and Breaking Governments: Cabinets and Legislatures in Parliamentary Democracies*. Cambridge: Cambridge University Press.
Lupia, A. and K. Strom. 1995. "Coalition Termination and the Strategic Timing of Elections," *American Political Science Review* 89: 648-665.
Madison, J. [1787] 1937. *The Federalist*: No. 10. New York: The Modern Library.

McKelvey, R. D. 1976. "Intransitivities in Multidimensional Voting Models and Some Implications for Agenda Control," *Journal of Economic Theory* 12: 472-482.

McKelvey, R. D. 1991. "An Experimental Test of a Stochastic Game Model of Committee Bargaining," in *Laboratory Research in Political Economy*, T. Palfrey, ed. Ann Arbor: Michigan University Press.

Mershon, C. 1994. "Expectations and Informal Rules in Coalition Formation," *Comparative Political Studies* 27: 40-79.

Plott, C. 1967. "A Notion of Equilibrium and its Possibility under Majority Rule," *American Economic Review* 57: 787-806.

Riker, W. 1962. *The Theory of Political Coalitions*. New Haven: Yale University Press.

Riker, W. 1982. *Liberalism against Populism*. San Francisco: W. H. Freeman.

Riker, W. 1986. *The Art of Political Manipulation*. New Haven: Yale University Press.

Riker, W. 1987. *The Development of American Federalism*. Boston: Kluwer.

Riker, W. 1993. "Rhetorical Interaction in the Ratification Campaigns," in *Agenda Formation*, W. Riker, ed. Ann Arbor: University of Michigan Press.

Schofield, N. 1978. "Instability of Simple Dynamic Games," *Review of Economic Studies* 45: 575-594.

Schofield, N. 1985. *Social Choice and Democracy*. Heidelberg: Springer Verlag.

Sen, A. 1970. *Collective Choice and Social Welfare*. Amsterdam: North Holland.

Sened, I. 1995. "Equilibrium in Weighted Voting Games in Two-Dimensional Spaces," *Journal of Theoretical Politics* 7: 283-300.

Smith, A. [1759] 1976. *The Theory of Moral Sentiments*. Oxford: Oxford University Press.

Smith, A. [1776] 1976. *An Inquiry into the Nature and Causes of the Wealth of Nations*. Oxford: Oxford University Press.

Strom, K. 1990. *Minority Government and Majority Rule*. Cambridge: Cambridge University Press.

Strom, K., E. C. Browne, J. P. Frendeis, and D. W. Gleiber. 1988. "Contending Models of Cabinet Stability: A Controversy," *American Political Science Review* 82: 923-941.

Strom, K., I. Budge, and M. Laver. 1994. "Constraints on Cabinet Formation in Parliamentary Democracies," *American Journal of Political Science* 28: 303-335.

von Neumann, J. and O. Morgenstern. 1944. *Theory of Games and Economic Behavior*. Princeton: Princeton University Press.

Foreword

Were groups of people merely extensions of more or less identical members, social choice would be simple. Any member or subset of members chosen at random would be able to articulate the interests of the whole. If there were apparent differences in expertise, everyone would agree that the most skilled in hunting, or witchery, or child care, *etc.* should decide, that is, should put his or her expertise to the service of everyone in the group.

But groups are, in fact, not at all like that. The interests of the individual members differ and no one member has exactly the same interest as the group itself. Even for the family, the most general purpose of all groups, we speak of its interests as separate from the interests of parents and siblings. And when we speak of more specialized groups with limited purposes—the church, the nation, the city, the labor union, the commercial association, the club, *etc.*—we specify ever more precisely just what restricted purposes each group is intended to serve. The reason we do so is that we recognize wide variations in the interests of members. Given these variations, members seldom have identical preferences, even about the stated purposes of the group itself, let alone about how to accomplish these purposes.

Consequently, social decisions are not easily arrived at because they must accommodate the wide variations in members' values and tastes. At one extreme, groups accommodate by requiring unanimity: no social choice is made unless everyone agrees. At the other extreme, groups accommodate by establishing dictatorship: one person decides for everybody. The difficulty with unanimity is that agreement is difficult to reach. In the Society of Friends, where dissidents are expected to re-examine their consciences, facility in decision depends wholly on the dissidents' will and skill in re-examination. In the Polish Diet, where each person had a veto, facility in decision is said to have depended, occasionally, on defenestration of dissidents. On the other hand, the difficulty with a dictator is that, when he or she ignores the values of other members, they often infer that membership is itself no longer worthwhile. Schism, runaways, immigration, police terrorism and civil war are thus characteristic features of dictatorship in various kinds of groups.

In between these extremes of unanimity and dictatorship, groups accommodate to diversity by requiring only that some intermediate number, larger than one but less than everyone, be necessary for decision. Rules of this intermediate sort set the scene for coalitions, that is, subsets of members, which are the subject of this book. Coalitions, defined as subsets, can, of course, be of any size, though usually we think of them as proper subsets with several members. (It is technically correct, but not particularly interesting, to speak of coalitions of one and of everyone.) Coalitions of the size required for decision are defined as winning (or decisive) and are the main focus of the essays printed here. Losing coalitions, or those that failed to develop into winners, are interesting for their impact on the future and their efforts to break up winning coalitions. but winning coalitions are themselves immediately interesting, for they are the ones that choose the alternatives to be pursued or enforced by the whole group.

From a practical viewpoint, the main feature of winning coalitions is that they are a means to enhance the force of their members. If a decision for a group is made by less than everyone, then a coalition of the appropriate size takes over the whole. There is both public and private advantage in this fact. The public advantage is that an intermediate rule avoids the immobilism of unanimity and the indifference of dictatorship. The private advantage is more delicate: When a winning coalition selects an alternative attractive only to its members, in effect these members utilize the name and resources of the whole group to enforce an only partially approved value. So long as the winning coalition selects an alternative within the (usually) ill-defined range of the goals of the whole group, then the non-members of the coalition are compelled, by their own continuing group membership and their own adherence to those goals, to recognize and accept the decision of the coalition. Thus a winning coalition deciding for the whole enhances the significance of its choice by subsuming as joint authors those who in fact reject it. Thus the private advantage of the method of decision by coalitions is that proper subsets of the whole group can enhance their influence or "power."

There is, it is true, one institution for decision making, namely the market, that does not utilize large coalitions and thus does not allow the winners to absorb the influence of the losers. In this idealized form of the economic world, coalitions are tiny, typically just two traders. A trader, it is said, "calls out" a wish to trade, and, if it reaches a receptive ear, a bargain is struck. The coalitions thus formed are not, of course, large enough to decide for the whole. So, conventionally, the decision for the whole is interpreted as the set of such bargains—at the equilibrium price—made by many coalitions. Since in this model every trader wins and, if everyone trades, everyone wins, winners cannot mulct the losers, as they do in institutions requiring decision-making by larger coalitions.

As we climb up from the agora, the marketplace, to the acropolis, the city center, where decisions are made on rules and rights and war and worship, we find that decisions require majorities and, often, supermajorities. No one has ever figured out how to operate a political system anarchically, that is, with numerous small decisive coalitions comparable to market coalitions. Even in oligarchies, it usually turns out that a majority or supermajority of oligarchs is necessary to make a decision stick. And so it is that political decisions are almost invariably made by unique winning coalitions, which enhance themselves by absorbing and redirecting the force of the losers.

This is why political life is so intense. Unique winning coalitions are, by their very nature, devices to sieze the usufruct of decision. Since the political method is decision by unique coalitions, it turns out that political life consists almost entirely of contests over the usufruct. Such contests involve force and intrigue, maneuver and manipulation. This is what gives politics its harsh persistent undertone of selfishness and exploitation.

This is also why we need to understand all the properties of coalitions and coalition-formation in order to appreciate and interpret politics. In the last generation, social scientists began to study coalitions in the abstract. This volume summarizes what we have learned. It is, I am pleased to say, a substantial amount. This volume also reveals how much more we must discover. It is enough to keep the next generation busy before we can really understand the way politics works.

William Riker
Rochester, New York, 1991

Contributors

David Austen-Smith
Northwestern University
Chicago, Illinois

Donald E. Campbell
College of William and Mary,
Williamsburg, Virginia

Francesc Carreras
Universidad Politecnica de Cataluna
Barcelona, Spain

Cheryl L. Eavey
The National Science Foundation
Washington, D. C.

Bernard Grofman
University of California
Irvine, California

Krishna K. Ladha
Washington University
St. Louis, Missouri

Michael Laver
Trinity College
Dublin, Ireland

Michel Le Breton
University of Aix-Marseille

Carol Mershon
University of Virginia
Charlottesville, Virginia

Gary Miller
Washington University
St. Louis, Missouri

Rebecca B. Morton
University of Iowa, Iowa City

Nicholas Noviello
University of California-Irvine

Guillermo Owen
Naval Postgraduate School
Monterey, California

Jan Potters
University of Amsterdam
The Netherlands

William Riker †
University of Rochester
Rochester, New York

Donald G. Saari
Northwestern University
Chicago, Illinois

Norman Schofield
Washington University
St. Louis, Missouri

Kenneth Shepsle
Harvard University
Cambridge, Massachusetts

Philip Straffin
Beloit College
Beloit, Wisconsin

Junichiro Wada
Yokohama City University

Frans van Winden
University of Amsterdam
The Netherlands

John Weymark
University of British Columbia
Vancouver

Yongsheng Xu
University of Durham

Collective Decision-Making:
Social Choice and Political Economy

1. Introduction: Research Programs in Preference and Belief Aggregation

Norman Schofield[1]

1.1 Preferences and Beliefs

Political economy and social choice both have their origins in the Eighteenth Century, in the work of Adam Smith (1759, 1776) during the Scottish Enlightenment and in the work of the Marquis de Condorcet (1785) just before the French Revolution.[2] Since then, of course, political economy or economic theory has developed apace. However, it was only in the late 1940's that social choice was rediscovered (Arrow 1951; Black 1948, 1958), and only relatively recently has there been work connecting these two fields. The connection between political economy and social choice theory is the subject matter of this volume.

Adam Smith's work leads, of course, to modern economic theory—the analysis of human incentives in the particular context of fixed resources, private goods, and a given technology. By the 1950's, the theorems of Arrow and Debreu (1954) and McKenzie (1959) had formally demonstrated the existence of Pareto optimal competitive equilibria under certain conditions on individual preferences. The maintained assumption of neoclassical economics regarding preference is that it is representable by a utility function and that it is private-regarding or "selfish". The first assumption implies that preference is both complete and fully transitive, in the sense that both strict preference (P) and indifference (I) are transitive (thus for example if x and y are indifferent as are y and z, then so are x and z). The private-regarding assumption means that each individual, i, has a choice space, X_i, say, on which i's preferences are defined. In some sense the collective choice space, X, is a subset (with appropriately defined feasibility constraints) of the Cartesian product $\Pi_i X_i$. Abstractly, the market is characterized by the existence of an equilibrium mapping $E : X \times D \to X$. Here D is an appropriate domain of preference profiles (defined perhaps by $D = \Pi_i D_i$, where D_i is used to characterize the set of permissible preferences for i). A point x within X in the domain of E describes

---

[1] Some of the arguments presented in this introductory chapter are based on research supported by NSF Grant SBR-94-22548 and presented at the 2nd International Meeting of the Society for Social Choice, Rochester, New York, July 1994. Iain McLean has been very helpful in sharing with me his published and unpublished work on Condorcet's manuscripts.

[2] A secondary theme of this introduction is the interplay of ideas between Smith, Condorcet and the Founding Fathers of the American Revolution. In this connection it is worth noting that Smith and Condorcet met in Paris in 1787 and that Sophie de Condorcet translated Smith's *Moral Sentiments* in 1795 (Badinter and Badinter 1988).

the initial allocations or resources of each of the individuals. This neo-classical equilibrium map should be viewed as a method of individual preference aggregation. That is, the model posits a certain form of rational behavior on the part of economic agents, where these agents are individuals rather than collections of agents. The natural generalization of the neo-classical model is non-cooperative game theory, the more abstract study of individually rational behavior. Both the neo-classical economic model and non-cooperative game theory are aspects of what I shall call the *Nash Research Program*, in honor of the key concept in this program, namely the Nash (1951) equilibrium.

Although the early proof of the existence of competitive equilibrium in the neo-classical model depended on the assumption of fully transitive preferences, later results by Bergstrom (1975), Gale and Mas-Collel (1975), Sonnenschein (1971) and others were able to weaken the assumption on preference by using a general theorem by Fan (1961). Fan's "fixed point" result considered a "strict" preference correspondence $P : X \to X$ on a topological vector space, X, and showed that if X was compact and P continuous then P would exhibit an equilibrium $E(P) = \{x \in X : P(x) \text{ is empty}\}$ as long as P satisifed the following "Fan condition": there is no x in X such that x belongs to the convex hull of $P(x)$. In essence all equilibrium results on a topological space depend on this result (see Bergstrom 1992). It is also important to understand the consequences when the Fan condition fails; not only may there be no equilibrium, but there will exist cycles. That is if there is some x_0 in X, such that x_0 belongs to the convex hull of $P(x_0)$, then by continuity of P, there exists a P−cycle $\{x_0, x_1, \ldots, x_r\}$ where $x_k \in P(x_{k-1})$ for $k = 1, \ldots, r$ yet $x_0 \in P(x_r)$.

In complex markets (for currencies, futures, derivatives, *etc.*) where the behavior of agents is driven not only by their preferences, but by their *beliefs* about the future behavior of prices, it is possible for the Fan condition to fail, and thus for there to be no equilibrium that can aggregate the agents' beliefs about the future.

One of the current important research areas in game theory is to determine how exactly preferences and beliefs interact. The "classical" formulation of Savage (1974) was to view preference as the primitive and to regard beliefs simply as probability assignments on acts to be deduced as the consequence of a utility representation of preference. However, there are many situations in which beliefs rather than preferences should be regarded as the primitive. For example, a collection of scientists, each with private information and a prior probability assessment of the truth of some empirical proposition, may pool their beliefs to generate a collective statistic of some form. Under certain "common knowledge" assumptions concerning the scientists' understanding of each other's modelling characteristics, the process of posterior probability assignment will converge (Aumann 1976; Geanakopolos and Polemarchakis 1982; McKelvey and Page 1986). These results, and other related work I view as belonging to a research program concerned with the aggregation (or convergence) of individual beliefs. I shall call this the *Aumann Research Program*.

One point that is worth emphasizing is that a Nash equilibrium, since it is an equilibrium in *preferences*, can be regarded as a compromise. However, an

Aumann equilibrium in *beliefs*, resulting from a process of belief convergence, gives an outcome (or collective belief) that is an agreement. Obviously enough these two types of equilibria can be very different. Our attitudes about the results of voting in a House of Representatives will depend on whether we feel the vote to be driven by conflicting preferences or by different judgments or beliefs about the best course of action. Recent technical results in game theory that attempt to model situations where both individual preferences and beliefs are involved suggest that, in general, the Fan condition will not hold at every point (x, b) in the collective action-belief space (Nyarko 1993; Nachbar 1995). Whether extreme indeterminacy (or chaos) can occur is, as yet, unclear. (I shall return later to the possibility of chaos.)

Although work in the Nash-Aumann research programs provides some justification for the use of the market to govern exchange of private goods, the results are not immediately applicable to political economies involving public goods. Such goods, of course, are both jointly produced and consumed, and the formal study of these processes lies in the domain of public finance and public choice theory. In a sense the key question in these disciplines is whether democratic political procedures, used to aggregate preferences for public goods, are compatible with market processes controlling the production and exchange of private goods.

Two separate attempts to enlarge the domain of political economy were made in the late 1940's and early 1950's by Black (1948; 1958) and Arrow (1951). Black's (1958) book, in fact, reintroduced two aspects of the work of Condorcet (1785) to modern audiences. Condorcet's earlier work on probability theory led him to what is now termed the Jury Theorem. Consider a society $N = \{1, \ldots, n\}$, or more particularly a *jury*, debating over a binary issue labelled $\{j, k\}$, say, where one of these two alternatives is true and the other false. For example we can interpret these options as the innocence or guilt of a defendant and without loss of generality suppose that k is truth (using $k = 1$ to denote this). Each individual, i, on the basis of private information chooses (or votes for) either j or k. If we denote $i's$ choice by χ_i, then it is possible, in principle, to assign a probability $Pr(\chi_i = 1)$ that i chooses the "true" option. Denote this probability simply by π_{ki}. Now let π_k be the average of $\{\pi_{ki}\}$; that is the expectation of $\overline{\chi} = \frac{1}{n}\sum \chi_i$. Assuming that $\{\chi_i : i \in N\}$ are statistically independent, then it is possible to compute the probability ξ_k that a majority of these n individuals chooses the truth. Condorcet provided an argument that as long as each individual is enlightened (in the sense that $\pi_{ki} > \frac{1}{2}$) then the probability, ξ_k, that the jury chooses the truth (by majority) exceeds π_k. In fact Condorcet made the additional assumption that π_{ki} are all identical, and essentially used the binomial theorem to argue that, in the limiting case with n very large, the probability ξ_k approaches unity. However Condorcet's deeper intuition was correct, in the sense that even with variable $\{\pi_{ki}\}$, as long as the choices are independent, and the average, π_k, is strictly greater than $\frac{1}{2} + \frac{1}{2n}$ then $\xi_k > \pi_k$. Moreover ξ_k approaches 1 in the limit (Boland 1989). Grofman and Feld (1988) have argued that Condorcet's Jury Theorem is one way to interpret Rousseau's notion of the "General Will". A recent close study (McLean and Hewitt 1994) of Condorcet's writings argues that he did indeed believe that the Jury Theorem captured the essence of the "General Will".[3] The last few decades have seen increasing attention paid to the Jury Theorem (Rae 1969; Schofield 1972; and the references in Chapter 19 of this volume). In contrast, Black's discussion of the Jury Theorem appeared to miss its significance, as might be inferred from his comment that "the probability of the correctness of a voter's opinion seems to be without definite meaning" (Black 1958: 163). However, in light of the recent realization that beliefs are at least as important as (but distinct from) preferences, it is perhaps appropriate to view Condorcet's efforts in this direction as part of a distinct research program. It is clear that the structure of the Jury Theorem does not model individual choice as such, but is concerned with the *collective* outcome. For this reason I shall identify work which examines belief aggregation through collective, rather than individual, choice as part of the *Condorcetian Research Program*.

Condorcet, in the *Essai* of 1785, was concerned to generalize the theorem to more than two alternatives and, in attempting to do this, he stumbled on what is now known as the "Condorcetian cycle". Suppose three members $N = \{1, 2, 3\}$ of a committee have strict preferences on $\{x_1, x_2, x_3\}$ where, for example, 1 prefers x_1 to x_2 to x_3, 2 prefers x_2 to x_3 to x_1, and 3 prefers x_3 to x_1 to x_2. Such a list $P = (P_1, P_2, P_3)$ of preferences for these individuals is called a profile. Using majority rule and taking pairwise comparisons the committee prefers x_1 to x_2 to x_3 to x_1 (a cycle). There is no majority motion (to use Black's term), since no alternative is unbeaten under majority rule. Black saw that if the preferences of the individuals were restricted in appropriate fashion, then Condorcetian cycles could not occur, and a majority motion could be guaranteed. For example, if we imagine the three alternatives to be ordered $x_1 > x_2 > x_3$ on a line, then restricting preferences to be "single-peaked" means that the above preference for the third voter violates the restriction, since the preference of x_3 over x_1 over x_2 is not singlepeaked, given $>$.

More generally, suppose that all preferences are convex (*i.e.*, for each individual, i, the set of alternatives, $P_i(x)$, preferred by i to x, is a convex set). If X is a compact interval on the real line, then this restriction guarantees existence of a majority motion (also called a voting equilibrium or *core*). However, if X is a compact subset of the plane $\Re^2$, then convexity of preference does not guarantee existence of a voting equilibrium. Figure 1 presents a two-dimensional case where each of three individuals have smooth convex preferences. In this case we can describe the preferences near the point x by the "gradient vectors" $\{p_1, p_2, p_3\}$, where p_i represents the most preferred direction of change for player i. It is evident that there exists a Condorcet cycle $\{x_1, x_2, x_3\}$ close to x. In fact, for *any* neighborhood V of x there exists a "local" Condorcet cycle contained in V (Kramer 1973). As Plott (1967) showed, the only possible situation that can guarantee that a point, x, be a core or voting equilibrium is when the point, x, is a "bliss point" of, say, individual 1 (in the sense that $P_1(x) = \emptyset$) and the two gradients p_2, p_3 point in

---

[3] Note however that Condorcet's biographers, Elizabeth and Robert Badinter (1988) quote Condorcet: "Contrairement à la philosophie des nombreux disciples de Rousseau, ce n'est pas la volonté générale, mais la Raison qui est le moteur du progrès humain."

opposite directions. As Black realized, the likelihood that preferences satisfy this property can be viewed, in some sense, as "infinitesimal" (Black 1958: 164). This intuition has been elaborated in a series of papers (see Chapter 8 below) analyzing deterministic voting models of committees. The essence of these results can be quickly seen in Figure 1.

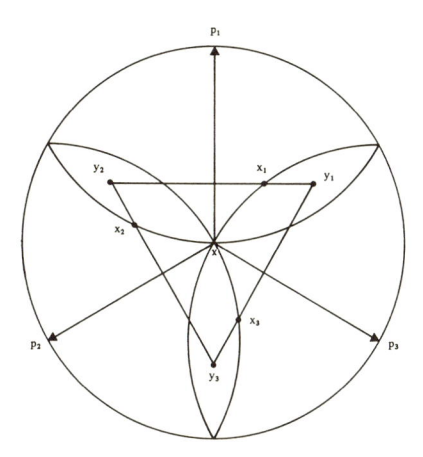

Figure 1. The failure of the Fan condition in two dimensions.

It is clear that, at x, the preferred set defined by majority rule and the profile P comprises three "win-sets" each one of which is associated with a single winning coalition. For example the point y_1 is preferred by both player 1 and 3 to x. The Fan Condition obviously fails at x, since the three points $\{y_1, y_2, y_3\}$ are all preferred to x and x belongs to the convex hull of those three points. It is then easy to show that the voting equilibrium, $E(P)$, is empty. To explore what can happen when the voting equilibrium is empty, let us use the gradient vectors $\{p_i\}$ to define for each pair $\{p_i, p_j\}$ a cone p_{ij}, as in Figure 2. It is evident from this figure that $p_{12} \cap p_{13} \cap p_{23} = \emptyset$. Suppose, on the other hand, for an arbitrary voting rule, $\mathcal{D}$, that at every point $x \in X$, the intersection $p_{\mathcal{D}}(x) = \cap \, p_M(x)$ is nonempty. Here $p_M(x)$ is the cone generated by the gradients $\{p_i(x) : i \in M\}$ at the point x, and the intersection is taken over the family of "decisive" coalitions (labelled $\mathcal{D}$). Then the Fan condition is satisfied and the Fan Theorem implies that $E(P)$ is non empty. This intersection condition, $p_{\mathcal{D}}(x) \neq \emptyset$, is very similar to the condition of "no unlimited arbitrage" recently shown to be sufficient for the existence of a competitive equilibrium (Chichilnisky 1993, 1995) for an abstract exchange economy. For a voting rule, $\mathcal{D}$, suppose that any subfamily $\mathcal{D}'$ of $\mathcal{D}$ consisting of at most $v = v(\mathcal{D})$ coalitions, has a voter, i say, in common. (For example, if $\mathcal{D}$ is majority rule, then $v \geq 2$.) Then clearly at any point $x \in X$, $p_i(x)$ belongs to $p_{\mathcal{D}'}(x)$, and so the intersection across $\mathcal{D}'$ is non-empty. By Helly's Theorem, if the dimension of the space is at most $v - 1$, then $p_{\mathcal{D}}(x)$ must be non-empty, at every point x, and the voting equilibrium must be non-empty (Schofield 1984). Thus, in both general equilibrium and spatial voting theories, a certain intersection property of cones is sufficient to guarantee existence of equilibrium. On the other hand, say "social diversity for $\mathcal{D}$" is satisfied at x iff $p_\mathcal{D}(x) = \emptyset$. (Chichilnisky, 1995, first used the phrase "social diversity" in this sense.) It can be shown that, for any rule $\mathcal{D}$ (satisfying $v(\mathcal{D}) < \infty$), if the dimension of X is strictly greater than a certain integer, $w(\mathcal{D})$, (where $w(\mathcal{D}) \geq v(\mathcal{D}) + 1$), then "social diversity for $\mathcal{D}$" is satisfied at nearly every point in X, for nearly every preference profile. But "social diversity" implies voting cycles. Thus the "Chaos Theorem" implies that ubiquitous cycles and non-existent equilibria are generic features of voting (McKelvey 1976; Schofield 1978a; McKelvey and Schofield 1986; Banks 1994; Saari 1995).

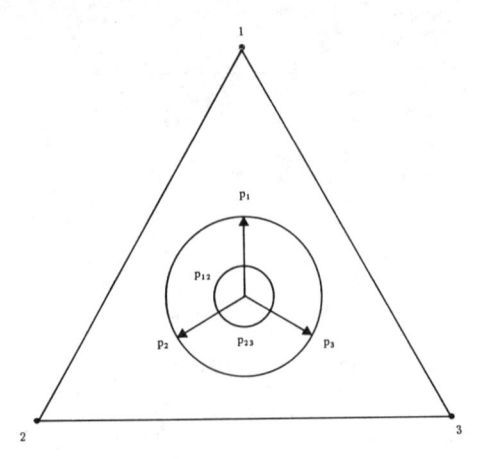

Figure 2. An empty intersection of the cones $\{p_{ij}\}$.

As intimated above, these models of committee voting based on preference are "deterministic". That is, it is assumed that voter i, in making a choice between two alternatives $\{x_j, x_k\}$, say, chooses x_j with probability 1 iff i prefers x_j to x_k and either does not vote, or chooses both x_j and x_k with probability $\frac{1}{2}$ each if i is indifferent between them. "Probabilistic" voting models, on the other hand, can be regarded as part of the Condorcetian program, since they posit that a voter, i, chooses x_k, say, with probability π_{ki} determined in some way by the beliefs (rather than the preferences) of the voter (see the various models in Enelow and Hinich 1984, Coughlin 1992). It is possible to formulate a probabilistic voting model based on Euclidean distance in the following way. Suppose voter i has an "ideal" point x_i (or a point believed by the voter to be the correct choice). Let $\delta_j = \| x_i - x_j \|$, $\delta_k = \| x_i - x_k \|$. Then a *quantal* model (McKelvey and Palfrey 1992) assumes that

$$\pi_{ki} = e^{-\beta \delta_k} \left(e^{-\beta \delta_k} + e^{-\beta \delta_j} \right)^{-1}, \text{ while } \pi_{ji} = 1 - \pi_{ki}.$$

(Here e stands for exponential.)

Probabilistic voting models suppose that the two positions $\{x_j, x_k\}$ are chosen by candidates $\{j, k\}$ so as to maximize their respective expected vote $\{\pi_j, \pi_k\}$. As the previous discussion of the jury theorem suggests, under the maintained assumption of independent voting, if candidate j maximizes expected vote, π_j, then this is tantamount to maximizing the probability that

j wins. Of course, the expected votes are functions of candidate positions and should be written $(\pi_j(x_j, x_k), \pi_k(x_j, x_k))$. A pure strategy Nash equilibrium $(PSNE), (x_j^*, x_k^*)$, is a pair of candidate positions that are mutual best responses, i.e., $\pi_j(x_j^*, x_k^*) \geq \pi_j(x_j, x_k^*)$ for all x_j, with strict inequality for some x_j (and a similar definition for x_k^*). Under certain assumptions the Nash equilibrium satisfies $x_j^* = x_k^*$ where both candidates adopt the mean of the distribution of voter ideal points.

In some sense the $PSNE$ can be thought of as a "belief optimum", given the distribution of information in the society, and particular assumptions on the way individuals form judgments. The probabilistic model suggests that two party competition by candidates (whose sole motivation is winning) generates a political outcome that has the highest probability of being "correct." Of course, there are many implicit assumptions in this chain of reasoning, not the least of which is the assumption of voter independence. An oddity of the "quantal" model is that even when candidate k chooses the ideal point of voter i (so that $x_k = x_i$), then the probability that i votes for k is less than 1. This could be corrected by choosing a model where $\pi_{ki} = \delta_j/(\delta_j + \delta_k)$. Here if $x_k = x_i$, then $\pi_{ki} = 1$. In such a model, however, it is easy to show that the $PSNE$ does not satisfy the convergence property $x_j^* = x_k^*$. Instead the candidates diverge and, in a sense, adopt "equilibrium" policies that are attractive to different subgroups in the society.

It should be obvious that representative politics involves both preferences and beliefs. Individuals have both beliefs about what is best for the society, and preferences that reflect their own particular economic or political interests. As long as voting reflects judgments alone, then it is possible to construct a model of probabilistic (or "Condorcetian") voting, such as the quantal model described above, and conclude on this basis that two-candidate competition leads to a belief consensus. However if voting also reflects preferences, then it is difficult to see how the chaos theorem for direct democracy can be avoided.

The inferences to be drawn for the design of political institutions can be very different depending on whether judgments or preferences are assumed to be the driving force behind politics. Condorcet's writings (McLean and Hewitt 1994) suggest that he believed that political representatives would restrain their passions in passing judgment. As architect of the "Girondin Constitution" of 1793, Condorcet proposed a unicameral house of representatives. However, this proposal was defeated by the Jacobins, and in March, 1794, Condorcet was declared an outlaw and died in hiding. It is interesting to speculate on the indirect effect Condorcet may have had on the development of the political institutions of the United States. It is known (Randall 1993) that Condorcet, Jefferson (and Thomas Paine) were friends while Jefferson was American Minister in Paris during 1785-89. Moreover Jefferson and Madison corresponded regularly, and one can see a distinctly Condorcetian chain of reasoning in *Federalist X*, written by Madison ([1787], see Bailyn 1993 for page references).

In contrasting a Democracy (by which Madison means a direct democracy) with a Republic (or representative democracy), Madison suggests that the key difference is the "greater number of citizens and extent of territory which may be brought within the compass of a Republican, than of a Democratic Government....it is this circumstance principally which renders factious combinations less to be dreaded in the former, than in the latter" [*Federalist X*: 410]. Clearly there is a suggestion here that the greater extent of the Republic will induce "heterogeneity in beliefs". We may interpret this to mean that pairwise voter correlations in choices are low. If the choices of the voters or representatives are close to independent, then the Jury Theorem holds. One interpretation of this would be that no faction or majority capable of acting against the "permanent and aggregate interests of the community" [*Federalist X*: 405] could persist.

Notwithstanding this interpretation, Madison seems to have been opposed to Condorcet's view that a unicameral house of representatives is the optimal design for a legislature. While the "checks and balances" implicit in the U.S. polity make little sense from the Condorcetian viewpoint, they are sensible in terms of the deterministic voting model. The fact that the President and supramajoritarian coalitions in the Legislature both have veto power in the U. S. polity essentially means that the integer $v(\mathcal{D})$, mentioned previously, is high. Thus a stable "legislative equilibrium" can exist (Hammond and Miller 1987). Unfortunately, if possible government policy has substantial redistributive components, then the underlying policy space may have even higher dimension. This suggests that legislatures will appear either to be "gridlocked" or "chaotic", depending on the dimensionality of the policy space.

Although it is suggestive that there is a formal connection between "diversity of preference" and the lack of equilibrium in both the competitive model of the economy and the spatial model of committee voting, the work that we have just discussed gives little insight into the underlying relationship between the economy and the polity. The genius of Arrow's (1951) work in social choice is that it attempts, in some sense, to provide an integrated approach to collective decision making. While "Arrovian" social choice takes individual preference as the underlying primitive, the focus of the theory is on collective decision-making rather than individual choice (as was the case in the Nash research program). To emphasize this difference, I shall identify social choice theory, as well as deterministic models of voting, as part of the *Arrovian Research Program*. To remind the reader, Table 1 sets out this four-fold partition.

Table 1.

	Individual	*Collective*
Beliefs	Aumann	Condorcet
Preferences	Nash	Arrow

One way to introduce social choice theory is to note that while the competitive economic model aggregates preferences, it does so on the restricted domain of private preferences. If the set of possible alternatives involves "public goods", then it can no longer be assumed that preferences are restricted in this fashion.

Arrow adopted an unrestricted domain assumption, namely that the class of permissible preference profiles, D, consists of all fully transitive preference orderings on the set of alternatives, X. In public economics it is often assumed that the choices available to society concerning the production of public goods can be valued in terms of a social welfare function—that is a preference that could, in principle, be defined in terms of a social utility, u, say. If this were possible, then standard economic techniques would be available to determine the optimal production of the public goods (given the relevant price structure at points on the transformation surface between the private economy and the "public goods" polity). However such a social preference must be *fully transitive*, since social indifference, induced from a social utility, must also be transitive. Arrow also adopted what is now called the "binary independence axiom", namely that the social preference between any pair $\{x,y\}$ of alternatives should be defined only in terms of the individual preference relations on $\{x,y\}$. For example, the deterministic voting processes considered above obviously satisfy this axiom. Arrow's impossibility theorem demonstrates that any social welfare function with unrestricted domain, satisfying the independence axiom and a unanimity or Pareto postulate, must be dictatorial (see Theorem 1 of Chapter 2 of this volume for a precise statement).

Of course, the requirement of full transitivity may be viewed as excessively strong. A weaker condition is the existence of a social *decision* function, σ, namely a way of defining a transitive strict social preference for every preference profile in the domain D. (Notice that the social indifference is no longer assumed to be transitive.) With the binary independence axiom and unrestricted domain, the social decision function must be *oligarchic*. In other words, however the function σ is defined, there will exist a family of σ-decisive coalitions, labelled $\mathcal{D}_\sigma$. If all members of a decisive coalition agree on the preferences between two alternatives $\{x,y\}$, say, then that they collectively control the social preference on $\{x,y\}$. Transitivity implies that $\mathcal{D}_\sigma$ is oligarchic: if two coalitions A, B are both σ−decisive, then so is their intersection, $A \cap B$. If, in addition, the social decision function satisfies the Pareto condition, then the whole society, N, must be σ−decisive. This essentially implies that any social decision function, σ, is determined by an *oligarchy* θ_σ, where θ_σ is a σ-decisive group belonging to every coalition in $\mathcal{D}_\sigma$. Of course the oligarchy could be the whole society, namely N. However, if it is necessary to restrict choice to some proper subset of the Pareto set for N, then this can only be done by choosing some proper subset θ_σ of N to be the oligarchy (see Kirman and Sondermann 1972). If $\{i\} = \theta_\sigma$ for some $i \in N$, then i is called an *Arrovian dictator* for the function σ.

A weaker rationality condition on σ is that social preference be *acyclic*. This "rationality" restriction is sufficient, under fairly weak conditions, to guarantee existence of a choice, $E_\sigma(P)$, namely an alternative that is unbeaten under the social preference $\sigma(P)$. For example, if X is a finite set of alternatives, or if X is a compact topological space and $\sigma(P)$ is a "continuous" social preference, then acyclicity of $\sigma(P)$ is sufficient to guarantee a choice (Walker 1977). However, to ensure acyclicity of $\sigma(P)$, it is necessary that σ (or $\mathcal{D}_\sigma$) be *collegial*: that is to say there must be some individual i (called a vetoer) who belongs to every σ−decisive coalition (Brown 1973). Suppose, on the contrary, that σ, or $\mathcal{D}_\sigma$, is not collegial (*i.e.*, there is no vetoer). To relate this to the situation of voting discussed earlier, suppose there is a minimal non-collegial subfamily $\mathcal{D}'$ of $\mathcal{D}_\sigma$. That is, $\mathcal{D}'$ consists of $v+1 = v(\mathcal{D}_\sigma)+1$ different coalitions, with nobody in common. By Nakamura (1979), if X is a finite set of cardinality at least $v+1$, then it is possible to construct a profile $\{P_1,\ldots,P_n\} = P$ on $\{x_1,\ldots,x_{v+1}\}$ such that $\sigma(P)$ is cyclic. Furthermore, if X is a topological vector space of dimension at least v, then there exists a continuous, convex profile $\{P_1,\ldots,P_n\} = P$ on X such that $\sigma(P)$ is cyclic on X (Schofield 1984; Strnad 1985). Indeed, the previous results on voting games suggest that, with an appropriate topology on preferences, the social preference $\sigma(P)$ will be cyclic for almost all preferences.

These abstract results on the cyclicity of the social preference function depend on particular assumptions on the nature of preferences and the topology imposed on preference profiles. For example, suppose D_H is the space of all continuous preference profiles on X endowed with the "Hausdorff" topology (see Chapter 8 for definitions). Without the restriction to convex preferences, the results of Rubenstein (1979), Cox (1984a) and Le Breton (1987) imply that if σ is non-collegial, then $\sigma(P)$ cycles "almost always". Similarly, if D_S is the space of all smooth convex preference profiles, endowed with a certain "smooth" topology (Schofield 1995a), and σ is non-collegial, then $\sigma(P)$ will be cyclic "almost always" if and only if the dimension of X exceeds some integer $w(\mathcal{D}_\sigma)$, where $w(\mathcal{D}_\sigma) \geq v(\mathcal{D}_\sigma)+1$. The term "almost always" refers to a subset D of D_S (or D_H, as appropriate) that is open dense with respect to the topology with which the space of profiles is endowed. Thus the results suggest that the subset $D_S \backslash D$ (or $D_H \backslash D$ as appropriate) on which σ is acyclic must be nowhere dense in the relevant topology. We may say, in more abbreviated fashion, that if σ is non-collegial then it is generically cyclic (whenever the appropriate dimension condition on X is satisfied).

1.2 A Brief Overview of the Volume

1.2.1 Social Choice

Part I of the volume is devoted to abstract "Arrovian" social choice theory. Chapters 2 and 3 focus on determining whether the unrestricted domain assumption is crucial to the inference that a method of social preference aggregation must be dictatorial or oligarchic. A key to the proof that a social welfare function must be dictatorial lies in the existence of Condorcet preference cycles in the class of permitted preference profiles. Le Breton and Weymark show in Chapter 2 that Arrow's Impossibility Theorem is valid for any social welfare function on "saturating preference domains". Such domains include preferences that are linear, strictly monotonic on the simplex, or those that are "Euclidean" (i.e., where $y \in P_i(x)$ iff $\| y - x_i \| < \| x - x_i \|$, and x_i is i's bliss point). To deal with the case of an exchange economy, Le Breton and Weymark consider the situation where each individual, i, has selfish preferences on a private choice space, X_i, and the collective choice space X is Cartesian ($X = \Pi_i X_i$). They show, under these assumptions, that there is an "Arrovian dictator" if the domain is "hypersaturating". Moreover this condition is satisfied whenever individual preferences are continuous and strictly monotonic on the strictly positive orthant of Euclidean space. Public or "private" choice domains generically satisfy either the saturating or hypersaturating conditions. In other words, it appears that a preference domain, for either public or private goods, does not admit an Arrovian dictator only if it is "nowhere dense" in an appropriate topology on the space of preference profiles. Note that this result is similar to, but not directly comparable with the genericity result on voting mentioned previously, since the voting result assumed that there was a common policy space X on which all preferences were defined.

Chapter 3 by Donald Campbell considers a continuous social decision function defined on preference domains large enough to include "free triples" (again these can be thought of as "Condorcet cycles"). Instead of assuming the Pareto condition, the social decision function, σ, satisfies a weaker property of "non-imposition". It is also assumed that the space of alternatives, X, is a connected topological space. These assumptions imply that there exists an "oligarchy", θ_σ, except that, in this case, some members of the oligarchy may have their preferences reversed in the social ranking. Campbell shows that this result is also true in economic environments (that is when X is "Cobb-Douglas"). Finally Campbell shows that if E is a social choice correspondence that maximises the social decision function, σ, and E satisfies an independence axiom due to Plott (1973), then σ must be oligarchic. He concludes by arguing that if σ can be implemented by a game form (whether cooperative or non-cooperative) then it must satisfy the Plott independence condition. Consequently, if a social welfare function can be implemented then it is either dictatorial or constant, and thus cannot be used to balance efficiency and equity considerations.

Whereas Chapters 2 and 3 deal with social welfare and decision functions, Chapter 4 by Yongsheng Xu reviews results on choice functions on universal preference domains. As noted above, acyclicity of the underlying preference relation allows the existence of a choice. A choice function, C, is a procedure for selecting a choice $C(V)$ from any set V. Starting with a choice function C it is possible that the base relation R_C induced by C on pairs of alternatives gives $C(V)$ as its choice on every set V. In this case C is said to be rationalizable. Xu shows how rationality properties imposed on R_C are equivalent to "choice theoretic" properties on C. As a corollary it is possible to obtain an Arrovian impossibility result: when the choice function satisfies universal domain, the Pareto condition, an independence axiom and strong choice theoretic properties, then it must be dictatorial.

In Chapter 5 Donald Saari returns to the 1784 debate on voting procedures between Borda and Condorcet (see McLean 1995). Borda argued that his technique based on counting always gave a method of ranking a finite number of alternatives, whereas Condorcet contended that the "Borda" count was open to extreme manipulation. Saari uses abstract tools of social choice theory to define a "dictionary" for each method of voting—that is a correspondence between all possible sets of profiles and all social preference rankings based on weighting voting vectors. For example, under plurality the weighting system is $(1, 0, 0)$, assigning one vote to the first placed alternative of any voter. Under

"Borda", the count $(3, 2, 1)$ assigns weight 3 to the first placed and weight 1 to the third-placed alternative. A "word" of the plurality dictionary, for example, could be $x > y, z > y, z > x$ yet $y > x > z$. Such a "word" clearly violates acyclity, transitivity, *etc.* Saari shows that almost any choice of weighting system gives the "universal" dictionary, where "chaos" (*i.e.*, anything) can occur. The Borda dictionary, which excludes "paradoxical" rankings, is the exception. However, the Borda count violates the binary independence axiom, since there is generally no connection between the Borda choice using the Borda count on a set V and the choice on a subset of V. Saari's findings suggest that any weighting voting system satisfying binary independence, or one of the choice theoretic rationality axioms will be chaotic. Conversely, while the Borda count gives a ranking on any set, and has a restricted dictionary, it is not rationalizable and violates choice theoretic conditions.

1.2.2 Elections and Committees

The essays in Part II of the volume examine voting in committees and elections. It is necessary to briefly distinguish here between these two kinds of voting procedures. In committee voting, the outcome is simply an alternative (in a set X), and depending on whether the model is intended to reflect preference or belief aggregation, the equilibrium (if one exists) is that alternative which is unbeaten (under deterministic voting) or which has the highest probability of winning or, at least, not losing (under probabilistic voting). Elections involve voting over candidates, and, to be formal, each candidate, j, should be described by a strategy set W_j, say. Obviously enough, part of a candidate's strategy will involve a declaration about intended policy (in the space X) and perhaps other choices on campaign expenditure (described by a set C_j, say). In general then $W_j = X \times C_j$. In the Downsian (1957) model it is assumed that $W_j = X$ for each j, and that the declarations can be interpreted as policy outcomes. A candidate, j, prefers to win ($u_j = 1$, say) rather than lose ($u_j = -1$). If it is assumed that voting is preference-based, then it is sensible for each voter, i, to choose sincerely (*i.e.*, to choose candidate j over candidate k if and only if $u_i(z_j) > u_i(z_k)$: here we use $\{z_j, z_k\}$ to represent the candidate "platforms" or declarations). Consequently the $PSNE$ for the candidates (if it exists) is to choose the voting equilibrium, or core. If we let $\mathcal{D}$ be plurality rule, then the integer $v(\mathcal{D})$, mentioned in Section 1.1, is at least 2. Thus a $PSNE$ can be guaranteed in one dimension if voters have single-peaked preferences. However, a fully developed model of elections must carefully specify the beliefs of voters (over the credibility of the candidates) as well as the preferences and beliefs of candidates. Such a model could involve aspects of all four of the research programs described in Section 1.1.

Chapter 6, by David Austen-Smith, develops a framework to extend the Downsian model to the multi-candidate, multiple constituency case (that is, with more than two candidates and more than a single constituency or district). As in the Downsian case, Austen-Smith assumes that X is a compact subset of the real line, and that each candidate, j, can be identified with a declaration z_j. Crucial to the analysis is a legislative outcome function λ

that specifies the policy outcome $\lambda(z_1, \ldots, z_t)$ when candidates $\{1, \ldots, t\}$ are elected to the legislature. Under these assumptions, no voter chooses sincerely (Moulin 1980). Austen-Smith goes on to discuss an important paper (Austen-Smith and Banks 1988) that models an election with three candidates. On the basis of these earlier results, he shows existence of a "subgame perfect" Nash equilibrium $\{z_1^*, z_2^*, z_3^*\}$, for the candidates, given the distribution of *voter* bliss points $\{x_1, \ldots, x_m\}$. In this model, given the declarations $\{z_1, z_2, z_3\}$, the voters choose strategically, a majority government coalition M forms, adopting a policy z_M. Each member j of M receives a payoff $b_j - (z_M - z_j)^2$, while any "party" outside M pays an election cost. The justification for the policy term $(-(z_M - z_j)^2)$ is that each government member is punished in future elections (either by not being re-elected or by facing diminishing electoral support) if "legislative outcomes fail to match electoral promises." The term b_j describes the "perquisites" or ministerial payoff that party j receives as a member of the governing coalition.

Notice that the terms "candidate" and "party" have been used more or less interchangeably in the above discussion. Clearly plurality voting systems, such as Britain's, involve candidates competing in different constituencies or districts, *and* parties deciding on overall policy objectives. Austen-Smith goes on to evaluate a number of multiple district models of two-party elections that attempt to address some of the questions raised by Robertson's (1976) work on British politics. A key assumption here is that party policy is a "selection" from the convex hull of the party's candidate's electoral positions. Under certain conditions, two-party electoral competition across multiple constituencies converges on the median of the constituency voter medians.

Austen-Smith's perspective is obviously based on the Nash research program. Even assuming that the policy space of political alternatives is one-dimensional, the analysis is extremely complex. Both voters and and candidates are assumed to behave rationally with respect to their policy preferences *and* to their beliefs about final outcomes. In a number of the results, the final outcome results from the unspecified collective behavior of political representatives within the legislature. This is necessary in order to link the strategies of the players to final outcomes and thus to utility payoffs. In the cases considered by Austen-Smith, X is assumed to be one-dimensional and voting is deterministic. The results from the theory of committee voting suggest that the legislative outcome will be well-defined. However the chaos results from spatial voting theory suggest, when X is of higher dimension, that legislative outcomes may be unpredictable.

Cheryl Eavey, in Chapter 7, reviews the experimental literature on committee voting, published in the period after 1978 once the relevance of the chaos theorem (McKelvey 1976; Schofield 1978a) was clear. In the case of a finite number of alternatives, using the "Condorcetian" procedure of binary comparison, it appears that the majority-rule voting equilibrium (or "core") does not perform well as a behavioral predictor. In experiments using the two dimensional spatial model with Euclidean preferences, it is necessary, of course, to distinguish between games with a core and those without one. The results by Fiorina and Plott (1978) and Hoffman and Plott (1983) strongly support the core. However, later experiments by Eavey (1991) suggest that the core is an imperfect predictor. One reason for this may be that the core examined in these games was structurally unstable (in the sense that any small perturbation of the given utility function rendered the core empty). Figure 3 illustrates this.

The five vertices of this figure represent the bliss points $\{x_1, \ldots, x_5\}$ of the five voters. Were x_5 located on the line joining x_2 with x_4, then it would be a core point. A small perturbation of colinearity produces Figure 3, where the core is empty. In fact the fifteen dots in this figure represent observations obtained in the Fiorina and Plott (1978) experiments. It is evident that the shaded star-shaped figure contains nine of the observations, while the other six observations are fairly close to the star. This star-shaped object is called the "heart" (Schofield 1995b) and has been proposed as a predictor for these voting games (Schofield 1978b). An alternative solution notion is the "uncovered set" (McKelvey 1986) of the majority preference correspondence P. (Again I do not distinguish between the preference profile P and the majority rule correspondence induced by P.) Define the covering correspondence, $\overline{P}$ of P, by $y \in \overline{P}(x)$ iff $y \in P(x)$ and $P(y) \subset P(x)$. The uncovered set is the choice of $\overline{P}$, namely $\{x : \overline{P}\{x\} = \emptyset\}$. Because of the set inclusion, $\overline{P}$ must be transitive, so $E(\overline{P})$ will be non empty under general conditions (Bordes, Le Breton and Salles 1992). In fact, it appears that the "heart" and the uncovered set are closely related, since the heart can be interpreted as the set of locally uncovered points (that is x is in the heart iff there is some neighborhood V of x, such that for no $y \in V$ is $y \in \overline{P}(x)$).

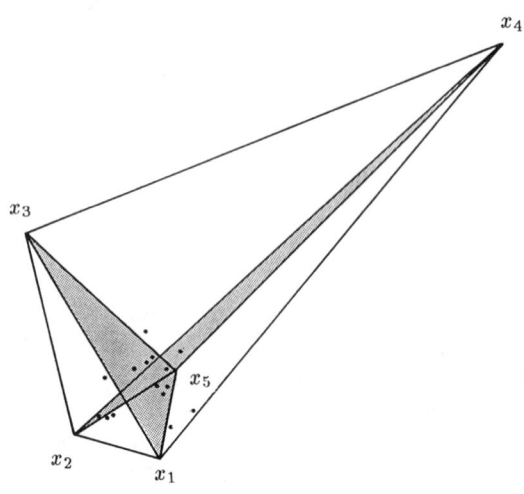

Figure 3. The heart of a five-person committee showing the Fiorina-Plott (1978) observations.

The heart is generally easy to compute; in Figure 3 it is the star "spanned" by the six "median" lines (for example the line joining x_2 and x_4 is median). Of the 55 observations over 5 experiments discussed by Eavey, I estimate 40 (or 73%) belong to the heart. Since the uncovered set is a subset of the heart,

I conclude that the success rate of the uncovered set is precisely the same.

Chapter 8 by Schofield attempts to integrate the two distinct models of elections and committee voting presented in Chapters 6 and 7. This chapter first defines the heart in spatial committee games, when voters have Euclidean preferences, and then argues that it can be used as a predictor of coalition formation in multiparty situations in Europe. Models of multiparty coalition formation typically assume that the list of party policy declarations or manifestos $\{z_1, \ldots, z_n\}$ coincides with the true bliss points, or most preferred policy points, $\{x_1, \ldots, x_n\}$, of the parties. (See for example Chapters 12 and 13 of this volume.) In contrast, Section 6 of Chapter 8 considers a model of coalition bargaining among three agents in two dimensions when the core is empty, and the declarations of the parties are chosen through an equilibrium process. Each party, i, makes an offer z_i and coalition $\{i,j\}$ forms with probability ρ_{ij}, inversely proportional to $\| z_i - z_j \|^2$, adopting the outcome $z_{ij} = \frac{1}{2}(z_i + z_j)$. The final outcome is a lottery across the three coalition possibilities. It is argued that, for every set of bliss points $\{x_1, x_2, x_3\}$, there exists a $PSNE$, $\{z_1^*, z_2^*, z_3^*\} = z^*$, in the choice of declarations or offers. The $PSNE$, z^*, results from the maximization of a von Neumann-Morgenstern expected utility function, U_i, for each party, i.

Just to illustrate, suppose the bliss points are actually colinear with $\{x_1, x_2, x_3\} = \{-1, 0, 1\}$. If each party makes a sincere declaration, $(x_i = z_i)$ it is easy to compute that $\{\rho_{12}, \rho_{13}, \rho_{23}\} = \{\frac{4}{9}, \frac{1}{9}, \frac{4}{9}\}$. Assuming Euclidean utility for party 1, so $u_1(x) = -\| x + 1 \|^2$, then gives "expected utility" of $U_1(\{-1, 0, -1\}) = -\frac{4}{9} + (-\frac{4}{9} \cdot \frac{9}{4}) + (-\frac{1}{9} \cdot 1) = -\frac{11}{9}$. On the other hand, if 1 makes the declaration $z_1 = 0$, then the coalition $\{1, 2\}$ forms with probability 1, and party 1 has expected utility $U_1 = -1$, resulting from the certain outcome $z_{12} = 0$. However, if $z_1 = \frac{1}{2}$, and the other two parties behave sincerely, then coalition $\{1, 2\}$ forms with probability close to .73 and chooses the outcome $z_{12} = -\frac{1}{4}$. The calculation shows $U_1 \simeq -.95$. Clearly given $(z_2, z_3) = (0, 1)$, there is a best response z_1^*, for 1 somewhere in the interior of the interval $[-1, 0]$. Indeed there is a $PSNE$ where all parties cluster in a neighborhood of the origin. In two dimensions this convergence need not occur. Although the conclusions of the model depend on the assumptions on coalition outcomes and probabilities, it is conjectured that the model is robust.

The motivation underlying this model is to provide an explanation why parties do not in fact converge to a "central" point of the electoral distribution, f. As we have noted previously, two-party competitive vote maximization models tend to give "convergent" $PSNE$. In the multiparty case $(n \geq 3)$ if the electoral response to the party declarations, z, is represented by a random variable $e^f(z)$ over $\Re^n$, then vote maximization by the parties leads, in equilibrium, to "coalescence" of some of the party positions (Nixon, et al., 1995). However, if parties are also concerned with the effect of their declarations on post-election coalition bargaining (that is on "coalition risk" as represented by a vector $\rho(z)$ of coalition probabilities) then they should balance the "centripetal" effects of electoral risk, $e^f(z)$ and the "centrifugal" effects of coalition risk $\rho(z)$.

The simple three-party model, proposed in Chapter 8, suggests that unique

$PSNE$ exist in this more general electoral/coalitional game. In particular if the policy space involves at least two dimensions, then the parties will, in equilibrium, make quite different declarations. This general model also suggests that if X is one-dimensional, or if government perquisites are far more important than policy preferences, then "Downsian" policy convergence occurs.

Whereas Chapter 6 assumes that the policy space, X, is uni-dimensional, and the legislative outcome is a *function* of the vector, z, of party declarations, Chapter 8 models the parties' pre-election beliefs concerning the eventual outcome as random variables defined over a higher dimensional state space and determined by the choice of z. Empirical analysis, such as presented in Part III of this volume, or experimental work (McKelvey 1991) could indicate how these beliefs are generated and sustained.

Chapter 9 by David Austen-Smith is a brief formal analysis of some of the properties of the heart. The heart of a committee is the equilibrium set $E(P_\mathcal{D}^*)$ defined by a certain preference correspondence $P_\mathcal{D}^*$ induced by the voting rule $\mathcal{D}$, and preference profile P. It seems that $P_\mathcal{D}^*$ is a sub-correspondence of the covering correspondence, so the uncovered set is contained in the heart. $P_\mathcal{D}^*$ is designed to capture the idea of efficient bargaining. Austen-Smith proposes two "refinements" of the heart, which under certain conditions, are subsets of the heart or of the uncovered set.

1.2.3 Coalitions

The six chapters of Part III of the volume examine coalition bargaining in a variety of multi-party parliamentary situations.

Chapter 10 by Schofield and Wada uses the concept of the bargaining set to predict the ministerial payoffs among the factions of the Liberal Democratic Party (LDP) in Japan. The bargaining set assumes that the "power" of each faction is determined by its ability to form coalitions with parties outside the LDP. The results suggest that the LDP is not a traditional party bound by common policy goals, but a loose coalition of "proto"-parties motivated primarily by the wish to gain ministerial rewards. The break up of the LDP in 1992 seems to provide some substantiation of this inference.

Carreras and Owen in Chapter 11 closely examine the bargaining between the parties that occurred in the Euskarian Parliament in the period November 1986 to January 1987, using an adaptation of the Shapley-Shubik power index.

In Chapters 12 and 13 Grofman and his co-authors, Straffin and Noviello, use varients of Grofman's proto-coalition model to discuss coalition formation in Norway, Denmark and Germany. Their work is essentially based on the model of committee voting with Euclidean preferences. The general idea is that, given the profile $\{x_1, \ldots, x_n\}$ of most preferred party positions, then that winning coalition M which exhibits the least variance var $\{x_i : i \in M\}$, is predicted to form. Clearly this rule gives a unique legislative outcome function (see Chapter 6). However the rule is of little value in predicting coalitions in Italy, where a wide variety of different governing coalitions may form after each election. To deal with this difficulty they propose a stochastic version of the model (incorporating error terms) and show that the rule performs much better than a number of cooperative game theory concepts that have been employed. One difficulty that they do not deal with is the following: if indeed government formation is specified by a legislative outcome rule that depends on the party bliss points $\{x_1,\ldots,x_n\}$, then parties will rationally choose declarations in an attempt to enter the governing coalition. This is a possibility that the Nash equilibrium model presented in Chapter 8 attempted to resolve. Nonetheless the results of Chapters 12 and 13 suggest that coalition formation in multiparty situations may fruitfully be modelled as a committee game, *once* the declarations and electoral responses are known.

In contrast to the cooperative game theory approach proposed in the chapters just mentioned, Chapter 14 by Laver and Shepsle develops a competitive model of ministerial government. Essential to the model is the notion of policy jurisdictions. The authors show existence of a subgame perfect Nash equilibrium allocation of ministeries.

The extraordinary characteristic of Italian politics is the brevity of the average coalition goverment. Nonetheless a dominant party, the Christian Democratic Party (DC), was in every government from 1946 to 1992. Schofield (1993) has suggested that the reason for the DC's dominance in government is that (up to 1992) it was always a core party (in the sense of being located at the core of the spatial policy game). Mershon argues in Chapter 15 that the DC was able to manipulate goverment formation by controlling, and increasing, the supply of ministerial payoffs. Cooperative game theory based on the notion of transferable value (or payoffs) has suggested that minimal winning coalitions will generally form (Riker 1962). Mershon's work suggests this inference is invalid in situations where the number and nature of ministerial payoffs can be manipulated by a powerful actor. The decades-long manipulation of coalition payoffs by the DC may well have contributed to the breakdown of the party system in 1993. As Schofield (1993) noted, the DC lost its core position after the 1992 election, and with loss of control, the corruption that was associated with ministerial manipulation may have contributed to the collapse of the system.

1.2.4 Political Economy

The chapters in Part IV of this volume focus, in varying degrees, on the application of formal models of social choice and voting, to the analysis of government policy making. Implicit in both Chapters 16 and 17 is the assumption that different groups in the society have conflicting preferences for government choice, and varying degrees of power. Instead of assuming, as in the voting models, that preferences are heterogeneous and that many different voting coalitions are possible, the models described in these two chapters essentially assume a situation with two groups. Chapter 16 by Potters and van Winden reviews various classes of models on the interaction between interest groups and government: one describes the influence that groups have on government; another uses campaign contributions as the mode of influence, while the information model concentrates on the strategic transfer of information between groups and government.

Rebecca Morton discusses and evaluates Rational Partisan Theory (RPT) in Chapter 17. In RPT, each party has a bliss point in a space of macroeconomic policies involving inflation and economic growth, and it is assumed implicitly that voters also have differing trade-offs between inflation and growth (or employment). Morton argues that it is crucial in these models to assume that there are random influences on voter preferences that cannot be predicted by parties or voters. It would seem that it is fundamental to these models to have a well-specified electoral model and to analyse more precisely the utility functions of the parties. For example, if we adopt the two party probabilistic model, then it would appear that parties would indeed tend to converge to a median voter position.

On the other hand, if parties do make a trade-off between their policy preferences and the electoral response to their declarations, then one might expect divergent party platforms (Cox 1984b). Of course, these inferences may only be valid in two party situations. RCT has made little effort to generalize the model to multiparty coalition situations, or to consider more carefully the basis of party motivations. It is evident that once an internally consistent model of electoral politics and party behavior is worked out, then this could be fruitfully applied to the analysis of macro-economic policy making.

The last two chapters of the volume present applications of the Condorcetian model, discussed above. As emphasized previously, making a choice between two different candidates or party platforms has many of the elements of choosing which of two hypotheses are true. Though each of the two parties, say D and R, propose different policies before an election, both will attempt to give plausible justification for their policies (based perhaps on both normative and efficiency reasons). The information received by a typical voter, i, say may be viewed as a message m_i. If m_i is far to the left then it would be reasonable for i to vote for D, and if m_i is to the right to vote for R.

Ladha, in Chapter 18, puts this in a simple context of deciding between two alternative hypotheses H_0, H_1, where "H_0" could be interpreted to mean that D offers "better" policy options. Ladha supposes that each i chooses a critical value κ_i, and selects H_0 (or votes for D) whenever $m_i \leq \kappa_i$, etc. Writing $\chi_i = 0$ or 1 for $i's$ voting choice, the majoritarian rule selects H_1 whenever $\sum \chi_i$ attains a majority. Ladha shows, under the assumption of voter independence, that the probability of "committing an error" approaches zero as the population size approaches infinity. Of course an alternative way to proceed is to perform the test using the sample mean $\frac{1}{n}\sum m_i = \overline{m}$. However in actual voting situations the two hypotheses compared by the individuals may be very different, so it would be difficult to use $\overline{m}$ to compare hypotheses. The Condorcetian technique, discussed above, is based instead on the expectation and distribution of $\overline{\chi} = \frac{1}{n}\sum \chi_i$ and may be thought of as a method for comparing hypotheses when there is uncertainty. Ladha's discussion suggests that voting may be a consistent technique for hypothesis testing under uncertainty.

Ladha and Miller in Chapter 19 examine the validity of the Jury Theorem under dependence. In other words, they consider the situation when $r_{ij} = Pr(\chi_i = 1; \chi_j = 1) \neq \pi_i \pi_j$ (where, as above, π_i is the probability that individual i makes the true choice, so $\pi_i = Pr(\chi_i = 1)$ and r_{ij} is the joint probability that both i and j make the correct choice). Let $\bar{r}$ be the average of r_{ij}. They show that, under certain conditions on $\bar{r}$, the probability, $\xi(n)$, that the majority makes the correct choice, exceeds $\bar{\pi}$ (the average of all π_i) and approaches 1 as $n \to \infty$. They give an example where adding an "uninformed" voter can increase $\xi(n)$. In their illustration, $\pi_1 = \pi_2 = .8$ and $r_{12} = .6$, so $\xi(2) = .6$ (since a majority requires two ayes). However, adding an informed voter with $\pi_3 = .4$ who is negatively correlated ($r_{13} = r_{12} = .2$) increases the "accuracy" of the group to $\xi(3) = 1$. No matter what signals the three individuals receive, if they vote on the basis of their signals, then two voters always choose the correct hypothesis. Ladha and Miller go on to consider situations where "political" factions are characterized by high inter-group correlations, and show that, other things being constant, social accuracy is maximized when factions are all of equal size. Consequently there is a correspondence between the fragmentation (Rae and Taylor 1970) of the faction structure and social accuracy. In a sense this inference supports the reasoning attributed to Madison in the previous discussion and contradicts the theoretical argument for a link between fragmentation and instability.

The discussion by Ladha and Miller suggests that in models of two party competition there may be a justification for using the expected vote $\bar{\pi}$ as a proxy for the probability, ξ, of winning. (See also Aranson, et al. 1974.) However, attempting to extend the argument to more than two hypotheses (or parties or candidates) must face the problem of cyclicity that Condorcet could not overcome. Clearly there is still much work to be done to integrate Condorcetian or probabilistic electoral models with those of party competition in coalitional situations, and to extend this framework to a fully developed theory that can relate factionalism to the "efficiency" of government.

The earlier work by Rae and Taylor (1970) provides an interesting empirical examination of Madison's thesis, by relating economic and political fragmentation to a measure of "tyranny". However their measure of "tyranny" is relative size of government and their finding of a negative correlation only hints at the complex interrelationships between economic diversity, fragmentation in beliefs, the electoral system, and government activity. Theoretical and empirical work of the kind described in this volume may lead, eventually, to a soundly based comparative political economy capable of addressing these questions.

References

Aranson, P., M. Hinich and P. Ordeshook. 1974. "Election Goals and Strategies: Equivalent and Non-equivalent Candidate Objectives," *American Political Science Review* 68: 135-152.

Arrow, K. J. 1951. *Social Choice and Individual Values*. New York: Wiley.

Arrow, K. and G. Debreu. 1954. "Existence of an Equilibrium for a Competitive Economy," *Econometrica* 22: 265-90.

Aumann, R. 1976. "Agreeing to Disagree," *Annals of Statistics* 4: 1236-39.

Austen-Smith, D. and J. Banks. 1988. "Elections, Coalitions and Legislative Outcomes," *American Political Science Review* 82: 405-422.

Badinter, E. and R. Badinter. 1988. *Condorcet: Un Intellectuel en politique.* Paris: Fayard.

Bailyn, B. 1993. *The Debate on the Constitution: Federalist and Antifederalist Speeches, Articles and Letters.* 2 volumes. New York: Viking.

Banks, J. 1994. "Singularity Theory and Core Existence in the Spatial Model," *Journal of Mathematical Economics* (forthcoming).

Bergstrom, T. 1975. "The Existence of Maximal Elements and Equilibria in the Absence of Transitivity." Typescript: Washington University.

Bergstrom, T. 1992. "When Non-transitive Relations Take Maxima and Competitive Equilibria Can't Be Beat," in *Economic Theory and International Trade,* W. Neuefeind and R. Riezman, eds. Berlin: Springer.

Black, D. 1948. "On the Rationality of Group Decision Making," *Journal of Political Economy* 56: 23-34.

Black, D. 1958. *The Theory of Committees and Elections.* Cambridge: Cambridge University Press.

Boland, P. J. 1989. "Majority Systems and the Condorcet Jury Theorem," *The Statistician* 38: 187-189.

Bordes, G., M. Le Breton, and M. Salles. 1992. "Gillies' and Miller's Subrelations of a Relation over an Infinite Set of Alternatives: General Results and Applications to Voting Games," *Mathematics of Operations Research* 17: 508-518.

Brown, D. 1973. "Acyclic Choice." Typescript: Yale University Press.

Chichilnisky, G. 1993. "Intersecting Families of Sets and the Topology of Cones in Economics," *Bulletin of the American Mathematical Society* 29: 189-207.

Chichilnisky, G. 1995. "Limited Arbitrage Is Necessary and Sufficient for the Existence of a Competitive Equilibrium with or without Short Sales," *Economic Theory* 5: 79-108.

Condorcet, M. J. A. N. de C., Marquis de. [1785] 1972. *Essai sur l'application de l'analyse à la probabilité des voix.* New York: Chelsea (orig. Paris: Imprimerie Royale).

Coughlin, P. J. 1992. *Probabilistic Voting Theory.* Cambridge: Cambridge University Press.

Cox, G. 1984a. "Non-collegial Simple Games and the Nowhere Denseness of the Set of Preference Profiles Having a Core," *Social Choice and Welfare* 1: 159-164.

Cox, G. 1984b. "An Expected Utility Model of Electoral Competition," *Quality and Quantity* 18: 337-349.

Downs, A. 1957. *An Economic Theory of Democracy.* New York: Harper and Row.

Eavey, C. 1991. "Patterns of Distribution in Spatial Games," *Rationality and Society* 3: 450-474.

Enelow, J. M. and M. J. Hinich. 1984. *The Spatial Theory of Voting: An Introduction.* Cambridge: Cambridge University Press.

Fan, K. 1961. "A Generalization of Tychonoff's Fixed Point Theorem," *Mathematische Annalen* 142: 305-310.

Fiorina, M. and C. Plott. 1978. "Committee Decisions under Majority Rule," *American Political Science Review* 72: 575-598.

Gale, D. and A. Mas-Colell. 1975. "A Short Proof of Existence of Equilibrium without Ordered Preferences," *Journal of Mathematical Economics* 2: 9-15.

Geanakoplos, J. and H. Polemarchakis. 1982. "We Can't Disagree Forever," *Journal of Economic Theory* 28: 192-200.

Grofman, B. and S. L. Feld. 1988. "Rousseau's General Will: A Condorcetian Perspective," *American Political Science Review* 82: 567-576.

Hammond, T. H. and G. Miller. 1987. "The Core of the Constitution," *American Political Science Review* 81: 1155-1174.

Hoffman, E. and C. Plott. 1983. "Pre-meeting Discussions and the Possibility of Coalition-Breaking Procedures in Majority Rule Committees," *Public Choice* 40: 21-39.

Kirman, A. and D. Sondermann. 1972. "Arrow's Impossibility Theorem, Many Agents and Invisible Dictators," *Journal of Economic Theory* 5: 267-278.

Kramer, G. 1973. "On a Class of Equilibrium Conditions for Majority Rule," *Econometrica* 41: 285-97.

Le Breton, M. 1987. "On the Core of Voting Games," *Social Choice and Welfare* 4: 295-305.

McKelvey, R. 1976. "Intransitivities in Multidimensional Voting Models and Some Implications for Agenda Control," *Journal of Economic Theory* 12: 472-482.

McKelvey, R. 1986. "Covering, Dominance and Institution-Free Properties of Social Choice," *American Journal of Political Science* 30: 283-314.

McKelvey, R. 1991. "An Experimental Test of a Stochastic Game Model of Committee Bargaining," in *Laboratory Research in Political Economy*, T. Palfrey, ed. Ann Arbor: Michigan University Press.

McKelvey, R. and T. Page. 1986. "Common Knowledge, Consensus, and Aggregate Information," *Econometrica* 54: 109-27.

McKelvey, R. and T. Palfrey. 1994. "Quantal Response Equilibria for Normal Form Games." Typescript: California Institute of Technology.

McKelvey, R. and N. Schofield. 1986. "Structural Instability of the Core," *Econometrica* 15: 179-88.

McKenzie, L. 1959. "On the Existence of General Equilibrium for a Competitive Economy," *Econometrica* 27: 54-71.

McLean, I. 1995. "The First Golden Age of Social Choice," in *Social Choice, Welfare and Ethics*, W. Barnett, H. Moulin, M. Salles and N. Schofield, eds. Cambridge: Cambridge University Press.

McLean, I. and R. Hewitt. 1994. *Condorcet: Foundations of Social Choice and Political Theory*. Adershot, England: Edward Elgar.

Moulin, H. 1980. "On Strategy-proofness and Single Peakedness," *Public Choice* 35: 437-55.

Nachbar, J. 1995. "Prediction, Optimization, and Rational Learning in Games." Typescript: Center in Political Economy, Washington University.

Nakamura, K. 1979. "The Vetoers in a Simple Game with Ordinal Preference," *International Journal of Game Theory* 8: 55-61.

Nash, J. F. 1951. "Non-Cooperative Games," *Annals of Mathematics.* 54: 289-295.

Nixon, D., D. Olomoki, N. Schofield, and I. Sened. 1995. "Multiparty Probabilistic Voting: An Application to the Knesset." Typescript: Center in Political Economy, Washington University.

Nyarko, Y. 1993. "Convergence in Economic Models with Bayesian Hierarchies of Beliefs." Typescript: New York University.

Plott, C. R. 1967. "A Notion of Equilibrium and its Possibility under Majority Rule," *American Economic Review* 57: 787-806.

Plott, C. R. 1973. "Path Independence, Rationality and Social Choice," *Econometrica* 41: 1075-1091.

Rae, D. 1969. "Decision Rules and Individual Values in Constitutional Choice," *American Political Science Review* 52: 349-366.

Rae, D. and M. Taylor. 1970. *The Analysis of Political Cleavages.* New Haven: Yale University Press.

Randall, W. S. 1993. *Thomas Jefferson: A Life.* New York: Holt.

Riker, W. 1962. *The Theory of Political Coalitions.* New Haven: Yale University Press.

Robertson, D. 1976. *A Theory of Party Competition.* London: Wiley.

Rubinstein, A. 1979. "A Note on the Nowhere Denseness of Societies Having an Equilibrium under Majority Rule," *Econometrica* 47: 511-514.

Saari, D. 1995. "The Generic Existence of a Core for q-rules." Typescript: Department of Mathematics, Northwestern University.

Savage, L. 1974. *The Foundations of Statistics.* New York: Dover.

Schofield, N. 1972. "Is Majority Rule Special?" in *Probability Models of Collective Decision Making*, R. Niemi and H. Weisberg, eds. Columbus, Ohio: Merrill.

Schofield, N. 1978a. "Instability of Simple Dynamic Games," *Review of Economic Studies* 45: 575-594.

Schofield, N. 1978b. "The Theory of Dynamic Games," in *Game Theory and Political Science*, P. C. Ordeshook, ed. New York: New York University Press.

Schofield, N. 1984. "Social Equilibrium and Cycles on Compact Sets," *Journal of Economic Theory* 33: 59-71.

Schofield, N. 1993. "Political Competition in Multiparty Coalition Governments," *European Journal of Political Research* 23: 1-33.

Schofield, N. 1995a. "The C^1-Topology on the Space of Preference Profiles and the Existence of a Continuous Preference Aggregator." Typescript: Center in Political Economy, Washington University.

Schofield, N. 1995b. "Existence of a Social Choice Functor," in *Social Choice, Welfare, and Ethics*, W. Barnett, H. Moulin, M. Salles and N. Schofield, eds. Cambridge: Cambridge University Press.

Smith, A. [1759] 1976. *The Theory of Moral Sentiments.* Oxford: Oxford University Press.

Smith, A. [1776] 1976. *An Inquiry into the Nature and Causes of the Wealth of Nations.* Oxford: Oxford University Press.

Sonnenschein, H. 1971. "Demand Theory without Transitive Preference with Applications to the Theory of Competitive Equilibrium," in *Preferences, Utility and Demand*, J. Chipman, L. Hurwicz, M. Richter and H. Sonnenschein, eds. New York: Harcourt, Brace, and Janovich.

Strnad, J. 1985. "The Structure of Continuous-Valued Netural Monotonic Social Functions," *Social Choice and Welfare* 2: 181-95.

Walker, M. 1977. "On the Existence of Maximal Elements," *Journal of Economic Theory* 16: 470-474.

Part I. SOCIAL CHOICE

2. An Introduction to Arrovian Social Welfare Functions on Economic and Political Domains

Michel Le Breton and John Weymark [1]

2.1 Introduction

A social welfare function assigns a social preference ordering to each admissible profile of individual preference orderings of a set of alternatives. Arrow (1963) required a social welfare function to satisfy the following list of axioms: *Weak Pareto* (if everyone strictly prefers one alternative to a second alternative, then so does society), *Binary Independence of Irrelevant Alternatives* (the social preference for a pair of alternatives depends only on the individual preferences for this pair), and *Nondictatorship* (nobody has his or her strict preferences always respected). Arrow's Theorem demonstrates that these axioms are inconsistent if the domain of admissible profiles of individual preference orderings is unrestricted and if there are at least three alternatives being ranked.[2]

This theorem has little direct relevance for economic problems. In economics, both the social alternatives and the individual preferences exhibit considerable structure. For example, alternatives could be allocations of private goods with individuals restricted to having selfish, continuous, monotonic, and convex preferences, or the alternatives could be vectors of public goods with individual preferences required to be continuous, monotonic, and convex. Similarly, in political science, voting models often assume that individuals have spatial preferences. In each of these examples, the domain of admissible profiles of individual preferences is restricted, in contrast to Arrow's Theorem in which it is assumed that the preference domain is unrestricted.

A preference domain for which a social welfare function exists that satisfies the three Arrow axioms is called *Arrow-consistent*. It is natural to enquire whether the preference domains encountered in economic and political problems are Arrow-consistent.

The first major result along these lines actually predates Arrow's contribution. We refer, of course, to Black's (1948) celebrated theorem about majority

---

[1] The authors would like to thank Ivan Alves and Jean Xie for preparing the diagrams.
[2] This version of Arrow's Theorem may be found in Chapter VIII of Arrow (1963). The original statement of the theorem in Arrow (1951) contains a minor error, a fact discovered by Blau (1957). Blau provided a correct statement of the impossibility theorem, but as noted by Arrow (1963), Blau's version of the theorem contains a redundant axiom.

rule. Black showed that majority rule yields social preferences which are orderings when the set of alternatives is a subset of the real line and there are an odd number of individuals with single-peaked preferences.[3] These structural restrictions on the set of alternatives and on the domain of preferences are satisfied in a number of political and economic applications, provided the set of alternatives is one-dimensional (such as the problem of a legislature choosing the amount of a single public good). It is not difficult to show that the method of majority rule satisfies all of the Arrow axioms on such domains.[4]

One of the innovative features of Arrow's (1951, 1963) monograph is that it shifted attention from the analysis of particular social aggregation procedures, such as majority rule, to the question of whether *any* social aggregation procedure can satisfy his set of *a priori* desirable principles. The fact that majority rule does not result in a social welfare function satisfying all of Arrow's axioms on a given restricted preference domain does not imply that the domain is Arrow-inconsistent; there may well exist some other social aggregation procedure which does satisfy the Arrow axioms on this domain. However, except for some brief remarks by Blau (1957), it was not until the late 1970's that a literature emerged which focused on the identification of preference domains which are either Arrow-consistent or Arrow-inconsistent. For public alternatives with every individual assumed to have the same set of admissible individual preferences, Kalai and Muller (1977) and Maskin (1979) showed that a preference domain is Arrow-consistent if and only if the corresponding two-person preference domain is Arrow-consistent. Further, they presented necessary and sufficient conditions for a domain to be Arrow-consistent. Analogous theorems for private alternatives with selfish preferences were established by Kalai and Ritz (1980). Unfortunately, these results were obtained with the maintained assumption that every individual exhibits a strict preference between any pair of alternatives.[5] As a consequence, these theorems are of limited applicability to economic and political problems when the alternatives include divisible goods.[6] For private alternatives, this limitation was overcome by Ritz (1983) who showed how the theorems in Kalai and Ritz (1980) may be modified to allow for indifference in preference. Ritz also weakened the assumption that the admissible preferences and sets of alternatives are the same for each individual. Ritz (1985) later extended his earlier work by considering a model in which there are both public and private alternatives. (This model can be specialized so that there are only public or only private alternatives.) As in his earlier article, indifference in preference was permitted. However, Ritz' characterization of Arrow-consistent domains for this model only covers

---

[3] See Arrow (1951, 1963) for a formal statement of Black's Theorem.

[4] For one-dimensional sets of alternatives, there is now a rather large literature concerned with developing restrictions on the preference domain for which majority rule has nice properties. See Gaertner (1991) or Sen (1970) for discussions of this literature.

[5] Extensions of these results may be found in Blair and Muller (1983) and Kim and Roush (1980, 1981).

[6] In the articles being discussed, there is no *a priori* structure placed on the set of alternatives except in the private alternatives case, where it is assumed that the set of social alternatives is the Cartesian product of the alternatives available to each individual. In particular, alternatives are not required to be vectors in a Euclidean space.

the case of two individuals. A brief survey of this literature may be found in Gaertner (1991).[7]

Simultaneous with these developments, a related literature appeared which had less ambitious objectives. Instead of attempting to completely characterize the preference domains which are Arrow-consistent given some background assumptions (*e.g.*, that there are private alternatives and selfish preferences), in this literature the objective was to develop conditions which are either sufficient or necessary (but not necessarily both) for a preference domain to be identified as either Arrow-inconsistent or Arrow-consistent. In addition, the Arrow-consistency of a number of domains found in economic and political applications was investigated. The models in this literature permit indifference in preference. The purpose of this article is to provide an introduction to this literature.

In Section 2.2, we consider the case in which alternatives are purely public. We begin Section 2.2 with a review of the pathbreaking contribution of Kalai, Muller, and Satterthwaite (1979). This article introduced a sufficient condition for a preference domain to be Arrow-inconsistent when individuals are required to have the same set of admissible preferences. The method of proof used to establish this result has been used extensively in the subsequent literature, so we examine this proof in detail. We also show that the Kalai-Muller-Satterthwaite condition is satisfied in a number of economic and political problems. In particular, we discuss Kalai, Muller, and Satterthwaite's finding that this condition is satisfied if there are two or more divisible public goods and individuals can have any continuous, strictly monotonic, and convex preference ordering. Then we show that the Kalai-Muller-Satterthwaite condition can be used to provide an alternative proof of Border's (1984) theorem that the domain of spatial preferences is Arrow-inconsistent when there are at least two divisible public alternatives. Applications of the Kalai-Muller-Satterthwaite condition to a problem studied by Le Breton (1986) in which the preferences satisfy the expected utility hypothesis and to the problem of aggregating inequality judgements studied by Le Breton and Trannoy (1987) are also considered. To conclude this section, we briefly consider the implications of dropping the assumption that everyone has the same set of admissible preferences.

In Section 2.3, we consider the case in which alternatives are purely private and individuals have selfish preferences. In this section, we review the main results in Bordes and Le Breton (1989). They developed a refinement of the Kalai-Muller-Satterthwaite condition which is sufficient for a private alternative domain to be Arrow-inconsistent. We use the Bordes-Le Breton condition to provide an alternative demonstration of the Border (1983) - Maskin (1976) theorem that the domain of selfish, continuous, monotonic, and convex preferences for private goods is Arrow-inconsistent if each individual consumption set is a positive orthant. We also discuss Border's finding that this preference domain is Arrow-consistent if each consumption set is some nonnegative

---

[7] The implications of these results for strategic social choice have also been considered in most of the articles discussed in this paragraph.

orthant.[8]

There are numerous extensions to the results we discuss in Sections 2.2 and 2.3. In Section 2.4, we provide a brief guide to this literature.

In discussing the various economic and political examples, we do not rigorously prove whether the preference domain is Arrow-inconsistent or not. Instead, we limit ourselves to heuristic arguments which give the main intuition of a formal proof. However, complete proofs are provided for all of the general results. The proofs of the propositions in Section 2.3 are, unfortunately, somewhat involved. Readers not interested in the complete technical details may safely omit reading these proofs, as we also set out the main arguments informally.

Before proceeding, it is worth stressing that our discussion is restricted to social welfare functions. We do not consider the social correspondence formulation of nonstrategic social choice nor do we consider strategic social choice.[9] On restricted domains, these topics have recently become active areas of research.[10]

2.2 Public Alternatives

We consider a finite set of individuals $N := \{1, \ldots, n\}$ with $n \geq 2$ and a universal set of alternatives X. $\mathcal{R}$ is the set of all (weak) orderings of X; i.e., $\mathcal{R}$ is the set of all reflexive, complete, and transitive binary relations on X. For each ordering R in $\mathcal{R}$, strict preference P and indifference I are defined in the usual way: (a) xPy iff xRy and not (yRx) and (b) xIy iff xRy and yRx. Each person has a preference ordering $R_i \in \mathcal{R}$ of X. A preference profile $\mathbf{R} = (R_1, \ldots, R_n)$ is an n-tuple of individual preference orderings of X. The collection of admissible profiles D, a nonempty subset of $\mathcal{R}^n$, is called the *preference domain*. Collective decisions are only required for profiles in the preference domain.

A *social welfare function* on D is a mapping $\sigma: D \to \mathcal{R}$ which assigns a social ordering $\sigma(\mathbf{R})$ of X to each admissible profile $\mathbf{R}$. In other words, for each admissible profile of individual orderings of the alternatives in X, there is a corresponding social preference ordering. To simplify the notation, henceforth $\sigma(\mathbf{R})$ is denoted as R.

Arrow's (1963) Theorem shows that it is impossible for a social welfare function to satisfy the following list of *a priori* desirable properties.

UNRESTRICTED PREFERENCE DOMAIN: $D = \mathcal{R}^n$.

---

[8] The basic idea underlying the example Border used to demonstrate this result appeared in an example in Blau (1957), a fact duly acknowledged by Border.

[9] A social choice correspondence assigns a subset of the feasible set of alternatives to each admissible preference profile and admissible feasible set.

[10] A recent article by Barberà and Peleg (1990) has been particularly influential in stimulating research on strategic social choice with restricted domains. In this article, the authors introduced a new technique for proving strategic impossibility theorems, a technique which can accommodate continuous preferences.

BINARY INDEPENDENCE OF IRRELEVANT ALTERNATIVES: *For all $x, y \in X$ and for all $\mathbf{R}^1, \mathbf{R}^2 \in D$, if $\mathbf{R}^1$ and $\mathbf{R}^2$ coincide on $\{x, y\}$, then R^1 and R^2 coincide on $\{x, y\}$.*

WEAK PARETO: *For all $x, y \in X$ and for all $\mathbf{R} \in D$, if $x P_i y$ for all $i \in N$, then $x P y$.*

NONDICTATORSHIP: *There is no individual $d \in N$ such that for all $x, y \in X$ and all $\mathbf{R} \in D$; if $x P_d y$, then $x P y$.*

A social welfare function is *dictatorial* if it does not satisfy Nondictatorship. Note that for a dictatorial social welfare function only the dictator's strict preferences need be respected. These axioms are well-known and need no discussion here. Theorem 1 provides a formal statement of Arrow's Theorem.

Theorem 1: *If $|X| \geq 3$, there is no social welfare function with an Unrestricted Preference Domain which satisfies Binary Independence of Irrelevant Alternatives, Weak Pareto, and Nondictatorship.*[11]

As noted in the introduction, an *Arrow-consistent domain* is a preference domain for which there exists a social welfare function satisfying Binary Independence of Irrelevant Alternatives, Weak Pareto, and Nondictatorship.[12] Analogously, if no social welfare function exists for which these three axioms are satisfied, then the preference domain is *Arrow-inconsistent*.

As a *maintained assumption*, we assume throughout this discussion that the set of admissible preference orderings of any one individual is independent of the preferences of the other individuals. That means that the preference domain can be expressed as the product of *individual preference domains* $D_i \subseteq \mathcal{R}$, $i \in N$.

CARTESIAN PREFERENCE DOMAIN: $D = \prod_{i=1}^{n} D_i$, *where $D_i \subseteq \mathcal{R}$ for all $i \in N$.*

If each person has the same set of admissible preferences, we say that there is a *common preference domain*.

COMMON PREFERENCE DOMAIN: *D is a Cartesian preference domain with $D_i = D_j$ for all $i, j \in N$.*

When the preference domain is common, we let D_* denote the individual

---

[11] There are many proofs of Arrow's Theorem in the literature. A standard proof may be found in Sen (1970). The proof in Blackorby, Donaldson and Weymark (1990) emphasizes the relationship between Arrow's theorem and traditional welfare economics.

[12] This terminology is due to Redekop (1991). This definition does not explicitly mention the set of alternatives X being considered. However, X can always be inferred from knowledge of the preference domain.

preference domain. In other words, we have $D_* = D_i$ for all $i \in N$. For a social welfare function σ on a common preference domain, although each person's preferences are required to be in D_*, the social preferences are merely required to be in $\mathcal{R}$.

Before considering further restrictions on the preference domain, we need to introduce some additional notation. Given a subset A of X, $\mathcal{R}|_A$ denotes the restriction of $\mathcal{R}$ to A, $D|_A$ denotes the restriction of D to A, and $\sigma|_A$ denotes the restriction of F to A. More precisely, $\sigma|_A$ is the social welfare function with domain D and range $\mathcal{R}|_A$ defined by $\sigma|_A(\mathbf{R}) := \sigma(\mathbf{R})|_A$.

In the theorems and examples we consider, it is necessary to determine how rich the preference domain is when restricted to certain subsets of X. The following kinds of sets of alternatives are used extensively.

TRIVIAL SUBSET: *A subset A of X is trivial with respect to D_i if $|D_i|_A| = 1$. The set A is trivial with respect to D if there is some $i \in N$ such that A is trivial with respect to D_i.*

TRIVIAL PAIR: *A subset A of X is a trivial pair with respect to D_i (resp. D) if it is a trivial subset with respect to D_i (resp. D) and $|A| = 2$.*

A subset is trivial (with respect to D) if there is some individual who has only one admissible preference ordering over this set of alternatives. A trivial pair is a trivial subset containing only two alternatives. Sets which are not trivial are called *nontrivial*. Note that a nontrival set with respect to D must be nontrivial for all individuals.

FREE SUBSET: *A subset A of X is free with respect to D_i if $D_i|_A = \mathcal{R}|_A$. The set A is free with respect to D if it is free with respect to D_i for all $i \in N$.*

FREE TRIPLE: *A subset of X is a free triple with respect to D_i (resp. D) if it is a free subset with respect to D_i (resp. D) and $|A| = 3$.*

A subset is free (with respect to D) if everyone's preferences are unrestricted on this set of alternatives. A free triple is a free subset containing three alternatives. A free subset (containing more than one alternative) is obviously nontrivial. However, a nontrivial set need not be free.

STRONG CONNECTION: *Two pairs A and B contained in X are strongly connected with respect to D_i (resp. D) if $A \cup B$ is a free triple with respect to D_i (resp. D).*

CONNECTION: *Two pairs A and B contained in X are connected with respect to D_i (resp. D) if there exists a finite sequence of pairs contained in X, $A_1, \ldots, A_r$, with $A_1 = A$ and $A_r = B$ such that A_j and A_{j+1} are strongly connected with respect to D_i (resp. D) for all $j = 1, \ldots, r-1$.*

In the subsequent discussion, when we refer to two pairs as being strongly connected or connected, we are implicitly assuming that this is relative to D. Note that two pairs which are strongly connected have exactly one alternative in common. For pairs that are strongly connected, the preference domain is unrestricted on their union. If two pairs of alternatives are connected, the preference domain need not be unrestricted on their union; it is only necessary that there exist a way to link the pairs together so that each adjacent pair in the chain is strongly connected. In general, two pairs A and B may be connected with respect to D_i for all $i \in N$ without being connected because there is not a *single* sequence of pairs which connects the pairs A and B in all of the individual preference domains D_i; *i.e.*, it may only be possible to connect A and B in i and j's preference domains using different intermediate pairs of alternatives. However, if there is a common preference domain, because the preference domain is Cartesian, any pairs which are connected (strongly connected) for any individual are obviously connected (strongly connected) for D.

Given a subset A of X, it follows that $\sigma|_A$ is a function on $D|_A$ if Binary Independence of Irrelevant Alternatives is satisfied. This insight plays a central role in the results discussed in this article. It implies that the structure of a social welfare function on A just depends on the restriction of the preference domain to A. In particular, with Weak Pareto and Binary Independence of Irrelevant Alternatives, if $D|_A = \mathcal{R}^n|_A$ and $|A| \geq 3$, then Theorem 1 (Arrow's Theorem) implies that $\sigma|_A$ is dictatorial; *i.e.*, there exists a dictator on A. Naturally, (when Weak Pareto and Binary Independence of Irrelevant Alternatives are satisfied) we may use the same line of reasoning for any other set of alternatives B to conclude that there is a dictator on B if $D|_B = \mathcal{R}^n|_B$ and $|B| \geq 3$. However, in general, the dictator on B need not be the same as the dictator on A. The following example, which appears in Fishburn (1976) and in Kalai, Muller, and Satterthwaite (1979), illustrates this point.

EXAMPLE 1: Let $N = \{1, 2\}$ and $X = \{x_1, x_2, x_3, x_4, x_5, x_6\}$. Let D be a common preference domain with $D_* = \{R \in \mathcal{R} \mid x_i P x_j$ for all $i = 1, 2, 3$ and for all $j = 4, 5, 6\}$. In this example, $\{x_1, x_2, x_3\}$ and $\{x_4, x_5, x_6\}$ are free triples. Hence, if σ is a social welfare function on D satisfying Binary Independence of Irrelevant Alternatives and Weak Pareto, there must exist a dictator on each of these free triples. However, the function σ defined by setting:

xRy iff xR_1y for $x, y \in \{x_1, x_2, x_3\}$,
xRy iff xR_2y for $x, y \in \{x_4, x_5, x_6\}$, and
xPy if $x \in \{x_1, x_2, x_3\}$ and $y \in \{x_4, x_5, x_6\}$

satisfies Binary Independence of Irrelevant Alternatives and Weak Pareto, but it is not dictatorial.

Because the domain in Example 1 is Arrow-consistent, one might conjecture that any smaller preference domain is Arrow-consistent as well. However, this conjecture is not correct, as Example 2 demonstrates.

EXAMPLE 2: Let $N = \{1,2\}$ and $X = \{x_1, x_2, x_3, x_4, x_5, x_6\}$. Let D be a common preference domain with $D_* = \{R \in \mathcal{R} \mid (a)\ x_i P x_j$ for all $i = 1,2,3$ and for all $j = 4,5,6$, (b) $x_4 P x_5$, and (c) $x_5 P x_6\}$. In this example, $\{x_1, x_2, x_3\}$ is the only free triple. By Arrow's Theorem, if σ is a social welfare function on D satisfying Binary Independence of Irrelevant Alternatives and Weak Pareto, then there is a dictator d on this triple. For any pair which is not a subset of $\{x_1, x_2, x_3\}$, everyone has the same strict preference, so by Weak Pareto everyone is dictatorial on these pairs. Hence, d is a dictator on X, and D is Arrow-inconsistent. However, the preference domain considered in Example 1 is a superset of D, and it is Arrow-consistent.[13]

For the set of alternatives considered in these two examples, the preference domain in Example 2 is a subset of the preference domain in Example 1 which, in turn, is a subset of the unrestricted preference domain $\mathcal{R}^n$. The first and third of these domains are Arrow-inconsistent, while the second is Arrow-consistent. In other words, enlarging an Arrow-inconsistent preference domain need not preserve the inconsistency and shrinking an Arrow-consistent preference domain need not preserve the consistency.

The reason why there is no dictator in Example 1 is that no pair of alternatives from either of the free triples is connected to any of the pairs contained in the other free triple. Connectedness is a common feature of the preference domains found in a number of economic and political models. When all nontrivial pairs are connected, there exists what Kalai, Muller, and Satterthwaite (1979) have called a *saturating preference domain*.

SATURATING PREFERENCE DOMAIN: *An individual preference domain D_i (resp. a preference domain D) is saturating iff (a) there exist at least two nontrivial pairs with respect to D_i (resp. D), and (b) any two nontrivial pairs are connected with respect to D_i (resp. D).*

The definition of a saturating preference domain used by Kalai, Muller, and Satterthwaite (1979) assumes that the preference domain is common. In generalizing their definition to an arbitrary Cartesian preference domain, we require all nontrivial pairs to be connected, rather than merely requiring each individual preference domain to be saturating. In general, our definition of a saturating preference domain is not equivalent to the requirement that each of the individual preference domains is saturating; as noted earlier, in the latter case, nontrivial pairs for different individuals may be connected using different sequences of pairs of alternatives. However, if there is a common preference domain, then our definition of a saturating preference domain is obviously equivalent to requiring the common individual preference domain D_* to be saturating.

The preference domain introduced in Example 2 is a common saturating preference domain. An unrestricted preference domain is one as well. In

---

[13] This example is taken from Kalai, Muller, and Satterthwaite (1979).

Michel Le Breton and John Weymark 33

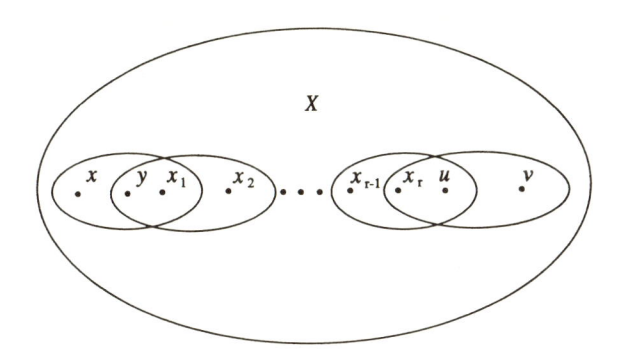

Figure 1. A saturating preference domain of free triples connected by the sequence $\{x, y, x_1\}, \{y, x_1, x_2\}, \ldots, \{x_r, u, v\}$.

fact, any preference domain, whether common or not, for which every triple is free must be saturating. Clearly, if every triple is free, then every pair is nontrivial. To show that any two pairs are connected is simple. Consider two pairs of alternatives $\{x, y\}$ and $\{u, v\}$ with $\{x, y\} \neq \{u, v\}$. For concreteness, suppose that $u \notin \{x, y\}$. Because every triple is free, these sets are connected by the pair $\{y, u\}$. It is also easy to verify that for any saturating preference domain, a nontrivial pair is also a free pair and it belongs to a free triple.[14]

For common saturating preference domains, Kalai, Muller, and Satterthwaite (1979) established the following key result.

Theorem 2: *If a social welfare function σ is defined on a common saturating preference domain and satisfies Binary Independence of Irrelevant Alternatives and Weak Pareto, then σ is dictatorial.*

Proof: By the definition of a saturating preference domain, there are at least two nontrivial pairs. Let $\{x, y\}$ and $\{u, v\}$ be any two such pairs of alternatives. Again by the definition of a saturating preference domain, these pairs are connected; *i.e.*, there exists a finite sequence of pairs of alternatives, say $\{x_1, x_2\}, \{x_2, x_3\}, \ldots, \{x_{r-1}, x_r\}$ such that $\{x, y, x_1\}, \{y, x_1, x_2\}, \{x_1, x_2, x_3\}$, $\ldots, \{x_{r-1}, x_r, u\}$, and $\{x_r, u, v\}$ are free triples. This sequence is illustrated in Figure 1.

By Arrow's Theorem (Proposition 1), there is a dictator on each of these free triples. Consider the first two free triples in this sequence. They have the pair $\{y, x_1\}$ in common. As a consequence, the dictator must be the same for both of these two free triples. By a similar reasoning, we can conclude that each adjacent pair of free triples in the sequence has a common dictator. Thus, there is a dictator on the set $\{x, y, x_1, \ldots, x_r, u, v\}$. Any other pair of nontrivial alternatives must be connected to $\{x, y\}$ (and to $\{u, v\}$). It then

---

[14] The statements in this paragraph are also valid for individual preference domains.

follows from the preceding argument that there is a single dictator on the set of all nontrivial pairs. Because there is a common preference domain, everyone has the same preferences on any trivial pair. Weak Pareto then implies that everyone is a dictator on the trivial pairs. Thus, there is a dictator on all of X.   Q.E.D.

This method of proof originated with Kalai, Muller, and Satterthwaite (1979) and variants of this proof have been used extensively to establish impossibility theorems on economic and political domains. This proof technique is now known as the "local" approach. The reason for this terminology is that the proof consists of first showing that there is a local dictator on a free triple of alternatives and then showing that this local dictator can be transformed into a global dictator (on the nontrivial pairs) by the connectedness implied by the assumptions on the preference domain.

In terms of applications with common preference domains, the problem remains of determining whether the preference domain is saturating or not. There are three main steps in this identification process: (1) identifying the nontrivial pairs, (2) identifying the free triples, and (3) determining how to connect the nontrivial pairs with free triples.[15] In practice, this last step is often the hardest, but in many interesting problems it is still relatively simple.

We now illustrate this procedure with some examples of common saturating preference domains. In these examples, the universal set of alternatives X is a connected subset of the m-dimensional Euclidean space $\Re^m$.[16]

EXAMPLE 3: Let X be any connected subset of $\Re^m$.[17] A preference ordering $R \in \mathcal{R}$ is *continuous* if for all $x \in X$, the sets $\{y \in X \mid yRx\}$ and $\{y \in X \mid xRy\}$ are both closed. Let D_* be the set of continuous preferences in $\mathcal{R}$. It is rather straightforward to show [for example, see Campbell (1992, Chapter 8)] that every triple is free. But we have already seen that if every triple is free, then the preference domain is saturating.

EXAMPLE 4: Before presenting the details of this example, we need a few more definitions. Suppose X is a connected subset of $\Re^m$. A preference ordering $R \in \mathcal{R}$ is *monotone* (resp. *strictly monotone*) if for all $x, y \in X$ such that $x >> y$ (resp. $x > y$), we have xPy. A preference ordering $R \in \mathcal{R}$ is *convex* if for all $x \in X$, the set $\{y \in X \mid yRx\}$ is convex.[18]

Now we turn to our example. Let X be $\Re^m_+$ with $m \geq 2$ and let D_* be the set of continuous, strictly monotonic, and convex preferences in $\mathcal{R}$.[19] In this

---

[15] This is the procedure used earlier to show that a preference domain is saturating if every triple is free.

[16] We let $\Re^m_+$ denote the nonnegative orthant and $\Re^m_{++}$ denote the positive orthant.

[17] In this example, X could be an arbitrary metric space instead of a Euclidean space.

[18] We use the following vector notation: (a) $x \geq y$ means $x_i \geq y_i$ for all $i = 1, \ldots, m$, (b) $x > y$ means $x_i \geq y_i$ for all $i = 1, \ldots, m$ with strict inequality for some i, and (c) $x >> y$ means $x_i > y_i$ for all $i = 1, \ldots, m$.

[19] If $m = 1$, there is only one possible individual preference ordering. Weak Pareto then makes everyone a dictator. Nondictatorship is clearly not appropriate on such a degenerate preference domain.

Michel Le Breton and John Weymark

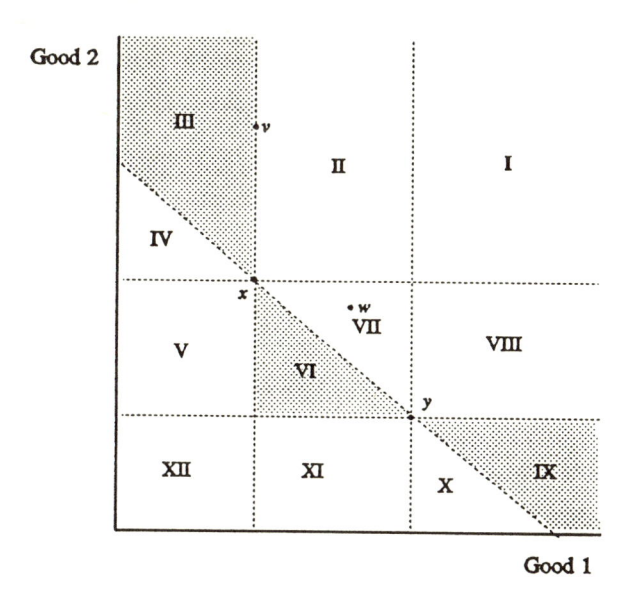

Figure 2. The shaded regions locate alternative spaces that are both monotonic and convex with respect to the indifference set, $\{x, y\}$. Regions I, II, V, VIII, XI, and XII are not monotonic and regions IV, VII, and X are not convex with respect to the pair $\{x, y\}$.

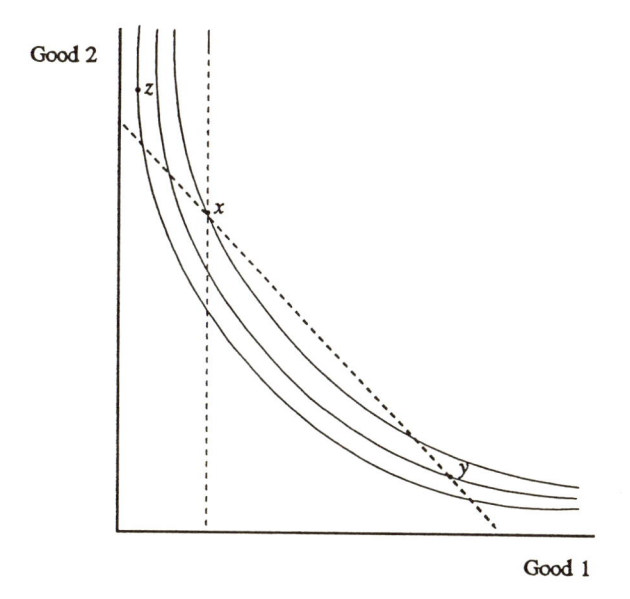

Figure 3. Preference ordering: $xPyPz$.

example, an alternative can be interpreted as being a vector of m public goods, with the individual preferences assumed to satisfy the usual regularity conditions found in microeconomic theory. Kalai, Muller, and Satterthwaite (1979) demonstrated that this preference domain is saturating. We sketch a proof for the case of $m = 2$.[20]

(1) First we identify the nontrivial pairs. Strict monotonicity of preference implies that any pair of alternatives $\{x, y\}$ with $x > y$ must be a trivial pair. It is easy to verify that if neither $x > y$ nor $y > x$ holds, then $\{x, y\}$ is nontrivial. Simple geometry can be used to confirm this fact. For example, the pair $\{x, y\}$ shown in Figure 2 is nontrivial.[21]

(2) We now identify the free triples. Consider the nontrivial pair $\{x, y\}$ shown in Figure 2. It is easy to check that $\{x, y, z\}$ is a free triple if and only if z is in one of the open regions marked III, VI, and IX. (If x is on the vertical axis, there is no region III. Analogously, if y is on the horizontal axis, there is no region IX.) Now consider the free triple $A = \{x, y, z\}$ shown in Figure 3. There are thirteen (weak) orderings of A. Suppose we want to confirm that there is an admissible preference ordering with xPy and yPz. In this case, using a preference ordering with indifference curves similar to those shown in Figure 3 will do. It is straightforward to check that for any of the other twelve orderings of A, there is an ordering R in D_* with $\mathcal{R}|_A$ coinciding with the prespecified ordering of $\{x, y, z\}$. Strict monotonicity prevents any alternative in the regions marked I, II, V, VIII, XI, and XII from being part of a free triple with x and y. Also requiring preferences to be convex precludes any alternative in the regions marked IV, VII, and X from being part of a free triple with x and y. For example, consider the w shown in Figure 2 and suppose we want to have xIy and yPw. This is obviously impossible with strictly monotonic, convex preferences, so $\{w, x, y\}$ is not a free triple.

(3) We now show how to connect nontrivial pairs. Consider the two nontrivial pairs $\{x, y\}$ and $\{u, v\}$ shown in Figure 4. All four of these alternatives have been chosen to be in the positive orthant. We introduce two new alternatives w and z, with w lying on the vertical axis and z lying on the horizontal axis. By choosing these points to be sufficiently far from the origin, the preceding argument shows that $\{u, v, z\}, \{v, z, w\}, \{z, w, x\}$, and $\{w, x, y\}$ are free triples. Thus, by simply considering the two additional alternatives w and z, we are able to connect $\{u, v\}$ with $\{x, y\}$ using the sequence of nontrivial pairs $\{u, v\}, \{v, z\}, \{z, w\}, \{w, x\}$, and $\{x, y\}$. When either of the nontrivial pairs $\{x, y\}$ or $\{u, v\}$ has an element on one of the axes, the connection is not so easy. First, such a nontrivial pair must be connected to a nontrivial pair in the interior of X and then the argument proceeds as above.

---

[20] Our discussion is very informal. See Kalai, Muller, and Satterthwaite (1979) for a rigorous treatment. Our sketch of the two-dimensional proof makes use of the essential ideas underlying a full m-dimensional proof.

[21] Note that if D_* includes all continuous, monotone, and convex preference orderings, i.e., strict monotonicity is relaxed to monotonicity, a pair such as $\{v, x\}$ in Figure 2 is no longer trivial.

EXAMPLE 5: To state this example, we need one more definition. Suppose X is a subset of $\Re^m$. A preference ordering $R \in \mathcal{R}$ is *linear* if there exists a $\pi \in \Re^m$ such that for all $x, y \in X, xRy$ iff $\pi x \geq \pi y$.[22]

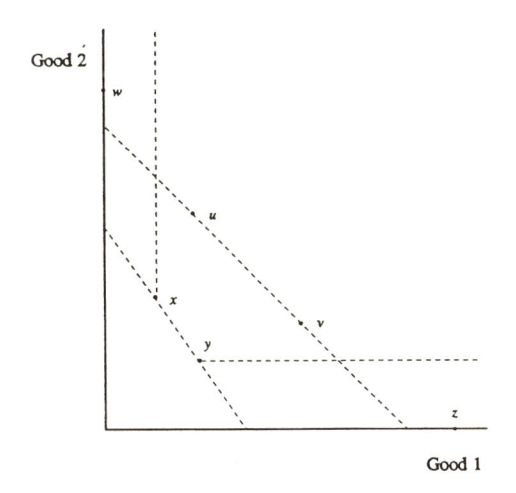

Figure 4. **Non-trivial pairs $\{u, v\}$ and $\{x, y\}$ connected by the sequence:** $\{u, v\}, \{v, z\}, \{z, w\}, \{w, x\}$ **and** $\{x, y\}$.

As our example, we let X be $\Re^m_+$ with $m \geq 3$ and D_* be the set of continuous, strictly monotonic, and linear preferences in $\mathcal{R}$. Kalai, Muller, and Satterthwaite (1979) have shown that this preference domain is saturating. We refer the reader to their article for details. In fact, Kalai, Muller, and Satterthwaite used linear preferences to perform the connection operations in their proof that the preference domain in the previous example is saturating when $m \geq 3$.

The assumption that $m \geq 3$ is essential. Kalai, Muller, and Satterthwaite (1979) showed that if $m = 2$, the preference domain considered in this example is Arrow-consistent, and, hence, it is not saturating.[23] Kalai, Muller, and Satterthwaite's proof of this result is constructive. Their social welfare function is defined as follows: for each profile of preferences in the domain, the social preference is set equal to the preference of the individual whose indifference curves have the median slope.[24]

---

[22] Note that a linear preference ordering is continuous and has hyperplanes (linear surfaces) for indifference contours. Unfortunately, the term *linear preference ordering* is also used in the literature to refer to an ordering for which no two distinct alternatives are indifferent.

[23] With a (strictly) monotone, linear preference ordering, the triple $\{x, y, z\}$ shown in Figure 3 is not free, as it is not possible to have all three elements of the triple indifferent to each other.

[24] Kalai, Muller, and Satterthwaite's (1979) discussion of the two-dimensional linear case is somewhat problematic. If there are an even number of individuals, their social welfare function is not well-defined as, typically, there are two median slopes. If the slope of the social indifference curves is always set equal to, say, the smallest median slope, an Arrow-consistent social welfare function is obtained. Other tie-breaking rules may not satisfy Binary Independence of Irrelevant Alternatives. See Bossert and Weymark (1993) for a

EXAMPLE 6: We let X be the $(m-1)$-dimensional unit simplex

$$S^{m-1} := \{x \in \Re_+^m \mid \sum_{i=1}^{m} x_i = 1\}$$

and we let D_* be the set of strictly monotonic, linear preference orderings in $\mathcal{R}$. The set X can be interpreted as being the set of lotteries over m outcomes or prizes; *i.e.*, an alternative x is a probability vector with x_i being the probability of obtaining the ith prize. The set of preferences D_* can then be interpreted as being the set of von Neumann-Morgenstern (1947) preferences. The vector π which characterizes the linear preference ordering R can be interpreted as a vector of von Neumann-Morgenstern (vNM) utilities for the m prizes; π_i is the vNM-utility of the ith prize. With this interpretation, xRy iff the expected utility of the lottery x is bigger than or equal to the expected utility of the lottery y. For $m \geq 3$, Le Breton (1986) has shown that this preference domain is saturating.[25] We outline the proof for the $m = 3$ case.[26]

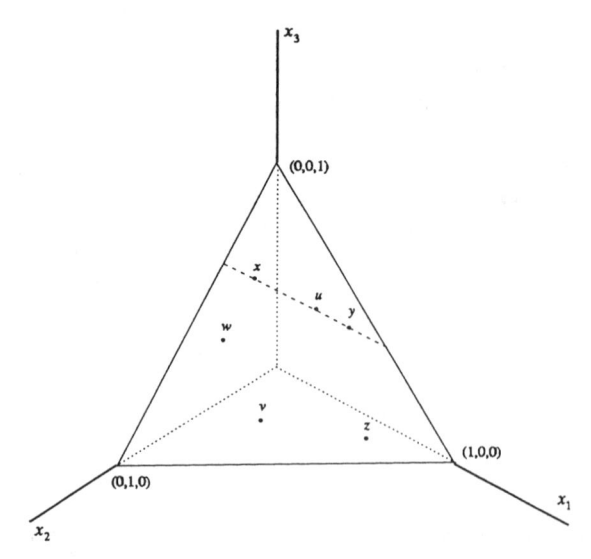

Figure 5. The preference set $\{xIyPz\}$ is a free triple, while the colinear (indifference) set $\{xIyIu\}$ is not.

---

detailed discussion of this two-dimensional problem. Kalai, Muller, and Satterthwaite's analysis of this case is based, in part, on Nitzan (1976).

[25] On a simplex, the assumption that preferences are strictly monotone is vacuous. In contrast, on the nonnegative orthant, strict monotonicity places considerable structure on the preferences. These facts help explain why the set of strictly monotone, linear preferences is saturating when the set of alternatives is the two-dimensional simplex, but it is not saturating when the set of alternatives is the two-dimensional nonnegative orthant.

[26] Again, the argument is easily extended to higher dimensions. When $m = 2$, each person has only three possible preference orderings.

(1) It is obvious that every pair is nontrivial.

(2) A triple $\{x, y, z\}$ is free if and only if its three elements are not colinear. For example, $\{x, y, z\}$ in Figure 5 is a free triple. If, for example, we want to find a linear preference ordering which has zPx and xIy, all of the indifference curves will be parallel to the dashed line through x and y with $(0, 1, 0)$ being the most preferred alternative in X. The other twelve possibilities are easy to check.[27] A colinear triple such as $\{u, x, y\}$ is not free; with linear preferences, if xIy, we must also have uIy.

(3) We now show how to connect nontrivial pairs. Consider the two pairs $\{x, y\}$ and $\{u, v\}$ shown in Figure 5. To make things interesting, we have chosen u so that it is colinear with x and y. It is clear that we can always choose two points w and z in X so that each of the following triples consists of points which are not colinear: $\{x, y, z\}, \{y, z, w\}, \{z, w, u\}$, and $\{w, u, v\}$. Figure 5 illustrates this construction. We connect $\{u, v\}$ with $\{x, y\}$ using the sequence of nontrivial pairs $\{x, y\}, \{y, z\}, \{z, w\}, \{w, u\}$, and $\{u, v\}$. Thus, we are able to connect the two nontrivial pairs $\{x, y\}$ and $\{u, v\}$ using only two additional alternatives, and this is the case even if any of the original alternatives lies on the boundary of X.

EXAMPLE 7: Suppose X is a connected subset of $\Re^m$. A preference ordering $R \in \mathcal{R}$ is *spatial* if there exists a point $\beta \in X$ such that for all $x, y \in X$, xRy iff $\|x - \beta\| \leq \|y - \beta\|$ where $\|\cdot\|$ denotes the Euclidean norm on X. The point β is known as an *ideal* or *bliss* point; it is a point of global satiation. With a spatial preference, alternatives are ranked by their Euclidean distance from the ideal point. Spatial preferences are used extensively by political scientists in formal voting models. In these applications, X is referred to as an *issue space*. The coordinates of X might, for example, measure the budgets for different categories of public expenditure (police, garbage collection, *etc.*) with voters assumed to have spatial preferences. Spatial preferences are also found in some economic models of public good provision. In these applications, the presence of a satiation point arises because attention is restricted to allocations satisfying a budget constraint. For introductions to spatial models, see Ordeshook (1986) or Enelow and Hinich (1984).[28]

For our example, we let $X = \Re^m$ and let D_* be the set of spatial preference orderings in $\mathcal{R}$.[29] Border (1984) has shown that Arrow's axioms are inconsistent on this preference domain if $m \geq 2$. However, Border's proof of this result is long and complicated. An alternative way of establishing Border's theorem is to first show that this preference domain is saturating. The impossibility theorem then follows from Theorem 2. This method of proof is

---

[27] If we want to have all three elements of the triple $\{x, y, z\}$ indifferent to each other, then there must be universal indifference over all lotteries in X.

[28] More precisely, what we are calling a spatial preferences is a *Euclidean* or *Type I* spatial preference. More generally, spatial preferences are convex preferences with a point of global satiation. In some applications, it is more natural to use some or all of this larger class of preferences.

[29] It is probably more realistic to let X be the nonnegative orthant. Choosing X to be all of $\Re^m$ simplifies the discussion.

due to Le Breton (1986). We outline Le Breton's proof that D_* is saturating for the case of $m = 2$.[30]

(1) It is obvious that every pair is nontrivial.

(2) As in the previous example, a triple $\{x, y, z\}$ is free if and only if its three elements are not colinear. To see why a colinear triple is not free, consider the pair of alternatives $\{x, y\}$ shown in Figure 6 and suppose that the triple is completed with a third alternative z (not shown) lying on the line through x and y. For these three alternatives, it is impossible to find a spatial preference for which xIy and yIz. To have xIy, the bliss point must lie on the line denoted ab; i.e., on the line through the point $\frac{(x+y)}{2}$ orthogonal to the line through x and y. Because, by assumption, z is distinct from x and y, if the bliss point is on ab, z can not be on the same indifference curve as x and y.

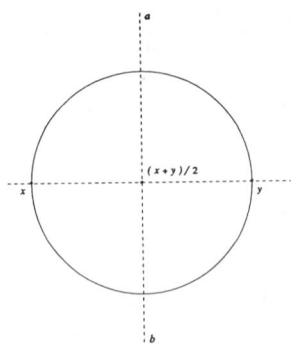

Figure 6. Any point z (not shown) that is a member of the perpendicular set ab defines a free triple $\{x, y, z\}$, unless z is colinear with xy; hence $z = xy \cap ab$ describes an indifference set $\{x, y, z\}$ and is not a free triple in the space $\mathcal{R}$ of alternatives.

We now suppose that the triple $\{x, y, z\}$ is not colinear. As before, we use the points x and y depicted in Figure 6. For each point z not on the line through x and y, we show that there is a spatial preference for which xPy and yPz. There are two cases to consider. First, we suppose that z lies outside the closed disk centered at $\frac{(x+y)}{2}$ that contains x and y on its boundary. In this case, we choose the ideal point β to lie on the line segment $[x, \frac{(x+y)}{2}]$. By choosing β sufficiently near the point $\frac{(x+y)}{2}$, it is clear that we have xPy and yPz. Second, we suppose that z lies in the closed disk and without loss of generality we can assume that z lies above the line segment $[x, y]$. Consider a preference ordering with a bliss point β on ab below the line segment $[x, y]$. By choosing β to be sufficiently far from $[x, y]$, the point z will lie outside the

---

[30] Again, our heuristic argument can be easily extended to higher dimensions. If $m = 1$, we have a domain of single-peaked preferences with each person's preference being symmetric relative to his or her peak (bliss point). In this case, it then follows from Black's (1948) Theorem on majority rule that the preference domain is Arrow-consistent if the number of individuals is odd.

circle centered at β through x and y. It then should be clear that if we choose a bliss point β' slightly to the left of β, then the corresponding preference ordering will have xPy and yPz. This construction is illustrated in Figure 7.

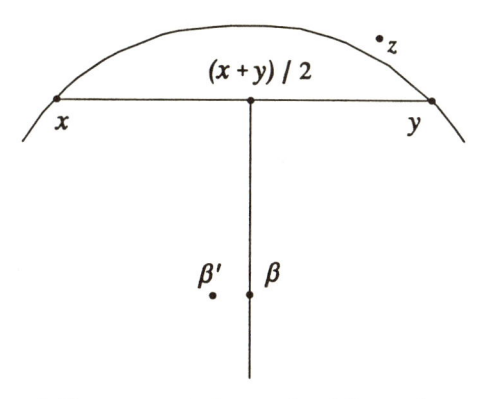

Figure 7. Let β and β' represent alternative bliss points of the preference field. Then the triple $\{z, x, y\}$ with the strict preference ordering: $xPyPz$ is the free triple closest (in this construction) to a bliss point of the set.

Except for the case in which all three alternatives are indifferent, a similar argument can be used to show that any of the other orderings of $\{x, y, z\}$ is possible with spatial preferences when the alternatives are not colinear. We leave the details of the arguments to the reader.

The case in which xIy and yIz is quite easy. Recall that the line ab in Figure 6 is the line through the point $\frac{(x+y)}{2}$ orthogonal to the line through x and y. Construct the analogous line cd (not shown) through the point $\frac{(x+z)}{2}$ orthogonal to the line through x and z. By placing the bliss point at the intersection of ab and cd, the corresponding preference has x, y, and z on the same indifference curve.

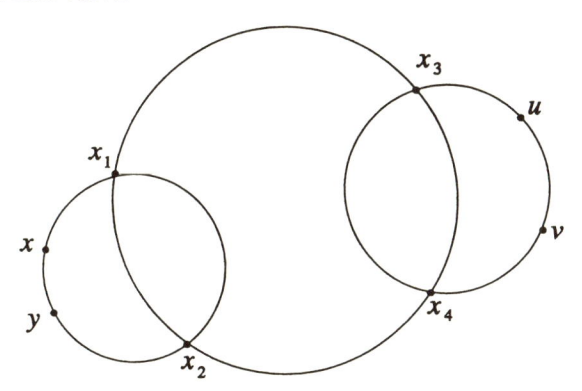

Figure 8. Nontrivial pairs $\{x, y\}$ and $\{u, v\}$, spatially connected by the sequence: $\{y, x_1\}, \{x_1, x_2\}, \{x_1, x_2\}, \{x_2, x_3\}, \{x_3, x_4\}$, and $\{x_4, u\}$.

(3) We now complete the argument by showing how to connect nontrivial pairs. Consider the two pairs $\{x,y\}$ and $\{u,v\}$ shown in Figure 8. Through x and y and through u and v we draw arbitrary circles, as in the diagram. We then draw a third circle so that it intersects each of the original circles twice, as illustrated. The connection is obtained using the sequence of nontrivial pairs $\{y,x_1\},\{x_1,x_2\},\{x_2,x_3\},\{x_3,x_4\}$, and $\{x_4,u\}$.

In each of the preceding examples, the connection step of the argument is quick and simple; *i.e.*, few intermediate pairs are needed to connect any two nontrivial pairs. Not all common saturating preference domains have such simple connection procedures. Example 8 provides another example of a common saturating preference domain, but in this case the connection process is long and complicated.

EXAMPLE 8: Suppose X is a connected subset of $\Re^m$. A preference ordering $R \in \mathcal{R}$ is *strictly Schur-convex* if for all $x,y \in X$, (a) xRy whenever $x = By$ for some bistochastic matrix B and (b) xPy whenever $x = By$ for some bistochastic matrix B and B is not a permutation matrix.[31]

For our example, we suppose that $X = S^{m-1}$ with $m \geq 3$ and we suppose that D_* is the set of continuous and strictly Schur-convex orderings of X.[32] The set X can be interpreted as being the set of all possible distributions of a unit of income, with D_* interpreted as being the set of inequality orderings of X.[33] For symmetric orderings on a simplex, strict Schur-convexity is equivalent to the Pigou-Dalton condition: an equalizing transfer from a richer to a poorer person results in a preferred distribution.[34] Le Breton and Trannoy (1987) have shown that the preference domain D_* is saturating on X. However, their demonstration that all nontrivial pairs are connected involves introducing a rather large number of intermediate pairs. We refer the reader to Le Breton and Trannoy's article for details of the proof that this preference domain is saturating.

We hope that these examples are sufficient to convince the reader that many interesting economic and political preference domains are common saturating preference domains when the alternatives are public in nature. It is not difficult to construct other examples of common saturating preference domains. Unfortunately, as we have seen, Theorem 2 demonstrates that all such domains are Arrow-inconsistent.

The assumption that the preference domain is common and saturating is merely sufficient, and not necessary, for the domain to be Arrow-inconsistent.

---

[31] A square matrix B is *biostochastic* if it is nonnegative and all of its row and column sums are equal to one. A biostochastic matrix whose entries are all zeroes or ones is a *permutation* matrix.

[32] If $m = 2$, each person has only one possible preference ordering.

[33] The details of this example are unchanged if there is any fixed amount of income $c > 0$ to distribute.

[34] In this application, a preference order $R \in \mathcal{R}$ is *symmetric* if for all $x,y \in X, xIy$ whenever $x = By$ for some permutation matrix B.

In Example 9, the preference domain is common, but not saturating; yet it is Arrow-inconsistent.

EXAMPLE 9: Let $N = \{1, 2\}$ and $X = \{x_1, x_2, x_3, x_4\}$. Let D be a common preference domain with $D_* = \{R \in \mathcal{R} \mid x_1 I x_4 \text{ or } x_1 P x_2 P x_4\}$. All of the pairs are nontrivial, but the pair $\{x_1, x_4\}$ is not connected to any other pair, so the preference domain is not saturating. Suppose that σ is a social welfare function on D satisfying Binary Independence of Irrelevant Alternatives and Weak Pareto. It follows from the fact that $\{x_1, x_2, x_3\}$ and $\{x_2, x_3, x_4\}$ are free triples with the two elements $\{x_2, x_3\}$ in common that there is a dictator d on every pair with the possible exception of $\{x_1, x_4\}$. On this preference domain, for any profile $\mathbf{R}$ with $x_1 P_d x_4$, it is also the case that $x_1 P_d x_2$ and $x_2 P_d x_4$. We have already established that for such a profile we must have $x_1 P x_2$ and $x_2 P x_4$. By the transitivity of social preference, it follows that $x_1 P x_4$; i.e., d is a dictator. Hence, D is Arrow-inconsistent.

Both Arrow's Theorem (Theorem 1) and the Kalai-Muller-Satterthwaite Theorem (Theorem 2) assume that the preference domain is not only saturating, but also that it is common. Example 10 shows that the common preference domain assumption is essential for these results; i.e., there exist saturating preference domains which are Arrow-consistent.

EXAMPLE 10: Let $N = \{1, 2\}$ and $X = \{x_1, x_2, x_3, x_4\}$. Let $D_1 = \{R_1 \in \mathcal{R} \mid x_4 P_1 x_i \text{ for } i = 1, 2, 3\}$ and $D_2 = \{R_2 \in \mathcal{R} \mid x_i P_2 x_4 \text{ for } i = 1, 2, 3\}$. Consider the social welfare function defined by setting xRy iff $xR_1 y$ when $x, y \in \{x_1, x_2, x_3\}$ and xPx_4 when $x \in \{x_1, x_2, x_3\}$. This social welfare function satisfies Binary Independence of Irrelevant Alternatives, Weak Pareto, and Nondictatorship. The preference domain D is saturating, but it is not common.

In this example, preferences are unrestricted on the set $A = \{x_1, x_2, x_3\}$ and any pair of alternatives in this set is nontrivial. All other pairs, i.e., pairs formed with x_4 as one of the alternatives, are trivial. On the trivial pairs, the two individuals have opposite strict preferences. The social welfare function makes person one a dictator on A and person two a dictator on all of the trivial pairs. For example, person two is a dictator on $B = \{x_3, x_4\}$. Although there are "local" dictators on A and B and these two sets overlap, because the intersection of these sets only contains a single alternative, there does not have to be a single dictator on their union. For the "local approach" to apply, the two sets must have at least two elements in common.[35]

Although the preference domain in Example 10 is Arrow-consistent, the social welfare function used to show the consistency is not very appealing; on every pair of alternatives, someone is a dictator. Furthermore, on every nontrivial pair, the same person is the dictator. Theorem 3 demonstrates that

---

[35] Example 10 is similar to the example used by Blau (1957) to show that the statement of Arrow's Theorem in Arrow (1951) is incorrect.

the latter property is a general feature of saturating preference domains.

Theorem 3: *If a social welfare function σ is defined on a saturating preference domain and satisfies Binary Independence of Irrelevant Alternatives and Weak Pareto, then there is an individual $d \in N$ who is a dictator on every nontrivial pair.*

Proof: Inspection of the proof of Theorem 2 reveals that the part of that proof dealing with nontrivial pairs makes no use of the assumption that the preference domain is common.[36]   Q.E.D.

We already know from Theorem 2 that the partial dictator found in Theorem 3 is a complete dictator if the preference domain is also assumed to be common. In fact, the somewhat weaker assumption of a *uniform preference domain* suffices for this result.

UNIFORM PREFERENCE DOMAIN: *A preference domain D is uniform if (a) the trivial pairs are the same for each individual preference domain D_i, for all $i \in N$, and (b) for every trivial pair $A \in X$, we have $D_i|_A = D_j|_A$, for all $i, j \in N$.*

Thus, if the preference domain is uniform, everyone has the same set of trivial pairs and everyone's preferences agree on these pairs. In Example 10, while the trivial pairs are the same for both people, on each trivial pair the two people disagree. Consequently, the preference domain in Example 10 is not uniform.

Theorem 4: *If a social welfare function σ is defined on a uniform saturating preference domain and satisfies Binary Independence of Irrelevant Alternatives and Weak Pareto, then σ is dictatorial.*

Proof: The proof of Theorem 4 is essentially the same as the proof of Theorem 2. Uniformity is used instead of commonality of the preference domain to show that everyone is dictatorial on the trivial pairs.   Q.E.D.

When the alternatives are purely public, economic and political preference domains are often saturating. Unfortunately, Theorems 2 and 4 show that all common saturating preference domains and all uniform saturating preference domains are Arrow-inconsistent. Furthermore, if the preference domain is both saturating and Arrow-consistent, Theorem 3 informs us that the social welfare function is dictatorial on every nontrivial pair of alternatives. It thus seems that restricting the preference domain does not provide a satisfactory way of escaping Arrow's dilemma when the alternatives are purely public.

---

[36] Note that in Theorem 3 the assumption that the preference domain is saturating cannot be replaced with the assumption that each person's individual preference domain is saturating, as we need to have nontrivial pairs connected by a common sequence of intermediate alternatives for our proof to be valid.

2.3 Private Alternatives

In the previous section, we restricted attention to problems in which the social alternatives are purely public. As a consequence, the analysis is not immediately applicable to problems with private goods. In this section, we suppose that social alternatives are allocations of private goods. Because there is no public dimension to the alternatives we are considering, the problem being analyzed in this section can be thought of as a polar case to the purely public goods case considered in the previous section. As we shall see, the techniques used to study public alternatives can be readily adapted to study private alternatives as well. However, to fully exploit the structure imposed on the problem by the private goods assumption, it is necessary to consider refinements of the notion of a saturating preference domain.

For the private domains we consider, X is a Cartesian set of alternatives.

CARTESIAN SET OF ALTERNATIVES: $X = \prod_{i=1}^{n} X_i$.

Thus, a social alternative is a vector $(x^1, \ldots, x^n)$ where $x^i \in X_i$ is the component of the social state relevant to person i. We refer to x^i as i's *consumption bundle* and to X_i as *i's consumption set*. In adopting this terminology, we are not requiring consumption bundles to be vectors in a Euclidean space, although that is in fact the case in the application we consider in detail. For subsequent reference, we define $x_{-i} := (x^1, \ldots, x^{i-1}, x^{i+1}, \ldots, x^n)$ and let $(y^i; x_{-i})$ denote $(x^1, \ldots, x^{i-1}, y^i, x^{i+1}, \ldots, x^n)$.[37]

As in the previous section, we maintain the assumption that D is a Cartesian preference domain. When the alternatives are private, we assume that individuals are selfish; *i.e.*, in comparing two social alternatives, each individual is only concerned with his or her own consumption. Formally, for each $i \in N$, a preference ordering $R_i \in D_i$ is *selfish* if there exists an ordering Q_i on X_i such that for all $x, y \in X, x R_i y$ if and only if $x^i Q_i y^i$ where x^i and y^i are i's consumption bundles in the alternatives x and y, respectively. We refer to Q_i as *i's induced private preference*.

SELFISH PREFERENCE DOMAIN: *For each $i \in N$, an individual preference domain D_i on a Cartesian set of alternatives X is selfish if R_i is selfish for all $R_i \in D_i$. A preference domain D on a Cartesian set of alternatives X is selfish if the individual preference domain D_i on X is selfish for each $i \in N$.*

Henceforth, for Cartesian sets of alternatives, we assume that the preference domain is selfish. For a selfish individual preference domain D_i, the set of induced private orderings of X_i corresponding to D_i is denoted by Q_i and is called *i's induced private preference domain*. Note that a pair of social alternatives x and y is nontrivial for person i with respect to D_i if and only

---

[37] The assumption that the set of alternatives has a Cartesian structure is not satisfied in all private goods problems. For example, if the set of social alternatives is the set of allocations in an Edgeworth box, the consumption bundles of the two individuals are restricted by an overall resource constraint.

if the corresponding pair of private consumption bundles x^i and y^i is nontrivial with respect to Q_i. Similarly, a triple of social alternatives $\{w, x, y\}$ is a free triple with respect to D_i if and only if the corresponding triple of private consumption bundles $\{w^i, x^i, y^i\}$ is free with respect to Q_i.

A selfish preference domain (provided each person is not indifferent between all alternatives) is obviously not common, nor even uniform. To see why a selfish preference domain is not uniform, consider the alternatives x, y, and $z = (x^i; y_{-i})$. By the Cartesian set of alternatives assumption, if x and y are in X, so is z. Suppose that xP_iy. By the assumption that preferences are selfish, it follows that zP_iy as well. But for all $j \neq i$, because preferences are selfish, y and z form a trivial pair for D_j with yI_jz. Thus, y and z are a trivial pair for D. Because there is a profile in which i's preference differs from that of the rest of society on a trivial pair for D, the domain D is not uniform. Consequently, Theorems 2 and 4, which show the Arrow-inconsistency of common saturating preference domains and of uniform saturating preference domains, are inapplicable to selfish preference domains.

However, Theorem 3, which shows that there is a dictator on every nontrivial pair when the social welfare function satisfies Binary Independence of Irrelevant Alternatives and Weak Pareto and the preference domain is saturating, is relevant to the study of selfish preference domains. In order to help identify saturating preference domains when there are private alternatives, it is useful to consider the concept of a *supersaturating preference domain*, which is a domain restriction introduced by Bordes and Le Breton (1989).

SUPERSATURATING PREFERENCE DOMAIN: *An individual preference domain D_i is supersaturating if (a) D_i is saturating and (b) for all nontrivial pairs x, y with respect to D_i in X, there exist $u, v \in X$ such that $u, v \notin \{x, y\}$ and $\{x, y, u\}, \{x, y, v\}, \{x, u, v\}$, and $\{y, u, v\}$ are free triples with respect to D_i.*[38] *A preference domain D is supersaturating if D_i is supersaturating for all $i \in N$.*

While Bordes and Le Breton (1989) introduced the concept of a supersaturating preference domain to study selfish preferences for private alternatives, preference domains for public alternatives can be supersaturating as well. For example, the domain of classical economic preferences for public goods considered in Example 4 is a supersaturating preference domain. Recall that in this example, X is $\Re_+^m$ with $m \geq 2$ and D_* is the set of continuous, strictly monotonic, and convex preferences in $\mathcal{R}$. We have already seen that this preference domain is saturating, so to establish that it is supersaturating it is sufficient to check that condition (b) is satisfied. We do this for the two-good case. Suppose that x and y are a nontrivial pair; *i.e.*, neither $x > y$ nor $y > x$. These alternatives are illustrated in Figure 9. We do not rule out the possibility that either x or y (or both) are on one of the axes. We pick u so that it is in the interior of the triangle formed by the points w, x, and y, as shown in the diagram. Our discussion of Example 4 shows that $\{x, y, u\}$ is a free triple.

---

[38] Bordes and Le Breton (1989) have shown that (a) and (b) are logically independent.

We pick v so that it lies below the line through u and y but above the lines through u and x and through w and y. By again appealing to our discussion of Example 4, we can conclude that $\{x, y, v\}, \{x, u, v\}$, and $\{y, u, v\}$ are free triples with respect to D_*. But that completes the demonstration that D_* is supersaturating (when $m = 2$).[39]

To help understand condition (b) in the definition of a supersaturating preference domain, we introduce the concept of a *self-cycle*.

SELF-CYCLE: *A sequence of pairs* $A_1, \ldots, A_r$ *in* X *is a self-cycle with respect to* D_i *(resp.* D*) if* $A_1 = A_r$ *and* A_j *and* A_{j+1} *are strongly connected with respect to* D_i *(resp.* D*) for all* $j = 1, \ldots, r - 1$.

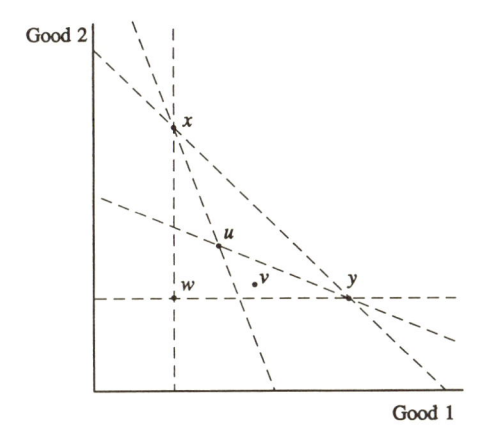

Figure 9. A supersaturating preference domain satisfying the conditions: (i) $u, v, x, y \in X$, (ii) all pairs are non-trivial, $u, v \notin \{x, y\}$ and (iii) the set of all free triples, $\{x, y, u\}, \{x, y, v\}, \{x, u, v\}$ and $\{y, u, v\}$, are strongly connected.

In other words, a self-cycle is a sequence of pairs connecting a pair of alternatives to itself. If condition (b) in the definition of a supersaturating preference domain is satisfied, then for each nontrivial pair of alternatives $\{x, y\}$ we can construct a self-cycle containing three distinct pairs and we can construct a self-cycle containing four distinct pairs. The first of these self-cycles is given by the sequence $\{x, y\}, \{y, u\}, \{u, x\}$, and $\{x, y\}$. The second of these self-cycles is given by the sequence $\{x, y\}, \{y, u\}, \{u, v\}, \{v, x\}$, and $\{x, y\}$. In both of these sequences, any two adjacent pairs form a free triple. For the domain of economic preferences for public goods considered in Example 4, Figure 9 illustrates these self-cycles. By combining an appropriate number of these two self-cycles, $\{x, y\}$ can be connected to itself with a self-cycle containing r pairs for any positive integer r except 2, 3, and 6.[40]

---

[39] We leave it to the reader to check which of the other preference domains considered in the previous section are supersaturating.
[40] The remarks in this paragraph apply *mutatis mutandis* to self-cycles for individual preference domains.

For private alternatives, because preferences are selfish, the induced private preference domain Q_i inherits many of the structural properties of the individual preference domain D_i.

Lemma 1: *If X is a Cartesian set of alternatives and D is a selfish preference domain, then for each $i \in N$, the individual preference domain D_i is saturating (resp. supersaturating) on X if and only if the induced private preference domain Q_i is saturating (resp. supersaturating) on X_i.*

Proof: We first show that i's preference domain D_i is saturating on X if and only if the induced private preference domain Q_i is saturating on X_i.

Suppose the induced private preference domain Q_i is saturating on X_i. By assumption, we can find two pairs of consumption bundles $\{x^i, y^i\}$ and $\{u^i, v^i\}$ (with $\{x^i, y^i\} \neq \{u^i, v^i\}$) which are nontrivial with respect to Q_i. Choose an arbitrary vector of consumptions z_{-i} for the rest of society. Let $x = (x^i; z_{-i}), y = (y^i; z_{-i}), u = (u^i; z_{-i})$, and $v = (v^i; z_{-i})$. Then $\{x, y\}$ and $\{u, v\}$ are two nontrivial pairs with respect to D_i. Now let x and y be any nontrivial pair for i in X. The corresponding private consumption bundles x^i and y^i are nontrivial for i in X_i and are thereby connected with respect to Q_i, because Q_i is saturating. For each intermediate private consumption bundle s^i used in a sequence connecting x^i and y^i, we can augment s^i with arbitrary consumptions for the rest of society and thus obtain a sequence of alternatives in X which connect x and y in D_i. Hence, i's preference domain D_i is saturating on X.

Now suppose i's preference domain D_i is saturating on X. Let $\{x, y\}$ be a nontrivial pair of social alternatives for i. Because D_i is saturating, there must exist a third social alternative z such that $\{x, y, z\}$ is a free triple for i. It then follows that the two pairs of consumption bundles $\{x^i, y^i\}$ and $\{x^i, z^i\}$ are distinct and nontrivial for i with respect to Q_i.[41] Let $\{x^i, y^i\}$ and $\{u^i, v^i\}$ be any two nontrivial pairs for i in X_i. As above, for an arbitrary z_{-i}, let $x = (x^i; z_{-i}), y = (y^i; z_{-i}), u = (u^i; z_{-i})$, and $v = (v^i; z_{-i})$. The pairs $\{x, y\}$ and $\{u, v\}$ are both nontrivial for i in X and are thereby connected with respect to D_i, because D_i is saturating. By projecting each alternative in the sequence connecting $\{x, y\}$ with $\{u, v\}$ into X_i we obtain a sequence connecting $\{x^i, y^i\}$ with $\{u^i, v^i\}$ in X_i with respect to Q_i. Hence, i's induced private preference domain Q_i is saturating on X_i.

A similar argument (*i.e.*, projecting social alternatives or augmenting private consumptions) shows that D_i satisfies condition (*b*) in the definition of a supersaturating preference domain if and only Q_i satisfies the corresponding condition for Q_i. Q.E.D.

The intuition for Lemma 1 is quite simple. Because preferences are selfish, an individual's ranking of a pair of alternatives is completely determined by the individual's preference for the corresponding consumption bundles. Hence,

---

[41] Note that if $\{x, y\}$ and $\{u, v\}$ are arbitrary distinct nontrivial pairs with respect to D_i, it may be true that $\{x^i, y^i\} = \{u^i, v^i\}$.

all of the richness in the individual preference domain D_i is embodied in the induced individual preference domain Q_i.

Example 11 shows that the private goods counterpart to the public preference domain considered in Example 4 is supersaturating.

EXAMPLE 11: To describe our example, we first need one more definition. Suppose X is both a Cartesian set of alternatives and a connected subset of a Euclidean space. For each $i \in N$, a selfish preference ordering $R_i \in \mathcal{R}$ is *strictly monotonic in own consumption* if the corresponding induced private preference Q_i is strictly monotonic on X_i.

In this example, X is a Cartesian set of alternatives. For all $i \in N$, we suppose that $X_i = \Re_+^{m(i)}$ where $m(i) \geq 2$. For all $i \in N$, we let D_i be the set of all selfish (for i), continuous, strictly monotonic in own consumption, and convex preference orderings on X. This preference domain is the classical domain of economic preferences for private goods. Our formulation of this domain permits individuals to be concerned with differing numbers of goods. If there are the same number of private goods for each person, then $m(i)$ is independent of i and each person has the same induced private preference domain Q_i.

It is a simple matter to show that each individual's preference domain D_i is supersaturating and thus that the overall preference domain D is supersaturating. Because the set of alternatives is Cartesian and individual preferences are selfish, by Lemma 1 D_i is supersaturating on X if and only if the induced private preference domain Q_i is supersaturating on X_i. But the induced private preference domain Q_i is formally the same as the public preference domain considered in Example 4. As we have already seen, this domain is supersaturating, from which it follows that D_i is supersaturating as well.

By definition, an individual preference domain D_i is saturating if it is supersaturating. In general, it does not follow that a preference domain D is saturating if it is supersaturating. However, if a preference domain D is both selfish and supersaturating, then it must also be saturating. The intuition for this result is as follows. Consider two nontrivial pairs $\{x, y\}$ and $\{w, z\}$. Because each person's preferences are saturating, for each individual there is a sequence of alternatives $S^i = \{x, y, s^{i1}, \ldots, s^{ir}, w, z\}$ connecting $\{x, y\}$ to $\{w, z\}$. If the sequences S^i are not initially the same length, because preferences are supersaturating, they can be made so by adding self-cycles to the beginning of the individual sequences. Using these equal-length individual sequences, we can construct a new sequence by letting i's consumption bundle in the jth alternative in the constructed sequence equal i's consumption bundle in the jth alternative in S^i. Because preferences are selfish, this single sequence connects the two nontrivial pairs for each individual, which shows that the preference domain D is saturating. This rather informal discussion is made precise in Theorems 5 and its proof.

Theorem 5: *Suppose X is a Cartesian set of alternatives. If the preference domain D is both selfish and supersaturating, then it is also saturating.*[42]

Proof: Because each of the individual preference domains is saturating, for each $i \in N$ we can find alternatives $w(i), x(i), y(i)$, and $z(i)$ in X such that $\{x(i), y(i)\} \neq \{w(i), z(i)\}$ and such that both pairs of alternatives are nontrivial with respect to D_i. Let $w = (w^1(1), \ldots, w^n(n))$, $x = (x^1(1), \ldots, x^n(n))$, $y = (y^1(1), \ldots, y^n(n))$, and $z = (z^1(1), \ldots, z^n(n))$. Because X is Cartesian, each of these four alternatives is in X. Because preferences are selfish, the pairs $\{x, y\}$ and $\{w, z\}$ are nontrivial with respect to D. Thus, there exist at least two nontrivial pairs with respect to D.

Now let $\{x, y\}$ and $\{w, z\}$ be any two nontrivial pairs with respect to D. From Lemma 1 and its proof, we know that for all $i \in N$, the induced private preference domains Q_i are supersaturating on X_i and the pairs of consumption bundles $\{x^i, y^i\}$ and $\{w^i, z^i\}$ are nontrivial with respect to Q_i. Because Q_i is saturating, we can connect $\{x^i, y^i\}$ and $\{w^i, z^i\}$ using a sequence S_i of pairs of consumption bundles starting with $\{x^i, y^i\}$ and ending with $\{w^i, z^i\}$. Because Q_i is supersaturating, we can find consumption bundles u^i and v^i in X_i such that $\{x^i, y^i, u^i\}, \{x^i, y^i, v^i\}, \{x^i, u^i, v^i\}$, and $\{y^i, u^i, v^i\}$ are free triples with respect to Q_i. Furthermore, $\{x^i, y^i\}$ is connected to itself using either the sequence of pairs (I): $\{x^i, y^i\}, \{y^i, u^i\}, \{u^i, x^i\}$, and $\{x^i, y^i\}$, or the sequence of pairs (II): $\{x^i, y^i\}, \{y^i, u^i\}, \{u^i, v^i\}, \{v^i, x^i\}$, and $\{x^i, y^i\}$.

Consider the sequences S_1 and S_2. Without loss of generality, we can suppose that S_1 is no longer than S_2. Suppose S_2 has k more pairs than S_1. If k is positive, we add self-cycles to the beginning of S_1 and S_2 until the two sequences are the same length. If $k = 1$, this is accomplished by adding one type-II self-cycle to the beginning of S_1 and by adding one type-I self-cycle to the beginning of S_2. If $k = 2$, we add two type-I self-cycles to the beginning of S_1 and add one type-II self-cycle to the beginning of S_2. If $k = 3$, we simply add one type-I self-cycle to the beginning of S_1. If $k > 3$, by first adding an appropriate number of type-I self-cycles to the beginning of S_1, the difference in the lengths of the two sequences can be made not to exceed three, and one of the preceding procedures can be used to equate the length of the sequences.

Now that the sequences for the first two individuals are the same length, we use similar operations to equalize the length of the sequences connecting $\{x^i, y^i\}$ and $\{w^i, z^i\}$ for $i = 1, 2, 3$. Continuing in like fashion, we equalize the lengths of the connection paths joining $\{x^i, y^i\}$ and $\{w^i, z^i\}$ for all $i \in N$. As a result, for each individual we have a sequence of consumption bundles $(x^i, y^i, s^{i1}, \ldots, s^{it}, w^i, z^i)$ containing $t + 4$ elements, with each adjacent pair in the sequence forming the intermediate pairs used to connect $\{x^i, y^i\}$ and $\{w^i, z^i\}$ with respect to Q_i. We now form a sequence of alternatives in X by combining these individual consumption bundles. That is, we form the sequence $\{x = (x^1, \ldots, x^n), y = (y^1, \ldots, y^n), s^1 = (s^{11}, \ldots, s^{n1}), \ldots, s^t = (s^{1t}, \ldots, s^{nt}), w = (w^1, \ldots, w^n), z = (z^1, \ldots, z^n)\}$. Each adjacent pair in this sequence is strongly connected, which shows that the pairs $\{x, y\}$ and $\{w, z\}$

---

[42] This theorem is based on Lemma 2 in Bordes and Le Breton (1989).

are connected in D. Hence, D is supersaturating.[43]   Q.E.D.

An immediate implication of Theorems 3 and 5 is that if a private preference domain is supersaturating, then there must be a dictator on every nontrivial pair if the social welfare function satisfies Binary Independence of Irrelevant Alternatives and Weak Pareto.

Theorem 6: *Suppose X is a Cartesian set of alternatives. If the preference domain D is both selfish and supersaturating and the social welfare function σ satisfies Binary Independence of Irrelevant Alternatives and Weak Pareto, then there is an individual $d \in N$ who is a dictator on every nontrivial pair of social alternatives.*

The usefulness of Theorem 6 is limited by the fact that a pair of social alternatives is nontrivial if and only if the corresponding pairs of private consumption bundles are nontrivial for each individual. For example, with the classical economic preferences for private goods considered in Example 11, the social alternatives x and y are a nontrivial pair if and only if for all individuals neither $x^i > y^i$ nor $y^i > x^i$. Because this domain satisfies the assumptions of Theorem 6, we know that there is a dictator on the nontrivial pairs. However, if we want to compare a pair of social alternatives in which even a single individual's consumption bundle is the same in both alternatives or in which some individual receives more of all goods in one of the two alternatives, then Theorem 6 tells us nothing about the social ranking.

At this point, it is natural to enquire whether it is possible for a preference domain to be Arrow-consistent when the set of alternatives is Cartesian and the preference domain is selfish and supersaturating. The answer is yes; the domain of classical economic preferences for private goods considered in Example 11 is Arrow-consistent. Using the essential idea underlying an example in Blau (1957), this consistency was shown in Border (1983). In Example 12, we present the social welfare function Border used to demonstrate this result.

EXAMPLE 12: In this example, the set of alternatives X and the preference domain D are the same as in Example 11 but with $n = 2$.[44] By construction, the set of alternatives is Cartesian and the preference domain is selfish. We have already established that the preference domain is also supersaturating. Consider the following four subsets of X: $A_1 = \{x \in X \mid x^1 \neq 0,$ and $x^2 \neq 0\}$, $A_2 = \{x \in X \mid x^1 \neq 0$ and $x^2 = 0\}$, $A_3 = \{x \in X \mid x^1 = 0$ and $x^2 \neq 0\}$, and $A_4 = \{0\}$. These four sets form a partition of X. In A_1 both people consume some of at least one good. In each of the other sets, at least one person receives nothing. The social welfare function σ is defined by setting:

---

[43] Note that this proof differs in some inessential details from the informal argument that precedes the statement of Theorem 5.
[44] It is a straightforward matter to extend this example to larger populations.

xRy iff xR_2y for $x,y \in A_1$ and for $x,y \in A_3$,
xRy iff xR_1y for $x,y \in A_2$, and
xPy if $x \in A_i$ and $y \in A_j$ with $i < j$.

This social welfare function is obviously nondictatorial. For example, we have person two dictating on alternatives in A_1. Person two is not an overall dictator because if $x \in A_3$ and $y \in A_2$, we have xP_2y because two's consumption is nonzero in A_3 but is zero in A_2, yet the social preference is yPx.

This social welfare function satisfies Weak Pareto because the social preference always agrees with the individual preference of at least one person. This fact is obvious if we compare two alternatives from the same cell in the partition. It is not difficult to verify this claim when the alternatives come from different cells. For example, if $x \in A_3$ and $y \in A_2$, the social preference coincides with person one's preference. The other cases are equally easy to check.

We leave it to the reader to confirm that Binary Independence of Irrelevant Alternatives is satisfied and that the social preferences are orderings.

To help understand the reason why domains like the ones considered in Examples 11 and 12 are Arrow-consistent, we introduce the notion of a trivial pair being *separable* for an individual.

SEPARABLE TRIVIAL PAIR: *A pair of alternatives $\{x,y\}$ in X which is trivial for i and for which xP_iy for all $R_i \in D_i$ is separable with respect to D_i if there exist $z \in X$ and $R_i' \in D_i$ such that $xP_i'zP_i'y$ and such that the pairs $\{x,z\}$ and $\{y,z\}$ are nontrivial for i.*

The concept of a separable trivial pair is implicit in Bordes and Le Breton (1989).[45] Informally, a trivial pair x and y is separable for person i if i is not indifferent between x and y and there is an admissible preference ordering for i and an alternative z such that z is on an indifference curve lying between the indifference curves through x and y and such that $\{x,z\}$ and $\{y,z\}$ are nontrivial pairs for i.

Bordes and Le Breton (1989) used the notion of a separable trivial pair to define a *hypersaturating preference domain*.

HYPERSATURATING PREFERENCE DOMAIN: *An individual preference domain D_i is hypersaturating if (a) D_i is supersaturating and (b) all trivial pairs $\{x,y\}$ with respect to D_i in X for which xP_iy for all $R_i \in D_i$ are separable for i. A preference domain D is hypersaturating if D_i is hypersaturating for all $i \in N$.*

---

[45] The inspiration for this concept comes from a closely related idea in Kalai and Ritz (1980).

With a hypersaturating preference domain, all nonindifferent trivial pairs are separable for each individual. The preference domains in Examples 11 and 12 are not hypersaturating because for each individual we can find trivial pairs consisting of two nonindifferent alternatives which are not separable. In Example 12, if $y = 0$, then for all $x \neq 0$, $\{x, y\}$ is a trivial pair for both individuals. For any alternative x in A_1, both people prefer x to y, but x and y can't be separated.

Lemma 2 provides the analogue to Lemma 1 for hypersaturating individual preference domains.

Lemma 2: *If X is a Cartesian set of alternatives and D is a selfish preference domain, then for each $i \in N$, the individual preference domain D_i is hypersaturating on X if and only if the induced private preference domain Q_i is hypersaturating on X_i.*

Proof: We know from Lemma 1 that D_i is supersaturating on X if and only if Q_i is supersaturating on X_i. By projecting alternatives in X to X_i and by augmenting commodity bundles in X_i to form alternatives in X, as in the proof of Lemma 1, it is easy to show that D_i satisfies condition (*b*) in the definition of a hypersaturating preference domain if and only if Q_i does as well.   *Q.E.D.*

Although the preference domain of classical economic preferences for private goods is not hypersaturating when each consumption set is a nonnegative orthant, it is hypersaturating if either the origin is removed from each person's consumption set or if all goods must be consumed in positive amounts.

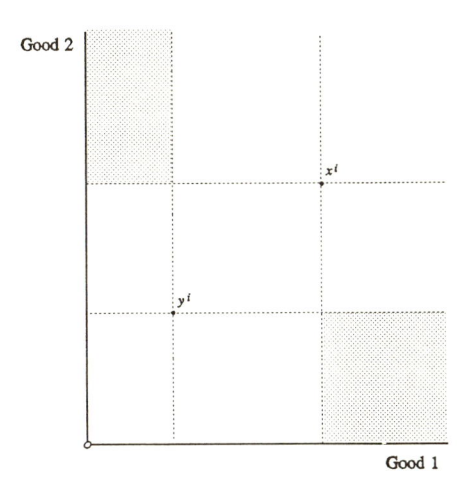

Figure 10. The trivial pair $\{x, y\}$ with the preference ordering $x_i p y_i$ is separable by any consumption bundle z_i located in the shaded regions.

EXAMPLE 13. In this example, X is a Cartesian set of alternatives. For all $i \in N$, we suppose that $X_i = \Re_+^{m(i)}\setminus\{0\}$ where $m(i) \geq 2$. We let D_i be the set of all selfish (for i), continuous, strictly monotonic in own consumption, and convex preference orderings on X. This preference domain is the classical domain of economic preferences for private goods considered in Example 11 but with the origin removed from each person's consumption set. For $n = 2$, the universal set of alternatives X is equal to the set A_1 in Example 12.

To show that this preference domain is hypersaturating, by Lemma 2 it is sufficient to show that the induced private preference domain $\mathcal{Q}_i$ is hypersaturating on $\Re_+^{m(i)}\setminus\{0\}$ for all $i \in N$. We already know from our discussion of Example 11 that $\mathcal{Q}_i$ is supersaturating. (Deleting the origin from the consumption set doesn't affect this argument.) We illustrate the rest of the proof that $\mathcal{Q}_i$ is hypersaturating for the case in which $m(i) = 2$. On X_i, the pair $\{x^i, y^i\}$ is trivial for i with x^i preferred to y^i if and only if $x^i > y^i$, as illustrated in Figure 10. The pair $\{x^i, y^i\}$ can be separated by any consumption bundle z^i in the shaded regions of the diagram. Note that if y^i is on one of the axes, then there is only one such region (whether or not x^i is on this axis as well).

EXAMPLE 14: This example is identical to Example 13 except that for all $i \in N, X_i = \Re_{++}^{m(i)}$; i.e., each consumption set is some strictly positive orthant. The reasoning used to show that Example 13 is hypersaturating also shows that this preference domain is hypersaturating.[46]

Border (1983) and Maskin (1976) have shown that the preference domain in Example 14 is Arrow-inconsistent. When there are two individuals, the universal set of alternatives in Example 13 is equal to the set A_1 in Example 12. Recall that the social welfare function in Example 12 is dictatorial on A_1. Theorem 7 shows that this is no accident. For a Cartesian set of alternatives and selfish preferences, Theorem 7 demonstrates that the preference domain is Arrow-inconsistent if it is hypersaturating. This result, which is due to Bordes and Le Breton (1989), is a private good analogue to the Kalai-Muller-Satterthwaite Theorem (Theorem 2) for public alternatives.

Theorem 7: *Suppose X is a Cartesian set of alternatives. If the preference domain D is both selfish and hypersaturating and the social welfare function σ satisfies Binary Independence of Irrelevant Alternatives and Weak Pareto, then σ is dictatorial.*

Proof: Because a hypersaturating preference domain is also supersaturating, it follows from Theorem 6 that there is a person d who is a dictator on all of the nontrivial pairs with respect to D. We show that d is a dictator on the trivial pairs as well.

Let $\{x, y\}$ be any trivial pair and $\mathbf{R} = (R_1, \ldots, R_n)$ be any profile in D for

---

[46] Bordes and LeBreton (1989) provided a number of other examples of hypersaturating preference domains with private alternatives.

which $xP_d y$. Partition N into the following subsets: $N_1 = \{i \in N \mid xP_i y\}$, $N_2 = \{i \in N \mid yP_i x\}$, and $N_3 = \{i \in N \mid xI_i y\}$. For each $i \in N$, consider the induced private preference Q_i on X_i corresponding to R_i. Note that the pair of consumption bundles $\{x^i, y^i\}$ need not be trivial for all i. By Lemma 2, the induced private preference domain Q_i is hypersaturating for i.

(a) For $i \in N_1$, we show that there exists a consumption bundle $z^i \in X_i$ such that $\{x^i, z^i\}$ and $\{y^i, z^i\}$ are nontrivial pairs for i and that there exists an induced private preference $Q'_i \in Q_i$ with x^i preferred to z^i and z^i preferred to y^i. Because Q_i is saturating for i, if $\{x^i, y^i\}$ is nontrivial for i, then, as we have previously seen, there must exist a consumption bundle z^i which forms a free triple for i with x^i and y^i. Hence, $\{x^i, z^i\}$ and $\{y^i, z^i\}$ are nontrivial pairs for i and the requisite preference ordering exists. If $\{x^i, y^i\}$ is trivial for i, the existence of such z^i and Q'_i follows immediately from that fact that Q_i is hypersaturating.

(b) For $i \in N_2$, a similar argument shows that there exists a consumption bundle $z^i \in X_i$ such that $\{x^i, z^i\}$ and $\{y^i, z^i\}$ are nontrivial pairs for i and that there exists an induced private preference $Q'_i \in Q_i$ with y^i preferred to z^i and z^i preferred to x^i.

(c) For $i \in N_3$, we show that there exists a consumption bundle $z^i \in X_i$ such that $\{x^i, z^i\}$ and $\{y^i, z^i\}$ are nontrivial pairs for i and that there exists an induced private preference $Q'_i \in Q_i$ with x^i indifferent to z^i and z^i indifferent to y^i. If $\{x^i, y^i\}$ is nontrivial for i, this result is proved using the same reasoning as in (a).

Before considering the other possibility, we first demonstrate that we can find a commodity bundle z^i such that $\{x^i, z^i\}$ is nontrivial. Note that there must exist a $w^i \in X_i$ and a $Q''_i \in Q_i$ such that x^i is not indifferent to w^i in Q''_i, otherwise Q_i would consist of the single preference ordering in which all commodity bundles are indifferent to each other, violating the assumption that Q_i is saturating for i. If $\{x^i, w^i\}$ is nontrivial for i, then we let $z^i = w^i$. If $\{x^i, w^i\}$ is trivial for i, it follows from the fact that Q_i is hypersaturating that $\{x^i, w^i\}$ is separable and z^i can be taken to be the commodity bundle used for the separation.

Returning to the main line of the argument, suppose $\{x^i, y^i\}$ is trivial for i (which includes the case in which $x^i = y^i$). Because $i \in N_3$, it follows that x^i is indifferent to y^i for all preference orderings in Q_i. This observation, the assumption that preferences are transitive, and the fact that $\{x^i, z^i\}$ is nontrivial together imply that $\{y^i, z^i\}$ is also nontrivial. On a saturating preference domain, a nontrivial pair is also free. Thus, we can find an induced private preference Q'_i with x^i indifferent to z^i. Because x^i is always indifferent to y^i for i, Q'_i is the requisite preference ordering.

We now combine the commodity bundles z^i for all $i \in N$ to form the social alternative $z = (z^1, \ldots, z^n)$. By construction, $\{x, z\}$ and $\{y, z\}$ are nontrivial pairs with respect to D. For each private preference Q'_i, let R'_i be the corresponding selfish preference on X. Let $\mathbf{R}' = (R'_1, \ldots, R'_n)$. Because $\{x, z\}$ and $\{y, z\}$ are nontrivial pairs, d is a dictator on these two pairs. Because $d \in N_1$, by construction we have $xP'_d z$ and $zP'_d y$ and so we must also have $xP'z$ and

$zP'y$. By the transitivity of social preference, it follows that $xP'y$. Binary Independence of Irrelevant Alternatives then implies that $xP_d y$; i.e., person d is a dictator. Q.E.D.

The basic logic of this proof is quite simple. We already know from Theorem 6 that there is a dictator d on the nontrivial pairs. For a trivial pair $\{x, y\}$, we show that there is an alternative z such that $\{x^i, z^i\}$ and $\{y^i, z^i\}$ are nontrivial pairs of consumption bundles for the induced private preference domain Q_i. If $\{x^i, y^i\}$ is nontrivial for i, the existence of z^i follows from the assumption that preferences are saturating. If $\{x^i, y^i\}$ is trivial for i, the existence of z^i follows from the assumption that preferences are hypersaturating. For example, for the preference domain used in either Example 13 or Example 14, if x^i and y^i are as depicted in Figure 10, then any consumption bundle in the shaded region of the diagram will do for z^i. Because preferences are selfish, we can then conclude that $\{x, z\}$ and $\{y, z\}$ are nontrivial pairs of social alternatives and d is a dictator on both of these pairs. To avoid an inconsistency with the assumption that social preferences are transitive, d must also be a dictator on $\{x, y\}$; i.e., person d is an overall dictator.

The classical domain of economic preferences for private goods is Arrow-consistent if the origin is included in the individual consumption sets, as in Examples 11 and 12. On this domain, the preceding argument does not apply whenever the pair $\{x, y\}$ includes the origin, as such a pair can not be separated. However, it follows from Theorem 7 and Example 13 that the only social welfare functions which satisfy all of the Arrow axioms on such domains are dictatorial on the subset of alternatives obtained by deleting the origin from each person's consumption set. In other words, only if at least one of the alternatives being compared has someone with zero consumption may this "almost dictator" have his or her strict preference overridden. Border's (1983) social welfare function in Example 12 has this property.

While this concentration of decision-making power in one individual is troubling enough, this is not the only problem with such social welfare functions; they are also poorly suited for generating social choices. Typically, determining a social preference is an intermediate step in choosing a social alternative. Given a preference profile, the social welfare function is used to determine a social preference and then this social preference is used to determine the socially-best alternative(s) in the feasible set of alternatives. In economic problems, a feasible set could be the set of feasible allocations for the economy. In standard economic models, the feasible set of allocations is compact, has a nonempty interior, and satisfies free disposal. For the economic domain used in Example 11, Campbell (1990a,b) has shown that there are no social welfare functions satisfying the Arrow axioms if we also require socially-best alternatives to exist for all compact subsets of alternatives. In particular, an impossibility theorem is obtained by requiring social preferences to be continuous on X.

Donaldson and Weymark's (1988) discussion of Border's (1983) example (Example 12) provides intuition for these results. They pointed out that with

Border's social welfare function, there are no socially-best alternatives in standard feasible sets of allocations, because there is always a discontinuity in the social preference on the boundary of the allocation space. For example, consider a two-person two-good exchange economy. Because the social welfare function satisfies Weak Pareto, we can restrict our search for socially-best alternatives to allocations in the Edgeworth box for this economy. For the social welfare function in Example 12, all points in the Edgeworth box excluding the two origins are socially preferred to person two's origin which in turn is socially preferred to person one's origin. However, for all points other than the two origins, transferring some of any good from person one to person two is a social improvement (provided person one remains with some consumption). Hence, there is no socially-best alternative.

It thus seems that with private alternatives, just like with public alternatives, restricting the preference domain does not provide a satisfactory way of avoiding Arrow's dilemma. Although the domain of classical economic preferences for private alternatives is Arrow-consistent when each individual has some nonnegative orthant for a consumption set, only unacceptable social welfare functions satisfy Arrow's axioms on this domain.

2.4 Extensions

The results discussed here have been extended in a number of directions. In this section, we briefly describe some of these extensions.

Redekop (1991) considered economic domains of preferences for public or private goods. He supposed that the individual preference domain D_i is a subset of the continuous and monotone preferences in the public good case and is a subset of the selfish, continuous, and monotone in own consumption preferences in the private good case. In either case, Redekop showed that a preference domain is Arrow-consistent only if it is nowhere dense in the Kannai topology. Roughly speaking, for an economic preference domain to be Arrow-consistent, the set of admissible preferences must be topologically small. Further results along these lines may be found in Redekop (1993a, 1993b).[47]

There is a large literature which examines the implications for Arrow's Theorem of weakening the assumption that social preferences are orderings and/or weakening (or eliminating) the Pareto principle. On an unrestricted domain, the results obtained from this line of enquiry are rather negative. Similar negative results have been obtained for restricted preference domains by Border (1983), Bordes and Le Breton (1989, 1990a), Nagahisa (1991) and Campbell (1990a,b; 1992). See also Chapter 3 of this volume and the further

---

[47] Redekop (1991) also proposed a variant of the local approach in which *strict free triples* are used instead of free triples. With a strict free triple, the preference domain includes every possible profile of strict preferences on the triple. For economic domains, Redekop showed that if $\{x, y, z\}$ is a strict free triple, then there is an $\varepsilon > 0$ such that all points in $B(x,\varepsilon) \times B(y,\varepsilon) \times B(z,\varepsilon)$ are free triples, where $B(w,\varepsilon)$ is an ε-neighborhood of w. This result follows from the continuity assumption on preferences.

references there.[48]

In Arrow's Theorem, it is assumed that there are a finite number of individuals. In many applications, such as overlapping generations models, the society is infinite. With an unrestricted preference domain and an infinite society, social welfare functions can be found which satisfy all of Arrow's axioms (although these social welfare functions have other unattractive features). Infinite societies with restricted preference domains have been considered by Campbell (1990a,b, 1992).

We have only considered sets of alternatives which are either purely public or purely private. Bordes and Le Breton (1990a), Redekop (1996), and Ritz (1985) have considered alternatives which have both public and private components.

For the private alternatives case, we assumed that the set of alternatives has a Cartesian structure. However, we noted that if the individual private consumptions are constrained *a priori* by an overall feasibility requirement, then the set of social alternatives is not Cartesian. Bordes and Le Breton (1990b) have considered non-Cartesian sets of indivisible private alternatives. Their analysis applies to such problems as the matching of graduating medical students to hospital residencies. Non-Cartesian sets of divisible private goods (generalized Edgeworth boxes) have been considered by Bordes, Campbell, and Le Breton (1992).

In each of these developments, the basic argument used by Kalai, Muller, and Satterthwaite (1979), what we call the "local approach", plays a central role in the analysis. It is now apparent that the critical assumption which permits the application of the local approach is Binary Independence of Irrelevant Alternatives.[49] However, Binary Independence of Irrelevant Alternatives precludes considering individual marginal rates of substitution (when they are well-defined) in deciding how to socially rank a pair of alternatives, as it is not possible to calculate marginal rates of substitution for the two alternatives being ranked without considering other "irrelevant" alternatives. In economic and political applications, it therefore seems appropriate to consider weaker formulations of Arrow's independence condition, formulations which permit marginal rates of substitution to be relevant features of an alternative. A start in this direction was made by Inada (1964, 1971).[50] Perhaps modifying Arrow's axioms in this way will provide a satisfactory way of avoiding social choice impossibilities on economic and political domains.

---

[48] Many of these restricted domain theorems assume that social preferences are continuous.

[49] Saari (1991) used a discrete version of a calculus argument to establish a number of social choice impossibility theorems, including a version of the result in Example 4 that the domain of classical economic preferences for divisible public goods is Arrow-inconsistent. While Saari did not use the local approach, an independence of irrelevant alternatives assumption is central to Saari's argument.

Donaldson and Roemer (1987) studied private goods environments in which the number of goods is variable. They considered a condition which relates the social rankings for each fixed number of goods to each other. They showed that a number of standard results which use an independence of irrelevant alternatives assumption still hold when their consistency condition is substituted for the independence assumption.

[50] See also Mayston (1980) and Saari (1991).

References

Arrow, K.J. 1963. *Social Choice and Individual Values.* Second Edition. New York: Wiley.

Barberà, S. and B. Peleg. 1990. "Strategy-Proof Voting Schemes with Continuous Preferences," *Social Choice and Welfare* 7: 31 - 38.

Black, D. 1948. "On the Rationale of Group Decision-Making," *Journal of Political Economy* 56: 23 - 34.

Blackorby, C., D. Donaldson, and J. Weymark. 1990. "A Welfarist Proof of Arrow's Theorem," *Recherches Economiques de Louvain* 56: 259 - 286.

Blair, D. and E. Muller. 1983. "Essential Aggregation Procedures on Restricted Domains of Preferences," *Journal of Economic Theory* 30: 34 - 53.

Blau, J.H. 1957. "The Existence of Social Welfare Functions," *Econometrica* 25: 302 - 313.

Border, K. 1983. "Social Welfare Functions for Economic Environments with and without the Pareto Principle," *Journal of Economic Theory* 29: 205 - 216.

Border, K. 1984. "An Impossibility Theorem for Spatial Models," *Public Choice* 43: 293 - 305.

Bordes, G. and M. Le Breton. 1989. "Arrovian Theorems with Private Alternatives Domains and Selfish Individuals," *Journal of Economic Theory* 47: 257 - 281.

Bordes, G. and M. Le Breton. 1990a. "Arrovian Theorems for Economic Domains: The Case Where There are Simultaneously Private and Public Goods," *Social Choice and Welfare* 7: 1 - 17.

Bordes, G. and M. Le Breton. 1990b. "Arrovian Theorems for Economic Domains: Assignments, Matchings and Pairings," *Social Choice and Welfare* 7: 193 - 208.

Bordes, G., D.E. Campbell, and M. Le Breton. 1992. "Arrow's Theorem for Economic Domains: The Case of the Generalized Edgeworth Box." Typescript: College of William and Mary.

Bossert, W. and J. Weymark. 1993. "Generalized Median Social Welfare Functions," *Social Choice and Welfare* 10: 17 - 33.

Campbell, D.E. 1990a. "Wilson's Theorem for Economic Environments and Continuous Social Preferences," *Social Choice and Welfare* 7: 315 - 323.

Campbell, D.E. 1990b. "Arrow's Theorem for Economic Environments and Effective Social Preferences," *Social Choice and Welfare* 7: 325 - 329.

Campbell, D.E. 1992. *Equity, Efficiency, and Social Choice.* Oxford: Clarendon Press.

Donaldson, D. and J.E. Roemer. 1987. "Social Choice in Economic Environments with Dimensional Variation," *Social Choice and Welfare* 4: 253 - 276.

Donaldson, D. and J. Weymark. 1988. "Social Choice in Economic Environments," *Journal of Economic Theory* 46: 291 - 308.

Enelow, J.M. and M.J. Hinich. 1984. *The Spatial Theory of Voting: An Introduction.* Cambridge: Cambridge University Press.

Fishburn, P.C. 1976. "Dictators on Blocks: Generalization of Social Choice Impossibility Theorems," *Journal of Combinatorial Theory, Series B* 20: 153 - 170.

Gaertner, W. 1991. *Domain Conditions in Social Choice Theory*. Chur: Harwood Academic Publishers, forthcoming.

Inada, K.-I. 1964. "On the Economic Welfare Function," *Econometrica* 32: 316 - 338.

Inada, K.-I. 1971. "Social Welfare Function and Social Indifference Surfaces," *Econometrica* 39: 599 - 623.

Kalai, E. and E. Muller. 1977. "Characterization of Domains Admitting Nondictatorial Social Welfare Functions and Nonmanipulable Voting Procedures," *Journal of Economic Theory* 16: 457 - 469.

Kalai, E., E. Muller, and M. Satterthwaite. 1979. "Social Welfare Functions when Preferences are Convex, Strictly Monotonic, and Continuous," *Public Choice* 34: 87 - 97.

Kalai, E. and Z. Ritz. 1980. "Characterization of the Private Alternatives Domains Admitting Arrow Social Welfare Functions," *Journal of Economic Theory* 22: 23 - 36.

Kim, K.H. and F.W. Roush. 1980. *Introduction to Mathematical Theories of Social Consensus*. New York: Dekker.

Kim, K.H. and F.W. Roush. 1981. "Effective Nondictatorial Domains," *Journal of Economic Theory* 24: 40 - 47.

Le Breton, M. 1986. *Essais sur les Fondements de l'Analyse Economique de l'Inégalité*. Thèse de Doctorat d'Etat: Université de Rennes 1.

Le Breton, M. and A. Trannoy. 1987. "Measures of Inequality as an Aggregation of Individual Preferences about Income Distribution: The Arrovian Case," *Journal of Economic Theory* 41: 248 - 269.

Maskin, E. 1976. "Social Welfare Functions for Economics." Typescript: Harvard University.

Maskin, E. 1979. "Fonctions de Préférence Collective Définies sur des Domaines de Préférence Individuelle Soumis à des Contraintes," *Cahiers du Séminaire d'Econométrie* 20: 153 - 182.

Mayston, D. J. 1980. "Where Did Prescriptive Welfare Economics Go Wrong?," in *Contemporary Economic Analysis*, Vol. 2. D.A. Currie and W. Peters, eds. London: Croom Helm.

Nagahisa, R. 1991. "Acyclic and Continuous Social Choice in T_1 Connected Spaces: Including its Application to Economic Environments," *Social Choice and Welfare* 8: 319 - 322.

Nitzan, S. 1976. "On Linear and Lexicographic Orders: Majority Rule and Equilibrium," *International Economic Review* 17: 213 - 219.

Ordeshook, P.C. 1986. *Game Theory and Political Science: An Introduction*. Cambridge: Cambridge University Press.

Redekop, J. 1991. "Social Welfare Functions on Restricted Economic Domains," *Journal of Economic Theory* 53: 396 - 427.

Redekop, J. 1993a. "Arrow-Inconsistent Economic Domains," *Social Choice and Welfare* 10: 127 - 148.

Redekop, J. 1993b. "Social Welfare Functions on Parametric Domains," *Social Choice and Welfare* 10: 107 - 126.

Redekop, J. 1996. "Arrow Theorems in Mixed Goods, Stochastic, and Dynamic Environments," *Social Choice and Welfare* 13: 95-112.

Ritz, Z. 1983. "Restricted Domains, Arrow Social Welfare Functions and Noncorruptible and Nonmanipulable Social Choice Correspondences: The Case of Private Alternatives," *Mathematical Social Sciences* 4: 155 - 179.

Ritz, Z. 1985. "Restricted Domains, Arrow Social Welfare Functions and Noncorruptible and Nonmanipulable Social Choice Correspondences: The Case of Private and Public Alternatives," *Journal of Economic Theory* 35: 1 - 18.

Saari, D.G. 1991. "Calculus and Extensions of Arrow's Theorem," *Journal of Mathematical Economics* 20: 271 - 306.

Sen, A.K. 1970. *Collective Choice and Social Welfare.* San Francisco: Holden-Day.

von Neumann, J. and O. Morgenstern. 1947. *Theory of Games and Economic Behavior.* Second Edition. Princeton: Princeton University Press.

3. Social Ranking of Allocations with and without Coalition Formation

Donald E. Campbell[1]

3.1 Introduction

This chapter provides an introduction to a number of recent results in axiomatic social choice theory for economic environments. It is the method of proof as much as the results themselves that I wish to highlight. By taking full advantage of the topological and algebraic structure of the economic allocation space, one obtains stronger impossibility theorems. Specifically, Arrow's independence axiom (IIA) alone implies that there are no efficiency-equity trade-offs. The only way to avoid the extreme inequity embodied in dictatorship and its variations is to employ a social choice rule that is completely unresponsive to individual preferences. This conclusion emerges when the social ranking is fully transitive. If it is only strict preference of the social preference relation that is required to be transitive, then Pareto optimality is the only welfare standard that neither ignores someone's preference scheme completely nor incorporates it into the social preference relation in a perverse way. The second result relies on a non-imposition condition in addition to Arrow's independence axiom.[2] Although the independence axiom is controversial, we show that its result is implied by a mild incentive compatibility condition. The implication holds regardless of any assumption that is made about the ability of coalitions to form.

Although the results reported here are sharper than usual, they do not supplant those discussed in this volume by Le Breton and Weymark. Their results take social choice theory in directions that I do not pursue. For example, the papers they cite by Bordes and Le Breton apply to a far wider range of situations than just the allocation of a fixed number of private goods. And Donaldson and Weymark (1988) place conventional economic restrictions on the feasible set as well as on individual preferences.[3] The present chapter demands a complete social ranking of the entire space of logically possible allocations of two private goods, and this leads to stronger results with weaker axioms. Undoubtedly, other theorems await discovery, and it is hoped that this summary will inspire a wider investigation.

It is implicit at every point that the social preference relation is continuous. When it is fully transitive as well, and the set of outcomes is a connected

---

[1] This research was financially supported by National Science Foundation, Grant No. SES 9007953.

[2] The independence axiom is the axiom introduced as Independence of Irrelevant Alternatives by Arrow in 1951.

[3] Another important paper in this vein is Le Breton and Weymark, 1991.

N_1 space, then Arrow's independence axiom implies that a nonconstant social decision function is either dictatorial, or inversely dictatorial. (Inverse dictatorship is defined by selecting a fixed individual and generating the social preference ranking by turning that person's preference ordering upside down.) A quasi-transitive relation is one for which only the strict (or asymmetric) part of the relation is required to be transitive; indifference may be intransitive. There do exist non-dictatorial social decision functions that satisfy the Pareto criterion, Arrow's independence axiom, and quasi-transitivity of social preference. For example, the Pareto aggregation rule, which places x above y in the social preference relation if and only if every individual ranks x above y. Of course, this rule is silent on efficiency-equity trade-offs. We are unable to offer a neat characterization of the family of social decision functions satisfying the independence axiom in the case of quasi-transitive social preference. Such a characterization would shed more light on the nature of efficiency-equity trade-offs. We will be concerned with the family of social decision functions satisfying quasi-transitivity, Arrow's independence axiom, and *strict non-imposition*. Strict non-imposition asserts that for arbitrary x and y, alternative x must rank above y socially in some situation–perhaps, but not necessarily, when everyone prefers x to y–unless the individual orderings of x and y are *a priori* restricted. (A typical *a priori* restriction arises when one allocation gives someone more of every good than another.) The basic quasi-transitivity theorem proves that strict non-imposition and Arrow's independence axiom imply that the social decision function is oligarchical, although one or more members of the oligarchy coalition may have their preference orderings inverted before they are incorporated into the group preference.

Our theorems provide clear but discouraging implications for the possibility of meaningful efficiency-equity trade-offs. (We return to this point at the end of the chapter.) In each case continuity of social preference is an important element of the hypothesis. It is a natural requirement when the alternatives to be ranked are members of a standard allocation space.

Section 2 of the chapter discusses the role played by the classical impossibility theorems in proving theorems about economic environments. These classical results are employed as lemmas in Section 3 to show how the results can be extended to connected spaces. Then the topological structure is used to sharpen them. Section 4 extracts critical connected subspaces from the basic allocation space of welfare economics. The theorems of Section 3 apply to these subspaces, and we show how to extend the results to the entire allocation space. Section 5 proves that Arrow's independence axiom is implied by a mild incentive compatibility condition when the framework of the social choice exercise is the standard resource allocation setting. This enables the main theorems to be restated in terms of incentive compatibility. The last section is a brief conclusion. A modest amount of notation must be introduced first.

X represents the space of logically possible outcomes. It is implicit throughout that X has at least three members. A topology is assumed for X, and if it is the discrete topology, then we have the framework of the classical contributions to social choice. When the space in question is the standard Euclidean space of allocations of two private goods we use Ω in place of X. A typical member x of Ω assigns the commodity vector $x(t)$ to individual t.

A preorder on X is a complete and transitive binary relation. A relation R is quasi-transitive if it is complete and its asymmetric factor P is transitive. R is continuous if the sets $\{y \in X|\ yPx\}$ and $\{y \in X|\ xPy\}$ are open. The inverse of a relation R is the relation $-R$, where $x(-R)y$ holds if and only if yRx.

$N = \{1, 2, ..., \tau\}$ represents the (finite) society. A profile is a function p from N into the set of continuous preorders, and $p(t)$ is the preorder assigned to $t \in N$ by p. A social choice domain is some specific set D of profiles. D is always a product set: $D = \prod_{t \in N} D_t$, where D_t is the set of preorders on X that are admissible for individual t. When the outcome space is Ω we let W represent the family of profiles of classical economic preferences on Ω: each $p(t)$ is selfish, monotonic, convex, and differentiable.

A *social decision function* is a function σ from the domain D into the set of continuous and quasi-transitive relations on X, and $\sigma(p)$ is the social preference relation specified by σ when individual preferences are represented by profile p. If $\sigma(p)$ is fully transitive for each profile p in the domain, then we say that σ is a social *welfare* function. A social welfare function is *null* if every alternative is socially indifferent to every other alternative at every profile. The social decision function σ satisfies *non-imposition* if for every pair of alternatives x and y, there is some $p \in D$ such that $\sigma(p)$ ranks x at least as high as y and there is some $p' \in D$ such that $\sigma(p')$ ranks y at least as high as x. (Non-imposition is applied at an early stage when it is not necessary to consider *a priori* restrictions; hence there is no need to incorporate them into the definition.)

Because our axioms do not rule out the possibility that an individual's preference ordering is inverted before it is brought to bear on the social preference scheme we will employ a fictitious 'anti-society'. Set $-N = \{-1, -2, ..., -\tau\}$ and let N^* be the union of N and $-N$. To every domain D for N we associate the domain D^* for society N^*. To each p in D there corresponds a unique p^* in D^*, namely the one satisfying $p^*(t) = p(t)$ for each t in N and $p^*(t) = -p(-t)$ for each $-t$ in $-N$. A coalition for society N^* is any subset S of N^* such that t does not belong to S if $-t$ does. To each social decision function σ defined for N and D we associate the social decision function σ^* for N^* and D^* by setting $\sigma^*(p^*) = \sigma(p)$.

The axioms that we impose on σ will automatically be satisfied by σ^*. Each of our theorems amounts to a proof that under the conditions imposed on σ there is an oligarchy $S \subset N^*$ underlying σ^*. In plain words, this means that there is an oligarchy underlying σ, but if $-t$ belongs to $S \cap -N$, then individual t's preference ordering is inverted before it is incorporated into the group preference scheme. Logically speaking, our lemmas and theorems apply to σ^* and D^* but there will be no confusion if we refer exclusively to σ and D; σ^* can be left off stage, although we will refer to the augmented society in stating the results. Note that σ is dictatorial if $S = \{t\}$ for some $t \in N$, and

σ is inversely dictatorial if $S = \{-t\}$ for some $t \in N$.

The contrived society N^* permits a very simple statement and proof of the following point of departure for impossibility theorems: If coalition $S \subset N^*$ is decisive for some ordered pair of distinct alternatives then S is decisive for all pairs of alternatives. As usual, we say that S is decisive for (x, y) if σ places x strictly above y in the social ranking whenever each member of S strictly prefers x to y. And S is (globally) decisive if it is decisive for all ordered pairs. In other words, x is socially preferred to y if every t in $S \cap N$ strictly prefers x to y, and every t in N such that $-t$ belongs to $S \cap (-N)$ strictly prefers y to x. A decisive coalition is an oligarchy if each of its members has veto power. Individual $t \in N^*$ has veto power if $\sigma(p)$ ranks x at least as high as y whenever t strictly prefers x to y.

Now we re-examine the basic impossibility theorems to see how the unrestricted domain assumption can be relaxed in a way that opens the door to results that bear on economic environments. The classical theorems to which we refer are the dictatorship theorems of Arrow (1963) and Wilson (1972), and the oligarchy theorem discovered independently by Gibbard (1969), Guha (1972), and Mas-Colell and Sonnenschein (1972).

3.2 Discrete Spaces

This section assumes the discrete topology for X. This means that continuity of social preference has no force. A domain has the *free triple property* if for every individual t, every three-element subset Y of X, and every preorder R on Y, there is some preorder R' in D_t that agrees with R over Y. Note that D^* has the free triple property if D does. For the classical theorems one can replace the assumption that the domain is the set of all profiles on X with the assumption that the domain has the free triple property, without having to modify any of the standard proofs. The free triple property is weaker than the unrestricted domain assumption. Suppose, for example, $X = \{w, x, y, z\}$ and D is the set of all profiles such that no individual ranks w as a most-preferred alternative. Then D has the free triple property. The distinction between an unrestricted domain and the free triple property has great significance for our treatment of allocation spaces and classical economic preferences.

The key step in the proofs of social choice impossibility theorems is the employment of the following *covering property*: For any two profiles, p and p' in the domain and any three alternatives x, y, z in X there is a profile p'' in the domain such that for each individual t the ordering $p''(t)$ agrees with $p(t)$ over $\{x, y\}$ and with $p'(t)$ over $\{y, z\}$. Clearly, both unrestricted domains and free-triple domains have the covering property. Consider the allocation space Ω and the domain W. Set $x(t) = (2, 2), y(t) = (2, 2)$, and $z(t) = (1, 1)$ for each t. Then $W(\{x, y, z\})$, the restriction of W to $\{x, y, z\}$, does not have the free triple property, but it does have the covering property because $W(\{x, y, z\})$ is a singleton. Consider a less trivial example. Set $x(1) = (2, 2), y(1) = (4, 1), z(1) = (3, 3)$ and $x(t) = (1, 4), y(t) = (4, 1), z(t) = (3, 3)$ for all $t \neq 1$. For everyone except person 1 the three alternatives may be arbitrarily ordered by an appropriate choice of a classical indifference map. As for person 1, preorders R and R' can be found in W_1 such that xPy and $yP'z$, but there is no R'' in W_1 such that $xP''yP''z$. Therefore $W(\{x,y,z\})$ does not have the covering property in this case. It will be necessary to proceed in a roundabout way in order to extend impossibility theorems to Ω and W. We first apply them to subspaces X for which $W(X)$ has the free triple property and then relate the subspaces in a way that produces the desired generalization.

Now we illustrate the key role played by the covering property. We prove four important but simple lemmas that will take us to the threshold of most of the celebrated impossibility theorems. The first result ties together the treatment of social decision functions and social welfare functions by proving that σ satisfies *strict* non-imposition if it is a non-null social welfare function satisfying non-imposition and Arrow's independence axiom. It is implicit throughout this section that X has at least three members.

The Non-imposition Lemma: *Let σ be a non-null social welfare function on a domain with the covering property. If σ satisfies Arrow's independence axiom and non-imposition, then σ satisfies strict non-imposition.*

Proof: There is some $p \in D$ and some $x, y \in X$ such that $\sigma(p)$ ranks x strictly above y, because σ is not null. Let z be any other alternative. By non-imposition there is some $p' \in D$ such that $\sigma(p')$ ranks y at least as high as z. By the covering property there is some profile p'' in D such that p'' and p exhibit the same individual orderings of x and y, and p'' and p' exhibit the same individual orderings of y and z. By the independence axiom $\sigma(p'')$ ranks x strictly above y and y at least as high as z. Transitivity of $\sigma(p'')$ implies that outcome x ranks strictly above z. Repeated application of this argument establishes strict non-imposition. $Q.E.D.$

The non-imposition lemma allows us to state the other lemmas in terms of social decision functions and the strict non-imposition condition. Now we prove one of the basic lemmas used in the more streamlined proofs of the classical theorems. See Sen (1986) for example.

The Extension Lemma: *Let σ be a social decision function on a domain with the free triple property. If σ satisfies Arrow's independence axiom and strict non-imposition, then coalition $S \subset N^*$ is decisive if it is decisive for some (x, y) such that $x \neq y$.*

Proof: Let z be any alternative distinct from x and y. We show that S is decisive for (x, z). Let p be any profile for which everyone in S strictly prefers x to z. If there is no such profile, then S is vacuously decisive for (x, z). There is some profile p' for which $\sigma(p')$ ranks y strictly above z by strict non-imposition. Let p'' be any profile such that for each t in $N, p''(t)$ and $p(t)$ agree over $\{x, z\}, p''(t)$ and $p'(t)$ agree over $\{y, z\}$, and everyone in S strictly prefers x to y under p''. Then $\sigma(p'')$ ranks x above y because S is decisive for (x, y)

and $\sigma(p'')$ ranks y above z by independence. Then $\sigma(p'')$ ranks x above z by quasi-transitivity and hence $\sigma(p)$ ranks x above z by independence. Similarly, one proves that S is decisive for (z,y). These two facts easily lead to a proof of the global decisiveness of S. Q.E.D.

The extension lemma goes a long way toward proving that the social decision function is oligarchical, but it is not the final step. If the Pareto criterion were in force, coalition T would be decisive even if individual 1 were a dictator. Identification of the smallest decisive coalition is essential. The next lemma does this, but it is necessary at this point to assume something stronger than the covering property, which does not guarantee any variability of individual preference. The free triple property is invoked.

The Reduction Lemma: *Let σ be a social decision function on a domain with the free triple property. If σ satisfies Arrow's independence axiom and strict non-imposition, then $S \cap S'$ is decisive if both $S \subset N^*$ and $S' \subset N^*$ are decisive.*

Proof: Let $x, y,$ and z be any three alternatives. Choose any profile p in D such that everyone in S strictly prefers x to y and everyone in S' strictly prefers y to z. Then $\sigma(p)$ ranks x strictly above y and y strictly above z by decisiveness of S and S' respectively. Then x ranks strictly above z by quasi-transitivity and thus $S \cap S'$ is decisive for (x,z) by independence. Then $S \cap S'$ is decisive by the extension lemma. Q.E.D.

We still do not know that a decisive coalition exists. In fact, if $\sigma(p)$ is merely quasi-transitive we can provide a counterexample.

EXAMPLE 1: Let X be any set endowed with the discrete topology. Set x above y socially if and only if person 1 prefers x to y and person 2 is indifferent.

This example will not generate continuous social preferences in most connected spaces. If x ranks above y socially then individual 2 is indifferent between x and y. If every neighborhood of y contains some alternative z that individual 2 strictly prefers to x then the social preference relation is not continuous, because x cannot be socially preferred to z. Proof of the existence of a decisive coalition when social preference is merely quasi-transitive is deferred to the next section dealing with connected spaces. It is easy to establish existence under full transitivity, as we now show.

The Existence Lemma: *Let σ be a non-null social welfare function on a domain with the free triple property. If σ satisfies Arrow's independence axiom and non-imposition, then either N or $-N$ is decisive.*

Proof: Choose a profile p such that some outcome x ranks above some outcome y according to $\sigma(p)$. Now choose a profile p' arbitrarily except that every

Donald E. Campbell   69

individual ranks both x and y strictly above z and p' and p agree with respect to the individual orderings of x and y. If $\sigma(p')$ ranks z strictly above y then $-N$ is decisive for (z,y) and hence for all pairs by the extension lemma. Otherwise, $\sigma(p')$ ranks x strictly above z, because x ranks above y which ranks at least as high as z. Then N is decisive. Q.E.D.

Now we can state Wilson's generalization of Arrow's theorem (Wilson 1972 and Arrow 1963).

Dictatorship Theorem 1 (Wilson): *Let σ be a nonnull social welfare function on a domain with the free triple property. If σ satisfies Arrow's independence axiom and non-imposition then it is dictatorial.*

Outline of proof: (See Campbell 1990b for details and extension to the infinite society case.) If N is decisive use the extension lemma to prove that an arbitrary subset of T is decisive if its complement is not. Repeated application of the reduction and extension lemmas will show that a singleton subset of N must be decisive. If N is not decisive then $-N$ is decisive by the existence lemma and hence a singleton subset of $-N$ is decisive by the reduction and extension lemmas. Q.E.D.

We remind the reader that we are proving theorems about σ^*, N^*, and D^*. Although D^* is not a product set, none of the proofs require the construction of new profiles from old profiles in a way that produces a violation of the equality $p^*(t) = -p^*(-t)$.

3.3 Connected Spaces

Now we assume that X is a connected T_1 space. This means that the assumption of continuous social preferences (which is implicit at every point) is restrictive. It also means that X is infinite and every nonempty open subset is infinite, unless X is a singleton in which case our theorems are obviously true. It also means that three-element subspaces are discrete and we can apply the lemmas of the previous section. The most important type of connected T_1 space that will be encountered in this chapter is a CD (Cobb-Douglas) subspace. To define this first choose for each $t \in N$ some subset X_t of $\Re^2_{++}$ such that $X_t = h_t[(0,1)]$ for some continuous one-to-one function h_t from the interval (0,1) into $\Re^2_{++}$ and for every distinct x, y, z in X_t we have

(i) $(x_1 - y_1)(x_2 - y_2) < 0$ and
(ii) $(x_2 - y_2)(z_1 - y_1) > (y_2 - z_2)(y_1 - x_1)$ if $x_1 < y_1 < z_1$.

Conditions (i) and (ii) imply that X_t is a strictly convex downward sloping curve. For example, $X_t = \{a \in E^2_{++} \mid \log a_1 + \log a_2 = 0\}$ has these two properties as well as being homeomorphic to $(0,1)$. The product $X = \Pi_{\{t \in T\}} X_t$ is almost what we require. However, for any t there will be distinct x, y, z in X such that $x(t) = y(t) = z(t)$, and therefore $D = W(X)$ does not have the free triple property. However, if we define the function $H : (0,1) \to \Omega$ by setting $H(\alpha) = \Pi_{t \in N}\, h_t(\alpha)$ then $Y = H(0,1)$ is connected as the continuous image of a connected set. If $x = H(\alpha)$ and $y = H(\beta)$ are distinct members of Y then $\alpha \neq \beta$ and hence $x(t) \neq y(t)$ for all $t \in N$. Therefore, $W(Y)$ has the free triple property. Sets constructed in this way are referred to as CD subspaces.

Almost all of the spaces that economists use to model individual decision making and resource allocation are connected T_1 spaces. Even this modest structure allows us to prove that a decisive coalition exists when social preference is quasi-transitive. An additional *regularity* assumption is required at this point, but it is a very modest one that is met in virtually every economic context. The domain D is regular if whenever individual t is indifferent between x and y under the preference scheme R then there is also an admissible preorder R' for t under which t is indifferent between z and y if and only if $z = x$ or $z = y$. (Because the regularity assumption is invoked in this paper primarily to obtain results for outcome spaces that are CD subspaces we can get away with a stronger and more manageable definition than would be appropriate for more general results such as those found in Campbell 1992c.) To establish the existence of a decisive coalition choose any two alternatives x and y and a profile p such that $\sigma(p)$ ranks x strictly above y. By regularity and Arrow's independence axiom we may assume that there is a neighborhood $v(x)$ of x such that $\sigma(p)$ ranks every $z \in v(x)$ strictly above y and no individual $t \in N^*$ is indifferent between y and any member of $v(x) - \{x\}$. Choose some $z \in v(x) - \{x\}$ and set $S = \{t \in N \mid t \text{ strictly prefers } z \text{ to } y\} \cup \{t \in -N \mid t \text{ strictly prefers } y \text{ to } z\}$. Then S is decisive for (z, y) and hence is globally decisive by the extension lemma. The intersection of all decisive coalitions is decisive by the reduction lemma. A standard argument shows that the members of a minimal decisive coalition have veto power. Therefore we have proved the following oligarchy theorem which generalizes Gibbard (1969), Guha (1972), and Mas-Colell and Sonnenschein (1972) by replacing the Pareto criterion with strict non-imposition. (See Campbell 1990a for the complete argument.) Q.E.D.

Oligarchy Theorem 1: *Let σ be a social decision function on a regular domain with the free triple property. If σ satisfies Arrow's independence axiom and strict non-imposition, then it is oligarchical.*

The topological assumption plays a modest role in proving this theorem; it allows us to prove that a decisive coalition exists. In the case of social welfare functions we are able to do this by calling on the assumption that social *indifference* is transitive. Transitivity of the symmetric factor always has far-reaching implications. When used in tandem with the assumption that X is a connected N_1 space, it leads to a substantial strengthening of Wilson's theorem. We can drop the supposition that σ satisfies non-imposition. There will be non-dictatorial social welfare functions that satisfy Arrow's independence axiom, but all of them are *constant*. In other words, the nondictatorial social welfare functions are completely unresponsive to individual preference. This means that the only way to avoid the extreme inequity of dictatorship is to abandon efficiency goals completely. In order to prove the theorem we need to define $\sigma|_Z$, the restriction of σ to the subset Z of X : Simply let $\sigma|_{Z(p)}$ be the restriction of $\sigma(p)$ to Z. If σ satisfies Arrow's independence axiom then $\sigma|_Z$ is well defined.

Dictatorship Theorem 2: *Let σ be a social welfare function on a domain D with the free triple property. If σ satisfies Arrow's independence axiom then it is dictatorial or constant.*

Outline of Proof: (See Campbell 1992a for details.) If σ is not constant then there are two alternatives x and y and two profiles p and p' such that $\sigma(p)$ ranks x above y and $\sigma(p')$ does not. Because $\sigma(p)$ is continuous and *fully transitive* and the space is connected there is some z such that $\sigma(p)$ ranks x above z and z above y. By the covering property there is some profile p'' such that p'' agrees with p over $\{z,y\}$ and p'' agrees with p' over $\{y,x\}$. Then $\sigma(p'')$ ranks z above y and y at least as high as x by the independence axiom. Then $\sigma(p'')$ ranks z above x by transitivity. Recall that $\sigma(p)$ ranks x above z.

By continuity of social preference there are neighborhoods $v(z)$ and $v(x)$ such that $\sigma(p'')$ [resp. $\sigma(p)$] ranks everything in $v(z)$ above [resp. below] everything in $v(x)$. Set $V = v(x) \cup v(z)$. Then $\sigma|_V$ satisfies non-imposition by transitivity and the covering property. Obviously, $\sigma|_V$ is not null. Therefore $\sigma|_V$ is dictatorial by the first dictatorship theorem. For concreteness, suppose that 1 is the dictator. Choose any x^* in V. Let G denote the set of x in X such that there exist two profiles p and p' with $\sigma(p)$ ranking x at least as high as x^* and $\sigma(p')$ ranking x^* at least as high as x. Obviously, $V \subset G$. By transitivity and the covering property $\sigma|_G$ satisfies non-imposition, so 1 is a dictator for $\sigma|_G$ by Wilson's theorem. If G is not closed, we will run into a contradiction at any point belonging to the complement of G *and* to the closure of G, because social preference is continuous. Therefore G must be closed. X is connected so the set $X - G$ is not closed if $X \neq G$. Then there will be some violation of continuity of social preference at a point in G that is a closure point of $X-G$. Therefore $X = G$ and σ is dictatorial. Q.E.D.

Oligarchy Theorem 1 can be strengthened by relaxing strict non-imposition. The next section provides an illustration for the realm of economic environments. The rest of this chapter shows how to apply the last two results to economic environments, and once the results are established Section 5 will strengthen them by replacing Arrow's independence axiom with a mild incentive compatibility requirement. Before treating economic environments we present an example that underscores the importance of continuity of social preference in Dictatorship Theorem 2.

EXAMPLE 2: Let X be the real interval $[0,2)$ and let D be the family of all profiles of continuous preorders on X. If $|x - y| = 1$ then the social ranking of x and y is determined by simple majority rule. If $|x - y| \neq 1$ then x ranks strictly above y in the social preference scheme if (i) $x - 1 > y \geq 0$ or $x > y - 1 \geq 0$, or (ii) $x > y$ and $x \geq 1$ and $y \geq 1$, or (iii) $x > y$ and $x < 1$ and $y < 1$.

Although this social welfare function is neither dictatorial nor constant, Arrow's independence axiom is satisfied and social preference is always transitive. Of course, social preference cannot always be continuous in a topology for which $[0, 2)$ is a connected T_1 space. But there is a more serious indictment of this social choice rule. Consider the space $[0, 2)^2$ of ordered pairs. This is a rectangle in $\Re_+^2$ with the Lebesgue measure 4. Connect the pairs with respect to which the social ranking is not imposed. What we get is two line segments comprising the set of pairs (x, y) in $[0, 2)^2$ such that $|x - y| = 1$, a set of measure zero. By employing Lebesgue measure in this way, Campbell and Kelly (1991) show that any social welfare function satisfying Arrow's independence axiom will either exhibit too much dictatorship or too much imposition.

3.4 Economic Environments

Let the outcome space X be the Euclidean space of allocations of two private goods, denoted by Ω. Each $x \in \Omega$ assigns the vector $x(t)$ to individual $t \in N$. Let W denote the set of profiles of classical economic preferences (selfish, monotonic, etc.) on Ω.

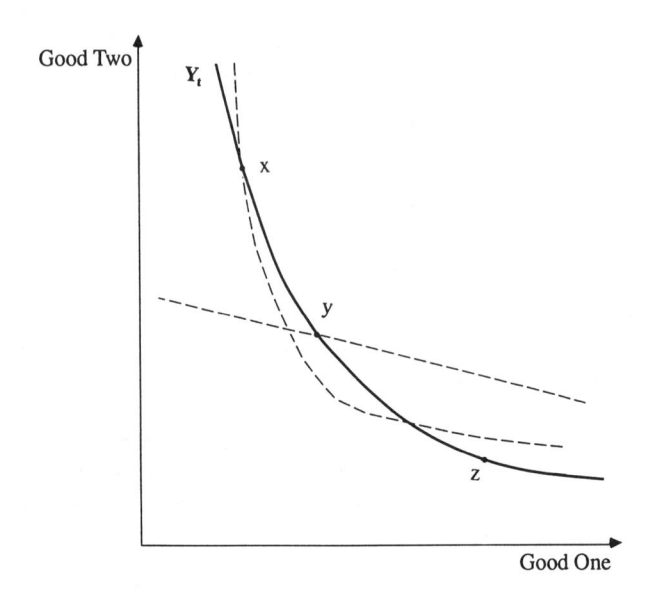

Figure 1

Donald E. Campbell 73

Consider the subspace Y_t of individual t's commodity space represented as the strictly convex downward sloping curve in Figure 1. It is easy to show that any three points in Y_t can be arbitrarily ordered by an appropriate choice of a classical indifference map on the entire commodity space. The broken curves are indifference curves belonging to distinct economic preference regimes, and they illustrate two of the thirteen logically possible preorders on a three-element set. Clearly, $W(Y)$ has the free triple property if Y is a CD subspace.

Therefore, a direct application of Dictatorship Theorem 2 and Oligarchy Theorem 1 gives us two stepping stones to the corresponding results for economic environments. [Note that $W(Y)$ is regular if Y is a CD subspace.]

Dictatorship Theorem 3: *If σ is a social welfare function on W satisfying Arrow's independence axiom and $Y \subset \Omega$ is a CD subspace then $\sigma|_Y$ is either constant or dictatorial.*

Oligarchy Theorem 2: *If σ is a social decision function on W satisfying Arrow's independence axiom and strict non-imposition and $Y \subset \Omega$ is a CD subspace then $\sigma|_Y$ is oligarchical.*

Now we connect various CD subspaces in a way that allows us to extend these two theorems to the entire allocation space Ω. Suppose that σ is a social welfare function on W satisfying Arrow's independence axiom and Y and Z are two CD subspaces that cross at x. Consider Figure 2. We can construct a new CD subspace X by connecting the part of Y_t above $x(t)$ to the part of Z_t below $x(t)$.

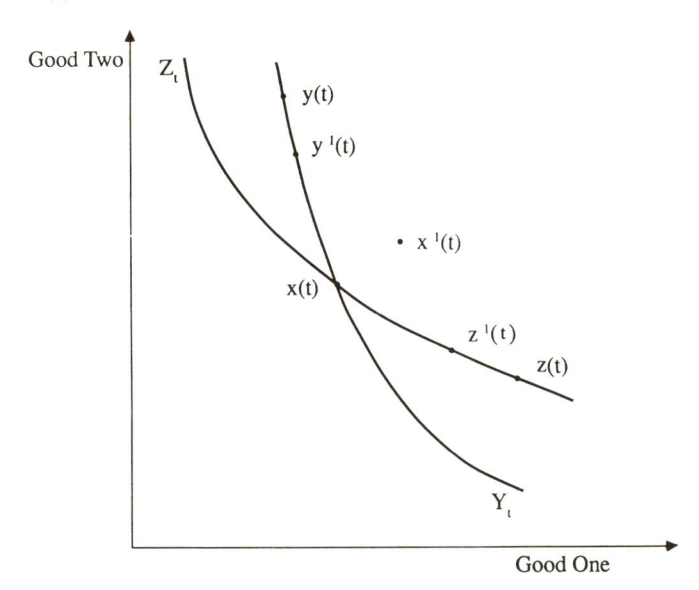

Figure 2

By Dictatorship Theorem 3 each of the social welfare functions $\sigma|_Y, \sigma|_Z$, and $\sigma|_X$ is either constant or dictatorial. Suppose that $t \in N^*$ is a dictator for $\sigma|_Y$. Choose two points $y, y^1 \in Y \cap X$. Person t dictates the social preference over $\{y, y^1\}$ because y and y^1 belong to Y. But then t must dictate $\sigma|_X$. The social welfare function $\sigma|_X$ is obviously not constant and therefore it is dictatorial by Dictatorship Theorem 3. The dictator must be person t because t dictates the ordering of y and y^1 which belong to X. And because X and Z have allocations in common, individual t must dictate $\sigma|_Z$ as well. Therefore, if t dictates $\sigma|_Y$ for CD subspace Y then t dictates $\sigma|_Y$ for *all* CD subspaces. This means that t dictates all pairs from Ω except perhaps pairs such as $\{x, x^1\}$ through which one cannot draw a strictly convex downward sloping curve for one or more individuals. Consider two such points represented in Figure 2. Person t will dictate the social ordering of x^1 and z because these allocations belong to some CD subspace. Similarly, t dictates the ordering of z and x. Choose profile $p \in W$ arbitrarily, except that t strictly prefers x^1 to z and z to x. Then $\sigma(p)$ ranks x^1 above z and z above x. Then x^1 ranks above x by transitivity, and hence x^1 ranks above x in the social preference scheme for all profiles by Arrow's independence axiom. Therefore, t dictates the ordering of x^1 and x. We have proved the dictatorship theorem for the domain W and the allocation space Ω.

Dictatorship Theorem 4: *If σ is a social welfare function on W satisfying Arrow's independence axiom then σ is either constant or dictatorial.*

In the same way we can use CD subspaces to prove the oligarchy theorem for economic environments. However, the oligarchy's jurisdiction may not extend to pairs in which one of the allocations assigns someone the zero commodity vector. We can have x and y tied in the social ranking associated with any profile if either x or y assigns some individual the zero vector. This will not produce a violation of strict non-imposition because in this case the individual's ranking of x and y is *a priori* restricted within the domain of economic preferences. And it will not contravene quasi-transitivity, because it only forces a violation of social *indifference*.

Oligarchy Theorem 3: *If σ is a social decision function on W satisfying Arrow's independence axiom and strict non-imposition then σ is oligarchical.*

The complete proofs may be found in Campbell (1992c). The results are proved for infinite societies and overlapping generations economies in Campbell (1991 and 1992d). The results are extended to economies with public goods in Campbell (1992e).

Campbell and Nagahisa (1991) prove Oligarchy Theorem 3 with a very weak unbiasedness condition substituting for strict non-imposition. The social decision function σ is unbiased if a (non-singleton) connected subspace Y does not contain any alternative that is socially best for all profiles in D or socially worst for all profiles in D whenever $D(Y)$ has the free triple property *and* for

Donald E. Campbell

each individual t and each $x \in Y$ there exist admissible preorders R and R' such that x is uniquely best in Y with respect to R and uniquely worst in Y with respect to R'.

Our theorems are quite strong, but they rest on the controversial independence axiom of Arrow. In the next section we show how independence can be replaced by a mild incentive compatibility condition without disturbing the conclusions.

3.5 Implementation

Let ϕ be a *social choice correspondence*. That is, for each profile p in W and each nonempty compact subset Z of Ω the correspondence identifies a set $\phi(p, Z)$ of socially best alternatives in Z. For each Z let $\Gamma_Z = (M_Z, g_Z)$ be a game form. To simplify, drop the subscript and let the feasible set Z be understood. M specifies a message (or strategy) set $M(t)$ for each agent t in N. And $m \in M$ conveys the message $m(t)$ transmitted by each agent t. For each m in M the outcome function g selects the outcome $g(m)$ in Z. Let E be the equilibrium correspondence: For each p in W, $E(p)$ denotes the set $\{g(m) | m$ is an equilibrium of Γ for profile $p\}$. We say that Γ *implements* the sub-correspondence $\phi(p, Z)$ if $E(p) = \phi(p, Z)$ for all $p \in W$. We remain vague about the equilibrium concept employed, because our proof that Arrow's independence axiom is implied by implementability is valid for a wide variety of noncooperative and *cooperative* solution concepts. As long as E is defined so that: (1) individual behavior is independent of individual preferences involving infeasible alternatives, *i.e.* involving alternatives not in Z, and (2) infeasible alternatives play no role in guiding the mechanism to an equilibrium, then we will have $E(p) = E(p')$ whenever p and p' specify the same individual preferences over Z, however they may differ outside of Z. In that case, implementability implies that $\phi(p, Z) = \phi(p', Z)$ whenever p and p' specify the same individual preferences over Z. We call this condition *Plott's independence axiom* (Plott 1976).

Now, let us apply this to social decision functions. Given σ, let $\phi(p, Z)$ denote the set $\{x \in Z |$ no $y \in Z$ ranks strictly above x according to $\sigma(p)\}$. Then ϕ is a social choice correspondence. To emphasize the dependence of ϕ on σ set $\phi = \max \sigma$. Campbell (1992b) proves the following proposition for social decision functions. The proposition refers to a fixed integer m, which should be thought of as a large finite number: finite for information processing considerations, but large in order to obtain a good approximation to the feasible set of allocations, which may be an Edgeworth box, *etc.*

Implementability Theorem: *Let m be any positive integer other than unity. If max $\sigma(\cdot, Z)$ satisfies Plott's independence axiom for every m-element subset Z of Γ, then σ satisfies Arrow's independence axiom.*

We can use the implementability proposition to rephrase the oligarchy and dictatorship theorems in terms of incentive compatibility.

Dictatorship Theorem 5: *Let m be any positive integer other than unity. If σ is a nonconstant social welfare function on W and max $\sigma(\cdot, Z)$ satisfies Plott's independence axiom for every m-element subset Z of Ω then σ is dictatorial.*

Oligarchy Theorem 4: *Let m be any positive integer other than unity. If σ is a social decision function on W satisfying strict non-imposition and max $\sigma(\cdot, Z)$ satisfies Plott's independence axiom for every m-element Z of Ω, then σ is oligarchical.*

Plott's independence axiom is implicit in the standard treatments of implementability: Maskin (1977), Kelly (1977), Strnad (1987), Saijo (1988), Matsushima (1988), Moore and Repullo (1988), Abreu and Sen (1990 and 1991), and Palfrey and Srivistava (1991) for example. This is also true of Maskin (1979), which explicitly allows for coalition formation. What makes the notion of implementability employed in this section quite restrictive is that the social choice correspondence is assumed to be rationalized by a social decision function. It is Arrovian in spirit because it requires a complete ranking of the allocation space Ω before any feasible set Z is presented for consideration. This really is the one restrictive axiom carried over from Arrow's seminal monograph. We have relaxed the transitivity assumption to quasitransitivity; of course that could be further weakened to acyclicity. Nagahisa (1990) presents some enlightening results under the acyclicity rubric without assuming the Pareto criterion, although he imposes a strong positive responsiveness condition.

3.6 Conclusion

We have shown that there are no meaningful efficiency-equity trade-offs if the social choice formula is based exclusively on *ordinal* individual preference information. This is quite clear in the case of transitive social preference. Either the social welfare function is without any vestige of equity because it is dictatorial, or it is constant and thus has no efficiency content. This is true even without invoking Arrow's independence axiom as long as a mild incentive compatibility condition is substituted and it is assumed that individual strategic behavior is a function only of the ordinal content of an individual's preference scheme.

In the case of quasi-transitive social preference, our results suggest that if the social decision function does not embody Pareto optimality as the welfare standard, then it is independent of the preferences of one or more individual or else it reflects some individual's preference ordering in a perverse way. In either case it fails an elementary test of equity. If it does lead to Pareto optimality then it is completely silent on distributional matters; it provides no guidance on efficiency-equity trade-offs.

References

Abreu, D., and Arunava Sen. 1990. "Subgame Perfect Implementation: A Necessary and Almost Sufficient Condition," *Journal of Economic Theory* 50: 285-299.

Abreu, D., and Aruvana Sen. 1991. "Virtual Implementation in Nash Equilibrium," *Econometrica* 59: 997-1022.

Arrow, K. J. 1951. *Social Choice and Individual Values.* New York: Wiley.

Arrow, K.J. 1963. *Social Choice and Individual Values,* Second Edition. New York: Wiley.

Campbell, D.E. 1990a. "Can Equity Be Purchased at the Expense of Efficiency? An Axiomatic Enquiry," *Journal of Economic Theory* 51: 32-47.

Campbell, D.E. 1990b. "Intergenerational Social Choice without the Pareto Principle," *Journal of Economic Theory* 50: 414-423.

Campbell, D.E. 1991. "Overlapping Generations Economies and Efficiency-Equity Trade-offs." Typescript: College of William and Mary.

Campbell, D.E. 1992a. "Transitive Social Choice in Economic Environments," *International Economic Review* 33: 341-352.

Campbell, D.E. 1992b. "Implementation of Social Welfare Functions," *International Economic Review* 33: 525-533.

Campbell, D.E. 1992c. *Equity, Efficiency, and Social Choice.* Oxford: Clarendon Press.

Campbell, D.E. 1992d. "Quasi-transitive Intergenerational Choice for Economic Environments," *Journal of Mathematical Economics* 21: 229-247.

Campbell, D.E. 1992e. "Public Goods and Arrovian Social Choice," *Social Choice and Welfare* 9: 173-183.

Campbell, D.E., and J. S. Kelly. 1991. "The Scope of Dictatorship and Responsiveness in Arrovial Social Choice." Typescript: College of William and Mary.

Campbell, D. E. and J. S. Kelly. 1993. "t or $1-t$. That is the Trade-off," *Econometrica* 61: 1355-1366.

Campbell, D.E., and R-I. Nagahisa. 1991. "A Simple Axiomatization of Pareto Optimality." Typescript: College of William and Mary.

Campbell, D. E. and R-I. Nagahisa. 1994. "A Foundation for Pareto Aggregation," *Journal of Economic Theory* 64: 277-285.

Donaldson, D., and J. Weymark. 1988. "Social Choice in Economic Environments," *Journal of Economic Theory* 46: 291-308.

Gibbard, A. 1969. "Social Choice and the Arrow Condition." Typescript: Harvard University.

Guha, A.S. 1972. "Neutrality, Monotonicity, and the Right of Veto," *Econometrica* 40: 821-826.

Kelly, J.S. 1977. "Strategy-proofness and Social Choice Functions without Single-valuedness," *Econometrica* 45: 439-446.

Le Breton, M., and J. Weymark. 1991. "Social Choice with Analytic Preferences." Typescript: University of British Columbia.

Mas-Collel, A., and H. Sonnenschein. 1972. "General Possibility Theorems for Group Decisions," *Review of Economic Studies* 39: 185-192.

Maskin, E.S. 1977. "Nash Equilibrium and Welfare Optimality." Typescript: M.I.T.

Maskin, E.S. 1979. "Implementation and Strong Nash Equilibrium," in *Aggregation and Revelation of Preference*, J.-J. Laffont, ed. Amsterdam: North-Holland.

Matsushima, H. 1988. "A New Approach to the Implementation Problem," *Journal of Economic Theory* 45: 128-144.

Moore, J., and R.L. Repullo. 1988. "Subgame Perfect Implementation," *Econometrica* 56: 1191-1220.

Nagahisa, R-I. 1991. "Acyclic and Continuous Social Choice in T_1 Connected Spaces: Including its Application to Economic Environments," *Social Choice and Welfare* 8: 319-332.

Palfrey, T. and S. Srivistava. 1991. "Nash Implementation Using Undominated Strategies," *Econometrica* 59: 479-502.

Plott, C.R. 1976. "Axiomatic Social Choice Theory: An Overview and Interpretation," *American Journal of Political Science* 20: 511-596.

Saijo, T. 1988. "Strategy Space Reduction in Maskin's Theorem: Sufficient Conditions for Nash Implementation," *Econometrica* 56: 693-700.

Sen, A.K. 1986. "Information and Invariance in Normative Choice," in *Essays in Honor of J.J. Arrow*, Vol. 1, *Social Choice and Public Decision-Making*, W.P. Heller, R.M. Starr, and D.A. Starrett, eds. Cambridge: Cambridge University Press.

Strnad, J. 1987. "Full Nash Implementation of Neutral Social Functions," *Journal of Mathematical Economics* 16: 17-37.

Wilson, R.B. 1972. "Social Choice Theory without the Pareto Principle," *Journal of Economic Theory* 5: 478-486.

4. Non Binary Social Choice: A Brief Introduction

Yongsheng Xu

4.1 Introduction

The purpose of this article is to provide a brief introduction to choice function approaches that examine Arrow's impossibility result. In Arrow's original formulation, the problem was to aggregate individual preferences into group preferences, while assuming that both individual and group preferences remained transitive and complete. It has long been recognized, however, that the transitivity of preferences is a strong assumption and in the theory of social choice less demanding properties are argued to be more reasonable.

One way to weaken the transitivity of preferences is to insist on the existence of those preference relations but to require less demanding properties such as quasi-transitivity (transitivity of strict preference relations) or acyclicity (the absence of cycles in preference relations). Alternatively, one can use choice functions as primitives, which may or may not be derived from an underlying preference relation. Of course, if choice functions satisfy some consistency conditions (for example, the contraction property α and the expansion property γ, see section 4.3), then there always exists an underlying preference relation from which these choice functions can be derived. In this case, there is no difference between the choice function approach and the preference relation approach. In general, however, choice functions fail to satisfy particular consistency conditions and as a consequence, an underlying preference relation does not exist. When this is the case, we may expect the results to be quite different. In Section 4.3, we discuss the exact relationships between choice functions and preference relations. Section 4.4 is concerned with the so-called non-binary approach to Arrow's problem and we give a version of the impossibility theorem. In Section 4.5, we use choice functions as primitives for both individuals and groups and consider the problem of the aggregation of individual choice functions into group choice functions.

4.2 Basic Notation and Definitions

Let X be a finite set of mutually exclusive social alternatives and let K be the set of all non-empty subsets of X. A choice function $C : K \to K$ assigns a non-empty subset $C(A)$ of A to every $A \in K$. Let $\mathcal{C}$ be the set of all choice functions.

For any choice function C on X, the *base relation* of C is the binary relation R_C on X defined as follows: For all $x, y \in X$, $xR_C y$ iff $x \in C(\{x,y\})$.

The asymmetric and symmetric part of R_C will be denoted as P_C and I_C, respectively.

A binary relation R on X is *transitive* iff for all $x, y, z \in X$, xRy and yRz imply xRz; it is *quasi-transitive* iff its asymmetric part is transitive; it is *triple acyclic* iff xPy and yPz imply xRz, where P is the asymmetric component of R. For all $A \in K$, define $C(A, R_C)$ as follows:

$$C(A, R_C) = \{x | x \in A \text{ and } \forall\, y \in A,\ xR_Cy\}.$$

Then a choice function is *rationalizable* iff

$$C(A) = C(A, R_C) \ \forall\, A \in K.$$

4.3 Consistency Conditions

In this section, we discuss the relationships between choice functions and preference relations. First, we give some standard consistency conditions.

Definition 1: A choice function C is said to satisfy:

1. *Property α* iff for all $A, B \in K, [A \subseteq B] \Longrightarrow [C(B) \cap A \subseteq C(A)]$;

2. *Property β* iff for all $A, B \in K$,
   $[\{x,y\} \subseteq C(A) \text{ and } A \subseteq B] \Longrightarrow$
   $[\{x,y\} \subseteq C(B) \text{ or } \{x,y\} \subseteq B - C(B)]$;

3. *Property γ* iff for all $A, B \in K, C(A) \cap C(B) \subseteq C(A \cap B)$;

4. *Property PI (Path Independence)* iff for all $A, B \in K$,
   $C(A \cup B) = C(C(A) \cup C(B))$.

Remark 1: Property α is the standard contraction, also known as the Chernoff condition. Properties β and γ are standard expansion conditions. Property PI was proposed by Plott (1973).[1]

Some choice functions may or may not be derived from an underlying preference relation. Consider the following choice functions:

$$C(\{x,y\}) = \{x,y\};\ C(\{y,z\}) = \{y\};\ C(\{x,z\}) = \{z\};\ C(\{x,y,z\}) = \{x\}.$$

It is clear that there is *no* underlying preference relation from which the above choice functions can be derived. However, the following result shows that if choice functions are restricted to some particular classes, then there is indeed an underlying preference relation associated with those choice functions and furthermore, the relation may possess certain properties, such as transitivity, or quasi-transitivity, or acyclicity.

---

[1] For the discussion of other consistency conditions and the connection with rationalizability, see, for example, Aizerman (1985), Moulin (1985), Sen (1986) and Suzumura (1983).

Theorem 1: *A choice function C is rationalizable and has*

1. *a triple acyclic base relation iff it satisfies properties α and γ;*
2. *a quasi-transitive base relation iff it satisfies properties PI and γ;*
3. *a transitive base relation iff it satisfies properties α and β.*

Proof:

1. **Sufficiency.** Suppose C satisfies α and γ. We need to show that:

    (a) for $A \in K, C(A) = C(A, R_C)$, and

    (b) R_C is triple acyclic.

    To show (a), note that α implies that if $x \in C(A)$, then $x \in C(\{x,y\})$ for every $y \in A$. Therefore, $xR_C y \ \forall \ y \in A$. Then $x \in C(A, R_C)$ follows from the definition of $C(A, R_C)$. Thus we have proved:
    $$C(A) \subseteq C(A, R_C). \qquad (4.3.1)$$
    For any $x \in C(A, R_C), xR_C y \ \forall \ y \in A$. Then, $x \in C(\{x,y\})$ for all $y \in A$ follows from the definition of R_C. If we assume γ, then $x \in C(A)$. Therefore:
    $$C(A, R_C) \subseteq C(A). \qquad (4.3.2)$$
    Combining (4.3.1) and (4.3.2), $C(A) = C(A, R_C)$.

    We now prove that α implies that R_C is triple acyclic.

    For all $x, y, z \in X$, let $xP_C y$ and $yP_C z$. We need to show that $xR_C z$, or $\{z\} \neq C(\{x,z\})$. Suppose to the contrary that $\{z\} = C(\{x,z\})$. Consider $C(\{x,y,z\})$.

    If $x \in C(\{x,y,z\}), \alpha$ implies $x \in C(\{x,z\})$, a contradiction;

    if $y \in C(\{x,y,z\}), \alpha$ implies $y \in C(\{x,y\})$, a contradiction;

    if $z \in C(\{x,y,z\}), \alpha$ implies $z \in C(\{y,z\})$, a contradiction.

    Hence, $C(\{x,y,z\}) = \emptyset$, a contradiction. Therefore, $\{z\} \neq C(\{x,z\})$.

    Necessity. Suppose C is rationalizable. We need to show that C satifies α and γ. Since C is rationalizable, $C(A) = C(A, R_C) \ \forall \ A \in K$.

    α : For all $A, B \in K, B \subseteq A$,
    $$x \in C(A) \Longleftrightarrow x \in C(A, R_C) \Longleftrightarrow xR_C y \ \forall \ y \in A.$$
    Therefore, $\forall \ b \in B, xR_C b$, that is, $x \in C(B)$.

    $\gamma : x \in C(A) \cap C(B) \Longrightarrow xR_C a \ \forall \ a \in A$ and $xR_C b \ \forall \ b \in B$.

    Therefore, $xR_C y \ \forall \ y \in A \cup B$, that is, $x \in C(A \cup B, R_C) = C(A \cup B)$.

2. **Sufficiency.** First, we show that path independence implies α. For all $A, B \in K$ with $A \subseteq B$, let $x \in C(B) \cap A$. Suppose, to the contrary, that $x \notin C(A)$. Consider $B = A \cup (B - A)$. Property PI implies that $C(B) = C(C(A) \cup C(B - A))$. Since $x \in C(B) \cap A$, it must be the case that $x \in A$. Therefore, $x \notin (B - A)$. Then by the definition of a choice function, $x \notin C(B - A)$. But we have supposed that $x \notin C(A)$. Consequently, $x \notin C(B)$, contradicting the fact that $x \in C(B)$. Hence, our assumption that $x \notin C(A)$ is false. Thus, property PI implies α. Then from Part 1 of Theorem 1, C is rationalizable.

Next, we show that property PI implies that R_C is quasi-transitive. Let $xP_C y$ and $yP_C z$, that is $\{x\} = C(\{x,y\})$ and $\{y\} = C(\{y,z\})$. Consider $C(\{x,y,z\})$. Path independence implies:

(a) $C(\{x,y,z\}) = C(\{x,y\} \cup \{y,z\}) = C(C\{x,y\}) \cup C(\{y,z\}) = C(\{x\} \cup \{y\}) = C(\{x,y\}) = \{x\}$, and

(b) $C(\{x,y,z\}) = C(\{x,y\} \cup \{z\}) = C(C(\{x,y\}) \cup C\{z\}) = C(\{x\} \cup \{z\}) = C(\{x,z\})$.

Therefore, $\{x\} = C(\{x,z\})$, so $xP_C z$.

Necessity. We need to show that if C is rationalizable and has a quasi-transitive base relation, then C satisfies properties PI and γ. From Part 1 of Theorem 1, if C is rationalizable, then γ is satisfied. So we need only check for property PI. Note that rationalizability of C implies $C(A) = C(A, R_C) \; \forall \; A \in K$.

For all $A, B \in K$, we need to show that $C(A \cup B) = C(C(A) \cup C(B))$. For any $x \in C(A \cup B) = C(A \cup B, R_C), x R_C y \; \forall \; y \in A \cup B$; in particular, $x R_C z \; \forall \; z \in C(A) \cup C(B)$. Therefore, $C(A \cup B) \subseteq C(C(A) \cup C(B))$.

Now, for any $x \in C(C(A) \cup C(B))$, we need to show that $x \in C(A \cup B)$, that is $x R_C a \; \forall \; a \in A$ and $x R_C b \; \forall \; b \in B$. Assume, to the contrary, that $x \notin C(A \cup B)$, i.e., there exists an $a_0 \in A \cup B$ such that $a_0 P_C x$.

First, assume that $a_0 \in A$. Then $x \notin C(A)$. However, since $x \in C(C(A) \cup C(B)), x R_C a \; \forall \; a \in A$. Therefore, $a_0 \notin C(A)$. That is, there exists an $a_1 \in A$ such that $a_1 P_C a_0$. Quasi-transitivity of the base relation now implies $a_1 P_C x$. By the repeated use of the above argument, it must be the case, since X is finite, that $C(A) = \emptyset$, a contradiction.

Assume next that $a_0 \in B$. This is similar to the above case. Therefore, our assumption that $x \notin C(A \cup B)$ is false. Hence, $x \in C(A \cup B)$. Consequently, $C(C(A) \cup C(B)) = C(A \cup B)$ and property PI is satisfied.

3. **Sufficiency.** We need to show that if C satisfies α and β then C is rationalizable and has a transitive base relation. First, we show that α and β imply γ, that is $C(A) \cap C(B) \subseteq C(A \cup B)$. Suppose, to the contrary, that there exists an $x \in C(A) \cap C(B)$ but $x \notin C(A \cup B)$. Then β implies $y \notin C(A \cup B) \ \forall \ y \in C(A)$ and $z \notin C(A \cup B) \ \forall \ z \in C(B)$; that is,

$$C(A) \cap C(A \cup B) = \emptyset = C(B) \cap C(A \cup B). \qquad (4.3.3)$$

However, α implies $C(A \cup B) \cap A \subseteq C(A)$ and $C(A \cup B) \cap B \subseteq C(B)$. This, together with (4.3.3) implies $C(A \cup B) = \emptyset$, a contradiction. Therefore, γ is satisfied. Thus, from Part 1 of Theorem 1, C is rationalizable.

Next, we show that if C satisfies α and β, then C has a transitive base relation. For all $x, y, z \in X$, let $xR_C y$ and $yR_C z$. We need to show $xR_C z$. Suppose, to the contrary, that $zP_C x$, that is, $\{z\} = C(\{x, z\})$. Consider $C(\{x, y, z\})$. Since C is rationalizable and $zP_C x, x \notin C(\{x, y, z\})$. If $y \in C(\{x, y, z\})$, then $yR_C x$, and since we have defined the preference relation as $xR_C y$, then $xI_C y$, or $\{x, y\} = C(\{x, y\})$. Then β implies $x \in C(\{x, y, z\})$, a contradiction. Hence, $y \notin C(\{x, y, z\})$. If $z \in C(\{x, y, z\})$, then $zR_C y$. Notice that $yR_C z$, therefore, $yI_C z$, or $\{y, z\} = C(\{y, z\})$. Then β implies $y \in C(\{x, y, z\})$, a contradiction. Therefore, $C(\{x, y, z\}) = \emptyset$, a contradiction. Hence, $\{z\} \neq C(\{x, z\})$, or $x \in C(\{x, z\})$. Therefore, $xR_C z$.

Necessity: We need to show that if C is rationalizable and has a transitive base relation, then C satisfies properties α and β. From Part 1 of Theorem 1, if C is rationalizable, then α is satisfied. So we only check for β. For all $A, B \in K$ with $A \subseteq B$ and any $x, y \in C(A)$, the rationalizability of C implies $xI_C y$. If $x \in C(B)$, that is, $xR_C z \ \forall \ z \in B$, then $yR_C z \ \forall \ z \in B$ follows from the transitivity of the base relation and the fact that $xR_C y$. Therefore, $y \in C(B)$. Similarly, it can be shown that if $x \notin C(B)$, then $y \notin C(B)$. Thus, β is satisfied. Q.E.D.

Therefore, rationalizability of choice functions is associated both with the contraction property α and the expansion property γ. The next theorem we present is concerned, not with rationalizability, but with characterizing the "rationality" of the base relation.

Definition 2: A choice function C is said to satisfy

1. *Property SS (Symmetric Substitution) iff for all $x, y \in X$,*
$[\{x, y\} = C(\{x, y\})] \Longrightarrow [x \in C(\{x, z\}) \Longleftrightarrow y \in C(\{y, z\})]$;

2. *Property WSS (Weak Symmetric Substitution) iff for all $x, y \in X$,*
$[\{x, y\} = C(\{x, y\})] \Longrightarrow [\{x\} = C(\{x, z\}) \Longrightarrow y \in C(\{y, z\})]$;

3. *Property AS (Asymmetric Substitution)* iff for all $x, y \in X$,
   $[\{x\} = C(\{x,y\})] \Longrightarrow [\{y\} = C(\{y,z\}) \Longrightarrow x \in C(\{x,z\})]$.

Remark 2: Properties SS and WSS were proposed by Baigent (1990). They embody the idea of "equal treatment" of preferences from any of the subsets of alternatives in K. On the other hand, property AS implies that there exists from the preference subsets in K an asymmetric preference (as its acronym suggests) for some alternative(s).

Theorem 2: *A choice function C has*

1. *a triple acyclic base relation iff it satisfies property (AS);*
2. *a quasi-transitive base relation iff it satifies properties (AS) and (WSS);*
3. *a transitive base relation iff it satisfies (AS) and (SS).*

Proof:

1. Straightforward.

2. **Sufficiency.** We need to show that if C satisfies (AS) and (WSS) then C has a quasi-transitive base relation. For all $x, y, z \in X$, let $xP_C y$ and $yP_C z$. From Part 1 of Theorem 2, $xR_C z$. If $xI_C z$, or $\{x,z\} = C(\{x,z\})$, then (WSS), together with $\{x\} = C(\{x,y\})$ would imply $z \in C(\{y,z\})$, a contradiction. Therefore, $xP_C z$.

   Necessity. Straightforward.

3. **Sufficiency.** We need to show that if C satisfies (AS) and (SS) then C has a transitive base relation. For all $x, y, z \in X$, let $xR_C y$ and $yR_C z$. There are four possibilities that are mutually exclusive and exhaustive.

   (a) $xI_C y$ and $yI_C z$: In this case, (SS) implies $xI_C z$;
   (b) $xI_C y$ and $yP_C z$: In this case, since $\{x,y\} = C(\{x,y\})$ and $\{y\} = C(\{y,z\}), (SS)$ implies $\{x\} = C(\{x,z\})$, that is, $xP_C z$;
   (c) $xP_C y$ and $yI_C z$: This case is similar to case (b) and we have $xP_C z$;
   (d) $xP_C y$ and $yP_C z$: Since (SS) implies (WSS), from Part 2 of Theorem 2, $xP_C z$.

   Necessity. Straightforward.

In the standard literature of social choice theory, the transitivity (quasi-transitivity or acyclicity) of the base relation is commonly understood to be associated with some kinds of contraction and/or expansion properties. Theorem 2 clearly shows that this perception is not quite accurate. Instead, the transitivity or quasi-transitivity of the base relation is associated with transitivity or quasi-transitivity of the base relation is associated with questions of "equal treatment" and "asymmetric substitutions", while the contraction and expansion conditions have to do with intersecting sets of K.

To conclude this section, we point out that identifying a choice function C as having a transitive base relation does not necessarily imply that C is rationalizable. Consider the following example:

$C(\{x,y\}) = \{x\}; C(\{y,z\}) = \{y\};$
$C(\{x,z\}) = \{x\}; C(\{x,y,z\}) = \{y\}.$

It is clear that the above choice function has a transitive base relation and yet is not rationalizable.

4.4 The Arrovian Problem

In this section, we shall give a version of a choice function approach to Arrow's impossibility result. Let $H = \{1,\ldots,n\}$ be a set of individuals where $n > 1$. Let R be a complete and transitive binary relation on X. The set of all such R's will be denoted as $\mathcal{R}$. Let $R_i \in \mathcal{R}$ be individual i's preference. A preference profile $p = (R_1,\ldots,R_n)$ is an n-tuple of individual preferences, one for each individual in H. A *social choice function* (SCF) $f : D \times K \longrightarrow K$ assigns a non-empty subset $f(p,A)$ of A to every $A \in K$ and every $p \in D$, where $D \subseteq \mathcal{R}^n$.

Definition 3: An *SCF* f satisfies

1. *Classical Domain (CD)* iff $D = \mathcal{R}^n$;

2. *Pareto Criterion (PC)* iff for all $x, y \in X$, and $\forall p \in D$,

   $$[xP_i y \; \forall \; i \in H] \Longrightarrow [\{x\} = C(\{x,y\})],$$

   where $C = f(p,\cdot)$;

3. *Independence of Irrelevant Alternatives (IIA)* iff for all $x, y \in X$, and $\forall \; p, p' \in D$,

   $$[xR_i y \Longleftrightarrow xR'_i y \; \forall \; i \in H] \Longrightarrow [C(\{x,y\}) = C'(\{x,y\})],$$

   where $C = f(p,\cdot)$ and $C' = f(p',\cdot)$;

4. *Nondictatorship (ND)* iff there is no individual $i \in H$ such that for all $p \in D$ and all $x, y \in X$,

   $$xP_i y \Longrightarrow [\{x\} = C(\{x,y\})],$$

   where $C = f(p,\cdot)$.

Remark 3: The above axioms are the counterparts of Arrow's axioms in the so-called non-binary approach and they do not need any further explanation.

Theorem 3: *If $\#X \geq 3$, then there is no SCF satisfying conditions (CD), (PC), (IIA) and (ND), and yielding choice functions satisfying (SS) and (AS).*

Proof: First, we introduce the following definition. $G \subseteq H$ is said to be decisive over a pair $\{x, y\}$, if and only if $xP_iy \ \forall \ i \in G \Longrightarrow \{x\} = C(\{x, y\})$ and $yP_ix \ \forall \ i \in G \Longrightarrow \{y\} = C(\{x, y\})$ where $C = f(p, \cdot)$.

The first step of the proof is to show that if $G \subseteq H$ is decisive over a pair, say $\{x, y\}$, then G is decisive over all pairs. Consider a preference profile $p : xP_iy$ and yP_iz and xP_iz for all $i \in G$, and yP_jz for all $j \in H - G$ and assume that G is decisive over $\{x, y\}$. Then $\{x\} = C(\{x, y\})$ follows from the assumption that G is decisive over $\{x, y\}$, and $\{y\} = C(\{y, z\})$ follows from (PC). Now, the transitivity of the base relation implies $\{x\} = C(\{x, z\})$. Assuming (IIA), the conclusion $\{x\} = C(\{x, z\})$ is derived from the fact that xP_iz for all $i \in G$ only. In a similar fashion it can be shown that if zP_ix for all $i \in G$, then $\{z\} = C(\{x, z\})$. Thus, G is decisive over $\{x, z\}$. By a similar argument, it can be proved that G is decisive over all pairs.

The next step is to show that if a group $G \subseteq H$ is decisive over a pair then either G_1 or G_2 is decisive over that pair, where G_1, G_2 are non-empty subsets of G with $G_1 \cap G_2 = \emptyset$. Suppose G is decisive over a pair $\{x, y\}$. Consider the following preference profile: xP_iy and zP_iy for all $i \in G_1$ and xP_jy and xP_jz for all $j \in G_2$. Then $\{x\} = C(\{x, y\})$ follows from the assumption that G is decisive over $\{x, y\}$. Consider $C(\{y, z\})$. There are two possibilities:

1. $\{z\} = C(\{y, z\})$. With the help of (IIA), in this case, G_1 is decisive over $\{y, z\}$. Then by application of the first step of the proof, G_1 is decisive over all pairs.

2. $y \in C(\{y, z\})$. The transitivity of the base relation implies $\{x\} = C(\{x, z\})$. Now, with the application of (IIA), G_2 is decisive over $\{x, z\}$. Again, by application of the first proof, G_2 is decisive over all pairs.

Notice that (PC) and (CD) imply that H is decisive over a pair $\{x, y\}$. We eventually arrive at the result, by repeated use of the first and the second steps in the finite set X, that there is one individual i such that i is decisive over all pairs of alternatives. Hence i is a dictator. Q.E.D.

In Theorem 3, the group choice function is required only to have properties SS and AS. From Theorem 2, SS and AS characterize the transitivity of the base relation, and the transitivity of the base relation does not necessarily imply that the choice function is rationalizable. Therefore, it is not really important whether or not a group choice function is rationalizable. The only thing that matters is the *transitivity* of the base relation. In view of this observation, Theorem 3 can be regarded as a stronger result than Arrow's original one.

4.5 Choice Aggregation Procedures

In this section, we shall consider the polar case of the Arrovian problem; that of aggregation of individual choice functions. For our purposes here, we assume that only the choice functions of individuals are known.[2] A choice profile $c = (C_1, \ldots, C_n)$ is an n-tuple of choice functions, one for each individual in H. A *choice aggregation procedure (CAP)* is a function $g : D \longrightarrow C$ where $D \subseteq C^n$. For any choice profile $c \in C^n$, any $A \in K$ and any $x \in A$,

$$N(x, A, c) \equiv \#\{i \in H : x \in C_i(A)\}.$$

A CAP g is *approval voting*[3] if and only if, for all $A \in K$, and $c \in C^n$,

$$C(A) = \{x \in A : N(x, A, c) \geq N(y, A, c) \ \forall \ y \in A\},$$

where $C = g(c)$.

To see *approval voting* more clearly, consider the following example.

EXAMPLE: Let $H = \{1, 2, 3\}$ and $A = \{x, y, z\}$. H can be interpreted as the set of voters and A as the set of candidates. Consider the following choice functions: $C_1(A) = \{x, y\}, C_2(A) = \{x\}, C_3(A) = \{y, z\}$. Then x is picked by persons 1 and 2, y by persons 1 and 3, and z by person 3 only. Approval voting will therefore pick the group choice consisting of both x and y, since both are chosen by two individuals.

Definition 4: A CAP g satisfies:

1. *Unrestricted domain (UD)* iff $D = C^n$;

2. *Neutrality (N)* iff for all $c, c' \in D$, all $A \in K$ and any permutation π on X, $C_i'(\pi(A)) = \pi(C_i(A)) \ \forall \ i \in H \implies C'(\pi(A)) = \pi(C(A))$, where $C = g(c)$ and $C' = g(c')$;

3. *Independence of Symmetric Substitutions (ISS)* iff for all $c, c' \in D$, all $j, k \in H$ and all $A \in K$ such that, for all $i \in H - \{j, k\}, C_i = C_i'$ and for all $B \in K - \{A\}, C_j(B) = C_j'(B)$ and $C_k(B) = C_k'(B)$. Then $x \in C_j(A)$ and $y \notin C_j(A), y \in C_k(A)$ and $x \notin C_k(A), C_j'(A) = (C_j(A) - \{x\}) \cup \{y\}$ and $C_k'(A) = (C_k(A) - \{y\}) \cup \{x\} \implies C(A) = C'(A)$, where $C = g(c)$ and $C' = g(c')$;

4. *Anonymity (A)* iff for all $c, c' \in D$, all $A \in K$, and any permutation δ on H, $[C_i'(A) = C_{\delta(i)}(A)$ for all $i \in H] \implies C'(A) = C(A)$, where $C = g(c)$ and $C' = g(c')$;

---

[2] We assume that individuals' choice functions are their true choice functions. For the problem of manipulation in the context of aggregating individual choice functions, see Baigent and Xu (1992).

[3] Approval voting is thoroughly discussed in Brams and Fishburn (1983).

5. *Positive Response (PR)* iff for all $c, c' \in D$, all $j \in H$ and all $A \in K$ such that, for all $i \in H - j$, $C_i = C'_i$, and for all $B \in K - \{A\}$, $C_j = C'_j$, if for all $x \notin C_j(A)$ and $C'_j(A) = C_j \cup \{x\}$ then $x \in C(A) \Longrightarrow \{x\} = C'(A)$, where $C = g(c)$ and $C' = g(c')$.

Remark 4: (UD) implies that there is no restriction on individual choice functions: they can be rationalizable, or they can have a transitive base relation, or they can be even very bizzare and very arbitrary. $(N), (A)$ and (PR) are very standard and do not need further explanation. (ISS) essentially embodies the idea that it does not matter "who votes for whom". For further discussion of the above axioms, see Baigent and Xu (1991).

Lemma 1: *If a CAP g satisfies (N) and (ISS), then for all $c \in D$, all $A \in K$ and all $x, y \in A$:*

$$N(x, A, c) = N(y, A, c) \Longrightarrow [x \in C(A) \Longleftrightarrow y \in C(A)],$$

where $C = g(c)$.

Proof: Consider any $c \in D$ and any $A \in K$, such that $x, y \in A$ and $N(x, A, c) = N(y, A, c)$. We need to show that $[x \in C(A) \Longrightarrow y \in C(A)]$, where $C = g(c)$.

Therefore, consider a permutation π on X such that, for all $w \in X - \{x, y\}$, $\pi(w) = w$, $\pi(x) = y$ and $\pi(y) = x$. Also, consider the sets:

1. $S_x = \{i \in H : x \in C_i(A) \text{ and } y \notin C_i(A)\}$;
2. $S_y = \{i \in H : y \in C_i(A) \text{ and } x \notin C_i(A)\}$;
3. $S_{xy} = \{i \in H : x \in C_i(A) \text{ and } y \in C_i(A)\}$.

If $S_x = \emptyset, S_y = \emptyset$ and $S_{xy} = \emptyset$, then $y \in C(A)$, where $C = g(c)$, follows from (N) immediately.

If $S_x = \emptyset, S_y = \emptyset$ and $S_{xy} \neq \emptyset$, then $y \in C(A)$ also follows from (N). If $S_x \neq \emptyset$, then $S_y \neq \emptyset$, and S_x and S_y contain the same number of individuals. This follows because $N(x, A, c) = N(y, A, c)$. A similar conclusion would follow from $S_y \neq \emptyset$. Assume that S_x and S_y each contain exactly one individual. In particular, assume $j \in S_x$ and $k \in S_y$, where $j \neq k$. Now consider the choice profile $c' \in D$ such that, for all $i \neq j, k$, $C_i = C'_i$, $C'_j(A) = (C_j(A) - \{x\}) \cup \{y\}$ and $C'_k(A) = (C_k(A) - \{y\}) \cup \{x\}$. Using (N) with π, it follows that $y \in C'(A)$, where $C' = g(c')$. Finally, it follows from (ISS) that $y \in C(A)$. An obvious extension of this argument applies to the cases in which S_x and S_y contain more than one individual. This completes the proof that $[x \in C(A) \Longrightarrow y \in C(A)]$. The converse is established in exactly the same way. Thus, the lemma is proved.   Q.E.D.

Therefore, if a CAP satisfies (N) and (ISS) and if x and y are chosen by the same number of individuals, then x and y should be treated "equally": if one is chosen by the group then the other must be in the group choice function. With the help of Lemma 1, we are able to prove the following theorem.

Theorem 4: *A CAP g satisfies (UD), (N), (ISS) and (PR) iff g is approval voting.*

Proof: The necessity part of the theorem is obvious; we prove only sufficiency. That is, we need to prove the following: if g satisfies all of the axioms, then for all $c \in D$ and all $A \in K$,

$$x \in C(A) \Longleftrightarrow [N(x, A, c) \geq N(y, A, c), \forall\, y \in A],$$

where $C = g(c)$.

We show first that $x \in C(A) \Longrightarrow N(x, A, c) \geq N(y, A, c)\; \forall\, y \in A$. Suppose, to the contrary, that there exists $y \in A$ such that $N(x, A, c) < N(y, A, c)$. Consider the case in which $N(x, A, c) + 1 = N(y, A, c)$. In this case, there exists an individual $k \in H$ such that $x \notin C_k(A)$ and $y \in C_k(A)$. Consider the choice profile $c' \in C^n$ such that, for all $i \in H - \{k\}, C'_i(A) = C_i(A)$ and $C'_k(A) = C_k(A) \cup \{x\}$. Since $x \in C(A), \{x\} = C'(A)$ now follows from (PR), where $C' = g(c')$. But for choice profile $c', N(x, A, c') = N(y, A, c')$. It follows from the lemma that $x \in C'(A)$ iff $y \in C'(A)$ and this contradicts $\{x\} = C'(A)$. Other cases in which $N(x, A, c) + 1 < N(y, A, c)$ may be dealt with by an easy extension of the above argument. Therefore, the original assumption is false.

Finally, we show that for all $c \in C^n$, all $A \in K$, and $x \in A$

$$[N(x, A, c) \geq N(x, A, y)\; \forall\, y \in A] \Longrightarrow x \in C(A),$$

where $C = g(c)$. Equivalently, we need to show that $x \notin C(A)$ implies that there exists $y \in A$ such that $N(x, A, c) < N(y, A, c)$. It must be the case that either $N(x, A, c) = 0$ or $N(x, A, c) > 0$. If $N(x, A, c) = 0$, then for any $i \in H$, consider $y \in C_i(A)$. It follows that $N(x, A, c) < N(y, A, c)$. For the case in which $N(x, A, c) > 0$, consider any $y \in C(A)$. It follows from the first part of the proof that $N(y, A, c) \geq N(x, A, c)$. If $N(x, A, c) = N(y, A, c)$, then it follows from the lemma that $x \in C(A)$, which contradicts $x \notin C(A)$. Therefore $N(x, A, c) < N(y, A, c)$. This completes the proof of the theorem. Q.E.D.

Since approval voting is characterized by $(UD), (N), (ISS)$ and (PR), and it satisfies (A), obviously (A) is implied by the other axioms. However, in contrast to May's characterization of simple majority rule (see May (1952)), approval voting is not characterized by $(UD), (N), (A)$ and (PR). To see this, for any $c \in C^n$ and any $A \in K$, define

$$M(A, c) = \{x \in A |\, (\exists\, i \in H)[(\forall\, j \in H), \#C_j(A) \geq \#C_i(A)\text{ and } x \in C_i(A)]\}.$$

That is, $M(A, c)$ is the set of all the alternatives that are chosen from A given profile c by some individual with one of the smallest choice sets. Let

g be approval voting, for all $A \in K$ and $c \in C^n$. Define g_0 as : $g_0(c)(A) = g(c)(M(A,c))$. It can be checked easily that g_0 satisfies $(UD), (N), (A)$ and (PR), but violates (ISS).

In Theorem 4, the axioms used are independent in the sense that, for any one of the four axioms, there exists a CAP that violates it but satisfies the remaining three. To see this, consider the following $CAPs$. For all $A \in K$ and $c \in C^n$,

1. $C(A) = \cap_{i \in H} C_i(A)$, where $C = g_1(c)$;

2. for given $x_0 \in A, C(A) = \{x_0\}$ if $x_0 \in A$ and $C(A) = g(c)(A)$ if $x_0 \notin A$, where $C = g_2(c)$ and g is approval voting;

3. for given $k \in H, C(A) = g(C_k(A))$, where $C = g_3(c)$ and g is approval voting;

4. $C(A) = \cup_{i \in H} C_i(A)$, where $C = g_4(c)$.

It is easy to check the following.

1. CAP g_1 violates (UD) but satisfies $(N), (ISS)$ and (PR);

2. CAP g_2 violates (N) but satisfies $(UD), (ISS)$ and (PR);

3. CAP g_3 violates (ISS) but satisfies $(UD), (N)$ and (PR);

4. CAP g_4 violates (PR) but satisfies $(UD), (N)$ and (ISS).

4.6 Conclusion

The implication of the requirement that a preference be a weak ordering on choice functions is two-fold; on the one hand, choice functions must be rationalizable, and on the other hand, the base relations must be transitive. However we have shown in Section 4.3 that the rationalizability of choice functions and the transitivity of the base relation are very different requirements.

The distinction is made clear by reformulating Arrow's original problem as one of aggregating individual preference into a group choice function. In Arrow's impossibility theorem, it is really the transitivity of the base relation that is responsible for the impossibility result. Rationalizability plays no role in establishing the negative result (Section 4.4).

Facing the difficulty of aggregating individual preferences into either group preference or group choice functions, we consider the problem of aggregating individual choice functions into a group choice function (Section 4.5). Here, we use individual choice functions as primitives and do not put any restrictions on the choice functions of either individuals or groups. In so doing, we propose several reasonable axioms for the exercise and axiomatically characterize approval voting. In this framework, it still might be interesting to examine how restrictions on individual choice functions and group choice functions affect aggregation procedures. For example, if individual choice functions are required to satisfy, say, property α, what should we expect from group choice functions under certain aggregation procedures?[4]

References

The author would like to thank Norman Schofield for useful comments and constructive suggestions.

Aizerman, M. A. 1985. "New Problems in the General Choice Theory: Review of a Research Trend," *Social Choice and Welfare* 2: 235-282.

Baigent, N. 1990. "Transitivity and Consistency," *Economic Letters* 33: 315-317.

Baigent, N. and Y. Xu. 1991. "Independent Necessary and Sufficient Conditions for Approval Voting," *Mathematical and Social Sciences* 21: 21-29.

Baigent, N. and Y. Xu. 1992. "Manipulability of Choice Aggregation Procedures and Quota Rules." Typescript: Tulane University.

Brams, S. J. and P. Fishburn. 1983. *Approval Voting*. Boston: Birkhauser.

May, K. O. 1952. "A Set of Independent, Necessary and Sufficient Conditions for Simple Majority Decisions," *Econometrica* 20: 680-684.

Moulin, H. 1985. "Choice Functions over a Finite Set: A Summary," *Social Choice and Welfare* 2: 147-160.

Plott, C. R. 1973. "Path Independence, Rationality and Social Choice," *Econometrica* 41: 1075-1091.

Sen, A. K. 1986. "Social Choice Theory," in *Handbook of Mathematical Economics*, Vol. 3, K. Arrow and M. Intriligater, eds. Amsterdam : North Holland.

Suzumura, K. 1983. *Rational Choice, Collective Decisions and Social Welfare*. Cambridge: Cambridge University Press.

---

[4] See Aizerman (1985) for some interesting results.

5. Election Relations and a Partial Ordering for Positional Voting

Donald G. Saari

5.1 Introduction

A basic objective of choice theory is obvious—we want to find an election procedure in which outcomes accurately reflect the "true" views of voters. In the quest for such a procedure positional voting methods have been widely employed and studied. They are easy to use and they also define a natural way to model the beliefs of voters, because they assign weights to voters' rankings of candidates. More precisely, a *positional voting vector* for k candidates, $\vec{w}^k = (w_1, w_2, \ldots, w_k = 0)$, $w_i \geq w_{i+1} \geq 0$, $w_1 > 0$, is a listing of specified weights where w_j points are assigned to a voter's jth ranked candidate. The election ranking of each candidate is determined by the number of points assigned to her, where "more is better". Thus, for example, the voting vector $(1, 0, \ldots, 0)$ corresponds to a plurality voting method, while $\vec{B}^k = (k-1, k-2, \ldots, 1, 0)$ defines the Borda Count (BC).

A basic issue, starting almost immediately after Borda introduced his BC procedure in the 1780's, is the choice of weights, w_j. Since there exist an infinite number of ways to define w_j, it is natural to wonder whether any particular choice is more "optimal" than another. Is it best to use the plurality voting vector $\vec{w}^3 = (1, 0, 0)$ ("vote only for the candidate you rank first"), the anti-plurality ranking $(1, 1, 0)$ ("vote for the two candidates you rank first and second"), a weighted ranking $(3, 1, 0)$ (assign three points to a top-ranked candidate, one to a second-ranked candidate, and none to a bottom ranked candidate), or what? Which method is *best* and why? Selecting a best method is the basic theme of this essay.

5.2 Who Cares?

Even though there are an infinite number of positional voting methods, it is reasonable to question whether the choice makes much difference. For a fixed profile, won't the election outcomes be essentially the same for all procedures? In other words, is this problem worth worrying about?

I answer these natural questions with an example and by reporting certain recent results. To construct the example, let 15 voters rank the three candidates, A, B, and C as

Number	Ranking
6	$A \succ C \succ B$
5	$B \succ C \succ A$
4	$C \succ B \succ A$

(1)

There is nothing spectacular about this profile, but a simple computation shows that the plurality ranking is $A \succ B \succ C$ with a tally of 6 : 5 : 4 while the anti-plurality outcome is the *reversed ranking* $C \succ B \succ A$, supported by the tally 15 : 9 : 6. So, which of the two distinctly conflicting outcomes best reflects the voters' true wishes?

The story continues; still other rankings emerge from the same profile. By varying the positional voting method, the following seven different election rankings all may be found in the single profile (1).

$\vec{w}^3$	Ranking
(1, 0, 0)	$A \succ B \succ C$
(8, 1, 0)	$A \succ B \sim C$
(7, 1, 0)	$A \succ C \succ B$
(13, 2, 0)	$A \sim C \succ B$
(6, 1, 0)	$C \succ A \succ B$
(5, 1, 0)	$C \succ A \sim B$
(2, 1, 0)	$C \succ B \succ A$

(2)

This worrisome example exposes only the tip of a very big iceberg! As the number of candidates increases, the number of rankings that can accompany a single profile escalates exponentially. Given ten candidates, for example, there is a profile with over 84 million possible rankings! (See Saari, 1992a for an explanation as well as a general discussion of this problem.) Moreover, each of the rankings yields distinctly different conclusions. Indeed, for each of the ten candidates, some methods show she is ranked first while others rank her last. We are faced then with the serious problem of determining which of the 84 million different rankings, providing wildly conflicting conclusions about the candidates, best reveals the views of the voters. Clearly the choice of a positional voting method is a very serious matter.

5.3 How to Choose a Positional Voting Method

There is an immense literature, dating from the 1780's, supporting one choice of a positional voting method over another. With only some exaggeration, much of this literature involves finding examples and/or specific properties to suggest that Procedure A is better than Procedure B. Then, members of the "Procedure B defense society" respond by arguing that the reverse is true. Primarily because of the lack of distinctive support for one procedure over another (even a lack of agreement about what election properties are most important), it is not surprising to find comments (*e.g.,* see Riker, 1982) to the effect that

> "The choice of a positional voting method is subjective."

In part, such remarks reflect the absence of a means to compare and rank classes of positional voting methods.

To respond to the above kinds of concern, a partial ordering of positional voting methods was recently developed. What makes this partial ordering interesting is that it introduces objective criteria for comparing and choosing positional voting methods. In this section, I define the partial ordering; in the next section I suggest the kinds of election relationships that emerge. Details and other election relationships can be found in the references.

5.4 What Should Be Compared?

As noted, the basic goal is to find a procedure that best captures voters' true wishes. But, because it is not clear how to measure these wishes, we are forced to compare procedures in terms of the properties they impose on election rankings. Such an approach, of course, invites a debate (well represented in the literature) over whether "The properties I choose are more relevant than the properties you prefer." To avoid this myopic approach of concentrating merely on particular election features, we compare instead the set of *all possible properties admitted by all possible positional voting methods*. This has been done, and I outline the approach here. I describe first how to obtain the set of all properties for election procedures.

Properties of election rankings are based on what kinds of election rankings are, and are not, admitted. This observation is not new; it is in the spirit of work that began with Borda (1784) and Condorcet (1784, 1785). Researchers since have discovered properties and axiomatic representations for certain procedures by describing the kinds of election rankings that can or cannot occur over different subsets of candidates. Indeed, it is not unusual to find arguments criticizing one procedure while promoting another that are based on differences in the election rankings that result from a specified profile.

A common method of this literature is to compare a procedure that ranks n candidates with one that ranks $\binom{n}{2}$ pairs of candidates. For example, if sincere pairwise rankings yield the outcomes

$$A \succ B, B \succ C, A \succ C,$$

then it is difficult to accept that the reversed ranking

$$C \succ B \succ A$$

could accurately reflect the views of the same set of voters. Consequently if a procedure admits this perverse listing of rankings for some profile then this fact should be construed as a negative feature of the procedure. It follows that any procedure that cannot admit this bothersome listing for *any* profile or this absence from the procedure should be construed as a positive property of the method. A natural measure of "positive properties" of positional election procedures, then, is the degree of inner consistency or predictability the method imposes upon the election rankings over different subsets of [all] candidates.

The above "election property" is based on just one particular listing of rankings. To find all other properties, we need to examine other kinds of listings; even those that we cannot imagine at the moment. More generally, to find *all* (single profile) properties admitted by a procedure, we need to find all possible listings of election rankings over all subsets of candidates that can be admitted by the procedure for some profile. Such a collection necessarily captures the complete list of election properties of a procedure, from which actual properties can be defined in terms of the kinds of election listings of rankings that have and have not been admitted. This theme is repeated and explained in more detail below.

As a practical example supporting the need to collect the listings of election rankings, suppose a departmental election for a tenure track position results in the ranking

$$c_1 \succ c_2 \succ \ldots \succ c_n.$$

This ranking suggests that c_1 is the candidate of choice and that c_{n-1} along with c_n are not highly regarded. Suppose a letter from c_{n-1} arrives immediately after the meeting announcing she has accepted a better job elsewhere. Because c_{n-1} is no longer available, the list of candidates that should have been ranked at the meeting is the subset $\{c_1, c_2, \ldots, c_{n-2}, c_n\}$. Do we need another election to determine whether c_1 remains the candidate of choice? I know of no department that would vote again, but, in fact, it is easy to construct profiles with an election ranking over the subset $c_n \succ c_{n-2} \succ \ldots \succ c_2 \succ c_1$ that is reversed; this ranking indicates that c_n, not c_1, is the *true candidate of choice*. Indeed, given the same voter preferences, the positions of c_1 and c_n as most preferred and least preferred are exactly reversed. The message is that the importance of understanding how the same voters rank different subsets of candidates under different procedures is revealed through the way we use and abuse election rankings. Again, the goal is to use this information to identify which procedures provide an acceptable level of consistency among election rankings. Only in this manner can we have hope for any degree of integrity in the election outcomes and in the way in which such procedures are used.

To implement this objective, we need to find the election rankings for each profile of all subsets with two or more candidates. Given $n \geq 3$ candidates, there are $2^n - (n+1)$ such subsets denoted as $S_1, S_2, \ldots, S_{2^n-(n+1)}$. For instance, given three candidates $\{A, B, C\}$, the $2^3 - (3+1) = 4$ subsets are $S_1 = \{A, B\}$, $S_2 = \{A, C\}$, $S_3 = \{B, C\}$, and $S_4 = \{A, B, C\}$. Next, assign a positional voting method to each subset of candidates. Denote this assignment process by the *system voting vector*

$$W^n = \left(\vec{w}^{|S_1|}, \ldots, \vec{w}^{|S_{2^n-(n+1)}|}\right),$$

where the voting vector $\vec{w}^{|S_j|}$ is assigned to S_j, $j = 1, \ldots, 2^n - (n+1)$. Finally, let B^n denote the system vector that assigns the Borda Count (*BC*) to each subset of candidates.

We have identified both the subsets of candidates and the positional election methods; what remains are the election rankings. For a profile p, let $f(p, W^n)$ specify the list of election rankings for the $2^n - (n+1)$ subsets of candidates obtained with the assigned positional voting methods specified by W^n. I call this listing of rankings, $f(p, W^n)$, a *word*.[1] To illustrate, if p is the profile from (1) and if the system vector of the three candidate subset is plurality ranked, or $W^3 = ((1,0),(1,0),(1,0),(1,0,0))$, then the computation from (2) shows that the *plurality word* for the profile is

$$f(p, W^3) = (B \succ A, C \succ A, C \succ B, A \succ B \succ C).$$

Alternatively, if both $B^3 = ((1,0),(1,0),(1,0),(2,1,0))$ (so the three-candidate subset is Borda ranked) and (2) are used, then the same profile defines the *Borda word*

$$f(p, B^3) = (B \succ A, \ C \succ A, \ C \succ B, \ C \succ B \succ A).$$

A *Dictionary*, $\mathcal{D}(W^n)$, is the collection of the words that emerge from all possible choices of profiles. (There are no restrictions on the numbers of voters.) Thus,

$$\mathcal{D}(W^n) = \{f(p, W^n) \,|\, \text{all choices of } p\}.$$

A dictionary, then, is the desired collection of all possible listings of election rankings (all possible words) that ever could occur for any choice of a profile. By examining what words are, and are not, in a dictionary, we can determine all possible (single profile) election relationships and properties.[2] For instance, it turns out that

$$(B \succ A, C \succ A, C \succ B, A \succ B \succ C) \notin \mathcal{D}(B^3).$$

The absence of this listing from the *BC* dictionary $\mathcal{D}(B^3)$ means that a three-candidate election outcome with a *Condorcet winner* (the candidate who wins all pairwise elections – C in the pairwise listings) is bottom-ranked and the

---
[1] This terminology is borrowed from symbolic dynamics or *chaos* as a convenient way to describe the results and to reflect the fact that the the development of this theory finds its roots and motivation from the theory of nonlinear dynamics. The connection is described in Saari 1987 and 1991b.

[2] Observe that with a dictionary, it becomes easy to analyze other types of procedures, such as agendas, run-off elections, etc. This is because we can ignore profiles; we just need to look up what words are available. Namely, the words become the primitives for the analysis. (See Saari, 1989, for a discussion and examples.)

Condorcet loser (the candidate who loses all pairwise elections – A in the listing) is top-ranked is impossible for the BC.

By examining what lists of rankings are and are not in $\mathcal{D}(B^n)$ (see Saari, 1990a), we can find all possible election properties of the BC. In this way, for instance, we find that the following familiar collection of BC properties holds for any value of $n \geq 3$. (Although Borda does not discuss these issues (see De Grazia 1953), I believe he knew about the following properties – at least for $n = 3$. Incidentally, the BC admits many other relationships; what follows is just a very small sample.)

1. A Condorcet winner never can be BC bottom-ranked.
2. A Condorcet loser never can be BC top-ranked.
3. A Condorcet winner always is BC ranked above a Condorcet loser.
4. If all pairwise rankings end in a tie, then the BC ranking is a complete tie.

It is worth repeating for emphasis that these election relationships are obtained by what words are in $\mathcal{D}(B^n)$ as well as by what listings are *not* in $\mathcal{D}(B^n)$. For instance, the last property holds for $n = 3$ because

$$(A \sim B,\ A \sim C,\ B \sim C,\ A \sim B \sim C) \in \mathcal{D}(B^3)$$

and because this is the only word in $\mathcal{D}(B^3)$ that starts with the rankings $A \sim B,\ A \sim C,\ B \sim C$. Thus, for example,

$$(A \sim B,\ A \sim C,\ B \sim C,\ A \sim B \succ C) \notin \mathcal{D}(B^3).$$

An easy way to create a listing of rankings is to choose an *initial ranking* of voters' choices over n candidates, say $c_1 \succ c_2 \succ c_3 \succ c_4 \ldots \succ c_n$, and then to assume the obvious restriction that this ranking is maintained in each subset of two or more candidates. It is not difficult to show that such a listing of *predictable outcomes* is a word common to all dictionaries. Namely, by considering profiles where all voters have similar preferences, it is not difficult to create a situation where the election outcome for each subset of candidates is the result of a given or initial ranking of, say, $c_1 \succ c_2 \succ \ldots \succ c_n$.

The set of *predictable words* are the kind of outcomes we hope for; they are the type naive observers may expect always to occur. (For example, by rigidly adhering to an election ranking of job candidates after some of the candidates have withdrawn, we are acting as though the profile has defined a predictable word.) All remaining words in a dictionary identify unpredictable situations, or the rankings of subsets of candidates that are *not* derivable from the initial ranking. Hence, a dictionary with many words identifies a corresponding system voting vector that admits *many* unpredictable election outcomes and paradoxes.

Conversely, because election relationships and properties are based on what listings of rankings are *not* admitted by a dictionary, we find that the size of a dictionary inversely measures the number of kinds of election relationships.

Donald G. Saari

The larger the dictionary, the fewer the kinds of election relationships. This observation leads to the following set theoretic way to compare system voting vectors.

Definition of PARTIAL ORDER: For two system voting vectors W_1^n and W_2^n, we say that W_2^n *is more coarse than* W_1^n, denoted as $W_1^n \triangleleft W_2^n$, iff

$$\mathcal{D}(W_1^n) \subset \mathcal{D}(W_2^n).$$

We say that W_1^n is equivalent to W_2^n, denoted as $W_1^n \square W_2^n$, iff

$$\mathcal{D}(W_1^n) = \mathcal{D}(W_2^n).$$

As already indicated, if $W_1^n \triangleleft W_2^n$, then W_2^n must admit more kinds of election paradoxes than W_1^n, and W_1^n admits more kinds of election properties.

5.5 Examples of Recent Results

The following is a sampler of the kinds of results that have been obtained by using this dictionary and partial ordering approach.

1. For $n \geq 3$, if W^n requires one or more sets of three or more candidates to be ranked by a method other than the BC, then

$$B^n \triangleleft W^n. \tag{3}$$

(See Saari, 1989, 1990a.) This relationship means that the BC enjoys more (single profile) election relationships than any other system vector. By using this result, we can add significant strength to the highlighted BC properties. Namely, by comparing dictionaries, it turns out that *the properties listed hold iff the BC is used to tally the subset of candidates!* In other words, for any other W^n, there are words in the dictionary $\mathcal{D}(W^n)$ that violate the specified properties. In fact, by examining the words in $\mathcal{D}(W^n)$, we arrive at the much stronger assertion that *only the BC admits relationships between the ranking of a set of candidates and the rankings of the pairs of candidates!* [3] Consequently, when a voting vector other than the BC is used with a set of $k \geq 3$ candidates, then the rankings of this set and the $\binom{k}{2}$ pairs of candidates can be chosen in an arbitrary fashion, and there exists a profile so that the chosen rankings are the actual election rankings.

As another implication of Assertion (3), suppose a system voting vector W^n admits a certain election property relating election rankings that is

---

[3] Axiomatic representations of systems are based on finding properties that separate a given system from others. So, by knowing that *any* BC property comparing the rankings of pairs and the full set separates the BC from other positional methods, it becomes easy to derive many new kinds of axiomatic representations for the BC; characterizations that differ distinctly from the one found by Young (1974). This is done in Saari (1990a,b).

so nice that it is used to promote the acceptance of W^n. According to the set inclusion property of Assertion (3), the BC either admits the same desired relationship or a much stronger one. In other words, because the BC dictionary is contained in all other dictionaries, the BC (the system vector B^n) maximizes the number and kinds of election relationships.

2. The universal set, $\mathcal{U}^n$, is the collection of all possible listings of rankings that can be constructed where the jth entry is a ranking of the candidates in S_j, $j = 1, \ldots, 2^n - (n+1)$. To illustrate, there are three ways to rank a pair and 13 ways to rank three candidates, so the universal set for three candidates, $\mathcal{U}^3$, has $(3)^3 13 = 351$ entries. The assertion is that for $n \geq 3$ and for almost all choices of a system vector W^n,

$$\mathcal{D}(W^n) = \mathcal{U}^n. \tag{4}$$

A stronger assertion holds for $n = 3$. Here, only the BC dictionary is a proper subset.

$$\mathcal{D}(W^3) = \mathcal{U}^3 \text{ iff } W^3 \neq B^3. \tag{5}$$

(See Saari, 1989 and 1990.)

Assertion (5) means, for example, that the paradoxical rankings in (2) (prohibited by the BC) *are* admitted by all other voting vectors! Assertion (5) also implies that only the BC can provide any relief from three-candidate election paradoxes. To indicate how much relief the BC offers, it turns out that $\mathcal{D}(B^3)$ has only about 38% of the 351 entries in $\mathcal{U}^3$. (All other methods, of course, admit 100% of the $\mathcal{U}^3$ entries.) Assertion (3) extends this comment about the favorable role played by the BC to all values of $n \geq 3$. In fact, the degree of freedom from paradoxes offered by the BC increases exponentially with the value of n. For example, $\mathcal{D}(B^6)$ has less than $1/10^{50}$ of the entries of $\mathcal{U}^6$, while most other choices of W^6 (Assertion 4) must admit all of the $\mathcal{U}^6$ entries. So, *anything can happen* for most systems!

As an example of the complications admitted by Assertion (4), it turns out that if W^n assigns the commonly used plurality method to all subsets of candidates, then $\mathcal{D}(W^n) = \mathcal{U}^n$. This set equality allows all imaginable ranking paradoxes, no matter how wild and improbable they may seem to be, to actually occur. As an extreme illustration, the assertion permits choosing a ranking for each subset of candidates with a random method (say, flipping a coin or checking the numbers from the weekly lottery). According to Assertion (4), there is a profile so that the sincere election ranking for each subset is the randomly selected one! As another example, there exist situations where the plurality election ranking for all n candidates is

$$c_1 \succ c_2 \succ \ldots \succ c_{n-1} \succ c_n,$$

but the plurality election ranking for any other subset is the obvious restriction of the reversed ranking

$$c_n \succ c_{n-1} \succ \ldots \succ c_2 \succ c_1.$$

When one recalls the above comments about how we use election rankings in practice (*e.g.*, if c_n drops out of consideration, often we don't have another election to rank the remaining candidates), these results and examples have to be troublesome.

3. On the positive side, *a theory has been developed to characterize all possible system voting vectors that admit election relationships!* Namely, there now exists a way to identify those system vectors where $\mathcal{D}(W^n)$ is a proper subset of $\mathcal{U}^n$; such procedures must admit election relationships. Some of the ideas along with the kinds of election relationships that arise are indicated below; for a complete description see Saari (1992a).

5.6 Some Partial Orderings

As asserted by (3) and (5), only the BC possesses election relationships for $n = 3$, so the only possible ordering is $B^3 \triangleleft W^3$. For more interesting partial orderings, we need $n \geq 4$ candidates; two examples in which $n = 4$ follow. While the details about the computational scheme used to order these system vectors are left to the references (Saari 1993a,b [II and III]), the two examples indicate what can happen. In each case, I encourage the reader to try to determine which system vectors admit election relationships before reading the answer; ambitious readers may try to find the ordering.

The first example compares four system voting vectors, including B^4. Each of the remaining three systems assigns common vectors $\vec{w}^3$ for each of four three-candidate sets and $\vec{w}^4$ for each of the four-candidate sets. The procedures are listed in the following table.

System Vector	$\vec{w}^3$	$\vec{w}^4$
W_1^4	$(1,0,0)$	$(3,1,0,0)$
W_2^4	$(1,1,0)$	$(3,3,2,0)$
W_3^4	$(3,1,0)$	$(3,1,1,0)$

(6)

Given the close similarity between the vectors $(3,1,0)$ and $(3,1,1,0)$, it is reasonable to suspect that the agreement about how top and second ranked candidates are treated forces W_3^4 to admit relationships among the election rankings of the three and four candidate sets. Conversely, there is no obvious relationship among the defining $\vec{w}^3$ and $\vec{w}^4$ for W_1^4 and W_2^4, so there is no reason to expect W_1^4 and W_2^4 to admit election relationships. However, such conjectures are wrong; according to the theory (Saari, 1992b, 1993a,b),

$$B^4 \triangleleft W_1^4 \square W_2^4 \triangleleft W_3^4 \tag{7}$$

and

$$\mathcal{D}(B^4) \subset \mathcal{D}(W_1^4) = \mathcal{D}(W_2^4) \subset \mathcal{D}(W_3^4) = \mathcal{U}^4. \tag{8}$$

The partial ordering (7) proves that both W_1^4 and W_2^4 must admit relationships among the election rankings of the subsets of candidates while W_3^4 does not. The last comment means, as above, that the rankings for the $2^4 - (4+1) = 11$ subsets of two or more candidates can be selected in an arbitrary fashion, and there exists a profile so that the W_3^4 election rankings of the eleven sets are the chosen ones. A consequence of $W_1^4 \square W_2^4$ is that for each profile defining a word in $\mathcal{D}(W_1^4)$, there is a profile leading to precisely the same word in $\mathcal{D}(W_2^4)$. These assertions are not obvious.

The above choice of system voting vectors defines a total ordering (7). One purpose of the following more ambitious comparisons involving twelve system voting vectors for $n = 4$ is to indicate that a total ordering need not always occur. (At this stage, the reader is not expected to understand why this partial ordering arises. In Section 5.7, I describe why some system vectors admit relationships while others do not.)

The first five system voting vectors assign $(3, 1, 0)$ to all three-candidate subsets, so they differ only in the assignment of $\vec{w}^4$ for the four-candidate subset which is given by

System Vector	Choice of $\vec{w}^4$
W_1^4	$(12, 7, 3, 0)$
W_2^4	$(15, 9, 4, 0)$
W_3^4	$(9, 5, 2, 0)$
W_4^4	$(3, 2, 1, 0)$
W_5^4	$(12, 8, 3, 0)$

The next five system voting vectors assign $(3, 1, 0)$ to all three-candidate subsets except $\{c_1, c_2, c_3\}$, so they differ both in the choice of a voting vector for $\{c_1, c_2, c_3\}$ and for the four-candidate subset.

The final two system vectors assign $(3, 1, 0)$ to all three-candidate subsets except $\{c_2, c_3, c_4\}$; here the BC is assigned. For the four-candidate set, W_{11}^4 assigns $(12, 7, 3, 0)$ while W_{12}^4 assigns $(9, 5, 2, 0)$.

Donald G. Saari 103

System Vector	Choice of $\vec{w}^3$	Choice of $\vec{w}^4$
W_6^4	$(2,1,0)$	$(12,7,3,0)$
W_7^4	$(2,1,0)$	$(3,2,1,0)$
W_8^4	$(2,1,0)$	$(9,5,2,0)$
W_9^4	$(1,0,0)$	$(9,5,2,0)$
W_{10}^4	$(1,0,0)$	$(15,9,4,0)$

So, how do these system voting vectors compare? By use of the theory (which involves several elementary linear algebraic relationships), this system defines the following four branches of the partial ordering:

$$
\begin{array}{l}
B^4 \triangleleft W_3^4 \triangleleft W_1^4 \ \square \ W_2^4 \triangleleft W_5^4 \\
B^4 \triangleleft W_7^4 \triangleleft W_4^4 \triangleleft W_5^4 \\
B^4 \triangleleft W_8^4 \triangleleft W_6^4 \triangleleft W_{10}^4 \triangleleft W_5^4 \\
B^4 \triangleleft W_{12}^4 \triangleleft W_{11}^4 \triangleleft W_5^4
\end{array}
\qquad (9)
$$

The associated listing of set containment of the dictionaries is given in the following diagram.

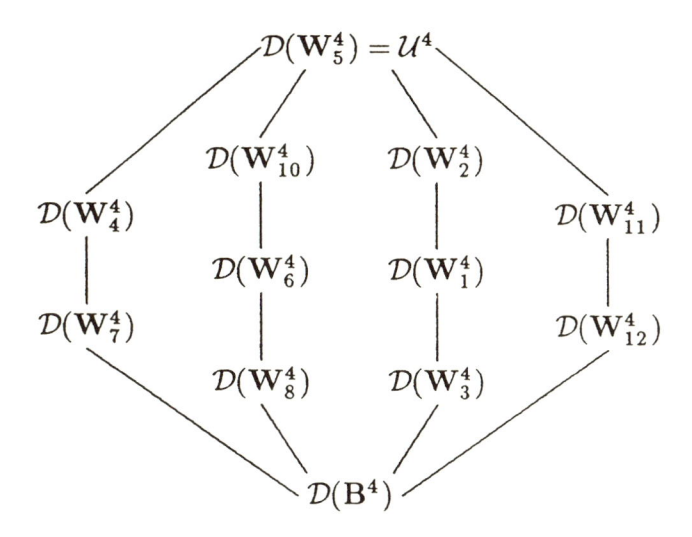

Figure 1. The partial ordering.

5.7 How Election Relationships Are Determined

An important aspect of this theory is that the dictionaries are not just abstract constructs; the entries of each dictionary can be characterized.[4] While the actual theory is left for the references, I now outline some of the basic ideas. (See Saari 1992b, 1993a,b for details and extensions.) The surprise is the elementary nature of the description! Indeed, armed with this outline, the reader should be almost ready to explain the partial orderings of the previous section.

To illustrate the ideas, start with $n = 3$ where only the BC vector $(2, 1, 0)$ can force election relationships. To understand the BC relationships, we need to interpret the choices of weights. (The ideas date back to Borda; see the historical part of the article by De Grazia, 1953.) By using $\vec{B}^3 = (2, 1, 0)$, the weight assigned by a voter to each candidate equals the sum of votes he would assign her over three pairwise majority vote elections (by using the voting vector $(1, 0)$). To see this, compare the following assignments of points for the preferences $\mathcal{A}_3 = c_1 \succ c_2 \succ c_3$.

Method	Set of candidates	$\{c_1\}$	$\{c_2\}$	$\{c_3\}$
Majority	$\{c_1, c_2\}$	1	0	
Majority	$\{c_1, c_3\}$	1		0
Majority	$\{c_2, c_3\}$		1	0
		--	--	--
BC	$\{c_1, c_2, c_3\}$	2	1	0

(10)

Thus the BC voting vector is the aggregated version of the pairwise majority voter ranking $(1, 0)$. Namely, with the *aggregated majority vote* interpretation, it becomes clear why the BC (not the plurality vote or any other procedure) is the "natural" extension of the pairwise majority vote. I underscore the dependency of the BC on the vector $(1, 0)$ by adopting the notation $\vec{B}^3 = \vec{w}^3(1, 0)$. The interesting fact is that this assignment phenomena extends to all values of $n \geq 3$. By this I mean that with $\vec{B}^n = (n-1, n-2, \ldots, 1, 0)$, a voter assigns each candidate the same number of points as he would over $\binom{n}{2}$ majority vote elections. Hence, I adopt the notation $\vec{B}^n = \vec{B}^n(1, 0)$.

Given the definition of w^n it is easily seen that when given 20 voters with the pairwise election results then the BC tally for this profile is the sum of the pairwise tallies, as the bottom line indicates.

---
[4]The entries are characterized, not listed, because there are too many of them. To see this, note that an earlier comment indicates that the number of entries in a six-candidate dictionary exceeds 10^{50}; so, to list them would require over 10^{46} volumes of about 500 pages each. Not many libraries would order a full set for different choices of W^6.

Donald G. Saari

Candidates	$\{c_1\}$	$\{c_2\}$	$\{c_3\}$
$\{c_1, c_2\}$	14	6	–
$\{c_1, c_3\}$	11	–	9
$\{c_2, c_3\}$	–	11	9
Total	25	17	18

(11)

It is also clear that desirable BC election relationships are preserved. For example, the condition that a Condorcet Winner cannot be BC bottom-ranked, *etc.*, is derived from the dependency of BC election outcomes upon the outcomes of pairwise contests in the electorate. The reason BC properties are maintained is obvious. For example, a Condorcet winner receives a superior vote tally in each pairwise election, so the sum of these points (her BC tally) must exceed the total for some other candidate. Candidate c_1, the Condorcet winner in Table 11, has a larger tally in both pairwise elections. Both values ensure that the BC sum (25) exceeds that of at least one other candidate. Similarly, the sum of pairwise comparisons, or the BC tally (18) of c_3, the Condorcet loser, must be lower than that of some other candidate. (But, as shown by Table 11, this sum need not be smallest! Thus, the Condorcet loser need not be BC bottom-ranked and a Condorcet winner need not be BC top-ranked.)

The goal is to extend this simple approach to other voting methods. In this manner, it turns out that all possible system vectors that admit election relationships can be determined (Saari 1992b, 1993a,b). The ideas are illustrated with the next simplest system which, as required by Assertion (3), must involve $n = 4$ candidates. To do this I mimic the above construction with a k-fold symmetry – a symmetry that captures distinctions among the elections of k-candidate subsets.

We begin with $k = 3$ and a voter with the ranking $\mathcal{A}_4 = c_1 \succ c_2 \succ c_3 \succ c_4$. Table 12 lists the number of points he gives to each candidate when $\vec{w}^3 = (w_1, w_2, 0)$ is assigned to each triplet of candidates.

Subset of candidates	$\{c_1\}$	$\{c_2\}$	$\{c_3\}$	$\{c_4\}$
$\{c_1, c_2, c_3\}$	w_1	w_2	0	
$\{c_1, c_2, c_4\}$	w_1	w_2		0
$\{c_1, c_3, c_4\}$	w_1		w_2	0
$\{c_2, c_3, c_4\}$		w_1	w_2	0
Totals	$3w_1$	$w_1 + 2w_2$	$2w_2$	0

(12)

By examining Table 12 and by extrapolating from the example of Table 11, it is reasonable to conjecture that *there is a relationship among the* $(w_1, w_2, 0)$ *positional election rankings of the four sets of triplets and the election ranking of*

$$\vec{w}^4 = \vec{w}^4 \vec{w}^3 = (3w_1, w_1 + 2w_2, 2w_2, 0). \tag{13}$$

The conjecture is true. Indeed, the derivation of $\vec{w}^4\vec{w}^3$ shows that it is the aggregated outcome of each of the four $\vec{w}^3$ elections – thus $\vec{w}^4\vec{w}^3$ is the natural extension of $\vec{w}^3$ from the subsets of triplets to the four-candidate subset.

Equation 13 explains why certain system vectors from Section 2 must admit election relationships. For example, given $\vec{w}^3 = (1,0,0)$, and Eq. 13, $\vec{w}^4((1,0,0) = (3,1,0,0))$. Thus, there must be a relationship among the plurality tallies of the three-candidate elections and the $(3,1,0,0)$ tallies of the four-candidate election. This explains why W_1^4 defined in Table 6 admits election relationships. Likewise, the computation $\vec{w}^4(1,1,0) = (3,3,2,0)$ explains why W_2^4, defined in Table 6, also admits election relationships. On the other hand, the computation $\vec{w}^4((3,1,0) = (9,5,2,0) \neq (3,1,1,0))$ provides us both the reason why W_3^4 of Table 6 does not admit election relationships and why in the twelve system vector example W_3^4, W_8^4, W_9^4, and W_{12}^4 do admit election relationships. (A different argument is needed to explain the partial ordering.)

To derive the election relationships, I mimic the examples of the BC in Tables 10 and 11. I calculate first the $\vec{w}^3$ tallies for each candidate for each of the four triplets in Table 12, and then sum them. The sums of the $\vec{w}^4\vec{w}^3$ tallies are derived directly from the profile. For instance, if the plurality tallies for a profile p are as given in the following table, then the totals on the bottom are the sum of the $(3,1,0,0)$ tallies of the four-candidate election. Thus, the *triplet-symmetry* generalization of the binary *Borda symmetry* must yield relationships among the $(3,1,0,0)$ ranking of the four-candidate subset of candidates and the plurality rankings of the triplets.

Subset of Candidates	$\{c_1\}$	$\{c_2\}$	$\{c_3\}$	$\{c_4\}$
$\{c_1, c_2, c_3\}$	8	7	5	
$\{c_1, c_2, c_4\}$	10	7		3
$\{c_1, c_3, c_4\}$	8		8	2
$\{c_2, c_3, c_4\}$		6	5	9
Totals	26	20	18	14

(14)

By examining how the election relationships for the BC-pairwise vote pair arise, one can guess what types of relationships arise with "$\vec{w}^4\vec{w}^3 - \vec{w}^3$" pairs. For instance, suppose c_j is $\vec{w}^3$ top-ranked whenever she is involved in an election of a subset of three candidates. (I called this a $\vec{w}^3$–Condorcet winner.) Mimicking the summation argument used to explain the BC, we must expect that she is not $\vec{w}^4(\vec{w}^3)$ bottom-ranked in the set of four candidates. This is the case. The reasoning is that any $\vec{w}^3$-Condorcet winner who wins all three of the $\vec{w}^3$ elections in which she is involved must garner more points in the aggregated $\vec{w}^4(\vec{w}^3)$ election than some other candidate. In other words, the tallies from her $\vec{w}^3$ victories add substantially to the terms in the summation of the four candidate tallies. A surprising extension is that *this assertion holds only if w^3 is used to tally all four sets of candidates and if $\vec{w}^4\vec{w}^3$ is used to tally the four candidate set* (Saari, 1992d). *For any other choice of a common voting vector for three candidate subsets, no relationships whatsoever exist!*

Using the above reasoning, we can list some of the resulting properties. The strong similarity of this list with the earlier sample of BC properties is not a coincidence; it is a basic consequence. On the other hand, the BC (where $\vec{w}^3 = (2, 1, 0)$) not only admits all of the following (new) properties, but also several others. For instance, the BC imposes a relationship among the rankings of the four three-candidate subsets, something that does not occur with any other $\vec{w}^3$.

1. A $\vec{w}^3$-Condorcet winner never can be $\vec{w}^4\vec{w}^3$ bottom-ranked.

2. A $\vec{w}^3$-Condorcet loser never can be $\vec{w}^4(\vec{w}^3)$ top-ranked.

3. A $\vec{w}^3$ Condorcet winner always is $\vec{w}^4\vec{w}^3$ ranked above a $\vec{w}^3$-Condorcet loser.

4. If all four $\vec{w}^3$ elections end in a three way tie, then the $\vec{w}^4\vec{w}^3$ outcome is a four way tie.

EXAMPLE: We have sufficient information to design several new, intricate comparisons of election rankings. For instance, let $n = 4$ and let $\vec{w}^4 = (3, 1, 0, 0)$ be used to tally the election for the set of candidates $\{c_1, c_2, c_3, c_4\}$. Let the BC ($\vec{B}^3 = \vec{w}^3(1,0) = (2,1,0)$) be used to tally the elections for the four sets of three candidates. As $(3, 1, 0, 0) \neq \vec{w}^4(2, 1, 0)$, *there need not be any relationship whatsoever among the election ranking of all four candidates with the BC election rankings from the four sets of triplets.* Thus there exists a profile p so that the $(3, 1, 0, 0)$ election ranking is $c_1 \succ c_2 \succ c_3 \succ c_4$, but each of the three-candidate BC election rankings is the natural restriction of the reversed ranking $c_4 \succ c_3 \succ c_2 \succ c_1$. In other words, even though c_1 is the BC-Condorcet loser, she wins the $(3, 1, 0, 0)$ election. This must be viewed as a counter-intuitive result.

Now consider what happens if instead of the BC, the plurality vote is used with the four sets of three candidates. In this situation, no profile exists that defines the above set of five rankings because $(3, 1, 0, 0) = \vec{w}^4(1, 0, 0)$. Thus, since the profile p ensures c_1 is the $(3, 1, 0, 0)$ top-ranked candidate in the set of all four candidates, it is impossible for her to be the plurality-Condorcet loser. Similar assertions apply to any $\vec{w}^4(\vec{w}^3) - \vec{w}^3$ pair.

When the BC is used in the three-candidate elections, we ensure the existence of other kinds of regularity among the election outcomes; *i.e.*, we obtain certain relationships that cannot occur with $(1, 0, 0)$ and $(3, 1, 0, 0)$ election outcomes. This is because the $(1,0,0)$ and $(3,1,0,0)$ election outcomes are not related to the outcomes of the pairwise elections; only the BC outcomes are. So, with the same profile p and the above BC ($\vec{B}^3 = \vec{w}^3(1,0)$) election outcomes for the four sets of three candidates, we know that it is impossible for c_4 to lose a pairwise election to any other pair of candidates; it is impossible for c_3 to lose to both c_1 and c_2. This is because if c_3 lost to both candidates, she would be a Condorcet loser in the subset $\{c_1, c_2, c_3\}$, so she could not be BC top-ranked in this subset. Likewise, if c_4 lost two of the pairwise elections, she would be the Condorcet loser for some subset of three candidates, and this would preclude her from being BC top-ranked in this subset. □

The approach of creating pairs of voting vectors extends to all integer values of s, n for $2 \leq s < n$. To do so, start with a voting vector $\vec{w}^s$ and the one-voter profile p_{A_n} (i.e., this voter has the ranking $A_n = c_1 \succ \ldots \succ c_n$). Next, determine the number of points he assigns to each candidate over the $\binom{n}{s}$ sets of s candidates with $\vec{w}^s$. The sum of points assigned to candidate c_j is the jth weight (or component) for voting vector $\vec{w}^n(\vec{w}^s)$, $j = 1, \ldots, n$. The voting vector $\vec{w}^n(\vec{w}^s)$ is the aggregated version of the voting vector $\vec{w}^s$, so the $\vec{w}^n(\vec{w}^s) - \vec{w}^s$ pair must reflect an s-fold symmetry among the election rankings, a symmetry ensured by using $\vec{w}^s$ to tally each of the $\binom{n}{s}$ sets of s candidates. (A compact formula for the entries of $\vec{w}^n(\vec{w}^s)$ is in Saari 1992b.) A small selection of the election relationships is the recurring list

1. A $\vec{w}^s$-Condorcet winner never can be $\vec{w}^n(\vec{w}^s)$ bottom-ranked.

2. A $\vec{w}^s$-Condorcet loser never can be $\vec{w}^n(\vec{w}^s)$ top-ranked.

3. A $\vec{w}^s$-Condorcet winner always is $\vec{w}^n(\vec{w}^s)$ ranked above a $\vec{w}^s$-Condorcet loser.

4. If all $\vec{w}^s$ elections end in a complete tie, then the $\vec{w}^n(\vec{w}^s)$ outcome is a complete tie.

(A formal study along with other relationships can be found in Saari 1992b, 1993a,b.)

The $\vec{w}^n(\vec{w}^s) - \vec{w}^s$ pairs do not exhaust all the ways there are to find positional voting methods with relationships among election rankings. To illustrate another possibility, let $n = 4$ and use the single voter profile p_{A_4} to compute the number of points assigned to each candidate in the four $\vec{w}^3$ elections of three candidates *and* in the six binary elections. The total number of points assigned to c_j defines the w_j values, $j = 1, \ldots, 4$, for the four-candidate voting vector

$$\vec{w}^4\left(\vec{w}^3, (1,0), \frac{1}{2}, \frac{1}{2}\right) = \frac{1}{2}(3w_1 + 3, 2w_2 + w_1 + 2, 2w_2 + 1, 0). \quad (15)$$

In defining this voting vector, equal emphasis $\{\frac{1}{2}, \frac{1}{2}\}$ is placed on both the points assigned to the candidates from the binary elections and to those assigned in elections with three candidates. With another ratio where, say, twice as much weight is placed on the triplets as on the binaries, we obtain the voting vector

$$\vec{w}^4\left(\vec{w}^3, (1,0), \frac{2}{3}, \frac{1}{3}\right) = \frac{1}{3}(6w_1 + 3, 4w_2 + 2w_1 + 2, 4w_2 + 1, 0). \quad (16)$$

(The new class of voting vectors can be used to explain why the remaining system vectors (from Section 4 and 6) admit election relationships.)

The relationships $\vec{w}^4((1,0,0),(1,0),\frac{1}{2},\frac{1}{2}))$ imposed among the election rankings are derived from a table that lists each candidate's election tally for each three-candidate plurality election and each pairwise election. The totals give the four-candidate election tallies. Because of the extra terms being added, it can be the case that c_1 is the Condorcet winner and $\vec{w}^4((1,0,0),(1,0),\frac{1}{2},\frac{1}{2}))$ is bottom-ranked; in this case she would have to have done poorly in the plurality elections.

To capture the election relationships, we need the added condition that the same candidate does well (or poorly) in *both* the three-candidate plurality and the pairwise majority elections. If the setting is restrictive in such a way that the same candidate is the Condorcet winner and the plurality–Condorcet winner, then the voting vector (14) ensures that she cannot be bottom-ranked when $\frac{1}{2}(6,3,1,0)$ is assigned to the four-candidate set. Such a relationship exists only when a BC or a $\vec{w}^4(\vec{w}^3)$– $\vec{w}^3$ pair is used.

To give a hint about some of the surprises that arise with this theory, let me note that the same voting vector $(6,3,1,0)$ can be derived when $(3,1,0)$ is assigned to three-candidate subsets and $(1,0)$ to the pairwise orderings. Then, it should be reasonable to expect that when c_j is both a $(3,1,0)$-Condorcet winner and a pairwise-Condorcet winner, she could not be $(6,3,1,0)$ bottom-ranked. *This expectation is false;* for many choices of profiles (Saari 1993b) she can be $(6,3,1,0)$ bottom-ranked. Instead, the operative relationship is

1. "if c_j is both a $(3,1,0)$-Condorcet winner and a pairwise Condorcet *loser*, then she cannot be $(6,3,1,0)$ bottom-ranked."

   A related relationship emphasizing the lack of respect shown to the Condorcet winner is:

2. "if c_j is a pairwise Condorcet winner and the $(3,1,0)$-Condorcet loser, then she cannot be top-ranked in a $(6,3,1,0)$ election. However, it is possible for c_j to be both the $(3,1,0)$-Condorcet winner and the pairwise Condorcet loser, and $(6,3,1,0)$ top-ranked!"

The assertion that losers in pairwise candidate comparisons can be winners in n-wise elections is highly counter-intuitive. The reason the advantage in a $(6,3,1,0)$ election transfers to a Condorcet loser from a Condorcet winner is that the voting vector $(6,3,1,0)$ is defined first by finding how many points voter p_{A4} assigns by the rule of comparison $(3,1,0)$ to each candidate in the three-candidate sets (which leads to the voting vector $(9,5,2,0)$), and then by *subtracting* the number of points assigned to each candidate from the pairwise elections. It is the subtraction effect that reverses the expected roles of the

Condorcet winner and loser in analyzing $(6, 3, 1, 0)$ elections. Consequently the Condorcet winner must stack up huge point totals in the $(3, 1, 0)$ elections if she is to counter the majority vote totals being subtracted.

All of the above is intended to indicate the kind of surprises (there are others) and relationships that exist among positional voting methods, and to suggest how these relationships are derived. Details can be found in the references.

References

Borda, J-C de. 1784. "Mémoire sur les élections par scrutin," *Mémoires de l'Académie Royale des Sciences Année 1781*: 657-65.

Condorcet, M. J. A. N., Marquis de. 1784. "Sur les élections par scrutin," *Histoire de l'Académie Royale des Sciences Année 1781*: 31-4.

Condorcet, M. J. A. N., Marquis de. 1785 [1972]. *Essai sur l'application de l'analyse à la probabilité des décisions rendues à la pluralité des voix*. New York: Chelsea (orig. Paris: Imprimerie Royale).

De Grazia, A. 1953. "Mathematical Derivation of an Election System," *Isis* 44: 42-51.

Riker, W. 1982. *Liberalism Against Populism*. San Francisco: W. H. Freeman.

Saari, D. G. 1987. "Chaos and the Theory of Elections," in *Dynamical Systems*, A. Kurzhanski and K. Sigmund, eds. Lecture notes in *Economics and Mathematical Systems*, Vol. 287. Berlin: Springer-Verlag.

Saari, D. G. 1989. "A Dictionary for Voting Paradoxes," *Journal of Economic Theory* 48: 443-475.

Saari, D. G. 1990a. "The Borda Dictionary," *Social Choice Welfare* 7: 279-317.

Saari, D. G. 1990b. "Consistency of Decision Process," *Annals of Operations Research* 23: 103-137.

Saari, D. G. 1991a. "Relationship Admitting Families of Candidates," *Social Choice and Welfare* 8: 21-50.

Saari, D. G. 1991b. "Erratic Behavior in Economic Models," *Journal of Economic Behavior and Organization* 16: 3-35.

Saari, D. G. 1992a. "Millions of Election Rankings from a Single Profile," *Social Choice Welfare* 9: 277-306.

Saari, D. G. 1992b. "Symmetry Extensions of 'Neutrality' I: Advantage to the Condorcet Loser," *Social Choice and Welfare* 9: 307-336.

Saari, D. G. 1993a. "Symmetry Extensions of 'Neutrality' II: Partial Ordering of Dictionaries," *Social Choice and Welfare* 10: 301-334.

Saari, D. G. 1993b. "Symmetry Extensions of 'Neutrality' III: The Vector Spaces." Typescript: Northwestern University.

Young, P. 1974. "An Axiomatization of Borda's Rule," *Journal of Economic Theory* 9: 43-52.

Part II. ELECTIONS AND COMMITTEES

6. Electing Legislatures

David Austen-Smith

6.1 Introduction

Policy outcomes in representative democracies arise out of legislative decision-making, and out of legislatures that consist of more than one elected official. The preferences of policy-oriented voters over possible representatives, therefore, will be induced both by their preferences over policy outcomes and the institutional structure of legislative decision-making. This observation is, I believe, fundamental to developing models, and to an understanding of the election of legislatures. Models of elected legislatures that assume, at the outset, individuals who vote on the basis of the policy positions of the available candidates, without regard to the legislative implications of their vote, misspecify both individual payoffs and the choice set.

The canonical spatial model of electoral competition presumes a degenerate legislative structure. Two Downsian parties (*i.e.*, candidates) compete, under simple plurality voting, for the right to *represent* a society of n individuals who are differentiated only by their preferences over policy outcomes. (In particular, the electorate is not partitioned into districts, each one of which elects a representative to some legislature.) Within this institutional setting, the party winning the election monopolistically selects the final policy outcome. If there is complete information (*e.g.*, Black 1958; Downs 1957: Ch. 8), then there is no loss of generality in identifying the parties with the policy outcomes they would implement if elected. In this case, voters' induced preferences over parties are trivially defined by their preferences over outcomes. When there is incomplete information (*e.g.*, Banks 1990; Enelow and Hinich 1984), voters' induced preferences over parties are defined by the composition of these preferences over outcomes and beliefs over what a party would implement if elected. Furthermore, whatever informational structure is assumed, the existence of only two competitors for an office that endows the winner with monopolistic control of the policy outcome is sufficient to yield sincere voting as the only sensible Nash equilibrium strategy.[1]

It is a recurrent theme of this essay that the simplicity of the induced preferences described above, and the reasonableness of sincere voting, are peculiar to models of single-district, two-party elections under simple-plurality rule. Although important, such models are generally not sufficient for analyzing the election of legislatures.

The plan of the essay is as follows. Section 6.2 introduces the basic framework used throughout, and Section 6.3 explores the implications of the sincere

---

[1] By *sensible* it is meant that no individual uses a weakly dominated strategy in equilibrium.

voting assumption for models of legislative elections.[2] In the light of the results of Section 6.3, Sections 6.4 and 6.5 review the extant (formal) theoretical literature on legislative elections. Since a legislature is understood throughout the essay to consist of at least two elected candidates, the review will not deal with models of multi-candidate, single-winner elections (*e.g.*, Cox 1985, 1987). Concluding remarks follow in Section 6.6.

6.2 Basic Framework

6.2.1 Individuals, Preferences, and Candidates

Let $N = \{1, ..., n\}$ be a finite set of voters. The set of feasible policy outcomes, X, is assumed to be isomorphic to a compact subset of the real line, $\Re$. Typically, we take X to be an interval. Let $U(X)$ be the set of strictly single-peaked preference orderings (*i.e.*, no flat spots) on X. Hereafter, the dependency of U on X will be left implicit. A preference profile for N is a list

$$u = (u_i)_N \in U^n,$$

where u_i describes individual i's preferences on X. For any $u_i \in U$, let $x_i = \text{argmax}_X u_i(\cdot) : x_i$ is individual i's *ideal point* in X. Individuals' preferences are common knowledge.

Let Ω be the set of discrete subsets of X. Any $C = \{z_1, ..., z_t\} \in \Omega$ is a set of *candidate platforms*. Typically, $|C| < \infty$. Unless explicitly stated otherwise, the terms *candidate platform* (generically indexed z_k) and *candidate* (generically indexed k) will be used interchangeably: this should cause no confusion.

For any $i \in N$ and collection of sets of candidates $\theta \in 2^\Omega \backslash \emptyset$, i's *(pure) voting strategy* on θ is a function:

$$\chi_i : \theta \to \Omega : \forall C \in \theta, \chi_i(C) \in C,$$

where $\chi_i(C) = z_k$ means individual i (with preferences u_i on X) casts his vote for candidate $z_k \in C$. Thus χ_i describes how i allocates his vote when faced with any set of candidates in θ. Given θ, let $\sum(\theta)$ be the set of pure voting strategies on θ, with generic element $\chi = (\chi_1, ..., \chi_n)$. For any $C \in \theta$, let $\chi(C) = (\chi_1(C), ..., \chi_n(C))$ be the list of votes on C induced by χ.

6.2.2 Legislative Election Structures

Given θ, a *legislative election structure for* θ consists of (1) a rule, ε_θ, governing which candidates get elected to the legislature as a function of individuals' voting strategies, and (2) a rule, λ_θ, describing how the elected candidates arrive at a final policy outcome.

Fix θ arbitrarily. An *election rule for* θ is a mapping,

---
[2] These sections draw heavily on Austen-Smith (1989).

$$\varepsilon_\theta : \theta \times \sum (\theta)^n \to \Omega,$$

such that $\forall (C, \chi) \in \Omega \times \sum (\theta)^n$, $C \supseteq \varepsilon_\theta(C, \chi)$. Call $\varepsilon_\theta(C, \chi)$, a *legislature*. Throughout, assume MAX $| \varepsilon_\theta(\cdot, \cdot) | \geq 2$, so any legislature may consist of at least two elected representatives. Let $v_k(\chi) = | \{i \in N \mid \chi_i = z_k\} |$. Then, for example, under the fixed-standard method studied in Greenberg and Weber (1985), $fs(m)$, the legislature generated by the strategy profile χ is defined by:

$$\varepsilon_\theta^{fs(m)}(C, \chi) = \{z_k \in C \mid v_k(\chi) \geq m\}.$$

Let E_θ be the set of election rules for θ.

A *legislative outcome function* (LOF) for θ is a mapping,

$$\lambda_\theta : \theta \times \sum(\theta)^n \to X.$$

For every possible legislature elected from θ, the LOF defines the legislative policy outcome. Strictly speaking, λ_θ is a reduced form of the legislative decision making process. In general, elected representatives will select strategies from some feasible set, and some prespecified set of rules will describe how any list of strategies (one for each legislator) is mapped into final outcomes. A complete theory of the legislative stage, therefore, would be explicit about such strategies, about how they are selected (*e.g.*, as equilibria of some non-cooperative game), and about the mapping from joint strategies to policies (Palfrey 1986). Here, all such detail is embedded in the composite map of λ_θ, taking the set of successful candidates, with their votes, into final outcomes. (However, where appropriate later, more detail on the structure of the LOF for particular models is provided.)

Notice that the outcome generated by any LOF is not restricted *a priori* to lie in the set of platforms espoused by the successful candidates in any election. For example, the final outcome may be some weighted average of the elected candidates' platforms. And notice that we allow the LOF to depend on voter strategies as well as on the positions of the elected set of candidates. This, for example, permits successful candidates' vote-shares to matter in legislative decision-making. Of course, the LOF may be constant across $\chi(C) \in C^n$ for any given legislature. For example, the median successful candidate rule, λ^μ, has the property:

$$\lambda_\theta^\mu(C^*, \chi) = \text{median } \{z_k \mid z_k \in C^*\},$$

where $C^* = \varepsilon_\theta(C, \cdot)$. Let L_θ be the set of LOFs for θ. A *legislative election structure for* $\theta \in 2^\Omega \setminus \emptyset$ is an ordered pair $(\varepsilon_\theta, \lambda_\theta) \in E_\theta \times L_\theta$. Typically, we are not interested in all logically possible legislative election structures. In this essay, we consider only structures which are anonymous (do not depend on the names of individual voters or candidates), efficient (do not select alternatives which are wanted by no one), and well-defined for any logically possible (finite) set of candidates.

Definition: An election rule ε_θ is:

1. *nontrivial* if $\forall\, C \in \theta, \forall\, z_k \in C,\ v_k(\chi(C)) > 0 \not\Rightarrow z_k \in \varepsilon_\theta(C, \chi(C))$;

2. *E − efficient* if $\forall\, C \in \theta, \forall\, \chi(C),\ z_k \in \varepsilon_\theta(C, \chi(C)) \Rightarrow v_k(\chi(C)) > 0$;

3. *anonymous* if it is symmetric with respect to candidates and voters.

Let $E_\theta^* = \{\varepsilon_\theta \mid \varepsilon_\theta \text{ is nontrivial, E-efficient, and anonymous}\}$.

Definition: Let $C^* = \varepsilon_\theta(C, \chi(C))$. A legislative outcome function λ_θ is:

1. *singleton* if $\forall\, C^* \in \theta, \forall\, \chi,\ |\lambda_\theta(C^*, \chi)| = 1$.

2. *L-efficient* if $\forall\, C^* \in \theta, \forall\, \chi,\ \lambda_\theta(C^*, \chi) \in$ the convex hull of $C^*[\text{con}(C^*)]$;

3. *L-anonymous* if it is symmetric with respect to elected candidates.

Let $L_\theta^* = \{\lambda_\theta \mid \lambda_\theta \text{ is singleton, L-efficient and L-anonymous}\}$.

Definition: For any θ, the legislative election structure $(\varepsilon_\theta, \lambda_\theta)$ is θ−*admissible* if $(\varepsilon_\theta, \lambda_\theta) \in E_\theta^* \times L_\theta^*$. If $\theta \equiv \Omega$, then $(\varepsilon_\Omega, \lambda_\Omega) \in E_\Omega^* \times L_\Omega^*$ is simply said to be *admissible*.

As remarked above, unless explicitly stated otherwise, this essay deals only with admissible legislative election structures. A justification for this is, firstly, that virtually all currently existing models of legislative elections are in fact admissible (exceptions include the multi-member party models discussed in Section 6.5, below); and, secondly, the defining properties of admissible structures are fairly appealing. If an election rule were not nontrivial, then a single vote for a candidate k would always be sufficient for k to be elected: this is extremely mild. Similarly, the efficiency conditions are weak. The anonymity conditions insure that individuals' names *per se* play no strategic role in determining the final outcome. This seems unexceptional at the election stage. At the legislative stage, however, it should be noted that L-anonymity not only says that names are irrelevant, but also rules out institutional features such as Presidential vetoes, and, as such, is restrictive. Likewise, the requirement that LOFs be singleton is quite demanding. Although at most one policy outcome can be implemented *de facto*, the assumption either constrains the implicit set of equilibria arising in any underlying legislative decisionmaking game to be unique, or insists that the selection to be made from any multi-valued set of equilibria is common knowledge *ex ante*. (The L-anonymity and the singleton properties are used principally to prove results reported in Section 6.3, below. However, the validity of the main proposition of Section 6.3 does not seem to depend crucially on either of these conditions.)

6.2.3 Reduced Forms

Given a set of candidates $C \in \theta$, an election rule, ε_θ, an LOF, λ_θ, and a vector of voting strategies χ, the final legislative outcome is given by $\lambda_\theta(\varepsilon_\theta(C, \chi(C)), \chi(C)) \in X$. Define the mapping,

$$\gamma_\theta : \theta \times \sum(\theta)^n \to X$$

by setting

$$\gamma_\theta(C, \chi) = \lambda_\theta(\varepsilon_\theta(C, \chi(C)), \chi(C)) \ \forall \ (C, \chi).$$

If $(\varepsilon_\theta, \lambda_\theta)$ is $\theta-admissible$, then γ_θ is anonymous (i.e., symmetric with respect to candidates and voters), and efficient (i.e. $\forall \ \chi, \gamma_\theta(C, \chi) \in \text{Con}(C)$ with $|\gamma_\theta(C, \chi)| = 1$). The mapping γ_c will be referred to as the *reduced form* of the legislative election structure for θ. Let, $\Gamma^* =$

$$\{\gamma_\Omega : \Omega \times \sum(\Omega)^n \to X \mid \gamma_\Omega(\cdot, \cdot) = \lambda_\Omega(\varepsilon_\Omega(\cdot, \cdot), \cdot), (\varepsilon_\Omega, \lambda_\Omega)) \in E^*_\Omega \times L^*_\Omega\}$$

be the set of reduced forms of admissible election structures.

Given any legislative election structure for θ, define i's indirect utility by,

$$w_i(\chi(C)) \equiv u_i(\gamma_\theta(C, \chi(C))), \forall \ C \in \theta, i \in N.$$

Thus w_i describes i's payoff under the legislative election structure $(\varepsilon_\theta, \lambda_\theta)$ as a function of the voting strategy vector χ; $w_i : \sum(\theta)^n \to \Re$.

This completes the description of the basic framework. Some important concepts are noticeably absent: in particular, candidate objectives and any notion of equilibrium. However, since these vary across models, their introduction is deferred until necessary.

6.3 The Assumption of Sincere Voting

It was claimed in the Introduction that an assumption of sincere voting is inappropriate for models of legislative elections. This claim is justified on theoretical grounds below, where it is argued that sincere voting in legislative elections constitutes rational behavior on the part of voters only if the legislative election structure is equivalent to a two-candidate, single-winner competition. Given such circumstances, it is hard to understand the rationale for (nondegenerate) legislative election structures. Furthermore, the assumption is questionable empirically (see Riker 1982, Section VI, for a brief review of the relevant literature): even in large electorates, individuals seem to vote strategically.

For this section, assume all individuals' preferences are Euclidean:

$$\forall \ i \in N, \forall \ y, z \in X; u_i(y) > u_i(z) \iff |x_i - y| < |x_i - z|.$$

Let U_e be the set of Euclidean preferences on X. For $u \in U^n_e$, preferences are effectively characterized by ideal points. Hence, we can replace such preference profiles by vectors of ideal points, $x = (x_i)_N \in X^n$. Because of the structure of voting strategies (cast a vote for a single candidate), assuming Euclidean preferences is not critical for the arguments to follow.[3]

Fix a collection of sets of candidates θ arbitrarily, and let the legislative election structure for θ be given.

Definition: Individual $i \in N$ votes *sincerely with respect to* C iff: $\chi_i(C) = z_k \Rightarrow [\not\exists\ z_{k\prime} \in C\backslash\{z_k\} \mid u_i(z_{k\prime}) > u_i(z_k)]$.

If i votes sincerely with respect to every $C \in \theta$, say that i adopts the *sincere voting strategy on* θ. Let χ_i^T denote i's sincere voting strategy on θ, and let $\chi_i^T(C)$ be i's sincere vote with respect to C.

The assumption that individuals necessarily vote sincerely with respect to C (for any C) is frequently invoked in models of legislative elections (*e.g.*, Sugden 1984; Greenberg and Weber 1985; Greenberg and Shepsle 1987). If voters are presumed to be rational and outcome-oriented, then this assumption is tantamount to claiming that sincere voting is a weakly dominant strategy.

Definition: The sincere voting strategy χ_i^T is *weakly dominant* under γ_θ for i if: $w_i(\chi_i^T, \chi_{-i}) \geq w_i(\chi_i, \chi_{-i})\ \forall\ \chi_i \neq \chi_i^T, \forall\ \chi_{-i}$, where $\chi_{-i} = (\chi_1, ..., \chi_{i-1}, \chi_{i+1}, ..., \chi_n)$.

Suppose that sincere voting is invariably a weakly dominant strategy for all individuals. What does this imply for the legislative election structure? To answer this question, we need one further concept.

Definition: A legislative election structure $(\varepsilon_\theta, \lambda_\theta)$ is *straightforward* if: $\forall\ x \in X^n, \forall\ i \in N;\ \chi_i^T$ is weakly dominant under the reduced form γ_θ.

When $(\varepsilon_\theta, \lambda_\theta)$ is straightforward, we say also that γ_θ is straightforward.

Theorem 1: *(Austen-Smith 1989). No admissible legislative election structure is straightforward.*

Essentially, this result is a corollary of a theorem due to Moulin (1980).

There are several ways to understand the result. Perhaps the most immediate is to consider an arbitrary legislative election structure $(\varepsilon_\theta, \lambda_\theta) \in E_\theta \times L_\theta$ for some family of candidates θ, with reduced form γ_θ. Then the following is true:

Theorem 2: *(Moulin 1980; Austen-Smith 1989).* γ_θ *is* θ*−admissible and straightforward* $\Leftrightarrow \exists$ *an order statistic* ρ *on* N *such that* $\forall\ u \in U_e^n\ \forall\ C \in \theta$,

$$u_{i(\rho)}(z_k) > u_{i(\rho)}(z_{k\prime})\ \forall\ z_{k\prime} \in C\backslash z_k \Rightarrow [z_k = \gamma_\theta(C, \chi)],$$

where $i(\rho) \in N$ *is the individual with the* ρ^{th}*−ranked ideal point.*

---
[3] The restriction to Euclidean preferences is in general strong. It is only for the arguments of this section that it is a convenience and not fundamental.

Theorem 2 says that if an assumption of sincere voting at the election stage in any legislative election model is justified on rationality grounds, then which candidates actually get elected to office is immaterial for legislative policy. It is the entire set of candidates competing for office that matters. Moreover, there exists an individual i^* such that if some candidate, c, adopts i^*'s ideal point, x_{i^*}, in the election, then (given that sincere voting constitutes rational behavior) x_{i^*} must be the final legislative outcome, whether c is elected to the legislature or not. So, for example, bargaining in legislatures to reach a compromise policy position is generally incompatible with sincere voting at the election stage. In effect, the multistage structure of a legislative election is irrelevant: whenever sincere voting is rational, a two-candidate race under an appropriately chosen $q-rule$ (i.e., a rule by which the candidate with at least q votes wins outright) generates *precisely* the same set of policy outcomes. An example illustrates these points.

EXAMPLE 1: Suppose there are seven voters and the policy space is $[0,1]$. Let the ideal points be, $x = (0, \frac{1}{5}, \frac{1}{5}, \frac{5}{7}, \frac{4}{5}, \frac{4}{5}, 1)$. Suppose there are three candidates competing for seats in a 2-member legislature, and suppose the election rule is the fixed-standard scheme (ε_θ^{fs}) with $m = 3$. Let the set of candidate platforms be $C = \{\frac{1}{5}, \frac{5}{7}, \frac{4}{5}\}$. Under sincere voting, individuals 1, 2 and 3 vote for $\frac{1}{5}$, individual 4 votes for $\frac{5}{7}$, and individuals 5, 6 and 7 vote for $\frac{4}{5}$. Therefore, the legislature is $C^* = \{\frac{1}{5}, \frac{4}{5}\}$. How is the final legislative outcome selected? Suppose the LOF is: if either elected candidate wins an overall majority of votes, then that candidate implements his electoral platform; otherwise the final outcome is a weighted sum of the elected candidates' platforms, with the weights being given by their respective vote-shares relative to the total votes going to elected candidates.[4] This LOF is certainly in L_θ^*. Under sincere voting, the final outcome is $\frac{1}{2}$. But if individual 4 votes strategically for $\frac{4}{5}$, given the others vote sincerely, the final outcome is $\frac{4}{5}$. And this improves 4's payoff over that achieved by sincere voting. To support sincere voting here, the final outcome essentially must be individual 4's ideal point. But then two-candidate simple majority voting generates the same outcome as the two-stage legislative election scheme.

The results reported above have two immediate implications for models of legislative elections. First, if the multi-stage legislative election structure is not vacuous (under complete information), then the assumption of sincere voting is problematic. Individual voting behavior should be deduced, not presumed. Second, to understand strategic behavior by candidates and (policy-oriented) voters at the election stage, the structure of the subsequent legislative stage needs to be specified explicitly. Different legislative structures induce different electoral behavior: if results on the election stage are to have content, the legislative stage cannot be treated as a *blackbox*.

For the remainder of the paper, unless explicitly stated otherwise, the domain of any election rule is taken to be Ω: subscripts Ω can therefore be ignored without ambiguity.

---

[4] See Ursprung (1980) for a similar example.

6.4 Single District Models

In general, parties and candidates are distinct: candidates for office may or may not be members of some party, and parties rarely consist solely of electoral candidates. In single district models, however, parties are typically assumed to be characterized by a single candidate for office (but see Aldrich 1983a, 1983b). Consequently, in this section, the terms candidate and party will be used interchangeably. Later, the two notions will be distinguished.

Greenberg and Weber (1985) examine a model of proportional representation under the fixed-standard election rule $(fs(m))$:

$$\varepsilon^{fs(m)}(C,\chi) = \{z_k \in C \mid v_k(\chi) \geq m\}.$$

Under this rule, the size of the legislature is variable and comprises all those candidates who receive at least m votes in the election, where $m > 0$ is some prespecified integer no greater than n, the size of the electorate. The feasible set X is assumed finite, and individuals' preferences–although single-peaked– are not necessarily symmetric on X. In the model, candidates are constrained to adopt distinct positions. Therefore, the feasible set of candidates, Ω, is the power set of X. The focus of attention is on the existence and structure of $fs(m)$-equilibria:

Definition: $C \in \Omega$ is an $fs(m)$-*equilibrium* if $\forall\ z_k \in X\ v_k(\chi^T(C)) \geq m$ iff $z_k \in C$.

Thus, an $fs(m)$-equilibrium is "a set of alternatives such that when the voters are faced with the choice among these alternatives, and when each voter votes for the alternative he prefers best in this set, each alternative receives at least m votes and, moreover, no new (potential) candidate can attract m voters by offering another alternative, in addition to those offered in the m-equilibrium" (Greenberg and Weber 1985, p. 696). The main result is:

Theorem 3: *(Greenberg and Weber 1985). For any m, $0 < m \leq n$, there exists an $fs(m)$–equilibrium.*

This result, which will be considered in more detail shortly, stands in contrast to that of Greenberg and Shepsle (1987), who study the fixed-number election rule in an environment otherwise identical to that of Greenberg and Weber. The fixed-number election rule $(fn(K))$, for $k \leq n$, is defined as:

$$\varepsilon^{fn(K)}(C,\chi) = \{z_k \in C \mid v_k(\chi) < v_{k'}(\chi),\text{ for } z_{k'} \in C' \subset C \text{ and } |C'| \leq K-1\}.$$

(If there are ties, it is assumed throughout that a fair random device casts a deciding *vote*.) Under the fixed-standard rule, the size of the legislature is variable. Under the fixed-number rule, however, the size of the legislature is predetermined at $K, 0 < K \leq n$.

Definition: C is an $fn(K)$–*equilibrium* if:

(1) $|C| = K$,
(2) $\forall z_k \in X \backslash C$, $v_k(\chi^T(C \cup \{z_k\})) \leq v_{k*}(\chi^T(C \cup \{z_k\}))$, $\forall z_k \in C$.

An $fn(K)$-equilibrium is therefore a set C of exactly K candidates, each adopting a distinct electoral platform such that no additional candidate could enter the election and gain more (sincere) votes than any candidate of C.

Theorem 4: *(Greenberg and Shepsle 1987).* $\forall K \geq 2 \; \exists \; u \in U^n$ *such that there exists no $fn(K)$-equilibrium.*

At first glance, Theorems 3 and 4 suggest that proportional representation systems using a fixed-standard election rule are likely to be more stable–at least at the electoral level–than those using a fixed-number rule. However, in the absence of a more complete specification of the legislative election game, this conclusion is premature. As they stand, the results refer to the abstract properties of particular preference aggregation mechanisms. For example, Theorem 3 answers the following question: Given an arbitrary $u \in U^n$, and given an integer m ($0 < m \leq n$), does there exist a subset C of X such that $\forall z_k \in C \; |\{i \in N : u_i(z_k) > u_i(z_{k'}) \; \forall \; z_{k'} \in C \backslash \{z_k\}\}| \geq m$, and $\exists$ no $z_j \in X \backslash C$ such that $|\{i \in N : u_i(z_j) > u_i(z_k), \; \forall \; z_k \in C\}| \geq m$?

Although the answer to this question (and the analogous one answered by Theorem 4) is important for the study of proportional representation, it does not, *per se*, address issues of electoral equilibrium. The difficulty is that the concepts of $fs(m)$-equilibrium and $fn(K)$-equilibrium are not behavioral. Substantive conclusions drawn from Theorems 3 and 4, therefore, must be treated cautiously.[5]

For a model of elections, voters and candidates need to be endowed (at least) with strategy sets. In Greenberg/Weber and Greenberg/Shepsle, voters' strategy sets are degenerate, and candidates for office are presumed to seek sufficient votes to win office: these restrictions are implicit in the formal definition of $fn(K)$-equilibrium and $fs(m)$-equilibrium.[6] Given these restrictions, the structure of the games for which $fn(K)$- and $fs(m)$-equilibria might define solutions does not seem particularly well-suited to legislative elections. To see this, recall Example 1 (Section 6.3). In that environment, the set $C = \{\frac{1}{5}, \frac{4}{5}\}$ is the unique $fs(3)$-equilibrium and the unique $fn(2)$-equilibrium. However, if candidates care about influencing policy and if sincere voting is rational, then a new candidate could enter at $\frac{5}{7}$ and induce $\frac{5}{7}$ as the legislative policy choice. This entrant would surely not get elected but, by the arguments of Section 6.3, for sincere voting to be rational the implicit legislative outcome function must nevertheless select $\frac{5}{7}$ as the final policy.[7] Consequently, for sin-

---

[5] In particular, remarks 3, 5 and 6 of Greenberg and Shepsle (1987): two of these are taken up when appropriate later.

[6] For instance, with sincere voting, no Nash equilibrium in candidate strategies exists if candidates attempt to vote-maximize under the fixed-standard or fixed-number rule.

[7] Greenberg and Weber argue that if the legislative outcome function were given by simple majority voting over con(C^*), then sincere voting is rational behavior. The example shows this to be incorrect: any alternative z lying between $\frac{1}{5}$ and $\frac{4}{5}$ is a median outcome, and thus a legitimate policy choice for the Greenberg/Weber legislature. But only $z^* \approx \frac{5}{7}$ insures

cere voting to be rational and for $fs(m)$- and $fn(K)$-equilibria to be germane for legislative elections, candidates must be presumed to seek office for reasons other than affecting policy. That there are nonpolicy reasons for getting elected is unexceptional; that such reasons can be the only ones is problematic. If elected candidates do in fact affect policy in the legislature then, by Theorem 1, sincere voting and rational voters cannot be jointly assumed: the legislative outcome function needs to be made explicit and appropriate voter (and candidate) behavior deduced. It is not sufficient to specify the election rule alone and impose sincere voting over candidates as a behavioral rule for voters.

A model similar in spirit to those of Greenberg, *et al.* is due to Robert Sugden (1984). He examines a normative principle of Free Association "as a game of strategy in which voters bargain and coalesce with one another in an attempt to influence the composition of the assembly" (p. 33). The principle, deriving from arguments of J. S. Mill (1861) among others, is that "citizens should be free to choose for themselves which constituencies they belong to" (Sugden, *ibid.*, p. 32). The analytical issue addressed is the extent to which particular forms of proportional representation implement this normative principle. His approach is ingenious. Sugden first describes a cooperative game without sidepayments in which individual voters can freely collude to elect some set of candidates. Then his "criterion for evaluating schemes of proportional representation is that, so long as the core of that game is not empty, the set of candidates who are elected [under the scheme] should be a member of the core" (p. 40). He concludes that under single-peaked preferences, a modified version of Single-Transferable Voting (STV) satisfies this criterion.

Unfortunately, when evaluating outcomes under STV, he assumes sincere voting over candidates, ignoring the legislative policy implications of such behavior. Similarly, in the game-theoretic model used as a benchmark–which is of special interest here–individuals are concerned about electing slates of candidates, and preferences over slates are induced without concern for the final policy outcomes generated from any elected legislature.

Sugden assumes a fixed number of candidates, t: hence, $C \in \Omega_t = \{C \in \Omega : |C| = t\}$. The election is by the fixed-standard rule, $fs(m)$. The standard m is set so that at most K candidates can be elected, and m is the Droop quota–the smallest integer exceeding $\frac{n}{(K+1)}$. Assume that $t > K$, and suppose (for convenience) that $\frac{(n+1)}{(K+1)} = m$ is integer. Then define a *slate* to be any subset A of C such that $|A| \leq K$. Preferences over slates are derived from the underlying (strict) preferences over candidates by:

Slate A is preferred to slate B by individual i iff either

(i) $\text{MAX}_{A \setminus (A \cap B)} u_i > \text{MAX}_{B \setminus (A \cap B)} u_i$, or
(ii) $A \supset B$.

If i prefers A to B according to this criterion, write $A >_i B$, etc.

---

sincere voting.

In the model, voters are allowed to abstain. But since this plays no role in the analysis, I assume here that everyone always votes. Thus, voter strategies are as specified in Section 6.2, above.

Definition: Fix $C \in \Omega_t$. A slate A in C is *blocked* under $fs(m)$ iff $\exists\, L, N \supseteq L$, and $\exists\, \chi_L = (\chi_i)_{i \in L}$ such that $\forall\, \chi_{-L} = (\chi_j)_{j \notin L}$, then $\forall\, i \in L$,

$$\varepsilon_{\Omega_t}^{fs(m)}((\chi_L, \chi_{-L})) >_i A.$$

The *core(C) under $fs(m)$* is the set of all slates in C that are not blocked under $fs(m)$.

Thus, only the voting game is considered. As in the models of Greenberg et al., candidate objectives are to obtain sufficient votes to insure election. (And note that core(C) is a so-called "beta" core.)

Recalling that individual preferences over X are single-peaked, rank-order ideal points so that $x_i < x_{i+1}$ for all $i < n$. For any $C \in \Omega_t$, let $C^{dq} = \{z_1, ..., z_K\}$ be the subset of C such that

1. $z_i = \text{argmax}_C\, u_{im}(\cdot)\; \forall\, z_i \in C^{dq}$;

2. $z_k \neq z_j\; \forall\, z_k, z_j \in C^{dq}$;

3. K = maximum number of seats in the legislature; and

4. m = Droop quota.

Since preferences are assumed strict (an implicit restriction on C), C^{dq} is uniquely defined for every C.

Theorem 5: *(Sugden 1984).* $\forall\, C \in \Omega_t$, the core (C) under $fs(m)$, where m is the Droop quota, is exactly C^{dq}.

It is instructive to compare Theorem 5 to Theorem 3. Theorem 3 guarantees the existence of at least one (and maybe several) $fs(m)$-equilibrium for any m and thus *a fortiori*, for the Droop quota. Theorem 5 asserts that under strategic and cooperative voting, there exists a unique equilibrium (or core) set of candidates under $fs(m)$. Where do they differ? The answer is straightforward. Sugden's equilibrium is defined for any arbitrarily fixed set of distinct candidate platforms: core(C) is a cooperative voting equilibrium concept relative to a given $C \in \Omega_t$. In contrast, Greenberg and Weber fix voting strategies: by definition of an $fs(m)$ equilibrium, voters (noncooperatively) vote sincerely, and so the focus of the $fs(m)$-equilibrium concept is candidate platforms relative to χ^T. Therefore, not every $fs(m)$-equilibrium (m = Droop quota) is necessarily a core slate, and not every core slate will be an $fs(m)$-equilibrium. However, consider the slate $C^{dq*} = (x_{1m}, ..., x_{Km})$, where m and K are defined as for Theorem 5, and x_{jm} is individual $jm's$ ideal point (with $x_i < x_{i+1}$ for all $i < n$). Then it is simple to check that C^{dq*} is both an $fs(m)$-equilibrium and a core(C) slate for any $C \supseteq C^{dq*}$.

Theorem 5 is driven by the assumption that preferences over slates are given by the induced relation, $>_i$. The assumption is very restrictive. Sugden recognizes this but argues that if a legislature is considered a forum for debate, and not a decision-making body, then it is a legitimate starting point from which to analyze proportional representation. However, legislatures, whatever else they may be, *are* decision-making bodies, and debate is simply one mechanism for influencing final policy decisions. From this perspective, it is natural to specify a legislative outcome function (which may well involve information transmission through debate) and induce preferences through this. And, once again, there is no reason *a priori* to suppose such preferences will be sincere.

Despite the objections, Sugden's approach through cooperative theory is important. Most democratic polities involve party activists—agents who, among other things, devote resources to organizing voting blocs. In legislative elections where the composition of the parliament as a whole matters for final outcomes, the ability to coordinate voting strategies among groups of voters is strategically valuable. Party activists promote such coordination, and one possible way to model such activist behavior is implicitly via a cooperative game at the electoral stage of the process. Of course, any set of voter strategies should be self-enforcing, and, therefore, an appropriate (cooperative) solution concept must subsume (noncooperative) Nash behavior. So, for example, although the core is the natural solution concept for the normative issue with which Sugden is concerned, some form of Strong Nash equilibrium might be more appropriate for positive theory.

The importance of being able to coordinate voting strategies in legislative elections with many parties was recognized clearly by Anthony Downs (1957). In chapter 9 of *An Economic Theory of Democracy*, Downs considers a two-stage model in which a multi-party legislature is elected via proportional representation (from a single district), and the elected representatives then use majority voting to determine a government. "Under these conditions, each voter's ballot does not support the policies of any one party. Instead it supports the whole coalition that party joins. Thus the meaning of a vote for any party depends upon what coalitions it is likely to enter, which in turn depends upon how other voters will vote" (Downs 1957, p. 163). Downs' model is described informally and not well-specified, (in particular, there is no explicit equilibrium concept). His conclusions are correspondingly rather vague and difficult to verify (*e.g.*, "(1) Though rational voting is more important in multiparty systems than in two-party systems, it is more difficult and less effective. (2) In systems normally governed by coalitions, voters are under pressure to behave irrationally..." (p. 143)). Nevertheless, Downs does invoke an explicit two-stage model of legislative elections, and is sensitive to the additional strategic considerations this involves.

Given a set of parties C contesting the election, the election rule he states (p. 144) is as follows. Take the aggregate electoral vote, n, and divide by K, the size of the legislature. Divide this number into each party's votes to obtain the number of legislative seats for that party. Since Downs ignores fractions, I shall refer to the weight (ω_k) of a party in the legislature rather

David Austen-Smith 125

than its number of seats, which may not be well-defined (see Balinski and Young 1982). Hence, for any party k, $\omega_k(\chi) = Kv_k(\chi)/n$. Unfortunately, Downs' scheme amounts to admitting any party with at least one electoral vote into the legislature. This is trivial. However, by requiring that a party obtain sufficient electoral votes to get a weight of at least one suggests the following, nontrivial, election rule:

$$\varepsilon^d(C,\chi) = \{z_k \in C \mid v_k(\chi) \geq n/K\}.$$

Once the legislature C^* is determined, it "selects a prime minister by majority vote and approves his government department heads as a group before they start to govern....there are no intermediate votes between the initial approval of a government and the next election, either by the legislature or by the voters" (p. 144). It is not clear from Downs' account whether he envisages a cooperative or a non-cooperative majority voting game in the legislature. The description of the process indicates a noncooperative model but, immediately following this description, he writes that "we ignore most of the problems caused by interparty negotiations within the legislature, since they are both too complex and too empirical to be handled here" (p. 145). This disclaimer suggests that Downs believes a cooperative model is more appropriate, but chooses to adopt a noncooperative voting framework in order to say anything at all. Certainly, the analysis following these statements makes most sense from the noncooperative perspective. So assuming this is indeed his approach, the legislative outcome is determined by weighted majority voting over C^*, with the weights given by $\omega(\chi) = (\omega_k(\chi))_{C^*}$. Thus,

$$\lambda^d(C^*,\chi) = \{z \in C^* \mid z \text{ is the outcome of (noncooperative) weighted majority voting over } C^*, \text{ with weights } \omega(\chi)\}.$$

The legislative election structure $(\varepsilon^d, \lambda^d)$ is admissible, and is therefore not straightforward (Theorem 1). Hence Downs' concern throughout the chapter is with individuals' voting decisions.

However, it is worth noting that if we take Downs' original specification of the (trivial) election rule–i.e., $\varepsilon^{d'}(\chi) = \{z_k \in c \mid v_k(\chi) > 0\}$–then the reduced form $\gamma^{d'}(\cdot,\cdot) = \lambda^d(\varepsilon^{d'}(\cdot),\cdot)$ *is* straightforward. In other words, given the noncooperative interpretation of Downs' legislative model and given the (trivial) election rule $\varepsilon^{d'}$, his concern with how rational individuals should vote is misplaced: their equilibrium voting strategies are sincere. Since I have argued that Downs, for analytical reasons, favors a noncooperative legislative voting model to select the government, it is necessary that his election rule be nontrivial for there to be an issue over electoral voting behavior in his model.

Downs does not resolve how voters should behave in any (voting) equilibrium. In the absence of a solution to this problem, parties' electoral strategies–choice of platform–cannot be pinned down, since the mapping taking a set of positions C into final party payoffs is then not well-defined. Following Downs' intuition, Austen-Smith and Banks (1988) develop a multi-stage legislative election model under proportional representation, in which voters are fully rational and final policy outcomes emerge as equilibria to a fully specified bargaining game.

In the models due to Greenberg et al., above, the number of parties who can enter the legislative election is constrained only by the cardinality of X (no two parties are allowed to share the same platform). Austen-Smith/Banks permit parties to adopt any position in X (including those already occupied by some other party), but assume that only three parties contest the election; hence, elections involve only $C \in \Omega_3$. The election rule is $fs(m)$, $3 \leq m < \frac{n}{3}, m$ and n odd.

The model is one of proportional representation and the weight of any party z_k in the post-election legislature is given by that party's vote-share, $v_k(\chi)/n$.[8] The importance of party weights lies in the specification of the legislative outcome function. Let C^* be the legislature (the set of parties with $v_k(\chi) \geq m$) and assume that any coalition in C^* with aggregate vote-share exceeding $\frac{1}{2}$ is winning, i.e., has control of the legislative decision-making process.[9] Call any winning coalition a government, and consider the following legislative bargaining game.

Suppose $|C^*| = 3$. If any party has a vote-share greater than $\frac{1}{2}$ then that party has monopolistic control of the legislature, and implements its electoral policy platform. If no party has such a majority, then the party with the highest vote-share is first given an opportunity to form a government. It does this by proposing a winning coalition, a policy, and a distribution of portfolios (discussed below). If the number of parties in the proposed coalition who agree to the proposal is sufficient to form a government, then that government forms and implements the specified policy. If a government fails to form, then the party with the second-highest vote-share is given the opportunity to form a winning coalition. Should this fail, the smallest party in the legislature attempts to form a government. And, finally, if no party is able to support a winning coalition, a *caretaker* government forms which is presumed to make the legislative decisions "equitably". Now suppose $|C^*| \leq 2$. Then if only one legislative party has the highest weight, then that party has monopolistic control of the legislature (even if it does not have an overall electoral majority). Otherwise, the process above is implemented. As before, ties in vote-shares are broken by a fair random device allocating a decisive vote prior to the start of the bargaining process.

This type of mechanism is common among multi-party legislatures. For example, it occurs by convention in Belgium and Italy, and by law in Israel.[10]

The payoffs to parties generated by this process are discussed shortly. Once these are specified, the process of forming a government described here generates a noncooperative sequential bargaining game, in which parties' opportunity costs from joining a proposed government are generated *endogenously*. Parties' strategies in this (legislative) game are proposals, *i.e.* triples

---

[8] So there is no abstention in the model. Also, voters are permitted to use mixed strategies; but this plays no role in equilibrium.

[9] As will become apparent below, if $C^* \leq 2$, this criterion is sufficient but not necessary for monopolistic legislative control.

[10] Parliaments of the World, Vol. II, (1986); Table 39.

(M, z_M, b_M), where M is a winning coalition, z_M is the policy position implemented by M, and b_M is the distribution of portfolios implemented by M.[11] The equilibrium concept used to solve the game is a subgame perfect Nash equilibrium: call any such equilibrium a C^*- legislative equilibrium. Then the LOF is,

$$\lambda^+(C^*, \chi) = \{y \in X \text{ such that } y \text{ is a component of some } C^*\text{-legislative equilibrium outcome.}\}$$

Modulo a technical tie-breaking rule, $\lambda^+ \in L_{\Omega_3}*$. Then, since $fs(m) \in E_{\Omega_3}*$ for $m \geq 3$, the legislative election structure is Ω_3-admissible.

Although voters are purely policy-oriented (as described in Section 6.2), parties care both about policy and about portfolios. A legislative party's portfolio is modelled as that party's share of some transferable resource, B. Thus: $b_{C*} = (b_k)_{k \in C^*} \in B^{|C^*|}$, $b_k \geq 0$ for all $k \in C^*$, $\sum_{C^*} b_k \leq B$. Fix a set of electoral positions for parties, $C = \{z_1, z_2, z_3\}$. Then party k's payoff from any outcome of the legislative bargaining game involving a policy $z \in X$ and a portfolio distribution $b \in B^3$ is given by:

$$U_k(C, B; \chi) = \begin{cases} b_k - (z - z_k)^2 & \text{iff } k \in C^* \\ -c & \text{otherwise} \end{cases}$$

where $c > 0$ is a cost paid by the party if it fails to be elected, i.e. $v_k(\chi) < m$. The assumption of quasi-linear preferences is a convenience, allowing, for any $C \in \Omega_3$ and any $\chi \in \sum (\Omega_3)^n$, explicit computation of the set of C^*-legislative equilibria. Before discussing this set, the key features of party payoffs need some justification.

The first important feature is that the portfolio is valuable: this is innocuous. That its value is independent of policy outcomes and of other parties' portfolios may not be so reasonable. Parties, for instance, might be expected to prefer holding a portfolio in a government which implements a relatively more-preferred policy, than one implementing a less-preferred position. Similarly, a party holding office in a government in which one of its coalition partners, say, is considered "ideologically unsound" by that party, is likely to value the office differently than otherwise. With such considerations, the trade-off between policy outcome and portfolio will be more complex. However, that there is a trade-off at all is the important observation (moreover, separability is not crucial to all of the properties of C^*-equilibria). In many formal treatments of legislative bargaining, the process is modelled as a cooperative game without side-payments (e.g., McKelvey, Ordeshook and Winer 1978; Schofield 1978, 1986). The solution concepts for such games generate families of coalitions and utility payoffs, rather than identifying particular coalition and policy outcomes. By introducing an institutional mechanism – the legislative bargaining game – along with a transferable resource – namely the portfolios – the trade-off between portfolio and policy can be exploited to generate unique equilibrium predictions.

---

[11] Strictly speaking, a party's strategy also involves an acceptance rule, describing when to agree to any proposal which includes the party as a member of the government.

The remaining key feature of party preferences is that a party's payoff declines as a function of the distance between its (strategically chosen) electoral policy platform, and the final outcome implemented by the government. As it stands, this is *ad hoc*. The motivation comes from parties and voters interacting over several elections. When there are repeated elections, individual voting strategies can be conditioned on the past behavior of parties. Consequently, voters can "punish" a currently elected party in subsequent elections to the extent that legislative outcomes fail to match electoral promises (platforms) (Austen-Smith and Banks 1989). However, since the game is not repeated, there is, strictly speaking, no mechanism in the Austen-Smith/Banks model by which these costs can be realized. Instead, there is an implicit assumption that the one-shot game of their model sufficiently approximates one play of a more complex repeated election game.

Given the above legislative bargaining game, if $|C^*| \leq 2$ or if $v_k(\cdot) \geq (n+1)/2$ then the C^*- equilibrium outcome is trivially given by the largest party's policy position, and that party takes all the portfolio.[12] In the more interesting case, the following is true:

Theorem 6: *(Austen-Smith and Banks 1988). For any $C \in \Omega_3$ and any χ such that $m \leq v_k(\chi) < (n+1)/2 \ \forall \ k$, there is a unique C^*- legislative equilibrium outcome (M^*, z_{M^*}, b_{M^*}) such that:*

(a) $M^* = \{k, j \in C \mid v_k(\chi) = max_C \{v_h(\chi)\}, v_j(\cdot) = min_C \{v_h(\chi)\}$,
(b) $z_{M^*} \in [z_k, \frac{(z_k + z_j)}{2}]$, *where k and j are defined in (a)*,
(c) $b_h = 0$ *if* $h \notin M^*$; $b_k > 0$; $b_j \geq 0$, *where k and j are defined in (a)*.

With the exception of the bound $\frac{(z_k+z_j)}{2}$ in (b), Theorem 6 does not depend on the quadratic specification of U_k. The result says that the winning coalition that forms the government is minimal winning (the coalition-of-the-whole does not form) but not minimum winning in the sense of Riker (1962). The second largest party gets excluded from the coalition because of its bargaining power relative to the smallest party: when the largest party seeks a coalition partner, it can extract relatively more surplus from the weakest member of the legislature. The result also implies that the government is not necessarily connected in the sense of Axelrod (1970): there is no reason to presume the positions of the largest and the smallest parties are adjacent in X.

In (b) and (c) of Theorem 6, the exact location of the final outcome, and the particular equilibrium distribution of portfolios, depend on B and on the entire list of candidate positions, C. With this information and with specified payoff schedules, (M^*, z_{M^*}, b_{M^*}) can be computed precisely as a function of voting strategies, χ. Since voters are rational, voting strategies in turn are a function of the policy platforms, C. Hence, given B, and C, Theorem 6 shows that the LOF $\lambda^+(\cdot, \chi)$ is a well-defined function of χ. This is crucial in specifying the behavior of voters and parties at the electoral stage of the

---

[12] Recall that in cases of equal vote-shares, a fair random device breaks the tie before the bargaining game begins.

process.

Definition: A *voting equilibrium* for the legislative election structure $(fs(m), \lambda^+)$ is an n-tuple $\chi^* \in \sum (\Omega_3)^n$ such that $\forall\, C \in N, \forall\, \chi_i$:

$$E[w_i(\chi^*(C))] \geq E[w_i(\chi_i, \chi^*_{-i}(C))],$$

where the expectation, E, is over $\lambda^+(\cdot, \cdot)$.

Thus a voting equilibrium here is simply a Nash equilibrium in which individuals vote on the basis of final legislative outcomes, and not on candidate positions *per se*.

As observed in the Introduction, with two-party, simple plurality elections, sincere voting at the electoral stage is the only sensible Nash voting equilibrium for any pair of policy positions: although there exist many Nash equilibria in voting strategies, χ, the sincere strategy vector, χ^T, is the unique undominated equilibrium. This is true largely because, under simple plurality voting, a party's legislative influence is monotonic in its electoral vote-share. Unfortunately, by part (a) of Theorem 6, this is not true with multi-party elections with proportional representation. And it turns out in this environment that no individual voting strategy, given $C = \{z_1, z_2, z_3\}$, is dominated. So using dominance arguments to refine the set of voting equilibria in legislative election games achieves nothing. However, since the strategic choice of policy platforms with which to contest the election will depend, *inter alia*, on how voters respond, the issue of voting equilibrium selection is important.

The refinement used in Austen-Smith/Banks is to require that *every* voter in an electoral equilibrium is pivotal. Let χ^{**} be the selected voting equilibrium. Then:

Definition: An *electoral equilibrium relative to* χ^{**} for the legislative election structure $(fs(m), \lambda^+)$, is any $C^o \in \Omega_3$ such that for every party k and every $z_k \in X$:

$$E[\pi_k(\chi^{**}(C^o))] \geq E[\pi_k(\chi^{**}(z_k, C^o \backslash z_k^o))],$$

where $\pi_k(\chi^*(\cdot)) \equiv U_k(\cdot, \cdot, \chi^*(C))$ is k's final payoff from the legislative bargaining process, and the expectation is over $\lambda^+(\cdot, \cdot)$.

An electoral equilibrium is a Nash equilibrium in policy positions when parties rationally take account of voter behavior and the subsequent legislative bargaining game. *Prima facie*, the refinement of voting equilibria offered above seems circular: in any electoral equilibrium, all voters are required to be pivotal, but the definition of electoral equilibrium is itself predicted on how voters will behave. However, there is no more difficulty here than that involved in solving a pair of simultaneous equations.

Given that voting strategies invariably constitute Nash responses, the refinement puts no restrictions on out-of-(electoral) equilibrium voting behavior. But it does isolate a relatively small class of party positions as electoral equilibria. And given this, the selection of any out-of-electoral equilibrium voting strategy is more-or-less determined by the natural requirement that such strategies provide incentives for parties to "move toward" an electoral equilibrium. (It is perhaps worth noting that sincere voting everywhere is not capable of supporting any electoral equilibrium.) Nevertheless, the general problem of voting equilibrium selection in multi-party legislative elections is nontrivial, and by no means solved. It is in this context that some form of cooperative model of voting–such as Sugden's (1984)–may prove valuable.

Assume that the distribution of voter preferences on X is symmetric, and that all voters have symmetric, strictly concave, utilities. For any $C = \{z_1, z_2, z_3\} \in \Omega_3$, label parties so that $z_1 \leq z_2 \leq z_3$. Then the set of electoral equilibria identified is:

Theorem 7: *(Austen-Smith and Banks 1988).* $C = \{z_1, z_2, z_3\} \in \Omega_3$ is an electoral equilibrium relative to χ^{**} for the legislative election structure $(fs(m), \lambda^+)$, iff:

(a) $z_2 = median \{x_1, ..., x_n\}$,
(b) $(z_2 - z_1) = (z_3 - z_2) \in [y, y\prime); y, y\prime \in \Re, y\prime > y > 0$.

Furthermore, there is a unique Pareto efficient equilibrium (relative to χ^{**}) at $\mid z_k - z_2 \mid = y, k = 1, 3$.

Electoral equilibria involve one party adopting the median voter's ideal point, and the remaining two parties locating symmetrically about this point. The bounds y and $y\prime$ are not arbitrary. To illustrate this result and to see where the bounds come from, consider the following example.

EXAMPLE 2: Suppose there are 101 voters, each with quadratic preferences on $X = [-200, 200]$. Let the ideal points be $x = (-50, ..., -1, 0, 1, ..., 50)$. Let the election rule be $fs(25)$, and assume party payoffs are given by the payoff, U_k. Then $y = 32$, $y\prime = 100$, and any $C = \{z_1, z_2, z_3\}$ such that $z_2 = 0$ and $-z_1 = z_3 \in [32, 100)$ is an electoral equilibrium. The possible final outcomes generated by some C^*-equilibrium to the legislative bargaining game when C is such a set of platforms, are:

$$\cup_\chi [\lambda^+(\cdot, \chi)] = \{z_1, z_2, z_3, z_{12}, z_{23}\},$$

where $z_{hk} = [z_h + z_k]/2$. In the χ^{**} voting equilibrium, individuals $i = 1, ..., 38$ vote for z_1; individuals $i = 39, ..., 63$ vote for z_2; and individuals $i = 64, ..., 101$ vote for z_3. Hence, $v_1(\chi^{**}) = v_3(\chi^{**}) = 38 > v_2(\chi^{**}) = 25$, and all voters are pivotal. Notice that in any electoral equilibrium for this environment, at least individuals $i = 36, 37, 38, 64, 65, 66$ do not use a sincere voting strategy at χ^{**} : as z_1 and z_3 move outwards toward (respectively) -100 and 100, the number of individuals voting strategically increases. By Theorem 6, the final policy outcome is $z_{M^*}(\chi^{**}) \in \{z_{12}, z_{13}\}$, with each outcome occurring with probability one-half.

If $\mid z_k - z_2 \mid \geq 100$, then the number of individuals who strictly prefer z_2 to any other alternative in $\cup_\chi[\lambda^+(\cdot, \chi)]$ exceeds 50. In this case, an overall majority of the electorate prefers that party 2 has monopolistic control of the legislature–there is no C^*-equilibrium outcome which is preferred by them. Consequently, the voting equilibrium selection made for this case is that everyone votes sincerely relative to C. This makes good sense, and prevents parties from being "too dispersed" in electoral equilibrium, relative to the distribution of voter preferences. And notice that the unique efficient electoral equilibrium is when the parties are minimally dispersed (within the set of equilibria): this is immediate from inspection of U_k. The inner bound y is generated implicitly by the requirement that at least $m = 25$ individuals must find it a best-response to vote for z_2, given that others' votes imply $v_1 = v_3$. In other words, these individuals must prefer the fair lottery over $\{z_{12}, z_{32}\}$ to a certain outcome of z_1 or z_3. Evidently, the closer a voter is to z_1 or z_3, the greater is his incentive (given risk-aversion) to vote for the relatively extreme party when he is pivotal. So the bound y is computed by finding the individual who is just indifferent between the lottery and a certain outcome of the platform of the extreme party closest to him or her.

There are three substantive features of electoral equilibria illustrated in Example 2 which are not special to the example. First, the middle party receives the smallest vote-share and the others receive the same share; second, not everyone votes sincerely, so that the distribution of vote-shares in the legislature does not reflect the distribution of voter preferences; and third, realized final policy outcomes are skewed away from the median and so do not reflect the relative weights of parties in the legislature. Virtually all advocates of proportional representation base their arguments on the premises that legislative representation will better reflect the diversity of electorate preferences, and that final policy outcomes will correspondingly reflect relative party weights in the legislature. The results of Austen-Smith and Banks suggest that this base is rather fragile.

To my knowledge, the papers above exhaust the set of formal models explicitly concerned with single-district legislative elections (as defined in the Introduction). Related work is due to Gary Cox (1984a,b), who studies an electoral model of multi-candidate, double-member districts. Cox's concern is not with the election of an entire assembly, but with how equilibrium candidate platforms under a double-member district system might differ from those under the canonic, single-member district, system. From this perspective, it is natural to maintain the implicit assumption of the canonic model; *viz.* that agents in a single district election behave as if there were only one district. By strengthening this assumption (as Cox does not) to presuming that there is indeed only one district in the polity, then the fact that more than one candidate is to be elected from the district makes Cox's electoral model "legislative" in the sense of this paper. However, voters' strategy sets are somewhat different than those considered up to now: with double-member districts, voters are permitted to vote for at most two candidates.[13]

For any $\theta \in \Omega$, let $\underline{\chi}_i : \theta \to \Omega^2$ such that $\underline{\chi}_i(C) \in (C \cup \emptyset)^2$ for each $C \in \chi$, describe individual i's voting strategy. Here, $\underline{\chi}_i(C) = \{z_k, \emptyset\}$ means i votes only for candidate z_k, and $\chi_i(C) = \{z_k, z_j\}$ means i votes for candidates z_k

---

[13] Sugden (1984), when discussing STV and not the cooperative game, allows for voters to record their entire preference ordering over a slate of candidates.

and z_j. Write $\underline{\chi}(C) = (\underline{\chi}_1, \underline{\chi}_2, ..., \underline{\chi}_n)$, etc. Individuals are assumed to have Euclidean preferences, so the analogue of sincere voting for any individual i in this environment is that i casts two votes, one for each of the two candidates closest to that voter's ideal point in X, on an interval (ties are broken by flipping a fair die). Let $\underline{\chi}^T$ be the strategy vector in which every individual uses this sincere strategy (given $u \in U_e^n$).

Cox (1984a) assumes $C \in \Omega_t, t = 3, 4$. For any candidate $k \in C$, define,

$$m_k(\underline{\chi}^T(C)) = \begin{cases} v_k(\underline{\chi}^T(C)) - \min\{v_j(\underline{\chi}^T(C))\}_{j \neq k}, & \text{iff } C \in \Omega_3 \\ v_k(\underline{\chi}^T(C)) - \text{med}\{v_j(\underline{\chi}^T(C))\}_{j \neq k}, & \text{iff } C \in \Omega_4 \end{cases}$$

to be k's *margin* under $\underline{\chi}^T$, given candidate platforms, C. "For the two winning candidates, this $[m_k(\cdot)]$ is their margin of victory. For the losing candidate[s], it indicates how many votes short of a seat he or she is [they are]" (Cox 1984a, p. 446). The election rule is $fn(2)$, where it is understood that in the definition of $\varepsilon_{\Omega t}^{fn(K)}$ the strategy vector χ is replaced by $\underline{\chi}$.

Definition: C^o is an $fn(2)$ Nash equilibrium for the double-member election game on $\Omega_t, t = 3, 4$, iff $C^o \in \Omega_t$ and, for every party k and every $z_k \in X$, $m_k(\underline{\chi}^T(C^o)) \geq m_k(\underline{\chi}^T(z_k, C^o \setminus z_k^o))$.

Given $u \in U_e^n$, let
$y_1 = \sup\{y \in X \mid 2 \mid \{i \in N \mid x_i \leq y_1\} \mid < \mid \{i \in N \mid x_i > y_1\}\}$, and let
$y_2 = \inf\{y \in X \mid 2 \mid \{i \in N \mid x_i \geq y_2\} \mid < \mid \{i \in N \mid x_i < y_2\}\}$.

Loosely speaking, y_1 and y_2 are the quantiles of order $\frac{1}{3}$ and $\frac{2}{3}$, respectively.

Theorem 8: (Cox 1984a). (a) $C^o \in \Omega_3$ is an $fn(2)$ Nash equilibrium iff $z_k^o = z^* \in [y_1, y_2], k = 1, 2, 3$. (b) Suppose n is odd. Then, $C \in \Omega_4$ is an $fn(2)$ Nash equilibrium iff $z_k^o = $ median $\{x_1, ..., x_n\}, k = 1, 2, 3$.

So in both cases (3 and 4 candidates), the classical Downsian convergence result reemerges. But, unlike the 4 candidate case in which the median voter defines the only equilibrium, with only 3 candidates many equilibria in addition to the median voter position are feasible. This last is a nice result, since in three candidate competition for a single-member district with sincere voting, no Nash equilibrium exists (see, *e.g.*, Cox 1987). But as a model of legislative elections, Theorem 8 suffers from the two familiar difficulties: no legislative outcome function is defined (so that voters vote over candidates, not policy outcomes); and voters are constrained to vote sincerely. In any $fn(2)$ Nash equilibrium parties converge, so one might argue that sincere voting is justified. But this would be wrong since the equilibria are supported by sincere voting at out-of-equilibrium party platforms. If we relax the requirement of sincerity, it is not evident that Theorem 8 obtains.

Cox is clearly aware of the problem of strategic voting. Cox (1984b) fixes a set of candidates C arbitrarily, and examines an arbitrary individual's (non-cooperative) strategic voting calculus. By taking C as given, the legislative outcome function can be left implicit: individuals' preferences over candidates can be assumed to be induced from candidate positions and some underlying

LOF. Cox explicitly adopts this interpretation of preferences. For the case of $C \in \Omega_3$ and voting strategies for each individual described by $\underline{\chi}_i$, the situation is "essentially equivalent to approval voting with three candidates; thus, voting in double elections with three candidates is 'sincere' in the same sense that approval voting is ... Nonetheless, it is shown that electoral choice in double (and approval) elections is inherently strategic in the sense that voters' beliefs about how others will vote affect their decisions..." (Cox, 1984b, p. 737).[14]

Having said this, however, it is worth pointing out that an individual's beliefs in Cox's analysis are arbitrarily assigned subjective estimates of others' behavior. Consequently, there is no guarantee that these beliefs are "rational" in the sense that, when all individuals play the strategies prescribed by their beliefs, everyone's beliefs are necessarily consistent with the observed electoral outcome. In other words, it is an open question within Cox's framework whether his conclusions hold in an appropriately defined Bayesian voting equilibrium. Nevertheless, earlier arguments (Theorem 1 ff.) suggest they will hold. And Cox finds some empirical evidence at an aggregate level to support the claim of strategic voting in double elections.

6.5 Multi-district Models

When the electorate is partitioned into several districts, with each district periodically electing representatives to a national legislature, it becomes necessary to distinguish "candidates" from "parties". A party comprises at least one candidate for office, and if different candidates of a given party contest distinct districts, then there is no reason *a priori* to assume that they would wish to fight an election on precisely the same platform. This in turn raises the question of what it is to be a party: a question I shall, to all intents and purposes, sidestep for the present.

Throughout this section, assume the electorate N is partitioned into a finite number, $1 < K \leq n$, of districts: $\mathcal{P}(N) = \{N_r\}_{r=1,\ldots,K}$; let $|N_r| = n_r$. Also assume that, in any legislative election, exactly two candidates contest each district under a single-member district, simple plurality election rule.[15] To define this formally, let $C_r = \{z_{ar}, z_{br}\} \in \Omega_2$ be the pair of *candidate* platforms offered in district $r \in \Delta = \{1, \ldots, K\}$. (As we shall see later, these may or may not be party platforms.) For any individual $i \in N_r$, i's voting strategy is a map, $\chi_i^r : \Omega_2 \to \Omega$, such that for all $C_r, \chi^r(C_r) \in C_r$. Let $\chi^r = (\chi_1^r, \ldots, \chi_{nr}^r)$, etc. Let $C = \cup_r C_r \in \Omega_{2K}$, and write $\chi = (\chi^r)_{r \in \Delta}$. Then the election rule assumed throughout Section 6.5 is:

$$\varepsilon^K(C, \chi) = \{(z_{pr})_{p \in \{a,b\}, r \in \Delta} \in \Pi_r\, C_r \mid \forall\, pr,\ v_{pr}(\chi^r) > v_{p'r}(\chi^r),\\ pr' \in \{a,b\}, p \neq p'\}.$$

---
[14] Approval voting is considered to be "sincere", if whenever you vote for some candidate k, you also vote for all candidates that you prefer to k.

[15] The question of candidate entry into an election is considered briefly in the concluding section.

While this rule[16] is prevalent among Anglo-American political systems, it is not the only election scheme used in multi-district polities; and the assumption of only two candidates per district is restrictive. However, to my knowledge, there are no formal multi-district analyses of rules other than simple plurality.[17] And results for multi-candidate elections with simple plurality voting, even in the single-district context, are delicate and hard to come by (Cox 1987). Consequently, since one rationale for studying models of legislative elections is to explore the robustness of conclusions derived from the canonic (two-candidate, single-district, simple plurality) model, the focus on ε^K is a natural starting point.

In Chapter 2 of *A Theory of Party Competition*, David Robertson (1976) sketches a multi-district model in which candidates all belong to various nationally-oriented parties, and legislative outcomes are determined by the party whose candidates win a majority of districts. Implicit in his discussion is that all electorally successful members of a party can be relied upon to vote as a bloc in the legislature, and that there are only two parties. If either of these assumptions were not met, Robertson's conclusion that "The official party policy [i.e., that of the national organizers] will be the one calculated to win a majority of constituencies, not the one which has majority support in the electorate at large" (p. 52), would be untenable. He is, however, explicit in arguing that rational voters in such polities will vote on the basis of *party* policy and not on the basis of *candidate* policy, whenever these are distinct. From the theoretical perspective this is clearly correct since, given the implicit assumptions just mentioned, it amounts to saying that voters vote over final policy outcomes and not over candidates' positions *per se*.

His model is not rigorous and his results are "broad brush" (*e.g.*, "No great degree of autonomy will be enjoyed by candidates in presenting policy" (p. 53)). Taking Robertson's cue, Austen-Smith (1984, 1986, 1987) examines a multi-district model of electoral competition under ε^K in which there exist exactly two parties or none, (*i.e.*, all candidates for legislative office run as independents).[18] A *party* is any set of candidates, each member of which shares a common label, (*e.g.*, Republican, Democrat, Conservative, Labour). If there are parties, these are labelled $p = a, b$, and it is assumed that each party consists of K candidates: thus, z_{pr} denotes the electoral platform adopted by the candidate of party p contesting district r. When there are no parties, the index p simply distinguishes the contestants for any district. For the moment, assume all candidates for office belong to one or other of the two political

---

[16] As usual, if vote-totals tie, a fair coin is flipped to determine the winner. Also, for convenience subscripts on election rules and *LOF*s throughout this section will be deleted.

[17] There does exist a theoretical literature on apportionment, however. But the analysis is exclusively axiomatic, and not strategic. See, for instance, Balinski and Young (1982).

[18] An earlier paper, Austen-Smith (1981), develops a multi-district model with many issues. To insure existence of an equilibrium (in the language developed below, a Downsian equilibrium), voting was assumed to be probabilistic in the sense of Hinich, Ledyard and Ordeshook (1972). As such, the structure is quite different from that of the rest of this essay. Moreover, probabilistic voting is essentially *ad hoc*. (And, for the enthusiast, be warned that the existence theorem in Austen-Smith (1981) is correct only if "quasi-concave" is strengthened to "concave".)

parties, p.

Under ε^K the legislature consists of K elected officials, one from each district. Assume (for expository convenience) that K is odd. A winning coalition in an elected legislature is any subset M of ε^K such that $M \geq \frac{(K+1)}{2}$. Let $\mathcal{D}(C,\chi) = \{M \mid \varepsilon^K(C,\chi) \subseteq M, \mid M \mid \geq \frac{(K+1)}{2}\}$ be the set of winning coalitions (governments) in the legislature given the set of candidates, C, and voter strategies, χ. Which particular government will form and what policy outcome it will implement depends on the details of legislative bargaining, *etc*. Unlike the single-district, multi-party environment, the assumption of many districts and two political parties suggests a natural approach to finessing problems of legislative coalition formation and bargaining.

Definition: A *constitution for party p* is a map, $g_p : \Omega_K \to X$, such that $\forall\ C \in \Omega_K, g_p(C) \in \text{con}(C)$.

A constitution for $p \in \{a,b\}$ defines how the list of the party's candidates' policy platforms are mapped into a legislative party policy, which is constrained to lie in the Pareto set of the party members' positions. Examples of party constitutions (*PC*s) are voting within the whole party (say, at conference), intra-party bargaining outcomes, dictatorship of the party leader, and so on and so forth. As defined, however, the party policy given by g_p is a function of all the party's candidates' electoral positions. So, for instance, the use of some within-party voting rule for which the franchise is extended only to the legislative (*i.e.*, winning) party members is excluded. This is an important substantive restriction. It amounts to assuming that once all party members have announced their platforms, $C^p \in \Omega_K$, the party is committed to implementing the policy $g_p(C^p)$ should it gain control of the legislature. Having said this, and although *PC*s are treated as exogenous here, various assumptions about party structure can be introduced through restrictions on the maps g_p.

For each party p, let $p(C,\chi)$ denote the set of party p candidates who get elected to the legislature, *i.e.*,

$$p(C,\chi) = \{y_{pr} \in C \mid v_{pr}(\chi^r) > v_{p\prime r}(\chi^r), p \neq p\prime\}.$$

Consider the following legislative outcome function:

$$\lambda^P(C,\chi) = \{z \in X \mid z = g_p(z_{p1},...,z_{pK}),\ p(C,\chi) \in \mathcal{D}(C,\chi)\}.$$

Since K is odd and all candidates belong to one of two parties, λ^p is well-defined.

Given party constitutions, the legislative election structure $(\varepsilon^K, \lambda^P)$ models two-party multi-district, first-past-the-post electoral systems in which legislative members of any party fully coordinate their legislative behavior to promote a given (through the *PC*) party policy position. (There is no presumption that at the electoral stage candidates similarly coordinate their strategic choices.) Empirically, this corresponds best to British-type parliamentary systems.

Although the LOF λ^P is anonymous with respect to parties, it is not anonymous with respect to candidates: party labels matter. Theorem 1, therefore, does not apply. Nevertheless, $(\varepsilon^K, \lambda^P)$ is not straightforward. This is evident: once party constitutions are defined, rational voters will (as Robertson observes) vote over *party policies*, and not candidate positions *per se*. Consequently, both of the following can hold for $i \in N_r$:

$$u_i(g_a(z_{a1}, ..., z_{aK})) > u_i(g_b(z_{b1}, ..., z_{bK})) \text{ and } u_i(z_{ar}) < u_i(z_{br}).$$

It is the first inequality which is relevant for a rational voting decision, not the second. Indeed, given the two parties' candidates electoral platforms, $C^a = \{z_{ar}\}_r$ and $C^b = \{z_{br}\}_{r\prime}$, and given the legislative election scheme $(\varepsilon^K, \lambda^P)$, all voters have a weakly dominant strategy: vote sincerely over party policies $\{g_a(\cdot), g_b(\cdot)\}$. This voting rule is left implicit hereafter.

Given candidates' electoral platforms, $C = (C^a, C^b)$, let the probability that party p wins r districts, given voter strategies χ, be

$$q_r^p(\chi(C^a, C^b)) \in [0, 1].$$

Definition: Party p is *Downsian* iff

(1) $z_{pr} = z_p, \forall r$
(2) $z_p = \text{argmax}_\chi \sum r \cdot q_r^p (\chi(z, C^{p\prime})), p\prime = a, b; p \neq p\prime$.

Downs (1957) assumes a single district polity, and makes an assumption on party structure, which "In effect...treats each party as though it were a single person" (p. 26). He then supposes that parties strategically select their electoral policy platforms to win control of the legislature. With no abstention, rational voting and simple plurality elections, winning control of the legislature amounts to maximizing votes. All of this is defensible in the single district framework. But in a multi-district model, parties necessarily consist of several candidates, and maximizing votes is not a sensible strategy for winning legislative control. The definition of a Downsian party above is the analogue, for the multi-district two party polity under $(\varepsilon^K, \lambda^P)$, to Downs' original conception. Part (1) of the definition says that the party is fully coordinated in its electoral strategy, given that voters are rational and vote on final outcomes under the legislative outcome function, λ^P. Part (2) of the definition says that the party's electoral platform is selected to win control of the legislature. Note that the PC for any Downsian party is immediate: since $z_{pr} = z_p$ for all $r, g_p(\cdot) \in \text{con}(C^p) \Rightarrow g_p(\cdot) = z_p$.

Definition: A *Downsian equilibrium* under $(\varepsilon^K, \lambda^P)$ is a pair $(z_a^*, z_b^*) \in X^2$ such that,

(1) $\forall r, z_{ar*} = z_a^*$ and $z_{br*} = z_b^*$;
(2) $\forall z \neq z_{p*}; \forall p = a, b$,
$\sum_r r \cdot q_r^p(\chi(z_{p*}, z_{p\prime*})) \geq \sum_r r \cdot q_r^p(\chi(z, z_{p\prime*}));$
$p\prime = a, b; p \neq p\prime$.

In the definition of a Downsian party, there is an alternative objective a party seeking legislative control under $(\varepsilon^K, \lambda^P)$ might adopt. Instead of assuming expected district maximization, we could suppose a party maximizes the probability of winning a simple majority of districts; *i.e.*, replace (2) in the definition of a Downsian party by,

$$(2') \; y_p = \mathrm{argmax}_X \; q^p_{\frac{(K+1)}{2}}(\chi(y_p, C^{p\prime})), \; p \neq p\prime.$$

However, given two parties and rational voters, it is not hard to check that in the one-dimensional environment assumed throughout, (z_a^*, z_b^*) is a Downsian equilibrium if and only if it is also an equilibrium in which (otherwise Downsian) parties choose z_p according to (2') rather than (2). So we lose no generality on this count by assuming, for Downsian parties, (2) rather than (2') hereafter.

Theorem 9: *(Austen-Smith 1987; Hinich and Ordeshook 1974)*.[19]
$(z_a^*, z_b^*) \in X^2$ *is a Downsian equilibrium under* $(\varepsilon^K, \lambda^P)$ *iff* $z_a^* = z_b^* = \mu^*$; *where* $\mu^* = \mathrm{median} \; \{\mu_r\}_r$, *and* μ_r *is the median voter's ideal point in district* N_r.

Theorem 9 is the natural generalization of Downs' classical result: Downsian parties in a multi-district polity with rational, final policy oriented voters, converge on the median of the medians. Now Robertson's basic model (1976) is essentially one of two party competition under $(\varepsilon^K, \lambda^P)$ in which both parties are Downsian.[20] This result, then, casts light on some of his claims. First observe that, because parties converge in equilibrium and because voters are purely final (*i.e.*, party) policy oriented, each party has a 50% chance of winning control of the legislature. Similarly, every candidate also has a 50% chance of winning his or her electorate. Hence, Robertson is not correct in claiming that "to allow that constituencies may not all have the same distribution of ideological opinions [*i.e.*, $\mu_r \neq \mu_{r\prime}$, all $r, r\prime$] is to entail that if party [p] is to fight an election on a constituency maximizing platform, some of its candidates are doomed to fight individual seats on platforms that cannot win" (p. 50). For this conclusion to be correct in equilibrium, voters cannot be purely final policy oriented. On the other hand, Robertson is right to argue that there will be tension between a party (*i.e.*, national organizers) and at least some of its office oriented candidates. Label districts so that $\mu_r < \mu_{r+1}$, all $r < K$. Then, say, given $z_a^* = \mu^*$, candidates of party b contesting districts $r > \frac{(K+1)}{2}$ have an incentive to move z_b^* to the right because this guarantees that they will win legislative office under the equilibrium voting strategy (sincere voting over party platforms). The assumption of a party being Downsian, however, implies that such candidates cannot do this (Robertson's view) or

---

[19] Hinich and Ordeshook (1974) examine a spatial model of the USA electoral college. The candidates in their model are isomorphic to Downsian parties. If it is assumed that all the colleges are of the same size, then Theorem 9 is a corollary to their result.

[20] Robertson is not only concerned with the impact of many districts on the Downsian model. He devotes a great deal of time to introducing party activism, campaign advertising, and so forth.

are not office oriented. Finally, since there is no reason to suppose median $\{x_1, ..., x_n\} = \mu^*$, there is no reason to suppose that "the winning electoral strategy [in the Downsian equilibrium] is that of the national median voter's preference" (*ibid.*).

Political parties do not have objectives. It is individuals who are purposive, and parties are collections of individuals. From this perspective, the (implicit) Downsian party constitution is extremely restrictive. Wider classes of party organization can be accommodated within $(\varepsilon^K, \lambda^P)$ legislative structures, and one of these is studied by Austen-Smith (1984).

Definition: A party p is *Type I* iff (1) $\forall\ pr$, g_p is continuous in $z_{pr} \in X$ and differentiable in $z_{pr} \in$ interior (X); and (2) every party candidate pr seeks to win his or her own district—in the absence of abstention, this amounts to within-district vote-maximization by pr.

So unlike the case with Downsian parties, candidates of Type I parties do not coordinate their electoral policy choices (save implicitly through the PC) to promote any party objectives *per se*.

For any subset of districts L in Δ, and any set of party p strategies $C^p \in \Omega_K$, let $C^{p \backslash L} = \{z_{ps} \mid s \notin L\}$.

Definition: A *Type I party equilibrium* under $(\varepsilon^K, \lambda^P)$ is a $2K$-tuple $(C^{a*}, C^{b*}) \in \Omega_{2K}, C^{p*} = \{z_{pr}^*\}_r$, such that for each $p \in \{a, b\}$, $\forall\ \{L \mid \Delta \supseteq L\}, \forall\ r \in L, \forall\ \{z_{ps}\}_L \in \Omega_{|L|}$, and when $p \neq p'$, $v_{pr}(\chi(g_p(\{z_{ps}^*\}_L, C^{p \backslash L^*}), g_p(C^{p'*}))) \geq v_{pr}(\chi(g_p(\{z_{ps}\}_L, g_{p'}(C^{p \backslash L'*})), g_{p'}(C^{p'*}))).$

A Type I party equilibrium is therefore a list of strategies, one for each candidate of each party, such that, given the policy platforms of all other candidates for office, no group of candidates within any particular party can coordinate their electoral policy platforms to improve their respective within-district vote totals. If $\mid L \mid\ =\ 1$, then this is simply a Nash equilibrium in which each candidate plays against the other party and against other members of his own party, via the PC. If $\mid L \mid\ >\ 1$, then the equilibrium concept is a form of Strong Nash equilibrium. On the one hand, it is somewhat stronger than Strong Nash since it requires that nobody benefits from any coalitional deviation. On the other hand, the only coalitions that are permitted to form are those involving candidates from within the same party. This last restriction seems natural in the present setting, in which candidates are exogenously endowed with a party affiliation and the party constitutions are prespecified. In the absence of these assumptions, the restriction is less reasonable. Finally note that although candidates of a Type I party are not constrained to offer identical electoral platforms, under the legislative outcome function λ^P (and given the definition of a party constitution), successful Type I party members (*i.e.*, those that get elected) still act as a bloc in supporting the party policy, $g_p(\cdot)$, in the legislature. Thus the voter strategies described earlier remain equilibrium (voting) strategies.

Suppose hereafter that voters' preferences are Euclidean, $u \in U_e^N$. The following result makes clear the tension between candidates' objectives and party structure mentioned by Robertson.

Theorem 10: *(Austen-Smith 1984).* $(C^{a*}, C^{b*}) \in \Omega_{2K}$ *is a Type I party equilibrium under* $(\varepsilon^K, \lambda^P)$ *iff,*

1. $g_a(C^{a*}) = g_b(C^{b*}) = z^*$;

2. $\forall\, p,\, \forall\, L \in \Delta\ s.t.\ [r \in L \Rightarrow \mu_r < (>) z^*], \forall\, \{z_{pr}\}_L$, $g_p(C^{p*}) \leq (\geq) g_p(\{z_{pr}\}_{L'}, C^{p \backslash L^*})$.

Theorem 10 claims that, as in Downsian party competition under $(\varepsilon^K, \lambda^P)$, *party* policies will converge in any Type I equilibrium, but in general the same is not true of *candidate* positions. In particular, candidates contesting districts with medians to the left of the common party position, z^*, will seek to move the party platform leftwards; and similarly for candidates competing for districts with medians to the right of z^*. Thus any Type I equilibrium will be associated with a dispersion of candidate positions within each party. And since there is no reason to expect the two parties' *PC* to be the same, there is likewise no reason to suppose that opposing candidates within districts converge–to the median or anywhere else. But despite this lack of convergence at the local level, each candidate in equilibrium continues to enjoy a 50% chance of winning office. Again, this is because rational voters vote over party policies and these do converge.

Unfortunately, Theorem 10 is not an existence result for Type I party competition under $(\varepsilon^K, \lambda^P)$. To insure that there is a suitable set of candidate positions satisfying both parts of the result, additional restrictions on party constitutions are required. For any set of candidate positions C^p, let $\underline{z}(C^p)$ be the average platform within the party; $\underline{z}(C^p) = (\sum_r z_{pr})/K$.

Definition: A party constitution g_p,

1. *discounts extremists* iff $\exists\, t_p(\mathcal{P}(N)) \in R_{++}$, such that $\forall\, r \in \Delta$, $\forall\, C^p = \{z_{pr}\} \cup C^{p \backslash \{r\}} \in \Omega_K$, $|\, z_{pr} - \underline{z}(C^p)\,| > t_p(\cdot) \Rightarrow \exists\, z \in X$ s.t. $|\, z - \underline{z}(C^p)\,| \leq t_p(\cdot)$, and $g_p(C^p) = g_p(z, C^{p \backslash \{r\}})$;

2. is *strongly symmetric* iff g_p is symmetric with respect to candidates, and $[C^p$ symmetrically distributed on $X] \Rightarrow [g_p(C^p) = \underline{z}(C^p)]$.

The first condition says that although a candidate is free to adopt as extreme a position as he or she wishes relative to other party members' positions, the *PC* will give no more weight to this position in arriving at the party platform than it would give to a less extreme position. And exactly what constitutes "extreme" depends on the partition of the electorate (in particular, the distribution of medians, $\{\mu_r\}$). Assuming a party constitution discounts extremists seems reasonable (although ideally it is something we would like to explain, not just assume). Assuming a party constitution is strongly symmetric is not so reasonable: it rules out, for instance, the presence of disproportionately influential members in the party.

Theorem 11: *(Austen-Smith 1984). Suppose g_p discounts extremists and is strongly symmetric, $p = a, b$. Then there exists a Type I party equilibrium under $(\varepsilon^K, \lambda^P)$. Moreover, the equilibrium is unique in party policies with $g_p(C^{p*}) = \mu^*, p = a, b$; but the equilibrium is not necessarily unique in candidate platforms.*

In any of the Type I equilibria under $(\varepsilon^K, \lambda^P)$ identified by Theorem 11, party platforms converge on μ^*, the median of medians $\{\mu_r\}$. Thus the final legislative outcome here exactly corresponds to that supported by Downsian party competition (Theorem 9): given rational policy oriented voters, the existence of self-seeking and (electorally) autonomous candidates is not necessarily incompatible with parties maximizing expected districts won.

However, this result does depend on assuming PCs discount extremists and are strongly symmetric. And although these conditions are not logically necessary for existence, they are minimally sufficient in the sense that, if either one is relaxed in the presence of the other, examples of polities for which no Type I equilibrium exists become easy to construct (Austen-Smith 1984, pp. 194-8). Essentially, the conditions insure a balance across candidates competing for districts with medians on opposite sides of μ^*. So one can interpret the Theorem as saying that within-party power must be evenly distributed to obtain stable electoral outcomes; in other words, disproportionately influential party members can be disruptive. Given this, Remark (3) of Greenberg and Shepsle (1987) must be treated cautiously. When discussing the implications of their result (Theorem 4, above), they write that "Since for every given society an [$fn(1)$-equilibrium] exists...a society choosing K legislators by first partitioning itself into K constituencies...and then empowering each constituency to choose a single representative produces an equilibrium..., whereas that same society choosing K legislators "at large" would not in general produce an equilibrium." The first part of this claim rests crucially on their assumption of sincere voting and the lack of any specification of a legislative outcome function. As Theorem 11 shows, even when the candidates are tied to one of two parties and these are such that there exist only two possible final outcomes $\{g_a(\cdot), g_b(\cdot)\}$, existence of an electoral equilibrium is generally not guaranteed by the method they suggest.

An example of a party constitution satisfying the conditions in Theorem 11, and for which the Greenberg/Shepsle claim is correct, is: $g_p(C^p) = $ median $[\{z_{p1}, ..., z_{pK}\}] \ \forall \ C^p, p = a, b$. This party constitution is easily checked to discount extremists and to be strongly symmetric. By Theorem 11, any $2K$-tuple (C^{a*}, C^{b*}) such that

(1) $\mu_r < (>) \mu^*$ implies $z_{pr}^* < (>) \mu^*, p = a, b$, and
(2) median $\{z_{a1}^*, ..., z_{aK}^*\} = $ median $\{z_{b1}^*, ..., z_{bK}^*\} = \mu^*$

is a Type I party equilibrium under $(\varepsilon^K, \lambda^P)$. But this case is special.

In addition to assumptions on party constitutions, the assumption that the legislative outcome function is λ^P also imposes structure on party organization. As remarked earlier, under λ^P elected party members are implicitly assumed to vote as a bloc in the legislature. In many circumstances, this is a reasonable assumption. However, even if the only two feasible policy positions that could be implemented by an elected legislature are given by the party positions, $\{g_a(\cdot), g_b(\cdot)\}$, it does not follow that any one party can guarantee all of its elected candidates will support the party platform. For instance, some successful candidate may have adopted an electoral platform z_{pr} which is some distance away from the party position, $g_p(\cdot)$. In this case, the candidate might abstain or even "cross the floor" and vote with the opposition. Theorem 11 can be generalized along these lines to apply to a somewhat wider class of party structures.

Let $S_p(C, \chi)$ be the set of elected candidates who support (vote for) the policy $g_p(C^p)$, given the total list of candidate positions, C, and voters' electoral strategies, χ. Define the legislative outcome function,

$$\lambda^Q(\cdot, \chi) = \{z_p \in \{g_a(\cdot), g_b(\cdot)\} \mid S_p(\cdot, \chi) > S_{p'}(\cdot, \chi)\}.$$

So λ^Q differs from λ^P only in that not all legislative party members necessarily vote for their party's platform in the legislature. In principle, recognizing that candidates may not support the party line once elected makes the voters' decisions that much more complex, which in turn complicates the candidates' strategic calculus. In some circumstances, however, these complications are inconsequential.

Theorem 12: *(Austen-Smith 1987). For every candidate pr, suppose that, conditional on being elected and conditional on voting at all in the legislature, the probability that pr will support $g_p(\cdot)$ is at least as great as the probability that his electoral opponent, p'r, will support $g_p(\cdot)$. Suppose also that the probability that pr will abstain in the legislature, conditional on being elected, is the same as the probability that p'r abstains. Then (C^{a*}, C^{b*}) is a Type I party equilibrium under $(\varepsilon^K, \lambda^Q)$ (naturally defined) iff (C^{a*}, C^{b*}) is a Type I party equilibrium under $(\varepsilon^K, \lambda^P)$.*

The first supposition on the likely legislative behavior of candidates is weak: it says that a given party member is more likely to support her own party than her electoral opponent is likely to support that same party. The second supposition is rather stronger, however.

The existence of two-party competition in multi-district legislative elections is a useful datum on which to support a nonstrategic view of legislative coalition-formation: there can be at most two coalitions, each one comprising the elected members of a given party. While this is theoretically convenient, and not a bad approximation to empirical reality in some polities (*e.g.,* Great Britain), it is unsatisfactory. Political parties are themselves coalitions, and a more complete theory will explain how they come to be and to develop the forms that they do (*cf.* Riker 1982). So while the party constitution approach may be a reasonable first cut at modelling multi-candidate parties in legislative elections, it is only a first cut. At the very least, the results above make clear exactly how important party structure is to understanding electoral competition with many districts.

This last observation is underscored in Austen-Smith (1986). In this paper, the election rule is still ε^K, but there are no parties: all candidates are independents. The legislature is implicitly modelled as a bargaining game in which the set of winning coalitions is $\mathcal{D}(\cdot,\cdot)$: call this the K-legislative bargaining game. An equilibrium to the game then consists of a winning coalition, $\mathcal{D} \in \mathcal{D}(\cdot,\cdot)$ and the policy z_M that coalition M implements. So the legislative outcome function is,

$\lambda^o(\cdot,\chi) = \{z$ is a component of some K-legislative bargaining equilibrium$\}$.

Unlike in Austen-Smith and Banks (1988), the structure of the K-legislative bargaining game being played is left unspecified. Instead, voters are presumed to form (rational) beliefs about which legislature will arise, and what the subsequent K-legislative bargaining equilibrium will be. Although this approach can be rationalized as a reduced form, it is basically *ad hoc*.

When deciding how to vote in this model, voters are implicitly choosing between gambles: the expected final outcome can differ in equilibrium across candidates within a given district. The convergence in (party) policies–and hence final legislative outcomes–associated with the deterministic models discussed above is not guaranteed here. Moreover, neither is the existence of a (Nash) equilibrium in candidate strategies. Taking Theorems 9, 11 and 12 together, it is clear that as the restrictions on party organization are relaxed, and candidates are given increasing degrees of freedom, ensuring the existence of equilibrium sets of candidate platforms becomes increasingly difficult. With the total absence of parties, it is therefore not too surprising that an existence theorem is elusive.

6.6 Concluding Remarks

6.6.1 The Legislature and Electoral Behavior

Representative democracy is inherently a multi-stage decision process. At a first stage, the electorate votes some set of candidates into legislative office; at a second stage, these agents select policy. As I argued in the Introduction, the canonic model of two candidates contesting a single district for monopolistic control of the legislature involves an essentially degenerate second stage. Since at most one candidate gets elected and that candidate simply implements his platform (whether it is known surely by the electorate, or expectationally), voters' strategic decisions are straightforward for any pair of candidate positions: *i.e.*, vote sincerely. Consequently, *ceteris paribus*, candidates' strategic choices are likewise fairly simple to compute. When the legislature consists of more than a single agent, things are not so clearcut. In particular, it is only in polities for which the two-stage process is policy-irrelevant (*i.e.*, equivalent to one-stage direct democracy) that sincere voting constitutes rational behavior (Theorem 2). In constructing models of legislative elections, therefore, it is crucial to specify the legislative decision-making mechanism explicitly: without this, it is logically impossible to derive rational voters' strategies when confronted with some set of electoral candidates. And without a well-defined voting equilibrium for any list of candidate platforms, candidates' strategies cannot be deduced, which in turn confounds any efforts to examine the comparative strategic and consequential properties of alternative electoral mechanisms.

Our theoretical understanding of legislative elections is as yet rudimentary. The literature is small and falls into one or other of two classes. In the first class, the legislature is elected from a national constituency by some form of proportional representation with several parties, and the final outcome is generated through legislative voting or bargaining. Unfortunately, the legislative decision-making mechanism is rarely specified and voters at the electoral stage are supposed to vote sincerely over candidates. In the second class of model, the legislature comprises the winning agents from each of K constituencies (districts), and the within-district electoral scheme is a two-candidate, simple-plurality, contest. Although the legislative decision-making mechanism is typically specified here, it is of a particularly restrictive form—by exploiting an observation that candidates in such polities generally belong to one or other of two parties, issues of legislative coalition forming are sidestepped by presuming coalitions coincide with party members who all act as a bloc once in the assembly. Moreover, party positions (as determined from candidate platforms) are taken to be well-defined and fixed when voters go to the ballot box.

From the above perspective, it is apparent that to make progress with either class of model requires a deeper understanding of the legislative stage of the decision-making process. Typically, legislative decision-making is modelled either as a cooperative game (*e.g.*, Schofield and Laver, 1987; Schofield, Grofman and Feld, 1988) or in terms of structure-induced equilibria (*e.g.*, Shepsle 1986). Both approaches provide real insights, but as yet neither seems sufficiently well-tailored for building more complete models of representative polities, *i.e.*, with integrated electoral and legislative stages. The difficulties with cooperative models relevant here are two-fold. First, the models generally fail to predict which winning coalition and/or final outcome will emerge, establishing instead families of coalition/outcome pairs satisfying some prespecified solution concept (*e.g.*, bargaining set, competitive solution, core). This feature makes it difficult to "fold back" to the electoral stage to determine parties' electoral strategies and rational (consequentialist) voting behavior. One way around the problem is to introduce some common knowledge randomization device to select which of the feasible (according to the solution concept being used) coalition/outcome pairs will be realized. But this is *ad hoc*.

The second, and more important, difficulty with cooperative models is that by focussing on coalitions as the unit of analysis, the theory begs issues of coalition organization, maintenance and so forth. For example, consider the classical one-shot, two-person prisoner's dilemma game. Even with costless communication, a noncooperative game-theoretic approach would predict mutual noncooperation, resulting in the Pareto-dominated outcome. Given costless communication, however, cooperative theory predicts that any outcome will be Pareto efficient since the coalition-of-the-whole can form: if there is an outcome to the game, a cooperative model would insist on mutual cooperation. In other words, the cooperative approach presumes that if a coalition can form and, as a group, do better for itself than otherwise, then that coalition will indeed form and act as a unit. This reasoning fails in the noncooperative setting because whatever it is the prisoners say to each other, it is unenforceable and this is known to both of them: thus prisoner A either believes prisoner B will cooperate, in which case A should renege, or that B will defect, in which case A should defect also.

Although cooperative theory can provide rationales for particular coalition/outcome pairs to occur, it fails to guarantee incentive-compatibility for the members of such coalitions, *i.e.*, given any predicted coalition/outcome pair, is it rational for each individual in the coalition not to defect from the coalition? In the context of legislative decision-making and government formation, these issues seem fundamental. However, having said this it may turn out that cooperative solutions can in fact be supported by fully noncooperative, strategic, behavior (as is the case, for example, with the Nash two-person bargaining solution which can be supported by Rubinstein's (1982) strategic bargaining model). It would be interesting to know to what extent there is such support, and, in particular, what are the game-forms which support cooperative solutions as noncooperative equilibrium outcomes.

Unlike cooperative models, structure-induced equilibrium models can unequivocally be framed as noncooperative games. They posit a set of legislators with given policy preferences, distributed across a variety of legislative committees with sundry agenda-control powers. Given these features, the models generate legislative decisions as equilibrium outcomes to a more-or-less explicit policy-setting game. To incorporate such models into a legislative election setting requires a theory of how elected representatives get allocated to committees. To date, such a theory is unavailable and it is this which makes it problematic simply to graft some structure-induced equilibrium model directly onto an electoral model. The general approach, however, is promising. Particular institutional rules for legislative decision-making induce particular game-forms for analyzing legislative behavior, which in turn generate well-defined equilibrium policy outcomes as functions of (*inter alia*) the elected representatives' preferences, platforms, *etc*. These functions can then be used by candidates and voters when making electoral decisions.

6.6.2 Candidate Entry and Payoffs

In almost all models of electoral competition, the number of competing candidates is taken as fixed. The number and locations of candidates in any election, however, are clearly endogenous to the legislative election scheme in operation (and not just the election rule).[21] Although there does exist some formal work on entry in a winner-takes-all setting (Brams and Straffin 1982;

---

[21] Consequently, analyses of the comparative properties of various election rules which assume the number of candidates is fixed are not very useful for constitutional design.

Palfrey 1984), the only explicit attempt to examine the entry question in a legislative election framework is due to Greenberg and Shepsle (1987). By construction, their concept of an $fn(K)$-equilibrium is intended as a notion of "entry stability". In such equilibria it is not in the interest of any potential candidate to enter the election, and no extant candidate would *(cet. par.)* choose to leave the election (since she is guaranteed electoral success under the assumption of sincere voting). However, as I argued in Section 6.4, the sincere voting assumption, coupled with a complete absence of any legislative decision-making mechanism, makes the status of the Greenberg/Shepsle results unclear. In particular, to interpret their (non)existence result (Theorem 4) as a positive statement on candidate entry under the fixed-number election rule is, I believe, inappropriate.

Whether or not candidates choose to enter an election is a positive question, the answer to which will depend on final payoffs to the relevant agents (voters and candidates). In a winner-take-all electoral scheme, it is enough to specify candidate payoffs in terms of votes, plurality, or probability of success. For whatever candidates' preferences might be with respect to policy or perquisites of office, once in power they have monopoly control over these variables. Consequently, the relevant objective is reducible to electoral success (even though voters' beliefs about the policies that any such candidate would implement if elected will influence behavior). In legislative elections as understood in this essay, however, it is not generally possible to reduce candidate objectives to some function solely of votes, and leave their underlying preferences more-or-less implicit: when elected, candidates do not have monopolistic control of legislative decisions. To solve for final policy and portfolio outcomes, therefore, it is necessary to specify the legislative preferences of elected candidates. Electoral success is instrumental to promoting legislative payoffs. Of course, a candidate might be wholly indifferent about legislative decision-making and seek office simply for its own sake. But even here, this is relevant information for the voters, since they cannot expect such a candidate to promote any particular legislative outcome, *e.g.*, his electoral platform, over another (but see Austen-Smith and Banks 1989).

6.6.3 Information

All of the models discussed earlier are models with full information. Although full information is a natural starting point, the existence of a multi-stage representative system may ultimately rest on the presence of incomplete and imperfect information. Legislative decisions are myriad. Policy issues arise more-or-less continuously, without being fully anticipated, and are not determined in any once-and-for-all legislative decision. Moreover, legislation is rarely an end in itself, but more often an attempt to influence final consequences. Exactly how legislation translates into consequences is subject to uncertainty. Electing a representative assembly, then, is one means by which authority for handling this uncertain stream of uncertain issues is delegated from the electorate at large to a subset of that electorate.[22]

The sort of informational concerns listed above involve imperfect information. Somewhat different concerns arise when information is incomplete–that is, when preferences or some other relevant innate feature of candidates or voters are not common knowledge. For example, at the electoral stage of the process, voters rarely know for sure the legislative intentions of any candidate. In this context, the informational role of party labels in national elections is well-recognized, if not fully understood. Party labels and electoral platforms can function as signals of what candidates will do conditional on being elected (Enelow and Hinich 1984; Banks 1990). Similarly, legislative decision-making games typically generate quite different sets of equilibria (and questions) when there is incomplete information than otherwise.

6.6.4 Multi-dimensional Issues

Finally, one-dimensional issue spaces are special. In the canonic model, assuming a single issue generates stability which typically is lost in moving to higher dimensional spaces. The relevance of incorporating a multi-dimensional issue space is evident. Unfortunately, since even with a single issue stability is hard to insure for legislative elections, the immediate prospect of successfully incorporating multiple issues is not good. At present the most promising approach to the problem is, I think, via the structure-induced equilibria route. By imposing sufficient institutional structure on agenda-setting, *etc.*, at the legislative stage, well-defined legislative equilibria can be supported in a multi-dimensional policy space. And once the legislative equilibrium correspondence is deduced, being able to fold back to generate equilibria at the electoral stage is more likely, since it is final outcomes that voters are concerned about. However, the disadvantage of the structure-induced equilibria approach – both in this context and elsewhere – is that in the absence of a general theory of institutional choice, models and results based on the approach are unlikely to be general. But we have to start somewhere.

References

Aldrich, J. 1983a. "A Downsian Spatial Model with Party Activism," *American Political Science Review* 77: 974-90.

Aldrich, J. 1983b. "A Spatial Model with Party Activists: Implications for Electoral Dynamics," *Public Choice* 41: 63-100.

Austen-Smith, D. 1981. "Party Policy and Campaign Costs in a Multi-Constituency Model of Electoral Competition," *Public Choice* 37: 389-402.

Austen-Smith, D. 1984. "Two-party Competition with Many Constituencies," *Mathematical Social Sciences* 7: 177-98.

---

[22] See Gilligan and Krehbiel (1987) for a model which suggests the importance and value of a committee structure to a larger assembly when there is imperfect information about the consequences of legislation.

Austen-Smith, D. 1986. "Legislative Coalitions and Electoral Equilibrium," *Public Choice* 50: 185-210.

Austen-Smith, D. 1987. "Parties, Districts and the Spatial Theory of Elections," *Social Choice and Welfare* 4: 9-23.

Austen-Smith, D. 1989. "Sincere Voting in Models of Legislative Elections," *Social Choice and Welfare* 6: 287-299.

Austen-Smith, D. and J. Banks. 1988. "Elections, Coalitions and Legislative Outcomes," *American Political Science Review* 82: 405-422.

Austen-Smith, D. and J. Banks. 1989. "Electoral Accountability and Incumbency," in *Models of Strategic Choice in Politics*, P. Ordeshook, ed. Ann Arbor: University of Michigan Press.

Axelrod, R. 1970. *Conflict of Interest*. Chicago: Markham.

Balinski, M. and P. Young. 1982. *Fair Representation*. New Haven: Yale University Press.

Banks, J. 1990. "A Model of Electoral Competition with Incomplete Information," *Journal of Economic Theory* 50: 309-325.

Black, D. 1958. *Theory of Committees and Elections*. Cambridge: Cambridge University Press.

Brams, S. and P. Straffin. 1982. "The Entry Problem in a Political Race," in *Political Equilibrium*, P. Ordeshook and K. Shepsle, eds. Boston: Kluwer-Nijhoff.

Cox, G. 1984a. "Electoral Equilibrium in Double Member Districts," *Public Choice* 44: 443-451.

Cox, G. 1984b. "Strategic Electoral Choice in Multi-member Districts: Approval Voting in Practice?" *American Journal of Political Science* 28: 722-38.

Cox, G. 1985. "Electoral Equilibrium under Approval Voting," *American Journal of Political Science* 29: 112-8.

Cox, G. 1987. "Electoral Equilibrium under Alternative Voting Institutions," *American Journal of Political Science* 30: 82-108.

Downs, A. 1957. *An Economic Theory of Democracy*. New York: Harper and Row.

Enelow, J. and M. Hinich. 1984. *The Spatial Theory of Voting: An Introduction*. Cambridge: Cambridge University Press.

Gilligan, T. and K. Krehbiel. 1987. "Collective Decision-making and Standing Committees: An Informational Rationale for Restricitve Amendent Procedures," *Journal of Law, Economics and Organization* 3: 287-386.

Greenberg, J. and K. Shepsle. 1987. "The Effect of Electoral Rewards in Multiparty Competition with Entry," *American Political Science Review* 81: 525-37.

Greenberg, J. and S. Weber. 1985. "Multiparty Equilibria under Proportional Representation," *American Political Science Review* 79: 693-703.

Hinich, M., J. Ledyard, and P. Ordeshook. 1972. "Nonvoting and the Existence of Equilibrium under Majority Rule," *Journal of Economic Theory* 4: 144-53.

Hinich, M. and P. Ordeshook. 1974. "The Electoral College: A Spatial Analysis," *Political Methodology* 1: 1-29.

McKelvey, R., P. Ordeshook, and M. Winer. 1978. "The Competitive Solution for n-person Games without Transferable Utility," *American Political Science Review* 72: 599-615.

Mill, J. S. [1861]. 1975. *Considerations on Representative Government*. Oxford: Oxford University Press.

Moulin, H. 1980. "On Strategy-proofness and Single Peakedness," *Public Choice* 35: 437-55.

Palfrey, T. 1984. "Spatial Equilibirum with Entry," *Review of Economic Studies* 51: 139-56.

Palfrey, T. 1986. "Comments," *Public Choice* 50: 211-19.

Parliaments of the World. 1986. Vol. II, 2nd edition. Aldershot: Gower.

Riker, W. 1962. *The Theory of Political Coalitions*. New Haven: Yale University Press.

Riker, W. 1982. "Perfect Equilibrium in a Bargaining Model," *Econometrica* 50: 97-109.

Robertson, D. 1976. *A Theory of Party Competition*. London: Wiley.

Rubinstein, A. 1982. "Perfect Equilibrium in a Bargaining Model," *Econometrica* 50: 97-109.

Schofield, N. 1978. "The Theory of Dynamic Games," in *Game Theory and Political Science*, P. C. Ordeshook, ed. New York: New York University Press.

Schofield, N. 1986. "Existence of a 'Structurally Stable' Equilibrium for a Noncollegial Voting Rule," *Public Choice* 51: 267-284.

Schofield, N., B. Grofman, and S. Feld 1987. "Bargaining Theory and Cabinet Stability in European Coalition Governments, 1945-1983," in *The Logic of Multiparty Systems*, M. Holler, ed. Dordrecht: Martinus-Nijhoff.

Schofield, N., B. Grofman, and S. Feld. 1988. "The Core and the Stability of Group Choice in Spatial Voting Games," *American Political Science Review* 82: 195-211.

Schofield, N. and M. Laver 1987. "Bargaining Theory and Cabinet Stability in European Coalition Governments: 1945-1983" in *The Logic of Multiparty Systems*, M. Holler, ed. Dordrecht: Martinus-Nijhoff.

Shepsle, K. 1986. "The Positive Theory of Legislative Institutions: An Enrichment of Social Choice and Spatal Models," *Public Choice* 50: 135-78.

Sugden, R. 1984. "Free Association and the Theory of Proportional Representation," *American Political Science Review* 78: 31-43.

Ursprung, H. 1980. "Voting Behaviour in a System of Concordant Democracy," *Public Choice* 35: 349-62.

7. Preference-Based Stability: Experiments on Cooperative Solutions to Majority Rule Games

Cheryl L. Eavey

7.1 Introduction

> Are we to believe that democratic institutions are fundamentally flawed, in the sense that no equilibrium in preferences is likely to occur, so that the outcomes of the political process are no more than accidental consequences of institutions or personalities? [*Schofield* 1995]

The issue of stability in majority rule voting games hinges on the existence or nonexistence of a game-theoretic solution for cooperative games known as the core, or set of undominated alternatives. The core is considered to be a "natural" equilibrium in that it guarantees that every coalition will achieve its maximum value given the actions of every other coalition. Thus, the core's claim to stability is unique: because it predicts outcomes that are rational for every coalition, coalitions should have no incentive to deviate from the core (Ordeshook 1986).

The problem, of course, is that for many n-dimensional preference configurations, the core simply does not exist. Taking the problem one step further, the chaos theorems of McKelvey and Schofield (McKelvey 1976; Schofield 1978; McKelvey and Schofield 1986) suggest that in the absence of a core, any point in the issue space may be reached given the appropriate agenda.

The absence of a natural equilibrium in majority rule games is highly disconcerting, and often at odds with real world observations of stable policy choices. One explanation for the observed stability revolves around institutions and the structural constraints imposed on majority rule processes. Consider an institution such as Congress. Although this body operates under majority rule, choices are mitigated by a variety of structural constraints, varying in complexity from a simple germaneness rule to the sprawling committee system. In the absence of a majority rule core, perhaps institutions induce stable outcomes.

Shepsle (1979) pioneered the search for institutional equilibria. His work suggests that institutional rules, such as jurisdictional arrangements and germaneness rules, may indeed produce equilibria. However, unlike the core in a majority rule game, his solution, the structure-induced equilibrium (SIE), predicts Pareto-dominated or inefficient alternatives. More recently, Hammond and Miller (1987; 1990) have examined the stability-inducing properties of such complex institutions as a bicameral Congress, the Congressional committee system and the executive veto. Their work is exciting because it suggests that these institutions, under certain conditions, will produce undominated or core alternatives.

But as the lead quote from Schofield suggests, some are uncomfortable with the notion that stability must be achieved through the imposition of structure. Thus, a second explanation for observed stability derives from cooperative solutions to majority rule games without a core. The absence of chaos in real world democratic processes may not be due to the role of institutions, but instead may indicate the existence of one or more alternative solutions to the core. And indeed, a number of solutions have been proposed for games without a core, including the competitive solution and the uncovered set. Although these alternative solutions lack the core's strong claim to stability, each satisfies a specific set of desirable criteria.

In this chapter, we will explore the experimental evidence on the predictive ability of the core and preference-based alternatives to the core. Overall, the outcomes from majority rule games exhibit considerable variability, even in games with a core alternative. Perhaps not surprisingly, when the core exists, the evidence supports the core as the most accurate predictor of committee outcomes, although the experiments also confirm that support is far from universal. As for solutions to noncore games, it would be premature to even attempt to select a "best" solution for these games based on the existing experimental evidence, given the scant attention paid to date to the experimental testing of solutions such as the uncovered set. However, there may be sufficient evidence to identify some of the advantages and/or disadvantages associated with each solution concept.

7.2 Majority Rule Games with a Core

The experiments described below are drawn from the economics and political science literature and examine the predictive value of the core for games without side-payments.[1] The methodology for these diverse experiments derives from Vernon Smith's induced-value theory (1976). Under the usual economic assumption that, *ceteris paribus*, more is preferred to less, players' preferences over alternatives are controlled by attaching a monetary value to each alternative. Once the preference profiles have been established, the core and any competing solutions to the core are then identified. The predictive value of the core is determined by the degree of correspondence between predicted and observed outcomes.

---

[1] For an analysis of the predictive ability of the core in side-payment games, see Michener and Yuen (1982) and Michener, *et al.* (1983).

7.2.1 Discrete Preferences

Consider the preferences given in Table 1. Discrete preferences, or preferences induced over a limited number of alternatives, provide the simplest settings for the experimental testing of game-theoretic solution concepts. The core has been the focus of a number of such experiments, and as we shall see, the experimental support for the core from these games is far from overwhelming.

The core is most simply defined as the set of undominated alternatives. Dominance relations are a function of preferences and control. Alternative X dominates alternative Y if a coalition with the authority to enforce its preferences strictly prefers X over Y (Isaac and Plott, 1978). Consider the preferences given in Table 1. The only undominated alternative in this profile is letter E. Moreover, E defeats every other alternative in a pairwise or binary comparison; thus, it is also the Condorcet winning alternative.

Table 1
Compensation Chart for Isaac/Plott
Majority Rule Games
(1978)

Players

1		2		3	
B	26.00	F	33.00	E	21.20
G	22.60	E	26.40	F	18.00
J	19.40	I	20.60	H	15.20
A	16.40	D	15.60	J	12.40
H	13.60	H	11.40	D	9.75
C	11.00	C	8.00	I	7.40
D	8.60	G	5.40	B	5.15
I	6.40	A	3.60	G	3.15
E	4.40	J	2.60	A	2.40
F	2.60	B	2.40	C	1.00

Isaac and Plott induced preferences in three players over the ten alternatives $A - J$ given in Table 1. The status quo point, or default option if a committee failed to make a choice, was D. Each player was given a chart listing the payoff values for each of the ten alternatives. Although players only received information on their own payoffs, they were allowed a verbal exchange of ordinal information.

Twelve experiments were conducted with the preferences given in Table 1 and a simple majority voting rule. The core, E, was the preferred choice of four committees, as was alternative H. Alternative F was selected two times, and B and D each received the support of a single committee. Isaac and Plott noted that committee members often supported alternative H for fairness reasons: "Option H had a definite appeal which was unnoticed by us until this series was conducted. As you "work down" the options ..., you see that H is the first option that all participants have in common" (Isaac and Plott, 1978, 304).

Table 2
Compensation Chart for Eavey/Miller Majority Rule Games
(1984)

Players

1		2		3	
E	19.60	I	22.00	B	23.50
F	15.40	H	17.10	C	16.10
G	12.20	J	13.15	A	13.20
D	6.20	E	12.45	G	12.20
A	5.40	G	12.20	D	5.70
I	4.60	D	5.30	F	4.10
J	3.35	F	3.70	E	2.65
C	2.70	B	2.95	H	2.45
H	2.10	A	1.20	J	1.50
B	1.20	C	0.85	I	0.75

As Eavey and Miller (1984) later observed, H is also the only alternative with a value of over $10.00 for all players. Would the core continue to be an attractive alternative if players had the option of selecting a dominated alternative that offered all players a "fair" return – say of $10.00 or more? Eavey and Miller examined this proposition in a series of majority rule experiments designed to parallel the experiments of Isaac and Plott. Preferences were induced in players over the ten alternatives given in Table 2. The core of this new game is still E; the fair alternative is G. Eavey and Miller argued that G is an attractive alternative for committees seeking a universalistic option: G has a value of $12.20 for all players, and although it requires a sacrifice from players 1 and 2, the benefits to player 3 are substantial. Eavey and Miller ran 10 experiments with these preferences and the Isaac/Plott instructions. The core was selected twice; the remaining committees selected the fair alternative.[2]

---

[2] One alternative explanation to fairness for the selection of letter G is envy. Perhaps player 2 supports alternative G because she resents player 1's dramatic gain (over $7.00) from the selection of E. Given the structure of information, we believe this explanation is less plausible than the fairness argument. Under conditions of common knowledge, envy is a

Their experimental results suggest that the predictive value of the core weakens when challenged by alternatives possessing fairness properties based on cardinal values. However, the core may be sensitive to features of the experimental setting unrelated to cardinal fairness. McKelvey and Ordeshook (1980) ran a series of vote trading experiments in which the core had a combined success rate of only 45%. In these games, five players were asked to make a decision on the passage of five separate "bills" represented by the letters $A - E$. The payoff value assigned to the passage of each bill was private information, although information was provided on the ordinal preferences of the other players.

Why did the core perform so poorly in these experiments? McKelvey and Ordeshook hypothesized that the attractiveness of the core was somehow linked to the structure of the experimental setting. Their instructions for the vote trading experiments did not specify the form of the vote; specifically, voting on bills could proceed either sequentially or simultaneously. Frequently, players disaggregated the bills, perhaps because it simplified the task or to gain a competitive advantage.

In a reformulation of these experiments, McKelvey and Ordeshook (1981) transformed the possible combinations of bills into 26 discrete alternatives $A - Z$. Players' rankings over these alternatives are displayed in Table 3. As in their earlier experiments, players were given full information on their own preferences and ordinal information on the preferences of the other players. The core of the transformed game was G, and the experimental results supported the core in all seven trials.

But what if the core was selected because of its fairness properties? In terms of the ordinal rankings given in Table 3, the core, G, was either at or above the median alternative for all players. Perhaps players supported the core because of its relative position across rankings and not because of the underlying dominance relation. In order to test this hypothesis, McKelvey and Ordeshook designed another series of experiments in which the core (now letter A) ranked below the median alternative for some players (see Table 4). In addition, they varied the communication conditions. In fourteen trials, players were given complete ordinal information as in the earlier games. However, in sixteen additional trials, players were given information only on their own preferences.

And indeed, support for the core dropped under the new preference profile. With the preferences given in Table 4, the core was selected only 60% of the time. Moreover, the rates of selection varied across communication conditions; specifically, the core was more successful in those games with incomplete ordinal information. When players received information on their preferences alone, the core was selected 75% of the time compared to a 43% success rate for games with complete ordinal information.

---

possible motive. But in this game, player 1 does not need to reveal his strong preference for alternative E in order to garner player 2's support. Player 3, however, does need to reveal his disdain for alternative E in order to convince the rest of the committee to support G.

Table 3
Preference Profile for McKelvey/Ordeshook Games with Core = G
(1981)

Players

1	2	3	4	5
X	Y	X	J	V
H	U	E	N	W,T
E	N	M	W	L,P
F,Q	L,S	Q	Z	G
B	B	G	G	Y,J,I,O
I,O	J,R	F,O,H	K,L,R	C
M	T	A	A	E,N
K,U	H,K	B,I	B,Y	A,D,U,K
R	I	D,R,W	M,O,V	B,M
G,P	G,Z	N,T	T,E	S,Z,F,Q
D,A	D,V	P,K	S,H	R,X
N	E	Z,C	C,Q	H
S,Z	F,P	U	U	
T,W	M,W	J,V,S	D,P,X	
C	C	Y	I	
J,Y	O,X	L	F	
V	A			
L	Q			

Table 4
Preference Profile for McKelvey/Ordeshook Games with Core=A
(1981)

Players

1	2	3	4	5
J	K	A	L	F
E	D	B	K	J
D	E	E	G	B
C	A	F	C	H
L	G	D	I	A
B	C	G	F	N
I	H	C	H	G
G	F	I	M	L
N	B	H	A	C
M	J	K	B	D
A	L	J	E	E
F	I	L	D	I
H	N	M	N	K
K	M	N	J	M

After further analysis, McKelvey and Ordeshook ruled out relative fairness as an explanation because the most popular alternative to the core, letter E, ranked low in the rankings for two people and thus obviously did not fit the criterion of a fair alternative. They concluded that they could best explain the experimental results by examining the specific dominance structure of each design. In the first design, where the core, G, was highly successful, there was no clear competitor to the core. Remove G from the rankings, and all the remaining alternatives comprise the top cycle. However, in the second design where the core, A, received less than universal support, the top cycle beneath A was smaller than in the first design, and of those alternatives in the top cycle below A, alternative E had a particularly strong claim to stability.

Analysis. If one looks solely at the experimental literature examining the core in majority rule games with discrete preferences, one might wonder why the core is considered to be the preeminent solution concept. The core seems to be vulnerable on a number of dimensions that are not addressed by cooperative game theory. McKelvey and Ordeshook's experiments identified two factors affecting the predictive ability of the core –the structure of the alternative space and the structure of the dominance relation below the core– that are not accounted for by the received theory. In addition, information seems to play a role: the core was less successful under complete ordinal information than incomplete ordinal information, although it isn't clear why that was the case.

The Isaac and Plott majority rule results hinted at, and Eavey and Miller's results confirmed, that three-person committees are attracted to alternatives that have a cardinal component of fairness. Yet the core, like many other cooperative solutions, is an ordinal solution concept; *i.e.*, the location of the core is completely determined by the ordinal preference rankings. As long as ordinal rankings are invariant, cardinal values are irrelevant for the purpose of defining the core. Yet in discrete experimental games, players appear to make decisions based upon cardinal information, even under information conditions that exclude the exchange of cardinal information.

How do we explain the prevalence of non-core results in discrete games? One explanation might be that for reasons of fairness, limited cognitive capabilities, or transaction costs, individuals are willing to incur some loss in their selection of an alternative. To the extent that this is true, perhaps we should adjust our solution concept accordingly. This is the approach taken by Salant and Goodstein (1990). Their solution concept, the selection set, is based on the assumption that committees will select non-core outcomes provided the loss associated with these outcomes is less than a specified threshold t (where $t \geq 0$) for each member of the winning coalition. When $t = 0$, the selection set coincides with the core; otherwise, the selection set contains that subset of alternatives (including the core) for which some bare majority of the committee would incur a loss of t or less.

Salant and Goodstein ran a total of 45 five-person experiments with discrete alternatives and a core outcome under varying rules of procedure and multiple payoff charts. From the data, they estimated the value of t using a maximum likelihood procedure, which established the threshold at $1.20. Holding t constant, they calculated the selection set for each set of preferences from their experiments as well as the experiments of other researchers.

The selection set captured considerable variation from the core in Salant and Goodstein's experiments. They identified high intensity preferences as those in which the selection set includes only the core point. Given high intensity preferences, the core was chosen over 90% of the time. However, with low intensity preferences, the core point was selected less than 51% of the time. Nevertheless, 83% of the non-core outcomes in games with low intensity preferences were in the selection set.

In addition, the selection set predicted well out of sample, capturing the fair outcomes of Eavey and Miller (1984). Recall that, in their experiments, the fair alternative, letter G, was selected 80% of the time by the experimental committees. Salant and Goodstein determined that G is the only alternative in Eavey and Miller's preference profile, other than the core, that is in the selection set.

Reformulations of the core, along the lines of the selection set, may capture the variation in outcomes observed in the discrete majority rule games. On the other hand, perhaps the problem lies not with the solution concept itself but with the experimental setting. Perhaps there is something about discrete games in general or committees of size three in particular that undermines the core's predictive ability. Complicate the experimental setting by moving (for example) to a two-dimensional issue space and these non-core results may disappear.

7.2.2 Spatial Preferences

In a 1990 review of the experimental literature on spatial models, McKelvey and Ordeshook wrote: "if preferences and alternatives are spatial, if a Condorcet winner exists, and if procedures imply a game-form (or "approximate game-form") that links this winner to the core, then that winner is the final outcome, either identically or approximately." And indeed, the experimental results from majority rule games with spatial preferences provide the strongest evidence in support of the core.

Consider the preference configuration given in Figure 1, henceforth referred to as the inside player/core design. As Plott (1967) has demonstrated, the existence of a core point in two dimensions is sensitive to the arrangement of ideal points. In this design, the core (39,68) coincides with the ideal point of the interior player, player 1. Notice that player 1 is located at the intersection of the indifference curves between players 2 and 4 and players 3 and 5. The existence of a core hinges on the location of the interior player. If player 1 is shifted ever so slightly off that point of intersection, then this preference configuration no longer contains a core outcome.

The inside player/core design served as the foundation for the now classic experiments of Fiorina and Plott (1978), as well as a number of other experiments on the core. Fiorina and Plott induced these preferences in five individuals via two-dimensional grids. Each individual was assigned an ideal point, or point of maximum value. The values of the remaining grid points were represented by concentric circular indifference curves emanating from a player's ideal point. Players were given full information on their own preferences, but were allowed to reveal only ordinal information to other players. Side payments were prohibited. The task of the committee was to select a point from the two-dimensional grid.

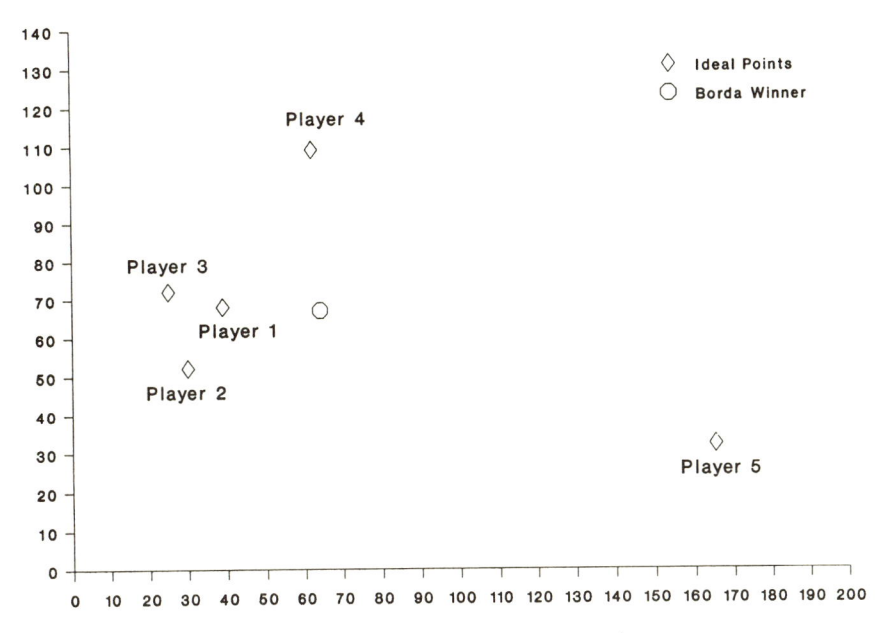

Figure 1. Inside Player/Core Design.

Fiorina and Plott also identified a fair solution for this design distinct from the core. The fair alternative was defined as the centroid point or point minimizing the sum of Euclidean distances from every player's ideal point. Computationally, it is simply the spatial average of all ideal points. The centroid point is located at the coordinates (64,67).

The rule was a variant on Robert's Rules of Order. The motion on the floor, or status quo point, was the point (200,140). Once recognized by the chair (a nonvoting role assigned to the experimenter), a player could offer an alternative proposal to the floor. The majority preferred alternative would become the new motion on the floor, and would itself be subject to amendment. Once a majority had consented to end debate and accept the current motion on the floor, the meeting adjourned.

Communication under this rule was subject to experimental manipulation. Under full communication, discussion was allowed and players were free to communicate anything except monetary values. Under no communication, players were restricted to procedural matters – making proposals and voting.

Payoff values were also manipulated to determine the effects of the magnitude of payoffs on outcomes (see Appendix A). Ideal points in the high payoff condition ranged from a high of $38.25 to a low of $9.45 compared with a high of $11.00 and a low of $6.00 for the low payoff condition. In addition, the rates of loss were somewhat steeper in the high payoff condition.

Fiorina and Plott ran a total of forty experiments with the inside player/core design. The breakdown across conditions is as follows: twenty high payoff experiments (ten with full communication and 10 with no communication) and twenty low payoff experiments (10 with full communication and 10 with no communication). The results were striking. First, the core was strongly supported in the high payoff experiments across communication conditions. This is not to imply that committees always select the point (39,68); in fact, only three of the twenty high payoff committees actually selected the core as the outcome of the game. But all twenty committees did select points either on or close (in spatial terms) to the core. The average outcome in the full communication games was (37,68) with a standard deviation of 5.2. In the no communication games, the average outcome was (38,69) with a standard deviation of 8.3. Thus, not only was the core outcome supported in these games (at least on average), but the degree of communication allowed within the context of Robert's Rules appears to have little effect on the selection of the core.

And what about the results from the low payoff variant? To quote Fiorina and Plott: "Given low payoffs, all the models work rather poorly with or without communication" (1978, 586). More specifically, although the core was selected as the outcome in four of the twenty low payoff experiments, it did not fare as well overall, and results appeared to be more sensitive to the level of communication. The average outcome under full communication was (47,72) with a standard deviation of 21.9, compared to an average outcome under no communication of (36,70) with a standard deviation of 17.3. Communication in these games seemed to facilitate a movement away from the core towards the extreme players, perhaps for reasons of fairness.

Fiorina and Plott conclude that "If the configuration of preferences is such that an equilibrium [read core] exists and if the preferences are strongly held, then, within narrow limits the committee's choice will be the equilibrium." (1978, 590). However, "when people are personally indifferent or near indifferent they try to be fair, thereby allowing the decision to be pulled further from them than the equilibrium outcome" (1978, 592). To paraphrase, if the stakes are high enough, people will behave in a self-interested fashion and the core will be an accurate predictor of committee outcomes; otherwise, the opportunity exists for individuals to respond to motivations other than self-interest, resulting in greater variation from the core.

Further evidence on the tension between a singleton core and a fair alternative is present in the experimental results of Laing and Olmsted (1978). Unlike the majority of experimental voting games, Laing and Olmsted were interested in the effects of a sequence of decisions on committee outcomes. They assembled nineteen 5-person committees, and asked them to select an alternative by

Cheryl L. Eavey

simple majority rule (where anyone could introduce an alternative for consideration at any time) for each of five different preferences configurations, one of which generated a singleton core prediction. In addition to the game-theoretic predictor, they identified an alternative model, the fair or "split-the-distance" alternative.

Overall, Laing and Olmsted concluded that the core was the superior solution concept: the average distance between observed and predicted outcomes was smaller for the core than for the split-the-distance alternative, based on an analysis of sixteen admissible outcomes. However, support for the core dissipated when controlling for committee style. Based on an analysis of committee discussions, Laing and Olmsted identified two distinct committee styles: competitive committees versus consensus-seeking committees. Consensus-seeking committees selected alternatives closer to the split-the-distance alternative, while competitive committees preferred alternatives closer to the core.

Despite the differences in experimental design, in many ways the experiments of Laing and Olmsted parallel those of Fiorina and Plott. Both used an inside player/core design with circular indifference curves, albeit with different ideal points and payoff functions. Both identified a fair alternative; indeed, the split-the-distance alternative of Laing and Olmsted is conceptually identical to the centroid point of Fiorina and Plott, and the two-dimensional Borda winner (Feld and Grofman 1988). Yet contrary to the results of Fiorina and Plott's high payoff experiments, Laing and Olmsted found support for the fair alternative. Perhaps we can attribute the behavior of consensus-seeking committees to the payoff structure used in Laing and Olmsted's game. Ideal points ranged from a low of $4.00 to a high of $12.00, with payoffs dropping $1.00 for each 10-unit movement away from a player's ideal point up to the $2.00 circle. Thus, their payoff structure appears comparable to Fiorina and Plott's low payoff variant, in which indifference or near indifference facilitated the selection of non-core outcomes.

On the other hand, it's impossible to say definitely given the procedural differences between the two sets of experiments. The sequencing of decisions might have led to coordination across games, or the differences in results might be due to information conditions.[3] Hoffman and Plott (1983) used the high payoff, full communication experiments of Fiorina and Plott as a baseline to examine the effects of coalition formation and less restrictive voting rules on outcomes. Using both the preference configuration and payoff functions of Fiorina and Plott (1978), Hoffman and Plott examined the predictive ability of the core under a simple majority rule procedure controlling for pre-meeting discussions. They found that pre-meeting discussions had little effect on outcomes under a Robert's Rules procedure: the core predicted equally well in both cases. However, significant deviations from the core were observed in the pre-meeting, simple majority rule variant compared with the other variants: the average outcome of ten trials was (35.7, 66.8) with a standard deviation of 6.81 in the x-dimension and 3.55 in the y-dimension. They suggest that

---

[3] Indeed, Laing and Olmsted omitted some trials from analysis specifically because of explicit agreements across trials.

these differences are due to differences in information conveyed by the various procedural rules; specifically, Hoffman and Plott argue that Robert's Rules procedures allow players to acquire more information about alternatives, thus dissolving coalitions formed around alternatives other than the core in pre-meeting discussions.

Analysis. The experimental results reported thus far support the core as the most accurate predictor of committee outcomes. Yet in many ways the evidence raises more questions than it answers. For example, was the core attractive because of the dominance relation or because of its spatial location? The alignment of preferences is crucial for the existence of a core in a two-dimensional issue space with circular indifference curves. The fact that the core necessarily coincides with the ideal point of an interior player certainly makes the core a good candidate for an obvious or Schelling (1960) point, so how do we know that the success of the core was due to its position in the dominance relation and not to its spatial location?

One approach to answering this question would be to create a situation with a non-obvious core point and then examine its success rate in experimental games. And that was precisely the tack employed by Berl, *et al.* (1978). Using city block preferences (or square indifference curves) in a two-dimensional space, they created a series of three-person games in which the core did not coincide with the ideal point of an inside player. Out of twelve trials with city block preferences, the core was never the outcome of a committee game. However, as in other games with spatial preferences, the results supported the core on average. This does not rule out the possibility that the core is a Schelling point in an inside player/core design, but it does suggest that there is an intrinsic attractiveness to the core.

Yet the fact that committees are attracted to the core does not limit them to selecting only core points. Indeed, more often than not, points spatially close to the core are selected instead of the core point. This suggests that a modified core solution, such as the selection set of Salant and Goodstein (1990), might be a more accurate predictor of committee outcomes than a singleton core. Consider the high payoff, full communication, no pre-meeting results of Fiorina and Plott and Hoffman and Plott. Figure 2 displays their results as well as the calculated selection set region for the threshold value of $1.20. In this case, the selection set fails to capture the variation in outcomes; specifically, the only non-core observation within the selection set region is the outcome (40,68) from Hoffman and Plott's simple majority rule trials.[4]

You may recall that the selection set successfully explained the variation in the discrete experiments of Eavey and Miller (1984). The failure of the selection set in the spatial case can be attributed to the very nature of the

---

[4] Salant and Goodstein (1990) report that 90% of the observed outcomes from Fiorina and Plott's (1978), high payoff, full communication experiments fall within the boundaries of the selection set. Those bounds were calculated from the payoff functions given in Fiorina and Plott. However, according to Charles Plott (personal communication, July 1992), two of the payoff functions (for players 2 and 5) were misspecified. The analyses reported in this chapter were based on the corrected payoff functions (given in Appendix *A*).

Cheryl L. Eavey

solution concept. Unlike the core, the selection set is a cardinally-based solution concept. Assuming a threshold of $1.20, if payoff functions are steep, so that the core is highly valued by all players, but alternatives spatially close to the core drop sharply in value, then the selection set will be a small subset of alternatives near the core (see Eavey, 1992). And this is precisely what occurred with the Fiorina and Plott payoff functions. The result was a small selection set, and little improvement over the core.

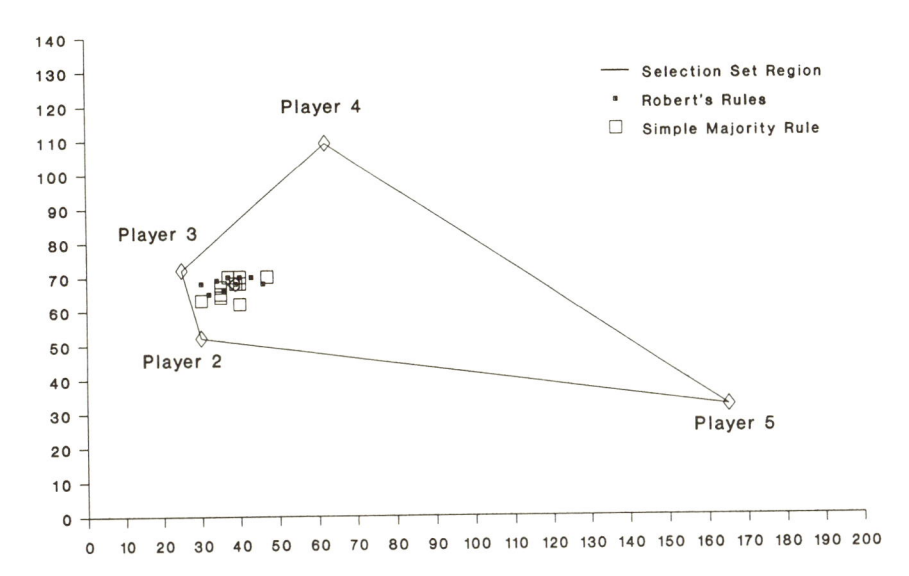

Figure 2. Experimental results of Fiorina/Plott (1978) and Hoffman/Plott (1983). Under Robert's Rules, two outcomes at (34,69).

And what about the effects of non-self-interested behavior on outcomes? Fiorina and Plott identified the magnitude of payoffs as a crucial variable for explaining deviations from the core. Indeed, in the high payoff, full communication variant of Fiorina and Plott, the centroid or fair alternative (64,67) received no support.

Most experimenters would agree that the magnitude of payoffs is an important variable: induce indifference and anything might happen. But what about the distributional aspect of the payoff functions? In experiments with discrete preferences, alternatives perceived as fair had the property of offering "something for everyone." As Eavey (1991) observed, in the Fiorina and Plott high payoff games, the centroid or fair alternative was worth only a few cents for the players closest to the core (players 1, 2 and 3) compared to a value of over $11.00 for the extreme players, players 4 and 5. Indeed, the only alternative which gave everyone at least $5.00 was the core.[5] Therefore, the only alternative which was fair in a cardinal sense (albeit weakly) was the core.

---

[5] In Eavey (1991), it was reported that there was no cardinally fair alternative in the Fiorina and Plott games. This conclusion was based on the payoff functions reported in the

162   *Preference-Based Stability*

Perhaps the core would not fare as well if the fair alternative were fair in a cardinal sense. In order to test this proposition, Eavey replicated the full communication, no pre-meeting experiments of Fiorina/Plott and Hoffman/Plott with a different set of payoff functions which, in terms of magnitude, corresponded to the high payoff functions of Fiorina and Plott (ideal points ranged from a high of $25.25 to a low of $15.75), but in addition created a region of fair alternatives emanating from the centroid point (64,67), which was valued at over $11.00 for all players (see Appendix A). The bounds of the fair region are subjective; they depend on how one defines the notion of "something for everyone." In this analysis, we will define the fair region as those alternatives which offered every player at least $5.00.

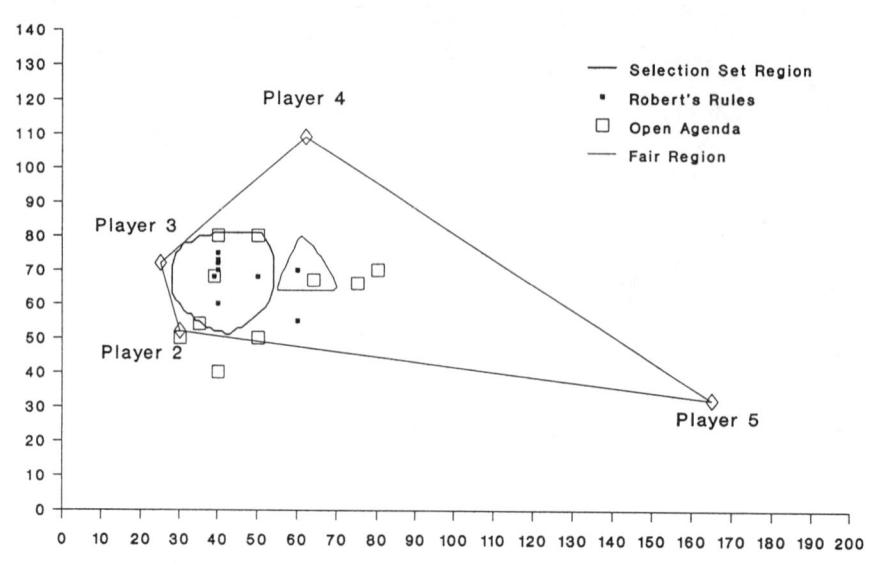

Figure 3. **Experimental Results of Eavey (1991). Under Robert's Rules, two outcomes at (40, 70).**

The results of Eavey's experiments under Robert's Rules and simple majority rule are displayed in Figure 3, and Table 5 summarizes the results from Figures 2 and 3. Notice that in trials under Robert's Rule, there is still a cluster of outcomes around the core point. However, the point (39,68) was the outcome of only one committee meeting, and points selected close to the core tend to favor one extreme player, player 4. Indeed, unlike the outcomes in the comparable Fiorina/Plott experiments, most of the noncore outcomes in these experiments appear to favor one or both of the extreme players. This interpretation of the results is supported by the structure of the coalition formation: eight of the ten committees formed larger than minimum winning coalitions

---

appendix of Fiorina and Plott (1978). All analyses reported in this paper were calculated with the corrected payoff functions.

supporting noncore alternatives, compared to one larger than minimum winning coalition in the Fiorina and Plott games.

Table 5
Summary Statistics and Mann-Whitney Test of Significance for Select Spatial Games

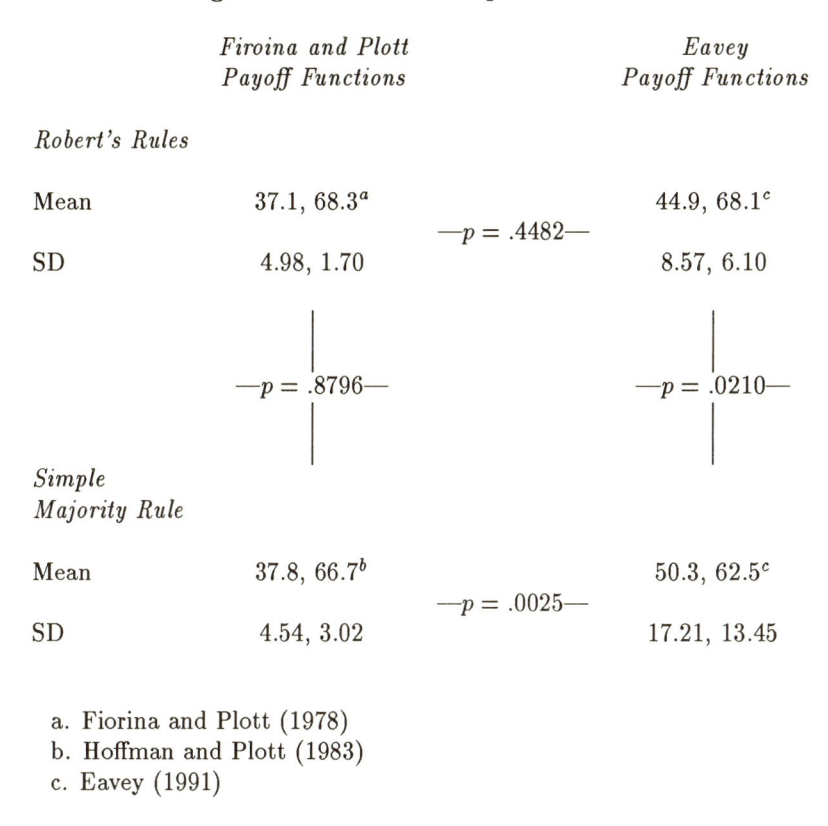

	Firoina and Plott Payoff Functions		*Eavey Payoff Functions*
Robert's Rules			
Mean	37.1, 68.3[a]		44.9, 68.1[c]
		—$p = .4482$—	
SD	4.98, 1.70		8.57, 6.10
	—$p = .8796$—		—$p = .0210$—
Simple Majority Rule			
Mean	37.8, 66.7[b]		50.3, 62.5[c]
		—$p = .0025$—	
SD	4.54, 3.02		17.21, 13.45

a. Fiorina and Plott (1978)
b. Hoffman and Plott (1983)
c. Eavey (1991)

However, the dispersion of outcomes increases in Eavey's experiments under simple majority rule. In these experiments, the core point was once again the outcome of only one committee meeting. Instead of selecting the core, a number of committees voted for alternatives that favored the extreme players. In one instance, the centroid point (64,67) was selected. However, committees also selected points beyond the fair region in an apparent attempt to appease player 5. And some committees appeared willing to satisfice and select the first acceptable alternative, as evidenced by the three-person coalitions opting for alternatives favoring player 2.

It does appear that the distribution of cardinal values affects the predictive ability of the core, especially in games with nonrestrictive voting procedures.

Further, the results of nonparametric tests of significance suggest that information plays an important, but secondary role to the underlying structure of cardinal values. If you recall, Hoffman and Plott argued that a restricted voting procedure allows players to acquire more information about the core, thus increasing the number of core or near core outcomes. Eavey's analysis suggests that while a restrictive voting procedure may increase the attractiveness of the core, it concomitantly decreases the likelihood of players exchanging the information necessary for locating a cardinally fair alternative. However, a more complete understanding of the role of information in shaping committee decision-making processes awaits further research.

Taken in their totality, the experimental results on majority rule games with a core suggest that the core is an imperfect predictor at best. Area solutions may be the best alternative to a singleton core. Salant and Goodstein's selection set, which was relatively unsuccessful in predicting outcomes in the experiments of Fiorina and Plott and Hoffman and Plott, was more successful with Eavey's design; eight of the ten Robert's Rules results lie within the selection set as do three of the ten simple majority rule outcomes. The success of the selection set in these games is largely due to its increased size. Since Eavey's payoff functions were designed to create a cardinally fair alternative at the point (64,67), payoff values dropped at a slower rate for points near the core in her experiments compared to the experiments of Fiorina and Plott and Hoffman and Plott, resulting in a larger selection set.

While the selection set may capture some of the deviations from the core, it still fails to predict directional movements toward the extreme players. Perhaps the conceptualization of loss embodied in the selection set is insufficiently complex to capture the trade-offs that result in movements away from core outcomes. On the other hand, the results indicate that the fair region is a poor predictor of committee outcomes. Indeed, if individuals are attempting interpersonal comparisons of utility, as Eavey presumes they are, then conditions of partial information ensure that these comparisons will be imperfect at best, and it is unlikely that the cardinally fair region will be an accurate predictor of outcomes.

The bottom line is that however unsatisfactory the core may be, it is still the solution concept to which all others are compared, and to date, there is no clearly superior alternative to the core. Moreover, once we move away from games with a core, our ability to predict outcomes becomes much more problematic.

7.3 Majority Rule Games Without a Core

A number of solutions have been proposed for games without a core outcome. As Ordeshook (1986) notes, many of these solutions have evolved in a progressive fashion, building upon and thus overlapping with, alternative solutions to noncore games. Although we will identify a number of alternative solutions to the core, one in particular has been examined extensively in experimental settings: the competitive solution.

As with most alternatives to the core, the competitive solution coincides with the core when it exists. However, the competitive solution predicts not only outcomes but also coalitions supporting outcomes (McKelvey, Ordeshook and Winer, 1978). Assume that coalitions form and compete in a bidding process for pivotal players. If we restrict coalitions to one proposal, the competitive solution consists of that set of alternatives (and their supporting coalitions) in which pivots are indifferent among competing proposals. All coalitions within the competitive solution are equally likely and proposals from outside the set should not be stable.

Table 6
Preference Profile for Competitive Solution
McKelvey and Ordeshook
(1980)

Players

1	2	3	4	5
N	J	B	L	B
J	O	H	E	A
F	M	A,F	D	E,G,H
I	E,F	I	A,G,O	K
K	I	K,M,D,J	M	D
G,O,H	K,D	G	I	M
D,M	G,B	E,C	K,B	O,C
B	H,C	L,N	F,C	L,N,J
A,C	L,N	O	N,J	F,I
L	A		H	
E				

Competitive Solution Proposals

A {3,4,5}
E {2,4,5}
F {2,3,4}
H {1,3,5}
O {1,2,4}

Consider the discrete preference profile given in Table 6. This preference profile does not contain a core outcome, but we can identify alternatives in the competitive solution, along with supporting coalitions. The five alternatives comprising the competitive solution are $\{A, E, F, H, \text{and } O\}$. Alternative A is supported by players 3, 4 and 5, and alternative F is supported by players 1, 2 and 3. The pivot, player 3, is indifferent between alternatives A and F. What if a coalition outside the competitive solution attempted to form? Players 3 and 5, for example, would both like the committee to select alternative B, their first choice, and they could offer to form a coalition around B with player 2. That coalition would not be stable, however, because players 1 and 4 could pull player 2 out of the $\{2,3,5\}$ coalition by offering her a more preferred alternative, letter O.

How has the competitive solution fared in the experimental setting? As with the core, the experimental evidence on the competitive solution is decidedly mixed. Further, the evidence suggests that some of the same variables that reduce the predictive ability of the core have an even more pronounced impact on the predictive ability of the competitive solution.

7.3.1 Discrete Preferences

The evidence from experiments with discrete preferences is a case in point. Remember that the selection of the core in discrete games was tied to a number of factors unrelated to the theory of the core, including the relative position of other alternatives in the dominance relation and the structure of the underlying cardinal payoffs. Consider again the ordinal preferences given in Table 6, and a slightly modified form of the preference chart in which G (an alternative not in the competitive solution) is raised to second, third and fourth place for players 5, 4 and 1 respectively. The competitive solution is invariant under either set of ordinal preferences. Yet it is conceivable that G may be more attractive under the modified preferences, due to its elevated position for three of the five players.

McKelvey and Ordeshook (1983) reported on fourteen trials with the preferences given in Table 6, and fifteen trials with the modified preference profile.[6] The voting rule was simple majority. Ordinal information was common knowledge, although discussion of cardinal values was strictly prohibited. However, these experiments had a slight twist to them compared to many other experimental designs. Instead of inducing one set of cardinal payoff charts for each player across trials, charts were randomly assigned to players. As a result, each trial was unique in terms of the distribution of cardinal values.

For the preferences given in Table 6, the experimental results strongly supported the predictions of the competitive solution; only two committees selected points outside the predicted set. However, those strong confirmatory results faded under the modified preference profile: in fifteen trials with the modified preferences, only four outcomes were in the competitive solution. Of the eleven outcomes outside the competitive solution, alternative G was the selection of nine committees.

And what about the role of cardinal values? The experimental design de-

---

[6]The experiments based on the preferences in Table 6 were originally reported in McKelvey and Ordeshook (1980) and reproduced in the 1983 paper.

scribed above ruled out the possibility of testing for cardinal effects. However, the design could easily be modified by simply changing the method of inducing preferences. And that was exactly the approach taken by McKelvey and Ordeshook (1983). In place of a randomization mechanism, they attached probability values to each alternative in Table 6, specifying the likelihood that each player would receive his 'stake,' or maximum payoff value.

McKelvey and Ordeshook ran thirteen experiments with one set of probability values and seventeen experiments with another set of probability values. The differences between the two sets of payoffs were minor; specifically, in the latter set, alternatives ranked at or directly below the competitive solution alternatives were closer in probability values to competitive solution values and thus were hypothesized to be more attractive to players. The result was that the success rate of the competitive solution varied with the assignment of cardinal values: when alternatives close to the competitive solution were more attractive, the competitive solution had a success rate of 64.7% compared to

Table 7
Preference Profile for the Competitive Solution
Miller and Oppenheimer
(1982)

Players

1		2		3		4		5	
F	14.25	C	14.25	B	14.25	E	14.25	A	14.25
C,B	13.30	E,F	13.30	A,F	13.30	A,C	13.30	E,B	13.30
D	12.25*	D	12.25*	D	12.25*	D	12.25*	D	12.25*
A	00.75	B	00.75	E	00.75	F	00.75	C	00.75
E	00.00	A	00.00	C	00.00	B	00.00	F	00.00

Competitive Solution Proposals

F $\{1,2,3\}$
C $\{1,2,4\}$
B $\{1,3,5\}$
E $\{2,4,5\}$
A $\{3,4,5\}$

*Alternative Values of D in $

8.50
6.72
4.20
2.10

a success rate of 84.6% under the alternative payoff functions. The discrete experiments of Miller and Oppenheimer (1982) underscore the role of cardinal values in the selection of competitive solution alternatives. The design for their experiments is deceptively simple. Consider the preferences given in Table 7. Five of the six alternatives (A, B, C, E, F) are elements of the competitive solution. The remaining alternative, D, is dominated by each of the competitive solution alternatives. Notice, too, that the value of D varies from a high of $12.25 to a low of $2.10.

If subjects play the game competitively, then we would expect committees to select alternatives in the competitive solution. But what if committees seek a universalistic, or something for everyone, alternative. Weingast (1979) argues that if the expected value of the universalistic alternative exceeds the expected value of playing the game competitively, committees will opt for the universalistic choice.

Miller and Oppenheimer (1982) ran twenty-five trials, five for each cardinal value of alternative D. They predicted (à la Weingast) that D would be the predominant choice in those situations in which the expected value of D was greater than the expected value of playing the game competitively; specifically, when D was valued at $12.25 and $8.40. However, when D is valued at anything less than $8.40, we should expect to see competitive behavior and the selection of competitive solution alternatives.

Miller and Oppenheimer's results suggest that the behavior of experimental committees is imperfectly captured by both Weingast's hypothesis and the predictions of the competitive solution. As anticipated, when the expected value of D was greater than the expected value of selecting a competitive solution, alternative D was the predominant choice (in nine out of ten trials). Conversely, when the expected value of selecting D was $2.10, the committees played competitively (in four out of five trials). However, when D's expected value was less than the competitive solution, but more than $2.10, committees selected D in eight of the ten trials.

Miller and Oppenheimer speculated that the obviousness of alternative D (in Schelling's (1960) sense) might be a factor in its selection, so they designed a comparable experiment which obviated the obviousness of D; specifically, the symmetry in preferences that is apparent in Table 7 was obscured by the introduction of three alternatives that were dominated by both the competitive solution alternatives and alternative D. The results confirmed the validity of the original design: D was the predominant outcome when it was valued at $12.25, but was not the choice of committees when valued at $2.10. These trials suggest that obviousness is not the operative factor here. However, we are left without a satisfactory explanation for the attractiveness of alternative D when the expected value of D is less than the expected value of playing competitively, but greater than the lowest assigned value of $2.10. And as Miller and Oppenheimer correctly state, it was impossible given their design to separate risk aversion from other plausible rationales for the attractiveness of D, such as fairness.

Cheryl L. Eavey

Analysis. As in games with core alternatives, the experiments discussed above highlight the role of factors unrelated to the received theory that impact on the selection of game-theoretic solution concepts. In the case of the competitive solution, we can identify the following factors: (1) the presence of highly ranked non-competitive solution alternatives, and (2) the structure of the underlying cardinal values. Given the differences in design across these experiments, it is difficult to ascertain possible interdependencies between these two factors. Both McKelvey and Ordeshook's experiments and Miller and Oppenheimer's experiments highlight the role of cardinal values in the selection of non-competitive solution alternatives, with the most pronounced effect occurring in the experiments of Miller and Oppenheimer. But in addition, Miller and Oppenheimer's "obvious point" experiments suggest that a highly ranked alternative is only attractive if it is also highly valued (in a cardinal sense). This result, however, raises a question for McKelvey and Ordeshook's experiments. To what extent was the failure of the competitive solution in their modified preference profile experiments a function of the elevated position of alternative G or the (unknown and changing) cardinal values associated with G?

In any event, these experiments demonstrate that, like the core, the competitive solution is an imperfect predictor of committee behavior for games with discrete preferences. The experiments with spatial preferences discussed below will uncover additional drawbacks to the competitive solution. Beyond that, they serve as a first cut for evaluating the empirical usefulness of alternative solution concepts such as the uncovered set.

7.3.2 Spatial Preferences

The competitive solution was first presented as a possible solution to games without a core in a 1978 article by McKelvey, Ordeshook and Winer. It was also this piece that provided the first empirical test of the new solution concept. The design used in their test is the now standard "house" design. Consider the preferences given in Figure 4. The five competitive solution points are located on the border of the interior pentagon. Each solution point is supported by a unique external coalition; for example, the point (70,105) is supported by the coalition of players 2, 3 and 4. Player 4 is the pivotal player. She is indifferent between this competitive solution point and a competing point (110,120) supported by players 1 and 5.

The procedures for this set of experiments generally followed those outlined for spatial games with a core. The voting rule was simple majority. Players were given both cardinal and ordinal information on their preferences and ordinal information on the preferences of the other players; specifically, ideal points were common knowledge as well as the shape (which was circular) of the indifference curves. And as in other experiments, players were prohibited from exchanging cardinal information.

The results of their experimental test are also presented in Figure 4. As you can see, there is a reasonably good correspondence between the experimental results and the predicted competitive solution points. In addition, McKelvey, et al. report that the only three-person coalitions that formed were those predicted by the competitive solution. Furthermore, the authors' note "that in no game was the coalition of the whole seriously considered, and the issue of equity or fairness arose explicitly in the bargaining only once (the idea of an equitable proposal was quickly rejected and never mentioned again)" (1978, 614).

These general conclusions were echoed by Ordeshook and Winer (1980) in a more extensive test of the competitive solution. Ordeshook and Winer were interested in the substantive question of coalition formation in parliamentary democracies. Thus, they induced preferences in players corresponding to known policy positions of political parties in Norway (for 1961 and 1969) and the German Democratic Republic (for 1969). In addition, players were given a voting weight in proportion to the number of seats each party was assigned. The resulting design included four different preference configurations, none of which contained a core outcome.

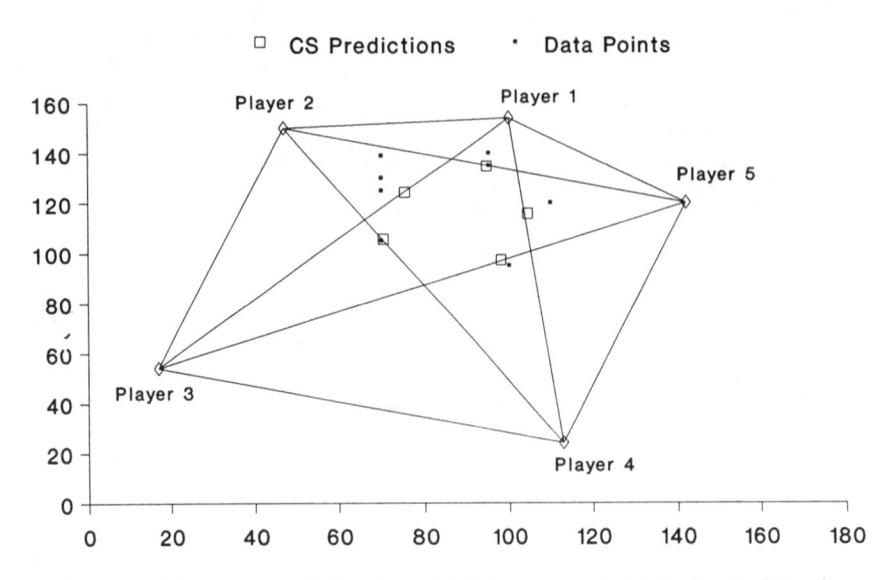

Figure 4. Experimental Results of McKelvey and Ordeshook (1978).

Ordeshook and Winer concluded, on the basis of 60 experiments (15 for each design), that the competitive solution was the best predictor (compared to minimum-variance hypotheses and an extension of bargaining set theory) of both outcomes and coalitions. However, they also observed a desire for equitable solutions on the part of the players which, at times, complicated the interpretation of their results. Nevertheless, Ordeshook and Winer dismiss these aberrations, arguing instead that altruistic concerns "are distortions of the preferences the experimenter seeks to induce and not evidence of the inappropriateness of a particular hypothesis or theory" (1980, 750).

Laing and Olmsted (1978), on the other hand, examined the predictive ability of the competitive solution versus a fair alternative, the split-the-distance alternative or Borda winner, for a number of different preference configurations, including the now familiar house, and a non-symmetrical variant on the house, the skew star. As stated earlier, Laing and Olmsted's procedures were unique in that committees made a sequence of choices, one for each design. Otherwise, experimental procedures followed those of McKelvey, *et al.* (1978).

The preference configuration and experimental results for Laing and Olmsted's house and skew star experiments are presented in Figures 5 and 6. Overall, Laing and Olmsted report that the competitive solution was very accurate in predicting which coalitions formed, as long as larger than minimum winning coalitions were not counted negatively. Moreover, they determined, based on average distance between observed and predicted outcomes, that the competitive solution was a more accurate predictor than the fair alternative or Borda winner, even when controlling for committee style (consensus-seeking versus competitive).

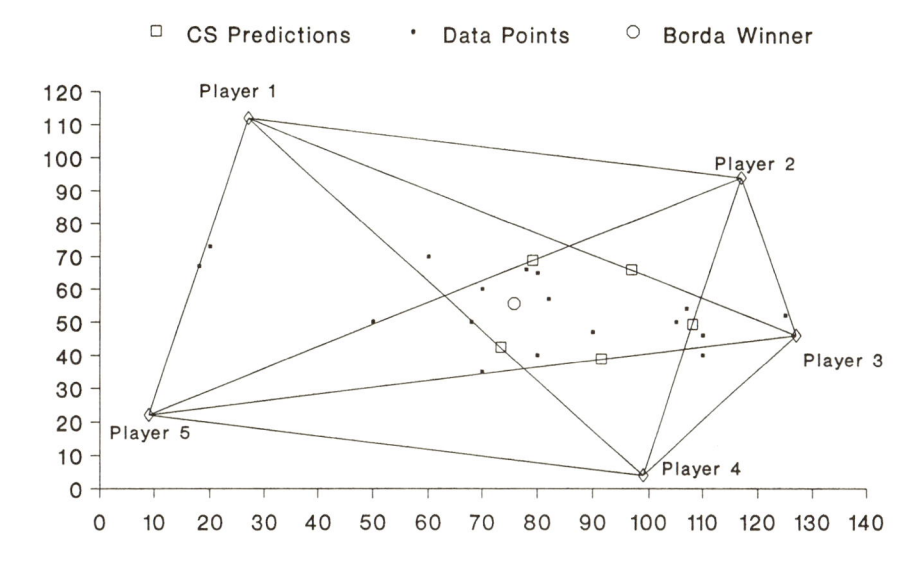

Figure 5. Experimental Results of Laing and Olmsted (1978).

Analysis. The results of McKelvey and Ordeshook (1978; displayed in Figure 4) and to a somewhat lesser extent, those of Ordeshook and Winer (1980; not shown) indicate a nice clustering of outcomes near the competitive solution points. Clearly, these outcomes are highly supportive of the predictive ability of the competitive solution. As in spatial experiments with a core, rarely, if ever, were outcomes exactly on the predicted points, but by now we should not find that observation surprising.

However, the results of Laing and Olmsted are somewhat disturbing. Even though the competitive solution was more accurate than the fair alternative or Borda winner, their trials exhibited far more variation in outcomes than realized in either McKelvey and Ordeshook or Ordeshook and Winer's experiments. Again, the differences in procedures make it difficult to generalize across experiments. In particular, as we've noted before, the sequencing of decisions in the Laing and Olmsted experiments may have generated some of the dispersion in outcomes.

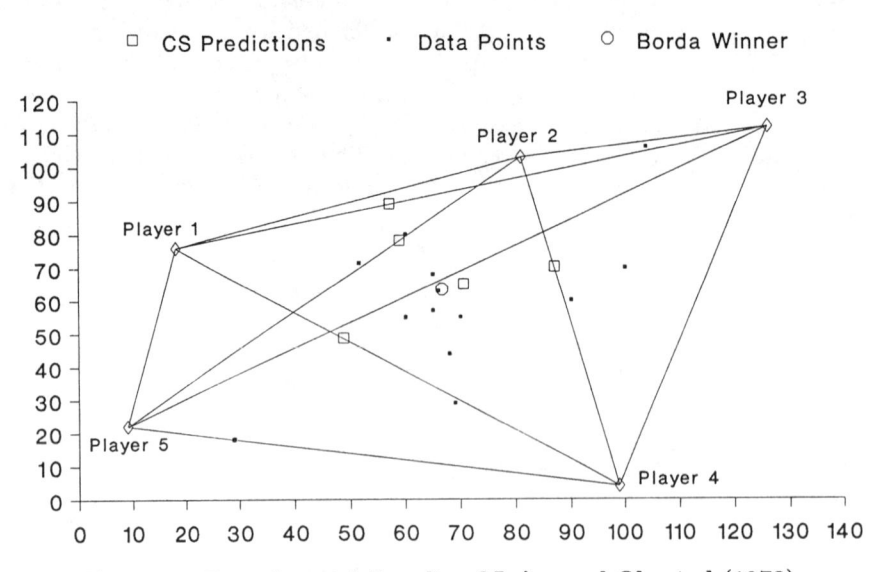

Figure 6. Experimental Results of Laing and Olmsted (1978).

On the other hand, we have seen from experiments with a core that cardinal values have been shown to play an important role in determining outcomes. Perhaps the structure of cardinal values can account for some of the observed differences across experiments. An analysis of the payoffs for McKelvey and Ordeshook's (1978) experiments indicates that the competitive solution alternatives were highly valued only for the coalition expected to support a given competitive solution point. For example, the competitive solution alternative supporting the coalition of players 3, 4 and 5 was valued at over $5.00 for those three players and under $1.50 for players 1 and 2. Given the cardinal structure of their alternative space, it makes sense that outcomes clustered near the competitive solution points.

In Laing and Olmsted's competitive solution games, ideal points ranged from $7.00 to $13.00, and payoff values dropped $1.00 for each ten-unit (eight-units in the skew star design) movement away from a players' ideal point. As we speculated in the discussion of payoff functions for spatial games with a core, payoffs of this type may generate indifference on the part of the players, and this indifference could account for the dispersion in outcomes observed in their games. Of course, neither Laing and Olmsted nor McKelvey and

Ordeshook were primarily concerned with the affect of the structure of cardinal payoff values on outcomes.

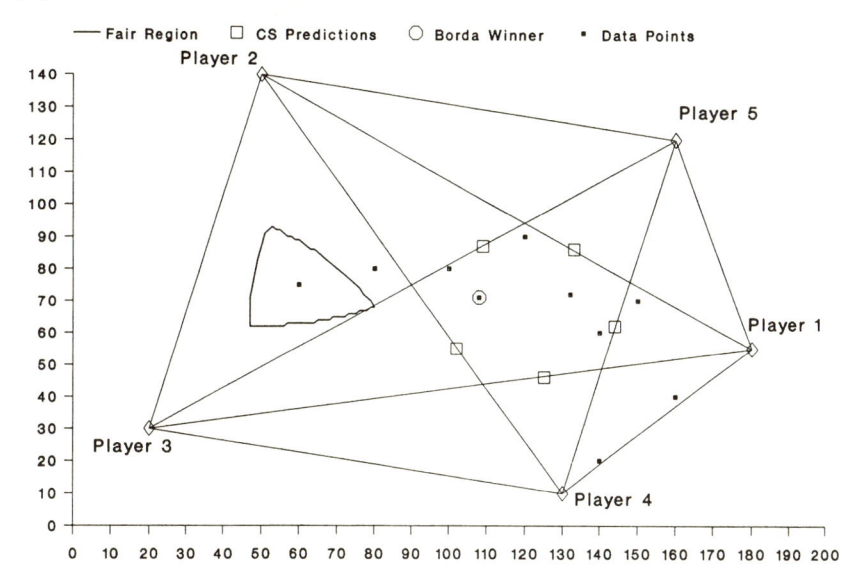

Figure 7. Experimental Results of Eavey (1991).

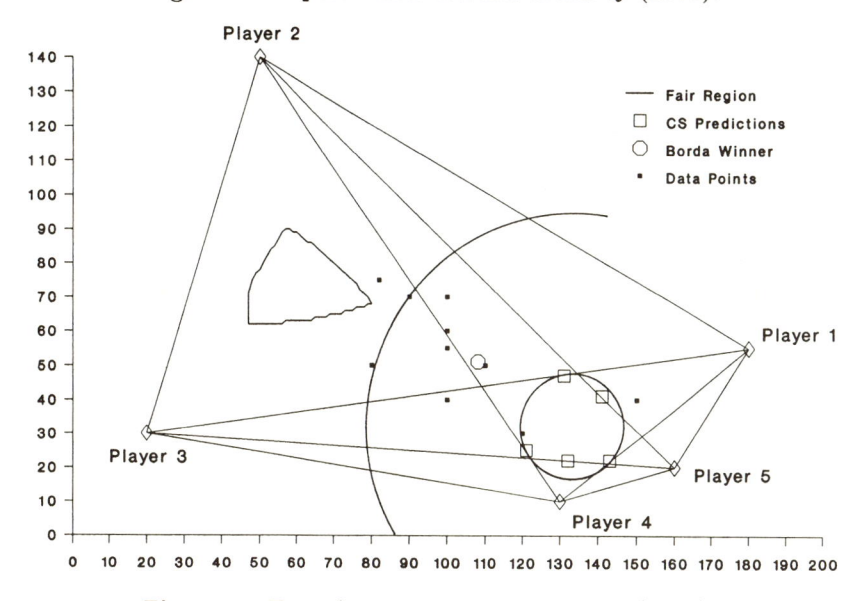

Figure 8. Experimental Results of Eavey (1991).

On the other hand, Eavey's (1991) experiments were designed explicitly to examine the predictive ability of the competitive solution versus a distinct and cardinally fair alternative under a simple majority rule procedure. Figures 7 and 8 display the ideal points, solution concepts and resulting outcomes from her house and skew star designs. Ideal points ranged from a low of $18.10 to a high of $30.50 (see Appendix B for specific functional forms). Eavey designated a fair region emanating from the point (60,75) – which had a value of over $9.00 for all players – and including all points with a value of $5.00 or more for all five players. By design, this region was outside the interior pentagon and to the left of the Borda winner, in the direction of the extreme players.

Eavey hypothesized that committees seeking fair (*i.e.*, something for everyone) alternatives would form greater than minimum winning coalitions supporting alternatives in or near the fair region. On the other hand, competitive committees were expected to form minimum winning coalitions supporting alternatives on or near the predictions of the competitive solution.

Table 8
Experimental Results from Eavey
(1991)

House		*Skew Star*	
Outcomes	Winning Coalition	Outcomes	Winning Coalition
160,40	1,4,5	150,40	1,4,5
140,60	1,4,5	120,30	1,4,5
140,20	1,4,5	100,40	2,3,4
132,72	1,4,5	110,50	2,3,4,5
100,80	1,2,4	100,70	1,2,3,5
150,70	1,2,4,5	100,55	1,3,4,5
120,90	1,2,4,5	90,70	1,2,4,5
108,71	1,2,4,5	80,50	1,3,4,5
60,75	1,2,3,5	100,60	1,2,3,4,5
80,80	1,2,3,4,5	82,75	1,2,3,4,5

The outcomes and supporting coalitions for both designs are given in Table 8. In terms of coalition formation, half of the committees with house preferences formed minimum winning coalitions while only three minimum winning coalitions formed in trials with skew star preferences. With the exception of a single trial, all observed minimum winning coalitions were predicted by the competitive solution. However, the (1,4,5) coalition was by far the most prominent minimum winning coalition. The competitive solution is premised on the belief that all external minimum winning coalitions are equally likely. Yet committee discussions from these experiments suggested (and the results confirmed) that the (1,4,5) coalition was perceived as the only viable three-person coalition. Indeed, only one experiment exhibited any semblance of competitive bidding for pivotal players; specifically, in one skew star game, the (2,3,4) coalition formed after the breakup of the (1,4,5) coalition. In that particular case, player 1 alienated player 4, who then willingly formed a coalition with players 2 and 3. In terms of outcomes supported by the (1,4,5) coalitions, a single outcome from the house design was very close to the predicted competitive solution point. Another outcome was half-way between the predicted outcome and another competitive solution point, while the last two were reasonably far away from the predicted point but within the set of Pareto optimal alternatives for those three players. However, in the skew star design, the (1,4,5) coalition supported outcomes that were closer to two other competitive solution points than the point predicted by the competitive solution for that specific coalition.

In every other experiment, larger than minimum winning coalitions formed. Note that these coalitions almost always included players 1, 4 and 5. Did these coalitions support outcomes which offered something for everyone? In the house design, only two of the five larger than minimum winning coalitions supported outcomes outside and to the left of the interior pentagon, one of which was in the fair region. Obviously, a strong case could not be made for Eavey's hypothesis given the results from this design.

However, the results from the skew star design are much cleaner. Although none of the outcomes were within the designated fair region, all of the seven larger than minimum winning coalitions supported alternatives outside and to the left of the interior pentagon. These outcomes were bounded on one side by the Borda winner and on the other side by the fair region. Clearly, the competitive solution fails to predict this sort of directional movement by larger than minimum winning coalitions toward the extreme players (players 2 and 3).

Taken as a whole, the evidence from spatial games underscores the conclusions drawn in light of experiments with discrete preferences; *i.e.*, the competitive solution is a reasonably good predictor of committee outcomes under a certain class of payoff functions. Like the core, the competitive solution is sensitive to the distribution of cardinal payoffs.

But compared to the results from games with a core, deviations from the competitive solution points seem somewhat more pronounced, at least in the spatial context. Moreover, Eavey's (1991) results highlight a potential problem with the competitive solution: given that there was no competitive bidding for pivots in these games and that the same minimum winning coalition formed over and over again, one could argue that the logic of the competitive solution holds only for a particular class of payoff functions. Indeed, the universality of this solution has been questioned before, but for different reasons. Laing and Olmsted (1978) were unable to determine the competitive solution points for one of their designs, leading McKelvey and Ordeshook (1990) to conclude that the solution was unsatisfactory as a general hypothesis (1990, 127).

But the competitive solution is not the only solution to games without a core. Indeed, there are several competing solutions, although none have been subject to rigorous testing in the experimental laboratory. However, we can present a cursory examination of these solutions, using data from some of the competitive solution experiments with spatial preferences.

A point alternative to the competitive solution is the Copeland winner or strong point. The Copeland winner is that alternative which "defeats or ties the greatest number of alternatives" in an issue space (Grofman, et al. 1987, 539). For Eavey's house and skew star designs (given in Figures 7 and 8), the Copeland winner is a centrally located point inside the interior pentagon; specifically, the point (123,67) in the house design and (133.5,30) in the skew star design. And as the results from these experiments clearly demonstrate, the Copeland winner receives no support in either of these designs.

However, the most promising solution concept, the uncovered set, is not a point predictor, but an area solution. An alternative is said to be stable if it is uncovered. Consider two alternatives: A and B. Alternative A covers alternative B if and only if alternative A is preferred by a majority to alternative B and also beats every alternative that B beats. Alternative A is then uncovered if and only if it is not covered by any other alternative (Miller 1980). The uncovered set is particularly attractive because not only does it exist in an institution-free environment, but it also has been shown to contain outcomes from a limited number of institutional settings, including two-candidate elections (McKelvey 1986).

Although it is difficult to calculate the exact bounds of the uncovered set for two-dimensional spatial games (Tovey 1993), we can determine the maximum bounds. The approach involves defining another solution concept, the yolk, in terms of median lines and then determining the boundaries of the uncovered set from the perimeter of the yolk. Consider the skew star preference configuration given in Figure 8. A median line divides the set of ideal points in half. So, for example, the contract curve between players 1 and 4 is a median line because three players (1, 4 and 5) are on or to the right of the line and four players (1, 2, 3 and 4) are on or to the left of the line. For a two-dimensional policy space, the yolk is the smallest circle that touches all median lines. The uncovered set, then, is no larger than a circle, concentric with the yolk, with a radius four times the radius of the yolk (McKelvey 1986).

Do the experimental results conform to the maximum bounds of the uncovered set? The results from McKelvey and Ordeshook's (1978) experiments are obviously within the outer bounds of the uncovered set. It also appears that Laing and Olmsted's (1978) results fall within these bounds. However, two of the outcomes from Eavey's skew star experiments lie outside the maximum bounds of the uncovered set.

7.4 Conclusion

Experimental work makes an important contribution to theoretical research by identifying those variables that in some sense delimit the predictive ability of game-theoretic solutions like the core. We are just beginning to delineate the conditions under which a majority rule core will successfully predict committee outcomes. Although we obviously have an imperfect understanding of these conditions, and further experimentation (and theorization) is needed, it is also obviously true that these conditions will not be met universally. Thus, even though the core may be the "best" solution, it is not a perfect solution, and at times may be a very poor predictor of committee outcomes.

Potentially, the same conclusion may be drawn for alternative solutions to the core. The problem at this moment is that many of these solutions have not been examined extensively in the experimental setting. And for those solutions which have been examined, the data are often inconclusive. For example, the Copeland winner received no support from the results of the house and skew star experiments of Eavey (1991), yet Grofman, *et al.* (1987) have shown that this solution is consistent with the data from a noncore experiment by Fiorina and Plott (1978). Obviously, this solution has not been the universal choice of committees. On the other hand, it's difficult to evaluate the potential usefulness of a solution when there has been no explicit test of the Copeland winner *per se* (only secondary analyses of existing data), and thus no attempt to reconcile the conflicting evidence.

Of the solutions discussed in this chapter for noncore games, the competitive solution has been subject to the most thorough examination in the experimental setting, and it has received some support. However, like the core, the attractiveness of the competitive solution appears to vary with changing experimental conditions that theoretically should have no effect on the predictive ability of this solution concept.

Is there a general solution for noncore games? The most likely candidate is the uncovered set. This solution is attractive from a theoretical perspective, and indeed may prove to be the most accurate predictor of committee outcomes for noncore games. Area solutions, by definition, capture more variation in outcomes than point predictors and, to the extent that individuals are imperfect maximizers of self-interested behavior, an area solution may be preferable to solutions that make point predictions. Certainly that is the rationale behind Salant and Goodstein's selection set. And the uncovered set, at least as indicated by its maximum boundaries, accounted for a substantial amount of variation in outcomes from the house and skew star experiments. However, a rigorous experimental test of the predictive ability of this solution concept awaits the precise specification of its perimeters.

To date, the experimental evidence suggests that we may not find a general solution that predicts equally well in all settings. To the extent that this conjecture is valid, then specifying the conditions under which a solution concept will or will not work becomes crucial. In addition, if non-self-interested motivations truly play a primary role in determining some subset of outcomes, then an understanding of the process, and not just the outcomes of decision making becomes much more important. The experimental setting provides the ideal environment for addressing these sorts of issues.

References

Berl, J.E., R.D. McKelvey, P.C. Ordeshook, and M.D. Winer. 1976. "An Experimental Test of the Core in a Simple N-Person Cooperative Nonsidepayment Game," *Journal of Conflict Resolution* 20: 453-476.

Eavey, C. L. 1991. "Patterns of Distribution in Spatial Games," *Rationality and Society* 3:450-474.

Eavey, C. L. 1992. "The Selection Set and Committee Games: A Comment on Salant and Goodstein." Typescript: Washington University.

Eavey, C. L. and G. J. Miller. 1984. "Fairness in Majority Rule Games with a Core," *American Journal of Political Science* 28: 570-586.

Eavey, C. L. and G. J. Miller. 1995. "Subcommittee Agenda Control," *Journal of Theoretical Politics* 7:125-156.

Feld, S. L. and B. Grofman. 1988. "The Borda Count in n-Dimensional Issue Space," *Public Choice* 59: 167-176.

Fiorina, M. and C. R. Plott. 1978. "Committee Decisions Under Majority Rule," *American Political Science Review* 72: 575-98.

Grofman, B., G. Owen, N. Noviello and A. Glazer. 1987. "Stability and Centrality of Legislative Choice in the Spatial Context," *American Political Science Review* 81: 539-552.

Hammond, T. and G. Miller. 1987. "Core of the Constitution," *American Political Science Review* 81: 1155-1174.

Hoffman, E. and C. Plott. 1983. "Pre-meeting Discussions and the Possibility of Coalition-Breaking Procedures in Majority Rule Committees," *Public Choice* 40: 21-39.

Isaac, M. and C. Plott. 1978. "Cooperative Game Models of the Influence of the Closed Rule in Three Person, Majority Rule Committees: Theory and Experiment," in *Game Theory and Political Science*, P. C. Ordeshook, ed. New York: New York University Press.

Laing, J. D. and S. Olmsted. 1978. "An Experimental and Game-Theoretic Study of Committees," in *Game Theory and Political Science, op. cit.*

McKelvey, R. D. 1976. "Intransitivities in Multidimensional Voting Models and Some Implications for Agenda Control," *Journal of Economic Theory* 12: 472-82.

McKelvey, R. D. 1986. "Covering, Dominance and Institution-Free Properties of Social Choice," *American Journal of Political Science* 30: 283-314.

McKelvey, R. D. and P. C. Ordeshook. 1980. "Vote-Trading: An Experimental Study," *Public Choice* 35: 151-184.

McKelvey, R. D. and P. C. Ordeshook. 1981. "Experiments on the Core: Some Disconcerting Results for Majority Rule Voting Games," *Journal of Conflict Resolution* 25: 709-724.

McKelvey, R. D. and P. C. Ordeshook. 1983. "Some Experimental Results That Fail to Support the Competitive Solution," *Public Choice* 40: 281-291.

McKelvey, R. D. and P. C. Ordeshook. 1990. "A Decade of Experimental Research on Spatial Models of Elections and Committees," in *Advances in the Spatial Theory of Voting*, J. M. Enelow and M. J. Hinich, eds. Cambridge: Cambridge University Press.

McKelvey, R. D., P. C. Ordeshook and M. D. Winer. 1978. "The Competitive Solution for N-Person Games Without Transferable Utility, With an Application to Committee Games," *American Political Science Review* 72: 599-615.

McKelvey, R. D. and N. Schofield. 1986. "Structural Instability of the Core," *Journal of Mathematical Economics* 15: 179-198.

Michener, H.A., K. Potter and M. Sakurai. 1983. "On the Predictive Efficiency of the Core Solution in Side-Payment Games," *Theory and Decision* 15: 11-28.

Michener, H.A. and K. Yuen. 1982. "A Competitive Test of the Core Solution in Side-Payment Games," *Behavioral Science* 27: 57-68.

Miller, G. J. and T. Hammond. 1990. "Committees and the Core of the Constitution," *Public Choice* 66: 201-227.

Miller, G. J. and J. A. Oppenheimer. 1982. "Universalism in Experimental Committees," *American Political Science Review* 76: 561-574.

Miller, N. R. 1980. "A New Solution Set for Tournaments and Majority Voting: Further Graph-Theoretical Approaches to the Theory of Voting," *American Journal of Political Science* 24: 68-96.

Ordeshook, P. C. 1986. *Game Theory and Political Theory.* Cambridge: Cambridge University Press.

Ordeshook, P. C. and M. Winer. 1980. "Coalitions and Spatial Policy Outcomes in Parliamentary Systems: Some Experimental Results," *American Journal of Political Science* 24: 730-752.

Plott, C. 1967. "A Notion of Equilibrium and Its Possibilities Under Majority Rule," *American Economic Review* 57: 787-806.

Salant, S. W. and E. Goodstein. 1990. "Predicting Committee Behavior in Majority Rule Voting Experiments," *Rand Journal of Economics* 21: 293-313.

Schelling, T. C. 1960. *The Strategy of Conflict.* London: Oxford University Press.

Schofield, N. 1978. "Instability of Simple Dynamic Games," *Review of Economic Studies* 45: 575-94.

Schofield, N. 1995. "Democratic Stability," in *Explaining Social Institutions*, J. Knight and I. Sened, eds. Ann Arbor: Michigan University Press.

Shepsle, K. 1979. "Institutional Arrangements and Equilibrium in Multidimensional Voting Models," *American Journal of Political Science* 23: 27-59.

Smith, V. L. 1976. "Experimental Economics: Induced Value Theory," *American Economic Review* 66: 274-279.

Tovey, C. 1993. "Some Foundations for Empirical Study in the Euclidean Spatial Model of Social Choice," in *Political Economy: Institutions, Competition and Representation*, W. Barnett, M. J. Hinich and N. Schofield, eds. Cambridge: Cambridge University Press.

Weingast, B. R. 1979. "A Rational Choice Perspective on Congressional Norms," *American Journal of Political Science* 23: 245-63.

Appendix A

Functional Forms for Payoff Values:
Inside Player/Core Design

Sub. No.	Fiorina-Plott (1978), and Hoffman-Plott (1983)	Eavey (1991)
1.	$9.45e^{-.153[(x-39)^2+(y-68)^2]^{\frac{1}{2}}}$	$18 - .19[(x-39)^2 + (y-68)^2]^{\frac{1}{2}}$, for $(x,y): 0 \leq [(x-39)^2+(y-68)^2]^{\frac{1}{2}} \leq 29$ $240e^{-.11[(x-39)^2+(y-68)^2]^{\frac{1}{2}}}$, for $(x,y): 29 < [(x-39)^2+(y-69)^2]^{\frac{1}{2}}$
2.	$27.75 - .102[(x-30)^2+(y-52)^2]^{\frac{1}{2}}$, for $(x,y): 0 \leq [(x-30)^2+(y-52)^2] \leq 12$ $172.5e^{-.169[(x-30)^2+(y-52)^2]^{\frac{1}{2}}}$, for $(x,y): 12 \leq [(x-30)^2+(y-52)^2]^{\frac{1}{2}}$	$17.45 - .15[(x-30)^2+(y-52)^2]^{\frac{1}{2}}$, for $(x,y): 0 \leq [(x-30)^2+(y-52)^2]^{\frac{1}{2}} \leq 37.20$ $520e^{-.11[(x-30)^2+(y-52)^2]^{\frac{1}{2}}}$, for $(x,y): 37.20 < [(x-30)^2+(y-52)^2]^{\frac{1}{2}}$
3.	$25.30 - .141[(x-25)^2+(y-72)^2]^{\frac{1}{2}}$, for $(x,y): 0 \leq [(x-25)^2+(y-72)^2]^{\frac{1}{2}} \leq 8$ $97.02e^{-.165[(x-25)^2+(y-72)^2]^{\frac{1}{2}}}$, for $(x,y): 10 \leq [(x-25)^2+(y-72)^2]^{\frac{1}{2}}$	$15.75 - .05[(x-25)^2+(y-72)^2]^{\frac{1}{2}}$, for $(x,y): 0 \leq [(x-25)^2+(y-72)^2]^{\frac{1}{2}} \leq 39.32$ $55e^{-.05[(x-25)^2+(y-72)^2]^{\frac{1}{2}}}$, for $(x,y): 39.32 < [(x-25)^2+(y-72)^2]^{\frac{1}{2}}$
4.	$38.25 - .1125[(x-62)^2+(y-109)^2]^{\frac{1}{2}}$, for $(x,y): 0 \leq [(x-62)^2+(y-109)^2]^{\frac{1}{2}} \leq 38$ $11931.75e^{-.165[(x-62)^2+(y-109)^2]^{\frac{1}{2}}}$, for $(x,y): 38 \leq [(x-62)^2+(y-109)^2]^{\frac{1}{2}}$	$25.25 - .29[(x-62)^2+(y-109)^2]^{\frac{1}{2}}$, for $(x,y): 0 \leq [(x-62)^2+(y-109)^2]^{\frac{1}{2}} \leq 42.05$ $1200e^{-.12[(x-62)^2+(y-109)^2]^{\frac{1}{2}}}$, for $(x,y): 42.05 < [(x-62)^2+(y-109)^2]^{\frac{1}{2}}$
5.	$26.50 - .05[(x-165)^2+(y-32)^2]^{\frac{1}{2}}$, for $(x,y): 0 \leq [(x-165)^2+(y-32)^2]^{\frac{1}{2}} \leq 122$ $(1.21)10^9 e^{-.145[(x-165)^2+(y-32)^2]^{\frac{1}{2}}}$, for $(x,y): 124 \leq [(x-165)^2+(y-32)^2]^{\frac{1}{2}}$	$19.95 - .05[(x-165)^2+(y-32)^2]^{\frac{1}{2}}$, for $(x,y): 0 \leq [(x-165)^2+(y-32)^2]^{\frac{1}{2}} \leq 107$ $5,000,000e^{-.12[(x-165)^2+(y-32)^2]^{\frac{1}{2}}}$, for $(x,y): 107 < [(x-165)^2+(y-32)^2]^{\frac{1}{2}}$

Appendix B

Functional Forms for Payoff Values:
House and Skew Star Designs

Sub. No.	House	Skew Star
1.	$30.5 - .22[(x-180)^2 + (y-55)^2]^{\frac{1}{2}}$, for $(x,y): 0 \leq [(x-180)^2 + (y-55)^2]^{\frac{1}{2}} \leq 54.5$ $55e^{-.02[(x-180)^2+(y-55)^2]^{\frac{1}{2}}}$, for $(x,y): 54.5 < [(x-180)^2 + (y-55)^2]^{\frac{1}{2}} \leq 80$ $11.10 - .01[(x-190)^2 + (y-55)^2]^{\frac{1}{2}}$, for $(x,y): 80 < [(x-180)^2 + (y-55)^2]^{\frac{1}{2}} \leq 129$ $48,000,000e^{-.12[(x-180)^2+(y-55)^2]^{\frac{1}{2}}}$, for $(x,y): 129 < [(x-180)^2 + (y-55)^2]^{\frac{1}{2}}$	$30.5 - .22[(x-180)^2 + (y-55)^2]^{\frac{1}{2}}$, for $(x,y): 0 \leq [(x-180)^2 + (y-55)^2]^{\frac{1}{2}} \leq 54.5$ $55e^{-.02[(x-180)^2+(y-55)^2]^{\frac{1}{2}}}$, for $(x,y): 54.5 < [(x-180)^2 + (y-55)^2]^{\frac{1}{2}} \leq 80$ $11.10 - .01[(x-180)^2 + (y-55)^2]^{\frac{1}{2}}$, for $(x,y): 80 < [(x-180)^2 + (y-55)^2]^{\frac{1}{2}} \leq 129$ $48,000,000e^{-.12[(x-180)^2+(y-55)^2]^{\frac{1}{2}}}$, for $(x,y): 129 < [(x-180)^2 + (y-55)^2]^{\frac{1}{2}}$
2.	$19.45 - .14[(x-50)^2 + (y-140)^2]^{\frac{1}{2}}$, for $(x,y): 0 \leq [(x-50)^2 + (y-140)^2] \leq 69$ $1200e^{-.07[(x-50)^2+(y-140)^2]^{\frac{1}{2}}}$, for $(x,y): 69 < [(x-50)^2 + (y-140)^2]^{\frac{1}{2}}$	$19.45 - .14[(x-50)^2 + (y-140)^2]^{\frac{1}{2}}$, for $(x,y): 0 \leq [(x-50)^2 + (y-140)^2]^{\frac{1}{2}} \leq 69$ $1200e^{-.07[(x-50)^2+(y-140)^2]^{\frac{1}{2}}}$, for $(x,y): 69 < [(x-50)^2 + (y-140)^2]^{\frac{1}{2}}$
3.	$18.10 - .12[(x-20)^2 + (y-30)^2]^{\frac{1}{2}}$, for $(x,y): 0 \leq [(x-20)^2 + (y-30)^2]^{\frac{1}{2}} \leq 64$ $1500e^{-.08[(x-20)^2+(y-30)^2]^{\frac{1}{2}}}$, for $(x,y): 64 < [(x-20)^2 + (y-30)^2]^{\frac{1}{2}}$	$18.10 - .12[(x-20)^2 + (y-30)^2]^{\frac{1}{2}}$, for $(x,y): 0 \leq [(x-20)^2 + (y-30)^2]^{\frac{1}{2}} \leq 64$ $1500e^{-.08[(x-20)^2+(y-30)^2]^{\frac{1}{2}}}$, for $(x,y): 64 < [(x-20)^2 + (y-30)^2]^{\frac{1}{2}}$
4.	$24.95 - .14[(x-130)^2 + (y-10)^2]^{\frac{1}{2}}$, for $(x,y): 0 \leq [(x-130)^2 + (y-10)^2]^{\frac{1}{2}} \leq 54$ $150e^{-.04[(x-130)^2+(y-10)^2]^{\frac{1}{2}}}$, for $(x,y): 54 < [(x-130)^2 + (y-10)^2]^{\frac{1}{2}} \leq 65$ $11.14 - .01[(x-130)^2 + (y-10)^2]^{\frac{1}{2}}$, for $(x,y): 65 < [(x-130)^2 + (y-10)^2]^{\frac{1}{2}} \leq 100$ $1450e^{.05[(x-130)^2+(y-10)^2]^{\frac{1}{2}}}$, for $(x,y): 100 < [(x-130)^2 + (y-10)^2]^{\frac{1}{2}}$	$24.95 - .14[(x-130)^2 + (y-10)^2]^{\frac{1}{2}}$, for $(x,y): 0 \leq [(x-130)^2 + (y-10)^2]^{\frac{1}{2}} \leq 54$ $150e^{-.04[(x-130)^2+(y-10)^2]^{\frac{1}{2}}}$, for $(x,y): 54 < [(x-130)^2 + (y-10)^2]^{\frac{1}{2}} \leq 65$ $11.14 - .01[(x-130)^2 + (y-10)^2]^{\frac{1}{2}}$, for $(x,y): 65 < [(x-130)^2 + (y-10)^2]^{\frac{1}{2}} \leq 100$ $1450e^{-.05[(x-130)^2+(y-10)^2]^{\frac{1}{2}}}$, for $(x,y): 100 < [(x-130)^2 + (y-10)^2]^{\frac{1}{2}}$
5.	$26.3 - .09[(x-160)^2 + (y-120)^2]^{\frac{1}{2}}$, for $(x,y): 0 \leq [(x-160)^2 + (y-120)^2]^{\frac{1}{2}} \leq 54$ $60e^{-.02[(x-160)^2+(y-120)^2]^{\frac{1}{2}}}$, for $(x,y): 54 < [(x-160)^2 + (y-120)^2]^{\frac{1}{2}} \leq 80$ $12.11 - .01[(x-160)^2 + (y-120)^2]^{\frac{1}{2}}$, for $(x,y): 80 < [(x-160)^2 + (y-120)^2]^{\frac{1}{2}} \leq 114$ $8.775E10e^{-.2[(x-160)^2+(y-120)^2]^{\frac{1}{2}}}$, for $(x,y): 114 < [(x-160)^2 + (y-120)^2]^{\frac{1}{2}}$	$26.3 - .13[(x-160)^2 + (y-20)^2]^{\frac{1}{2}}$ $(x,y): 0 \leq [(x-160)^2 + (y-20)^2]^{\frac{1}{2}} \leq 50$ $23.7 - .08[(x-160)^2 + (y-20)^2]^{\frac{1}{2}}$, for $(x,y): 50 < [(x-160)^2 + (y-20)^2]^{\frac{1}{2}} \leq 54.9$ $100e^{-.03[(x-160)^2+(y-20)^2]^{\frac{1}{2}}}$, for $(x,y): 54.9 < [(x-160)^2 + (y-20)^2]^{\frac{1}{2}} \leq 70$ $12.25 - .018[(x-160)^2 + (y-20)^2]^{\frac{1}{2}}$, for $(x,y): 70 < [(x-160)^2 + (y-20)^2]^{\frac{1}{2}} \leq 119$ $(16,000,000e)^{-.12[(x-160)^2+(y-20)^2]^{\frac{1}{2}}}$, for $(x,y): 119 < [(x-160)^2 + (y-20)^2]^{\frac{1}{2}}$

8. The Heart of a Polity

Norman Schofield [1]

8.1 Rational Choice Models of Electoral Politics

Arrovian classification results applied to voting theory have created a serious obstacle to constructing a rational choice theory of representative politics. A natural framework within which to work is one where the electorate has preferences that can be described in terms of a domain X, called the policy space, representing the possible creation and distribution of public goods in the political economy. In the most general context X would be a manifold described by a transformation possibility frontier between the private goods economy and the "public goods" economy.

Significant work has been done (Denzau and Parks 1983) to show the existence of a joint political economy equilibrium. Here the task was to show that the conditions for a general equilibrium in the economic domain were compatible with existence of a political equilibrium in the polity. It was known that as long as the political domain, X, was one-dimensional, then there would exist a political equilibrium (at the "median" voter position). If all political competition were fundamentally one-dimensional (based on a left-right dimension, say, or characterized by tax-rates) then a combined political economy equilibrium would exist. Moreover the political equilibrium could be found by "binary Downsian competition" between two office-seeking parties competing against each other to secure a majority of the votes (Downs 1957).

Unfortunately for this model, results by Plott (1967), Kramer (1973), McKelvey (1976), Schofield (1978, 1983) and finally McKelvey and Schofield (1986, 1987) showed that any democratic voting rule is generically unstable as long as the dimension is sufficiently high. "Generically" refers to an open dense set of profiles in a topological space of all smooth, utility profiles on the manifold X (full definitions of this term and related concepts can be found in Section 8.2). For example if majority rule is used, and the society has an odd number of voters, and if an equilibrium (or majority "core") exists in two dimensions, then it will disappear under the slightest perturbation of the utility profile. In three dimensions endless cycling both within and outside the Pareto set is almost always possible. Initially it was thought that the result was an artefact of the mathematical model used, in the sense that "generic" referred to utilities rather than preferences, and that the instability resulted from the introduction of non-convex perturbations. However this "voting paradox" has been shown to be "generic" in a topological space of smooth preferences, and even of convex preferences, when X is a vector space (Schofield 1995a).

---
[1] This chapter is based on work supported by NSF Grants SBR-8808405/9422548.

These results are, however, only applicable to models of *direct democracy* or "committees," where no political representation is involved. We cannot draw any immediate inferences about the behaviour of representative democracies in general.

Over two decades of research on studying rational choice models of representative democracy have given us some understanding of the relationship between the type of assumptions made and the possibility of political equilibrium. Results are somewhat different depending on whether or not electoral risk is assumed. If there are two political agents simply competing for votes in a situation where they are unsure of the electoral response, then there will generally be a Nash equilibrium in the sense that there are "best" positions to pick that maximize the candidates' expected vote totals, given their beliefs (see Hinich and Ordeshook 1970; Enelow and Hinich 1984; Coughlin 1992 for full details of the "binary Downsian model of electoral politics"). Even if these agents have policy preferences, then one might expect an equilibrium (Cox 1984a). However, in the second case there is a problem of "credible commitment" (see Section 8.4). Why should voters trust these political agents?

In response perhaps to experimental evidence, reviewed in McKelvey and Ordeshook (1990), that committee voting is not unstable in two dimensions, considerable research effort has been devoted to the notion of the *uncovered set* (Miller 1980; McKelvey 1986). This set always belongs to the Pareto set of the voters, and converges to the voting core (if one exists). See Cox (1987) and the discussion in Section 8.2. Two justifications for the uncovered set have been given: (*a*) if two vote-maximizing parties compete against each other, then arguments can be made why they would converge to the uncovered set; (*b*) in large "committees" such as Congress, where voting is not entirely governed by party discipline, certain kinds of sophisticated voting behavior by representatives in response to "amendment procedures" can lead into the uncovered set (Shepsle and Weingast 1984). With respect to (*b*) it has been observed (Ordeshook and Schwartz 1987) that most amendment procedures (particularly those generally used in Congress) do not have the required property. This observation has somewhat weakened the justification for using the uncovered set as an equilibrium notion.

My intention here is to present an outline of an integrated theory of multiparty competition (where "multi" means at least three). Unfortunately the uncovered set cannot be used directly since this set depends for its definition on the underlying preference relation obtained from the voting rule. Since coalitions are the "agents" in a multiparty system, an appropriate equilibrium notion must be based on behavior by coalitions. In Section 8.2 I define an equilibrium notion called the *heart*. It is Paretian and satisfies a continuity property (called lower hemi-continuity) that implies convergence to the core. Section 8.3 gives a number of illustrations and empirical examples of the heart, to justify the argument that this notion captures the essence of political bargaining in a situation where parties are concerned about policy.

Section 8.4 reviews models of two party competition and argue that a direct generalization to a vote or seat-maximization model is implausible in the multi-party case. Instead I argue that a natural model is one where parties compete with each other by presenting *manifestos* to the electorate. These manifestos have a dual purpose. In the period prior to the election, they give the electorate a basis for evaluating the parties. I assume implicitly that each profile of manifestos ($z = (z_1, \ldots, z_n)$ in the case of n parties) gives rise to a response by the electorate that can be described in one of two ways. If there is no electoral uncertainty, then the "electoral map" gives an allocation $e(z) = (e_1(z), \ldots, e_n(z))$, specifying the shares of the seats to the parties. This generates a "political heart", written $\mathcal{HD}(z)$, defined by the set of winning coalitions. (That is, $\mathcal{D}(z)$ consists of those coalitions that win once the seat shares, $e(z)$, are known.) After the election, bargaining then takes place between the parties within the heart. Section 8.5 analyzes a particularly simple version of this model, when there are only three parties and $\mathcal{D}(z)$ is fixed. In this simple model, the parties need not consider electoral response in choosing their manifestos. However, the model assumes that they will be committed to these declarations and analyses the relationship between their choices of manifestos and their likely coalition partners. The probabilities that various coalitions form are described by a vector, $\rho(z)$, defined by the profile of declarations. Schofield and Parks (1993) have shown that there is a pure strategy Nash equilibrium in this game. The expectation of the equilibrium outcome, across the three possible coalition governments, belongs to the Pareto set of the three parties. Finally, Section 8.6 suggests how to incorporate the electoral connection. With electoral risk, the response of the electorate is described by a list of probabilities $\xi(z) = (\ldots, \xi_t(z)), \ldots)$, where $\xi_t(z)$ is the probability that a coalition structure, $\mathcal{D}_t$, occurs, given the declaration, z, of manifestos. The assumption here is that the number of seats won by each party is less important than the post-election set of winning coalitions. Again the parties assume that they are committed to their declarations. With a joint choice, z, each party calculates the probability $\xi_t(z)$ that $\mathcal{D}_t$ occurs, and evaluates this state of the world using a "policy" selection g_t of the heart. More generally, the overall outcome $g(z)$ is described by a game form g_ξ which specifies how coalitions form and what perquisites are allocated to members. A von Neumann-Morgenstern utility function is used by each party to evaluate z.

The notion of a Nash equilibrium for such a game can be developed. It is conjectured that, under general conditions, a pure strategy Nash equilibrium exists. It is hoped that later research will substantiate this conjecture and demonstrate the nature of the relationship between the political equilibrium and the electoral distribution of preferences.

8.2 The Voting Paradox, the Uncovered Set, and the Heart in a Committee

Arrow's Theorem (1951) and later research showed that *any* social choice mechanism, σ, can be "badly behaved" whenever it satisfies minimal democratic principles. The result should, properly speaking, be viewed as a classification theorem, since the large class of results that have been obtained make fairly clear the relationship between the assumptions on σ and its properties. To some extent the theorem creates formidable theoretical difficulties for the development of a discipline of political economy founded on a rational choice model of human behavior. To understand these difficulties it is worthwhile reviewing the structure of the classification theorem.

The primitive in *discrete* social choice theory is an array or *profile* of individual preferences $P = (P_1, \ldots, P_n)$ on a set of alternatives, X. Social preference $\sigma(P)$ is simply a social ordering determined by P and the normative properties imposed on σ. A key property of $\sigma(P)$ is that there exists some non-empty choice set, or "core," $E(\sigma(P))$, of outcomes unbeaten under $\sigma(P)$. Moreover the choice should belong to the Pareto set of the preference profile. If P_N is the unanimity preference relation, then $E(P_N)$ stands for the Pareto set. A sufficient condition for a non-empty choice set is that $\sigma(P)$ always be acyclic. That is, it is impossible for there to exist a cycle of the form $x_1 \sigma(P) x_2 \sigma(P) \ldots x_n \sigma(P) x_1$. Any social choice mechanism σ gives rise to a class of coalitions, called $\mathcal{D}_\sigma$, that are decisive under σ. In other words, if all members of a decisive coalition agree, then it can control an outcome. $\mathcal{D}_\sigma$ is called *collegial* if some set of individuals belongs to every coalition in $\mathcal{D}_\sigma$. This set of individuals is called the *collegium* of $\mathcal{D}_\sigma$. An individual in the collegium is also called a *vetoer*. If no vetoer exists, then $\mathcal{D}_\sigma$ is called non-collegial. When $\mathcal{D}_\sigma$ is non-collegial, it is *classified* by an integer $k = k(\sigma)$ called the Nakamura number (1979). This integer is simply the cardinality of the smallest subfamily of $\mathcal{D}_\sigma$ which is non-collegial. In other words if we take $(k-1)$ different coalitions from $\mathcal{D}_\sigma$, then they have a member in common. (For majority rule, in general, $k = 3$. However for the $\frac{3}{4}$-rule, k is clearly 4.)

If σ has a non-collegial family $\mathcal{D}_\sigma$ of decisive coalitions, then it is always possible to find a profile P such that $\sigma(P)$ is cyclic. While this does not necessarily imply that the choice set $E(\sigma(P))$ is empty, it does mean that there is no general reason for presuming that the choice exists. A further point to note is that any cycle that exists will involve at least k different alternatives. For example if σ is a majority voting rule, then the Nakamura number is generally three. Thus a voting rule will, in general, be well-behaved if (and only if, in some sense) there are not more than two alternatives.

For the case of a voting rule σ, defined entirely by a class of coalitions $\mathcal{D}$, we now write $P_\mathcal{D}$ for the social preference induced by σ on the profile P. It is notationally clearer to regard $P_\mathcal{D}$ as a function $P_\mathcal{D} : X \longrightarrow 2(X)$ from X to the power set $2(X)$ (*i.e.*, all subsets of X). Thus $y \in P_\mathcal{D}(x)$ iff there exists some $M \in \mathcal{D}$ such that y is preferred to x by all members of M. Another way of writing this is that $P_\mathcal{D} = \cup \{P_M : M \in \mathcal{D}\}$ where P_M is the preference for coalition M. We write $k(\mathcal{D})$ for the Nakamura number of the rule, $\mathcal{D}$. The set $E(P_\mathcal{D})$ is usually called the *core* of the voting rule $\mathcal{D}$ at the profile P.

The first classification result states that if there are at least $k(\mathcal{D})$ alternatives, then it is possible to construct a profile, P, on these alternatives such that $E(P_\mathcal{D})$ is empty. Attempts to examine the frequency of the voting paradox were obliged to make ad-hoc assumptions on the relative frequencies of different preferences. The Arrovian classification theorem in this form does not give cause for concern for the development of a formal political economy, since it could easily be the case that no real society exhibits the particular preference profile required to construct social preference cycles. However one aspect of the theorem due to Gibbard (1973) and Satterthwaite (1975) suggested that social choice mechanisms would either be dictatorial or "manipulable" if preferences were "rich enough". The natural question then was: how rich does the domain of preferences have to be for Arrow's theorem to be relevant?

To put some structure on preferences it is natural to let X be a convex topological (vector) space. In this case we may require continuity and convexity properties on preference, before determining whether well-behaved social preference can be constructed. In this "category" of continuous convex preference, an Arrovian classification result again obtains. In this case the voting rule $\mathcal{D}$ will always exhibit an equilibrium, $E(P_\mathcal{D})$, as long as the dimension of the space, X, is no greater than $k(\mathcal{D}) - 2$ (see Greenberg 1979; Schofield 1984; Strnad 1985). On the other hand if the dimension of X is at least $k(\mathcal{D}) - 1$ then a continuous, convex profile, P, can be found such that $E(P_\mathcal{D})$ is empty and $P_\mathcal{D}$ cycles. Again this is a possibility theorem–a profile P can be *found* which generates cycles.

Rubinstein (1979), Cox (1984b), and Le Breton (1987) all attempted to answer the question "how often will $P_\mathcal{D}$ cycle"? A natural way to answer this question is to put a topology on the set $P(X)^N$ of profiles $P = \{P_1, \ldots, P_n\}$ for the society N. This can be done by considering the graph of a preference P_i and defining an ϵ-neighborhood, $V_\epsilon(P_i)$, to consist of all preferences whose graphs are within ϵ (in the so-called Hausdorff metric) of the graph of P_i. The set of preference profiles $P(X)^N$ is then given the product topology. Call this the *Hausdorff* topology on preference profiles.

A set V in $P(X)^N$ is *dense* iff for any profile, P, not in V, then any open neighborhood of P intersects V. In general a property ψ of profiles is *generic* with respect to a topology if it is true for an open dense set of profiles (in this topology). Rubinstein (1979), Cox (1984b), and Le Breton (1987) have shown essentially that the property $\psi = \{E(P_\mathcal{D}) = \emptyset\}$ is *generic* in this topological space $P(X)^N$, endowed with the Hausdorff topology.

Notice that there is no dimension constraint in this result. The apparent contradiction between the results of Greenberg, *et al.* and Rubinstein, *et al.* is because of the possibility of non-convex preference. Even though P is a convex profile, P, exhibiting a choice $E(P_\mathcal{D})$, there will exist a profile P' in any ε-neighborhood of P in the Hausdorff topology, but involving non-convex preferences, such that $E(P'_\mathcal{D})$ is empty.

The problem with the Hausdorff topology is that it is coarse in the sense that its open sets are "large". It is possible that, for a finer topology on $P(X)^N$, with more open sets, the set of profiles $\{P : E(P_\mathcal{D}) = \emptyset\}$ would not be open-dense. Then the property $\psi = \{E(P_\mathcal{D}) = \emptyset\}$ need not be generic with respect to the finer topology.

Results relevant to this concern were obtained by McKelvey (1976), Schofield (1978), and McKelvey and Schofield (1986, 1987). Consider now the set of smooth utility profiles, $U(W)^N$, endowed with the Whitney topology. In this topology two utilities are close if their values and all gradients are close. Then the instability aspect of the *classification theorem*, is that for any non-collegial rule $\mathcal{D}$, there exists an integer $w(\mathcal{D})$ satisfying $k(\mathcal{D}) - 1 \leq w(\mathcal{D})$, which also classifies σ and $\mathcal{D}$ in the following sense. If the dimension of X (namely $dim(X)$) is at least $w(\mathcal{D})$, then the property $\{E(P_{\mathcal{D}}(u)) = \emptyset\}$ is *generic*, in the Whitney topology $U(W)^N$. Here $P_{\mathcal{D}}(u)$ is the preference relation defined by the rule, $\mathcal{D}$, using the preference profile $P(u)$ induced, in the obvious way, from the utility profile, u. Properly speaking, $dim(X) \geq w(\mathcal{D})$ is sufficient for generic emptiness of the core in the interior of X, while $dim(X) \geq w(\mathcal{D}) + 1$ guarantees generic emptiness of the core in the boundary of X. Moreover, the property that cycles go almost everywhere in X is also generic if the dimension is at least $w(\mathcal{D}) + 1$. These two properties are together called the *generic voting paradox* for smooth utilities. Note that if $\mathcal{D}$ is majority rule, then $w(\mathcal{D}) = 2$ or 3 depending on whether n is odd or even (Schofield 1983). Saari (1995) has recently obtained a tight bound for $w(\mathcal{D}_q)$ in the case of a q-rule, $\mathcal{D}_q$, where $\mathcal{D}_q$ contains all coalitions of size q and above. In particular, he shows that if $dim(X) \leq w(\mathcal{D}_q) - 1$, then $\{u : E(P_{\mathcal{D}}(u)) \neq \emptyset\}$ contains an open set in $U(W)^N$. These results on the generic voting paradox for utilities imply a similar result for smooth preferences. Let $W(X)^N$ be the space of all smooth utility profiles whose components have isolated, non-degenerate critical points. Then there is a natural operation $P : W(X)^N \longrightarrow \mathcal{T}(X)^N \subset P(X)^N$, where $\mathcal{T}(X)^N$ is the space of preferences obtained from such utilities (endowed with a topology induced from $U(X)^N$). As before if u is a utility profile, then $P(u)$ is the appropriate preference profile. It has recently been shown (Schofield 1995a,b) that the classification result involving $w(\mathcal{D})$ is generic in the topological space $\mathcal{T}(X)^N$. In other words the set of smooth preference profiles

$$\{P(u) \in \mathcal{T}(X)^N : E(P_{\mathcal{D}}(u)) = \emptyset\}$$

is open dense as long as $dim(X) \geq w(\mathcal{D})$. Moreover, generically, $P_{\mathcal{D}}(u)$-cycles can go almost anywhere. An important feature of this result is that the topology used on $\mathcal{T}(X)^N$ makes use of information encoded in the gradients of the underlying utility representation. For this reason we call this the C^1-topology on $\mathcal{T}(X)^N$ and write $\mathcal{T}_1(X)^N$ when this topology is used. "C^1" refers to "continuous first differentials". If gradient information is not used, then the topology is based on the C^O-topology for smooth utilities, and in this case we write $\mathcal{T}_O(X)^N$. Again C^O means continuous, but without reference to the values of differentials. The Hausdorff topology, discussed previously, is equivalent to the use of $\mathcal{T}_O(X)^N$. It can be shown that the Rubinstein-Cox-Le Breton result is not true in the "finer" topology $\mathcal{T}_1(X)^N$, without a dimension constraint (Schofield 1995a). One case that is useful to analyse is when preferences are Euclidean. In this case the two topologies, $\mathcal{T}_O(X)^N$ and $\mathcal{T}_1(X)^N$ are identical. We say a preference P_i is *Euclidean* on X (where the vector space, X, is endowed with a Euclidean metric $\| \ \|$) iff there exists some "bliss" point x_i such that

$$y \in P_i(x) \text{ iff } \| y - x_i \| < \| x - x_i \|.$$

Such preferences are used frequently in spatial voting theory because they have a simple geometric structure. Indeed there is a more profound reason for considering preferences of this kind. If P_i has a bliss point at x_i, then any utility function u_i which represents the preference P_i has a gradient $du_i(x)$ at x which is a function of the vector $(x_i - x)$. Consequently if u_i and u'_i are "Euclidean" utility functions which have bliss points, x_i and x'_i, which are close, then u_i and u'_i will also be close in the C^1-topology. Thus the C^0- and C^1-topologies are identical (homeomorphic) in the case of Euclidean preferences.

Consequently, the space of Euclidean preferences with the C^1-topology can be identified with the product space $X^N = \Pi_{i=1}^n X_i$, where each X_i is a copy of X and X^N has the Euclidean topology. It follows, from the generic voting paradox for utilities, that in a topolgical space of Euclidean preferences, $\{P \in X^N : E(P_\mathcal{D}) = \emptyset\}$ is open dense as long as $dim(X) \geq w(\mathcal{D})$, for $\mathcal{D}$ non-collegial. In other words, the classification of $P_\mathcal{D}$ for smooth utilities implies a similar classification for Euclidean preferences. As a consequence, the space, X^N, of such profiles can be viewed as a *model* for $T(X)^N$.

A corollary of this is that if it is possible to "solve" the generic voting paradox in X^N, then it is possible to solve it in $U(X)^N$. In light of the above discussion, the Rubinstein–Cox–Le Breton result is not valid for Euclidean preferences, without the dimension constraint given by $w(\mathcal{D})$. Consequently the voting paradox does not occur for the rule, $\mathcal{D}$, in dimension below $k(\mathcal{D})-2$. The problem only becomes relevant in dimension $w(\mathcal{D})$ or above.

In an effort to solve the voting paradox, a number of authors have developed the notion of the *uncovered set* (Miller 1980; Shepsle and Weingast 1984; McKelvey 1986). Let $P : X \longrightarrow 2(X)$ be a preference correspondence on X, representing the social preference. Define the *covering correspondence*, $\overline{P}$ of P by $\overline{P} : X \longrightarrow 2(X)$ where $y \in \overline{P}(x)$ iff $y \in P(x)$ and $P(y) \subset P(x)$. The uncovered set, $\overline{E}(P)$, of the correspondence P is $\overline{E}(P) = \{x \in X : \overline{P}(x) = \emptyset\}$. Because of the set inclusion, $\overline{P}$ will be acyclic. If X is compact and $\overline{P}$ is "continuous" then $\overline{E}(P)$ will be non-empty. (Bordes, *et al.* 1992).

Cox (1987) has shown that the uncovered set satisfies three crucial properties. Suppose $\mathcal{D}$ is the majority voting rule with n odd. Let P be a Euclidean preference profile (actually the following result is valid if each P_i is obtained from "quasi-concave" utility functions, u_i with single bliss point x_i).

The uncovered set at the profile P, for majority rule, $\mathcal{D}$, is $\overline{E}_\mathcal{D}(P) = E(\overline{P}_\mathcal{D}) = \{x \in X : \overline{P}_\mathcal{D}(x) = \emptyset\}$. Then $\overline{E}_\mathcal{D}$ is

1. non-empty and "Paretian" : $\emptyset \neq \overline{E}_\mathcal{D}(P) \subset E(P_N)$;

2. "core-like" : if $E(P_\mathcal{D}) \neq \emptyset$, then $\overline{E}_\mathcal{D}(P) = E(P_\mathcal{D})$;

3. "convergent to the core" : if $P \longrightarrow P'$ and $E(P'_\mathcal{D}) \neq \emptyset$ then $\lim_{P \to P'} \overline{E}_\mathcal{D}(P) = E(P'_\mathcal{D})$.

Actually Cox proved a weaker version of (3), namely convergence (in terms of bliss points) to a point core. The convergence property (3) would follow from (2) and the "lower hemi-continuity" of the correspondence $\overline{E}_\mathcal{D}$.

A correspondence $\mathcal{H}$ between two topological spaces X, Y is lower hemi-continuous (*lhc*) iff for any open set V in Y, the set $\{x \in X : \mathcal{H}(x) \cap V \neq \emptyset\}$ is open in X. From *lhc*, if $x_n \longrightarrow x$ in X, then $\mathcal{H}(x_n) \longrightarrow \mathcal{H}(x)$ in Y. I now wish to propose an alternative equilibrium notion to $\overline{E}_\mathcal{D}$ which satisfies (1), (2) and *lhc* (and thus (3)). Although the definition is given in terms of Euclidean preferences, all the results are valid for more general "convex" preferences derived from smooth quasi-concave utilities (see Schofield 1995b). Moreover the definitions and results are valid for any voting rule, $\mathcal{D}$.

The key to constructing the covering correspondence $\overline{P}$ is that $\overline{P}$ is a sub-correspondence or "reduction" of P in the sense that $y \in \overline{P}(x) \implies y \in P(x)$. However if $y \in P(x)$ but $P(y) \not\subset P(x)$ then $y \notin \overline{P}(x)$.

We proceed in a similar way to reduce $P_\mathcal{D}(x)$. Note that $y \in P_\mathcal{D}(x)$ iff $y \in P_M(x)$ for some M in $\mathcal{D}$. So $P_\mathcal{D} = \cup \{P_M : M \in \mathcal{D}\}$. Consider a single coalition M. It is impossible to reduce P_M in the above way because if $y \in P_M(x)$ and $z \in P_M(y)$, then by transitivity of individual preference, $z \in P_M(x)$. So $\overline{P}_M = P_M$. However we can construct a reduction $\tilde{P}_M$ of P_M called the *efficient* preference for the coalition. Suppose that $y \in P_M(x)$ for some y, x. Suppose further that there exists no point $z \in X$ with $z \in P_M(y)$ and $\| z - x \| = \| y - x \|$. Then define $y \in \tilde{P}_M(x)$. On the other hand if $\exists z \in X$, with $z \in P_M(y)$ and $\| z - x \| = \| y - x \|$ then $y \notin \tilde{P}_M(x)$.

Figure 1(a) illustrates the definition in the case when $M = \{1, 2\}$ and the individuals have Euclidean preferences. The spherical indifference curves for $\{1, 2\}$ through x are labelled I_1, I_2. Let $P = P_{\{1,2\}}$ and $\tilde{P} = \tilde{P}_{\{1,2\}}$. Now $y_3 \in P(x)$. However $y_2 \in P(y_3)$ and y_2, y_3 are on the sphere $S = S(x : \| y - x \|)$ with center x and radius $\| y - x \|$. Thus $y_3 \notin \tilde{P}(x)$. Notice that y_1, y_2 both lie in S. However 2 prefers y_2 to y_1 while 1 prefers y_1 to y_2. Clearly all points on the arc in S between y_1 and y_2 belong to $\tilde{P}(x)$.

The same argument holds in Figure 1(b). Here $y_3 \notin \tilde{P}(x)$ because $y_3 \notin P(x)$, while 1 and 2 disagree over their preferences for y_1 and y_2.

In Figure 1(a) the preference for y_3 over x is "inefficient" in some sense. A more abstract argument can be made for eliminating points such as y_3 from $P(x)$, but the formalism requires the idea of preference cones. See Austen-Smith (Chapter 9 of this volume) for the technical definitions. The general idea is simply that, since Euclidean preference is denominated in distance, it is appropriate for coalitions, choosing to move from x, to compare like with like, namely points such as $\{y_1, y_2, y_3\}$ equidistant from x. Now define

$$\tilde{P}_\mathcal{D} = \cup \{\tilde{P}_M : M \in \mathcal{D}\}$$

by $y \in \tilde{P}_\mathcal{D}(x)$ iff $y \in \tilde{P}_M(x)$ for some M belonging to $\mathcal{D}$. $\tilde{P}_\mathcal{D}$ is the *efficient* preference for the rule $\mathcal{D}$ at the profile P. It can be shown (Schofield 1995b) that $P_\mathcal{D}(x) = \emptyset$ iff $\tilde{P}_\mathcal{D}(x) = \emptyset$, for any "convex" preference profile, P. Thus $E(P_\mathcal{D}) = E(\tilde{P}_\mathcal{D})$. Consequently if the core for $P_\mathcal{D}$ exists then so does $E(\tilde{P}_\mathcal{D})$. What happens if $E(P_\mathcal{D}) = \emptyset$?

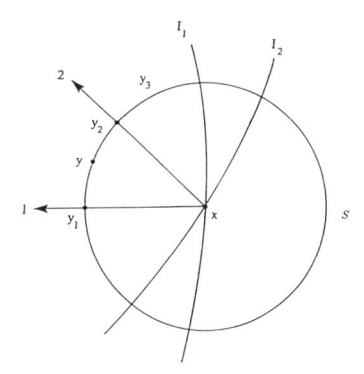

Figure 1(a)

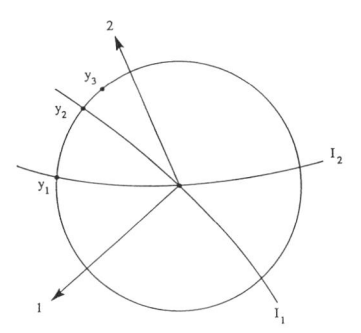

Figure 1(b)

Define $\Gamma(\tilde{P}_\mathcal{D})$ in the following way: $x \in \Gamma(\tilde{P}_\mathcal{D})$ iff $\exists$ at least three vectors $\{v_i : i = 1, 2, 3\}$ such that each $v_i \in \tilde{P}_\mathcal{D}(x)$ and

$$x = \sum_{i=1}^{n} \lambda_i v_i,$$

where $\lambda_i \geq 0$, but not all are zero.

From previous results (Schofield 1984) it is known that if $\Gamma(\tilde{P}_\mathcal{D}) = \emptyset$, then $E(\tilde{P}_\mathcal{D}) \neq \emptyset$, whenever X is a compact convex set. (In fact, for a Euclidean profile, the emptiness of Γ is a necessary and sufficient condition for non emptiness of E.) Now define the *heart*, $\mathcal{H}_\mathcal{D}$ for the profile, P, and rule, $\mathcal{D}$, by $\mathcal{H}_\mathcal{D}(P) = E(\tilde{P}_\mathcal{D}) \cup \text{clos } \Gamma(\tilde{P}_\mathcal{D})$.

(For technical reasons it is necessary to ensure $\mathcal{H}_\mathcal{D}(P)$ is closed, and clos just means take the closure.) It then follows (Schofield 1993a, 1995b) that $\mathcal{H}_\mathcal{D}$ is:

1. non-empty and Paretian : $\emptyset \neq \mathcal{H}_\mathcal{D}(P) \subset E(P_N)$;

2. core-like : if $E(P_\mathcal{D}) \neq \emptyset$ then $\mathcal{H}_\mathcal{D}(P) = E(P_\mathcal{D})$;

3. lower hemi-continuous.

If we identify a Euclidean preference profile P by the list of bliss points, $\{x_1, \ldots, x_n\}$ then $\mathcal{H}_\mathcal{D}$ is a closed correspondence $\mathcal{H}_\mathcal{D} : X^N \longrightarrow 2(X)$.

Because $\mathcal{H}_\mathcal{D}$ is lower hemi-continuous, if the sequence $\{P_k = (x_{1k}, \ldots, x_{nk})\}$ converges to $P' = (x'_1, \ldots, x'_n)$ and the profile P' has a core, then $\mathcal{H}_\mathcal{D}(P_k)$ also converges to this core.

It is known from previous results that cycles may occur under $\tilde{P}_\mathcal{D}$, but in a certain sense they can occur only within $\Gamma(\tilde{P}_\mathcal{D})$. If we modify $\tilde{P}_\mathcal{D}$ to a subpreference $P_\mathcal{D}^*$ of $\tilde{P}_\mathcal{D}$ in the following way, then no cycles can occur.

Define $P_\mathcal{D}^*$ by $y \in P_\mathcal{D}^*(x)$ iff $y \in \tilde{P}_\mathcal{D}(x)$ and $y \notin \mathcal{H}_\mathcal{D}(P)$. Then it can be shown that, for any point $x_0 \notin \mathcal{H}_\mathcal{D}(P)$ and any sequence $\{x_1, \ldots, x_r\}$ with $x_k \in P_\mathcal{D}^*(x_{k-1})$ for $k = 1, \ldots, r$, then the distance between x_r and $\mathcal{H}_\mathcal{D}(P)$ is strictly less than the distance from x_0 to $\mathcal{H}_\mathcal{D}(P)$. Thus $P_\mathcal{D}^*$ converges to the heart. That is to say, $\mathcal{H}_\mathcal{D}(P)$ is an "attractor" for the preference correspondence $P_\mathcal{D}^*$. (It should also be emphasized that it is assumed in this model that $P_\mathcal{D}^*$ is based on continuous "preference paths". See Schofield (1978) for the original definition.)

We have now constructed a preference correspondence $P_\mathcal{D}^*$ that is a subpreference of both the efficient preference $\tilde{P}_\mathcal{D}$ and the social preference $P_\mathcal{D}$. Further $P_\mathcal{D}^*$ exhibits no cycles and it converges to the heart, (a subset of the Pareto set). Indeed if the core is non-empty, then it converges to the core. The preference $P_\mathcal{D}^*$ has all the desirable properties of the covering correspondence but more importantly it is based on "efficient" behavior by coalitions.

I conjecture that the correspondence $\mathcal{P}_\mathcal{D}^*$ is a sub-correspondence of the covering correspondence, that is $P_\mathcal{D}^*(x) \subset \overline{P}_\mathcal{D}(x)$ for all x, (at least in the case of Euclidean preferences). More precisely if $x \notin \mathcal{H}_\mathcal{D}(P)$ so that $y \in P_\mathcal{D}^*(x)$ for some $y \in X$, then it is easy to show that for any neighborhood V of x there exists $y' \in V$ such that $y' \in P_\mathcal{D}^*(x)$. Moreover y' also covers x. Thus $P_\mathcal{D}^*$ is a "localization" of the covering relation. It appears therefore that $\mathcal{H}_\mathcal{D}(P)$ can be interpreted as the set of points that are locally uncovered. The advantage of this equilibrium notion is that determining whether a point lies in the heart or not is a local problem. Determining whether a point lies in the uncovered set is a global problem and almost impossible to solve when $n > 3$. It should be noted that the heart is formally defined for a situation where each individual, i, in the voting procedure has well-defined preferences on the space, X. This means that the concept is formally appropriate only for spatial models of direct democracy, or of a *committee*.

However it has been traditional in examining coalition bargaining in multiparty situations to suppose that parties do have well-defined policy preferences. Section 8.3 assumes that parties do indeed have "spatial" or policy preferences and uses the heart to analyse the outcomes of coalition negotiation.

8.3   The Heart in Multiparty Politics

To illustrate the concept of the heart, consider Figure 2 which presents estimates of party position of the five parties in Sweden in 1976 for a two-dimensional policy space, X. The spatial map is drawn from my own factor

Norman Schofield   193

analysis of data made available by Holmstedt and Schou (1987). The left-right dimension concerns economic policy, while the north-south dimension is defined by non-economic welfare concerns. With 349 seats, a majority is 175. Because the space of Euclidean profiles is a model space, we can without great loss of generality assume each party has Euclidean preferences, based on a bliss point, as in Figure 2.

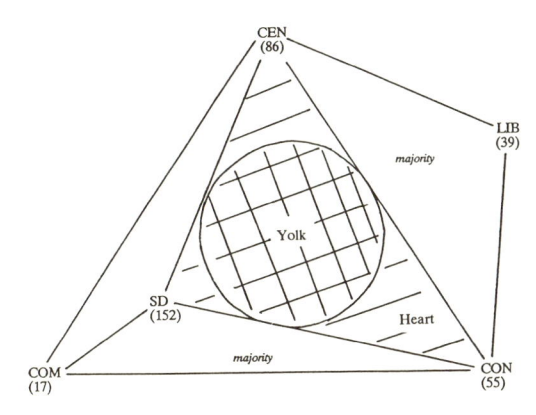

Figure 2. Sweden in 1976.

The Social Democrats (SD) with 152 seats face a bourgeois coalition of three parties (Center, Liberals and Conservatives) controlling 180 seats. We can represent the pattern of winning coalitions by three important majorities, namely $\{SD, CON\}, \{SD, CEN\}$, and $\{CEN, LIB, CON\}$. The two majorities involving the SD can be represented by "median" lines through the SD position, while the bourgeois majority is described by one median line, $\{CEN, CON\}$. The majorities they describe bound a triangular area (shaded in Figure 2) with vertices $\{SD, CEN, CON\}$. This area can easily be shown to be the heart of this game. It is also easy to see that if the party positions move continuously, then the heart will also change shape, continuously.

Table 1.
SEAT STRENGTHS IN SWEDEN

	Seats			Weight	
	1973	1976	1979	1973	1976
Communist Left (COM)	19	17	20	1	1
Social Democrats (SD)	156	152	154	5	4
Center Party (CEN)	90	86	64	2	2
Liberals (LIB)	34	39	38	2	2
Conservatives (CON)	51	55	73	2	2
Total	350	349	349	7/12	6/11

We can contrast this figure with the situation in 1973 where the SD had 156 seats and a majority of 176 was required (see Table 1 and Figure 3). In this case the median lines all pass through the SD position. That is, there is no majority coalition, M, such that the compromise set for M (namely the convex hull $\{x : i \in M\}$ of the bliss points) excludes the SD position. Consequently the core is precisely the SD position. By definition the core and the heart are identical. Given the information on party weights, and the estimates of party position, SD can be termed a "core party". Most importantly, this core property is "structurally stable" (Schofield 1986) since it is insensitive to (small) errors in the estimates of party positions.

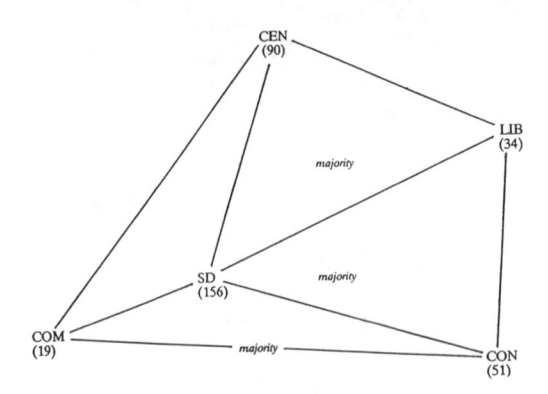

Figure 3. Sweden in 1973.

We may give some theoretical and substantive reasons why two dimensions appear important in coalition bargaining. In 1973 the SD formed a minority (non-majority) one-party government. This would be predicted by the fact that it is in the core position in the two-dimensional space. However a one-dimensional model (based on the economic dimension alone) would predict a two party coalition $\{SD, CEN\}$ since this two party group comprises the one-dimensional core. In fact in this period the SD had strongly committed the "country to a large scale expansion of nuclear generating capacity" (*Keesing Contemporary Archives* 28056), and the Center Party equally strongly objected. This cleavage was important in characterizing the second dimension. In 1976 the SD and Communist Left lost their blocking capability and the three-party bourgeois government formed, lasting (except for a minority liberal party government in 1978-79) until 1982. As we have emphasized, differences of policy opinions between SD and CEN made the bourgeois coalition likely once it obtained a majority. However this coalition was not *inevitable*. Between 1951 and 1957 the two party coalition, $\{SD, CEN\}$, did govern, even though the three-party bourgeois group controlled a majority after the election of 1956. A natural one-dimensional core model would have predicted a minority SD government up to 1956 and a minority Center Party government after 1956.

These observations imply that a model incorporating at least two dimensions is necessary for predicting government formation in Sweden. There is a further important inference. In a three-dimensional policy space it is "generically" the case that no party can occupy a core position (see Schofield 1989) unless it controls a majority of the seats. Yet in Sweden the SD party has on numerous occasions formed a minority government without control of a majority. Often, of course, the SD had the tacit support of the Communist Left, but this support could not always be assumed. This gives some theoretical justification for the inference that in Sweden the underlying policy space is neither one nor three-dimensional but two-dimensional.

If we accept the logic of this model, then it follows that a minority one-party government can only occur in two dimensions, in a stable fashion when a "dominant" party occupies the core position. Theoretical results (Schofield 1995c) have shown that any "smaller" party cannot occupy a "structurally stable" core position, in two dimensions. The terms "dominant" and "smaller" are defined technically, and refer not just to the number of seats, but to the minimum integer weights that specify the winning coalition structure. A voting rule $\mathcal{D}$ has an integer representation iff there is a representation of $\mathcal{D}$ by a quota, q, and a "profile" of minimum integer weights $\{q : w_1, \ldots, w_n\}$ such that $\sum_{i \in M} w_i \geq q$ iff $M \in \mathcal{D}$. Then say party i is "larger" than j (or j is "smaller" than i) iff $w_i > w_j$. Party i is dominant if $w_i > w_j$, for all $j \neq i$. See Table 1 for the "quotas" and minimum integer weights for the parties in 1973 and 1976. Clearly SD is "dominant" and the rest are "smaller" in both years.

However, as we noted previously, the coalition $\{COM, SD\}$ after the 1973 election is blocking (in the sense that it can deny the bourgeois group a majority) whereas in 1976 and 1979 it is not blocking. Schofield (1995c) introduced the term "strongly dominant" to characterize a party that was not only dominant but could be a member of such a two-party blocking coalition. Using results by McKelvey and Schofield (1987), it was shown that only a strongly dominant party, such as the SD in 1973, could stably occupy a core position in two dimensions. Since we know that the SD is not strongly dominant in 1976 and 1979, we can infer that it is impossible for it to occupy a core position in a stable fashion. It is this reasoning, I believe, that can provide an understanding of why relatively small shifts in election results can produce the big shift from a minority government to a majority coalition. Since a one-dimensional model always exhibits a core, it cannot account for a shift of this kind.

We can use Figure 2 to contrast the heart and the uncovered set. The easiest way to characterize the uncovered set is in terms of the *yolk*—the smallest ball that touches all median lines. In this case it is clear that the yolk is a ball located between the SD position and the $\{CEN, CON\}$ median in Figure 2. The uncovered set is known to lie inside a ball centered on the yolk, with radius no more than four times that of the yolk. Since the larger ball includes the entire Pareto set (the quadrilateral $\{COM, CEN, LIB, CON\}$), we only know the uncovered set lies inside the Pareto Set. The heart on the other hand is the triangle $\{SD, CEN, CON\}$. This triangle seems most relevant to the understanding of coalition bargaining in Sweden. Consequently there is an underlying prediction made by the heart that one of its three "bounding" coalitions will form. As we saw in the 1976 situation, these three bounding coalitions are $\{SD, CON\}, \{SD, CEN\}$ and $\{CEN, LIB, CON\}$. The heart is offered here as a general equilibrium concept suitable for analyzing coalition bargaining in multi-party systems.

The hypotheses implicit in this example can now be set out more formally. We use the terms minority for non-majority, minimal winning for majority with no surplus party, and surplus for majority but non-minimal. A "core party" is one that occupies the core of the spatial voting game generated by the various party weights and positions.

A. Theoretical Propositions:

1. In a one-dimensional policy space there will always exist a core party. This follows because $k(\mathcal{D}) \geq 3$ for any weighted majority rule. It is possible for the core party to be the smallest party.

2. In dimension $w(\mathcal{D}) - 1$, if there is a core party, then its position must belong to the core in any one-dimensional subspace. If a "smaller" party occupies the core in this dimension, then it is unstable with respect to perturbations in position. Consequently only a "strongly dominant" party (if one exists) can stably occupy the core position.

3. No "structurally stable" core is possible in dimension $w(\mathcal{D})$. Generically the heart will consist of either a star-shaped or convex set within the Pareto set.

4. In general $w(\mathcal{D}) \leq 3$ for weighted voting rules requiring a simple majority of the seats. However, if one party has a blocking majority of the seats, then $w(\mathcal{D}) = \infty$. (A blocking majority for a party is a sufficient number of seats so that no other group of parties controls a simple majority of the seats.)

5. With three parties, none of whom has a blocking majority, then $w(\mathcal{D}) = 2$. Moreover, with an odd number of parties, all with identical minimum integer weight, then $w(\mathcal{D}) = 2$.

6. If the core is empty then the dominant party will always occupy a position on the boundary of the heart. In particular in a situation where three parties all have equal minimum integer weight, so no one blocks, then, generically, all three are on the heart boundary.

B. Empirical Hypotheses:

7. Any government that forms will include the core party (if one exists). In particular if a minority one party government forms, then it will comprise the party at the core position.

8. If there is no core (and so at least two dimensions), then one of the coalitions bounding the heart will form. In particular a single party minority government is impossible.

C. Deduced Hypotheses:

9. If the policy space is one-dimensional then it is possible for a smaller party to form a minority government, excluding the dominant party, as long as the smaller party is at the core. In any case, every government includes the core party.

10. If the policy space is two dimensional, and a "stable" one-party minority government (with no other party support) occurs, then it must comprise the strongly dominant party.

11. If the policy space is three-dimensional, then a "stable" one-party minority government cannot occur, except when that party has a blocking majority.

D. Plausible Hypotheses:

12. If the policy space is two dimensional but the core is usually empty, then minority governments will be unusual. If $w(\mathcal{D}) = 2$, then minimal winning governments will be typical.

13. If the policy space is two dimensional and $w(\mathcal{D}) = 3$, but there is a dominant party nearly always at the core position, then that party will tend to "control" coalition politics.

14. If the policy space is two dimensional, and a "dominant" party usually occupies the core position, then, in specific instances when the core is empty, this "dominant" party will be excluded from government.

This is a complex set of hypotheses, incorporating both theoretical results on the core and heart, and some empirical hypotheses. The "plausible" hypotheses (12-14) do not follow directly, but they are consistent with the general model. These hypotheses can be evaluated in terms of the data presented in Table 2. These data are assembled from Schofield (1993b) and show coalition types for twelve post-1945 European polities. Column 1 in this table enumerates the number of single party minority governments that have formed. In brackets (in this column) is the number of single party minority governments comprising a "smaller" party.

In contradiction to hypothesis 10, in Denmark a smaller party, Venstre (Liberals) formed a one party minority government in 1947 and in 1973. In both cases however there was tacit support from right wing parties such as the Conservatives. Moreover in 1947 and 1975 the supported minority Venstre government gave way to a supported minority SD government. On the usual left-right economic dimension Venstre was not at a core position. It is likely that the situation was one of two dimensions with an empty core.

In Sweden the three party bourgeois coalition (Center, Conservatives and Liberals), described above, resigned in October 1978 as a result of serious disagreements on nuclear energy policy. The Liberals took over as a (very) minority goverment. After an election in September 1979 the three party coalition reformed. This event contradicts hypotheses (9) and (10), since the liberal party is usually assumed to be to the right of the median or core position on economic policy. It is possible however that the disagreements over nuclear policy were so extreme as to temporarily overwhelm the ability of the bourgeois parties to compromise. It is plausible therefore that the Liberals were at the median position on a nuclear policy dimension, positioned between the Social Democrats on one side and the Center and Conservative parties on the other.

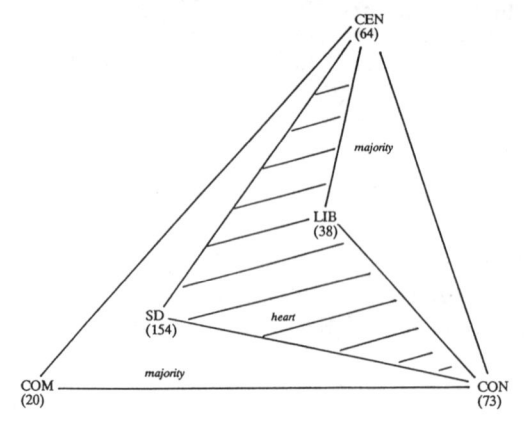

Figure 4. Sweden in 1979.

Figure 4 presents estimates of the positions of the parties based on their manifestos during the 1979 election. It is evident that LIB shows a change in position from 1976 to one nearer SD. The heart has changed shape from 1976 (it is shown shaded again in Figure 4). In fact a possible inference from this Figure is that the Liberals were considering an alliance with SD in the period 1978 to 1979.

The data on single party governments in Table 2 does seem to give quite strong confirmation that two dimensions are relevant, particularly in the Scandinavian countries. No confirmation is provided that only one-dimension is relevant.

In empirical work reported in Schofield (1993b), factor analysis of party manifestos based on data collected by Budge, et al. (1987) was used to estimate party positions. In Austria, Germany, and Luxembourg the party system is such that $w(\mathcal{D}) = 2$, so core positions cannot be expected in non-majority situations. Table 2 shows that single party minority governments are rare in the first six countries listed in the table. Notice that minimal winning coalitions are very frequent in these countries.

Table 2.
COALITION TYPES IN EUROPE

	Single Party Min.	Other Min.	Minimal Winning	Surplus	Maj.	Total
Austria		1	6		6	13
Belgium	1(0)	1	15	4	1	22
Germany			10		2	12
Luxembourg			9	1		10
Iceland	1(0)	1	10	2		14
Netherlands		3	6	8		17
Denmark	12(2)	6	2			19
Norway	7(0)	1	3		4	15
Sweden	9(1)	1	5		1	16
Finland	4(0)	6	5	17		32
Ireland	4(0)	1	3		4	12
Italy	7(0)	7	3	18		35

(Taken from Schofield, 1993b.)

In Belgium and the Netherlands a Center party tends to "dominate" politics. In the Netherlands the Christian People's Party (KVP) or its successor, the Christian Democratic Appeal (CDA), are estimated to be at the core position after six of the eleven elections for which manifesto data (Dittrich 1987) are available. Either the CDA or KVP has been in every government. This gives some confirmation for hypothesis (13). It is possible that there is, in fact, only one relevant dimension in the Netherlands, and the KVP (CDA) occupies the core position. The non-occurrence of single party minority government suggests however that two dimensions are important.

Hypothesis (14) is intended to capture the essence of the political game in the Scandinavian countries. As we have seen in Sweden a left-wing Social Democrat Party faces a bourgeois coalition. When the bourgeois coalition fails to attain a majority, then an SD minority (or majority) government typically forms. This phenomenon also seems to characterize both Denmark and Norway.

In Belgium the situation is somewhat more complex. Before 1961 the instability integer, $w(\mathcal{D})$, is two, and as one would expect, two party minimal winning coalitions tend to form. After 1961, increasing complexity in coalition politics meant that the Christian Social Party (CS) tended to occupy a core position. It has been in every coalition government since then. As Table 2 shows, coalitions tend to be minimal winning or surplus. In some sense we can argue that the $KVP(CDA)$ in the Netherlands and the CS in Belgium dictate the nature of coalition politics. It is interesting that one party minority governments based on these core parties are rare in these two countries. Dodd's (1976) arguments on conflict cleavage might suggest that conflict between the left and right in the Scandianvian countries creates the context for minority one-party governments, whereas in Belgium and the Netherlands, a large centrist party is able to provide the context for coalition negotiation.

The situation in Ireland is extremely interesting. Over the years Fine Gael has gained strength over Fianna Fail. Until 1982 Fianna Fail governments were common. As discussed in Laver and Schofield (1990: Chapter 1) the results of the March 1987 election resulted in a hung Dail. Fianna Fail had 81 seats out of 166 but wished to form a minority one party government. Two independents voted for Fianna Fail, and at the election for Taoiseach, a third independent, Gregory, abstained, giving Fianna Fail a blocking majority and thus control of government. On a one-dimensional model Fianna Fail would be placed at the core position, and thus the "minority" government just described might be expected. However earlier in 1981 a minority two party coalition of Fine Gael and Labor formed against Fianna Fail. It would seem logical, as a consequence, to infer that there is more than one dimension in Irish politics, and that the relevant second dimension in some sense characterizes an extreme form of political antagonism between the two major parties. In fact the factor analysis by Mair (1987) does suggest that a second dimension (interpretable as "Irish Unity") separates the two major parties. With three significant parties one might expect $w(\mathcal{D})$ to be 2. However the large number of independents in the Dail makes it possible for one of the two larger parties to form a minority government, particularly if they have support of a small group of independents such as the Farmers. A reasonable inference, then, is that Irish politics is compatible with the two dimensional model of the heart presented here.

Italy is even more interesting. Until the last election in 1992 the Christian Democrat Party (DC) occupied the core position on both dimensions (Schofield 1993b), these being left-right (economic) and north-south (technology versus social harmony: see Mastropaolo and Slater 1987). As Table 2 illustrates every imaginable kind of coalition has occurred, all including the DC. It now appears that because of its political dominance, the DC was able to use its strategic core position to obtain economic resources so as to maintain its political power. The fragmentation that occurred in the 1992 election brought new parties into being (the Northern League, Anti-Mafia group, *etc.,*) and split the Communist Party. As a result the DC was, for the first time since the 1940's, no longer in control of the core position. (See Figure 11 in Schofield, 1993b.) Since 1993 of course Italian politics (or at least the names of the parties) have been dramatically transformed. It no longer seems to be the case that even the large party, Forza Italia, is in the core position (see Schofield 1995c for a brief discussion).

In this analysis, I have emphasized that a theoretical model based on the existence, or otherwise, of a core position is important for interpreting multiparty coalition politics. I have assumed in this section that the positions and political strengths of the parties are known (they are common knowledge) and that they effect coalition bargaining in the manner described. Moreover, throughout this description, I have focussed on the political control that a party has if it occupies a core position. In the Swedish example it was argued that the SD would be able to implement a minority government if and only if it happened to occupy the core position. If the political rewards from occupying such a position are high, then one might expect parties to attempt to position themselves at the core. It is this possibility of maneuvering in policy space that we shall explore in the next section. Moreover since we have based the analysis on spatial maps derived from manifesto data, we must present a model of how parties choose these manifestos.

8.4 Models of Party Competition and Electoral Politics

Section 8.1 referred to the "binary Downsian model of electoral politics" where two candidates (or parties) compete against each other in order to win office. Neither is interested in policy *per se*, but each chooses a policy and promises the electorate to implement it, if elected. The Classification Theorem governs the behavior of such a model. With a finite electorate and using majority rule, $\mathcal{D}$, we know $w(\mathcal{D}) = 2$ or 3 depending on whether the size of the electorate is odd or even. If there is more than one dimension to policy, there is no reason to expect a Nash equilibrium in this political game.

As we have noted, the uncovered set has been proposed as a choice concept applicable to such a game. If $y \in \overline{P}_\mathcal{D}(x)$ then any point z that beats y also beats x. In some sense the point x is "weakly dominated" by z. Nonetheless in general there is no "pure strategy" Nash equilibrium.

It is worth reviewing the general class of models of electoral competition to see how they predict candidate choice under *risk*. Suppose therefore that candidates $1,2$ choose "declarations" or "manifestos" z_1, z_2 $(\in X)$ respectively to present to the electorate. Suppose further that it is impossible to say definitely whether z_1 beats z_2 or vice versa. "Risk" means that there are "common knowledge" probability functions $\xi_1, \xi_2 : X \times X \longrightarrow \Re$ where $\xi_i(z_1, z_2)$ is the probability that i wins when $1,2$ pick $\{z_1, z_2\}$ respectively. The outcome is a finite lottery $g(z_1, z_2) = \{(z_1, \xi_1(z_1, z_2)), (z_2, \xi_2(z_1, z_2))\}$ which we can regard as a point in $\hat{X}$, the set of all finite lotteries on X. The expectation is $\underline{Ex}[g(z_1, z_2)] = \xi_1(z_1, z_2) z_1 + \xi_2(z_1, z_2) z_2 \in X$. We can also include the possibility of a tie, by supposing that, with probability $1 - \xi_1 - \xi_2$, both candidates obtain the same number of votes. Then each party can use a von Neumann-Morgenstern utility function, U_i, to evaluate $g(z_1, z_2)$. That is

$$U_i(g(z_1, z_2)) = \xi_1(z_1, z_2) u_{i1}(z_1, z_2) + \xi_2(z_1, z_2) u_{i2}(z_1, z_2) + (1 - \xi_1 - \xi_2) u_{i3}(z_1, z_2).$$

Eq. 1

In the Downsian case, the candidates (or parties) are concerned simply to win. In this case we can assume that party 1 receives 1, say, if it wins the election (*i.e.*, $u_{11}(z_1, z_2) = 1$) whereas it receives -1 if it loses ($u_{12}(z_1, z_2) = -1$). For a draw, $u_{13} = 0$. Under certain conditions there will exist a Nash equilibrium. More formally, the strategy space for party i is a copy X_i of X.

The ith best response correspondence is

$$R(U_i) : X_j \longrightarrow 2(X_i)$$

where $R(U_i)(z_j) = \arg\max_{z_i \in X} \{U_i(g(-, z_j))\}$.

This just means i chooses z_i to maximize $U_i(g(,))$ given that the opponent plays z_j.

The joint best response correspondence is

$$R(U_1, U_2) : X_1 \times X_2 \longrightarrow 2(X_1 \times X_2)$$

where each plays best response to the other. A pure strategy *Nash equilibrium* (*PSNE*) is a fixed point of the correspondence $R(U_1, U_2)$.

In case there is no *PSNE*, there will generally be a mixed strategy Nash equilibrium (*MSNE*) where each party plays a mixed strategy in $\tilde{X}$ (see Kramer 1978).

In the case of deterministic voters, the win functions ξ_1, ξ_2 will take values of $0, 1$ or $\frac{1}{2}$ (in the case of a draw). It is important to note that this case can be viewed as a degenerate version of the probabilistic model. However in the absence of a core point in the distribution of voter preferences, there will be no *PSNE* in the candidate game with deterministic voters. Moreover the "win" functions $\{\xi_1, \xi_2\}$ will be discontinuous in the candidate strategies $\{z_1, z_2\}$. For this reason the uncovered set has been proposed as a "solution set" for the two-candidate game with determininstic voters. However since it appears that the uncovered set lies inside the heart, chaotic or cyclic behavior by candidates is possible.

In the probabilistic model on the contrary, the assumptions on voter behavior (Enelow and Hinich 1984; Coughlin 1992) are sufficient to ensure that the win probabilities are continuous in the candidate strategies. Indeed in these models it is usual to use, not the win probabilities (ξ_1, ξ_2) but the expected votes $\{\pi_1(z_1, z_2), \pi_2(z_1, z_2)\}$. Under conditions of voter independence these two models give the same Nash equilibria (see Aranson, *et al.* 1974 and the chapter by Ladha in this volume). However the work by Ladha and Miller (this volume) can be interpreted to imply that the probability of winning and expected vote do not give equivalent candidate objective functions when voter choices are statistically dependent. To obtain *PSNE* it is usually assumed that the *voter* probability functions have a convenient form (see the discussion in Chapter 1 of this volume), so as to guarantee that the best response functions $\{R_1, R_2\}$ are quasi-concave.

In a sense then the analysis of two party models of this kind come down to an examination of the equilibrium correspondence

$$E_g : U(X_1 \times X_2) \times U(X_1 \times X_2) \longrightarrow 2(\tilde{X}_1 \times \tilde{X}_2).$$

Here, the notation $U(X_1 \times X_2)$ is meant to represent the class of utility functions defined on both z_1 and z_2. That is $E_g(U_1, U_2)$ is obtained by finding the fixed points of the best response correspondence $R(U_1, U_2)$, thus giving the set of $MSNE$ for the game form g. Typically, of course, these models are posed in the context of a distribution, f, of voters and the equilibrium outcome is one where both parties choose the same point.

While the above model gives an elegant description of electoral politics, it is not evident that two party competition does, in fact, produce "Downsian convergence" as suggested by the probabilistic model.

There are many empirical situations of two parties competing in a way that suggests that they both wish to win, yet with little indication of convergence in declarations. If the parties are indeed "Downsian", then the probabilistic model in such a case must be invalid. The model could be modified by considering different voter probability functions $\{\pi_{ij}, \pi_{ik}\}$ or by assuming voter dependency. A different possibility is to suppose that parties' utility functions depend on the policy outcomes. Cox (1984a) for example, assumes that each party i has a bliss point x_i in X where its "political preferences" are maximised. Normally it is assumed that $u_i(z) = -\frac{1}{2} \| z - x_i \|^2$.

The expected utility model can now be written

$$U_1(g(z_1, z_2)) = \xi_1(z_1, z_2)(u_1(z_1) + \gamma_1) + \xi_2(z_1, z_2)u_1(z_2) +$$
$$(1 - \xi_1 - \xi_2)(u_1(\tfrac{(z_1 + z_2)}{2}) + \tfrac{\gamma_1}{2}). \qquad (Eq.2)$$

and similarly for party 2.

In this model party 1 presents a "manifesto" z_1 to the electorate, promising that this policy position will be played should i win the election. The prize γ_1 is the "perquisite" of government. In the event of a draw, we can assume (as we have in Eq. 2) that the parties agree to implement the policy $\frac{z_1+z_2}{2}$ and to split the perquisite.

In this case the equilibrium correspondence can be written:

$$E_g : U(X) \times U(X) \longrightarrow 2(\tilde{X}_1 \times \tilde{X}_2)$$

since the fundamental parameters concern the policy preferences, and these are described by utility functions with domain X. (Of course, nothing is changed by linear transformations of utilities, so we should regard $U(X)$ as the space of von Neumann-Morgenstern "preferences" over finite lotteries on X.) In the usual applications however the preferences are assumed to be Euclidean. Without great loss of generality, therefore, we may write

$$E_g : X_1 \times X_2 \longrightarrow 2(\tilde{X}_1 \times \tilde{X}_2)$$

for the equilibrium map.

Note that this model has two features. It is "policy-seeking" in the sense that the utilities u_i are dependent on policy bliss points $\{x_i\}$ and the policy outcome. It is "office-seeking" since each party gains an award, or perquisite, γ_i from winning. We can contrast the pure policy-seeking model (when each $\gamma_i = 0$), with the pure office-seeking or "Downsian" model when $u_i(z_i) = 0$. The model is set up with electoral risk, but we could instead define it in terms of uncertainty–namely probability distributions over win probabilities.

There is one serious difficulty with all policy-seeking models such as this. Having won the election with declaration z_i, why would party i implement policy z_i rather than its preferred policy x_i? This suggests that in the full equilibrium analysis each party should compare implementing z_i against the later electoral costs of implementing x_i instead. From the point of view of the electorate, why should they believe candidate i will implement its declaration z_i if it wins? A number of interesting papers (Austen-Smith and Banks 1989; Banks 1990; Banks and Sundaram 1990, 1993) have tackled this problem. Notwithstanding these attempts, I believe this problem of credible commitment by parties is not yet resolved. On the contrary, I believe a case can be made that the uncertainty involved in the degree of credible commitment should be incorporated into the win probabilities ξ_i, ξ_j. This becomes very complex however, because there would need to be a strong component of common knowledge in the beliefs by parties about the electorate, and in the beliefs by the electorate about the parties. This we might describe as *political culture*.

Attempts to develop this model in the multiparty context are suggestive, and the model I propose can be regarded as a natural generalization. Suppose that the set $N = \{1, \ldots, n\}$ of parties transmits a *message profile* $z = (z_1, \ldots, z_n)$ to the electorate, where z_i is intended to represent the information that party i chooses to transmit to the electorate about its intentions. For simplicity I shall assume that the message from party i is simply an "ideal point", z_i, with the implicit assumption that i will act after the election as though it had Euclidean policy preferences based on z_i. However, I shall also assume that the "true" party preferences (based on a "bliss" point, x_i) are unknown to the voters. Electoral preferences are described by a distribution, f of voter "bliss" points.

Under deterministic voter behavior, the electoral response is described by an electoral map $e^f : X^N \longrightarrow \Delta_N$ where $e^f(z) = (e_1(z), \ldots, e_n(z))$ gives the vector of seat shares to each party. Since $\sum_{i=1}^{n} e_i(z) = 1$, the image of the electoral map is in the $(n-1)$ dimensional simplex Δ_N.

David Austen-Smith argues (in Chapter 6 of this volume) that a fully developed model of voter behavior should analyze voter strategies as functions not only of the declarations, z, but of the legislative outcome function. For the present I shall assume that e^f results from "sincere" voter strategies.

Eaton and Lipsey (1975) considered a version of the "Downsian" model where each party has a utility function $u_i(z) = e_i(z)$. That is each party attempts to maximize the number of seats it controls. In general the best response correspondence $R(u_1, \ldots, u_n) : X^N \longrightarrow 2(X^N)$ has no fixed point (Shaked 1975) when the dimension is 2 and $n = 3$. Consequently there may be no $PSNE$. Many authors have attempted to show existence of equilibrium where the parties in parliament attempt to keep out intruders (Greenberg and Weber 1985; Greenberg and Shesple 1987; Palfrey 1984; Shepsle 1991; see also Chapter 6 of this volume for a more detailed discussion.)

The general difficulties with existence of equilibrium in this model and its variants are two-fold: (i) discontinuity; and (ii) non-convexity in induced preference. A discontinuity can occur at a message profile $z = (z_1, \ldots, z_n)$ where $z_i = z_j$ for all i, j. In this case it is reasonable to assume $e_i(z) = e_j(z) = \frac{1}{n}$, for all i, j. Clearly a small perturbation to $z' = (z'_1, \ldots, z'_n)$ can result in discontinuous change in $e_i(z')$. Dasgupta and Maskin (1986) have argued that this is not a fundamental problem. They propose a *standard smoothing* procedure. That is consider a profile $z' = (z'_1, \ldots, z'_n)$ with $z'_i = z'_j$. Then it is possible to smooth away the discontinuities by defining a new continuous outcome function $\bar{e}$ with $\bar{e}(z) = e(z)$ for any $z \notin V_\epsilon(z')$, an ϵ-neighborhood of z', but also satisfying $\bar{e}(z') = e(z')$. Moreover the pure strategy (or mixed strategy) Nash equilibria determined by e and $\bar{e}$ coincide. Dasgupta and Maskin (1986) showed that mixed strategy Nash equilibria exist in a general class of such models.

Even assuming the relevance of the model, what precisely is the interpretation of a mixed strategy Nash equilibrium? The more general question however is: Why would parties in a multiparty context attempt to maximize seats?

It is difficult to believe that parties have no policy preferences, and no ideological positions to maintain. If they do have policy preferences, then there is a cost to them of presenting a policy proposal to the electorate simply to gain seats. Of course they need seats to obtain representation in the Parliament, so there is an implicit trade-off between policy choice and electoral advantage, which the pure multiparty office-seeking or Downsian models do not address. There is also a serious difficulty in using a variant of Cox's (1984a) mixed policy-seeking office-seeking model. In a multiparty parliamentary system, it is very uncommon for any party to gain a straight majority of the seats. Data presented in Schofield (1993b) indicate that only 17 majority party situations occurred out of 216 governments in twelve European countries examined in the period from 1945 until 1987. To determine whether a Nash equilibrium exists in the selection of party manifestos we must model a dependence of u_i on z that is not simply based on the number of seats won by the party.

One modelling strategy, adopted by Baron (1989, 1991), is to assume that each party declares its "true" bliss point. He considers a model where there are three parties. Each party, i, has true Euclidean preference with bliss point x_i, which it declares. The outcome is a finite lottery

$$g(x) = \{y_1, \rho_1(x); \ y_2, \rho_2(x); \ y_3, \rho_3(x)\}.$$

Here $x = (x_1, x_2, x_3)$ are the three bliss points and $y_i(x)$ is an outcome associated with coalition $\{j, k\}$ that occurs with a probability $\rho_i(x)$ that is structurally determined by x and by exogeneous parameters.

The problem with this model is that it may not be incentive compatible. In particular since g is defined for any manifesto profile $z \in X^N$ and U_i can be defined as the von Neumann-Morgenstern expected utility function obtained from the underlying Euclidean preferences, it is likely, for party 1, say, that there exists $z_1 \in X$ such that

$$U_1(z_1, x_2, x_3) > U_2(x_1, x_2, x_3).$$

In a later paper Baron (1993) considered a variant of this model, where the parties are "endogenous". He assumed that parties are collections of voters, who choose declarations so as to maximize average electoral utility (via $g(z)$) within the group. This is an ambitious model, but I believe it misses the essential feature of principal agent relations in representative politics.

An influential paper by Austen-Smith and Banks (1988) dealt with the problem in an ingenious fashion. The space is one-dimensional and there are three parties. Once the profile of declarations $z = (z_1, z_2, z_3)$ is selected, then given the electoral map $e^f : X^3 \longrightarrow \Delta_3$ there is a unique outcome $g(z)$ specifying the governing coalition M, a policy point z_M and perquisites $\{\gamma_i : i \in M\}$. Knowing g, the electorate chooses in an equilibrium fashion. (See Chapter 6 of this volume for a full discussion.) Thus both the electorate and the parliamentary parties make choices that are in equilibrium with each other. However, though the preferences of the electorate are exogenous, the party preferences are endogenous. In particular, the outcome $g(z)$ is evaluated by party i (if it enters the government coalition M) using the endogenous utility $u_i = - \| z_i - z_M \| + \gamma_i$. That is, the declaration, z_i, chosen by i is used as the "induced" bliss point by that party. The problem of credible commitment by i to z_i does not arise.

In the next section of the chapter, I construct a model that is based on parties' "exogenous" policy preferences and focuses on the existence of a Nash equilibrium in coalition bargaining.

8.5 Coalition Bargaining in a Committee

This section attempts to construct a multiparty model of coalition bargaining that is a natural generalization of the work, described in Section 8.4, of Austen-Smith and Banks, Baron and Cox.

We consider first of all the case of three parties $N = \{1, 2, 3\}$ and X a compact, convex subset of $\Re^2$. Once an adequate model is obtained in this case then extending it to large n and more general X should, in principle, be easy. We also ignore the electoral connection (for the moment). That is $\mathcal{D}$ is fixed and equal to $\{\{1,2\}, \{2,3\}, \{1,3\}\}$. Thus the framework is based on a model of spatial voting in a committee. However it can be viewed as resembling Austria or Germany where any two party coalition can form a government. Because $w(\mathcal{D}) = 2$ as we have seen, the core (if it ever exists) is unstable. Each party, i, has "true policy preferences" defined by a "policy" utility function $u_i(z) = -\frac{1}{2} \| z - x_i \|^2$, where z is an outcome in X. Note that each bliss point, x_i, is chosen by a process not considered by the model. If party i forms a government with j, then i receives a perquisite γ_{ij}, and the political utility function is separable in policy and perquisites.

We may therefore regard the model as an adaptation of spatial voting, but incorporating certain fixed benefits $\{\gamma_{ij}\}$ that are allocated to members of the final winning coalitions. The innovation of this model is that, instead of supposing that some geometrically defined set of outcomes in X is possible from coalition bargaining, it proposes that each party makes an offer (a "declaration" of proposed policy). The "legislative outcome" resulting from a vector $z = (z_1, z_2, z_3)$ of declarations is a finite lottery $g(z)$ across coalition-policy outcomes and distributions of perquisites. This defines a game, which may or may not have a $PSNE$. Unlike the models of electoral competition, involving electoral risk, this model involves coalitional risk. That is, each two party coalition, M, forms with probability, ρ_M, where ρ_M is inversely related to the "distance" between the declarations of the coalition members. Some empirical evidence for such an assumption is implicit in the discussion below in Chapters 12 and 13, of the "proto-coalition model".

Assumptions of the 3-Party Model.

1. Once party i chooses a declaration $z_i \in X$ it acts in negotiation with other parties as though it had a Euclidean preference given by $u'_i(z) = -\frac{1}{2} \| z - z_i \|^2$. That is, it is committed to z_i in coalition bargaining. The declaration, z_i, may be viewed as an offer to the other parties.

2. Once the profile $z = \{z_1, z_2, z_3\}$ is declared, then the policy outcome is a lottery $g(z) = \{(\rho_M, z_M) : M \in \mathcal{D}\}$ where $z_M = \frac{1}{|M|} \sum_{i \in M} z_i$ and $\rho_M(z)$ is the probability that coalition M forms.

3. For each $M = \{i, j\}$ if $z_i \neq z_j$ then $\rho_M(z)$ is inversely proportional to $\| z_i - z_j \|^2$. For each z, the sum $\sum \{\rho_M(z) : M \in \mathcal{D}\} = 1$.

4. The three functions $\rho_M : X^3 \longrightarrow [0, 1]$ are smoothed near any point z such that $z_i = z_j$.

5. Each profile choice $z \in X^3$ determines an outcome $g_\gamma(z) \in \tilde{X}_\Delta$ where $\tilde{X}_\Delta$ is the space of finite lotteries over policy outcomes and perquisites. That is, $g_\gamma(z) = \{(\rho_M, z_M, \gamma_M)\}$ where γ_M is a specified vector of perquisites to members of M. It is assumed here that the perquisites to the two members $\{i, j\}$ of M are exogenously specified. This assumption could easily be modified. We also write $g(z) = \{(\rho_M, z_M)\}$ for the *policy lottery outcome* in $\tilde{X}$. Each party, i, evaluates the outcome $g_\gamma(z)$ by a von Neumann-Morgenstern utility function $U_i : \tilde{X}_\Delta \longrightarrow \Re$, which is separable in policy preferences and perquisites and based on the true Euclidean policy preferences.

6. Each party, i, chooses a best response to the choices z_j, z_k of the parties by maximizing U_i. That is, i's best response is given by a correspondence $R_i : X_j \times X_k \longrightarrow X_i$ where X_j and X_k are the strategy spaces of j, k (namely copies of X).

7. The pure strategy Nash equilibrium (if one exists) is a fixed point of the joint response correspondence

$$R_{123} : X^3 \longrightarrow 2(X^3).$$

As before the $MSNE$ belongs to $2(\tilde{X}^3)$. The smoothing operation of (4) is carried out to avoid the discontinuities observed by Dasgupta and Maskin (1986) near the diagonal. This problem is easy to avoid by constraining $\rho_{ij}(z) \leq 1 - \epsilon$, for some $\epsilon > 0$ in a neighborhood of any profile z with $z_i = z_j$, and by smoothing the ρ_{ij} in a neighborhood of a profile with $z_1 = z_2 = z_3$. (See Schofield and Parks, 1993, for details.)

Notice in this model that we have assumed a specific game form $g_\gamma : X^3 \longrightarrow \tilde{X}_\Delta$. This one seems very natural to analyze coalition bargaining. Based on the declarations of intended policies, z_i, z_j by two parties, they choose a compromise position to implement in case they form a government. Moreover in the *symmetric* case when $\| z_1 - z_2 \| = \| z_2 - z_3 \| = \| z_1 - z_3 \|$, then each of the three two-party coalitions are equally likely, so that $\rho_{ij} = \frac{1}{3}$.

To analyze this game we need to determine the properties of the equilibrium map

$$E_g : X^3 \longrightarrow 2(\tilde{X}^3),$$

which takes a profile of bliss points (x_1, x_2, x_3) to the $MSNE$.

Let $\gamma = \{\gamma_{ij} : i, j = 1, 2, 3\}$ be the pattern of party perquisites in the various government coalitions. For each Euclidean profile, represented by the profile of bliss points $x = (x_1, x_2, x_3) \in X^3$, does there exist a fixed point $E_g(x)$ to the joint response correspondence? If there is no $PSNE$, then there may be an $MSNE$, $E_g(x) \in \tilde{X}^3$.

Schofield and Parks (1993) have recently shown analytically that a $PSNE$ exists for particular profiles in X^3, when the game form has certain features.

Definition 1:

1. Say three points $\{z_i, z_j, z_k\}$ each in $\Re^m$ are $\epsilon-$ *bounded in linearity* if

   $$min_{\lambda_j, \lambda_k \in \Re} \{\| z_i - \lambda_j z_j - \lambda_k z_k \|\} \leq \epsilon.$$

   If $\epsilon = 0$ the points are *colinear*.

2. Say three points $\{z_i, z_j, z_k\}$ are $\epsilon-$ *bounded in symmetry* if

   $$max_{i,j,k} | \| z_i - z_k \| - \| z_j - z_k \| | \leq \epsilon$$

   where $max_{i,j,k}$ means across all permutations of i, j, k. If $\epsilon = 0$ then the three points are *symmetric*.

3. Say three points $\{z_1, z_2, z_3\}$ are $\epsilon-$ *convergent* if there exists a ball, B, of radius ϵ, and center in the convex hull of $\{z_1, z_2, z_3\}$ which contains all three.

Theorem 1: *In the three party model of coalition formation on $\Re^2$, with zero perquisites, then there exists $\epsilon > 0$ such that*

1. when the bliss points $x = (x_1, x_2, x_3)$ are ϵ-bounded in linearity there exists a unique $PSNE$, $E_g(x)$. Moreover $E_g(x) = (z_1, z_2, z_3)$ such that these points $\{z_1, z_2, z_3\}$ are ϵ'-convergent, for some ϵ' dependent on ϵ,

2. when the bliss points are ϵ-bounded in symmetry, there exists a unique $PSNE$, $E_g(x)$. Moreover $E_g(x) = (z_1, z_2, z_3)$ such that $\{z_1, z_2, z_3\}$ are ϵ'-bounded in symmetry for some ϵ' dependent on ϵ. In particular, if $\epsilon = 0$, then $\{z_1, z_2, z_3\}$ are symmetric and $\| z_i - z_j \| = 2 \| x_i - x_j \|$ for each pair i, j.

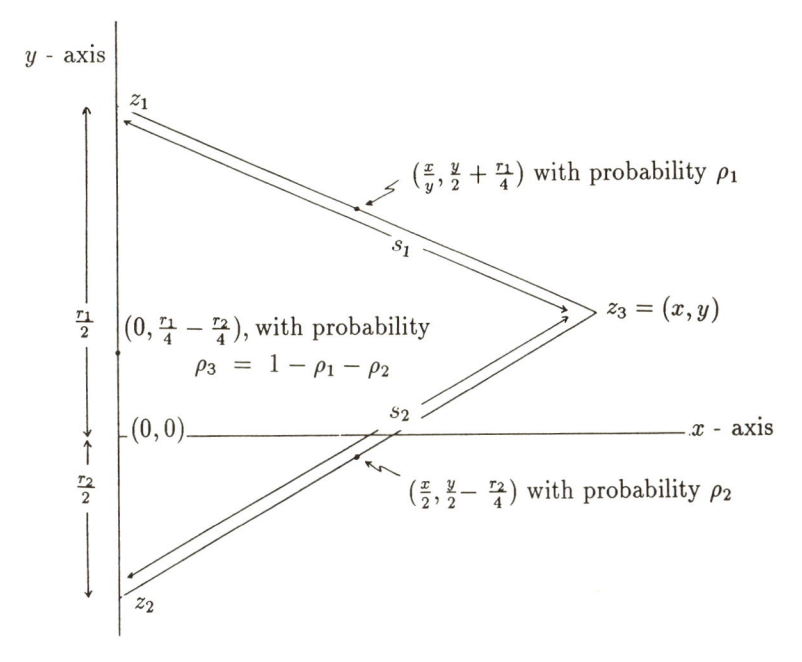

Figure 5. Lottery of three possible legislative outcomes, given three party manifesto positions (z_1, z_2, z_3).

To illustrate this result, consider Figure 5 which presents an example where three parties have adopted positions (z_1, z_2, z_3) and coordinates are chosen so that $z_1 = (0, \frac{r_1}{2})$, $z_2 = (0, -\frac{r_2}{2})$, $z_3 = (x, y)$. (It is hoped that coordinate x is not confused with the bliss point x_i.) For convenience suppose that the bliss point for party 3 is at $(L, 0)$. Now consider the best response problem from the point of view of party 3. To simplify notation, let us write ρ_1 for ρ_{31}, ρ_2 for ρ_{32} and $1 - \rho_1 - \rho_2$ for ρ_{12}. Remember γ_{3i} is the perquisite to party 3 if coalition $\{3, i\}$ forms. From the point of view of party 3, the outcome $g_\gamma(z)$, resulting from the joint declaration, z, consists of three possibilities:

1. policy $\frac{z_1 + z_3}{2} = (\frac{x}{2}, \frac{y}{2} + \frac{r_1}{4})$ and perquisite γ_{31}, with probability ρ_1

2. policy $\frac{z_2 + z_3}{2} = (\frac{x}{2}, \frac{y}{2} - \frac{r_2}{4})$ and perquisite γ_{32}, with probability ρ_2, and

3. policy $\frac{z_1+z_2}{2} = (0, \frac{r_1-r_2}{4})$ and no perquisite with probability $1-\rho_1-\rho_2$.

Notice that $\| z_1 - z_2 \| = \frac{1}{2}(r_1+r_2)$. Let us write $s_i = \| z_3 - z_i \|$ for $i = 1, 2$. Thus

$$\rho_i = \left(\frac{1}{s_i^2} + \frac{1}{s_j^2} + \left(\frac{2}{r_1+r_2}\right)^2\right)^{-1} \frac{1}{s_i^2}.$$

Clearly ρ_1, ρ_2 can be effected by choice of x and y. If we write $U(x, y)$ for the von Neumann Morgenstern expected utility for 3 in terms of the choice variables $(x, y) \in \Re^2$, and u for this party's true Euclidean utility, then the response problem for 3 is to maximise

$$U(x, y) = \rho_1 \left\{ u\left(\tfrac{z_1+z_3}{2}\right) + \gamma_{31} \right\} + \rho_2 \left\{ u\left(\tfrac{z_2+z_3}{2}\right) + \gamma_{32} \right\} +$$
$$(1 - \rho_1 - \rho_2) \left\{ u\left(\tfrac{z_1+z_2}{2}\right) \right\}.$$

Notice the similarity of this equation to Eq. 2 governing two party competition (Cox 1984a).

Parks and Schofield (1993) have calculated "best response" by taking partial derivatives. These give "optimality" equations in x and y. Taking $\frac{\partial U}{\partial x} = 0$ gives

$$\frac{\rho_1+\rho_2}{2}\left(L - \frac{x}{2}\right) - 2x\left(\frac{\rho_1^2+\rho_2^2}{\bar r^2}\right)\left(\frac{\gamma_{31}+\gamma_{32}}{2} + Lx - \frac{x^2}{4} - \epsilon\right) = 0 \quad (Eq.3)$$

where $\bar r = \frac{r_1+r_2}{2}$ and $\epsilon = \frac{r^2}{16}$.

Equation $\frac{\partial U}{\partial y} = 0$ gives $y(\rho_2 + \rho_2) =$

$$-\frac{1}{2}(\rho_1 r_1 - \rho_2 r_2) - 8y\left(\frac{\rho_1^2}{\bar r^2} + \frac{\rho_2^2}{\bar r^2}\right)\delta + 4\left(\frac{r_1\rho_1^2}{\bar r^2} - \frac{r_2\rho_2^2}{\bar r^2}\right)\delta, \quad (Eq.4)$$

where $\delta \simeq \frac{\gamma_{31}+\gamma_{32}}{2} + u(\frac{x}{2}, \frac{y}{2}) - u(0, \frac{r_1-r_2}{4})$.

These rather difficult non-linear equations can be easily solved in the case $r_1 = r_2 (= r)$. Then $\rho_1 = \rho_2$ and by symmetry the optimal solution for y is $y^* = 0$. If $\gamma_{31} = \gamma_{32} = 0$, then the equation in x becomes

$$\rho\left\{\left(L - \frac{x}{2}\right) - \frac{2x\rho^2}{r^2}\left(Lx - \frac{x^2}{4} - \frac{r^2}{16}\right)\right\} = 0. \quad (Eq.5)$$

To solve this equation, consider the case $L = \beta r, x = ar$. We obtain

$$\rho\left\{\left(\beta - \frac{a}{2}\right) - 2a\rho\left(a\beta - \frac{a^2}{4} - \frac{1}{16}\right)\right\} = 0. \quad (Eq.6)$$

Now $\rho = \frac{r^2}{2r^2+s^2} = \frac{1}{\frac{9}{4}+a^2}$ since $s^2 = (\frac{r}{2})^2 + x^2$. Assuming $\rho \neq 0$, gives a quadratic expression in a, β with solution

$$a = \frac{1}{2}\left(-\frac{1}{\beta} \pm \sqrt{\frac{1}{\beta^2} + 9}\right). \quad (Eq.7)$$

Thus if $L \gg r$, so that $\beta \gg 1$, then $x^* = \frac{3r}{2}$. Notice that there is only one positive solution, so that $U(x,0)$ is concave on the positive x-axis.

Note however that if $x = \frac{3r}{2}$, then $s^2 = (\frac{r}{4})^2 + x^2 > r^2$. Thus best response produces a divergence of the position of party 3 from the positions of parties 1 and 2. To examine the symmetric case further, suppose that $\beta \simeq 1$. It is easy to show that if $\beta = \frac{\sqrt{5}}{2}$, then $a = \beta$. In particular, if $\beta \in (\frac{\sqrt{5}}{2}, \infty)$, then $a \in (\frac{\sqrt{5}}{2}, \frac{3}{2})$ with $a < \beta$, while if $\beta \in (0, \frac{\sqrt{5}}{2})$, then $a > \beta$, but $a \in (0, \frac{\sqrt{5}}{2})$. If $\beta = \frac{1}{\sqrt{3}}$, then $a = \frac{\sqrt{3}}{2}$, and $s^2 = r^2$.

Given z_1, z_2 there is a 1-1 relationship between the bliss point $(\beta r, 0)$ and the best response $(ar, 0)$. In particular if $L = \frac{r}{\sqrt{3}}$, then $x^* = \frac{\sqrt{3}r}{2}$ and the best response is to set $s = r$.

Consequently, if the bliss points are symmetric then the joint best response will also be symmetric. Further analysis shows that there exists a pure strategy Nash equilibrium $\{z_1, z_2, z_3\}$ related to the bliss points $\{x_1, x_2, x_3\}$ by
$\| z_i - z_j \| = 2 \| x_i - x_j \|$.

For bliss points close to symmetry, transversality arguments show that the $PSNE$ is again unique and also close to symmetric.

Suppose now that the declarations are $z_i = (0, y_i)$ with $y_1 < y_2 < y_3$. For such colinear points it is possible to compute $\frac{\partial U}{\partial y}$. Then $\frac{\partial U}{\partial y}$ is maximized at $x^* = 0$, with y^* equal to the midpoint of $\{y_1, y_2, y_3\}$. Simulation of this optimization problem when the bliss points are close to colinear shows that the unique Nash equilibrium occurs when all three parties choose positions in some ϵ'-neighborhood of the middle bliss point.

The conclusion from this analysis is somewhat surprising. For bliss points near to symmetric, divergence in declared positions occurs. However if the bliss points are close to colinear, then a form of Downsian convergence occurs.

It is also possible to determine the effects on the Nash equilibrium when government perquisites are added.

Theorem 2: *In the 3-party model of government formation, if government perquisites $\{\gamma_{ij}\}$ are of the same order of magnitude as policy disagreements $(\| x_i - x_j \|^2)$ then there exists a unique ϵ-convergent pure strategy Nash equilibrium, where ϵ is dependent on $\{\gamma_{ij}\}$.*

To illustrate this consider Eq. 3 with an additional perquisite term given by $\gamma_{31} = \gamma_{32} = r^2$. Then Equation 7 becomes

$$a = \frac{1}{2}\left(-\frac{3}{\beta} \pm 3\sqrt{\frac{1}{\beta^2} + 1}\right).$$

If $\beta = \sqrt{3}$ then $a = \frac{\sqrt{3}}{2}$. Consequently if $\gamma_{ij} \simeq r^2$, all i,j, then the best response correspondence is a contraction mapping which has a unique

Nash equilibrium. The greater the magnitude of the perquisites, the greater the degree of convergence (*i.e.*, the smaller is ϵ).

It is conjectured that these two results hold for a general form of this model involving n parties, where the probabilities ρ_M are inversely proportional to the variance of $\{z_i : i \in M\}$. It is also possible that such a model could be used to explain the formation of parties. In simulation of this game, Schofield and Parks (1993) found, in the case of zero perquisites, that parties "close" to one another tend to converge, while parties far from the others diverge. Thus, in Nash equilibrium, there is a complex pattern of convergence and differentiation.

On the other hand, if perquisites dominate, as in the office seeking "Downsian" model, convergence always occurs.

We can think of these results in more general terms. The construction of the game form g_γ gives, for each z, a finite lottery $g_\gamma(z)$ in the space $\tilde{X}_\Delta$. Moreover, since $\mathcal{D}$ is fixed, the heart $\mathcal{H}_\mathcal{D}(z)$ is the triangle with vertices $\{z_1, z_2, z_3\}$. Each possible policy outcome under the game form belongs to $\mathcal{H}_\mathcal{D}(z)$, so the *policy lottery outcome*, namely $g(z) \in \tilde{X}$, belongs to $\tilde{\mathcal{H}}_\mathcal{D}(z)$, the space of finite lotteries over the set $\mathcal{H}_\mathcal{D}(z)$. As z varies, then $g(z)$ varies continuously with $\tilde{\mathcal{H}}_\mathcal{D}(z)$. Since $\mathcal{H}_\mathcal{D}$ is lower hemi-continuous, so is $\tilde{\mathcal{H}}_\mathcal{D}$ (Schofield 1993a). Thus we see that $g : X^3 \longrightarrow \tilde{X}$ is a *continuous selection* of the correspondence $\tilde{\mathcal{H}}_\mathcal{D} : X^3 \longrightarrow 2(\tilde{X})$. Notice also that the expectation of g at the Nash equilibrium outcome always belongs to the Pareto set (the convex hull of $\{x_1, x_2, x_3\}$).

Combined analysis and simulation give the following:

Theorem 3: *In the 3-party model:*

1. *If perquisites are identically zero, then the expectation of the policy outcomes, in Nash equilibrium, namely $\underline{Ex}[g(E_g(x))]$ belongs to the Pareto set of the profile $x = \{x_1, x_2, x_3\}$.*

2. *If all perquisites exceed some level $\overline{\gamma}$, determined by the bliss points $\{x_1, x_2, x_3\}$ then all $PSNE$ outcomes in $g(E_g(x))$ belong to the Pareto set of the profile. (Since $\mathcal{D}$ is fixed, the Pareto set is simply $\mathcal{H}_\mathcal{D}(x)$.)*

To see how to extend this model to one where there is dependence on electoral response to n parties, let $\mathcal{D}(z)$ be the electorally-determined set of decisive coalitions at the profile, z, of declarations. Let $g(z)$ be the lottery of coalitionally determined policy outcomes. It is natural to assume that $g : X^N \longrightarrow \tilde{X}$ is a continuous selection of the heart correspondence $\tilde{\mathcal{H}}\mathcal{D} : X^N \longrightarrow 2(\tilde{X})$. Here $\tilde{\mathcal{H}}\mathcal{D}(z)$ is the set of finite lotteries across the heart, as defined by z and $\mathcal{D}(z)$. The previous result that $\mathcal{H}_\mathcal{D}$ is *lhc* can be extended to show the correspondence $\tilde{\mathcal{H}}_\mathcal{D}$ is *lhc* (Schofield 1993a) and so we do know that there does exist such a selection, g.

For example, if the declaration profile z gives rise to a distribution of seats such that one party (say SD) is the core, then $g(z) = \{z_{SD}\}$ the declaration of that party. If in fact a minority SD government forms, then the vector γ of perquisites would assign all the cabinet positions to that party.

The next section suggests how to extend this model to deal with electoral risk.

8.6 The Heart and Electoral Politics

In Section 8.3 we argued that the heart gave a theoretical way to interpret coalition bargaining in multiparty systems such as those of a number of European countries. However there was an apparent problem to resolve. The heart was defined earlier in terms of true preferences (and bliss points), whereas the empirical evidence was obtained from factor analytical methods applied to party manifestos or policy declarations. In Section 8.5 we considered a three-party competitive model involving no electoral competition. Instead parties chose declarations to which they were committed in policy bargaining. We assumed that these declarations were chosen in Nash equilibrium under a common knowledge assumption about the game form, g_γ, mapping from declarations to the lottery of outcomes, in $\tilde{X}_\Delta$. Reasons were given why the Nash equilibrium correspondence

$$E_g : X^N \longrightarrow 2(X^N)$$

from Euclidean profiles to equilibrium outcomes would be single-valued for general N and "reasonable" g.

The heart model of Section 8.3 describes post-election party bargaining when seat strengths, represented by $\mathcal{D}$, are known. On the other hand the competitive model of Section 8.5 describes pre-election behavior when $\mathcal{D}$ is assumed fixed. Note that we showed in Section 8.5 that the expected value of the equilibrium outcome always belongs to the Pareto set of the true bliss points (x_1, x_2, x_3). Moreover the policy components of the equilibrium, $z^* = E_g(x)$, always belongs to the "lottery" heart of the declarations $\tilde{\mathcal{H}}\mathcal{D}(z^*)$.

To develop a model of n−party competition we proceed as folllows. Once the vector of policy declarations $z = (z_1, \ldots, z_n)$ is known then each voter, v, responds by a probability vector $\pi_v(z) = (\pi_{v1}(z), \ldots, \pi_{vn}(z))$, where $\pi_{vi}(z)$ is the probability that v chooses party i. Let $(\overline{\pi}_1, \ldots, \overline{\pi}_n)$ be the vector of expected votes for each party. Of course the vote for each party is now a random variable defined by a probability distribution. With at least three parties it is no longer possible to say whether one party or the other wins. However if we let $\{\mathcal{D}_t\}$ be the class of possible winning coalition structures, then we can construct a probability distribution over $\{\mathcal{D}_t\}$. Specifically, let $\xi_t(z)$ be the probability that the winning coalition structure, $\mathcal{D}_t$, results from the profile of declarations, z, given the electoral response $\{\pi_v(z)\}$. Let $\{\xi_t(z)\}$ be this list of probabilities defined at z. For example in the case of two parties $\{i, j\}$, $\{\mathcal{D}_t\} = \{\{i\}, \{j\}, \{i, j\}\}$ where $\{i, j\}$ means that i and j draw.

In the case of three parties $\{i, j, k\}$ clearly $\{\mathcal{D}_t\} = \{\{i\}, \{j\}, \{k\}, \{i, j\}, \{j, k\}, \{i, k\}\}$ since either one or two parties must win under majority rule. It is possible, of course, to have more complex winning coalition structures, but this formulation obviously generalizes the simple two-party case.

Note however that, in the two party case, maximizing π_i and maximizing the probability of winning are equivalent. In the multiparty case it appears necessary to consider the probabilities rather than expected vote. To pursue the existence of equilibria, I shall assume that ξ_t are continuous functions of the vector, z, of declarations. This implicitly makes certain assumptions on voter behavior, which we leave unspecified in the present work (see however Nixon, et al., 1995, and David Austen-Smith's discussion in Chapter 6).

Given a coalition structure, $\mathcal{D}_t$ at the policy vector z, let $g_{\gamma(t)}(z)$ be the "legislative" outcome. That is, $g_{\gamma(t)}(z)$ defines a specific policy lottery, $g_t(z)$, giving probabilities $\{\rho_M\}$ and outcomes $\{z_M\}$ associated with each coalition $M \in \mathcal{D}_t$. Moreover $g_{\gamma(t)}(z)$ defines for each M an allocation γ_M of perquisites to each member of M. Now let $\tilde{X}_\Delta$ be the set of finite lotteries over the policy space X and the simplex, Δ, of distributions of perquisites.

We may put electoral risk and coalition risk together in the form of a general model of n-party competition.

Assumptions of the General n-Party Model.

1. The electoral response ξ to a joint policy declaration $z = (z_1, \ldots, z_n)$ is an assignment $\{\xi_t(z) : t = 1, \ldots, T\}$ of probabilities, one to each possible decisive structure, $\mathcal{D}_t$. Let Δ_T be the $(T-1)$ dimensional unit simplex. Then the map $\xi : X^N \longrightarrow \Delta_T : z \longrightarrow (\xi_1(z), \ldots, \xi_T(x))$ is continuous and common knowledge.

2. The outcome function is a continuous map $g_\xi : X^N \longrightarrow \tilde{X}_\Delta$ defined from ξ by $g_\xi(z) = \{(\xi_t(z), g_{\gamma(t)}(z)) : t = 1, \ldots, T\}$.

Here $g_{\gamma(t)}(z)$ specifies the legislative outcome given the declarations of the parties and given the decisive structure $\mathcal{D}_t$.

We shall also assume, as we did in Section 8.5, that $g_{\gamma(t)}(z)$ is "separable" between policy outcomes and perquisites, and that the policy component $g_t : X^N \longrightarrow \tilde{X}$ is a continuous selection from the heart correspondence, $\mathcal{H}\mathcal{D}_t : X^N \longrightarrow 2(\tilde{X})$. That is, if coalition structure $\mathcal{D}_t$ occurs after the election, then $g_{\gamma(t)}(z)$ selects certain coalition outcomes from $\mathcal{H}\mathcal{D}_t(z)$. In this way we deal both with electoral risk (represented by ξ) and political or coalitional risk (ρ represents the indeterminacy underlying coalition formation). Because of the assumption of von Neumann-Morgenstern utility functions, the lottery outcome $g_\xi(z)$ can be evaluated by each party.

In principle it is possible to impose quite a general form on the coalition policy outcomes. The structure of the model attempts to generalize both the pure two party model of electoral risk proposed by Cox (1984a) and the pure three-party model of coalitional risk proposed by Baron (1989).

A Nash equilibrium of the electoral game at the profile $x = (x_1, \ldots, x_n)$ is just an equilibrium of the game form g_ξ. In general a $PSNE$ may not exist, but because of the assumptions on the continuity of each ξ_t and g_ξ there will exist an $MSNE$, described by an equilibrium map $E_{g_\xi} : X^N \longrightarrow \tilde{X}^N$. If we extend g_ξ to the domain $\tilde{X}^N$, then the equilibrium outcome is the lottery $g_\xi(E_{g_\xi}(x)) \in \tilde{X}_\Delta$. This in turn defines an expectation $\underline{Ex}[g(E_{g_\xi}(x)]$ for the policy outcome.

The model is rather complex but the idea is less difficult. Each party (1, say) may make reasonable guesses as to the declarations $\{z_2, \ldots, z_n\} = z_{-1}$ of the other parties. For each possible choice of z_1, it estimates what the range of likely electoral responses $\{\xi_t(z)\}$ will be. For each t it considers how its own choice, z_1, will affect coalition bargaining over policy outcomes and perquisites. It aggregates across t and chooses z_1 accordingly. Of course, with such a complex game there may be many Nash equilibria. However the uniqueness of the $PSNE$ in the three-party game gives some hope that, at least generically, there will be a unique pure strategy Nash equilibrium in this game.

Suppose we consider the degenerate case examined in Section 8.5, where $t = 1$, so there is only one decisive coalition structure, namely the family comprising the three different two party coalitions. We have shown that the equilibrium outcome has expected value within the Pareto set. This suggests that in general the expected value of the equilibrium outcome under the game form g_ξ also lies inside the Pareto set of the parties. Current research seeks to substantiate these claims through computer simulation.

We may conjecture that a system of beliefs, regarding the electoral map ξ, and a system of known perquisites γ pertaining to government will give a unique outcome (in expectation) within the Pareto set of the parties' bliss points. Since this outcome is determined by ξ, it makes sense to ask what is the relationship between the expected policy outcome and the distribution of voters' preferences. If we let f be a distribution of voter bliss points, then we can define the electoral heart $\mathcal{H}(f)$ induced by this electoral distribution under plurality rule.

Implict in the discussion of Section 8.2 is the conclusion that decision-making under direct democracy, (with electoral prefrences represented by f) would lead to an outcome within $\mathcal{H}(f)$. Moreover for a large electorate, the results of Schofield and Tovey (1992) suggest that $\mathcal{H}(f)$ will be small relative to the electoral Pareto set. Politics is *efficient* if the expectation of the multiparty equilibrium policy outcome belongs to $\mathcal{H}(f)$.

8.7 Conclusion

The general model proposed here is that, in the pre-election environment, parties choose a Nash equilibrium to a game form g_ξ that represents their beliefs about electoral response, coalition policy outcome, and party perquisites from government. In stable regimes, parties would have a fairly good understanding of the game form, and in general might only need to consider two or three possible decisive structures. As we have emphasized, a key to the various possibilities will be whether or not one of the parties can present a core policy declaration.

In the context of such a model, there are a number of obvious questions:

1. How will the game change if new parties enter?

2. How will the equilibrium change if the pattern of perquisites is changed?

3. Is the pattern of convergence of "close" parties and divergence of "distant" parties that we observed in the three party case generic in the n–party case?

4. Under what conditions is this political game efficient?

5. Given that the game form g_ξ is a generalized version of the two party game, can we draw any general conclusion about the differences between two party and multiparty systems?

6. Can this model be used to describe how parties form in the first place?

7. In the post-election state $\{\mathcal{D}_t, z\}$, can the coalition probabilities $\{\rho_M\}$, coalition outcomes $\{z_M\}$ and perquisites $\{\gamma_M\}$ be determined endogenously? It is assumed in the model just presented that these are exogenously (or "historically") determined. As suggested, in stable regimes parties could form expectations of these outcomes. It is obvious however that in unstable situations parties will, in all likelihood, use a crude method of estimation to guess at post election events.

A useful goal for work on coalitions in multiparty systems would be to obtain information of the parameters of the general model (see for example the chapters in Part III of this volume).

The approach outlined here has attempted to integrate three rather different classes of political models. In Sections 8.2 and 8.3 we have considered coalition politics essentially as committee games, assuming that each party has well-defined policy preferences on X. The empirically-based discussion seems to give some credence to the notions of the core and heart. In Section 8.5 we considered again a committee of three parties, and proposed a model where parties make proposals, knowing that the outcome will be a lottery across coalitional compromises. Results on existence of a Nash equilibrium in such a game were presented. Finally Section 8.6 suggested how electoral risk could, in theory, be included in the model. Implicit in the model building is the assumption that parties do care about policy, and are not content simply to make declarations that maximize expected vote. A justification for this assumption is empirical work, just completed, on the multiparty system of Israel. Nixon *et al.* (1995) using data on electoral preferences and party declarations have statistically fitted a probabilistic voting model for the recent election of 1992. It turns out that the Nash equilibrium in the expected vote maximization model would have resulted in the coalescence of the parties into two groups, essentially based on the two large parties, Labor and Likud. Since the parties kept their separate identities and did not converge, this suggests that policy and electoral considerations are both important. The same argument would appear valid for all European multiparty polities.

There is a more general point to be made. On the one hand, all "Downsian" competitive electoral models, whether probabilistic or deterministic, exhibit "centripetal" tendencies towards convergence of party positions. On the other hand, the coalition model presented in Section 8.5 is based on cooperative, spatial voting theory. The very simple two dimensional model, presented in Section 8.5, exhibited a countervailing or "centrifugal" tendency towards divergence. The remaining fundamental research problem is to relate the nature of the electoral system (and other political institutional rules) to the balance attained between these two "forces" in a society, and to account for the formation of parties in different contexts. (See Cox 1990, for the effects of different electoral systems on these forces in the special case of a unidimensional policy space.)

It is possible, of course, that there can be situations where no "equilibrium" exists, or where it is unstable. Recent events in Russia, Italy and Japan, for example, may remind us that equilibria can persist for many years and then collapse. My view is that an integration of the analytical framework of cooperative game theory (as presented in section 8.2 for example) and of non-cooperative equilibrium theory provides the best hope for understanding the complexities of democratic politics.

References

Aranson, P., M. Hinich and P. Ordeshook. 1974. "Election Goals and Strategies: Equivalent and Non-equivalent Candidate Objectives," *American Political Science Review* 68: 135-152.

Arrow, K. 1951. *Social Choice and Individual Values*. New York: Wiley.

Austen-Smith, D. and J. Banks. 1988. "Elections, Coalitions and Legislative Outcomes," *American Political Science Review* 82: 405-422.

Austen-Smith, D. and J. Banks. 1989. "Electoral Accountability and Incumbency," in *Models of Strategic Choice in Politics*, P. C. Ordeshook, ed. Ann Arbor: University of Michigan Press.

Banks, J. 1990. "A Model of Electoral Competition with Incomplete Information," *Journal of Economic Theory* 50: 309-325.

Banks, J. and R. Sundaram. 1990. "Incumbents, Challengers, and Bandits: Bayesian Learning in a Dynamic Choice Model." Typescript: University of Rochester. '

Banks, J. and R. Sundaram. 1993. "Adverse Selection and Moral Hazard in Repeated Elections," in *Political Economy: Institutions, Competition, and Representation*, W. Barnett, M. J. Hinich and N. Schofield, eds. Cambridge: Cambridge University Press.

Baron, D. 1989. "A Non-Cooperative Theory of Legislative Coalitions," *American Journal of Political Science* 33: 1048-1084.

Baron, D. 1991. "A Spatial Bargaining Model of Government Formation in Parliamentary Systems," *American Political Science Review* 85: 137-164.

Baron, D. 1993. "Government Formation and Endogenous Parties," *American Political Science Review* 87: 34-47.

Bordes, G., M. Le Breton and M. Salles. 1992. "Gillies' and Miller's Sub-relations of a Relation over an Infinite Set of Alternatives: General Results and Applications to Voting Games," *Mathematics of Operations Research* 17: 508-518.

Budge, I., D. Robertson, and D. H. Hearl, eds. 1987. *Ideology, Strategy and Party Change: A Spatial Analysis of Post-War Election Programmes in Nineteen Democracies.* Cambridge: Cambridge University Press.

Coughlin, P. 1992. *Probabilistic Voting Theory.* Cambridge: Cambridge University Press.

Cox, G. 1984a. "An Expected-Utility Model of Electoral Competition," *Quality and Quantity* 18: 337-349.

Cox, G. 1984b. "Non-Collegial Simple Games and the Nowhere Denseness of the Set of Preference Profiles Having a Core," *Social Choice and Welfare* 1: 159-164.

Cox, G. 1987. "The Uncovered Set and the Core," *American Journal of Political Science* 31: 408-422.

Cox, G. 1990. "Centripetal and Centrifugal Incentives in Electoral Systems," *American Journal of Political Science* 34: 903-945.

Dasgupta, P. and E. Maskin. 1986. "The Existence of Equilibrium in Discontinuous Economic Games, I: Theory, II: Applications," *Review of Economic Studies* 53: 1-42.

Denzau, A. and R. Parks. 1983. "Existence of Voting Market Equilibria," *Journal of Economic Theory* 30: 243-265.

Dittrich, K. 1987. "The Netherlands 1946-1981," in *Ideology, Strategy and Party Change, op cit.*

Downs, A. 1957. *An Economic Theory of Democracy.* New York: Harper and Row.

Eaton, C. and R. Lipsey. 1975. "The Principle of Minimum Differentiation Reconsidered: Some New Developments in the Theory of Spatial Competition," *Review of Economic Studies* 42: 27-50.

Enelow, J. M. and M. J. Hinich. 1984. *The Spatial Theory of Voting: An Introduction.* Cambridge: Cambridge University Press.

Gibbard, A. 1973. "Manipulation of Voting Schemes: A General Result," *Econometrica* 41: 587-601.

Greenberg, J. 1979. "Consistent Majority Rules over Compact Sets of Alternatives," *Econometrica* 41: 285-297.

Greenberg, J. and S. Weber. 1985. "Multiparty Equilibria under Proportional Representation," *American Political Science Review* 79: 693-703.

Greenberg, J. and K. Shepsle. 1987. "The Effect of Electoral Rewards in Multiparty Competition with Entry," *American Political Science Review* 81: 525-537.

Hinich, M. J. and P. C. Ordeshook. 1970. "Plurality Maximization vs. Vote Maximization: A Spatial Analysis with Variable Participation," *American Political Science Review* 64: 772-791.

Holmstedt, M. and T. L. Schou. 1987. "Sweden and Denmark: 1945-1982: Election Programmes in the Scandinavian Setting," in *Ideology, Strategy and Party Change, op cit.*

Keesing's Contemporary Archives, 1945-1993. Bristol: Longmans.
Kramer, G. 1973. "On a Class of Equilibrium Conditions for Majority Rule," *Econometrica* 41: 285-297.
Kramer, G. 1978. "Existence of Electoral Equilibrium," in *Game Theory and Political Science*, P. Ordeshook, ed. New York: New York University Press.
Laver, M. and N. Schofield. 1990. *Multiparty Government.* Oxford: Oxford University Press.
Le Breton, M. 1987. "On the Core of Voting Games," *Social Choice and Welfare* 4: 295-305.
Mair, P. 1987. "Ireland 1948-1981: Issues, Parties, Strategies," in *Ideology, Strategy and Party Change, op cit.*
Mastrapaolo, A. and M. Slater. 1987. "Italy: 1946-1979; Ideological Distances and Party Movements," in *Ideology, Strategy and Party Change, op cit.*
McKelvey, R. D. 1986. "Covering, Dominance, and Institution-Free Properties of Social Choice," *American Journal of Political Science* 30: 283-314.
McKelvey, R. D. and P. C. Ordeshook. 1990. "A Decade of Experimental Research on Spatial Models of Elections and Committees," in *Advances in the Spatial Theory of Voting*, J. M. Enelow and M. J. Hinich, eds. Cambridge: Cambridge University Press.
McKelvey, R. and N. Schofield. 1986. "Structural Instability of the Core," *Journal of Mathematical Economics* 15: 179-98.
McKelvey, R. and N. Schofield. 1987. "Generalized Symmetry Conditions at a Core Point," *Econometrica* 55: 923-33.
Miller, N. 1980. "A New Solution Set for Tournaments and Majority Voting," *American Journal of Political Science* 24: 68-96.
Nakamura, K. 1979. "The Vetoers in a Simple Game with Ordinal Preference," *International Journal of Game Theory* 8: 55-61.
Nixon, D. C., D. Olomoki, N. Schofield, and I. Sened. 1995. "Multiparty Probabilistic Voting: An Application to the Knesset." Typescript: Washington University.
Ordeshook, P. C. and T. Schwartz. 1987. "Agendas and the Control of Political Outcomes," *American Political Science Review* 81: 180-199.
Palfrey, T. 1984. "Spatial Equilrium with Entry," *Review of Economic Studies* 51: 139-156.
Parks, R. and A. Denzau. 1983. "Existence of Voting-Market Equilibria," *Journal of Economic Theory* 30: 243-265.
Plott, C. 1967. "A Notion of Equilibrium and its Possibility under Majority Rule," *American Economic Review* 57: 787-806.
Rubinstein, A. 1979. "A Note on the Nowhere Denseness of Societies Having an Equilibrium under Majority Rule," *Econometrica* 47: 511-514.
Saari, D. 1995. "The Generic Existence of a Core for q-rules." Typescript: Northwestern University.
Satterthwaite, M. A. 1975. "Strategy- Proofness and Arrow's Conditions: Existence and Correspondence Theorems for Voting Procedures and Social Welfare Functions," *Journal of Economic Theory* 10: 187-217.

Schofield, N. 1978. "Instability of Simple Dynamic Games," *Review of Economic Studies* 45: 575-594.

Schofield, N. 1983. "Generic Instability of Majority Rule," *Review of Economic Studies* 50: 695-705.

Schofield, N. 1984. "Social Equilibrium and Cycles on Compact Sets," *Journal of Economic Theory* 33: 59-71.

Schofield, N. 1986. "Existence of a 'Structurally Stable' Equilibrium for a Non-collegial Voting Rule," *Public Choice* 51: 267-284.

Schofield, N. 1989. "Smooth Social Choice," *Mathematical and Computer Modelling* 12: 417-435.

Schofield, N. 1993a. "Party Competition in a Spatial Model of Coalition Formation," in *Political Economy, op cit.*

Schofield, N. 1993b. "Political Competition in Multiparty Coalition Governments," *European Journal of Political Research* 23: 1-33.

Schofield, N. 1995a. "The C^1-Topology on the Space of Preference Profiles and the Existence of a Continuous Preference Aggregator." Typescript: Washington University.

Schofield, N. 1995b. "Existence of a Social Choice Functor," in *Social Choice, Welfare, and Ethics*, W. Barnett, H. Moulin, M. Salles and N. Schofield, eds. Cambridge: Cambridge University Press.

Schofield, N. 1995c. "Coalition Politics: A Formal Model and Empirical Analysis," *Journal of Theoretical Politics* 7: 245-281.

Schofield, N. and R. Parks. 1993. "Existence of Nash Equilibrium in a Spatial Model of n-Party Competition." Typescript: Washington University.

Schofield, N. and C. Tovey. 1992. "Probability and Convergence for Supra-Majority Rule with Euclidean Preferences," *Mathematical Computer Modelling* 16: 41-58.

Shaked, A. 1975. "Non-existence of Equilibrium for the Two-Dimensional Three-Firm Location Model," *Review of Economic Studies* 42: 51-56.

Shepsle, K. 1991. *Models of Multiparty Competition.* London: Harwood.

Shepsle, K. and B. Weingast. 1984. "Uncovered Sets and Sophisticated Voting Outcomes with Implications for Agenda Institutions," *American Journal of Political Science* 28: 49-74.

Strnad, J. 1985. "The Structure of Continuous-Valued Neutral Monotonic Social Functions," *Social Choice and Welfare* 2: 181-195.

9. Refinements of the Heart

David Austen-Smith

9.1 Introduction

The preceding chapter by Schofield develops the concept of the *heart* for general committee games when preferences are Euclidean. Among other things, he uses it to analyse parliamentary bargaining in multiparty polities. The formal defintion of the heart, $\mathcal{H}_\mathcal{D}$, provided in Schofield (1993, 1995) for general preferences and a given voting rule, $\mathcal{D}$, are reviewed in Section 9.2, and the application of the heart as a general solution concept are considered in Section 9.3. Two refinements (or subsets) of the heart called $\mathcal{S}_\mathcal{D}$ and $\mathcal{IS}_\mathcal{D}$ are proposed in Section 9.4. Section 9.5 concludes the chapter.

9.2 Chaos and the Heart

Let N be the finite set of voters and $X \subseteq \Re^m$ the feasible issue space. Each voter $i \in N$ has smooth preferences over X. At each $x \in X$, and for each $i \in N$, let

$$h_i(x) = \{v \in \Re^m \mid p_i(x) \cdot v > 0\},$$

where $p_i(x)$ is i's gradient vector at x. Thus $h_i : X \to X$ describes i's preferences on X, and the relevant preference profile for N can be summarized by the vector, $h = (h_1, \ldots, h_{|N|})$. For any coalition $M \subseteq N$, define the *preference cone for M at x* to be $h_M(x) = \cap_{i \in M} h_i(x)$. Figure 1 illustrates the definition for $M = \{1, 2\}$ at $x \in \Re^2$.

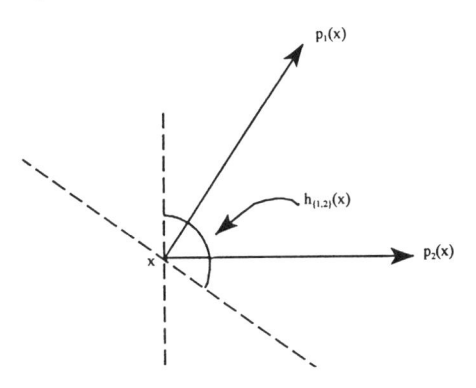

Figure 1. The preference cone $h_{\{1,2\}}(x)$.

A *voting rule* is implicitly defined by a given set of decisive coalitions, $\mathcal{D}$: say alternative y is socially preferred to alternative z iff there exists a decisive coalition in $\mathcal{D}$, all of whose members strictly prefer y to z. Assume $\mathcal{D}$ is proper ($M \in \mathcal{D}$ implies $N\backslash M \notin \mathcal{D}$) and monotonic ($M \in \mathcal{D}$ and $M \subset M'$ implies $M' \in \mathcal{D}$). Schofield's (1985) model is one of continuous social choice. Therefore define $\forall\ x \in X$, a *preference field* $h_\mathcal{D}$ on X by

$$h_\mathcal{D}(x) = \cup_{M \in \mathcal{D}}\ h_M(x),$$

with the interpretation that, given the status quo x, when $v \in h_\mathcal{D}(x)$, then v is a direction in which a decisive coalition of voters would like to move. By definition of decisiveness, this coalition can insist on leading x in the direction v, and so x cannot be a chosen point under the implicit voting rule. Conversely, if no such v exists, then no decisive coalition can agree on a direction of change, and x is a stable point relative to $h_\mathcal{D}$; specifically, define the *critical core* to be

$$E(h_\mathcal{D}) = \{x \in X|\ h_\mathcal{D}(x) = \emptyset\}.$$

Say that there is a *local cycle* about x if, for any open neighbourhood, V, of x, there exists a sequence of alternatives $< y_1, y_2, \ldots, y_T >$, all in V, such that $y_1 = y_T = x$, and each alternative is socially preferred to the immediately preceding alternative. Now let,

$$\Gamma(h_\mathcal{D}) = \{x \in X\ |\ \exists\ \text{a local cycle about } x \text{ under } h_\mathcal{D}\}.$$

Finally, let $k(\mathcal{D})$ be the Nakamura number for the voting rule implictly defined by $\mathcal{D}$.[1] Then if $\mathcal{D}$ is noncollegial, (so $k(\mathcal{D}) < \infty$), there exists an instability integer, $w(\mathcal{D})$ for $\mathcal{D}$, with $w(\mathcal{D}) \geq k(\mathcal{D}) - 1$, such that the following two statements are generically true (*cf.* Chapters 1 and 8 of this volume).

1. $m \geq w(\mathcal{D})$ implies $E(h_\mathcal{D}) = \emptyset$;

2. $m \geq w(\mathcal{D}) + 1$ implies $\Gamma(h_\mathcal{D})$ is open dense in X.

In other words, virtually no points in the social choice process are stable ones, and it is typically possible to construct continuous social preference cycles to cover the entire feasible set.

EXAMPLE 1: Let $N = \{1, 2, 3\}$; $\mathcal{D} = \{M \subseteq N : |M| \geq 2\}$. Assume that individual preferences are Euclidean. In this case, $k(\mathcal{D}) = 3$ and $w(\mathcal{D}) = 2$.

(a) Consider $X = \Re^2$. $E(\cdot) = \emptyset$, but since $w < k(\mathcal{D}), \Gamma(\cdot)$ is not open dense in X; rather, $\Gamma(\cdot)$ coincides with the interior of the Pareto set. (Because preferences are Euclidean, the Pareto set is the convex hull of the bliss points, labelled 1, 2, 3 respectively. The Pareto set is labelled $\Delta(1, 2, 3)$. See Figure 2.) To see why this is so, consider, alternatively, the point y outside the Pareto set. (See Figure 2.) Because $m = 2$, all the gradient vectors lie in the same plane and point toward the Pareto set; in particular, $h_\mathcal{D}(y)$ lies in an open halfspace in $\Re^2$ and there is no room to construct a local cycle

---

[1] If $\cap_\mathcal{D} M \neq \emptyset$ then $k(\mathcal{D}) = \infty$; otherwise, $k(\mathcal{D}) = \min\{|\ \mathcal{D}'\ | : \mathcal{D}' \subseteq \mathcal{D}$ and $\cap_{\mathcal{D}'} M = \emptyset\}$

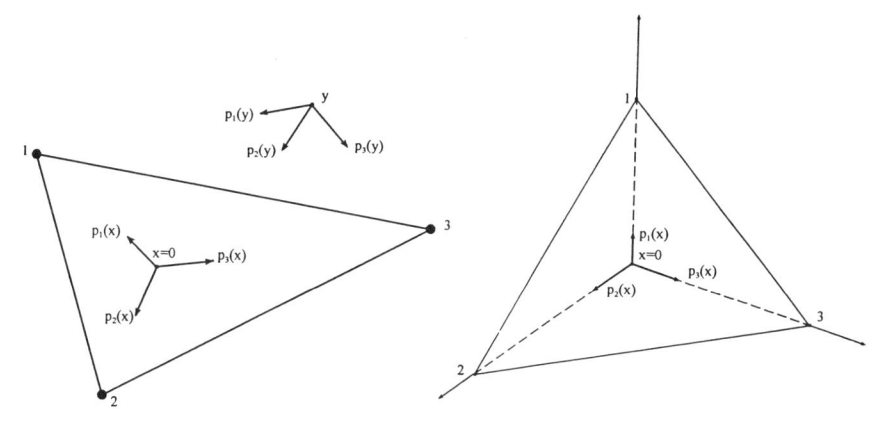

Figure 2. $\Gamma(h_D) = \text{Int } \Delta(1,2,3)$ in two dimensions.

Figure 3. $\Gamma(h_D) = X$ in three dimensions.

about y. So $y \notin E(\cdot) \cup \Gamma(\cdot)$. It is clearly possible, however, to construct a local cycle about any point in the interior of the Pareto set.

(b) Consider $X = \Re^3$. Again, $E(\cdot) = \emptyset$. Since in this case $k(\mathcal{D}) = m$, $\Gamma(\cdot)$ is open dense in X. To see why points off the Pareto surface now lie in $\Gamma(\cdot)$, consider Figure 3, which examines the situation at $x = 0$. Although all three gradient vectors lie in the same halfspace containing the Pareto set, it is no longer the case that $h_D(0)$ lies in an open halfspace. Indeed, for any two-person coalition, say $\{1,3\}$, the gradient vectors lie in a two-dimensional subspace, yet the preference cone $h_{\{1,3\}}(0)$ is a three-dimensional subset of $\Re^3$. (See Figure 4.) Consequently, it is possible to construct a local cycle about 0 by exploiting this additional degree of freedom on directions of change for any coalition (see Kramer 1973 for details). Geometrically, one can find a two-dimensional plane containing the point $x = 0$ that has a nonempty intersection with each $h_{\{i,j\}}(0), i \neq j$ and $i,j = 1,2,3$. Projecting the gradient vectors onto this plane then yields a picture corresponding to Figure 2 above.

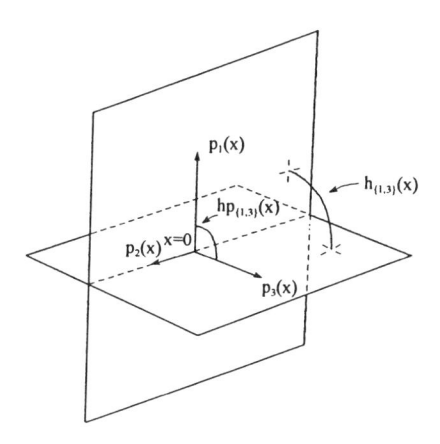

Figure 4. Preference cones at $x = 0$ in three dimensions.

Fix a coalition $M \in \mathcal{D}$ and a point $x \in X$ such that $h_M(x) \neq \emptyset$. Then we can think of coalition M's problem as choosing the direction in which social choice is to be moved away from x. Given the local, rather than global, focus of the model, it is natural to assume that whatever the intra-coalition bargaining process might be, the decision eventually reached, say $v \in \Re^m$, should be both *individually rational* (i.e., $v \in h_M(x)$) and *locally efficient* for M (i.e., $\forall\ v' \in h_M(x) \backslash v, \exists\ i \in M$ such that $p_i(x) \cdot v' < p_i(x) \cdot v$). It follows immediately that if the coalition's choice v satisfies both these requirements, then necessarily,

$$v \in h_M(x) \cap p_M(x) \equiv hp_M(x);$$

where

$$p_M(x) = \{v \in \Re^m |\ v = \sum_M \alpha_i p_i(x), \alpha_i \geq 0\ \forall\ i \in M, \sum_M \alpha_i = 1\}.$$

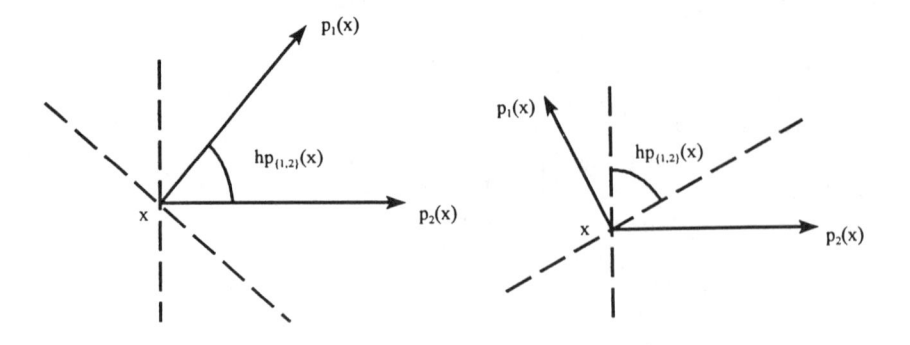

Figure 5. Canonic cases for $hp_{\{1,2\}}(x)$ in $\Re^2$.

Figure 4 above illustrates the difference between $h_{\{1,3\}}(0)$ and $hp_{\{1,3\}}(0)$ for $X \subseteq \Re^3$. Figure 5 illustrates the two canonic cases for $X \subseteq \Re^2$.

Define the *efficient preference field*, $hp_\mathcal{D}$, on X by,

$$hp_\mathcal{D}(x) = \cup_{M \in \mathcal{D}}\ hp_M(x).$$

Clearly, $\forall x \in X, hp_\mathcal{D} \subseteq h_\mathcal{D}(x)$. Just as for the preference field $h_\mathcal{D}$, we can define the sets,

$$E(hp_\mathcal{D}) = \{x \in W\ |\ hp_\mathcal{D}(x) = \emptyset\};$$

$$\Gamma(hp_\mathcal{D}) = \{x \in X\ |\ \exists\ \text{a local cycle about } x \text{ under } hp_\mathcal{D}\}.$$

Then Schofield (1993) defines the *heart* $\mathcal{H}_\mathcal{D}$, at the profile h, by

$$\mathcal{H}_\mathcal{D}(h) = E(hp_\mathcal{D}) \cup \text{clos}\ \Gamma(hp_\mathcal{D}).$$

Because $E(hp_\mathcal{D}) \cup \Gamma(hp_\mathcal{D}) \neq \emptyset$, the heart always exists and coincides with the critical core when this exists (Schofield 1995). Note that by (1) and (2) above, generically it will be the case that $E(h_\mathcal{D}) \cup \text{clos } \Gamma(h_\mathcal{D})$ is open dense in X in dimension $w(\mathcal{D}) + 1$ and above. In contrast, Schofield shows that not only is the heart $\mathcal{H}_\mathcal{D}(h)$ non-empty, but that $\mathcal{H}_\mathcal{D}(h)$ is a subset of the Pareto set for any profile h defined by smooth convex preferences.

To see why the social choice process induced by the efficient preference field $hp_\mathcal{D}$, unlike that induced by the preference field $h_\mathcal{D}$, is not chaotic, consider Figure 4 once again. As discussed above, to generate a local cycle about $x = 0$, it is necessary to exploit the fact that $h_\mathcal{D}(0)$ does not lie in a halfspace. And given that the only restriction on the direction a coalition can move is individual rationality, $v \in h_M(0)$, this is certainly possible. However, if local efficiency for M is also required, $v \in hp_M(0)$, then the permissible moves away from 0 (i.e., characterized by $hp_\mathcal{D}$) all lie in a halfspace containing the Pareto set. In terms of the earlier geometric intuition, it is no longer possible to find a two-dimensional plane containing 0 that simultaneously intersects every $hp_{\{i,j\}}(0)$. Hence it is the requirement of local efficiency on intracoalition bargaining that guarantees Pareto optimality of the heart.

For arbitrary (proper and monotonic) $\mathcal{D}$ and arbitrary (smooth) preference profiles, the geometric structure of the heart is not readily apparent. However, if $\mathcal{D}$ is majoritarian[2] and preferences are Euclidean, then Schofield shows that the heart can be characterized as the set of points bounded by median hyperplanes,[3] and is thus an easily computed starshaped subset of the Pareto set.

9.3 The Heart as a Solution Concept

For spatial (majoritarian) voting games, the core is a most attractive solution concept. Unfortunately, the core is typically empty in such games and, as a consequence, there is an ongoing search for a suitable predictor that generally exists. Given the attractiveness of the core, any proposal for an acceptable solution concept must, I claim, satisfy at least three requirements. First, it must coincide with the core when the core exists; second, it must be "close to" the core when the distribution of voter preferences is "close to" supporting a core; and third, it must have a behavioural motivation. As remarked in the previous section, the heart satisfies the first requirement. From this perspective, there is nothing to choose between the Heart and any of the other contenders for a solution concept (in particular: the uncovered set, the yolk and the minmax set).[4] But this is not true with respect to the two remaining desiderata.

---

[2] That is, the implicit voting rule is a q–rule : x is socially preferred to y iff at least q voters strictly prefer x to y. $\mathcal{D}$ is simple majoritarian if (assuming $|N|$ odd) $q = (|N|+1)/2$).

[3] For supramajority rules, a "median" hyperplane is defined by having a winning coalition set of ideal points contained in one closed halfspace bounded by the hyperplane.

[4] (i) A point $x \in X$ is *covered* if there exists some $y \in X$ that beats x, and everything that beats y also beats x. The *uncovered set* is the set of points that are not covered. (ii) The *yolk* is the ball of minimum radius that intersects all median hyperplanes. (Note that this definition is only meaningful for Euclidean preferences and simple majority rule.) (iii) For

Although exactly what is meant by "close to" is subject to various technical specifications, the central idea is simply that of continuity. Suppose we start with a distribution of voter preferences that supports a core and then perturb this distribution slightly so that the core vanishes. Then the requirement is that the solution concept under consideration approximately coincides with the pre-perturbation set of core outcomes. For quasi-concave preferences and majority rule, McKelvey (1986) and Cox (1987) have shown that the uncovered set, and therefore the yolk, satisfy such a requirement; and the example of Kramer and McKelvey (1984) dramatically shows that the minmax set fails to do so. Schofield (1995, Theorem 2) proves that the heart does have the requisite continuity property. (Note that Schofield uses a "fine" smooth topology on preferences and proves the result for an arbitrary voting rule.) For the special case of majority rule and Euclidean preferences, the theorem follows directly from the results of McKelvey and Cox by virtue of the definition of the heart as the set of points bounded by median hyperplanes.

By construction, the heart has a good behavioral foundation. Given the family of decisive sets determining social preference, the heart is defined exclusively in terms of outcomes resulting from a process of intracoalitional bargaining, constrained only to be individually rational and locally efficient. The behavioural motivation for the uncovered set or minmax set, on the other hand, is fairly weak. To the extent that such exists, it is entirely indirect; a variety of majoritarian processes (*e.g.*, amendment agendas with fixed sets of alternatives, sequential elections with myopic vote-maximizing candidates) have been demonstrated to lead to outcomes located within one or the other of these sets. These results certainly justify focusing on the set as places to look for predictions about where majoritarian outcomes are likely to be found, but they fall short of providing a satisfactory basis for a generally acceptable solution concept. Neither of these two sets, for example, has any sort of independent justification, and neither has (yet) been fully characterized by the set of outcomes generated by a given majoritarian social choice process.

In sum, therefore, the heart fulfills all three desiderata for an acceptable solution concept. However, I claim the conditions are necessary, not sufficient, and there are some reservations about the heart.

First, although the heart surely has a behavioural basis, this basis is not strategic insofar as the focus on local, directional, changes precludes any decisive coalition from implementing discrete changes. Yet by definition of decisiveness, such changes are in principle admissible and individual preferences are well-defined on X. (And it is not hard to see that in majoritarian systems, the natural global version of the heart essentially coincides with the Pareto set.)[5] Normatively, requiring social choice processes to exhibit some

---

any $x \in X$, let $n(yx)$ denote the number of voters who strictly prefer y to x; let $n(x) = \min \{n(yx)|y \in X\}$. The *minmax set* is the set $\{x \in X : n(x) \leq n(z)$ for all $z \in X\}$.

[5] Let $u_i : X \to \Re$ be i's utility function on X. For any $M \subseteq N$, let P_M be the Pareto set for $M \subseteq N$ in X; let the set of Pareto improvements for coalition M from policy y be:

$$P_M(y) = \{x \in X|\ u_i(x) > u_i(y)\ \forall\ i \in M\}.$$

Let the set of Pareto efficient moves from y be the subset of $P_M(y)$ defined by :

David Austen-Smith

kind of continuity properties seems natural; if voter preferences are smooth on $X \subseteq \Re^m$ and one preference profile is "close to" another, then the social choice predicated on the former profile should likewise be "close to" that predicated on the latter. But this does not justify assuming that strategic behaviour by individuals operating under any particular voting rule should be continuous. Similarly, any empirical observation that social choice in a multiparty majoritarian system does indeed seem to behave in a fairly continuous fashion, is something to be explained rather than assumed. On the other hand, given that the focus of analysis is on the local structure of social choice in a spatial setting, Schofield's view of bargaining as being strictly about incremental changes is reasonable. Further, the fact that Schofield develops a "local bargaining" justification for the heart does not preclude the concept being supported by a fully strategic (global) model. The core, for example, is both the set of stationary points for the local process described by the preference field $h_\mathcal{D}$, and is also the undominated Nash equilibrium set of outcomes for a two-candidate plurality voting game.

Second, even though the uncovered set is not particularly satisfactory as a solution concept, it certainly has some attractive properties and seems to characterize some outcomes from a wide class of social choice processes (McKelvey 1986). As such, it would be desirable for a solution concept to lie within the uncovered set. Unfortunately, the heart can contain outcomes not in the uncovered set. Figure 6 illustrates this claim. In the example, the three voters have Euclidean preferences on $\Re^2$, and the voting rule is simple majoritarian. The heart is the entire Pareto set but the point y is covered, by x.

Third, although Schofield argues, using both empirical and hypothetical examples, that the heart is likely to be a small centrally located subset of the Pareto set when there are large numbers of voters, his principal motivation in developing the heart is to use it as a predictor for coalition formation in multiparty parliamentary systems. And in such systems, the relevant parliamentary players are often the parties and these are relatively few. So the heart may be large here, attenuating its value as the appropriate solution concept for parliamentary environments. The game with three players in Figure 6 is a good example.

Given the appeal of the heart from a local bargaining perspective, the last two reservations concerning its properties suggests looking for some kind of refinement for the concept. Two such refinements are offered in the following section, both of which exploit Schofield's idea of placing restrictions on the local coalitional bargaining process.

$$\hat{P}_M(y) = \{x \in P_M(y) \mid \forall\, z \in P_M(y)\setminus\{x\}, \exists\, j \in M \text{ s.t. } u_j(x) > u_j(z)\}.$$

Analogously, to define the local case define: $\hat{P}_\mathcal{D}(\cdot) = \cup_\mathcal{D} \hat{P}_M(\cdot)$. Then the *Global Heart* is $E(\hat{P}_\mathcal{D}) \cup \text{clos } \Gamma(\hat{P}_\mathcal{D})$, where

$$\Gamma(\hat{P}_\mathcal{D}) = \{x \in W \mid \exists\, < y_0, y_1, \ldots, y_T > \text{ s.t. } x \equiv y_0 \equiv y_T \text{ and } \forall\, t \geq 1,\ y_t \in \hat{P}_\mathcal{D}(y_{t-1})\}.$$

It is fairly easy to check that when the core is empty, the global heart is defined by $\cup P_M$, with the union being over all minimum winning coalitions. So in simple majority voting, the global heart is either the core or the Pareto set.

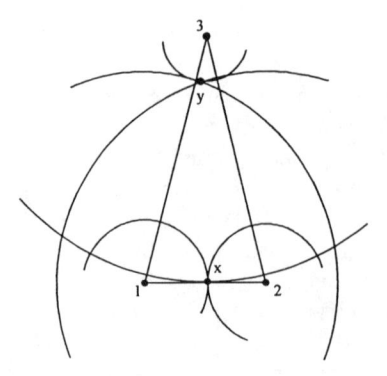

Figure 6. Heart = $\Delta(1,2,3)$; x covers y.

9.4 Two Refinements of the Heart

The first refinement is prompted by the fact that the heart need not lie within the uncovered set. Figure 7 reproduces the point y marked in Figure 6 above and describes the optimal preference cones $hp_{\{i,j\}}(y)$ for each of the minimum winning coalitions. It is clearly possible to construct a local cycle about y under $hp_\mathcal{D}$, and so y is a member of the Heart. However, it is evident that there is a direction in which the decisive coalition $\{1,2\}$ can move that both members of the coalition strictly prefer to *any* admissible move available to either member in any other decisive coalition. So it seems reasonable to extend the local bargaining perspective and to argue that of the three possible coalitions that could move social choice away from y, the coalition $\{1,2\}$ will form: both 1 and 2 can do strictly better here than either of them could possibly do by forming a coalition with player 3.

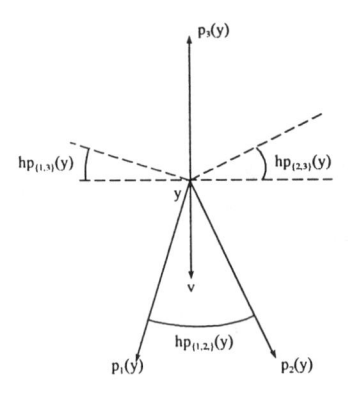

Figure 7. $p_i(y) \cdot v \geq p_i(y) \cdot u$ for all $u \in hp_{\{i,3\}}(y), i = 1, 2$.

More generally, the first refinement focuses on the best that individuals can do by joining any decisive coalition: if there is a decisive coalition that can adopt a direction of policy change that is at least as good for all coalition members as the *best* each member could hope for by joining *any* other coalition, then this is the coalition that will form. Formally, fix $\mathcal{D}$ and $x \in X$. For all $i \in N$, let $M_i = \{M \in \mathcal{D} | i \in M\}$. Let

$$\begin{aligned} \mathcal{D}(x) = \{M \in \mathcal{D} \mid &\exists v \in hp_M(x), \\ \text{s.t. } &\forall i \in M, \forall M' \in M_i \setminus \{M\}, \\ &p_i(x) \cdot v \geq \sup_{u \in hp_{M'}(x)} p_i(x) \cdot u\}. \end{aligned}$$

In words, a coalition M is a member of $\mathcal{D}(x)$ if and only if there is some local move away from x with the property that each member $i \in M$ weakly prefers this move to any feasible move from x that any other coalition containing i might select. Let,

$$\mathcal{C}(x) = \begin{cases} \mathcal{D}(x) & \text{if } \mathcal{D}(x) \neq \emptyset. \\ \mathcal{D} & \text{otherwise,} \end{cases}$$

and define the subfield $hp_\mathcal{C}$ of the optimal preference field by, $\forall x \in X$,

$$hp_\mathcal{C}(x) = \cup_{M \in \mathcal{C}(x)} hp_M(x).$$

Finally, define,

$$\mathcal{S}_\mathcal{D}(h) = E(hp_\mathcal{C}) \cup \text{clos } \Gamma(hp_\mathcal{C}).$$

By definition, $\emptyset \neq \mathcal{S}_\mathcal{D}(h) \subseteq \mathcal{H}_\mathcal{D}(h)$. Indeed, as the following claim implies, $\mathcal{S}_\mathcal{D}(h)$ is a well-behaved subset of the heart.

Theorem 1: *If $\{p_i(x) : i \in N\}$ all lie in an open half space, then $hp_\mathcal{C}(x)$ also lies in an open halfspace.*

Proof: Let $\mathcal{C}(x) \neq \mathcal{D}$, and without loss of generality, assume all decisive coalitions are minimum winning. If $|\mathcal{C}(x)| = 1$, we are done, so assume $|\mathcal{C}(x)| > 1$. Since $\mathcal{D}$ is proper, $\forall M, M' \in \mathcal{D}, \exists i \in M \cap M'$. Hence, for every $M, M' \in \mathcal{C}(x), hp_M(x) \cup hp_{M'}(x)$ lie in a common halfspace, say $\mathcal{U}$. By definition of $\mathcal{C}(x), \exists v \in hp_M(x)$ and $\exists v' \in hp_{M'}(x)$ such that for $i \in M \cap M'$,

$$\text{(a)} \begin{cases} p_i(x) \cdot v &\geq \sup_{u \in hp_{M'}(x)} p_i(x) \cdot u \geq 0 \\ p_i(x) \cdot v' &\geq \sup_{u \in hp_M(x)} p_i(x) \cdot u \geq 0. \end{cases}$$

Hence, $p_i(x) \cdot v = p_i(x) \cdot v'$. Now suppose the claim to be false. Then $\exists M'' \in \mathcal{C}(x)$ such that $hp_{M''}(x)$ does not lie in $\mathcal{U}$. Since $\mathcal{D}$ is proper, $\exists j \in M \cap M''$. If $p_i(x) = \alpha p_j(x)$ for some $\alpha > 0$, we are done; so suppose these gradient vectors are distinct. Then $\exists v'' \in h_{M''}(x)$ such that,

$$\text{(b)} \begin{cases} p_j(x) \cdot v &\geq \sup_{u \in hp_{M''}(x)} p_j(x) \cdot u \geq 0 \\ p_j(x) \cdot v'' &\geq \sup_{u \in hp_M(x)} p_j(x) \cdot u \geq 0. \end{cases}$$

Hence, $p_j(x) \cdot v = p_j(x) \cdot v''$. By definition of $M, M' \in \mathcal{C}(x)$, it follows that either $p_i(x) \notin hp_M(x) \cup hp_{M'}(x)$ or $p_i(x) \in hp_M(x) \cap hp_{M'}(x)$. Suppose the former is true. Then by individual rationality, (a) and (b) imply

$$p_i(x) \cdot v > (=) 0 \iff p_j(x) \cdot v = (>) 0.$$

Without loss of generality, suppose $p_i(x) \cdot v > 0$ and $p_j(x) \cdot v = 0$. But then either $M'' = \{j\}$, in which case, by definition of $M'' \in \mathcal{C}(x)$, $v = \alpha_j p_j(x)$, $\alpha_j > 0$; or $hp_{M''}(x) = \emptyset$; or $j \notin M''$. All three possibilities yield a contradiction. Therefore, we must have $p_i(x) \in hp_M(x) \cap hp_{M'}(x)$; in which case (a) yields $v = v' = \alpha_i p_i(x), \alpha_i > 0$. Hence, (b) and $p_i(x) \neq p_j(x)$ together imply $p_j(x) \notin hp_{M''}(x) \cup hp_M(x)$. By definition of $M, M'' \in \mathcal{C}(x)$, either $p_j(x) \notin hp_M(x) \cup hp_{M''}$ or $p_j(x) \in hp_M(x) \cap hp_{M''}(x)$. Therefore, $p_j(x) \in hp_M(x) \cap hp_{M''}(x)$, and (b) implies $v = v'' = \alpha_j p_j(x), \alpha_j > 0$. Since $p_i(x)$ and $p_j(x)$ are not colinear, we have the desired contradiction and the result is proved. Q.E.D.

Let UC denote the uncovered set of X; and for any $M \subseteq N$, let P_M denote the Pareto set for M in X. The proposition can be interpreted to mean that $\mathcal{S}_\mathcal{D}$ lies within the Pareto set P_N.

Theorem 2: *If $|N| = 3$, preferences are Euclidean and $\mathcal{D}$ is simple majoritarian, then $\mathcal{S}_\mathcal{D}(h) \subseteq UC \subseteq \mathcal{H}_\mathcal{D}(h)$.*

Proof: If there is a core $(E(h_\mathcal{D}) \neq \emptyset)$, then all three sets evidently coincide. So assume there is no core. Then with $\mathcal{D}$ majoritarian and $|N| = 3$, $\mathcal{H}_\mathcal{D}(h) = P_N$ (Schofield 1993) and $UC \subseteq P_N$, (e.g., McKelvey 1986). It remains to check the first inclusion claimed in the proposition. Suppose $\mathcal{S}_\mathcal{D}$ is not a subset of UC. Then, because $\mathcal{S}_\mathcal{D}$ and UC both lie in P_N, $\exists\, y \in \mathcal{S}_\mathcal{D}(h) \cap (P_N \backslash UC)$. Let $B(x)$ denote the set of points in X that defeat x under $\mathcal{D}$; and let $P_i(x)$ denote the set of points strictly preferred to x by $i \in N$. Since $|N| = 3$ and preferences are Euclidean,

$$\exists\, x \in P_i(y) \cap P_j(y) \cap P_{\{i,j\}},$$

such that x covers y. By definition of covering, $B(x) \subset B(y)$. Hence,

$$B(x) \subseteq P_i(y) \cap P_j(y).$$

Moreover, since $x \in P_{\{i,j\}}$, Euclidean preferences imply for $k \neq i, j$,

$$B(x) \cap P_{\{i,k\}} \neq \emptyset, \text{ and } B(x) \cap P_{\{j,k\}} \neq \emptyset.$$

Therefore, $P_{\{i,j\}} \subset P_i(y) \cap P_j(y)$. Euclidean preferences therefore yield,

$$hp_{\{i,j\}}(y) = p_{\{i,j\}}(y), \text{ and}$$
$$hp_{\{l,k\}}(y) \subset p_{\{l,k\}}(y),$$

$l = i, j$; $k \neq i, j$. Hence $\mathcal{C}(y) = \{i, j\} \neq \mathcal{D}$; in which case $y \in \mathcal{S}_\mathcal{D}(h)$. Q.E.D.

Figure 8 illustrates this result for the example of Figure 6, above.

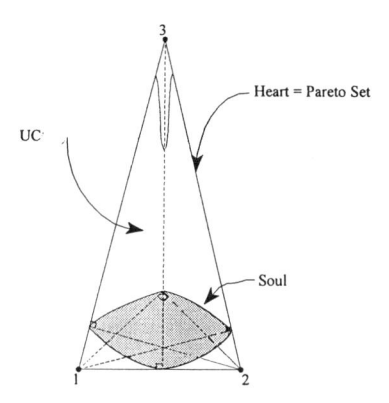

David Austen-Smith

Figure 8. $\mathcal{S}_\mathcal{D}(\cdot,\cdot)$ refines the Heart.

Unfortunately, Proposition 2 cannot be extended beyond $|N| = 3$; it is tedious but straightforward to construct counterexamples. However, even in such cases $\mathcal{S}_\mathcal{D}(h)$ can still refine the heart somewhat, in which case it may prove useful for small $|N|$. It is, however, very weak and in general has little bite when there are moderate or large numbers of voters.[6] The reason for its weakness lies in the focus on the best that individuals can hope to achieve in local coalitional bargaining. This is easily seen in Figure 9, which describes a five-voter example with Euclidean preferences and simple majority rule.

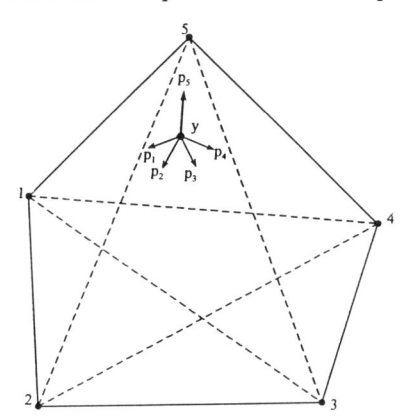

Figure 9. $\mathcal{H}_\mathcal{D}(h) = \mathcal{S}_\mathcal{D}(h)$ is the pentagon.

Here, the heart and $\mathcal{S}_\mathcal{D}(h)$ coincide. Consider a point like y. For y not to be a member of $\mathcal{S}_\mathcal{D}(h)$ either or both of the coalitions $M = \{1,2,3\}$ and $M' = \{2,3,4\}$ must be in $\mathcal{C}(y) \neq \mathcal{D}$. Now notice that $\{p_2(y), p_3(y)\} \subset hp_M(y) \cap hp_{M'}(y)\}$. Therefore there is no direction of movement that, say, M could take that can simultaneously make both voters 2 and 3 better off than in coalition

---

[6] Of course, as Schofield argues, with large enough numbers of voters, the heart itself is small and so likewise will $\mathcal{S}_\mathcal{D}(h)$ be small.

M'; and similarly if the roles of M and M' are reversed. Hence, $\mathcal{C}(y) = \mathcal{D}$ and $y \in \mathcal{S}_\mathcal{D}(h) = \mathcal{H}_\mathcal{D}(h)$. An alternative approach to finding a refinement is to consider the *worst* that players can do in any coalition, rather than the best. At y in Figure 9, it is evident that the worst players 2 and 3 can do if either joins a coalition that includes voter 5, is "zero" (*i.e.*, inf $p_i(y) \cdot u = 0$). On the other hand, in either coalition M or M', 2 and 3 are assured of a strictly positive change in utility for any move in the relevant preference cone. If these voters are sufficiently risk-averse, then we can argue that a coalition involving voter 5 will not form to move social choice from y. More generally, if there are two possible coalitions that include some individual such that, in one coalition, the *worst* direction of change that could be adopted is nevertheless a strictly utility-increasing change and, in the second coalition, the worst such change leaves the individual indifferent, then the second coalition will not form.

To formalize the suggestion above, for any $x \in X$ let

$$\mathcal{D}^*(x) = \{M \in \mathcal{D} | \forall i \in M, \inf_{u \in hp_M(x)} p_i(x) \cdot u > 0\};$$

$$\mathcal{C}^*(x) = \begin{cases} \mathcal{D}^*(x) \text{ if } \mathcal{D}^*(x) \neq \emptyset; \\ \mathcal{D} \text{ otherwise,} \end{cases}$$

and define a subfield $hp_{\mathcal{C}^*}$ of the optimal preference field by, $\forall\, x \in X$,

$$hp_{\mathcal{C}^*}(x) = \cup_{M \in \mathcal{C}^*(x)}\, hp_M(x).$$

Now define,

$$\mathcal{IS}_\mathcal{D}(h) = E(hp_{\mathcal{C}^*}) \cup \text{ clos } \Gamma(hp_{\mathcal{C}^*}).$$

Theorem 3: *If $\mathcal{D}$ is majoritarian, then $\mathcal{IS}_\mathcal{D}(h) \subseteq \mathcal{S}_\mathcal{D}(h)$.*

Proof: If there is a core, then the result is trivial; so assume there is no core. Suppose $x \in \mathcal{IS}_\mathcal{D}(h)$ but $x \notin \mathcal{S}_\mathcal{D}(h)$. Then $\exists\, M \in \mathcal{C}(x) \neq \mathcal{D}$ such that

$$\inf_{u \in hp_M(x)} p_i(x) \cdot u = 0$$

for some $i \in M$. By definition of $hp_M(x)$, therefore, $\exists\, j \in M \backslash \{i\}$ such that $p_i(x) \cdot p_j(x) \leq 0$. Generically, this inequality is strict; so assume $p_i(x) \cdot p_j(x) < 0$. Since $M \in \mathcal{C}(x) \neq \mathcal{D}$, there exists no $M' \in M_k \backslash M$ such that $p_k(x) \in hp_{M'}(x), k \in \{i, j\}$. By $\mathcal{D}$ majoritarian, $M_k \backslash M \neq \emptyset, k \in \{i, j\}$. In particular $\exists\, \hat{M} \in M_i$ with $j \notin \hat{M}$; and $\exists\, \overline{M} \in M_j$ with $i \notin \overline{M}$. By $x \in \mathcal{IS}_\mathcal{D}(h)$, we can choose $\hat{M}$ and $\overline{M}$ so that $hp_{\hat{M}}(x) \neq \emptyset$ and $hp_{\overline{M}}(x) \neq \emptyset$. Hence,

$$\sup_{u \in hp_{\hat{M}}(x)} p_i(x) \cdot u > 0; \text{ and}$$
$$\sup_{u \in hp_{\overline{M}}(x)} p_j(x) \cdot u > 0.$$

By $\mathcal{D}$ proper, $\hat{M} \cap \overline{M} \neq \emptyset$ and so $hp_{\hat{M}}(x) \cup hp_{\overline{M}}(x)$ lie in an open half-space. By construction, $k \in \hat{M} \cap \overline{M}, k = i, j$; and, therefore, $p_i(x) \cdot p_j(x) < 0$ implies for $u \in hp_M(x)$,

$[p_i(x) \cdot u \geq \sup_{u \in hp_M(x)} p_i(x) \cdot v] \Rightarrow [p_j(x) \cdot u < \sup_{v \in hp_M(x)} p_j(x) \cdot v];$

and this contradicts $i, j \in M \in \mathcal{C}(x) \neq \mathcal{D}$. Q.E.D.

That the set-inclusion can be proper is demonstrated in Figure 10, which reproduces Figure 9. Here, as argued above, the heart and $\mathcal{S}_\mathcal{D}(h)$ coincide; however, $\mathcal{IS}_\mathcal{D}(h)$ excludes the "corners" of $\mathcal{S}_\mathcal{D}(h)$.

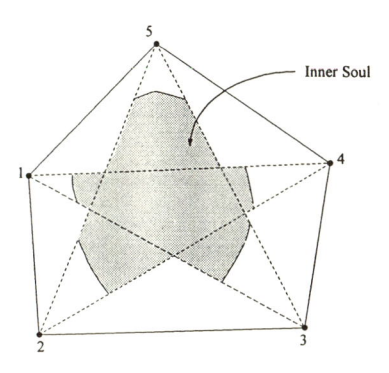

Figure 10. $\mathcal{IS}_\mathcal{D}(\cdot)$ refines $\mathcal{S}_\mathcal{D}(\cdot) \equiv$ Heart.

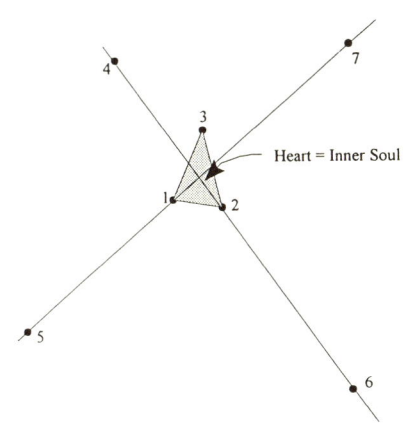

Figure 11. Heart $= \mathcal{S}_\mathcal{D}(\cdot) = \mathcal{IS}_\mathcal{D}(\cdot)$.

Given that the heart is starshaped when preferences are Euclidean and $\mathcal{D}$ is majoritarian, a reasonable conjecture in the light of Figure 10 is that $\mathcal{IS}(\cdot)$ is invariably a proper refinement of the heart in such environments. Unfortunately, it turns out that this is not the case. Figure 11 describes a seven voter counterexample for $X \subseteq \Re^2$ and simple majority rule; the heart and $\mathcal{IS}_\mathcal{D}(\cdot)$ coincide here. The example is clearly somewhat special, and it remains an open issue as to the extent of such cases. However, the following result gives a sufficient condition for $\mathcal{IS}_\mathcal{D}(\cdot)$ to provide a strict refinement of the heart in two-dimensional policy spaces (which Schofield suggests is typically sufficient for a spatial analysis of contemporary parliamentary democracies). For any set A, let ∂A and con A denote the boundary and convex hull of A, respectively.

Theorem 4: *Assume preferences are Euclidean; $\mathcal{D}$ is simple majoritarian; and $X \subseteq \Re^2$. If the core is empty and if $\partial P_N = \partial(\operatorname{con} \mathcal{H}_\mathcal{D}(h))$, then $\mathcal{IS}_\mathcal{D}(h) \subset \mathcal{H}_\mathcal{D}(h)$.*

Proof: Since $|N|$ is finite, ∂P_N is a convex polyhedron in $\Re^2$. Given $\partial(\operatorname{con}\mathcal{H}_\mathcal{D}(h)) = \partial P_N$, every vertex of ∂P_N is an (outer) vertex of $\mathcal{H}_\mathcal{D}(h)$. Let V denote the set of such vertices and let $x \in V$. Then there exist two median lines, $\mu(x)$ and $\mu'(x)$, such that

1. $x \in \mu(x) \cap \mu'(x)$;

2. $\mu(x) \cap \partial P_N \setminus \{x\} = y \in V$, $\mu'(x) \cap \partial P_N \setminus \{x\} = y' \in V$;

3. y and y' are adjacent in ∂P_N.

Thus x is the apex of the triangle formed by two median lines and an edge of ∂P_N. Moreover, since $y, y' \in V$, both y and y' are apexes of such triangles with one side given by (respectively $\mu(x), \mu'(x)$), and (at least) one on the other side given by distinct median lines (respectively) $\hat{\mu}(y), \hat{\mu}(y')$). See Figure 12, to which the subsequent argument refers. (Note that one or more of the median lines may coincide with an edge of ∂P_N; suppose $|N| = 3$, for example.) For every vertex of ∂P_N there is some $i \in N$ with an ideal point at that vertex. Therefore there exist $i, i', j, j' \in N$ with gradient vectors as illustrated in Figure 12. Since $\{x, y, y'\}$ form the vertices of a triangle, either $p_i(y) \cdot p_j(y) > 0$ or $p_{i'}(y') \cdot p_{j'}(y') > 0$ or both. Without loss of generality, assume $p_i(y) \cdot p_j(y) > 0$, and let $k \in N$ have the gradient vector at y illustrated in Figure 12 (such a k exists since this vector lies in ∂P_N). Because $y \in V \subset \partial P_N, \forall\, l \in N$,

(6) $p_l(y) \neq 0 \Rightarrow p_l(y) = \alpha_l p_k(y) + \beta_l p_j(x); \alpha_l, \beta_l \geq 0, \alpha_l + \beta_l > 0$.

Therefore, by definition of a median line, $\exists\, M \in \mathcal{D}$ such that $p_M(y) \subseteq p_{\{i,j\}}(y)$; hence $hp_M(y) \neq \emptyset$. Consider a point $z \in \mathcal{H}_\mathcal{D}(h) \cap N_\epsilon(y)$, where $N_\epsilon(y)$ is an open ball centered at y with radius ϵ. Because preferences are smooth, for ϵ sufficiently small, $hp_M(z) \neq \emptyset, p_M(z) \subseteq p_{\{i,j\}}(z)$, and $p_i(z) \cdot p_j(z) > 0$. Moreover, $z \in \mathcal{H}_\mathcal{D}(h)$ and no core implies $z \in \Gamma(hp_\mathcal{D})$. So for ϵ sufficiently small, (6) and smooth preferences imply $\exists\, M' \in \mathcal{D}$ such that $hp_{M'}(z) \subset p_{M'}(z)$; in which case, by $\mathcal{D}$ proper, $\exists\, l \in M \cap M'$ such that $\inf_{u \in hp_{M'}(z)} p_l(z) \cdot u = 0$. But then $C^*(x) \neq \mathcal{D}$, and by Theorems 1 and 3, $z \notin \mathcal{IS}_\mathcal{D}(h)$. Q.E.D.

David Austen-Smith   235

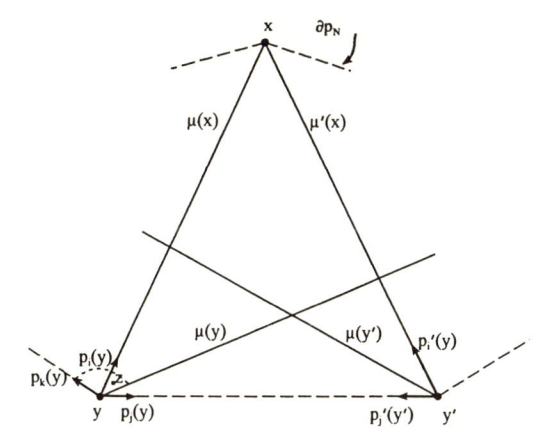

Figure 12. Proof of Theorem 4.

9.5 Conclusion

With sufficient institutional structure on the coalition-formation process, sharp predictions can be derived about which coalitions and which policies will arise in a particular parliamentary setting. Unfortunately, the predictions from such institutionally rich models tend to be highly sensitive to the institutional detail. On the one hand, this is not a problem; it has become a commonplace that "institutions matter," and indeed they do. But on the other hand, institutionally rich models do not constitute good general explanations, for they beg the questions of where the institutions come from and why they survive. Moreover, from a post-WW II European perspective, it is true that while the variance in institutional structure across the democracies is high, the policy outcomes are nevertheless very "centrally located" by virtually any measure (Laver and Schofield 1990). So to provide a general explanation of coalition formation and policy outcomes in parliamentary democracies, it seems essential to look for as institutionally poor a theory as possible (although, of course, given what is now known about the abstract properties of voting rules, some institutional detail is essential). The only structure (other than the basic spatial framework) that Schofield imposes is that change is incremental and intracoalitional bargaining is individually rational and locally efficient for any coalition. While I have suggested that the acceptability of insisting on incremental change is moot, the assumptions on the coalitional bargaining process are innocuous. That they lead to a clear, "centrally located" prediction–that all outcomes will be in the heart–is striking. But the local bargaining approach to social choice and the heart itself are, I think, surely worth serious attention and further work.

References

Cox, G. 1987. "The Uncovered Set and the Core," *American Journal of Political Science* 31: 408-22.

Kramer, G. 1973. "On a Class of Equilibrium Conditions for Majority Rule," *Econometrica* 41: 285-97.

Kramer, G. and R. McKelvey. 1984. "The Relationship between the Generalized Median and Minmax Sets," *Social Choice and Welfare* 1: 243-44.

Laver, M. and N. Schofield. 1990. *Multiparty Government: The Politics of Coalition in Europe*. Oxford: Oxford University Press.

McKelvey, R. 1986. "Covering, Dominance and Institution-free Properties of Social Choice," *American Journal of Political Science* 29: 69-95.

Schofield, N. 1985. *Social Choice and Democracy*. New York: Springer-Verlag.

Schofield, N. 1993. "Party Competition in a Spatial Model of Coalition Formation," in *Political Economy: Institutions, Competition and Representation*, W. Barnett, M. J. Hinich and N. Schofield, eds. Cambridge: Cambridge University Press.

Schofield, N. 1995. "Existence of a Smooth Social Choice Functor," in *Social Choice, Welfare and Ethics*, W. Barnett, H. Moulin, M. Salles, and N. Schofield, eds. Cambridge: Cambridge University Press.

Part III. COALITION GOVERNMENTS

10. Bargaining in the Liberal Democratic Party of Japan

Junichiro Wada and
Norman Schofield [1]

10.1 Introduction

Since its establishment in 1955 and until August 1993, the Liberal Democratic Party (*LDP*) was the ruling party in the Japanese government.[2] However, there is a consensus among researchers that the *LDP* was not a single party in this period, but a coalition of different factions.[3] Indeed each faction in the *LDP* has its own office, its own account system, and its own councillors, as if it were a party. Ishikawa (1978, 1984) has suggested that work on Japanese politics be analyzed from the viewpoint of the *LDP* as a governing coalition consisting of different factions. The size of many of the *LDP* factions (see Tables 1, 2, and 3) was in fact about the same as the size of many of the opposition parties, supporting the conceptual framework Ishikawa prescribes.

In the lower house elections, almost all constituencies choose between three to five legislators, which means that the *LDP* generally has some candidates in each district. Under the Single-Non-Transferable-Voting (SNTV) rule *LDP* candidates compete for the same conservative voters. It is very difficult for the party to support all *LDP* candidates running in such an election. Consequently, an *LDP* candidate runs in lower house elections only with the support of his or her own faction. It is also not unusual for a new conservative candidate to run, not as an *LDP* candidate, but as an independent. After winning an election an Independent candidate typically joins the *LDP*. The leader of a faction is interested in candidates who can win and so make his faction larger. This advantage gives the faction a better chance of winning the election for the leader of the *LDP* or the prime minister.

Factions are most prominent during the election of the leader of the *LDP* and during cabinet formation. Many students of Japanese politics have noticed that the mechanism of *LDP* coordination has changed over the years.

---

[1] This chapter is based on work supported by NSF Grants SES-88-208405 and SBR 94-22548. The authors thank Gregory Densen for research assistance.

[2] In 1983 it formed a coalition government with the New Liberal Club (*NLC*), but *NLC* members had belonged to the *LDP* before, and almost all of them returned to the *LDP* later.

[3] Leiserson (1968), Ishikawa (1978, 1984), Sato and Matsuzaki (1986), Kanazashi (1989), Inoguchi (1990, 1991), Kohno (1991, 1992).

Until the late 1970's, some of the *LDP* factions did not lend their support to the cabinet. Since then, however, and until about 1992 the *LDP* factions have tended to vote as a block for the candidacy of the *LDP* leader for the position of prime minister. In particular all *LDP* factions received portfolios, or ministerial positions, in the cabinet, and the number allocated to each faction has tended to be close to proportional to the size of the faction. Inoguchi (1991) has termed this a shift from Minimum-Winning to Wall-to-Wall coalition formation.[4] This shift appears to have coincided with a shift from "policy preferences", particularly since about 1978. In other words, disagreements between the factions over policy objectives in the context of elections for the leader, and in constituency elections, became increasingly muted.

Why did such a cooperative structure become the rule? Kanazashi (1989) views the shift in terms of the preference for stability, but he has not explained the mechanism for achieving stabilization. Yoda (1985) suggests two factors. He observes that the animosities between the politicians who had previously been bureaucrats and the politicians who started out as politicians have disappeared. However, the dissolution of the struggle in this group may be a reference point rather than the essence of the power game in the *LDP*. Yoda's second explanation is the bureaucratization of the organization. However, this is the result rather than the cause of the nature of *LDP* bargaining. Inoguchi (1990) argues that the phenomenon of the "bandwagon" has become increasingly important (by "bandwagon" he means the tendency of small factions to support the dominant faction). But it may be irrational for the dominant faction to wish to encourage the bandwagon effect. Since the number of cabinet portfolios is constant, yielding some of these positions to small factions can result in a loss of power for the dominant faction.

We suggest that the change in the process of cabinet formation, from Minimum-Winning to Wall-to-Wall, is due to a change in "the rules of the game". In other words, during the 1970's and 1980's the policy positions of the opposition parties were closer to the positions of the *LDP* than before. As a consequence, the *LDP* factions were able to conceive of aligning with non-*LDP* parties. It is argued here that the bargaining game between the *LDP* factions can be interpreted in terms of their willingness to use the threat of exit from the *LDP* coalition. (See Tables 1-3 for faction and party strengths during 1983-90.)

From 1978 to 1992 we propose that the *LDP* should be regarded as a supramajoritarian coalition, which was able to maintain itself because of the existence of stable solutions to the bargaining problem over portfolio distributions. However, since the bargaining solution depends on factional strength, and this is the result of factional competition in multimember districts, the power of the factions depended on their ability to raise contributions. The reoccurrence of bribery scandals involving former prime ministers Tanaka and Takeshita, and others, introduced policy disagreements between the factions over appropriate electoral methods *and* corruption. This in turn fractured the bargaining "equilibrium" over portfolios. Once the bargaining equilibrium was

---

[4] See Riker (1962) for work on minimal winning coalitions.

lost, the potential for the collapse of the LDP was realized.

The collapse of LDP dominance started with allegations of corruption against Kanemaru Shin, leader of the largest LDP faction (called Takeshita, after its previous leader: see Table 3). Kanemaru Shin resigned in September 1992 both from the leadership of the faction and his seat in the Diet. The resignation set off a power struggle between Kanemaru's protegé, Ozawa Ichiro, and Obuchi Keizo. In December, Ozawa and over 30 other Diet members broke away from the Takeshita faction. The prime minister, Miyazawa, was obliged to call for an election on July 18, 1993. During July more LDP members broke away, eventually forming three new parties: the Japan Renaissance Party (JRP), the Japan New Party (JNP) and Harbinger. In the election the combined LDP factions won only 223 seats, while the three new parties took 103 seats. Ozawa Ichiro, now leader of the JRP, brokered the appointment of Hosokawa Morihiro (leader of JNP) as the prime minister in August 1993 with the support of the non-LDP parties. Allegations of corruption against Hosokawa brought about the collapse of the anti-LDP coalition in April 1994, and the appointment of Tsutomo Hata (of the JRP) as prime minister. As of August 1995, Tomiichi Murayama (leader of the Social Democrats) is prime minister with the support of the LDP. It seems that Japan could be entering a period of high political instability.

We are not in a position, as yet, to test the hypothesis that it was policy conflicts that broke the LDP coalition, but we can test the hypothesis that between the three elections of 1983, 1986 and 1990, the LDP factions acted as though they were bargaining only over cabinet positions. More precisely we demonstrate that a formal solution notion, known as the "bargaining set" (which is designed to model bargaining over transferable benefits), does explain the distribution of cabinet posts among the LDP factions after these three elections. This analysis complements other work by Schofield and Laver (1985, 1987) on portfolio distribution in European multiparty politics. (See also Laver and Schofield 1990.)

10.2 The Bargaining Set and the Kernel

The definitions of the kernel and bargaining set used here are taken from Schofield (1978, 1982, 1987). See also Owen (1982) and Shubik (1981, 1982).

For a simple weighted majority game with transferable value, the value of a "winning coalition" is defined in the following way. Each player i from the set $N = \{1, \ldots, n\}$ is assigned a weight $w(i)$. The weight of coalition M is $w(M) = \sum_{i \in M} w(i)$. A coalition M is in the set $\mathcal{D}$ of winning coalitions iff $w(M) > \frac{1}{2}$. The value of M, or $v(M)$, is defined to be $v(M) > 0$ iff $M \in \mathcal{D}$, while $v(M) = 0$ iff $M \notin \mathcal{D}$.

Definition 1: For a general transferable value game v, and coalition M, let $V(M)$ be the subset of $\Re^n$ defined as follows: $x \in V(M)$ iff

(i) $x_j = 0$ for all $j \notin M$;
(ii) $x_i \geq 0$ for all $i \in M$;
(iii) $\sum_{i \in M} x_i = v(M)$.

A *payoff configuration* is a pair (x, M) where M is a coalition and $x = (x_1, \ldots, x_n)$ belongs to $V(M)$.

The bargaining set formalizes the concept of power in a transferable value game by focussing on the ability of a player (or group) to *object* to other players in the same coalition.

Definition 2: $T_{LJ} = \{A \subset N : L \subset A \text{ and } J \cap A = \phi\}$.

Definition 3: Let (x, M) be a payoff configuration and L, J two disjoint subsets of the coalition M.

1. *An objection* by L against J with respect to (x, M) is a payoff configuration (y, C) such that

    (a) $C \in T_{LJ}$
    (b) $y_i > x_i$ for all $i \in L$
    (c) $y_i \geq x_i$ for all $i \in C$.

2. *A counter objection* by J against L's objection (y, C) is a payoff configuration (z, D), with

    (a) $D \in T_{JL}$
    (b) $z_j \geq x_j$ for all $j \in J$
    (c) $z_j \geq y_j$ for all $j \in D$.

3. An objection (y, C) by L against J with respect to (x, M) is said to be *justified* if there is no counter objection by J to (y, C). If L has a justified objection against J with respect to the payoff configuration, (x, M) then write $Lp(x)J$.

Definition 4:

1. A payoff configuration, (x, M), is called B_1-stable if to any objection by individual i against an individual $j \in M\setminus\{i\}$, there is a counter objection by j. Let $B_1(M)$ be the set of B_1-stable payoff vectors for M. $B_1(M)$ is called the B_1-*bargaining set* for M. Thus,
$B_1(M) = \{x \in v(M) : (x, M) \text{ is } B_1\text{- stable}\}$.

2. A payoff configuration, (x, M), is called B_2-stable if to any objection by an individual i against a subgroup $J \subset M\setminus\{i\}$, there is a counter objection by J. Let $B_2(M)$ be the set of B_2-stable payoff vectors for M.

$B_2(M)$ is called the B_2-*bargaining set* for M. Thus, $B_2(M) = \{x \in V(M) : (x, M) \text{ is } B_2\text{-stable}\}$.

Note that by definition $B_2(M) \subset B_1(M)$.

Theorem 1: (Billera, 1970). $B_1(M)$ *is always non-empty.*

Since $B_1(M)$ often includes "counter intuitive" payoff configurations and $B_2(M)$ is often empty, Schofield (1978) introduced a bargaining set $B_*(M)$, which always exists and is "in between" B_2 and B_1.

Definition 5:

1. Define $ip_*(x)j$ iff

    (a) $x_j > 0$

    (b) $ip(x)K$ for some $K \subset M$ with $K \in T_{ji}$, but j cannot "block" this objection, in the sense that there is no $L \subset M$ with $L \in T_{ij}$ such that $L \cap K \neq \phi$ and $jp(x)L$.

2. $B_*(M) = \{x \in V(M) : ip_*(x)j \text{ for no } i, j \text{ in } M\}$.

Note that if $ip(x)K$ for no K containing j, then $ip_*(x)j$ is impossible, so $B_2(M) \subset B_*(M)$. Moreover if $ip(x)j$, then j cannot "block" this objection, so that $ip_*(x)j$. Hence $B_*(M) \subset B_1(M)$.

The existence proof technique of Billera (1970) can be used to show that $B_*(M)$ is non empty for each coalition M, in a game with transferable value (see Schofield, 1978).

An earlier solution concept for games with transferable value is the *kernel* (Aumann, Peleg and Rabinowitz, 1965).

Definition 6:

1. For a payoff configuration, (x, M), and coalition C, define the *excess* of C over x to be

$$e_x(C) = v(C) - \sum_{i \in C} x_i.$$

2. For L, J disjoint subsets of M define the *surplus* of L over J to be

$$S_{LJ}(x, M) = max\{e_x(C) : C \in T_{LJ}\}.$$

3. Say L *outweighs* J with respect to (x, M) iff

    (a) $S_{LJ}(x, M) > S_{JL}(x, M)$

    (b) it is not the case that $x_j = 0 \; \forall \; j \in J$.

4. A payoff configuration, (x, M), is called K_1-stable if no individual i in M outweighs another $j \in M\setminus\{i\}$. Write $K_1(M)$ for the set of K_1-stable payoff vectors for M. This set is called the K_1-*kernel* for M.
Thus $K_1(M) = \{x \in v(M) : (x, M) \text{ is a } K_1\text{-stable payoff configuration}\}$.

5. A payoff configuration (x, M) is called K_2-stable if no individual in M outweighs any group $J \subset M\setminus\{i\}$. The set of K_2-stable payoff vectors for coalition M is called the K_2-*kernel* for M, and written $K_2(M)$.

Theorem 2: (Schofield, 1982) *For each winning coalition, M, in a transferable value game, the following inclusions hold:*

1. $K_2 \subset K_1 \subset B_1$

2. $K_2 \subset B_2 \subset B_* \subset B_1$.

These five "solution" concepts all depend on the notion that, given a system of voting weights, then a payoff configuration (x, M) is stable iff no player (or faction) has a justified objection against another faction (or group of factions). A justified objection may be thought of as a threat by the initiating faction, which if implemented, would reduce the final payoff of one of the other factions. The idea behind the K_2 kernel and B_2-bargaining set is to permit the possibility of threats by a faction against a group of factions, making it more difficult for the group to counter. This has the effect of reducing the size of the set of stable payoffs. In most side payment games, however, both K_2 and B_2 are empty.

On the other hand, the B_1-bargaining set often includes counter-intuitive "stable" payoffs. In particular, the empirical analysis of Schofield and Laver (1985, 1987) showed that the K_1-kernel often underestimates the bargaining power of large factions or parties. Since K_1 is a subset of B_1, this implies that B_1 implicitly underestimates the power of large factions. The modified B_*-bargaining set was invented so that it both exists, and reduces the size of the predicted stable set of payoffs.

For example Table 1 shows that the Tanaka faction in the LDP in 1983, with weight 63 (seats) out of 269 for the LDP coalition, (that is 23%), has a kernel prediction of 3 ministries out of 21 (that is 14%). In fact the Tanaka faction gained six ministries out of 21. However, the actual portfolio allocation to the Tanaka faction is identical to the B_*-bargaining prediction. This "underprediction" by the kernel is because the implicit notion of power underlying the kernel identifies almost all the LDP factions as equally powerful.

A prediction for payoffs in transferable value games made before the bargaining concepts were developed is due to Gamson (1961). Gamson proposed that each player in a coalition receive a payoff proportional to the ratio of the player weight divided by the coalition weight. Since the Tanaka faction has 63 seats out of the 269 seats controlled by the LDP coalition in 1983, its ratio is thus 23%. The Gamson payoff prediction is 23% of the 21 ministeries, or 4.9 (which we can take to be 5 when rounded to an integer). Moreover, the Gamson predictions in Tables 1 through 3 underestimate the payoff to the largest faction, while the B_*-bargaining prediction is generally very close to the actual payoff configuration. Notice that the B_*-bargaining set can easily be computed for discrete payoffs (such as portfolios) which is an advantage over other power indices (such as the Shapley-Shubik index discussed in Chapter 11 of this volume).

10.3 Data and Results

To illustrate the relevance of the bargaining set and the kernel in analyzing the game of portfolio allocation in the LDP, we use the number of the lower house members of each faction as the "weight" of the faction. We consider independents as one faction ("Independents") in our computations, because independents usually later become members of LDP factions. We regard the number of ministerial positions assigned to each faction as the payoff. The total number of portfolios is 21 (so $v = 21$ for any winning coalition).

We also considered two possible definitions of winning coalition, namely the simple majority of the Diet seats (256 for the 1983 election or 257 for the 1980 and 1990 elections) and a "supra" or "stable" majority of 271 seats. As Tables 2 and 3 suggest, using the "stable" majority increases the "power" of smaller factions. We also considered the possibility that the JCP (the Communist Party) was not considered as a possible coalition partner in the bargaining process. This had no effect on the payoff prediction for 1983. For 1986, however, the Independents, treated as a faction, were unable to form a winning coalition excluding both the JCP and a significant proportion of the other LDP factions. For this reason B_* (under this assumption) predicts that the Independents receive zero payoff. The fact that they did obtain one portfolio gives some evidence (albeit circumstantial) that the JCP was, in fact, a potential coalition partner.

For the 1983 elections, the New Liberal Club (NLC) gained the Home Affairs portfolio, even though its B_2 (and thus B_*) prediction was zero. The NLC at that point was not formally an LDP faction, and it is reasonable to suppose that the particular portfolio was viewed as a necessary "bribe" to the NLC to give the LDP a functioning majority in the Diet. As the data in these tables suggests the kernel does a poor job of predicting the pattern of portfolio distribution, while B_* is fairly accurate in general. Indeed if the payoffs are identified with portfolio allocations assigned to the Lower House, together with the three principal LDP executive positions, then B_* gives an almost exact prediction. This suggests that the B_*-bargaining model based on objection and counter-objection captures some of the nature of inter-factional negotiation. The inference then is that LDP factions did in fact consider the possibility of joining parties outside the LDP coalition.

10.4 Conclusion

LDP portfolio allocations are close to the proportionality prediction of Gamson, but they also reflect the effects of pure bargaining as modelled by B_*. This suggests that intra-LDP bargaining involved little or no policy disagreements during the period in question.

Nakamura (1987) has suggested that the difference between the Japanese polity and the situation in Italy is that factions within the dominant Christian Democratic Party (DC) in Italy may threaten to break away to form a new governing coalition with other parties. Indeed, it is plausible that the "political game" in Italy until 1992 was characterized by the exercise of threats of this kind by the larger DC factions so as to maintain power through the control of the principal portfolios. Our analysis here suggests that a similar phenomenon occurred in Japan, but within the LDP in the period 1983-1990. One difference, of course, between the two polities is that the support of other parties had to be sought by the DC in Italy (see Chapter 15 of this volume) whereas the LDP in Japan was able to control a majority (with the "Independents" in 1983, and without them in 1986 and 1990). A further difference is that loss of one-party dominance was brought about by a new party (the Northern League) in Italy, but by one of the LDP factions in Japan.

However, in both cases the pursuit of cabinet positions appears to have become associated with a degree of political corruption, and this fueled demands for electoral change. In Italy, the demand has been for a change away from proportional representation (PR) towards plurality (simple majority) in single member districts. In Japan, the expected change is to a mixed system with perhaps 300 Diet members chosen in a single member districts, and about 200 chosen by a proportional representation system based on party lists. This proposed Japan system is a compromise between the desire for PR by small parties, and the hope by the LDP that single member districts will reduce LDP factionalism (Wada 1994). However such a mixed PR–plurality system was the one adopted in Russia in the last election. The consequence of such a mixed system in Russia was a very large number of independents, a highly factionalized polity, and a high degree of political disorder (see Schofield 1995 for a brief discussion). It is still unclear whether the Japanese polity will be able to make the transition to a stable multiparty regime based on a representative and fair electoral system.

References
English:

Aumann, R. J., B. Peleg and P. Rabinowitz. 1965. "A Method for Computing the Kernel of N-Person Games," *Mathematics of Computation* 19: 531-551.

Billera, L. J. 1970. "Existence of General Bargaining Sets for Cooperative Games without Side Payments," *Bulletin of the American Mathematical Society* 76: 275-379.

Gamson, W. 1961. "A Theory of Coalition Formation," *American Sociological Review* 26: 373-81.

Inoguchi, T. 1990. "The Emergence of a Predominant Faction in the Liberal Democratic Party: Domestic Change in Japan and their Security Implications," Typescript: Tokyo University.

Kohno, M. 1992. "Rational Foundations for the Organization of the Liberal Democratic Party in Japan," *World Politics* 44: 369-397.

Laver, M. and N. Schofield. 1990. *Multiparty Government*. Oxford: Oxford University Press.

Leiserson, M. 1968. "Factions and Coalitions in One-Party Japan: An Interpretation Based on the Theory of Games," *American Political Science Reveiw* 62: 70-87.

Owen, G. 1982. *Game Theory*. 2nd ed. New York: Academic Press.

Riker, W. 1962. *The Theory of Political Coalitions*. New Haven: Yale University Press.

Schofield, N. 1978. "Generalized Bargaining Sets for Cooperative Games," *International Journal of Game Theory* 7: 183-199.

Schofield, N. 1982. "Bargaining Set Theory and Stability in Coalition Governments," *Mathematical Social Sciences* 3: 9-31.

Schofield, N. 1987. "Bargaining in Weighted Majority Voting Games," in *The Logic of Multiparty Systems*, M. Holler, ed. Dordrecht: Martinus Nijhoff.

Schofield, N. 1995. "Coalition Politics: A Formal Model and Empirical Analysis," *Journal of Theoretical Politics* 7: 245-281.

Schofield, N. and M. Laver. 1985. "Bargaining Theory and Portfolio Payoffs in European Coalition Governments, 1945-83," *British Journal of Political Science* 15: 143-164.

Schofield, N. and M. Laver. 1987. "Bargaining Theory and Cabinet Stability in European Coalition Governments, 1945-1983," in *The Logic of Multiparty Systems*, M. Holler, ed. Dordrecht: Martinus-Nijhoff.

Shubik, M. 1981. "Game Theory Models and Methods in Political Economy," in *Handbook of Mathematical Economics*, Vol. 1, K. J. Arrow and M. D. Intriligator, eds. Amsterdam: North-Holland.

Shubik, M. 1982. *Game Theory in the Social Sciences*. Cambridge: MIT Press.

Wada, J. 1994. *The Japanese Election System*. Unpublished Ph.D. Dissertation: University of Maryland.

Japanese:

Inoguchi, T. 1991. "Jiminto Kenkyu no Fukugouteki Shiten," *Leviathan* 9: 7-31.

Ishikawa, M. 1978. *Sengo Seiji Kozoshi*. Tokyo: Nihon Hyoronsha.

Ishikawa, M. 1984. *Deta Sego Seijishi*. Tokyo: Iwanami.

Kanazashi, M. 1989. "Habatsu-Jiminto wo Ugokasumono," in *Nihon no Seiji*, Y. Sone, ed. Nihon Keizai Shinbunsha.

Kohno, M. 1991. "Jiminto-Soshiki Riron Karano Kento," *Leviathan* 9: 32-54.

Nakamura, A. 1987. "Seito to Habtsu," *Seito to Demokurashii*, in Y. Iizaka N. Tomita, and N. Okazawa, eds. Tokyo: Gakuyo Shobo.

Sato, S. and T. Matsuzaki. 1986. *Jiminto Seiken*. Tokyo: Chuo Koron Sha.

Yoda, H. 1985. "Jiminto Habatu to Nakaku Keisei," *Kokyo Sentaku no Kenkyu* 6: 71-86.

Appendix

Table 1. The 37th General Election in 1983 (27 December)

	Tanaka	Suzuki	Nakasone	Fukuda	Komoto	Indep.	NLC	Nakogawa
Lower House Seats	63	50	50	42	28	22	8	6
Portfolios*	Fin. Hlth. Agri. Posts Adm. (Env.)	Just. Const. Def. (Sci.)	Pr. M. Trade Secret. (Hokkai)	Foreign Educ. Transp. Gen. Mg.	Labor Econ.		Home	
Payoff a	6	4	4	4	2	0	1	0
Payoff b	6	4	3	5	2	0	1	0
Kernel	3	3	3	3	3	3	1.5	1.5
B_2	Empty							
B_*	6	4	4	4	2	1	0	0
Gamson	5	4	4	3	2	2	$\frac{1}{2}$	$\frac{1}{2}$

Non-LDP Parties	Seats
NLC: New Liberal Club (associated LDP faction)	8
JSP: Japan Socialist Party	114
CGP: Clean Government Party	59
JCP: Japan Communist Party	39
DSP: Democratic Socialist Party	27
SDF: Social Democratic Federation	3

Notes: (*) Portfolios allocated in Nakasone's 2nd cabinet; those in parentheses are in the Upper House; (a) number of portfolios assigned to factions in both Lower and Upper Houses; (b) number of portfolios in Lower House plus major executive positions in LDP.

Table 2. The 38th General Election in 1986 (22 July)

	Tanaka	Nakasone	Suzuki	Fukuda	Komoto	Indep.
Lower House Seats	87	62	60	56	28	13
Portfolios[*]	Vice Pr. Trade Transp. Secret. Nat. Land Env. (Just.) (Hlth.)	Pr. M. Foreign Posts Const. (Labor)	Fin. Home Def.	Educ. Agri. Sci.	Econ	Gen. Mg.
Payoff a	8	5	3	3	1	1
Payoff b	7	4	4	4	1	1
Kernel	5.25	5.25	5.25	5.25	0	0
B_2 (c)	6.5	4.5	4.5	3.5	1	1
B_2 (d)	7	4	4	3	3	0
B_2 (e)	7	4	4	4	1	1
Gamson	6	4	4	4	2	1

Non LDP Parties	Seats
NLC	6
JSP	86
CGP	57
JCP	27
DSP	26
SDF	4

Notes: (*) Portfolios allocated in Nakasone's 3rd cabinet; bracketed offices are in upper house; (a) and (b) are as defined in Table 1; (c) computed under simple majority, including JCP; (d) computed under simple majority, but excluding JCP; (e) computed under stable majority, including JCP.

Table 3. The 39th General Election in 1990 (28 February)

	Takeshita (Tanaka)	Miyazawa (Suzuki)	Abe (Fukuda)	Watanabe (Nakasone)	Komoto	Indep.
Lower House Seats	71	63	62	53	26	15
Portfolios*	Fin. Educ. Constr. Home Nat. Land (Just.)	Hlth. Gen. Mg. Def. Econ Pl.	Foreign Trans. Labor (Agr.)	Trade Posts Hokkaido (Sci.)	Pr. M. Sec. Env.	
Payoff a	6	4	4	4	3	0
Payoff b	6	5	4	3	3	0
Kernel	4.2	4.2	4.2	4.2	2.1	2.1
B_2	Empty					
B_* (c)	6	5	4	3	2	1
B_* (d)	6	5	4	3	2	1
B_* (e)	6	4	4	4	3	0
Gamson	5	4.5	4.5	4	2	1

Non LDP Parties	Seats
JSP	141
CGP	46
JCP	16
DSP	14
PS(Progressive Party)	5

Notes: (*) Portfolios assigned in the Kaifu cabinet; bracketed offices are in Upper House; (a), (b) are defined as in Table 1; (c) stable majority with or without JCP; (d) stable majority including JCP; (e) stable majority excluding JCP.

11. An Analysis of the Euskarian Parliament

Francesc Carreras and

Guillermo Owen[1]

11.1 Introduction

The object of this article is to examine the Euskarian Parliament (in the Basque country) after the elections held on 30 November 1986. From the time of the election until 21 January 1987, the parties had to bargain with each other to form a winning coalition, since no one of them held an absolute majority.

A brief political description of the parties involved is as follows: There is, first of all, a left-wing party associated with PSE (the socialist party of Felipe González). Next there is a large Basque "nationalist" grouping split into four subgroups. Finally there is a small representation of the center-right and center parties. The classical left-to-right axis must thus be combined, in this case, with an orthogonal axis ranging from centralism to nationalism (see Figure 1).

We adopt the hypothesis that a number of pairs of parties cannot join in coalition. These "pair rejections" include Herri Batasuna (HB) and, the Coalicion Popular (CP) say, as well as the PSE and the CP. A second feature of this "political game" was the high probability that HB (the political arm of the Basque organization ETA) would walk out of Parliament: this had indeed happened in the two previous legislatures.

We shall modify the formal structure of Parliament by considering the most obvious pair rejections. Taking the modified structure as our starting point, evaluations of the utility that each feasible coalition offers to its members will allow us to find the stable coalitions. The evaluations will be taken as solutions to the problem of the formation of a governing coalition.

The effect of HB's absence will also be considered. Finally, the theoretic results will be compared with the actual behavior of the parties.

We use standard techniques of game theory, including: (1) the structure of simple and weighted majority games; (2) the classical Shapley-Shubik (1953, 1954) index of power; (3) Owen's (1977) modification to games with *a priori* unions. We call this the coalition value. (See the Appendix, as well as the references, for details.)

---

[1] Guillermo Owen's research was supported by National Science Foundation, Grant 085-03676, Division of Decision and Management Sciences. This collaboration was made possible by a grant from the joint Spanish-U.S.A. committee for cooperation in cultural matters.

As a matter of internal consistency it should be emphasized that the coalition value, under the trivial coalition structure, coincides with the Shapley-Shubik index of the game.

11.2 Formal Structure

75 seats were contested in the third Euskarian regional elections, which took place on November 30, 1986. A 70% participation from a roll of over a million and a half registered voters gave the following result:

Composition of the Euskarian Parliament, 1986-90

	Party*	Seats
PSE	Partido Socialista de Euskadi	19
PNV	Partido Nacionalista Vasco	17
EA	Eusko Altarsuna	13
HB	Herri Batasuna	13
EE	Euskadiko Ezkerra	9
CP	Coalición Popular	2
CDS	Centro Democrático y Social	2
Total		75

* We designate each party in the text that follows by its initials.

Our estimate of the political positions of these parties is shown in Figure 1. It is included here only for descriptive purposes.

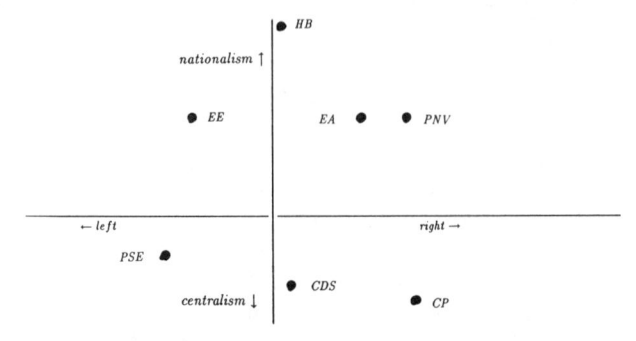

Figure 1. Policy positions of the Euskarian parliament parties following the election of November 30, 1986.

EA had recently formed as a dissident group of the PNV : this explains why the positions of the two parties (in Figure 1) are so near. In general, however, no strict meaning should be given to the distance between the points in this diagram.

The required majority in Parliament is 38, so that the *formal structure* of the Parliament is a majority game on the seven-player set

$$N = \{PSE, PNV, EA, HB, EE, CP, CDS\},$$

represented by the "quota" $q = 38$ and the system of weights:

$$\{38; 19, 17, 13, 13, 9, 2, 2\}.$$

Assuming that this game has transferable value, we may define the "characteristic function" $v(M) = 1$ for any "winning" coalition, M, with 38 or more votes, and $v(M) = 0$ for all other coalitions. Let $\mathcal{W}$ represent the set of winning coalitions.

Looking at this as a simple game, we note that it is proper, strong, and without dummies. There are 12 minimal winning (MW) coalitions:

PSE, PNV, EA	PSE, EA, EE
PSE, PNV, HB	PSE, HB, EE
PSE, PNV, EE	PNV, EA, HB
PSE, PNV, CP	PNV, EA, EE
PSE, PNV, CDS	PNV, HB, EE
PSE, EA, HB	EA, HB, EE, CP, CDS.

Most of these are ternary coalitions, and include PSE, PNV, or both. Only the last one does not, and it seems very unlikely to form because of its size.

We can order the players according to their "strength" as follows:

$$CDS \equiv CP < EE \equiv HB \equiv EA < PNV \equiv PSE.$$

The ranking $<$ on the parties is determined by the minimum integer weights (see Chapter 8 of this volume) defined by $\mathcal{W}$. Although HB has more seats than EE, their minimum integer weights are identical. To see why, note that for any winning coalition $C \cup \{HB\}$, excluding EE, the coalition $C \cup \{EE\}$ is also winning.

Table 1. Shapley-Shubik Index, for $\mathcal{W}$ and $\mathcal{D}$

Party	Seats	$\mathcal{W}$	$\mathcal{D}$
PSE	25.33%	25.24%	23.33%
PNV	22.67%	25.24%	31.67%
EA	17.33%	15.24%	23.33%
HB	17.33%	15.24%	3.33%
EE	12.00%	15.24%	15.00%
CP	2.67%	1.90%	0.00%
CDS	2.67%	1.90%	3.33%

The second column gives the fraction of seats occupied by each party. The Shapley-Shubik power index is based on $<$ and gives a numerical expression of this strength (see the third column of Table 1). We note an equivalence between PSE and PNV, in spite of the two seat difference, and the equivalence of EE, EA, and HB. Note finally that CP and CDS are attributed a minimal amount of power, as they just avoid being dummies (they are only in one minimal winning coalition in $\mathcal{W}$).

Because of the assumption that $v(M) = 1$ for each winning coalition, the Shapley-Shubik indices sum to 1. We may regard these indices as predictions of overall payoffs in the TV game, $\mathcal{W}$. (See the Appendix for the formal definition of the index.)

11.3 Modified Structure

One way to introduce new information into the description of the Parliament is to exclude the least feasible coalitions, *i.e.*, assign to them null probability of formation. This is a delicate task, because disinformation about one's preferences is a common stratagem in political bargaining. We have tried to be very cautious in selecting the infeasible coalitions, taking into account: (1) the previous behavior of each party; and (2) opinions expressed in public interviews, after the elections, by their leaders and spokesmen. In any case, we put more emphasis on the method than on our particular opinion as to political affinities.

We have selected the following very clear "pair" rejections, expressed as a binary, irreflexive and symmetric relations:

PSE/HB, PSE/CP, HB/EE, HB/CP.

Accordingly, null probability will be given to the minimal winning coalitions containing any of these pairs. We are then led to consider the *modified structure* of the game, *i.e.*, the game defined by the six remaining minimal winning (MW) coalitions:

PSE, PNV, EA   *PSE, EA, EE*
PSE, PNV, EE   *PNV, EA, HB*
PSE, PNV, CDS *PNV, EA, EE.*

As expected, the "unlikely" coalition of five parties has been excluded.

We might perhaps have considered other rejections, such as HB/CDS, but this would have had no effect on our current list of admissible minimal winning coalitions. Any excess in restrictions would, moreover, produce a modified structure very different from the real one, and thus a very different description of the situation. This is dangerous because instead of a more realistic analysis we might tend toward a more illusory one.

Briefly, what is important is which coalitions are excluded, rather than the reason for this. In the Euskarian case we have followed the method of rejections rather than a graph of affinities, since rejections seemed to us clearer than affinities (the two methods are not equivalent).

A question now arises: if certain minimal winning coalitions have been affected by pair rejections, can a "supra" majority winning coalition be accepted if it contains a rejecting pair? For example, the supra-majority coalition $\{PSE, PNV, EA, HB\}$ contains the MW coalition $\{PSE, PNV, EA\}$ but also contains the pair rejection PSE/HB. Should this coalition be acceptable?

The answer is yes. So long as a coalition contains, *as subset*, some acceptable minimal winning coalition, it should be acceptable also as a winning coalition. The reason we make this assumption is as follows. The modified structure is a simple game, but it is not possible to represent this as a weighted majority game, *i.e.*, no weights and quota can be found giving exactly these six minimal winning coalitions. However, the game is non-collegial, and can be designated by the symbol $\mathcal{D}$. It is easy to see that the Nakamura number, $k(\mathcal{D})$, of $\mathcal{D}$ is 4 (see Chapter 8 for the definition of $k(\mathcal{D})$). We shall use the Shapley-Shubik index (or coalition value) for each of the coalitions in $\mathcal{D}$. To do this, we require that $\mathcal{D}$ be "monotonic", so that if $M \in \mathcal{D}$, then $M' \in \mathcal{D}$ for any M', a superset of M. This explains our assumption on "acceptability".

This is still a proper game, since any two coalitions in $\mathcal{D}$ have non-empty intersection. However the game is not strong, since there are coalitions $M, M\setminus N$, neither of which belong to $\mathcal{D}$. While there are no vetoers (the collegium of $\mathcal{D}$ is empty) there is a blocking coalition[2] $B = \{PSE, PNV\}$, since the coalition $N\setminus B$ does not belong to $\mathcal{D}$. CP becomes a dummy, since it belongs to no minimal winning coalition in $\mathcal{D}$.

We now obtain only a partial ordering of strength, increasing from left to right:

$$CP \; < \; \begin{matrix} HB \\ CDS \end{matrix} \; < \; EE \; < \; \begin{matrix} PSE \\ EA \end{matrix} \; < \; PNV$$

The Shapley-Shubik index, compatible with this ordering, is given in the fourth column in Table 1. Notice that the class $\mathcal{D}$, of "acceptable" coalitions is less rich than $\mathcal{W}$, and this is reflected in the fact that $k(\mathcal{D}) = 4$, while $k(\mathcal{W}) = 3$.

Although the index gives the power more accurately than the partial ordering, equality of value does not mean absolute equivalence (substitutability) of two parties, but merely the existence of an automorphism (in this case interchanging PSE with EA and HB with CDS) which equates players with equal power.

Comparing the final two columns in Table 1 we note PNV's improved position (it now ranks first, even though PSE has more seats), EA's increase in power to a second position equivalent to that of PSE, the expected regression of HB (because of so many rejections), and the annulment of CP in contrast with CDS's advance.

---

[2] Editor's note: Using the estimates of party positions given in Figure 1, it is easy to show that the "heart" (*cf.* Chapter 8) for $\mathcal{D}$ is generated by the positions of $\{PSE, PNV, EA\}$.

11.4 Evaluation of Coalitions

A player (in this case a party) who is bargaining to enter a coalition cannot threaten to join another one if the latter is given null probability of forming. That is why the modified structure will be our starting point in the theory of alliances. This is important, since the coalition index takes the original game into account.

We will consider only minimal winning coalitions, and not oversized ones or minorities. Our interest is in the six minimal winning coalitions selected in Section 11.3.

If one of these coalitions forms, it controls 100% of the power. The coalition value divides this power among its members in the ratio of the Shapley-Shubik indices. We note that these are all ternary coalitions (with three members). Let A, B, and C be three parties in a coalition. We shall represent the possible results as:

$$
\begin{aligned}
A + B &\quad + \quad C \\
(A + B) &\quad + \quad C \\
(B + C) &\quad + \quad A \\
(A + C) &\quad + \quad B
\end{aligned}
$$

to indicate that they agree simultaneously in the first case, while in the other cases a protocoalition of two parties is formed, which later invites the third party to join. Obviously there are only four ways for a ternary coalition to form, and we can compute the Shapley-Shubik index for each coalition, and for each method of formation (see the Appendix for the formal technique).

Table 2 shows the coalitional value (as a percentage) in each case (for each way of forming a coalition) under the modified structure $\mathcal{D}$. For simplicity, we have rounded to the nearest percentage point.

In general, the parties in a coalition receive a higher value than the Shapley-Shubik index. In most cases, a party is better off joining a protocoalition of the two other parties. There are, however, exceptions: note PSE does worst in $PSE + (PNV + EA)$. In fact, PSE's best outcome with PNV and EA will be obtained if it first forms a protocoalition with one of them. On the other hand, the opposite situation holds for PSE with PNV and CDS : PSE would prefer to be invited by $PNV + CDS$ or, at the very least, to join all three simultaneously, rather than to initiate contacts.

Note also that coalitions 2 and 6 give isomorphic tables, as do coalitions 3 and 5. This is as expected, because of the equivalence of PSE and EA and of CDS and HB.

If we consider instead the interval of values that each party can obtain by entering a coalition, regardless of the way it forms, a new and more compact table is obtained. The idea is then to find, for each party, its best interval. The result is given in Table 3.

The differences being relatively small, some comments are in order. Coalition 1 is of no interest to its members, because all are clearly better off in other coalitions. Coalitions 2 and 6 would be profitable for only one of its members (PNV in both cases). Coalition 4 is perhaps less easy to exclude.

Table 2. Values of the Coalition Index for $\mathcal{D}$

	Coalition	PSE	PNV	EA	HB	EE	CDS
	Shapley-Shubik Index	23	32	23	3	15	3
1.	PSE + PNV + EA	30	39	31			
	(PSE + PNV) + EA	37	46	17			
	PSE + (PNV + EA)	17	46	37			
	(PSE + EA) + PNV	37	26	37			
2.	PSE + PNV + EE	31	47			22	
	(PSE + PNV) + EE	33	50			17	
	PSE + (PNV + EE)	23	52			25	
	(PSE + EE) + PNV	35	40			25	
3.	PSE + PNV + CDS	40	49				11
	(PSE + PNV) + CDS	37	46				17
	PSE + (PNV + CDS)	46	46				8
	(PSE + CDS) + PNV	37	55				8
4.	PSE + EA + EE	39		39		22	
	(PSE + EA) + EE	37		37		25	
	PSE + (EA + EE)	42		37		21	
	(PSE + EE) + EA	37		42		21	
5.	PNV + EA + HB		49	40	11		
	(PNV + EA) + HB		46	37	17		
	PNV + (EA + HB)		55	37	8		
	(PNV + HB) + EA		46	46	8		
6.	PNV + EA + EE		47	31		22	
	(PNV + EA) + EE		50	33		17	
	PNV + (EA + EE)		40	35		25	
	(PNV + EE) + EA		52	23		25	

Table 3. Value Intervals for $\mathcal{D}$

Coalition	PSE	PNV	EA	EE	HB	CDS
1	17-37	26-46	17-37			
2	25-35	40-52		17-25		
3	37-46	46-55				8-17
4	37-42		37-42	21-25		
5		46-55	37-46		8-17	
6		40-52	23-35	17-25		

Strictly speaking, however, it seems that coalitions 3 and 5 show a very special characteristic: each one gives each of its members its best position. This is important as it implies a high degree of stability: if one of these coalitions forms, none of its members will be interested in going elsewhere. This offers, it seems to us, a great guarantee of durability.

Coalitions 3 and 5 are not only isomorphic in the sense described above, but appear optimal for PNV and the best either for PSE and CDS or for EA and HB.

These two optimal coalitions, $\{PSE, PNV, CDS\}$ and $\{PNV, EA, HB\}$, are suggested as the most rational coalitions to form the Euskarian government. In these two cases, each of the three parties would prefer to be invited to join as a third member, and thus they will probably form symmetrically, (*i.e.*, simultaneously).

We shall return to this result after discussing the effect of HB's absence.

11.5 The Absence of HB

During the negotiation process, there was a high probability that HB would (as in the previous two legislatures) decide not to participate in the Parliament. We now consider this possibility, with a consequent modification of all the steps of our analysis.

First of all, there are now 62 seats, with 32 required for a majority. The *formal structure* of Parliament is then the weighted majority game

$$[32; 19, 17, 13, 9, 2, 2]$$

on the 6-player set $N' = \{PSE, PNV, EA, EE, CP, CDS\}$.

As a simple game, this is proper, strong, and without dummies. We shall designate it $\mathcal{W}'$. There are six minimal winning coalitions

PSE, PNV	PNV, EA, EE
PSE, EA	PNV, EA, CP
PSE, EE, CP, CDS	PNV, EA, CDS.

Two binary coalitions and a quaternary one have appeared. The first two will be important, but the quartenary coalition disappears as soon as we incorporate the pair rejection PSE/CP. Let the modified game be designated $\mathcal{D}'$.

The ranking for both $\mathcal{W}'$ and $\mathcal{D}'$ is now

$$CDS \equiv CP \equiv EE < EA \equiv PNV < PSE$$

and the Shapley-Shubik indices for $\mathcal{W}'$ and $\mathcal{D}'$ are presented in the second and third columns of Table 4.

The game, $\mathcal{D}'$, is again proper but not strong: $\{PNV, EA\}$ is a losing but blocking coalition under $\mathcal{D}'$ but there are no veto players or dummies. Note

Table 4. Shapley-Shubik Index, without HB.

Party	$\mathcal{W}'$	$\mathcal{D}'$
PSE	36.67%	35.00%
PNV	26.67%	30.00%
EA	26.67%	30.00%
EE	3.33%	1.67%
CP	3.33%	1.67%
CDS	3.33%	1.67%

Table 5. Values of the Coalition Index for $\mathcal{D}'$, (without HB)

Coalition	PSE	PNV	EA	EE	CP	CDS
Shapley-Shubik Index	35	30	30	2	2	2
1. PSE + PNV	54	46				
2. PSE + EA	54		46			
3. PNV + EA + EE		46	46	8		
(PNV + EA) + EE		44	44	12		
PNV + (EA + EE)		57	37	6		
(PNV + EE) + EA		37	57	6		
4. PNV + EA + CP		46	46		8	
(PNV + EA) + CP		44	44		12	
PNV + (EA + CP)		57	37		6	
(PNV + CP) + EA		37	57		6	
5. PNV + EA + CDS		46	46			8
(PNV + EA) + CDS		44	44			12
PNV + (EA + CDS)		57	37			6
(PNV + CDS) + EA		37	57			6

that CP, a dummy in the presence of HB, escapes that status in the present situation.

We note that HB's absence (in $\mathcal{W}'$) favors PSE and EA and weakens PNV and EE. The PSE/CP rejection (in $\mathcal{D}'$) further favors EA and weakens EE. Observe how EE is dramatically weakened by HB's refusal to participate.

In this case, the modified structure $\mathcal{D}'$ can be represented as a weighted majority game, namely

$$[9; 5, 4, 4, 1, 1, 1].$$

Note also that there are 12 automorphisms of the modified structure, giving rise to several identical partial tables, as shown in Table 5.

The intervals are presented in Table 6. (Of course for the binary coalitions we obtain a single number rather than an interval). The differences are not so clear in this case. The major problem is for PNV and EA. Would each of them prefer the safe 46% level in its binary coalition rather than take a risk of 37% while trying to obtain 57% in a ternary one?

Table 6. Value Intervals for $\mathcal{D}$, without HB

Coalition	PSE	PNV	EA	EE	CP	CDS
1	54	46				
2	54		46			
3		37-57	37-57	6-12		
4		37-57	37-57		6-12	
5		37-57	37-57			6-12

Given that the 57% level would only be reached by being invited as a third member to a ternary coalition, it seems more natural to select the binary one as a better position for PNV and EA. We might include, at a lower level of likelihood, the coalition $PNV + EA + EE$, selected from among the ternary coalitions because of its greater homogeneity (all being Basque nationalists). This coalition has another positive aspect: HB's absence could prove temporary rather than permanent. The last two coalitions would lack a majority if HB were to rejoin the Parliament, whereas the preferred ones would be safe.

These optimal coalitions:

$PSE + PNV$
$PSE + EA$
$(PNV + EA + EE)$

are selected as the most likely coalitions in this case.[3] The last of them, should it form, would probably form symmetrically, *i.e.*, all entering at the same time.

---
[3] Editor's note: It is interesting that the heart for $\mathcal{D}'$ is a subset of the heart for $\mathcal{D}$ and is based on these three coalitions.

11.6 Conclusion and Final Comments

We have modified the formal structure of the Euskarian Parliament by means of some likely pair rejections; this modified structure has served as the basis for our analysis of coalitions. The coalition index has given us a criterion of stability, allowing us to select some coalitions as the most likely ones to form. Two cases have been considered and these are the results:

(a) The most stable coalitions among all the parties in the Parliament, are:

$$PSE + PNV + CDS$$
$$PNV + EA + HB$$

(b) In HB's absence, the most stable coalitions are:

$$PSE + PNV$$
$$PSE + EA$$
$$PNV + EA + EE.$$

We can compare our analysis with the actual formation of the government in 1987. In the last days of January, EA and EE formed a protocoalition and tried to capture PSE. In the final negotiations PSE did not agree, and $EA + EE$ decided to present a candidacy for a minority cabinet.

On February 23, PSE and PNV reached an agreement to form a coalition.

During this time HB announced that it would participate in Parliament. The decisive plenum to elect the *lendakari* (president) was adjourned from 20 to 26 February since the Spanish government would not allow HB's candidate to leave prison (to attend the session) on the earlier date.

On February 26 there were two candidates, one from HB, the other from $PSE + PNV$. After presenting their party's program (in support of ETA), HB's candidate and the party members walked out of the Chamber. Mr. José Antonio Ardanza (PNV) did not need a second ballot to be elected: in the first ballot he received (of course) the PNV and PSE votes, plus the 2 from CDS—a bare majority of 38.

Thus, HB's absence allows the $PSE+PNV$ coalition to govern easily, with 36 of 62 votes in Parliament. They can count, moreover, on the additional support of CDS, should HB choose to return. The actual behavior of the parties seems to agree closely, then, with the results of our analysis.

References

Carreras, F. 1984. "A Characterization of the Shapley Index of Power via Automorphisms," *Stochastica* 8: 2: 171-179.

Hart, S., and M. Kurz. 1983. "Endogenous Formation of Coalitions," *Econometrica* 51: 1047-1064.

Owen, G. 1977. "Values of Games with *a priori* Unions," in *Mathematical Economics and Game Theory*, Henn and Moeschlin, eds. Berlin: Springer Verlag.

Owen, G. 1986. "Values of Graph-Restricted Games," *SIAM J. Alg. Disc. Meth.* 7: 210-220.

Shapley, L. S. 1953. "A Value for n-Person Games," in *Contributions to the Theory of Games, II, Annals of Mathematics Studies*, No. 28, Kuhn and Tucker, eds. Princeton: Princeton University Press.

Shapley, L. S., and M. Shubik. 1954. "A Method for Evaluating the Distribution of Power in a Committee System," *American Political Science Review* 158: 787-792.

Winter, E. 1992. "The Consistency and Potential for Values of Games with Coalition Structures," *Games and Economic Behavior* 4: 132-144.

Appendix: The Coalition Value

Let v be the characteristic function of a game with a set of players $N = \{1, 2, ..., n\}$. Let $T = \{T_1, ..., T_\tau\}$ be a partition of N. Following Owen (1977), we shall call the sets $\{T_j\}$ *a priori unions*. The interpretation is that the members of each of these unions have a reasonably serious prior commitment to collaborate in playing the game. There is nothing, however, to force them to do so, *i.e.*, they are free to break up a union if they feel that their partners are making unreasonable demands. Moreover, it is understood that the unions are likely to bargain with other unions to form larger coalitions, should that seem profitable.

We wish, now, to assign a value $\Omega[v; T] = \{\ldots \Omega_i[v;T] : i \in N\}$ to the game v with the given coalition structure. We do this using axioms very similar in spirit to those of Shapley (1953).

We first of all define the *quotient game* $v^* = v/T$ with player set $C = \{1, 2, ..., \tau\}$ by $v^*(H) = v\left(\cup_{j \in H} T_j\right)$, *i.e.*, v^* is just the game played among the unions. Then we have:

Axiom 1: *If K is any carrier of the game, the total value attributable to K is $v(K)$.*

Axiom 2: *The value treats players symmetrically.*

Axiom 3: *The value treats the unions symmetrically.*

Axiom 4: *If T_j is one of the unions, then the total value attributed to T_j depends only on the quotient game v/T.*

Axiom 5: *If v and $v\prime$ are two games with the same player set N and the same a priori unions T, then the value of game $v + v'$ (with the same unions) is the sum of the values in games v and v'.*

(The reader is invited to read Owen (1977) or Hart and Kurz (1983) for an exact rendering of the axioms.)

It can be shown that, over the space of all games with finite carrier, there exists a unique value $\Omega[v, T]$ satisfying the five axioms. For $i \in T_j$, this is given by

$$\Omega_i[v,T] = \sum_{S \subset M} \sum_{K \subset T_j} \frac{s!(\tau - s - 1)! \, k! \, (t_j - k - 1)!}{\tau! \, t_j!} [v(Q \cup K \cup (i)) - v(Q \cup K))]$$

where $Q = \cup_{h \in S} T_h$, and s, k, and t_j are the cardinalities of S, K and T_j respectively.

As is well known, the (ordinary) Shapley value can be obtained by taking all possible permutations of the set N of players, assigning equal probabilities $\frac{1}{n!}$ to each of these, and then assigning to player i the expected value of $v(S \cup \{i\}) - v(S)$, where S is the set of players preceding i under a given permutation.

It turns out that the coalition value Ω can also be expressed in terms of permutations. The difference is that instead of considering all $n!$ permutations of the set N, we consider only the $\tau! t_1! ... t_\tau!$ permutations which keep the members of each of the unions T_j together. As an example, suppose that in a 5-person game, the *a priori* unions are $\{\{1,2,3\},\{4,5\}\}$. In that case, there will be 24 permissible permutations (orderings). For example, $2-1-3-4-5$ and $5-4-3-1-2$ are permissible, whereas $4-1-2-3-5$ is not permissible (the union $\{4,5\}$ is not together in the last ordering).

The union-building process may, moreover, be continued to higher levels by introducing the concept of *nested unions*: within a union, there may be a closer bloc (say, a clan), and within this bloc there may be even closer sets (say, families). The process can be continued indefinitely, subject only to the obvious constraint that single players cannot be further subdivided.

Where these nested unions exist, the coalition value can be further generalized. An axiomatic development, though possible (see Winter, 1992), is actually somewhat messy. The expression in terms of permutations is, however, quite straightforward: only those permutations are permissible which keep each of the distinguished coalitions (unions, clans, families, *etc.*,) together.

As an example, we consider once again the 5-person game, with nested union structure $\{\{2,\{1,3\}\},\{4,5\}\}$, which differs from our previous example in that the union $\{1,2,3\}$ contains an inner bloc $\{1,3\}$. In this case, there will be 16 permissible permutations; here, $5-4-2-1-3$ is permissible, but $3-2-1-5-4$ and $1-3-4-5-2$ are not permissible: the former splits up the inner bloc $\{1,3\}$, whereas the latter splits up the union $\{1,2,3\}$.

12. Extending a Dynamic Model of Protocoalition Formation

Bernard Grofman[1]

12.1 Introduction

With some loss of historical accuracy, we may think of there having been two generations of research on formal models of coalition formation. The first generation (see, *e.g.*, Browne 1971; Koehler 1972; Rohde 1972a, 1972b; Leiserson 1968; Dodd 1976) was inspired by Riker's seminal statement of the minimal winning coalition hypothesis (Riker 1962; Gamson 1961).[2] The second generation of models has focused on policy-driven motivations. The best known of these models is Axelrod's (1970) notion of undimensionally "connected" coalitions (*cf.* Leiserson 1970a, 1970b; Hinckley 1972; Rohde 1972c). DeSwaan (1970, 1973) proposed a closely related notion of "policy distance minimizing" coalitions. Similar approaches are also found in Morgan (1976) and in Browne, Gleiber and Mashoba (1984). The early emphasis on minimum winning coalitions has been found inadequate both empirically (Browne 1971; Taylor and Laver 1973)[3] and theoretically. For example, Grofman (1984) has argued that real world coalition politics is very unlikely to be zero sum in nature, and thus a key assumption of Riker's (1962) work is inappropriate to the cabinet coalition context. More generally, several authors (see Luebbert 1986; Franklin and Mackie, 1984; Schofield 1984) have made very similar points about the inability of most coalitional models of cabinet formation to account for the substantial number of minority and supra-minimal coalitions or to accommodate the dramatic differences in coalitional types across countries.

Minority governing coalitions are common in a number of countries, and are actually the predominant type in some countries (*e.g.*, Norway, Sweden, Denmark) (see Luebbert 1983; Taylor and Laver 1973; Schofield 1993a), while they never or almost never occur in other countries (*e.g.*, Israel, the Netherlands, Belgium, Germany). Luebbert (1983), Straffin and Grofman (1984) and Franklin and Mackie (1983, 1984), among others, have suggested that the political cultures of various countries may result in parties in different countries

---

[1] This article is a revision and extension of Grofman (1982). Figures 1-4 are reproductions or adaptations of those presented in that article.

[2] Riker's own (1962) formulation gave rise to two quite distinct hypotheses: one is the "minimal winning coalition" hypothesis; the second is the assertion that the winning coalition which will form will be one with the least resources (that is the smallest total number of seats) needed to win. The set of such "least resource" coalitions will, of course, be a (not necessarily proper) subset of the set of minimal winning coalitions.

[3] Also, the empirical evidence is such that the "least resource" hypothesis can clearly be rejected, as can the "fewest actor" hypothesis.

assigning different relative weights to their concerns for ideology and power. Luebbert (1983) points out that countries differ in the opportunities "politicians have for party cooperation inside and outside the cabinet context." This in turn has implications concerning the set of potentially winning coalitions that parties wish to join, because differences in political systems affect the feasibility of parties' options to combine *de jure* opposition with *de facto* cooperation. Luebbert also reminds us that party leaders must retain the support of parliamentary party and extra-parliamentary activists and must maintain party unity—achievements sometimes best accomplished from outside a governing coalition. Such observations suggest another failing of most coalitional models—an inability to allow for the possibility of a party choosing to be in a role supporting the governing coalition (*cf.* Lijphart, 1984).

Still another type of limitation of many coalitional models is their plethora of predicted coalitions. While there are statistical models that do allow one to compare the predictive fit of models that make unique or relatively few predictions with those offering many potential outcomes (see, *e.g.*, Winer 1979; Franklin and Mackie 1984), it would be useful if every model made relatively specific predictions. On the other hand, there are situations where there is a unique coalitional prediction but a multiplicity of real-world outcomes. In Italy, for example, coalitions form, then dissolve, and are replaced by other coalitions without any new election taking place or any change in the number of seats held by parties in the parliament. Models such as those of Grofman (1982), which make unique predictions, have been criticized (Rapoport and Weg 1986) for exactly this reason. However, in most countries, cabinet coalitions do almost always remain in place until a new election, and in such cases a model that makes a unique prediction is desirable. Thus, it would seem desirable to identify different models as being appropriate either for different situations, or to have a single model which somehow can "tell" when (in what countries, and in what contexts) it ought to make a unique prediction and when there must be multiple predictions (*cf.* Luebbert 1986). Alternatively, when multiple coalitions form even though seats are unchanged, it is possible to introduce stochastic error to account for the likelihood that party locations are known only imprecisely or are subject to "random" fluctuation (Straffin and Grofman 1984; Grofman, Straffin and Noviello, this volume).

A final important limitation of applications of most of the earliest models of coalition formation is that their use is limited to cases with one-dimensional policy spaces. Many European party systems can best be characterized in multidimensional terms (Budge, Robertson, and Hearl, 1987). Recent models which are applicable to multi-dimensional as well as undimensional policy spaces include the "competitive solution" (McKelvey, Ordeshook and Winer 1978; Winer 1979; Ordeshook and Winer 1980); game-theoretic models that use bargaining set notions (Aumann and Maschler 1964; Schofield 1982; Schofield and Laver 1985) or the concept of the core of voting games (Schofield 1986; Schofield, Grofman and Feld 1986; Schofield and Laver 1987; Laver and Schofield 1990; Schofield 1993a,b); the inertial model of Owen and Grofman (1984); Grofman's (1982) model of protocoalition formation; and Rapoport and Weg's (1986) multi-criterion approach. A useful review of the properties of a number of some of these "third generation" models is found in Straffin and Grofman (1984) and Schofield (1993a).

In this paper, I explicate the properties of one simple policy-driven dynamic model (Grofman 1982) of protocoalition formation in the multidimensional context and then offer a modified form of this model which I believe substantially improves its predictive power. I compare the predictive power of the original model, which yields a unique prediction for each situation, to that of several other coalition models; then I consider how the model might be modified to cope with multiple coalitions arising from a single election (using data from Italy). The modified protocoalition model addresses the objection of Luebbert (1983) to models which require winning coalitions to form (and thus cannot cope with minority government).

I also wish to argue in this paper for the importance of using standing coalitions, *not* governing coalitions, as the best data source with which to test policy-driven models of cabinet formation. The reason that supporting parties are usually omitted from consideration in tests of coalition formation models is that cabinet membership symbolizes for a party a commitment to publicly participate in the governing coalition, and an explicit bargain among the parties in the governing coalition as to the coalition's membership and division of cabinet responsibilities. Cabinet and subcabinet posts are customarily taken to be the currency in which parties are rewarded for their agreement to participate in the governing coalition. Thus, absence of a party from the governing coalition is taken to indicate absence of a party from the winning coalition. However, if we take the "spoils of victory" to be not simply jobs but, at least equally importantly, government policies to one's liking, then we can take support in a vote of confidence to indicate a party's preference for continuing the policies of the governing coalition. Parties which offer such support are obviously benefiting from the governing coalition, even if they do not wish for themselves (or the parties in the governing coalition do not wish to give them) cabinet or sub-cabinet posts. It is the standing coalition rather than the governing coalition which is most likely to be ideologically-connected, because idiosyncratic factors may keep a given party out of the governing coalition, even though its ideological position makes it very likely, because of policy similarities, to support the governing coalition in a vote of confidence.

12.2 A Dynamic Model of Protocoalition Formation

In some Western European countries (*e.g.*, Italy, France, and Denmark) there appears to be strong support for the view that ideologically connected coalitions predominate. (See Axelrod 1970; Damgaard 1969; Rosenthal 1969; Morgan 1976; DeSwaan and Mokken 1980.) That the predominance of such connected coalitions is due to some form of policy/ideological diversity minimization is, I believe, also well supported—although the evidence here is more indirect. (See the discussions in DeSwaan 1973; Flanagan 1973; Budge and Farlie 1978.) Certainly the notion that political parties seek to join a coalition whose policy and/or ideological center is one from which they are not too far distant is an intuitively plausible one. Operationalizing such a notion however can be done in different ways. In this paper I use the dynamic model of protocoalition formation in m-space postulated in Grofman (1982).

In this use of the model, it is assumed that political parties are locatable as points in some m-dimensional space with metric properties.[4] Each political party is assumed to evaluate the relative desirability of potential coalition partners in terms of the distances of other parties from itself. I assume that each party is a potential member of a protocoalition, and that each party or protocoalition seeks to attract others into a coalition with it so as to eventually form a winning coalition. (Later I shall modify this assumption slightly.) Parties will not in general all be of equal weight. The weight of a party is assumed to be the number of seats it has in the legislature. I posit a multistage process of protocoalition formation. At stage 1 each political party attempts to form a protocoalition of itself and the party nearest to it in m-space. Nearness is defined in terms of proximity based on weighted distance, $\frac{dw_j}{w_i+w_j}$; i.e., the proximity of actor i with weight w_i to actor j with weight w_j, when these two are separated by a distance d. Hence, although distance is of course symmetric, proximity is not symmetric, except for the special case where $w_i = w_j$.

If and only if party i is the party closest to party j and party j is also the party closest to party i, where closeness is in terms of weighted distance, do the two join together in a protocoalition.[5] The reason for using a proximity measure which is a function of both distance and (relative) weight is simple. I believe that the position between a strong (high-weight) actor and a weak (low-weight) actor that the protocoalition will adopt in m-space will reflect the relative weights of the actors and thus will be closer to the stronger than the weaker actor's ideal policy position. The proximity measure captures the notion that if weak actor i joins strong actor j, then i must move further from his ideal point than j does from his ideal point; i.e., the proximity of i to j is a measure of the distance actor i would "travel" if he were to join a protocoalition with actor j.

If no winning coalition is formed at stage 1, stage 2 begins. Once a protocoalition is formed, it is assumed to act as a single party, although determining the center of gravity of subsequent larger protocoalitions it may enter will be based on the weight of the parties in it. Parties that do not form pairs are "isolate" protocoalitions. At stage 2, the process I have discussed for stage 1 continues at the protocoalition level; i.e., each protocoalition seeks to merge with exactly one protocoalition. Protocoalition I joins protocoalition J if and only if the center of gravity of protocoalition I in ideological space is closest

---

[4] The protocoalition model is potentially applicable to coalition processes in a variety of areas in addition to cabinet formation.

[5] I assume, for simplicity, that distances are sufficiently "finely" measured so as to eliminate the possibility of ties.

to the center of gravity of protocoalition $I + J$, *and* if the center of gravity of the protocoalition J is closest to the center of gravity of protocoalition $I + J$. If no winning coalition is formed, stage 3 begins. The process continues until a winning coalition is formed.

The model posited above emphasizes the reciprocity required for a coalition to form—both partners must have no other coalitions which they prefer to join and which it is feasible for them to join. We may illustrate this model of protocoalition formation with a simple example in unidimensional space. Let n (the number of parties) be 5, and let K (the resources needed for a winning coalition) be a simple majority, where all parties begin with equal weight.

$$\overline{A \qquad\qquad\qquad B \quad C \quad D \qquad\qquad\qquad E.}$$

Consider the parties arrayed in ideological space as above:

Stage 1: B and C join together as do D and E. A is left "isolate," since its "natural" protocoalition partner B prefers to join a protocoalition with C.

Stage 2: The protocoalitions of $B + C$ and $D + E$ coalesce to form a winning coalition. A remains isolated since its "natural" protocoalition partner $B + C$ prefers to merge with $D + E$.

This example leads us to assert two interesting results:

Result 1: The process of protocoalition formation posited above need not lead to a minimal winning coalition.

Of course, if the center of gravity of each of the coalitions $A + B + C$ and $B + C$ were closer than the center of gravity of the coalition $(B+C)+(D+E)$, then a minimal winning coalition $(A + B + C)$ would form. Such a coalition would form if the distance between A and the midpoint of $B + C$ were less than $\frac{3}{2}$ the distance between the midpoints of $B + C$ and $D + E$. Because $B + C$ is a two-person protocoalition, the protocoalition $B + C$ is twice as important (has twice the weight) as the protocoalition A in determining the center of gravity of the coalition $A + (B + C)$.

Result 2: The process of protocoalition formation posited above need not lead to a winning coalition whose center of gravity is the median party, C, in the overall space; nor must the median party be the party closest to the coalition's center of gravity.

Indeed, in the example I have given, in no possible winning coalition is the center of gravity located in the median party, C. In the coalition $A+(B+C)$, B is closer to the coalition's center of gravity than is C; and in coalition $(B + C) + (D + E)$, D is closer to the coalition's center of gravity than is C.

In the protocoalition model it is demonstrated that

Result 3: The process of protocoalition formation posited above must ultimately lead to a winning coalition and can never lead to deadlock;[6] and

Result 4: In unidimensional space, the process of protocoalition formation posited above necessarily generates connected protocoalitions; *i.e.*, if two parties, I and K, are to be found in some protocoalition, any parties "between" them in the space must always be in the protocoalition.

In order to see if Result 4 can be generalized to the m-dimensional case, we require a notion of "connectedness" applicable to m-space. In unidimensional space, a (proto)coalition can be said to be connected when it includes all actors on any line segment connecting any two members. A natural generalization of this to m-space follows:

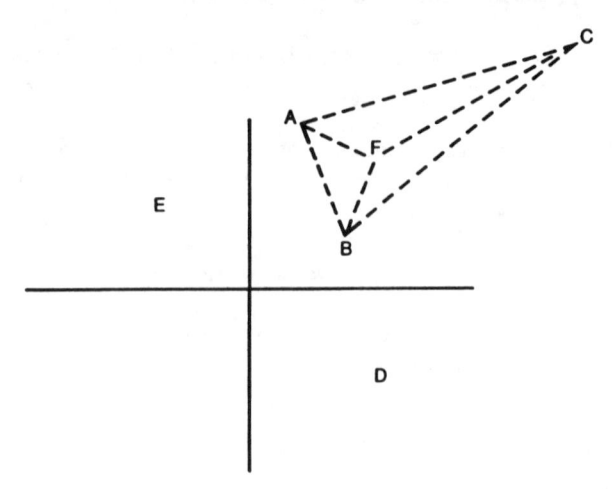

Figure 1. Model of m-connectedness.[7]

Definition: A (proto)coalition shall be said to be connected in m-space (or, equivalently, m-connected) when it includes all actors in or on any convex hull defined by any $m + 1$ members of the (proto)coalition.

As far as I am aware, this generalization of the connectedness notion was first proposed by the protocoalition model. I believe the only author previous to Grofman (1982) to have looked at connectedness in m-space was Rosenthal (1969), who used a graph theory model in which connected subgraphs indicate relative closeness in an otherwise ordinal and unidimensional space. Of course for $m = 1$, "m connectedness" is simply "connectedness".

Our definition of m-connectedness can be made clear by a simple two-

---

[6] Grofman proved this result for $n = 3, 4$, and 5. The general case result given in Grofman (1982) was independently derived by Philip Straffin and Christopher Nevison. See Straffin and Grofman (1984).

[7] From Grofman, B., 1982, p. 81.

Bernard Grofman   271

dimensional example with six actors (see Figure 1) taken from Grofman (1982).

In this example the coalition $\{A, B, C, F\}$ is 2-connected, since there are no actors not themselves members of the coalition in any of the 3 convex hulls defined by any 3 of the 4 actors in the coalition (see Figure 1). On the other hand, the coalition $\{A, B, C\}$ would not be 2-connected, since Actor F is not a member though he is within the convex hull defined by A, B, and C.

It is important to see that m-connectedness need not imply $(m - 1)$-connectedness. If we look at the actors in the two-dimensional example in Figure 1 above and consider their projections onto the one-dimensional space defined by the x-axis, we obtain a unidimensional alignment as follows:

<u>E A B F D C</u>.

Although the coalition $\{A, B, F, C\}$ is connected in two-dimensional space, it is not connected in the one-dimensional space defined by the projections onto the x-axis, or in the one-dimensional space defined by projections onto the y-axis, where the coalition alignment is <u>C A F E B D</u>.

This example leads us to consider another extension of the connectedness notion. We may define full-connectedness as follows.

Definition: A (proto)coalition shall be said to be fully connected in m-space (or simply, fully-connected) when it is j-connected for all integers: $0 < j \leq m$.

In the example given in Figure 1, $\{A, B, E, F\}$ would be a fully connected (proto)coalition, while $\{A, B, C, F\}$ would not be.

"m"-connectedness and full-connectedness are, I believe, concepts of considerable potential empirical importance, since if a coalition is not m-connected, there are, given ideological location, "natural" members of the coalition who are not part of it. Such actors might be expected to vociferously seek their "natural" rewards or to force some kind of coalition realignment. Similarly, if a (proto)coalition is not fully connected, there necessarily exists a dimension (or dimensions) of choice which has the possibility of splitting the coalition, since for choices contained in such a dimension(s), some coalition members will be closer to actors outside the coalition than to actors within it.

12.3 Three Illustrative Tests of the Protocoalition Model

Grofman (1982) provides some illustrative tests of his proto-coalition model using data on two-dimensional party arrays from three countries; Norway (1961, 1965, 1969), Denmark (1971, 1973), and Germany (1969, 1972).[8]

---

[8] Tables 1, 2, 3 of Chapter 13 of this volume compare the results of the proto-coalition model with three other coalition models. These tables also show the results of modifying the model by making the formation process stochastic. See these tables for the full names of the various parties.

In each case elections were chosen on the basis of the availability of a spatial map of party locations, produced by country-specialist scholars.

Norway. For all three elections in Norway, the winning coalitions are correctly predicted by the model. They are 2-connected, minimal winning, and connected in 1-space with respect to projections onto the x-axis, but not with respect to the y-axis. Moreover, the model gives rise to a considerably more focused prediction than others in the literature. For example, there are four other minimal winning coalitions that could have formed in 1965 and 1969 and five in 1961. The coalition predicted is the unique minimal resources coalition in 1965 and 1969 and one of the two such in 1961. It is one of the minimal winning coalitions with the fewest actors in 1961 but is not a member of that set in 1965 and 1969. (See Table 1, Chapter 13 of this volume.)

Clearly, no model is any better than the data used to generate it, and identifying parties' spatial locations has hitherto been an inexact science, although this should change with the availability of the data from the Party Manifesto Project (Budge, Robertson and Hearl 1987). In this chapter, however, I have replicated the analysis (first performed in Grofman 1982) of these three Norwegian elections using other spatial representations of the Norwegian party system and obtained virtually identical results. I used the model to predict the 1969 cabinet coalition from a two-dimensional representation for 1969 survey data on voters given by Converse and Valen (1971) and to predict the 1961 and 1963 coalitions from a two-dimensional representation based on a nonmetric scaling analysis performed by Groennings (1970) on 1963 survey data. My predictions remained unchanged, and only with the Groennings (1970) spatial representation am I able to find even a different protocoalitional dynamic. Thus, at least in the Norwegian case the model does not appear unduly sensitive to alternative methods in specifying party space. This is particularly important because in the Groennings (1970) array the Labor Party is actually shown as (slightly) closer to the Liberals than to the Socialist People's Party, and the protocoalition model (based on weighted distance) does not predict a Liberal-Labor coalition.

Table 1. Legislative Seat and Coalition Outcomes
In Norway in 1961, 1965, and 1969

	SocP	Lab	Chr	Lib	Cen	Con
			1961			
No. of seats	2	74	15	14	16	29
Observed coalition	*	*				
			1965			
No. of seats		68	13	18	18	31
Observed coalition			*	*	*	*
			1969			
No. of seats		74	14	13	20	29
Observed coalition			*	*	*	*

Bernard Grofman

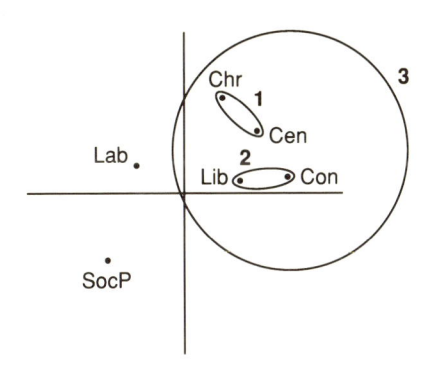

Figure 2. Perceived Party Locations in Norway, 1965—Two-Dimensional Solution. (Adopted from Converse and Valen, Figure 4, p. 134.) Numbered circles represent the stages of protocoalition formation in both 1965, and 1969. In 1961 the process requires only one stage—union between the Socialist People's Party and the Labor Party. (The Communist Party has been omitted because it was not seen as a viable coalition partner.) See Table 1, Chapter 13 for party names.

Denmark. In Denmark, for 1971, treating the parliamentary support coalition as the winning coalition, the Grofman (1982) prediction is confirmed by the data. The coalition predicted is among five possible minimal winning coalitions. It is also the unique minimal resource coalition and one of the minimal winning coalitions with the least possible number of parties. For Denmark in 1973 (again treating the support party as part of the standing coalition) the protocoalition model again yields a confirmed prediction which is distinct from that of any other coalition models and far more specific than that of most other coalition theory models (See Table 2).[9]

Table 2. Legislative and Coalition Outcomes
In the 1971 and 1973 Elections in Denmark (Winer, 1979).

	SP	Com	SD	Tax	Prog	CtrD	RdL	Con	ChP	AgL
1971										
No. of seats	17		70				27	31		30
Coalition	*		*							
1973										
No. of seats	11	6	46	5	28	14	20	16	7	22
Coalition					*	*	*	*	*	*

---

[9] In 1971 and 1973, eighty-eight seats were needed to form a majority government in Denmark. In 1971 only five parties obtained seats in the legislature, and the cabinet "coalition" consisted of a one-party minority government. However, the minority party, the Social Democrats, had the parliamentary support of the Socialist People's Party, and I have treated those two parties as in a coalition together, and as effectively comprising a minimal winning coalition.

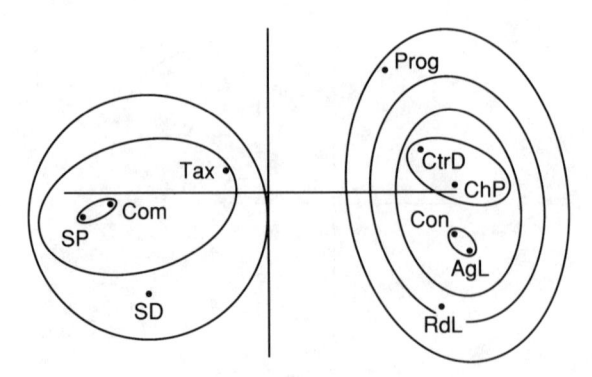

[Figure 3 diagram]

Figure 3. Perceived Party Locations in Denmark, 1973. (Spatial configuration from Rusk and Borre (1974, Figure 3, p. 341). Ellipses represent protocoalition formation stages after the 1973 election. (Adapted from Grofman 1982.)

In 1973 all ten parties held legislative seats, with the Agrarian Liberals forming a one-party minority government. However, by 1974 five other parties were providing parliamentary support for key elements of the Agrarian Liberal program, especially its economic policy. I have treated these parties as in a coalition together. I might note that the Progress Party was the last to join the support coalition and only joined on certain issues.

The coalitions predicted by the model were 2-connected. If we look at the projections onto the x-axis, the predicted coalitions were connected in 1-space as well as in 2-space; but this is not true if we look at projections onto the y-axis. (See Figure 3.)

Germany. For Germany, the protocoalition model gives rise to identical predictions for 1969 and 1972. The coalition I predict is 2-connected; it is connected in 1-space with respect to the x axis but not with respect to the y axis. For both elections the prediction of a specific minimal winning coalition is confirmed by the data. In both years there are three other possible minimal winning coalitions. (See Table 3 of Chapter 13 for the predictions of the various coalition models for both of the German elections.) Despite the limited number of actors, and the rather simple spatial array, most other models come up with multiple predictions.

I do not, however, wish to make too much of the German results, since in 1972 the FDP ran as the incumbent partner of the SPD, and I am using 1972 voter perceptions to locate the parties. Moreover, even in 1969 the $SPD - FDP$ coalition might have been seen by many of the voters to be predetermined. Furthermore, it is misleading in this period to really treat the CDU and CSU as independent parties.

Table 3. Legislative Seats and Coalition Outcomes
In the 1969 and 1972 Elections
In Germany (Winer 1979)

	1969			
	SPD	FDP	CSU	CDU
No. of seats	237	31	49	201
Observed coalition	*	*		
	1972			
No. of seats	230	41	48	177
Observed coalition	*	*		

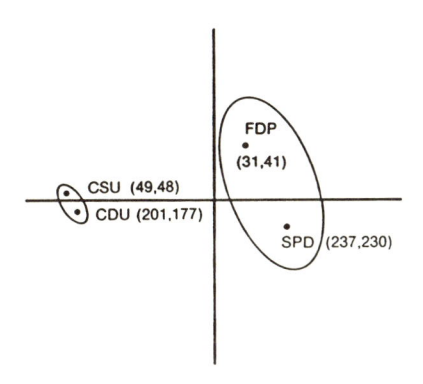

Figure 4. Perceived Party Locations in the Federal Republic of Germany, 1969. (Spatial configuration from Winer 1979 and Grofman, 1982, p. 85.)

The data for Germany, Denmark and Norway considered above strongly support the basic point that ideological factors and not just coalitional resources or number of actors are important in determining coalitional alignments. Indeed, I believe this point to be more important than the fact that the proto-coalition model predicted these coalitions perfectly, since some other, as yet unknown, policy-driven model might in principle have done likewise, even though it posited a quite different form of protocoalitional dynamics.

I now wish to briefly consider how the unique predictions of the protocoalition model might be modified to deal with situations such as Italy, where no unique coalitional prediction can be correct, because a given parliamentary lineup is compatible with several different successive patterns of coalitional alliances as governments rise and fall without a new election being called.

12.4 Italian Cabinet Coalitions 1946-1982

Table 1 presented in Chapter 15 of this volume shows the data on Italian cabinet coalitions from 1946 through 1992. We use the definition of a distinct cabinet coalition as one which occurs either after a general election, or after a change in prime minister, or after a change in the party composition of the cabinet, or after a resignation of a prime minister followed by a re-formation of the same governing coalition. We examine the period 1946-1982, during which time there are 44 distinct coalitions, even though there were only nine elections. We take the members of the standing coalition to be the governing coalition (*i.e.*, the parties represented in the cabinet) when that is a majority coalition, and the governing plus support coalition otherwise (those parties without cabinet seats who regularly support the governing coalition on votes of confidence and on other important policy matters). Using the maps I have constructed (available upon request from the author, adapted from Marradi 1982 and Morgan 1977), I find 37 of the 44 post-WWII standing coalitions to be connected on the left-right dimension (x-axis) but only 6 to be connected on the clerical-secular dimension (y-axis). Only 3 standing coalitions are minimal winning.[10]

For Italy, with an average of over 3 distinct coalitions occurring during each election period, to generate a single prediction from the protocoalition model seems a waste of time, since, at best, it will be right less than one third of the time, even if every coalition it predicted actually formed. Also, the party-space configurations I used are sufficiently subjective and *ad-hoc* that assuming they possess the accuracy required to calculate the nearest neighbors in the protocoalitional model seems misguided. Nonetheless, I have gone through the exercise in an informal manner, and it appears that in seven of the nine election years at least one of the obtained outcomes was predicted by the protocoalition model. (See the next chapter, where this analysis is extended to the case where party locations are subject to a stochastic disturbance.)

The protocoalition model posits that parties seek to join a coalition whose ideological center is one from which they are not too far distant, and that once a group of parties has coalesced into a protocoalition, its policy will represent a compromise among the preferred policy positions (on each dimension) of the protocoalition partners–probably weighted to favor the stronger parties. Clearly, under those assumptions, parties not already in the protocoalition whose ideal points are within or near the convex hull defined by the locations of the protocoalition members have every reason either to join the protocoalition, or, if (for a variety of reasons) publicly joining the coalition may not be desirable or even possible.[11] One can still expect such parties to support

---

[10] I find the predictive success of the Axelrod (1970) connected coalition model for postwar Italy to be somewhat less than other authors (*e.g.*, DeSwaan, 1973; Morgan, 1976) have reported, because I (following Marradi, 1982) count rightist parties such as the Liberal Party in 1946-47 and the Republican Party in 1969-70 and 1976 as potential coalition members whose absence, with respect to the left-right dimension, can make a coalition non-connected. Also, the practice of counting support parties as part of the standing coalition if the governing coalition is not a winning coalition leads us to label the Tambroni government of 1960 as non-connected. (See Table 2, Chapter 15, for the names and acronyms of the Italian parties, and Table 1, Chapter 15, for coalition type and duration.)

[11] Some parties are not considered "coalition-worthy" ("Koalitionsfahig," Damgaard, 1973). This "conventio exclusandum" (Georgio Freddi, personal communication) limits the feasible space of coalition-making. Also some parties may not wish to have cabinet representation because they wish to maintain an identity with the voters as parties *not* responsible for whatever mess the current government may be in.

the policies of the coalition to which they are internal. The policies of that coalition are likely to be close to their own preferred positions so that they will find the coalition a generally compatible one. Moreover, their participation can only enhance the likelihood that policies close to the ones they most prefer will be followed. Thus, in Italy, if a 2-dimensional representation of party space is reasonable, I would expect that 2-connected standing coalitions would form. All 44 standing coalitions in post-WWII Italy are 2-connected. Moreover, this is not a vacuous prediction, since there were often a number of winning coalitions (coalitions sometimes closer to minimal winning) that could have formed after the 1976 election but would not have been 2-connected, *e.g.*, a coalition of the Socialists, Republicans and Christian Democrats.

Thus, even if the specific predictions of the proto-coalition model are of only limited value in the case of Italy, the general notion of 2-connectedness seems to have some relevance.

12.5 Conclusions

The principal problem with the cabinet coalition literature is that it is three literatures, not one: (1) a literature on models of coalition formation, (2) a literature on the distribution of coalition payoffs, and (3) a literature on cabinet duration. Each of these literatures contains a number of excellent articles or books, but there is no overarching theoretical framework which ties coalitional structures, payoffs, and longevity together. In my view such a theory will need to recognize that parties are concerned not merely with being in a winning coalition, but also are concerned both with particular discrete payoffs in terms of portfolios and with expected policy outcomes. Moreover, only if we recognize the multiple options that parties may have (*e.g.*, to be in the governing coalition, to be in the support coalition, to be in opposition) and the mixed incentives that favor or disfavor each option, along with the previous history of coalitional alignments, can we understand the dynamics of the coalition process in terms of long-term choices.

References

Aumann, R. J. and M. Maschler. 1964. "The Bargaining Set for Cooperative Games," *Annals of Mathematical Studies* 52: 443-476.

Axelrod, R. 1970. *Conflict of Interest: A Theory of Divergent Goals with Applications to Politics.* Chicago: Markham.

Browne, E. 1971. "Testing Theories of Coalition Formation in a European Context," *Comparative Political Studies* 4: 391-413.

Browne, E. and J. Dreijmanis. 1982. *Coalitions in Western Democracies.* New York: Longman.

Browne, E., D. W. Gleiber, and C. Mashoba. 1984. "Evaluating Conflict of Interest Theory: Western European Cabinet Coalitions, 1945-1980," *British Journal of Political Science* 14: 1-32.

Budge, I. and D. Farlie. 1977. *Voting and Party Competition.* New York: Wiley.

Budge, I. and D. Farlie. 1978. "The Potentiality of Dimensional Analyses for Explaining Voting and Party Competition," *European Journal of Research* 6: 203-223.

Budge, I. and V. Herman. 1978. "Government Coalition Formation: An Empirically Relevant Theory," *British Journal of Political Science* 8: 459-477.

Budge, I., D. Robertson, and D. Hearl, eds. 1987. *Ideology, Strategy and Party Movement: Spatial Analyses of Party Electoral Programmes in Twenty Democracies.* Cambridge: Cambridge University Press.

Converse, P. E. and H. Valen. 1971. "Dimensions of Change and Perceived Party Distances in Norwegian Voting," *Scandinavian Political Studies* 6: 107-151.

Damgaard, E. 1969. "The Parliamentary Basis of Danish Governments: Patterns of Coalition Formation," *Scandinavian Political Studies* 4: 30-58.

Damgaard, E. 1973. "Party Coalitions in Danish Law-making, 1953-1970," *European Journal of Political Research* 1: 35-66.

DeSwaan, A. 1970. "An Empirical Model of Coalition Formation as an N-person Game of Policy Minimization," in *The Study of Coalition Behavior*, S. Groennings, E.W. Kelley and M. Leiserson, eds. New York: Holt, Rinehart and Winston.

DeSwaan, A. 1973. *Coalition Theories and Cabinet Formations.* Amsterdam: Elsevier.

DeSwaan, A. and R. Mokken. 1980. "Testing Coalition Theories: The Combined Evidence," in *Politics as Rational Action*, L. Lewin and E. Vedung, eds. Dordrecht: Reidel.

Dodd, L. 1976. *Coalitions in Parliamentary Government.* Princeton, N.J.: Princeton University Press.

Felker, L. 1981 "Conflict of Interest Theory and Specific Systems: Postwar Italy and Weimar Germany," *Comparative Political Studies* 14: 357-370.

Flanagan, S. C. 1973. "Theory and Method in the Study of Coalition Formation," *Journal of Comparative Administration* 5: 267-314.

Franklin, M. N. and T. T. Mackie. 1983. "Familiarity and Inertia in the Formation of Governing Coalitions in Parliamentary Democracies," *British Journal of Political Science* 13: 275-298.

Franklin, M. N. and T. T. Mackie. 1984. "Reassessing the Importance of Size and Ideology for the Formation of Governing Coalitions in Parliamentary Democracies," *American Journal of Political Science* 28: 275-298.

Gamson, W. A. 1961. "A Theory of Coalition Formation," *American Sociological Review* 26: 373-382.

Groennings, S. 1970. "Patterns, Strategies and Payoffs in Norwegian Coalition Formation," in *The Study of Coalition Behavior (op cit.).*

Grofman, B. 1982. "A Dynamic Model of Protocoalition Formation in Ideological N-space," *Behavioral Science* 27: 77-90.

Grofman, B. 1984. "The General Irrelevance of the Zero Sum Assumption in the Legislative Context," in *Coalitions and Collective Action*, M. Holler, ed. Wurzberg: Physica Verlag.

Hinckley, B. 1972. "Coalitions in Congress: Size and Ideological Distance," *Midwest Journal of Political Science* 16: 197-207.

Koehler, D. 1972. "The Legislative Process and the Minimal Winning Coalition," in *Probability Models of Collective Decision Making*, R. G. Niemi and H.F. Weisberg, eds. Columbus, Ohio: Merrill.

Laver, M. and N. Schofield. 1990. *Multiparty Government: The Politics of Coalition in Europe.* Oxford: Oxford University Press.

Leiserson, M. 1968 "Factions and Coalitions in One-party Japan," *American Political Science Review* 57: 770-787.

Leiserson, M. 1970a. "Game Theory and the Study of Coalition Behavior," (*op cit.*)

Leiserson, M. 1970b. "Power and Ideology in Coalition Behavior," *(op cit.)*

Lijphart, A. 1984. "New Approaches to the Study of Cabinet Coalitions," *Comparative Political Studies* 17: 155-129.

Luebbert, G. M. 1983. "Coalition Theory and Government Formation in Multiparty Democracies," *Comparative Politics* 15: 235-249.

Luebbert, G. M. 1986. *Comparative Democracy: Policy Making and Governing Coalitions in Europe and Israel.* New York: Columbia University Press.

Marradi, A. 1982. "Italy: From 'Centrism' to Crisis of the Center-left Coalitions," in *Coalitions in Western Democracies*, E. Browne and J. Dreijmanis, eds. New York: Longman.

McKelvey, R., P. Ordeshook, and M. Winer. 1978. "The Competitive Solution for N-person Games with Transferable Utility with an Application to Committee Games," *American Political Science Review* 72: 599-615.

Morgan, M. J. 1976. *The Modelling of Governmental Coalition Formations: A Policy-Based Approach with Interval Measurement.* Unpublished dissertation, University of Michigan.

Ordeshook, P. C. and M. Winer. 1980. "Coalitions and Spatial Policy Outcomes in Parliamentary Systems: Some Experimental Results," *American Journal of Political Science* 24: 730-752.

Owen, G. and B. Grofman. 1984. "Coalitions and Power in Political Situations," in *Coalitions and Collective Action*, M. Holler, ed. Wurzburg: Physica-Verlag.

Rapoport, A. and E. Weg. 1986. "Dominated, Connected, and Tight Coalitions in the Israeli Cabinet," *American Journal of Political Science* 30: 577-598.

Riker, W. 1962. *The Theory of Political Coalitions.* New Haven: Yale University Press.

Rohde, D. W. 1972a. "A Theory of the Formation of Opinion Coalitions in the U.S. Supreme Court," in *Probability Models of Collective Decision Making, (op cit.).*

Rohde, D. W. 1972b. "Policy Goals, Strategic Choice and Majority Opinion Assignments in the U.S. Supreme Court," *Midwest Journal of Political Science* 16: 652-682.

Rohde, D. W. 1972c. "Policy Goals and Opinion Coalitions in the Supreme Court," *Midwest Journal of Political Science* 16: 208-224.

Rosenthal, H. 1969. "Voting and Coalition Models in Election Simulation," in *Simulation in the Study of Politics*, W.D. Coplin, ed. Chicago: Markham.

Rusk, J. G. and O. Borre. 1976. "The Changing Party Space in Danish Voter Perceptions, 1971-73," in *Party Identification and Beyond*, I. Budge, I. Crewe and D. Farlie, eds. New York: Wiley.

Schofield, N. 1982. "Bargaining Set Theory and Stability in Coalition Governments," *Mathematical Social Sciences* 3: 9-31.

Schofield, N. 1984. "Political Fragmentation and the Stability of Coalition Governments in Western Europe," in *Coalitions and Collective Action, (op cit.)*.

Schofield, N. 1986. "Existence of a 'Structurally Stable' Equilibrium for a Noncollegial Voting Rule," *Public Choice* 51: 267-284.

Schofield, N. 1993a. "Political Competition and Multiparty Coalition Governments," *European Journal of Political Research* 23: 1-33.

Schofield, N. 1993b. "Party Competition in a Spatial Model of Coalition Formation," in *Political Economy: Institutions, Competition and Representation*, W. Barnett, M. Hinich and N. Schofield, eds. Cambridge: Cambridge University Press.

Schofield, N., B. Grofman, and S. L. Feld. 1988. "The Core and the Stability of Group Choice in Spatial Voting Games," *American Political Science Review* 82: 195-211.

Schofield, N. and M. Laver. 1985. "Bargaining Theory and Portfolio Payoffs in European Coalition Cabinets, 1945-1983," *British Journal of Political Science* 15: 143-164.

Schofield, N. and M. Laver. 1987. "Bargaining Theory and Cabinet Stablity in European Coalition Governments 1945-1983," in *The Logic of Multiparty Systems*, M. Holler, ed. Dordrecht: Martinus-Nijhoff.

Straffin, P. and B. Grofman. 1984. "Parliamentary Coalitions: A Tour of Models," *Mathematics Magazine* 57: 259-274.

Taylor, M. and M. Laver. 1973. "Government Coalitions in Western Europe," *European Journal of Political Research* 1: 205-248.

Winer, M. 1979. "Cabinet Coalition Formation: a Game-theoretic Analysis," in *Applied Game Theory*, S. Brams, A. Schotter, and G. Schwodiauer, eds. Wurzburg: Physica-Verlag.

13. The Sequential Dynamics of Cabinet Formation, Stochastic Error, and a Test of Competing Models

Bernard Grofman, Philip Straffin, and Nicholas Noviello [1]

13.1 Introduction

Axelrod (1970) introduced the idea of connected coalitions in one dimension. Grofman (1982) provided a straightforward generalization of that idea to the multidimensional case and offered a multistage model of protocoalition formation in an m-dimensional ideological space which gave rise to the prediction of a unique *m-connected* winning coalition.

Players in the Grofman framework are myopic, and results resemble those of a "clustering" model. In his model minimal winning coalitions also usually form. Peleg (1981) provides a game-theoretic model of coalition formation in which, when there is a single major (weakly dominant) player, only those coalitions weakly dominated by that player will form.

Rapoport and Weg (1986) synthesized the approaches of Peleg (1981) and Grofman (1982) to improve both models, borrowing the idea of a dominant player from Peleg and the idea of m-connected coalitions from Grofman. The principal difficulty of Peleg's approach is that it generates embarrassingly many coalitions as its predictive set. Another limitation of the model is that it fails to make use of the notion of m-dimensional connectedness. Grofman's prediction of a unique government, claimed by the author (1982) to be a major advantage of the protocoalition model is criticized by Rapoport and Weg. "[T]he prediction set of any model of coalition formation that incorporates the notion of ideological diversity and measures ideological proximities by Euclidean distances should include more than a single element. The size of this prediction set should be inversely related to the goodness of fit of the spatial configuration." Rapoport and Weg find a second difficulty with the application of the Grofman model to the case of Israel. "[T]he multistage model of

---

[1] This research was supported by NSF Grant SES-85-06376, Decision and Management Sciences, to the first-named author. We are indebted to Dorothy Gormick for bibliographic assistance. We are especially indebted to Amnon Rapoport for making the raw data of his Israeli study available to us. An earlier version of this paper was presented at the Conference on European Cabinet Coalition Formation, European University Institute, Fiesole, Italy, May 24-29, 1987.

protocoalition that Grofman proposes, which may be appropriate for cabinet negotiations conducted secretly, sequentially, and bilaterally, seems inappropriate for the coalition formation process in the Knesset, since it ignores the particular role assigned to the dominant party..." of initiating the process of coalition formation.

We agree with these objections. Indeed, in a published review essay (Straffin and Grofman, 1984) previous, though unknown to Rapoport and Weg (1986), virtually identical points on cabinet coalition models were made. In particular, Straffin and Grofman (1984, emphasis ours) assert:

> At the very least *the inexactness of placement methods should caution us against claiming precision in prediction...*,
>
> 1. There may be inconsistencies in the spatial placements obtained by different analysts using the same or different methods;
> 2. although Euclidean distance has usually been used as the measure of ideological proximity, other metrics... might have an equal or better claim to validity;
> 3. there may be some logical circularity in deriving likely coalitions from spatial placements, since parties might be perceived as similar *because* they have often been in coalitions together.

Also, Straffin and Grofman (1984, emphasis ours) make the point that

> It probably does not make sense to ask for a unique best model. Some of the models have parties concerned mainly with power, some mainly with ideology. The game theory models posit careful rational consideration of alternatives, the protocoalition model relies on more shortsighted behavior. *We will likely find that different models work best in different situations.*

For some countries and some time periods (*e.g.*, Italy or Israel in much of the post World War II period), even though there is no new election and thus no change in seats (and also, often, no particular reason to believe that the ideological locations of parties have shifted), a cabinet coalition may come to an end and a new one replace it (albeit sometimes with only minimal changes in which parties are in the cabinet and which parties support it). Any model which predicts a unique coalition to form cannot easily account for why there could be shifts in coalitions without any changes in legislative representation. For any country where multiple coalitions form, the unique predictions of the protocoalition approach would *ipso facto* seem doomed to failure.

Grofman (Chapter 12 of this volume), however, proposes a simple modification to the protocoalition model to permit it to make multiple predictions based on stochastic perturbances of the party location spatial map or changes in the relative weights a party attaches to each dimension. There are several justifications for introducing stochastic error. First, there are inevitably errors in the estimated party locations in any spatial map. If those locations are approximately correct, introducing noise tells us how robust the model predictions are likely to be. Second, over time, exogenous events occur which may provide the equivalent of a "shock" to the system resulting in small movements in party locations.

Introducing stochastic error in the protocoalition model rescues it, in principle, from the difficulties of a deterministically unique prediction. However, the model still suffers from the second difficulty noted by Rapoport and Weg, namely that it is not well-suited to a situation in which a single (major) party is asked to initiate cabinet coalition formation.

13.2 Sequential Protocoalition Formation

To deal with situations such as those in many countries (including Israel) where a given party is initially designated to form the cabinet, we propose a new model of sequential protocoalition formation in which the designated party (usually the party with greatest legislative strength) makes one-at-a-time offers to other parties, which may be either refused or accepted, to join the government. In this model we posit that the designated party makes offers to parties in order of their (weighted) ideological proximity to it. Once the first party accepts the designated party's offer to join a proto-coalition, the new proto-coalition makes offers to parties in order of their (weighted) ideological proximity to it, and so on, until a winning coalition is formed. In this model, a party, j, will choose to join a proto-coalition, I, if and only if the ideological center of gravity of the new proto-coalition is closer to the ideological location of j than is the center of gravity of the complementary protocoalition $P - I$, where P is the entire set of parties in the space. (See the Appendix for a more formal expression of the sequential protocoalition algorithm.)

In this paper we further specify the properties of the sequential model of protocoalition formation described above and provide two illustrative tests of the predictive power of this model and the protocoalition model, both with and without the addition of stochastic noise.

The first test uses the spatial maps of Germany (1969 and 1972), Norway (1971 and 1973), and Denmark (1961, 1965, and 1969) (see Figures 2, 3, and 4 of Chapter 12) to develop predictions based on the protocoalition model, by admitting the possibility of stochastic error in the location of party positions in the two-dimensional policy space.

The second test uses the spatial maps of 52 Israeli experts and observers of 1980 Israeli party politics used by Rapoport and Weg (1986). These maps are used to predict the cabinet outcome of the 1981 Israeli election under both the protocoalition model and the new sequential model described in this paper. The predictions of each model are compared to Rapoport and Weg's model predictions of dominated, connected and tight (DCT) coalitions.

Table 1

Comparisons of the Predictions of the Eight Models of Coalition Formation

Predicted Cabinet Coalitions

Year	Observed Support Coalition	Proto-coalition Model	Stoch. Coalition Model	Seq. Coalition Model[†]	Barg. Set	Min. Win.	Comp. Sol.
			Norway[2]				
1961	1,6	1,6	1,6	1,6	1,2 1,3 1,4 1,5 1,6	1,2 1,3 1,4 1,5 1,6 2,3,4,5,6	1,5 1,6 2,3,4,5,6
1965 and 1969	2,3,4,5	2,3,4,5	2,3,4,5	2,3,4,5	1,2 1,3 1,4 1,5	1,2 1,3 1,4 1,5 2,3,4,5	1,4 1,5 2,3,4,5
			Denmark[3]				
1971	1,5	1,5	1,5	1,5	1,5 1,2 1,3 1,4	1,5 1,2 1,3 1,4 2,3,4,5,6	1,5 1,6 2,3,4,5
1973	2,3,4,6,7,8	2,3,4,7,8	2,3,4,6,7,8	2,3,4,5,6,7,8	not calculated	2,3,4,6,7 etc.	2,3,4,6,7 2,3,4,6,8
			Germany[4]				
1969 and 1972[a]	3,4	3,4	3,4	3,4	3,4 1,4 2,4	3,4 1,4 2,4 1,2,3	3,4 2,4

(†) largest party is asked to initiate the coalition process.

Our empirical findings are quite interesting:

(1) For the Danish, German, and Norwegian elections previously studied (in Chapter 12), with the exception of Denmark in 1971, both the stochastic version of the protocoalition model (with random noise of up to 20%) *and* the deterministic form of the new sequential proto-coalition model predict perfectly the observed coalitions, regardless of which party is asked to initiate the coalition formation process in the sequential protocoalition model. In Denmark in 1971 the observed winning coalition (the Social Democrats supported by the Socialist People's party) is predicted by the new sequential model if we require the largest party to initiate the coalition formation process. Otherwise, the complementary coalition is predicted. The protocoalition model predicts a minority coalition on round one of bargaining, and the complementary majority coalition if the process continues until round three. Since these six elections were also perfectly predicted by the original deterministic form of the protocoalition model, we see, for these particular spatial maps, that the model's predictions can be very robust to even substantial (random) perturbations of party locations. Also, even though the protocoalition model and our present sequential model are very different, we cannot use these elections to decide between them, since both models fit the data equally well. We show a comparison of our results with those of other models in Table 1. The table compares the predictions of the stochastic and sequential models with those of the bargaining set (Aumann and Maschler 1964), minimal winning coalitions (Gamson 1961; Riker 1962), and the competitive solution (see McKelvey, Ordeshook and Winer 1978).

Footnotes: Table 1

[2] Source of the spatial mapping of Norway: Converse and Valen (1971: Figure 4, p. 134). See also Ordeshook and Winer (1980).

	1961	1965	1969
1 = Labor (Social Democrat)	74	68	74
2 = Conservatives	29	31	29
3 = Center	16	18	20
4 = Christian People's Party	15	13	14
5 = Liberals	14	18	13
6 = Socialist People's Party	2	0	0

[3] Source of the spatial mapping of Germany: Rusk and Borre (1974: Figure 3).

	1971	1973		1971	1973
1 = Social Democrats	70	40	6 = Progressive Party	0	28
2 = Conservatives	31	16	7 = Center Democrats	0	14
3 = Agrarian Liberals	30	22	8 = Christian People's Party	0	7
4 = Radical Liberals	27	20	9 = Communists	0	6
5 = Socialist People's	17	11	10 = Single Tax Party	0	5

[4] Source of the spatial mapping of Denmark: Winer (1979), and Ordeshook and Winer (1980); (a) in 1972 there is also a competitive solution for {1, 2, 3}.

	1969	1972		1969	1972
1 = Christian Social Union CSU	49	48	3 = Free Dem. FDP	31	41
2 = Christian Dem. CDU	201	177	4 = Social Dem. SPD	237	230

(2) For the 1981 Israeli election, using the set of 52 spatial maps, the stochastic versions of both the protocoalition model and our present sequential model, like the Rapoport and Weg (1986) DCT model, have as their prediction the actual Likud-Tami-Mafdal-Agudat-Tehiya coalition which formed after three months following an initial coalition involving Likud, Tami, Mafdal, and Agudat only. Moreover, both the deterministic form of the protocoalition model and, when we require (as is the case in Israel) that the largest party initiate the coalition formation process, the new sequential protocoalition model gives a correct prediction for each of the composite maps generated by pooling the data points from each of the three sets of observers and for all 52 observers (students (21), legislators (24), and journalists (7)) consulted by Rapoport and Weg.

For each of the 52 maps and four composite maps (one for each of the three groups, and one for all 52 observers), we show (Table 2) the Israel 1981 predictions of the *deterministic* protocoalition model. In Table 3[5] we show the predictions of the new sequential model described in the Appendix. The column entries give the relative frequencies of the predictions.

Table 2. Predictions of the
Protocoalition Model for the 1981 Israel Cabinet Coalition

	Legislators (24)	Journalists (7)	Students (21)	Total (52)	Composite Maps (4)
EFGHJ	.08 (2)			.04 (2)	
EFGHIJ	.21 (5)	.28 (2)	.14 (3)	.19 (10)	
AEFEHIJ	.13 (13)			.06 (3)	
FGHIJ*	.21 (5)	.43 (3)	.52 (11)	.37 (19)	1.00 (4)
ABCDEGH	.04 (1)			.02 (1)	
BCDEHI	.04 (1)			.02 (1)	
AFGHI	.04 (1)			.02 (1)	
BCDG	.04 (1)			.02 (1)	
ABCDEGI	.04 (1)			.02 (1)	
ABCDGHIJ	.04 (1)			.02 (1)	
BCFGHIJ		.05 (1)		.02 (1)	
EFGHI			.05 (1)	.02 (1)	
DFG			.05 (1)	.02 (1)	
ABCDEGIJ			.05 (1)	.02 (1)	

* = model prediction. (See also Table 3.)

A	Hadash	4	E	Jelem	2	I	Agudat	4
B	Shinui	2	F	Likud	48	J	Tehiya	3
C	Katz	1	G	Tami	3			
D	Labor	47	H	Mafdal	6			

[5] The 52 Spatial Maps reported in Rapoport and Weg (1986) are the sources for Tables 2 and 3.

For the protocoalition model, we see that the actual Likud-Tami-Mafdal-Agudat-Tehiya Coalition is the choice of all three sets of subjects and of the group of 52 as a whole (though it is only tied for first place among the legislators). Moreover, it is the clear choice in each of the four composite maps which "smooth out" the individual variations in the assigned location of the importantly, again it is *the* choice in the composite maps. Thus, both the protocoalition model and the present sequential dynamics model do as well as the Rapoport and Weg DCT model for this Israeli data set, *i.e.*, effectively, all three models perform perfectly.

13.3 Discussion

The fact that the predictions of the deterministic and stochastic protocoalition models of cabinet formation are the same suggests that the political divisions in these countries are in some important sense "robust". In other words, even (random) error in locating parties does not substantially affect predictions as to which sets of parties will ultimately coalesce. Visual inspection of the two-dimensional spatial maps used by Grofman (1982) (reproduced in Chapter

Table 3. Predictions of the Sequential Model for the 1981 Israel Cabinet Coalition

	Legislators (24)	Journalists (7)	Students (21)	Total (52)	Composite Maps (4)
EFGHJ	.17 (4)	.14 (1)	.10 (2)	.13 (7)	
AFHI	.04 (1)			.02 (1)	
FGHIJ*	.46 (11)	.71 (5)	.48 (10)	.50 (26)	1.00 (4)
EFHIJ	.13 (3)		.10 (2)	.10 (5)	
FHIJ	.04 (1)	.14 (1)		.04 (2)	
FGHJ	.04 (1)				.02 (1)
AFGHI	.04 (1)			.02 (1)	
EFGHI	.04 (1)		.05 (1)	.04 (2)	
EFG	.04 (1)			.02 (1)	
BCFHIJ			.10 (2)	.04 (2)	
CFHIJ			.05 (1)	.02 (1)	
ABCDHIJ			.05 (1)	.02 (1)	
FGHI			.05 (1)	.02 (1)	
FGH			.05 (1)	.02 (1)	

* = Model prediction.

12 of this volume) suggests why this might be so. Essentially, these maps provide pictures in each of these three countries of a bipolar political universe

position of the FDP shifts over time relative to the SPD and CDU/CSU points.)

In the 1981 Israel example, the fact that the composite maps yield the correct predictions under both the original protocoalition as well as the stochastic model suggests that we might be able to think of the 52 individual maps as "approximations" to the "true" configuration, but contaminated by noise.

In the previous chapter, Grofman identified three (not necessarily chronological) "generations" of research on cabinet coalition formation. The first generation of research, (*e.g.*, Riker 1962; Schofield 1976) treats the goal of coalition actors as maximizing payoffs in terms of portfolios and other perquisites of power. In such models, even ideological opposites will join if in so doing they create a minimal winning (or minimal resource) coalition. The second generation of models emphasized ideological proximity. The seminal model of this "generation" of research is, of course, Axelrod (1970), but there is other work by DeSwaan (1973), *etc.*

We regard Rapoport and Weg (1986) as the first of the "third generation" of coalition research. What distinguishes third generation research on coalitions is that it combines the concern for power (of the first generation of research) with the concern for ideological proximity (of the second generation), with a recognition of the *diversity of actual coalition formation processes in different countries*. In Israel, in particular, the largest party has the first opportunity to form the cabinet. A model which fails to take into account this key institutional fact is very apt to make inaccurate predictions. The third generation of coalition models can be thought of as reflecting the spirit of the "new institutionalism" emphasis in public choice (see *e.g.*, Shepsle 1979; Feld and Grofman 1988). The sequential model of coalition dynamics described in the Appendix to this paper is also a "third generation" model, as is recent work discussed in Chapter 6 of this volume. We believe that this new generation of coalition research offers the possibility of major advances in both predictive power and theoretical understanding as compared to earlier work without an "institutional" focus.

13.4 Properties of the Sequential Model of Protocoalition Formation

Grofman (1982) and Straffin and Grofman (1984) specify a number of properties of the model of protocoalition formation. For example: (1) the model must always identify a unique winning coalition, *i.e.*, no deadlock is possible; (2) for parties located in a single dimension the predicted winning coalition must be connected, but the same is not true if the parties' issue-space is multidimensional (although in practice, in m-dimensions the model almost always generates m-connected coalitions); and (3) the predicted winning coalition need not be minimal winning. In this section of the paper we provide some analogous results for the sequential model of protocoalition formation.

Lemma 1: In one dimension, there is always a party that can get someone to say YES to it, since an extreme party q will say YES to the party p such that the distance $d(q, \{pq\})$ between q and the center of gravity of the proto-coalition, is minimal. (See the Appendix for definitions of the notation.)

Proof. Choose the coordinate system such that the location of party q, $L_q = O$ and $L_p \geq L_q$ for all p, and let w_i = the weight (or number of seats) of party i. The required condition is that

$$\frac{w_p L_p}{w_p + w_q} \leq \frac{w_{p'} L_{p'}}{w_{p'} + w_q} \; \forall \; p' \neq p, q.$$

Hence

$$\frac{w_p L_p}{w_p + w_q} \leq \frac{\sum w_{p'} L_{p'}}{\sum w_{p'} + (n-2) w_q} \leq \frac{\sum w_{p'} L_{p'}}{\sum (w_{p'} + w_q)}$$

(where the summation is over all $p' \neq p, q$).

PROPOSITION 1: In one dimension the sequential model of protocoalition formation may break down without reaching a coalition of winning size, but only at the "knife-edge" where there are two equal blocks.

EXAMPLE 1: (The numbers in parentheses are weights.)

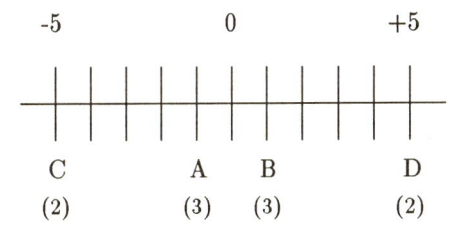

```
        -5              0              +5
        ┼┼┼┼┼┼┼┼┼┼┼
        C           A  B              D
        (2)        (3)(3)            (2)
```

Here if A or C begin, AC will form but neither B nor D will join it. If B or D begin, BD will form but neither A nor C will join it. In such circumstances we would predict a grand coalition or a minority government to form.

PROPOSITION 2: Even in one dimension, not all parties will say YES to all proposals, and there may be one or more parties which cannot get any other parties to say YES; *i.e.*, there may be a party with whom no other party will join directly in a coalition.

EXAMPLE 2:

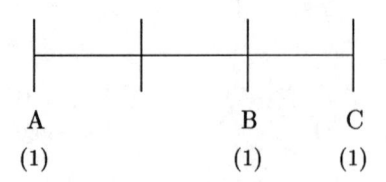

```
    A          B    C
   (1)        (1)  (1)
```

Neither B nor C will say YES to A. However, B will say YES to C, and conversely.

PROPOSITION 3: Even in one dimension, centrist coalitions need not always form.

EXAMPLE 3:

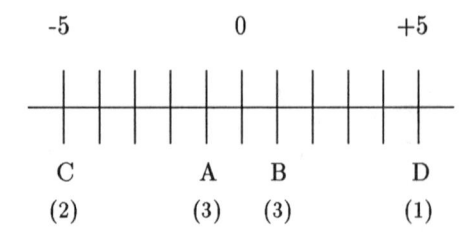

```
   -5              0           +5

    C           A   B          D
   (2)         (3) (3)        (1)
```

Note that even though A is the party which B would ask first if B were forming a coalition, if B is asked by A, B will say NO.

PROPOSITION 4: The result of the sequential model of protocoalition formation need not be a minimal winning coalition.

EXAMPLE 4:

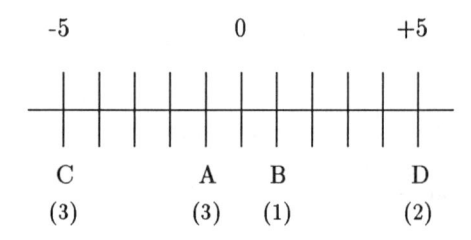

```
   -5              0           +5

    C           A   B          D
   (3)         (3) (1)        (2)
```

B will join A, then D will join AB, but ABD is nonminimal, even though it is minimal connected winning.

PROPOSITION 5: Even in one dimension, disconnected winning coalitions are possible.

EXAMPLE 5:

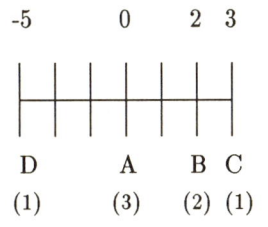

```
       -5       0     2  3
        ├───┼───┼───┼──┤
        │   │   │   │  │
        D       A     B C
       (1)     (3)   (2)(1)
```

A will ask B, who will say NO: then A will ask C, who will say YES, resulting in AC, a coalition which is not connected. Of course, if a party other than A begins the process, connected coalitions may form. For example, B will ask C, who will say YES, then ABC results. Similarly C will ask B, who will say YES, again leading to ABC. However, D can't get anyone to say YES.

PROPOSITION 6: If there is more than one dimension, there may be parties who will not say YES to anyone (as well as in Proposition 2, parties who cannot get anyone to say YES). See Figure 1.

EXAMPLE 6:

$$
\begin{array}{ccc}
 & A & \\
 & (1,0) & \\
C & & D \\
(-3,0) & & (3,0) \\
 & B & \\
 & (-1,0) &
\end{array}
$$

Figure 1. *An example to illustrate Proposition 6. All parties have equal weight.*

In Figure 1, A and B will not say YES to either singleton actor. C and D cannot get anyone to say YES. However, C will say YES to A; then ABC forms. In like manner, by symmetry, C will say YES to B, leading again to ABC. Similarly, D will say YES to either A or B, leading to ABD.

References

Aumann, R. J. and M. Maschler. 1964. "The Bargaining Set for Cooperative Games," *Annals of Mathematical Studies* 52: 443-476.

Axelrod, R. 1970. *Conflict of Interest: A Theory of Divergent Goals with Applications to Politics*. Chicago: Markham.

DeSwaan, A. 1973. *Coalition Theories and Cabinet Formation: A Study of Formal Theories of Coalition Formation as Applied to Nine European Parliaments after 1918*. Amsterdam: Elsevier.

Feld, S. L. and B. Grofman. 1988. "Majority Rule Outcomes and the Structure of Debate in One-Issue-at-a-Time Decision Making," *Public Choice* 59: 239-252.

Converse, P. E. and H. Valen. 1971. "Dimensions of Change and Perceived Party Distances in Norwegian Voting," *Scandinavian Political Studies* 4: 107-151.

Grofman, B. 1982. "A Dynamic Model of Proto-Coalition Formation in Ideological N-Space," *Behavioral Science* 27: 77-90.

McKelvey, R., P. Ordeshook, and M. Winer. 1978. "The Competitive Solution for N-person Games with Transferable Utility with an Application to Committee Games," *American Political Science Review* 72: 599-615.

Ordeshook, P. C. and M. Winer. 1980. "Coalitions and Spatial Policy Outcomes in Parliamentary Systems: Some Experimental Results," *American Journal of Political Science* 24: 730-752.

Peleg, B. 1981. "Coalition Formation in Simple Games with Dominant Players," *International Journal of Game Theory* 10: 11-33.

Rapoport, A. and E. Weg. 1986. "Dominated, Connected, and Tight Coalitions in the Israeli Knesset," *American Journal of Political Science* 30: 577-596.

Rapoport, A. and E. Golan. 1985. "Assessment of Political Power in the Israeli Knessett," *American Political Science Review* 79: 673-692.

Riker, W. H. 1962. *The Theory of Political Coalitions*. New Haven: Yale University Press.

Rusk, J.G. and 0. Borre. 1976. "The Changing Party Space in Danish Voter Perceptions, 1971-73," in *Party Identification and Beyond*, I. Budge, I. Crewe and D. Fairlie, eds. New York: Wiley.

Schofield, N. 1976. "The Kernel and Payoffs to European Government Coalitions," *Public Choice* 26: 29-51.

Shepsle, K.A. 1979. "Institutional Arrangements and Equilibrium in Multidimensional Voting Models," *American Journal of Political Science* 23: 27-59.

Straffin, P. and B. Grofman. 1984. "Parliamentary Coalitions: A Tour of Models," *Mathematics Magazine* 57: 259-274.

Winer, M. 1979. "Cabinet Coalition Formation: A Game-Theoretic Analysis," in *Applied Game Theory*, S. Brams, A. Schotter, and G. Schwodiauer, eds. Vienna: Physica-Verlag.

Appendix

Sequential Protocoalition Formation Algorithm

We define a collection P of parties, such that each party p is characterized by weight w_p and location L_p. For each subset $S \subset P$, let

$$w_S = \sum_{p \in S} w_p \text{ and } L_S = \frac{\sum_{p \in S} w_p L_p}{\sum_{p \in S} w_p}.$$

Denote by $d(p,q)$ the Euclidean distance between L_p and L_q, and analogously for coalitions. Let the number of votes needed to win be $K =$

$$\left\lceil \sum_{p \in P} \frac{w_p}{2} \right\rceil;$$

where $\lceil x \rceil$ is the least integer bound of x, i.e., $\lceil x \rceil$ is the smallest integer such that $x < \lceil x \rceil$.

The Sequential Protocoalition Algorithm:

1. If any protocoalition has weight $\geq K$, STOP, Else:

2. Referee asks a party p (not already asked in this round) to form a coalition.

3. "p" ranks other party, q, by the distance $d(p, \{pq\})$.

4. p works down the list asking the closest other party to join in a coalition. A party q, when asked by p, says YES if and only if
$d(q, pq) \leq d(q, P - \{p\})$.

5. As soon as some party says YES, that round finishes and a new round starts with a new protocoalition $\{pq\}$ in place of p and q.

6. If no party says YES to p and there is a party who has not yet been asked in this round to form a coalition, return to Step 1 and begin again, after dissolving any protocoalitions that may have formed.

7. If all parties have been asked, STOP and signal DEADLOCK.

14. Subgame-Perfect Portfolio Allocations in Parliamentary Government Formation

Michael Laver and

Kenneth Shepsle

14.1 Introduction

In parliamentary democracies based on a first-past-the-post electoral formula, legislative majorities are manufactured by an election. Ordinarily a single party captures a majority of parliamentary seats, enabling it to form a government. Post-election government formation is normally *pro forma* at the parliamentary level, though it undoubtedly involves much intraparty strategic behavior.

In contrast, in those parliamentary democracies based on some version of a proportional-representation electoral formula, a legislative majority is rarely manufactured. In these circumstances a carefully choreographed political dance is staged in which the monarch or head of state asks some party to attempt to form a government. If it fails, the head of state designates some other party as *formateur*. The process continues until some *formateur's* proposal for a government obtains an affirmative investiture vote in parliament. (This vote may be explicit, or implicit in the sense that a no-confidence motion is *not* put and carried.) If no party succeeds, the constitution stipulates some reversion outcome, one that varies from country to country. In some, a caretaker government takes office, possibly followed shortly thereafter by new elections. In others, the status quo government remains in power.

The present paper offers a strategic model of government formation in parliamentary democracies. It grows out of earlier work by the present authors (Laver and Shepsle 1990a,b; 1991, 1993a,b) and Austen-Smith and Banks (1990). At the center of this analysis is a precise conceptual view of what a government is, on the one hand, and the process by which one is formed, on the other. (See also Laver and Shepsle, 1994, 1996.) Each of these is elaborated in the next two parts of the paper. In Section 14.4, we analyze a finite, extensive-form, noncooperative spatial game that captures some of the essentials of our formulation. Since it is probably most plausible to think of the political world as 'without end,' our finite extensive form game is, at best, a suggestive vehicle for displaying some central ideas. It is not the last word and, after suggesting some modest general properties of the finite game in Section 14.5 of this chapter, we turn in Section 14.6 to some ways to transform our model into a repeat-play game.

Before beginning we should mention two other game-theoretic approaches to government formation phenomena. Baron (1991), like us, employs a noncooperative spatial game approach. His model differs from ours in three important respects. First, he is less concerned with the formation of a government than with the equilibrium spatial policy that emerges from the formation process. In contrast, we see the government as the intermediate instrument determining policy; it is the government, on the one hand, and the rational expectations of all agents about the policies that will be implemented by this government, on the other, that characterize the equilibrium. Second, and relatedly, he allows any point in the policy space to be available to the agents as final government policy. As in Austen-Smith and Banks (1990), our model does not allow agents this capacity to commit credibly to any point in the space. Finally, Baron's model is a repeat-play game, a variation on which we report in the final section of this paper.

Schofield has written on coalition bargaining in multiparty parliaments for many years. (See, for example, Chapter 8 of this volume.) His recent work, displaying its empirical power, is found in Schofield (1993a, 1993b), and his general approach is summarized in Laver and Schofield (1990). In contrast to the models of Austen-Smith and Banks, Baron, and us, his derives from cooperative spatial voting theory. He is therefore less concerned than us with an explicit treatment of the sequential process of coalition formation. Instead, his theoretical focus is on the balancing forces that stabilize particular outcomes as the natural equilibria of bargaining.

It should be underscored that all of these approaches share a number of familial resemblances. They all take the spatial formulation and a strategic capacity of the actors as fundamental. While they differ in several respects, collectively they hold out the promise, somewhere down the theoretical road, of more thorough-going integration.

14.2 Government Formation

We briefly report our formal set-up; it is more extensively elaborated in our previously cited papers. We begin with a Euclidean policy space, $\Re^m$, the basis vectors of which are policy or issue dimensions. These basis vectors are partitioned into *jurisdictions*, each of which comprises a domain of responsibility for a government ministry. The party or politician with ministerial authority is said to hold the *portfolio* for that jurisdiction. Each party is described by a policy position (a point in $\Re^m$), Euclidean preferences over various policy outcomes (circular iso-policy contours), and an exogenously given weight w_i (the proportion of parliamentary seats it possesses). Parties are taken to be policy-motivated in the sense that their government formation behavior is driven by their policy preferences. Thus, these parties are not Downsian—they are not motivated exclusively by a desire for an official role in government.

A *government* is an allocation of portfolios to parties supported (in a manner to be specified below) by a parliamentary majority. If party i holds all the portfolios, and $w_i > \frac{1}{2}$, then i constitutes a single-party majority government.

If $w_i \leq \frac{1}{2}$, then i is a *single-party minority government*. If more than one party holds portfolios, then they comprise a *coalition government*; they are a *majority* or *minority* (coalition) government depending upon whether the sum of participant weights exceeds one-half or not. Let us emphasize that *the government is the set of parties holding portfolios*. The government need not be identical to the set of parties supporting it in parliament.[1]

In our model parties in the parliament are policy-oriented, but do not select policies directly. They select a government—an allocation of policy portfolios. Since they are policy-oriented, parties must be able to forecast the policy implications of their choices. We assume that a specific *policy forecast* is associated with each particular allocation of portfolios among parties. This forecast is a belief, commonly held by all the actors, about subsequent ministerial policy choices in each jurisdiction. Here we make a simplifying assumption: actors forecast that each government minister will implement the ideal policy of her party on policy dimensions within her jurisdiction.[2] For example, if there is a five-dimensional policy space and there are three jurisdictions (the first two two-dimensional and the third one-dimensional) controlled by parties A, B, and C, respectively, then the common forecast for this government is $x = (A_1, A_2, B_3, B_4, C_5)$, where X_i is the ideal point component of party X on dimension i.[3]

A distinguishing feature of our model, made clear by the preceding discussion, is that there is more to a government than its party composition. The *distribution* of jurisdiction-specific authority is central to our argument. Thus, when a government engages in a 'cabinet reshuffle,' but its party composition remains invariant, this is nevertheless an entirely new government in our view, for jurisdiction-specific authority has been reallocated.

If there are J jurisdictions and n parties, then there are n^J feasible portfolio allocations, each associated with a unique policy forecast. In our government formation game, this *lattice*, L, of policy forecasts constitutes the feasible set of policy outcomes, each one 'implemented' by assigning jurisdictional authority to specific parties. Figure 1 displays the lattice L for two unidimensional jurisdictions and three parties. The three party ideals are the single-party governments and the remaining six points are coalition governments, where AB, for example, means that party A is allocated the horizontal portfolio and party B the vertical. (Ignore the indifference contours for now.)

---

[1] Nearly every theory of coalition government, including those of Baron and Schofield, fail to make this distinction. Instead, they regard the government as consisting of all parties supporting it in an investiture vote.

[2] From the assumption of Euclidean preferences, policy preferences are separable by jurisdiction. Thus, a party's optimum policy in any jurisdiction is invariant to choices in other jurisdictions.

[3] As Baron (1991) correctly observes, ours is not a model of *cabinet* government, since the cabinet has no existence independent of individual ministers. Rather, ours may be taken as a model of *ministerial* government. It may be generalized in two ways. First, we may maintain our ministerial focus, but deny the minister unilateral authority; in this circumstance a minister must bargain with her senior civil servants. Second, we may depart from unilateral ministerial authority by providing an independent role for the cabinet. Both of these generalizations are taken up in Laver and Shepsle (1991c).

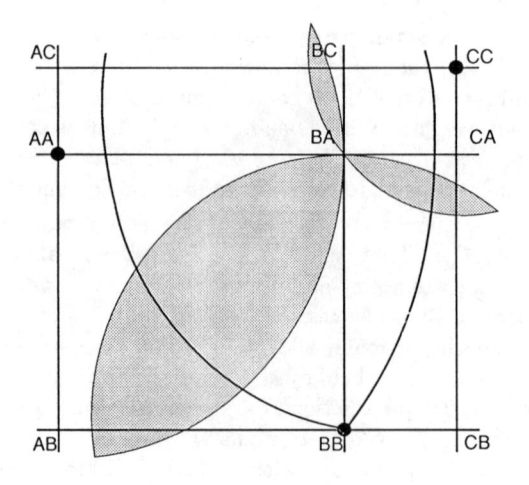

Preference Orderings

A	B	C
AA	BB	CC
AC	CB	CA
AB	BA	BC
BA	CA	BA
BC	AB	CB
BB	BC	BB
CA	CC	AC
CC	AA	AA
CB	AC	AB

Figure 1. Forecast of a three-party feasible set of policy outcomes.

To examine equilibrium the conventional winset machinery is employed. Let $P_i(x)$ be the set of points in $\Re^m$ preferred by i to $x \in \Re^m$. A point $y \in \Re^m$ is in the *winset of* x, $W(x)$, if the combined weight of the parties for which $y \in P_i(x)$ exceeds one-half. A portfolio allocation leading to policy x is an *empty winset equilibrium (EWE)* if and only if $x \in L$ and $W(x) \cap L = \emptyset$. That is, an EWE is a portfolio allocation the policy forecast of which is preferred by a majority to the policy forecast associated with any other portfolio allocation. In effect, an EWE is a conventional spatial equilibrium restricted to L. Given the generic cyclicity of majority rule in conventional spatial settings (McKelvey 1976, 1979; McKelvey and Schofield 1987), it is noteworthy that many spatial distributions nevertheless yield EWEs. In Figure 1, BA is an EWE since no coalition of majority weight prefers any other lattice point to it. In the context of unidimensional jurisdictions, an extension of Kadane's division-of-the-question theorem (Kadane 1972) establishes that the dimension-by-dimension median of L is the unique EWE or no point is. In what follows, whenever the dimension-by-dimension median has an empty winset, we label it m**.

An additional feature of the institutional setting of most multiparty governments suggests that this definition of equilibrium is incomplete. In every political system with which we are familiar, a party may not be forced into government against its will. Each *participant* in a prospective government must give assent to her participation. She may not be dragooned into a prospective government and thus may deny parliamentary consideration of that proposed government if she does not wish to participate in it. Consequently, an equilibrium government may be sustained because of vetoes cast by participants in prospective alternatives, even if that equilibrium government does not possess an empty winset. In Figure 1, BB is a single-party minority government. Every point in $W(BB)$ includes party B as a participant and, therefore, requires her assent. Thus, at BB, no point in L is preferred by a majority that cannot potentially be vetoed by one of its participants. Under some strategic circumstances BB may be an equilibrium.

In the next part we formulate an extensive form game that seeks to capture some elements of government formation. To summarize our theoretical conceptualization to this point, a government is to be regarded here as a portfolio allocation. Associated with each portfolio allocation is a policy forecast, understood here to entail each minister exercising complete discretion in her jurisdiction and unable to commit credibly to anything other than her ideal point. Strategically, majorities have the ability to remove a government, replacing it with an alternative, or to sustain it in power. Individual parties may veto any proposed government in which they participate.

Before turning to our extensive form game, we add one further conceptual development. In Figure 1, *Party B* is in the enviable position of being able to veto every alternative in the winset of its ideal point. We call a party with this capability *strong*, and label its ideal point s*.

14.3 A Game-Theoretic Formulation of Government Formation

At the outset of our model, at time zero, there is an incumbent or status quo government. We assume that a government is in place at all times, its ministers attending to day-to-day policymaking in their respective ministries. An incumbent government may not resign until a replacement for it is selected. If no replacement is selected, then it remains in place.[4]

After an election, or on any other occasion of government formation, the first step is for the head of state to select a sequence of *formateurs*. In effect, he selects one of the $n!$ party orderings, though it is quite compatible

---

[4] In effect, this means that the status quo may not be vetoed by its participants; incumbent ministers may not 'turn in their badges' until replaced. In Laver and Shepsle (1990a) several alternatives to this assumption are suggested.

with our approach if his discretion is strictly delimited.[5] The first party in the sequence proposes an allocation of portfolios among parties. Based on the common-knowledge policy forecast associated with this proposal and its rational expectations about what will occur conditional on its actions, each participant in the proposal is given an opportunity to exercise its veto.[6] If some participant does so, then the next *formateur* in the sequence is asked to propose a government. If no veto is forthcoming, then the proposal for a new government goes to an investiture vote in parliament. If a parliamentary majority votes in favor of the proposal, then this government is formed and the game ends. If a parliamentary majority votes down the proposal, then the next *formateur* in the sequence is asked to propose a government. If, in sequential order, no *formateur*'s proposal succeeds, then the status quo government remains in power and the game ends. Once a government forms, whether it is a new portfolio allocation or the status quo allocation, it serves for a fixed term. This bargaining sequence is given for three parties in Figure 2.[7]

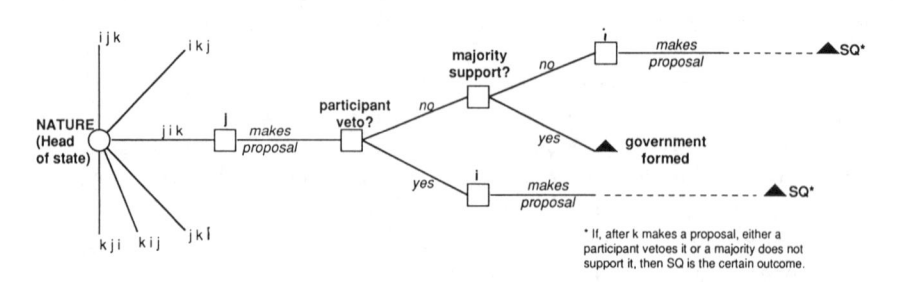

Figure 2. Three party bargaining sequence of government proposals.

Throughout, the following are common knowledge: (1) each actor's preferences among policy outcomes; (2) the common policy forecast associated with each prospective government; (3) the *formateur* sequence, once selected by the head of state; (4) the actual proposal made at each step; (5) whether a participant veto has been cast; (6) the results of any investiture vote; and (7) the general structure of the process as given in Figure 2.

In equilibrium, we require strategies to satisfy the requirement of *subgame perfection* determined by backward induction. The finiteness of the game and the common-knowledge assumptions given above produce well-defined equilibria (modulo occasions of indifference in a decisive actor). We assume that the process takes place over a duration sufficiently short that we need not worry about time preferences; the pie does not shrink.

---

[5] For example, the head of state may be required to select parties in the order of their parliamentary strength. Alternatively, the head of state may select the *formateur* sequence stochastically (with selection probabilities possibly related to parliamentary strength).

[6] The sequence in which each participant indicates whether or not it will exercise its veto does not affect our results, so we suppress this detail.

[7] This bargaining sequence is similar to that employed by Austen-Smith and Banks (1988).

14.4 Subgame Perfect Portfolio Allocations

To provide some intuition, we begin by analyzing a simple setting in which there are three parties and two unidimensional jurisdictions. It turns out that the outcome of strategic behavior depends on whether or not there is a strong actor. A strong actor, it will be recalled, is a party that is in a position to veto any point in the winset of its ideal; that is, it is a participant in every government in the winset of the policy that would result if it formed a single-party government.

14.4.1 Configuration with a Strong Party

In Figure 1, in which the lattice L consists of nine points, the dimension-by-dimension median, BA, is the unique EWE, and party B is a strong actor (that is, it is a participant in all the portfolio allocations, BA and BC, preferred by parliamentary majorities to its ideal). Euclidean preferences are unnecessary to many of our results and are employed mainly for intuitive purposes. What matters is each actor's preference ordering over lattice points; so long as these preference orderings remain invariant, it does not matter what metric induces them.

Any of the nine lattice points may identify the incumbent government. The head of state may select any of the six *formateur* sequences. There are, then, 54 possible settings, each of which is associated with a unique subgame perfect portfolio allocation. In equilibrium, this portfolio allocation is proposed by the first *formateur*, is not vetoed by any participant, and is then approved by a parliamentary majority. It is, however, conditioned by what would happen (off the equilibrium path) if a different choice were made by a decisive actor.

A systematic examination of each of the 54 settings is given in Appendix 1. Several will be considered in the text to display the model at work, as well as to highlight the effect of assuming the government formation game to be finite.

Suppose that $SQ = AA$ and the head of state chooses the *formateur* sequence ABC. Thus, A gets to make the first proposal. If it fails, then it is B's turn to propose. If it fails, then it is C's turn. Finally, AA remains the portfolio allocation if C's proposal fails. With the backward induction methodology, we, naturally, work backwards. It is common knowledge that, should the process get to C, it will propose (and cannot commit to do otherwise) the superior cabinet in its preference ordering preferred, both by the cabinet's participants and by a parliamentary majority, to AA. Party C will propose CC, since this obviously avoids a participant veto, and is preferred by B and C to AA; neither B nor C can do any better at this point in the process than to invest a CC government with authority. Given this forecast of C's behavior, B proposes (and, likewise, cannot commit to do otherwise) the superior cabinet in its preference ordering preferred, both by the cabinet's participants and by a parliamentary majority, to CC. Party B will propose BB, since it, too, avoids a veto and is preferred by A and B to CC. Given these forecasts of B and C proposal actions, A's optimal proposal is also BB.[8] This will not be vetoed by B and will be approved in an investiture vote. We thus have the unusual circumstance of an incumbent minority government (Party A) proposing to form an alternative government in which it does not participate.

It turns out (see Table 1) that, for $SQ = AA$, *any formateur* sequence yields BB as the subgame perfect equilibrium (SPE). At some point in any of the *formateur* sequences, one of the actors will either propose BB or an alternative that can be beaten by BB. If the latter, then an actor moving earlier will have an incentive to propose BB. Thus, if B moves last (as in *formateur* sequences ACB and CAB), then it will propose BB (since this defeats AA); because B is strong, no earlier mover can improve upon BB. If A or C is last, then they will propose AA and CC, respectively, which are also beatable by BB—thus BB will be proposed by someone moving earlier. In sum, for any sequence starting from an SQ of AA, BB will emerge at some point and cannot be displaced.

As Table 1 indicates, for only three of the nine status quo commencement points is it possible to arrive at a subgame perfect portfolio allocation other than BB. $SQ = BA$ is obviously one of those. The BA portfolio allocation, as suggested above, is m**: no alternative portfolio allocation is preferred to it by any parliamentary majority. It, like BB, constitutes an absorbing state that can only be disturbed by a change in party preferences or by a change in party weights that gives some party a majority.

Table 1
Strong-Party Subgame Perfect Portfolio Allocation

Order of Offers	AA	AB	AC	BA	BB	BC	CA	CB	CC
ABC	BB	BB	BB	BA	BB	BA	BB	BB	BB
ACB	BB	BB	BB	BA	BB	BA	BB	BB	BB
BAC	BB	BB	BB	BA	BB	BB	BA	BB	BB
BCA	BB	BB	BB	BA	BB	BB	BA	BB	BB
CAB	BB	BB	BB	BA	BB	BA	BB	BB	BB
CBA	BB	BB	BB	BA	BB	BB	BA	BB	BB

(Column header: *Status Quo*)

---

[8] In practice, any other proposal by A will either be vetoed or defeated in parliament and B will then propose BB. So, in a sense, it does not matter what A does and A might just take a flyer. If, however, in cases of indifference like this one, we posit a small cost associated with making a losing proposal, then the behavior in the text follows.

$SQ = BC$ is another status quo government from which it is possible for a government other than BB to form. BA emerges as a subgame perfect portfolio allocation in three of the *formateur* sequences, namely those in which some agent has an incentive to propose BA early in the sequence. Similarly, for $SQ = CA$, there are three *formateur* sequences in which BA prevails.

Thus, in *this* three-party example, either the strong actor's ideal or m** is subgame perfect for every set of initial conditions. This is not, however, true in general for the finite government formation game. Even when there is a strong party and an empty winset point (m**), there are configurations yielding neither m** nor the strong party's ideal as the subgame perfect equilibrium.

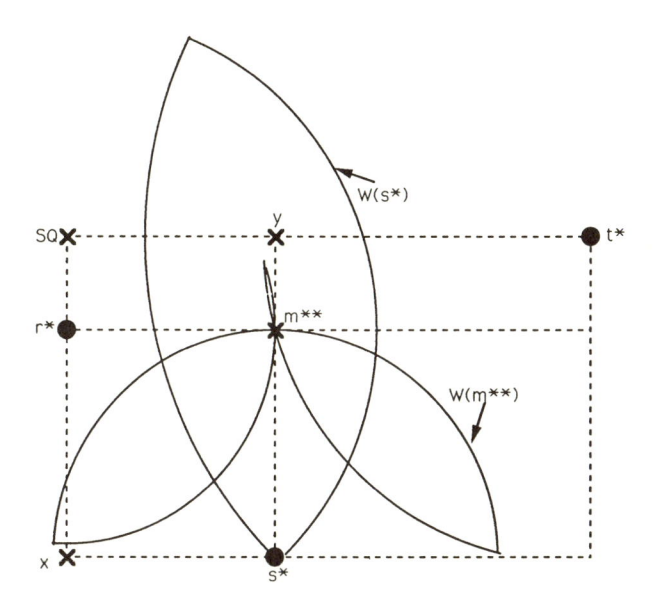

Figure 3. Three party configuration of preferences with dimension by dimension median m^{**} and strong party preference s^*.

This can be seen in the following example. In Figure 3 there are three parties, R, S, and T, with ideals, r*, s* and t*, respectively. The dimension-by-dimension median has an empty winset, labeled m** in the figure. Party S is strong. Suppose we have $SQ = RT \in W(s^*)$ and the *formateur* sequence is RST. The optimal choice for party T is y. Note that $y \in W(s^*)$. Party S, second in the sequence, cannot, therefore, propose s*. Its subgame perfect proposal is $x \in W(s^*)$. This allows party R, going first, to propose r*. Thus the SPE is neither m** nor s*, even though both exist.

The failure of either s* or m** to prevail in general is a function of the *finiteness* of the government formation game. If the government formation game repeats—that is, if a no-confidence motion and a proposal for a new government were always in order—then it would not be possible for party R in the previous example to propose r* (indeed, each actor's equilibrium strategy would change). This is because r* is vulnerable to a no-confidence vote. In the repeat-play version of the game, we are able to prove that, whenever s^* and m^{**} exist, the stationary subgame perfect equilibrium is either s^* or an element of $W(s^*)$. Moreover, if it is the latter, it will always be an element of $W(s^*)$ that party S prefers at least as much as m^{**}.[9] The finite case, therefore, provides occasions when a *deviant* equilibrium (such as r*) may arise, because that government, once installed, is *guaranteed* a fixed term in office.

14.4.2 Configuration with No Strong Party.

In Figure 4 we display a three-party configuration with no strong actor. The $B-C$ majority prefers a variety of portfolio allocations to AA, many of which do not involve party A, and therefore, cannot be vetoed by it. The $A-C$ majority prefers CC to BB, so party B cannot veto an allocation in the winset of its ideal. Finally, the $A-B$ majority prefers AB to CC, so party C cannot veto an allocation in the winset of its ideal. Thus, no actor is strong. BC is the dimension-by-dimension median and, as may be easily determined, has an empty winset.

Preference Orderings

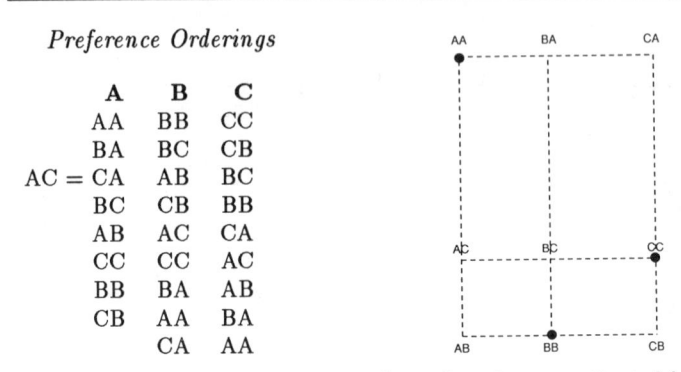

	A	B	C
	AA	BB	CC
	BA	BC	CB
AC = CA		AB	BC
	BC	CB	BB
	AB	AC	CA
	CC	CC	AC
	BB	BA	AB
	CB	AA	BA
		CA	AA

Figure 4. Three party configuration of preferences for cabinet allocations, with no strong party.

As Table 2 reveals, in the absence of a strong actor there is considerably more variety in subgame perfect portfolio allocations.[10] Three allocations are never subgame perfect (see Table 3), but each of the other six are subgame perfect for some status quo government and *formateur* ordering. However, except for BC, which is an absorbing state and does emerge frequently when other allocations are the status quo, for no other status quo portfolio allocation is the subgame perfect portfolio allocation *formateur*- sequence invariant. Thus, we obtain no apparent regularity in outcomes. The details are given in Appendix A.2.

---

[9] These results are reported in another paper, currently in draft form, in which the repeat-play game is analyzed more fully.

[10] To add an additional twist in this case, one of the actors is indifferent between two portfolio allocations, thereby affecting its strategic behavior in several instances.

Table 2
Nonstrong-Party Subgame Perfect Portfolio Allocation

	\multicolumn{9}{c}{Status Quo}
Order of Offers	AA	AB	AC	BA	BB	BC	CA	CB	CC
ABC	CA	BC	CC	CA	AC*	BC	AC*	AC*	AC*
ACB	AB	AB	AB	AB	AB	BC	AB	AB	BC
BAC	BB	BC	BB	BB	BB	BC	BB	AC*	BB
BCA	AB	BC	BB	AB	AB	BC	AB	BC	BC
CAB	CC	CC	CC	CC	CC	BC	CC	CC	CC
CBA	CC	BC	CC	CC	AC*	BC	CC	CC	CC

Table 3
Possible Subgame Perfect Portfolio Allocations For Each Status Quo Government and No Strong Party

	\multicolumn{9}{c}{Subgame Perfect Portfolio Allocations}
Status Quo Portfolio	AA	AB	AC	BA	BB	BC	CA	CB	CC
AA		X		X			X		X
AB		X				X			X
AC		X		X					X
BA		X			X		X		X
BB		X	X		X			X	X
BC						X			
CA		X	X	X			X		X
CB		X	X			X	X		X
CC			X		X	X	X		X

14.5 Prospects for Generalization

In Figure 3 *SPE*s are not restricted to s* or m** because there is a lattice point $x \notin W(s*)$ that party S prefers to m**. In some *formateur* configurations, as just demonstrated, this fact will yield an $SPE \neq s^*$, m**. The geometric conditions yielding these 'deviant' equilibria, either in the three-party, two-unidimensional-jurisdictions case or in more general circumstances, are not particularly enlightening. Given our more sweeping conclusion for the repeat-play government formation game alluded to above, however, it is worth indicating, for this *finite* setting, when the resulting equilibrium will be s* or m**.

Let the sequence in which parties make proposals be $1, 2, ..., m$. Let party S, the strong party, be ranked *ith* in this sequence. First we define the binary relation Q on $L \times L$. We say that xQy if and only if $x \in W(y)$ and $x >_j y$ for all j that are allocated portfolios in x.[11] We define x^k, party k's subgame perfect proposal, recursively as follows:

$x^m = argmax_{x \in L} \{u_m(x) : x \, Q \, SQ\}$

For any $j < m$,

$x_j = argmax_{x \in L} \{u_j(x) : x^j \, Q \, x^{j+1}\}$.

Several simple results follow from this setup. First, if SQ = m** or s*, then the SPE is m** or s*, respectively. The former follows since $W(m^{**}) = \emptyset$, so no successful proposal to alter SQ is possible. The latter follows because any proposal preferred to SQ by a majority will be vetoed by party S.

Second, and more generally, if x^j = m** or s*, for any j, then the SPE is m** or s*, respectively. That is, if at any point in the sequence m** or s* is an optimal proposal by an actor, then that point will, from the same logic as in the previous paragraph, be the SPE.

Third, if $x^{i+1} \notin W(s^*)$, then s* is the SPE. If the party succeeding the strong party in the proposal sequence is commonly forecast to propose an alternative outside the winset of s*, then a parliamentary majority will support s* at the preceding stage.

Finally, as the example associated with Figure 3 illustrates, it is only when proposer $i + 1$ proposes an alternative in $W(s^*)$ that there is the potential for deviation from the general tendency we have identified (*viz.*, that the SPE is s* or m**). That such potential can be realized is provided by the example. It should be mentioned in qualification, however, that there is nothing inevitable about a deviation under the condition just identified. If some proposer earlier than position i has an incentive to propose either s* or m**, then, by our second result, this alternative will be the SPE.

14.6 Motions of No Confidence: Repeat-Play Government Formation

The finite government formation game with complete and perfect information, as in any extensive-form game of this genre, yields an equilibrium in the first proposal. The engine of backward induction is sufficient to create a new government at the first branch of the game tree. But, as we have noted at several junctures, this formulation is at variance with most real-world government formation processes. Baron (1991) has adapted the Baron-Ferejohn (1989) closed-rule bargaining model to accommodate some of these features.

---

[11] In Laver and Shepsle (1990a), Q is the 'contending' relation.

In Baron's model, as we noted in the introduction, a proposer (rather than a proposer *sequence*) is randomly selected to make a proposal. If his proposal fails to obtain a parliamentary majority in an investiture vote, then the game repeats with a newly recognized proposer. However, if a proposal succeeds, then the game ends. In comparing Baron's model to ours, it may be seen that he has taken a step in the direction of repeat play–the game continues until a successful proposal is made. *But the game does not repeat once a new government is installed.*

In our repeat-play formulation, we adopt the Baron approach, but modify it in several ways. First, actor proposals are *governments* (that is, portfolio allocations), associated with which are common-knowledge policy forecasts; thus, each proposal must be associated with an element of L. Second, we require that a proposal obtain the consent of its participants; thus, participants have strategic veto rights. Third, our government formation game repeats after *successful* proposals as well as after failed attempts; thus, once a government is installed, it is subject to subsequent motions of no confidence.

We have not fully worked out the implications of this model. We can say, however, that in those political circumstances in which there exists a strong party (with ideal point s^*), on the one hand, and an empty-winset multidimensional median (m^{**}), on the other, the stationary subgame perfect equilibrium is either s^* or an element of $W(s^*)$. We intend to report the details of this theorem in a subsequent paper.

References

Austen-Smith, D. and J. Banks. 1988. "Elections, Coalitions, and Legislative Outcomes," *American Political Science Review* 82: 405-422.

Austen-Smith, D. and J. Banks. 1990. "Stable Governments and the Allocation of Policy Portfolios," *American Political Science Review* 84: 891-906.

Baron, D. 1991. "A Spatial Bargaining Theory of Government Formation in Parliamentary Systems," *American Political Science Review* 85: 137-165.

Baron, D. and J. Ferejohn. 1989. "Bargaining in Legislatures," *American Political Science Review* 83: 1181-1206.

Kadane, J.B. 1972. "On Division of the Question," *Public Choice* 13: 47-54.

Laver, M. and N. Schofield. 1990. *Multiparty Government: The Politics of Coalition in Europe*. Oxford: Oxford University Press.

Laver, M. and K. Shepsle. 1990a. "Coalitions and Cabinet Government," *American Political Science Review* 84: 873-890.

Laver, M. and K. Shepsle. 1990b. "Government Coalitions and Intraparty Politics," *British Journal of Political Science* 20: 489-507.

Laver, M. and K. Shepsle. 1991. "Divided Government: America is not *Exceptional*," *Governance* 4: 250-269.

Laver, M. and K. Shepsle. 1993a. "A Theory of Minority Government in Parliamentary Democracy," in *Games in Hierarchies and Networks*, F. W. Scharpf, ed. Boulder, Colo.: Westview Press.

Laver, M. and K. Shepsle. 1993b. "Agenda Formation and Cabinet Government," in *Agenda Formation*, W. Riker, ed. Ann Arbor: University of Michigan Press.

Laver, M. and K. Shepsle. 1994. "Cabinet Government in Theoretical Perspective," in *Cabinet Ministers and Parliamentary Government,* M. Laver and K. Shepsle, eds. Cambridge: Cambridge University Press.

Laver, M. and K. Shepsle. 1996. *Making and Breaking Governments.* Cambridge: Cambridge University Press.

McKelvey, R. D. 1976. "Intransitivities in Multidimensional Voting Models and Some Implications for Agenda Control," *Journal of Economic Theory* 12: 472-482.

McKelvey, R. D. 1979. "General Conditions of Global Intransitivity in Formal Voting Models," *Econometrica* 47: 1085-1111.

McKelvey, R. D. and N. Schofield. 1987. "Generalized Symmetry Conditions at a Core Point," *Econometrica* 55: 923-933.

Schofield, N. 1993a. "Political Competition and Multiparty Coalition Governments," *European Journal of Political Research* 23: 1-33.

Schofield, N. 1993b. "Party Competition in a Spatial Model of Coalition Formation," in *Political Economy: Institutions, Competition, and Representation,* W. Barnett, M. Hinich and N. Schofield, eds. Cambridge: Cambridge University Press.

Appendices

In these appendices we provide a description of the subgame perfect equilibrium path for each of the six *formateur* orderings and nine possible incumbent governments (status quos). We distinguish two circumstances, depending upon whether a strong actor exists or not. In each presentation below, for each ordering and status quo, we give the equilibrium proposal for an actor if the formation sequence should reach it. We present these proposals *in reverse order* of the *formateur* sequence in order to display the backward-induction logic. The entry in the last column, the offer of the party listed first in the *formateur* sequence, is the subgame perfect portfolio allocation.

A.1 Configuration with a Strong Party

I. SQ = AA

Formateur Sequence	Proposal of Party in Formateur Sequence		
	Ranked		
	3rd	*2nd*	*1st*
ABC	CC	BB	BB
ACB	BB	BB	BB
BAC	CC	AB	BB
BCA	AA	CC	BB
CAB	BB	BB	BB
CBA	AA	BB	BB

II. SQ = AB

Formateur Sequence	Proposal of Party in Formateur Sequence		
	Ranked		
	3rd	2nd	1st
ABC	CB	BB	BB
ACB	BB	BB	BB
BAC	CB	BB	BB
BCA	AB	CA	BB
CAB	BB	BB	BB
CBA	AB	BB	BB

III. SQ = AC

Formateur Sequence	Proposal of Party in Formateur Sequence		
	Ranked		
	3rd	2nd	1st
ABC	CC	BB	BB
ACB	BB	BB	BB
BAC	CC	AB	BB
BCA	AA	CC	BB
CAB	BB	BB	BB
CBA	AA	BB	BB

IV. SQ = BA

BA wins under all formateur sequences since it is the EWE.

V. SQ = BB

BB wins under all formateur sequences.

VI. SQ = BC

Formateur Sequence *Proposal of Party in Formateur Sequence*

	Ranked		
	3rd	2nd	1st
ABC	BC	BA	BA
ACB	BA	BA	BA
BAC	BC	AB	BB
BCA	AB	CB	BB
CAB	BA	BA	BA
CBA	AB	BB	BB

VII. SQ = CA

Formateur Sequence *Proposal of Party in Formateur Sequence*

	Ranked		
	3rd	2nd	1st
ABC	CA	BB	BB
ACB	BB	BB	BB
BAC	CA	BA	BA
BCA	BA	BA	BA
CAB	BB	BB	BB
CBA	BA	BA	BA

Note: If allocation AB were slightly closer to party B's ideal than CA, then BB would be the subgame perfect allocation in each formateur sequence in this case (without altering any other result).

VIII. SQ = CB

Formateur Sequence *Proposal of Party in Formateur Sequence*

	Ranked		
	3rd	2nd	1st
ABC	CC	BB	BB
ACB	BB	BB	BB
BAC	CC	AB	BB
BCA	BB	BB	BB
CAB	BB	BB	BB
CBA	BB	BB	BB

IX. SQ = CC

Formateur Sequence	Proposal of Party in Formateur Sequence		
	Ranked		
	3rd	2nd	1st
ABC	CC	BB	BB
ACB	BB	BB	BB
BAC	CC	AB	BB
BCA	AB	CB	BB
CAB	BB	BB	BB
CBA	AB	BB	BB

A.2 Configuration with No Strong Party

I. SQ = AA

Formateur Sequence	Proposal of Party in Formateur Sequence		
	Ranked		
	3rd	2nd	1st
ABC	CC	AB	CA
ACB	BB	CC	AB
BAC	CC	AB	BB
BCA	AA	CC	AB
CAB	BB	CC	CC
CBA	AA	BB	CC

Note 1: In the ABC formateur sequence, neither B nor C can improve on this result, even though they jointly prefer a large number of alternative portfolio allocations, because B, going second, cannot commit not to propose AB.

Note 2: In the ACB formateur sequence, the outcome is Pareto inferior. BC is preferred by all parties to AB. But if A proposes BC, party C cannot commit not to veto it and then move CC.

II. SQ = AB

Formateur Sequence	Proposal of Party in Formateur Sequence		
	Ranked		
	3rd	2nd	1st
ABC	BC	BC	BC
ACB	B	CC	AB
BAC	C	BC	BC
BCA	C	BC	BC
CAB	B	CC	CC
CBA	C	BC	BC

III. SQ = AC

Formateur Sequence	Proposal of Party in Formateur Sequence		
	Ranked		
	3rd	2nd	1st
ABC	CB	BB	CC
ACB	BB	CC	AB
BAC	CB	AB	BB
BCA	AC	CB	BB
CAB	BB	CC	CC
CBA	AC	BB	CC

Note: In the *ABC formateur* sequence, party *C* cannot propose *CC* if the sequence reaches the last move; but at the first move, party *A* must propose *CC* to avoid BB!

IV. SQ = BA

Formateur Sequence	Proposal of Party in Formateur Sequence		
	Ranked		
	3rd	2nd	1st
ABC	CC	AB	CA
ACB	BB	CC	AB
BAC	CC	AB	BB
BCA	BA	CC	AB
CAB	BB	CC	CC
CBA	BA	BB	CC

V. SQ = BB

Formateur Sequence	Proposal of Party in Formateur Sequence		
	Ranked		
	3rd	2nd	1st
ABC	CC	AB	AC or CA
ACB	BB	CC	AB
BAC	CC	AB	BB
BCA	CC	CC	AB
CAB	BB	CC	CC
CBA	CC	AB	AC or CA

VI. SQ = BC

BC is the outcome in all formateur sequences, since BC is the EWE.

VII. SQ = CA

Formateur Sequence	Proposal of Party in Formateur Sequence		
	3rd	*2nd*	*1st*
ABC	CC	AB	AC or CA
ACB	BB	CC	AB
BAC	CC	AB	BB
BCA	CA	CC	AB
CAB	BB	CC	CC
CBA	AC or CA	BB	CC

Note 1: In the CBA formateur sequence, neither party C nor party B can forecast what A will do if the sequence reaches it, because A is indifferent between AC and CA. Nevertheless, both C's and B's optimal proposal is invariant to the manner in which this indifference is resolved.

Note 2: In the other formateur sequence with A moving last (BCA), despite A's indifference between CA and AC, it cannot propose AC, since party C would exercise its veto (given that it prefers CA).

VIII. SQ = CB

Formateur Sequence	Proposal of Party in Formateur Sequence		
	3rd	*2nd*	*1st*
ABC	CC	AB	AC or CA
ACB	BB	CC	AB
BAC	CC	AB	AC or CA
BCA	AB	BC	BC
CAB	BB	CC	CC
CBA	AB	BB	CC

IX. SQ = CC

Formateur Sequence	Proposal of Party in Formateur Sequence		
	3rd	*2nd*	*1st*
ABC	CC	AB	AC or CA
ACB	AB	BC	BC
BAC	CC	AB	BB
BCA	AB	BC	BC
CAB	AB	CA	CC
CBA	AB	BB	CC

Note: In the CAB formateur sequence, party A's indifference between AC and CA has an interesting effect. In the table, the backward induction argument yields AB as party B's move if the proposal process reaches the final stage. With this rational expectation, party A is indifferent between proposing AC and CA. It is in this condition of uncertainty about A's likely subsequent move that party C, proposing first, must move. If party C expected party A to propose AC, then its optimal proposal is CB (which party B would support since it prefers CB to AC). If, on the other hand, party C expected party A to propose CA, then its optimal response is CC (which party B again would support since it prefers CC to CA). Party C clearly would rather propose CC, if it could be confident that party B would support it. But B's support depends upon whether it prefers CC to the lottery over CA and AC (since it is uncertain of what party A would do if B chose not to support CC). We have made the not implausible assumption that party B prefers CC for certain to the lottery over AC and CA.

15. The Costs of Coalition: The Italian Anomaly

Carol Mershon

15.1 Introduction

The record of Italian governments displays a pattern that is deeply perplexing. As Figure 1 shows, cabinets in Italy from 1946 to 1992 both changed and remained the same. The Christian Democratic Party (*DC*) always held governing power. Yet almost no government managed to stay in office for more than a few years and many governments collapsed after only a few months. Italy exhibited the lowest turnover rate of any parliamentary democracy (Strom 1990a)[1] and yet had, except for the defunct French Fourth Republic, the most short-lived governments (King, *et al.*, 1990). How can instability coexist with stability in this way? How can governments break up at such low cost and with so few apparent effects?

In posing and pursuing these questions, I am guided by the game-theoretic literature on coalitional behavior. My question about (in)stability reflects a central – perhaps *the* central – result in this literature: that voting games in multidimensional policy space under simple majority rule are subject to endless cycles among alternative decisions (*e.g.*, McKelvey 1976, 1979; Schofield 1983). Given these predictions, it is a mystery why real-world legislative decision-making exhibits substantial stability. Efforts to comprehend the inconsistency between predictions of chaos and empirical observations of decisional stability have stimulated the development of entire schools of spatial theory. Such efforts inform my study. But I move beyond extant theoretical and empirical research in order to deal with an anomaly that to date has not been adequately explored and understood: the combination of stability and instability found in Italy.

My question about costs, too, is rooted in the body of work on coalitions. An implicit but widely shared assumption of coalition theorists is that government coalitions, once installed, can withstand much internal tension because their members want to avoid the costs associated with destroying a coalition. As Figure 1 suggests, however, such costs seem to be very limited in Italy before 1992. Why? The available literature clarifies the question but does not provide an answer to it.

The answer offered here is that politicians' purposive actions can reduce the costs of coalition. I argue that the costs of making, breaking, and main-

---

[1] Strom (1990a) defines the turnover or alternation rate as "the proportion of legislative seats held by parties changing status between government and opposition," averaged across a country's governments.

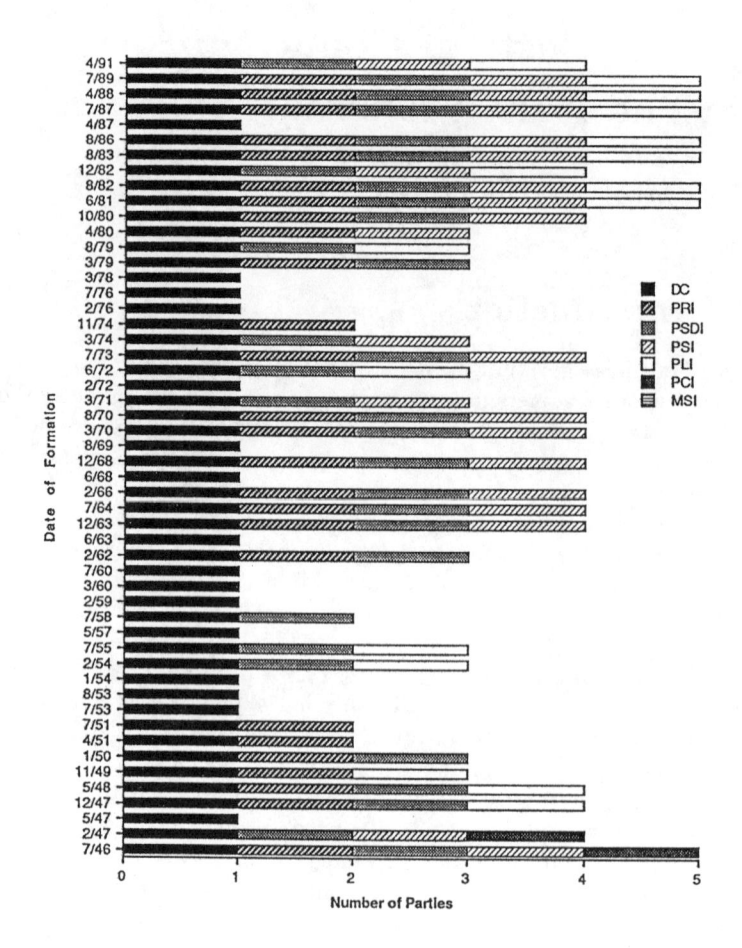

Figure 1. The Composition of Italian Governments, 1946-1992. See Table 2 below for the acronyms of the Italian parties. For simplicity, this figure always depicts the *PSI* and *PSDI* as separate parties, even though they were united under a different name before 1947 and between 1963 and 1966.

taining coalitions depend on political institutions and on the array of parties and voters in policy space. Institutional and spatial conditions structure politicians' opportunities and attempts to lower costs. Under some conditions, as I demonstrate, coalitions are cheap and politicians can easily make coalitions even cheaper. The first section of the chapter distinguishes several kinds of costs attached to coalitions and advances an explanation for variations in those costs across party systems. The second part shows that my explanation accounts for features of Italian politics that are otherwise inexplicable. The conclusion considers cross-national applications of the argument.

15.2 Explaining Cost Reduction in Coalition Bargaining

In the extensive literature that pits game-theoretic predictions against cross-national evidence on real governments, Italy routinely emerges as an outlier case. In particular, spatial theory expects stability only when a core exists,[2] in contrast to decisional instability or "cyclicity" in the absence of a core. These predictions fit oddly with the conjunction of perpetual incumbents and short-lived cabinets observed in Italy, for the *DC* qualifies as a core party from 1946 to 1992 (Schofield 1993). Moreover, the Italian anomaly raises questions about how political actors view the costs and benefits of sealing, keeping, and severing alliances. (For discussion of the discrepancies between theoretical expectations and Italian outcomes, see Mershon 1995a.)

Coalition theories of all sorts assume that expected costs push politicians away from some behaviors and expected benefits pull them toward others. The reasoning often runs that politicians, in a game among parties, fear loss of office or a diminished influence on policy and so are deterred from undoing governments. For a few analysts, parties, in a game with voters, pay a price for governing. While the notion of costs in coalition theories is always implicit, the mechanisms that generate variations in costs are rarely specified and modeled. The alternative framework I propose here thus draws from, and revises, existing studies of coalitions.

The essence of my argument is that political actors do not just react to the "prices" of coalition bargains: they attempt to set those prices. I assume that actors pursue gains, that they project beyond the short term, and that, if they anticipate losses, they do what they can to cut their losses. Actors will not always avoid what they identify as a costly course of action but will at times follow that course and try to lower the costs of doing so. I assume that actors face uncertainty and imperfect information, and that all care to some extent about office, policy, and votes (Strom 1990b). The relative priority given these objectives varies, but no political actor is utterly unmoved by the prospect of holding office, just as none is completely oblivious to policy or electoral concerns.

The game of bargaining over governments is also a game of maneuvering around or modifying the costs that coalitions entail. Political actors incur costs when they build a coalition, since they must award ministerial portfolios to other parties. Moreover, as spatial theory emphasizes for parties outside the core, parties must compromise on policy positions in order to come up with the government's program. Partners in a new government look ahead to the electoral benefits or burdens that governing will bring (Strom 1990a). As Axelrod (1970) reasons, potential allies spend time and effort in negotiating to overcome differences. Similarly, it is costly to sustain a coalition. As allies proceed in governing, they divide the spoils of office, uphold old policy agreements and strike new ones, make decisions that do not please all voters,

---

[2] The core is a policy position that cannot be overturned, given the overall configuration of actors' sizes and positions (*e.g.* McKelvey and Schofield 1987; Schofield 1986, 1993).

Table 1. Italian Governments, 1946-1993[3]

Government	Date Formed	Date Resigned	Parties in Cabinet	Seats in Chamber (%)	Size*
1. De Gasperi II	7/46	1/47	DC + PCI + PSI + PRI	81	S
2. De Gasperi III	2/47	5/47	DC + PCI + PSI	67	S
3. De Gasperi IV	5/47	12/47	DC	37	Min
4. De Gasperi V	12/47	5/48	DC + PSDI + PRI + PLI	58	S
5. De Gasperi VI	5/48	10/49	DC + PSDI + PRI + PLI	64	S
6. De Gasperi VII	11/49	1/50	DC + PRI + PLI	58	S
7. De Gasperi VIII	1/50	4/51	DC + PSDI + PRI	60	S
8. De Gasperi IX	4/51	7/51	DC + PRI	55	S
9. De Gasperi X	7/51	6/53	DC + PRI	55	S
10. De Gasperi XI	7/53	7/53	DC	45	Min
11. Pella	8/53	1/54	DC	45	Min
12. Fanfani I	1/54	1/54	DC	45	Min
13. Scelba	2/54	6/55	DC + PSDI + PLI	50	MW[a]
14. Segni I	7/55	5/57	DC + PSDI + PLI	50	MW[a]
15. Zoli	5/57	6/58	DC	45	Min
16. Fanfani II	7/58	1/59	DC + PSDI	49	Min
17. Segni II	2/59	2/60	DC	46	Min
18. Tambroni	3/60	7/60	DC	46	Min
19. Fanfani III	7/60	2/62	DC	46	Min
20. Fanfani IV	2/62	5/63	DC + PSDI + PRI	51	MW
21. Leone I	6/63	11/63	DC	41	Min
22. Moro I	12/63	6/64	DC + PSI + PSDI + PRI	61	S
23. Moro II	7/64	1/66	DC + PSI + PSDI + PRI	61	S
24. Moro III	2/66	6/68	DC + PSI + PSDI + PRI	61	S
25. Leone II	6/68	11/68	DC	42	Min
26. Rumor I	12/68	7/69	DC + PSI-PSDI + PRI	58	S
27. Rumor II	8/69	2/70	DC	42	Min
28. Rumor III	3/70	7/70	DC + PSI + PSDI + PRI	58	S
29. Colombo I	8/70	3/71	DC + PSI + PSDI + PRI	58	S
30. Colombo II	3/71	1/72	DC + PSI + PSDI	57	S
31. Andreotti I	2/72	2/72	DC	42	Min
32. Andreotti II	6/72	6/73	DC + PSDI + PLI	50	MW[a]
33. Rumor IV	7/73	3/74	DC + PSI + PSDI + PRI	59	S
34. Rumor V	3/74	10/74	DC + PSI + PSDI	57	S
35. Moro IV	11/74	1/76	DC + PRI	45	Min
36. Moro V	2/76	4/76	DC	42	Min
37. Andreotti III	7/76	1/78	DC	42	Min
38. Andreotti IV	3/78	1/79	DC	42	Min
39. Andreotti V	3/79	3/79	DC + PSDI + PRI	46	Min
40. Cossiga I	8/79	3/80	DC + PSDI + PLI	46	Min
41. Cossiga II	4/80	9/80	DC + PSI + PRI	54	S
42. Forlani	10/80	5/81	DC + PSI + PSDI + PRI	57	S
43. Spadolini I	6/81	8/82	PRI + DC + PSI + PSDI + PLI	58	S
44. Spadolini II	8/82	11/82	PRI + DC + PSI + PSDI + PLI	58	S
45. Fanfani V	12/82	4/83	DC + PSI + PSDI + PLI	56	S
46. Craxi I	8/83	6/86	PSI + DC + PSDI + PRI + PLI	58	S
47. Craxi II	8/86	3/87	PSI + DC + PSDI + PRI + PLI	58	S
48. Fanfani VI	4/87	4/87	DC	37	Min
49. Goria	7/87	3/88	DC + PSI + PSDI + PRI + PLI	60	S
50. De Mita	4/88	5/89	DC + PSI + PSDI + PRI + PLI	60	S
51. Andreotti VI	7/89	3/91	DC + PSI + PSDI + PRI + PLI	60	S
52. Andreotti VII	4/91	4/92	DC + PSI + PSDI + PLI	56	S
53. Amato	6/92	4/93	PSI + DC + PSDI + PLI	53	MW

and bargain among themselves. Governing parties also meet costs when a coalition breaks apart. At least until a new coalition emerges, the ex-partners may be threatened with removal from office, handicapped in their efforts to influence policy, and open to accusations of ineffectiveness or irresponsibility, which could cost them votes. Maneuvers to destroy a coalition, unless unilateral from start to finish, carry bargaining costs as well. Thus actors engaged in a coalition risk or incur office, policy, electoral, and bargaining costs at distinct stages in the coalition's history.

Throughout the history of a coalition, actors can lower its costs by choosing to manipulate various levers, such as office benefits, information, reputation, and rules. When building a coalition, actors can increase the number of portfolios; they can limit public information about policy compromises so as to ease agreement inside the coalition; and they can delegitimize opponents so as to escape or dilute voters' blame. To diminish bargaining costs, actors can devise rules to guide the process of bargaining. Once installed, a coalition is sustained at relatively low cost if allies expand spoils and emphasize special-interest legislation. Along similar lines, actors can take steps to curtail risks when a coalition breaks up.

Are choices of this kind equally open and viable in all political settings? Obviously not. Building on existing themes in the literature, I argue that the sizes and positions of parties in policy space, the distribution of voters' preferences in policy space, and political institutions (in particular, electoral laws, legislative rules, and links between the executive and the legislature) affect how costly it is to break, make, and maintain coalitions and affect which cost-reduction strategies actors are likely to see as available and potentially successful (Laver and Schofield 1990; Strom 1990b). Spatial and institutional conditions are hypothesized to influence costs directly. For instance, when a government falls, a party occupying the core of policy space faces a relatively low risk of not regaining office. The anonymity afforded legislators by a secret ballot means that they can sabotage a government with little fear of losing office, antagonizing voters, or complicating bargaining. Spatial and institutional conditions are also hypothesized to influence costs indirectly by structuring the opportunities actors have to try to lower costs.

The Italian-specific version of this general argument is that particular spatial and institutional conditions in Italy lower the costs associated with breaking and building coalitions and favor strategies that further reduce these costs. Italy's coalitions are not easily sustained, since breakups cause little damage.

---

[3] *Notations in Table 1*: (*) Size of government is defined as follows: minimal winning (MW) coalitions would lose their parliamentary majority if any member party were to withdraw from them; (a) connotes coalitions that control exactly half of the seats (whose winning status is thus ambiguous). Surplus majority coalitions (S) are larger than minimal winning. Minority governments (Min) do not control a parliamentary majority.

See Table 2 below for the acronyms of the parties.

Because this logic is put into practice, I claim, Italy displays ephemeral governments and yet permanent incumbents. The Italian pattern is personified in Giulio Andreotti, a Christian Democrat who has held posts in 36 governments since 1947, including seven turns as Prime Minister.

15.3 Assessing the Costs of Coalition in Italy

My test of these assertions focuses here on two kinds of costs, electoral and office. (For a fuller treatment, see Mershon 1995a.) To perform the test, I need to measure when governments begin and end. In Table 1, I count a new cabinet with each change of party composition, parliamentary election, change of prime minister, and accepted resignation of the cabinet.[4] I calculate electoral payoffs as mean changes in parties' percentage shares of the vote between pairs of consecutive elections to the Chamber of Deputies. To tap office costs, I count the number of ministers and undersecretaries per party in a cabinet and take averages across cabinets. I also determine the percentage share of all ministries and undersecretaryships each party controls and compute the ratio between that share and the party's share of all Chamber seats held by a government.

The Pursuit of Cost-Reduction Strategies. A brief point should be made before investigating the impact of spatial and institutional conditions on the costs of coalition. A variety of moves taken by Italian politicians could reasonably be interpreted as attempts at reducing those costs (for details, see Mershon 1995a). For example, written guidelines for portfolio distribution were developed in the summer of 1968. From the timing and content of the guidelines and the declarations made by the guidelines' authors, I infer that the rules were invented in a deliberate attempt to cut bargaining costs in building coalitions. Moreover, Italian politicians have devised informal rules about party alliances in cabinets, creating patterns in government composition that are known as "formulae" (centrism from 1947 to 1963, center-left coalitions from 1963 to 1976, national solidarity from 1976 to 1979, and five-party coalitions from 1979 to 1992). The coalition formulae narrow the range of unsettled issues in coalition bargaining and also perpetuate expectations that politicians who undo one cabinet will be able to re-enter negotiations for the next and try to improve on portfolio assignments or policy influence (Mershon 1994). Still another cost-reduction strategy – the expansion of offices – finds ample illustration below.

The Impact of Spatial and Institutional Conditions on Costs and Cost-Reduction Strategies. If spatial and institutional conditions do influence costs and cost-reduction strategies, then parties should differ in the costs they incur and the strategies they implement. If spatial and institutional conditions shift over time, then costs and strategies should also show some change. I assess

---

[4] These criteria replicate those used for Italy by Strom (1990a) and others who have borrowed Strom's data (King, et al. 1990; Warwick and Easton 1992). I differ from Laver and Schofield (1990), who use only the first two criteria. By each set of criteria, Italy has the most short-lived governments of any extant parliamentary democracy.

this logic in two steps. I first outline the posited influences on electoral costs and trace the electoral costs incurred. I then turn to the office costs attached to coalitions.

Voters' Preferences. Religion and class have powerfully shaped vote choices in postwar Italy (*e.g.*, Barnes 1977; Galli and Prandi 1970). Indeed, limits on policy voting inform a well-known typology of Italian electoral behavior (Parisi and Pasquino 1979) that distinguishes a vote of opinion, motivated by a broad interest in policy; a vote of belonging, affirming an enduring allegiance to either the Catholic or Communist subculture; and a vote of exchange, awarded in return for patronage goods. Mannheimer and Sani (1987) use a 1985 survey to estimate that subcultural voters constitute 60% of the *DC* electorate, 67% of the *PCI* electorate, and only 30% of all other parties' electorates. Other data suggest that exchange voters form sizable proportions of the *DC* and *PSDI* electorates, that opinion voters predominate in the *PLI* and *PRI* electorates, that the *PSI* draws opinion and exchange voters, and that socioeconomic change has recently eroded the subcultural vote and augmented the opinion vote (Caciagli 1988; Cazzola 1985).

Electoral Laws. As Table 2 indicates, from 1946 until 1993 a relatively pure version of proportional representation made a place for small parties in the Italian Parliament and assigned a small bonus of parliamentary seats to large parties. The long-standing provision for preference voting in Chamber races directed politicians' attention to the utility of attracting personal followings through the distribution of spoils (Zuckerman 1979).[5]

The Sizes and Positions of Parties in Policy Space. Content analyses of party manifestos show two leading dimensions of party competition in Italy: a socioeconomic left-right dimension and a technocracy-social harmony dimension subsuming Catholicism (Mastropaolo and Slater 1987). The array and strength of parties in this policy space established the *DC* as a core party from 1946 to 1992. The 1976 elections made the *PSI* "pivotal," for it became the essential ally in any *DC*-based coalition capable of commanding a majority while excluding the *PCI*. The *DC*'s sizable losses in the 1992 elections ended its status as a core party (Schofield 1993); and in 1992 the *PSI* lost pivotal status.

The Electoral Costs of Building and Sustaining Coalitions. Italy's governing parties have suffered smaller electoral losses than have governing parties in many other democracies (Strom 1990a). Table 3 disaggregates electoral costs by party and distinguishes between a party's presence in office on election eve and its role in all governments formed from one election to the next.

Electoral payoffs for all governing parties in Italy have depended on spatial conditions and the segmentation of the electorate. An incumbent party for five decades, the *DC* has scored slight electoral gains when it has governed alone on election eve, and it has lost the least votes when it has governed with allies for most of the time between elections. This two-part finding supports the

---

[5] As a result of a 1991 referendum, voters could cast only one preference vote in the 1992 elections instead of the three or four allowed previously. Below I discuss this change and the overhaul of electoral laws enacted in 1993.

Table 2. Italian Electoral Results, 1946–1992: Votes and Seats Won in Elections to the Chamber of Deputies.

Party	1946	1948	1953	1958	1963	1968	1972	1976	1979	1983	1987	1992
Parties' percentage shares of valid votes
Rete	–	–	–	–	–	–	–	–	–	–	–	1.9
Leghe	–	–	–	–	–	–	–	–	–	–	1.3	8.7
Verdi	–	–	–	–	–	–	–	–	–	–	2.5	2.8
DP	–	–	–	–	–	–	–	1.5	0.8	1.5	1.7	–
PDUP	–	–	–	–	–	–	0.7	w/DP	1.4	w/PCI	–	–
PSIUP	–	–	–	–	–	4.4	1.9	–	–	–	–	–
PR	–	–	–	–	–	–	–	1.1	3.5	2.2	2.6	–
RC	–	–	–	–	–	–	–	–	–	–	–	5.6
PCI [a]	18.9		22.6	22.7	25.3	26.9	27.2	34.4	30.4	29.9	26.6	16.1
PSI [c]	20.7[c]	31.0[b]	12.7	14.2	13.8		9.6	9.6	9.8	11.4	14.3	13.6
PSDI [c]	–	7.1	4.5	4.6	6.1	14.5[c]	5.1	3.4	3.8	4.1	3.0	2.7
PRI	4.4	2.5	1.6	1.4	1.4	2.0	2.9	3.1	3.0	5.1	3.7	4.4
DC	35.1	48.5	40.1	42.3	38.3	39.1	38.7	38.7	38.3	32.9	34.3	29.7
PLI	6.8	3.8	3.0	3.5	7.0	5.8	3.9	1.3	1.9	2.9	2.1	2.8
UQ	5.3	–	–	–	–	–	–	–	–	–	–	–
PM-PNM	2.8	2.8	6.9	4.8	1.7	1.3			–	–	–	–
MSI	–	2.0	5.8	4.8	5.1	4.5	8.7[b]	6.1[b]	5.3	6.8	5.9	5.4
Other	6.0	2.3	2.8	1.7	1.3	1.5	1.3	0.8	1.8	3.2	3.3	6.3
Seats of major parties (number)
Leghe	–	–	–	–	–	–	–	–	–	–	1	55
RC	–	–	–	–	–	–	–	–	–	–	–	35
PCI [a]	104		143	140	166	177	179	227	201	198	177	107
PSI [c]	115	183[b]	75	84	87		61	57	62	73	94	92
PSDI [c]	–	33	19	22	33	91[c]	29	15	21	23	17	16
PRI	23	9	5	6	6	9	15	14	15	29	21	27
DC	207	305	263	273	260	266	266	263	261	225	234	206
PLI	41	19	13	17	39	31	20	5	9	16	11	17
MSI	–	6	29	24	27	24	56[d]	35[d]	31	42	35	34
TOTAL	556	574	590	596	630	630	630	630	630	630	630	630[e]

Leghe	Northern/Lombard Leagues	PR	Radical Party	DC	Christian Democrats
Rete	Network (anti-Mafia)	RC	Communist Refoundation	PLI	Liberal Party
Verdi	Greens	PCI [a]	Communist Party	UQ	Everyman's Party
DP	Proletarian Democracy	PSI [c]	Socialist Party	PM-PNM	Monarchist Party
PDUP	Party of Proletarian Unity	PSDI [c]	Social Democratic Party	MSI	Ital. Soc. Movement
PSIUP	Socialist Party of Proletarian Unity	PRI	Republican Party		

Sources: Farneti 1983; Rhodes 1988; *Corriere della Sera*, 8 April 1992.

Notations: (a) Democratic Party of the Left in 1992; (b) Joint slate; (c) Parties were united before 1947 and between 1963 and 1966; (d) Seats won with Monarchists; (e) Rete controlled 12 seats, Verdi 16 and others 13. Dashes indicate that a party did not contest the election in question.

Table 3.
Electoral Costs by Government Status, 1948-1992
(Mean change in % share of total votes)

	PSI	PSDI	PRI	DC	PLI
Status immediately before election					
One-party government	na	na	na	+0.8	na
Coalition government	-0.9	+0.04	-0.5	-1.2	-0.4
Opposition	-0.6	-0.9	+0.4	na	-0.3
Predominant status between elections					
One-party government	na	na	na	-2.2	na
Coalition government	-0.08	-0.8	+0.2	-0.1	+0.4
Opposition	-1.3	+0.95	-0.2	na	-0.8
Coalition govt, 1979-92	+1.3	+0.4	+0.5	+2.9	+0.3

Note: The baseline year is 1946 for all parties except the *PSDI*, which first contested elections in 1948.

Sources: Calculations based on electoral data reported here in Table 2, and government status data contained in Table 1.

Notations: (na): not applicable.

notion that exchange voters respond strongly to spoils delivered by a single governing party, and that multi-party governments blur responsibility and spread blame. The losses the *DC* has posted in coalition since 1979 also deserve notice. The *DC* became more vulnerable with the erosion of the subcultural vote, the rise in opinion voting, more intense interparty competition for spoils growing out of the *PSI*'s pivotal position, and less favorable conditions for the ideological delegitimization of opponents.

As Table 3 displays, the *DC*'s habitual allies – with one exception – have received more votes when they have held opposition rather than governing status immediately before elections. The Social Democratic exception reflects its pool of exchange voters (Strom 1990a). The *PRI* has benefited more from pre-electoral opposition than has the *PLI*, for its more centrist position has allowed the *PRI* to attract more opinion voters dissatisfied with government policy (Mannheimer and Sani 1987). The costs of governing in coalition on election eve have tended to be offset by advantages accruing from longer-term governing roles. That is, the *PSI*, *PRI*, and *PLI* have performed better when they have shared governing power rather than joined the opposition for most of the span since the preceding election. The leftmost and rightmost governing parties, the *PSI* and *PLI*, have suffered more from interelectoral opposition than have the *PSDI* and *PRI* and have spent more time in opposition. The *PSDI* has operated in opposition even less than the *PRI*. When the *PSDI*'s dominant interelectoral status was opposition, it campaigned on its prospective role in coalitions (Galli and Prandi 1970; Leonardi 1981). From 1979 to 1992, all of the *DC*'s allies have reaped electoral benefits from participation in coalitions. These gains have been greatest for the *PSI*, whose rightward moves have captured opinion voters and whose pivotal contributions to *DC*-based majorities have helped it to tap and deliver spoils. Overall, then, the parties identified as the *DC*'s allies under coalition formulae have usually won electoral credit for brief exits from coalition and have banked on re-entering government, looking for additional credit.

Table 4.
Office Payoffs by Type of Government, 1946-1992 (Means)

	One-party governments	All coalitions	Coalitions incl. PSI	Post-1976 coalitions incl. PSI
	Percentage shares (means)			
DC share of ministers	94.4%	61.0%	55.3%	52.1%
DC share of undersecretaries	99.1%	64.2%	55.3%	54.2%
	Ratios of ministerial shares to government seat shares* (means)			
For DC ministers	0.94	0.82	0.83	0.78
For DC undersecretaries	0.99	0.85	0.83	0.81
	Number of posts (means)			
DC ministers	20	15	15	15
DC undersecretaries	36	29	29	33

Sources: Calculations based on portfolio data in Petracca (1980) and *Corriere della Sera*, various issues; and electoral data reported here in Table 2.

Notations: (*) government seat share = a party's % share of the seats in the Chamber controlled by all governing parties.

The Office Costs of Building Coalitions and Strategies for Managing Office Costs. Table 4 measures the office price that the *DC* has paid when it has governed with coalition partners. In one-party governments, the *DC* has occasionally awarded a few posts to independent experts. In coalition, the *DC* has sacrificed this near monopoly on cabinet slots. The *DC* has relinquished a greater percentage of offices when the coalition has embraced the medium-sized *PSI*, and still more when the *PSI* has made a pivotal contribution to the government's majority. The division of portfolios between the *DC* and its allies illustrates a finding from cross-national portfolio studies: The largest party in a coalition obtains a share of senior cabinet posts that is somewhat smaller than that party's share of the parliamentary seats controlled by the government (Browne and Franklin 1973; Laver and Schofield 1990; Schofield and Laver 1985). The disadvantage that the *DC* has met is only slightly less pronounced for shares of undersecretary posts. Intervals of one-party government have thus compensated the *DC* for disproportionate shares of portfolios surrendered to allies at other times (Marradi 1982).

The last two rows of Table 4 spotlight actual numbers of offices. In these terms, the *DC* has spent less to construct coalitions than might be expected – and much less than pure office-driven theory would predict. On average, it has cost the *DC* nothing in numbers of cabinet slots to include the *PSI* in a coalition, even when the *PSI* has been pivotal. Indeed, *DC* undersecretaries have been more numerous in coalitions containing a pivotal *PSI* than in other types of coalitions.

As Figure 2 reveals, portfolio inflation is the cost-management strategy producing these outcomes. Offices – especially undersecretaryships – are like balloons, inflated when needs arise. The number of allies changes, but the number of Christian Democrats in government remains remarkably stable.

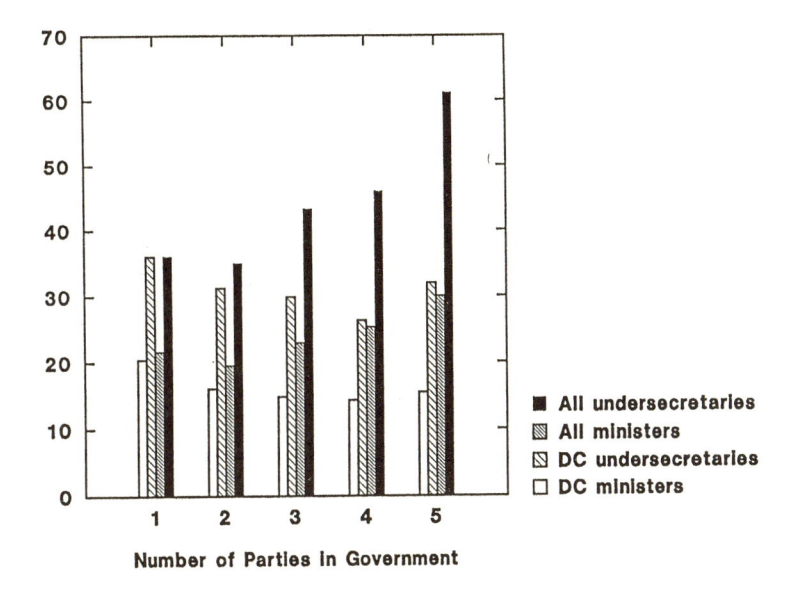

Figure 2. Office Payoffs by Number of Parties in Government, 1946-1992 (means).

The distinction between ministers and undersecretaries is worth weighing. As coalitions have expanded from two parties to three to four and then to five parties, the number of ministers has been pumped up steadily and the number of undersecretaries has risen rather unevenly. The largest boosts in undersecretaries separate two- from three-party coalitions and four- from five-party coalitions. Why? No two-party coalition has included the *PSI* and all five-party coalitions have governed when the *PSI* was pivotal. The competition for office between the *DC* and the *PSI* drives portfolio inflation in coalitions.

As Figure 3 shows, the steepest increases in ministerial and undersecretary posts have occurred when the *PSI* has re-entered government after a sojourn in the opposition (in the early 1960s, when center-left coalitions were prepared and then implemented, and in the early 1980s, when five-party coalitions were instituted). Those hikes have enabled the *DC* to protect or even add to its portfolios. Why have undersecretaryships been more elastic balloons than senior cabinet posts? Undersecretaries are arguably less visible to voters and imply a less permanent, more flexible, commitment of resources. Moreover, in "an informal division of ministerial labour, he [an undersecretary] is left free to distribute the patronage of the ministry in his constituency" (Allum 1973). The secret ballot has made it "necessary ... to satisfy the greatest possible number of deputies," and coalition builders have used undersecretary posts as a convenient currency with which to gratify deputies and buy loyalty (Dogan 1984). Since parliamentary rules require that members of government – both ministers and undersecretaries – step down from parliamentary committees (Nocifero and Valdini 1992), increases in cabinet posts have the advantage of enlarging access to committee positions for parliamentarians without cabinet responsibilities. Members of multiple committees are well equipped to pipe narrow benefits to clienteles.

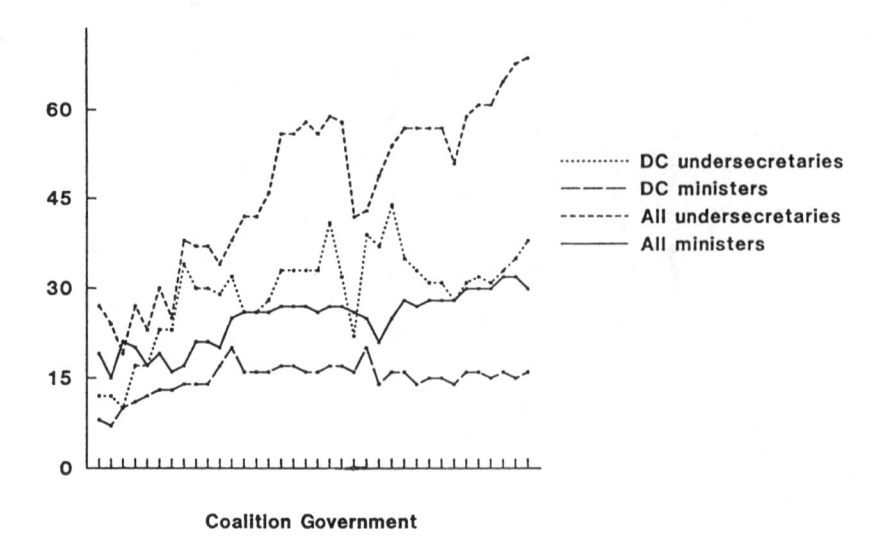

Figure 3. Office Payoffs in Coalition Governments, 1946-1992.
Governments are ordered chronologically and numbered as in Table 1.

Parliamentary Rules. The Italian Parliament has standing, specialized committees whose powers to take final action on legislation make them "mini-parliaments" (Hellman 1992). The committees have handled the bulk of legislation – about two-thirds of the legislative proposals in a 1963-1972 sample and 54% of enacted laws from 1987 to 1992 (Di Palma 1977; Nocifero and Valdini 1992). Both within and outside committees, governing parties have typically sought to avert upsets by including the major opposition parties in the preparation of legislative proposals. This practice has furnished defense against the secret ballot, which was required on final votes in the Chamber until 1988 and gave shelter to governing parties' parliamentarians who voted against government bills.

Links between the Executive and the Legislature. According to a noted constitutional lawyer, "No modern parliament raises so many negative conditions for a government; no government is weaker in parliament than the Italian" (Andrea Manzella, quoted in Spotts and Weiser 1986). The Constitution stipulates that a government takes office when its ministers swear loyalty to the Republic before the president, but further requires that the new government submit to a vote of confidence in both chambers of Parliament within ten days of its inauguration. If a government fails on either vote, it must resign – a fate met by five governments to date. Governments that pass votes of investiture meet other obstacles. No rule has ever assigned the government direct responsibility for setting the legislative calendar. Until 1971, there were no ceilings in either chamber on the number of bills that private members could propose (Baldassare 1985). Governments can attempt to compel parliamentary majorities to emerge through the provision for executive decrees, which expire unless enacted by Parliament within sixty days of their issue.

The Electoral Costs of Destroying Governments. To assess how the rules just reviewed have influenced the costs of breaking coalitions, I again disaggregate by party and track trends over time. I also identify which parties were responsible for cabinet collapses.[6] The *DC* contributed to the demise of 31 governments between 1946 and 1992, the *PSI* to 32 falls, the *PSDI* to 18, the *PRI* to 16, and the *PLI* to 8.

The Christian Democrats and Socialists have made far more governments fall than have Italy's other habitual governing parties. Not only are the *DC* and *PSI* bigger and thus able to push more effectively against governments, but they have also benefited electorally from knocking down governments. Yet, as Table 5 shows, distinctions separate the *DC* and *PSI* in this regard. The *DC* has gained at the polls when it has helped to upset most cabinets between two successive elections, whereas the *PSI* has contained its losses when it has toppled governments. Since acquiring pivotal status in 1976, the *PSI* has won votes despite – or due to – its responsibility for terminating every government formed after 1974. The *DC*, in contrast, has suffered for its role in government falls since 1976.

The electoral payoffs for demolishing governments, like those for creating governments, have reflected spatial conditions and the segmentation of the electorate. For decades the *DC* undid governments with impunity, since loyal subcultural voters have long dominated the *DC* electorate, and exchange voters have long expected a continuing flow of spoils from the large, centrally located *DC*.[7] Cabinet dissolutions have cost the *DC* votes since 1976 because,

---

[6] This identification relies primarily on *Keesing's Contemporary Archives*, a source often used in coalition studies (*e.g.*, Budge and Keman 1990; Dodd 1976; Strom 1990a). In the few cases where *Keesing's* supplied inadequate information, I coded *Facts on File*, the *Corriere della Sera*, and/or *L'Espresso*.

[7] The *DC*'s drop when not responsible for cabinet collapses rests on one datum: the difference between 1948, when voters rallied around the *DC* at the onset of the Cold War, and 1953, when controversy over a majoritarian electoral law repulsed some voters.

as noted earlier, subcultural voting has waned, opinion voting has increased, the pivotal *PSI* has put up stiffer competition for spoils, and ideological justifications for delegitimizing opponents have had less force. Since 1976, further, responsibility for breakups has become more of an electoral liability for the *PSDI* and *PRI* and more of an electoral advantage for the *PSI*. Some voters seem to have defected in response to perceived disruptions of policy (particularly opinion voters amongst the *PRI* supporters), while others have defected in response to potential complications in patronage (the *PSDI*'s exchange voters). Still other voters have rewarded the pivotal *PSI* for its capacity to influence policy and tap spoils, a capacity exhibited and exploited in government falls (Mannheimer and Sani 1987). The rightmost *PLI* has been exposed to relatively severe electoral punishment for dismantling cabinets, which helps to explain why it has risked punishment relatively rarely. On the whole, though, these differences across parties are small. No party courts electoral disaster when it causes a government to fall.

Table 5.
Electoral Costs by Responsibility for Government Collapse, 1948-1992 (Mean change in % share of total votes)

Predominant role in collapses between elections	PSI	PSDI	PRI	DC	PLI
Responsible	-0.03	-0.5	-0.1	+0.3	-0.8*
Not responsible	-1.7	-0.4	+0.06	-8.4*	-0.3
Responsible, 1976-92	+1.0	-1.1	-0.8*	-2.3	-0.8*

Note: The baseline year is 1946 for all parties except the *PSDI*, which first contested elections in 1948.
Sources: Calculations based on coding of information in *Keesing's Contemporary Archives* and on electoral data in Table 2 above.
Notations: (*) Change is based on one inter-electoral period only.

The Office Costs of Destroying Governments and Strategies for Managing Office Payoffs. As typically measured, the office price of ending governments is negligible in Italy. As Table 6 reports, all five governing parties have received a weighted share of senior cabinet posts that stays roughly steady, on average, whether or not they have overthrown the preceding government. The same statement holds true for weighted shares of undersecretary posts. Not a single pair of ratios in the top two rows of Table 6 is significantly different. This finding runs counter to conventional assumptions about the office costs of breakups. It becomes even more remarkable when average numbers are considered. The total of cabinet posts has varied little according to whether or not the *PSDI, PRI*, and *PLI* have pulled down the prior government. But a government's ministers and undersecretaries, on average, are significantly more numerous after the Socialists have sabotaged, as compared to sustained, its predecessor. With the *PSI*'s percentage of offices unaltered and the number of all offices up, more Socialists fill cabinet slots. Office benefits go to the *PSI* after it eliminates a government – above all when the *PSI* is pivotal. Along similar lines, but only since 1976, a constant share and a significantly larger total of offices mean that more Christian Democrats attain cabinet positions after the *DC* topples a government. In this sense, too, the competition between the *DC* and *PSI* drives portfolio inflation. Since 1976, the *PSI* has decided the government's fate with astonishing frequency. At the same time, the contest between the *DC* and the pivotal *PSI* has altered the ties between the executive and the legislature. Cabinets have met increased difficulties in relying on parliamentary majorities. As one sign of those difficulties, the first

Table 6. Office Payoffs by Responsibility
for Government Collapses, 1946-92 (Means)

	PSI		PSDI		PRI		DC		PLI	
	\multicolumn{10}{c}{Was party responsible for collapse at time t - 1?}
	no	yes	no	yes	no	yes	no	yes	no	yes
	\multicolumn{10}{c}{Ratios of party's ministerial shares to government seat shares^a (means)}
Offices at time t										
Ministers	1.30	1.23	1.84	1.84	3.00	2.25	0.89	0.83	2.09	2.12
Undersecretaries	1.39	1.34	1.70	1.53	1.85	1.55	0.91	0.89	2.16	1.85
	\multicolumn{10}{c}{Number of posts (means)}
All ministers	21	25^c	24	23	23	25	23	24	24	24
All undersecretaries	35	49^c	44	44	41	48	42	45	44	44
	\multicolumn{10}{c}{Number of posts 1976-92 (means)}
All ministers	na	27	27	30	28	26	26	30^b	27	28
All undersecretaries	na	56	55	61	55	56	53	62^b	55	59

Sources: Calculations based on portfolio data in Petracca 1980 and *Corriere della Sera*, various issues; and on coding of information in *Keesing's Contemporary Archives*.
Notations: (a) Government seat share is as defined in Table 4. (b) $p < 0.5$ (separate variances t-test). (c) $p < .001$ (separate variances t-test). (*na*): not applicable.

government with a Socialist premier – Craxi I, a surplus coalition – saw defectors reduce its support to a minority on 163 occasions (Di Scala 1988). As a consequence of such challenges, executive decrees have become much more common since 1976 (Della Sala 1987; Nocifero and Valdini 1992). These changes have generated reactions in turn. Legislation in August 1988 limited the conditions under which executive decrees could be issued; and in October 1988 the Chamber radically circumscribed use of the secret ballot (Barrera 1989).

Clinching Evidence. The April 1992 parliamentary elections marked a profound shift in spatial and institutional conditions in Italy. The Lombard League and the anti-Mafia Network recast dimensions of party competition and campaigned against corruption. The *DC*'s support dipped below 30%, which meant that the *DC* no longer qualified as a core party (Schofield 1993). The 1992 elections were the first national elections held after the secret ballot was restricted in Parliament, the single preference vote introduced, and the *PCI* transformed into the Democratic Party of the Left (*PDS*). According to my argument, some change in the costs of coalition and cost-reduction strategies should have ensued.

The first post-election coalition joined the same four parties that governed on election eve. But the allies were led by Italy's second Socialist premier, their coalition had minimal winning size, and they divided among themselves a total of 60 portfolios. The pre-election coalition contained 99 portfolios. The second post-election government was headed by Italy's first non-party premier, Carlo Azeglio Ciampi, who almost succeeded in allying with the *PDS*, Greens, and *PRI*; last-minute disagreements left him with a four-party minimal winning coalition,[8] a new edition of its predecessor that allotted an unprecedented share of portfolios (out of 62) to non-party experts. Clearly, Italian politicians can no longer easily offset the office costs of constructing governments. In August 1993, pressured by referendum results and Ciampi's exhortations, Parliament passed new electoral laws, which combined plurality and proportional rules for Chamber and Senate elections and imposed a four-percent threshold for representation in the Chamber.

Held under the new laws, the March 1994 elections produced even more sweeping change: the end of fifty years of uninterrupted *DC* incumbency. Public outrage at widespread corruption inflicted devastating losses on the Popular Party (as the *DC* renamed itself in January 1994) and the *PSI*; undone by corruption, the *PLI* and *PSDI* did not even contest the elections. In May, media magnate Silvio Berlusconi became premier. His government embraced Forza Italia, the movement he founded in early 1994; the Lombard/Northern League; the National Alliance, the renamed MSI; and the Centrist Union (*UDC*) and the Christian Democratic Center (*CCD*, a right-wing splinter from the *DC*). The coalition contained 64 portfolios and by one standard had minimal winning size.[9] Berlusconi resigned in December 1994 when the Lombard/Northern League withdrew. In January 1995 economist Lamberto Dini became Italy's second non-party premier, guiding a cabinet made up of 55 ministers and undersecretaries—and, for the first time in postwar Italy, not a single member of Parliament. The Dini government passed its vote of

---

[8] Even though a Republican Senator was undersecretary to the Premier, the *PRI* did not consider itself a member of the coalition and abstained on the cabinet's vote of investiture. *Corriere della Sera*, 29 April to 13 May 1993. Table 1 records the very few minimal winning coalitions formed in Italy. For discussion, see Mershon 1995a.

[9] The Berlusconi government qualifies as a minimal winning coalition if electoral alliances (the Freedom Alliance and the Good Government Alliance) are counted as its component units. If parliamentary parties are counted as the units comprising the coalition, it has surplus status and a superfluous member in the *CCD*.

investiture thanks to support from the *PDS*.

15.4 Conclusions

In postwar Italy until 1992 transitory cabinets were staffed by permanent incumbents. These exceptional outcomes pose vexing questions when viewed in light of game-theoretic predictions. What explains the strange combination of instability and stability found in Italy? How can governments break up at such low cost?

The framework I develop accommodates this anomaly. The evidence indicates that in Italy particular spatial and institutional conditions curbed the costs of assembling and dismantling coalitions and encouraged strategies that lowered costs further. When policy space and institutions were redefined in the early 1990s, costs and outcomes in Italian coalition politics were transformed.

The reasoning in this chapter is formulated in general terms, but is evaluated only against the Italian experience. A cross-national test of the argument would involve comparisons across parties, across sets of governments, and across time—comparisons analogous to those made here for Italy. A preliminary report on ongoing cross-national research (Mershon 1995b) compares five countries that present a range of electoral and parliamentary institutions and also differ in configurations of parties and voters in policy space. The findings suggest that, not only for Italy but for Finland, Ireland, the Netherlands, and Norway as well, spatial and institutional environments shape the costs of coalition that parties face and structure parties' efforts to deflate those costs. For instance, the country that most nearly resembles Italy in spatial terms, the Netherlands, displays relatively long-lived governments. Dutch institutions, working through their influence on the costs of coalition, account for the difference in outcomes.

Additional cross-national research is needed to establish a firmer empirical basis for these claims. To judge from the evidence now available, the explanation advanced here accounts for Italy's extremes and for the degrees of stability found in other parliamentary democracies.

References

Allum, P. A. 1973. *Italy – Republic without Government?* New York: Norton.

Axelrod, R. 1970. *Conflict of Interest: A Theory of Divergent Goals with Applications to Politics.* Chicago: Markham.

Balboni, E. 1988. "I nodi istituzionali di una difficile crisi di governo," in *Politica in Italia. I fatti dell'anno e le interpretazioni.* Edizione '88. P. Corbetta and R. Leonardi, eds. Bologna: Il Mulino.

Baldassare, A. 1985. "Le 'performances' del Parlamento italiano nell'ultimo quindicennio," in *Il sistema politico italiano*, G. Pasquino, ed. Bari: Laterza.

Barnes, S. 1977. *Representation in Italy: Institutionalized Tradition and Electoral Choice.* Chicago: University of Chicago Press.

Barrera, P. 1989. "La prima riforma istituzionale: la nuova disciplina dell'attivita' di governo," in *Politica in Italia. I fatti dell'anno e le interpretazioni.* Edizione '89. R. Catanzaro and R. Y. Nanetti, eds. Bologna: Il Mulino.

Browne, E. C. and M. Franklin. 1973. "Coalition Payoffs in European Parliamentary Democracies," *American Political Science Review* 67: 453-464.

Budge, I. and H. Keman. 1990. *Parties and Democracy: Coalition Formation and Government Functioning in Twenty States.* Oxford: Oxford University Press.

Budge, I., D. Robertson, and D. Hearl, eds. 1987. *Ideology, Strategy and Party Change: Spatial Analyses of Post-War Election Programmes in 19 Democracies.* Cambridge: Cambridge University Press.

Caciagli, M. 1988. "Quante Italie? Persistenza e trasformazione delle culture politiche subnazionali," *Polis* 2: 429-457.

Calise, M. and R. Mannheimer. 1982. *Governanti in Italia: Un trentennio repubblicano, 1946-1976.* Bologna: Il Mulino.

Cazzola, F. 1985. "Struttura e potere del Partito socialista italiano," in *Il sistema politico italiano,* G. Pasquino, ed. Bari: Laterza.

Della Sala, V. 1987. "Governare per decreto. Il governo Craxi e l'uso dei decreti-legge," in *Politica in Italia. I fatti dell'anno e le interpretazioni.* Edizione '87. P. Corbetta and R. Leonardi, eds. Bologna: Il Mulino.

Di Palma, G. 1977. *Surviving without Governing.* Berkeley: University of California Press.

Di Palma, G. 1979. "The Available State: Problems of Reform," *West European Politics* 2: 149-165.

Di Scala, S. M. 1988. *Renewing Italian Socialism: Nenni to Craxi.* New York and Oxford: University of Oxford Press.

Dodd, L. C. 1976. *Coalitions in Parliamentary Government.* Princeton: Princeton University Press.

Dogan, M. 1984. "Come si diventa ministro in Italia: le regole non scritte del gioco politico," in *Il sistema politico italiano tra crisi e innovazione,* Centro studi P. Farneti. Milan: Franco Angeli.

Farneti, P. 1983. *Il sistema dei partiti in Italia 1946-1979.* Bologna: Il Mulino.

Franklin, M. N. and T. T. Mackie. 1984. "Reassessing the Importance of Size and Ideology for the Formation of Governing Coalitions in Parliamentary Democracies," *American Journal of Political Science* 28: 672-691.

Galli, G. and A. Prandi. 1970. *Patterns of Political Participation in Italy.* New Haven: Yale University Press.

Guarnieri, C. 1989. "Strutture e processi decisionali," in *Scienza politica,* L. Morlino, ed. Torino: Fondazione Giovanni Agnelli.

Hellman, S. 1992. "Italian Politics in Transition," in *European Politics in Transition,* 2nd ed. M. Kesselman and J. Krieger, eds. New York: D.C. Heath.

Herman, V. 1976. *Parliaments of the World: A Reference Compendium.* Berlin and New York: De Gruyter.

Katz, R. S. 1985. "Preference Voting in Italy: Votes of Opinion, Belonging, or Exchange," *Comparative Political Studies* 18: 229-249.

Katz, R. S. 1986. "Intraparty Preference Voting," in *Electoral Laws and their Political Consequences.* B. Grofman and A. Lijphart, eds. New York: Agathon.

Keesing's Contemporary Archives. 1945-1993. Bristol: Longman.
King, G., J. E. Alt, N. E. Burns, and M. Laver. 1990. "A Unified Model of Cabinet Dissolution in Parliamentary Democracies," *American Journal of Political Science* 34: 846-871.
LaPalombara, J. 1987. *Democracy: Italian Style.* New Haven: Yale University Press.
Laver, M. and N. Schofield. 1990. *Multiparty Government: The Politics of Coalition in Europe.* Oxford: Oxford University Press.
Leonardi, R. 1981. "The Victors: The Smaller Parties in the 1979 Italian Elections," in *Italy at the Polls, 1979: A Study of the Parliamentary Elections*, H. R. Penniman, ed. Washington, DC: American Enterprise Institute.
Leonardi, R. and D. A. Wertman. 1989. *Italian Christian Democracy: The Politics of Dominance.* New York: St. Martin's Press.
Lewis-Beck, M. S. 1986. "Comparative Economic Voting: Britain, France, Germany, Italy," *American Journal of Political Science* 30: 315-346.
Lewis-Beck, M. S. 1988. *Economics and Elections: The Major Western Democracies.* Ann Arbor: The University of Michigan Press.
Lijphart, A. 1984. *Democracies: Patterns of Majoritarian and Consensus Government in Twenty-One Countries.* New Haven: Yale University Press.
Mannheimer, R. and G. Sani. 1987. *Il mercato elettorale. Identikit dell'elettore italiano.* Bologna: Il Mulino.
Manzella, A. 1991. *Il parlamento,* nuova edizione. Bologna: Il Mulino.
Marradi, A. 1982. "From 'Centrism' to Crisis of the Center-Left Coalitions," in *Government Coalitions in Western Democracies*, E. C. Browne and J. Dreijmanis, eds. London: Longman.
Mastropaolo, A. and M. Slater. 1987. "Italy 1947-1979: Ideological Distances and Party Movements," in *Ideology, Strategy and Party Change, op. cit.*
McKelvey, R. D. 1976. "Intransitivities in Multidimensional Voting Models and Some Implications for Agenda Control," *Journal of Economic Theory* 12: 472-482.
McKelvey, R. D. 1979. "General Conditions for Global Intransitivities in Formal Voting Models," *Econometrica* 47: 1085-1111.
McKelvey, R. D. and N. Schofield. 1987. "Generalized Symmetry Conditions at a Core Point," *Econometrica* 55: 923-933.
Mershon, C. 1994. "Expectations and Informal Rules in Coalition Formation," *Comparative Political Studies* 27: 40-79.
Mershon, C. 1995a. "The Costs of Coalition: Coalition Theories and Italian Governments." Typescript: University of Virginia.
Mershon, C. 1995b. "The Costs of Coalition: A Five-Nation Comparison." Presented at the annual meeting of the European Consortium for Political Research, Bordeaux.
Nocifero, N. and S. Valdini. 1992. *Il palazzo di vetro. Il lavoro dei deputati italiani nella decima legislatura.* Firenze: Vallecchi.
North, D. C. 1990. *Institutions, Institutional Change and Economic Performance.* Cambridge: Cambridge University Press.

Parisi, A. and G. Pasquino. 1979. "Changes in Italian Electoral Behavior: The Relationships between Parties and Voters," *West European Politics* 2: 6-30.

Pasquino, G. 1981. "The Italian Socialist Party: Electoral Stagnation and Political Indispensability," in *Italy at the Polls, 1979, op.cit.*

Petracca, O. M. 1980. *Storia della prima repubblica.* Milano: Mondo Economico.

Pollio Salimbeni, A. 1989. "Presidente per la sesta volta," *L'Unita'.* 23 July, p. 4.

Powell, G. B. Jr. 1982. *Contemporary Democracies: Participation, Stability, and Violence.* Cambridge, Ma.: Harvard University Press.

Pustetto, M. B. 1991. *Il manuale del candidato politico.* Milano: Bridge.

Rhodes, M. 1988. "Craxi e l'area laico-socialista. Terza forza o tre forze?" in *Politica in Italia. I fatti dell'anno e le interpretazioni.* Edizione '88. P. Corbetta and R. Leonardi, eds. Bologna: Il Mulino.

Riker, W. H. 1962. *The Theory of Political Coalitions.* New Haven: Yale University Press.

Schofield, N. 1983. "Generic Instability of Majority Rule," *Review of Economic Studies* 50: 696-705.

Schofield, N. 1986. "Existence of a 'Structurally Stable' Equilibrium for a Noncollegial Voting Rule," *Public Choice* 51: 267-284.

Schofield, N. 1993. "Political Competition and Multiparty Coalition Governments," *European Journal of Political Research* 23: 1-33.

Schofield, N., B. Grofman, and S. L. Feld. 1988. "The Core and the Stability of Group Choice in Spatial Voting Games," *American Political Science Review* 82: 195-211.

Schofield, N. and M. Laver. 1985. "Bargaining Theory and Portfolio Payoffs in European Coalition Governments 1945-83," *British Journal of Political Science* 15: 143-164.

Spotts, F. and T. Wieser. 1986. *Italy: A Difficult Democracy.* Cambridge: Cambridge University Press.

Strom, G. S. 1990. *The Logic of Lawmaking: A Spatial Theory Approach.* Baltimore: The Johns Hopkins University Press.

Strom, K. 1990a. *Minority Government and Majority Rule.* Cambridge: Cambridge University Press.

Strom, K. 1990b. "A Behavioral Theory of Competitive Political Parties," *American Journal of Political Science* 34: 565-598.

Tarrow, S. 1990. "Maintaining Hegemony in Italy: 'The softer they rise, the slower they fall'!" in *Uncommon Democracies: The One-Party Dominant Regimes,* T. J. Pempel, ed. Ithaca: Cornell University Press.

Tsebelis, G. 1990. *Nested Games: Rational Choice in Comparative Politics.* Berkeley: University of California Press.

Venditti, R. 1981. *Il manuale Cencelli.* Roma: Editori Riuniti.

Warwick, P. and S. T. Easton. 1992. "The Cabinet Stability Controversy: New Perspectives on a Classic Problem," *American Journal of Political Science* 36: 122-146.

Wertman, D. 1977. "The Italian Electoral Process: The Elections of June 1976," in *Italy at the Polls, op. cit.*

Zuckerman, A. 1979. *The Politics of Faction.* New Haven: Yale University Press.

Part IV. POLITICAL ECONOMY

16. Models of Interest Groups: Four Different Approaches

Jan Potters and Frans van Winden

16.1 Introduction

Many students of political economy have stressed the importance of interest groups for the formation of public policy. Empirical studies seem to confirm this alleged importance. These studies, however, typically focus on the relationship between the presence and characteristics of groups, on the one hand, and the policies that result on the other hand, leaving out the behavior and interaction in between;[1] in this respect they resemble the structure-performance approach in industrial organisation. Neglected are the determinants of the level and kind of activities of groups and the explanation of the influence of these activities on public policy.

Lack of data is, of course, a major obstacle for the incorporation of interest group activity in empirical models. However, in order to gain insight—and to guide the collection of adequate data—one could proceed deductively and develop theoretical models and hypotheses. Since interest group politics refer to situations with strong strategic features, game theory seems a particularly appropriate modelling tool here, *cf.* Elster (1986), Johansen (1979), and van Winden (1988).

The present paper reviews and discusses the game-theoretical literature of interest groups. Attention is focused on two central problems, regarding the way in which these models determine and explain (a) the level and kind of interest group activity, and (b) the influence of interest groups on government policy. In this regard, special attention will be given to formal aspects, in contrast with the more interpretative surveys of Mitchell and Munger (1991) and Tollison (1982).

The relevant literature can by and large be divided into four approaches depending on whether they employ an *influence function*, a *vote function*, or a *composite utility function* or focus on the *transmission of information*. These four approaches will be dealt with in Sections 16.2 through 16.5, respectively, followed by some concluding remarks in Section 16.6. As the last two approaches have received little or no attention in other surveys of interest groups models,[2] they will play a relatively prominent role in the present survey. Nevertheless, it should be clear that this brief discussion cannot do full

---

[1] See, e.g., Kau and Rubin (1979), Mueller and Murrell (1986), Pincus (1979), Plotnick (1986), Renaud and van Winden (1988), and Salamon and Siegfried (1977).

[2] See Kolman (1992), Mitchell and Munger (1991), Morton and Cameron (1992), and Tollison, (1982).

justice to all the details and the results of these studies.

16.2 Models with an Influence Function

The basic idea behind most models on interest groups, such as those on rent-seeking, is that the political process can be treated as a kind of market. The 'goods' supplied by politicians and bureaucrats in this 'political market' are certain policies (regulation, transfers, public goods). The interest groups are the demanders of these goods and the 'price' of the goods is the (monetary equivalent of the) amount of pressure by the groups directed towards the polity. A characteristic aspect of these models is the use of an *influence function*, to represent the 'supply' of government policies.[3] The following, rather general, setup is inspired by Becker (1983, 1985).

There are two groups (lobbies), L^1 and L^2, of size n^1 and n^2, respectively. Regarding a certain governmental decision variable x, it is assumed that L^1 favors an increase of x and L^2 favors a decrease of x.[4] The level of x is assumed to be determined by an influence function I, which relates the variable x to the pressure $(p^i, i = 1, 2)$ produced by the two groups and a vector z of exogenous variables:

$$x = I(p^1, p^2, z)$$

with

$$I_1 := \frac{\partial I}{\partial p^1} > 0,$$

and

$$I_2 := \frac{\partial I}{\partial p^2} < 0.$$

The level of pressure p^i by L^i depends on the amount of resources y^i it spends on the production of pressure and the extent to which it is able to control free riding. It is assumed that a large group has more problems controlling free riding and hence can produce less pressure:

$$p^i = p^i(y^i, n^i),$$

with

$$p_y^i := \frac{\partial p^i}{\partial y^i} > 0,$$

and

$$p_n^i := \frac{\partial p^i}{\partial n^i} < 0,$$

---

[3] See, *e.g*, the models of Congleton (1983), Feenstra and Bhagwati (1982), Findlay and Wellisz (1983), Fisher (1992), Levy (1989), Michaels (1989), Mitra (1989), Rodrik (1986), Tullock (1980), Rogerson (1982), Wellisz and Wilson (1986), and Wong (1989). Furthermore, see Cairns (1989) for a dynamic model and Coggins, *et al.* (1991) for a general equilibrium model.

[4] In the rent-seeking literature x is usually the probability that the rent (*e.g.*, a monopoly right or license) is obtained by L^1, and $1 - x$ the probability that the rent is given to L^2. Furthermore, the 'groups' considered usually are individual firms. Consequently, $n^1 = n^2 = 1$, and free-rider problems (see below) can be ignored.

and
$$p_{yn}^i := \frac{\partial p_y^i}{\partial n^i} < 0.$$

Spending resources implies a cost. So, with respect to the utility functions $v^i(x, y^i)$ of the (representative individual of the) groups, $i = 1, 2$, it is assumed that:

$$v_y^i := \frac{\partial v^i}{\partial y^i} < 0;$$

$$v_x^1 := \frac{\partial v^1}{\partial x} > 0;$$

$$v_x^2 := \frac{\partial v^2}{\partial x} < 0.$$

The equilibrium level of resources spent by the groups are now determined by assuming non-cooperative (Nash-Cournot) behavior. Each group maximizes its utility function, taking the action of the other group as given. Hence, for $i = 1, 2$:

$$\frac{dv^i}{dy^i} = v_x^i I_i p_y^i + v_y^i = 0.$$

If the second-order conditions are satisfied, the first-order conditions determine the strategies (best reply functions) σ^i of each group, that is, the resources spent by one group as a function of the resources spent by the other group: $y^1 = \sigma^1(y^2)$ and $y^2 = \sigma^2(y^1)$. Solving for y^1 and y^2 gives the Nash equilibrium.[5] In turn, the equilibrium values of (y^1, y^2) determine the equilibrium values of pressure (p^1, p^2) and the equilibrium value of $x = I(p^1, p^2, z)$.

In the literature this setup is mainly used to study the social costs of pressure and rent-seeking. Many studies are concerned with understanding to what extent the gain of rents to rent-seekers is dissipated in the competition to obtain the rent.[6] Although the issue is of great importance from a welfare-theoretic point of view, it does not provide much insight into the positive-theoretic issues addressed in this survey.

An important asset of the model, from a positive-theoretic point of view, is that it nicely disentangles the pressure process by making a meaningful distinction between (1) an individual member's contribution, y^i/n^i, (2) a group's total outlays on the production of pressure, y^i, (3) the actual pressure produced by a group, $p^i(y^i, n^i)$, and (4) the influence resulting from the combination of pressures produced by the two groups, $I(p^1, p^2, z)$. This distinction, for instance, can be used to show that the impact of a group's size on the

---

[5] It is noted that an exogenous increase in the amount of resources spent by one group can either increase or decrease the amount of pressure by the other group, as it can be derived that sign$(d\sigma^1/dy^2) = -$sign$(d\sigma^2/dy^1)$ =sign(I_{12}), if I is twice continuously differentiable.

[6] See, e.g., Delorme and Snow (1990), Hillman and Katz (1984, 1987), Tullock (1980, 1989). Becker (1983, 1985) is mainly concerned with the mutual impact of the deadweight (efficiency) costs due to x and the competition between the interest groups.

pressure process is not at all a trivial matter. This is especially so, if the vector of exogenous variables z contains the size of the groups, that is, if the size of the groups somehow 'counts' in the political process.

As will be shown now, these features of the model allow for the derivation of some interesting comparative-static results regarding the amount of pressure produced by a group. In this regard, it is useful to make a distinction between (a) the case that x is a *private* good (or bad) to the individual members of a group, and (b) the case that x is a *public* good (or bad) to the members of a group. The competition between the groups is not essential for these results but complicates their derivation. To simplify matters it will, therefore, be assumed that $I_{12} = I_{21} = 0$, implying that the best reply function of one group is independent of the level of resources spent by the other group. Furthermore, we shall focus on interest group L^1, the one that considers x a *good*. The results for the group that considers x a *bad*, L^2, are similar.

First, case (a) is considered, where x is a private good to the individual members, and it is assumed that the benefits and costs, x and y^1, are shared equally among them. Furthermore, it is assumed that utility is linear in x and y: $v^1(x, y^1) = x/n^1 - y^1/n^1$ (as in Becker 1983, 1985) where x is the amount of money to be redistributed from L^2 to L^1). The first-order condition for a Nash equilibrium is simply $I_1 p_y^1 = 1$, and the second-order condition holds if it is assumed that there are decreasing returns in the production of both pressure and influence ($p_{yy}^1 < 0$ and $I_{11} < 0$).

A first comparative-static result is that the level of pressure of a group increases if the group becomes more efficient in its production or if the policymaker becomes more susceptible to its pressure. To see this suppose that there is an exogenous upward shift in p_y^1 or I_1 (inducing not too large a shift in p^1 and I). Then the first-order condition, $I_1 p_y^1 = 1$, implies that y^1 must rise.

The next result concerns the impact of a group's size on the level of pressure. For its derivation it will be assumed that a group's size 'counts' in the political process. Specifically, it is assumed that the marginal influence of the group's pressure is increasing in its size, that is, $I_{1n} := \partial I_1/\partial n^1 > 0$. Totally differentiating the first-order condition with respect to p^1 and n^1 and rearranging terms gives:

$$\frac{dp^1}{dn^1} = -\frac{(I_{11}p_n^1 + I_{1n})p_y^1 + I_1 p_{yn}^1}{I_{11}p_y^1 + I_1 p_{yy}^1/p_y^1}.$$

Since the denominator is negative, it is found that $dp^1/dn^1 > 0$ if and only if $(I_{11}p_n^1 + I_{1n})p_y^1 + I_1 p_{yn}^1 > 0$. This condition need not hold because $p_{yn}^1 < 0$, due to the free rider problem. However, we could say that pressure by a group is 'more likely' to increase with its size if I_{1n} is large, that is, if the marginal influence of a group's pressure varies significantly with its size. It may perhaps be expected that a group's size has a stronger impact on its marginal influence in the legislative branch of government than in the executive branch, due to the legislature's dependence on electoral support. Therefore, an interesting, albeit somewhat loose, interpretation of this second comparative-static result is that large groups, contrary to small groups, are more likely to direct their pressure at legislators than at bureaucrats.

To derive a third result, case (b) is considered, where the public good x is consumed equally by all members of L^1, that is, $v^1(x, y^1) = x - y^1/n^1$. The first-order condition for an equilibrium is $I_1 p_y^1 n^1 = 1$. Differentiating with respect to p^1 and n^1 yields:

$$\frac{dp^1}{dn^1} = -\frac{(I_1/n^1 + I_{11}p_n^1 + I_{1n})p_y^1 + I_1 p_{yn}^1}{I_{11}p_y^1 + I_1 p_{yy}^1/p_y^1}.$$

Now it is seen that $dp^1/dn^1 > 0$ if and only if $(I_1/n^1 + I_{11}p_n^1 + I_{1n})p_y^1 + I_1 p_{yn}^1 > 0$. Since $I_1 p_y^1/n^1 > 0$, $dp^1/dn^1 > 0$ is, ceteris paribus, 'more likely' to hold than in case (a) where x is a private good to the members of L^1. An interesting interpretation of this result is that larger groups are more likely to produce pressure in the pursuit of public goods (*e.g.*, defense, environmental protection, tariffs) than in the pursuit of private goods (such as transfers) that have to be divided among a large number of group members (*cf.* Rodrik 1986).

The models that use an influence function will now be evaluated in light of the problems, mentioned in the introduction, concerning the determination and explanation of the level and kind of activities and their impact on government policy. First of all, it was seen that these models can be used to derive some interesting comparative-static results, regarding the determination of the *level* of pressure activities. An interest group was seen to spend more resources on pressure if it becomes more efficient in the production of pressure and if the policymaker becomes more susceptible to this pressure. Moreover, these models suggest that small (large) groups are more likely to direct their efforts towards the executive (legislative) branch and that they are more likely to vie for rents, that have a private (public) good characteristic.

However, the models exhibit two important limitations. One is that the production process of pressure is treated as a black box, in the sense that it is simply assumed that pressure is produced by spending resources. The *kind* of activities involved are not specified. Another major limitation is that the influence of the pressure by the interest groups is assumed but *not explained*. The government is not modelled as a player but is assumed to behave mechanistically in response to pressure. The focus is solely on the demand side, that is, on the behavior of interest groups.[7]

16.3 Models with a Vote Function and Campaign Contributions

The single activity by interest groups that is most intensively studied is contributing to the political campaigns of parties and candidates. The main reason for this is not the undisputed importance of this activity, but the relative

---

[7] An exception is Appelbaum and Katz (1987), where a political candidate in setting the size of a rent x makes a trade-off between the bribes (y_1) received from producers (L_1) and the electoral punishment (y_2) by voters (L_2). In this sense, the model is close to the type of models dealing with campaign contributions, which are discussed in the next section.

abundance of data, in particular on the so-called Political Action Committees in the U.S. These data can and have been employed to test the implications of two competing theoretical models on campaign contributions.

In the first set of models the main behavioral assumption is that contributions by an interest group to a party's campaign elicit a favorable policy position by the party. (See Aranson and Hinich 1979, and Welch 1989.) In the second set of models the crucial assumption is that a particular party will receive more votes in the election when it spends more money on its political campaign. Hence, an interest group contributes to the campaign of a favored party in order to increase the expected number of votes.[8] The essentials of both types of models will be discussed below. Attention will be focussed on versions of the models with only one interest group. Generalizations to more groups are possible, but do not add much to the issues at stake in the present survey.

A basic version of the first type of models is the following. Let $v(x) - y_1 - y_2$ denote an interest group's utility function, with y_j the contribution to the electoral campaign of party $G_j (j = 1, 2)$ and x the extent to which the policy that will be implemented after the elections is favorable to the interest group. It is assumed that $v' > 0$ and $v'' < 0$. The important assumption is that party G_j will implement a policy, x_j, when in office, which is more favorable to the interest group the more the group has contributed to the party's campaign, that is, $x_j = F_j(y_j)$, with $F_j' > 0, F_j'' < 0$. Furthermore, it is assumed that the probability π_j that party G_j is elected is fixed, with $\pi_1 = 1 - \pi_2$. Hence, the group's expected benefits from contributing to the campaign of party G_j are maximized if $\pi_j v' F_j' = 1$. The model has two main implications: (1) the interest group may contribute to the campaigns of *both* parties; (2) the group's optimal contribution y_j to party G_j is increasing in π_j. A group contributes more to the campaign of a party or candidate if the latter is more likely to win the election:

$$\frac{dy_j}{d\pi_j} = -\frac{v' F_j'}{\pi_j [v''(F_j')^2 + v' F_j'']} > 0.$$

Evidently, the use of an influence function (here, F) to represent the transformation of donations into the party's platform makes this type of model very similar to the models presented in the previous section.

In the second type of model, it is assumed that an interest group takes the (expected) policy positions of the parties as given, and that campaign contributions are aimed at influencing the election outcome. The following game-theoretic version has one interest group, L, and two parties or candidates, G_1 and G_2.

Let the utility function of the interest group again be given by $v(x) - y_1 - y_2$. It is assumed that party G_j implements policy x_j once in office, and that L takes these policy positions as given. Let $\pi_1 = \pi$ be the probability that G_1 wins the election, and $\pi_2 = 1 - \pi$ the probability that G_2 wins. It is

---

[8] See Austen-Smith (1987), Brock and Magee (1980), Edelman (1992), Hillman and Ursprung (1988), Magee and Brock (1983), Ursprung (1990), and Wilson (1990).

assumed that π is a function of D, the difference in the expected percentage of votes for G_1 and G_2:
$$\pi = \pi(D),$$
with
$$\pi' > 0,$$
and
$$sign\ (\pi'') = -sign\ (D).$$

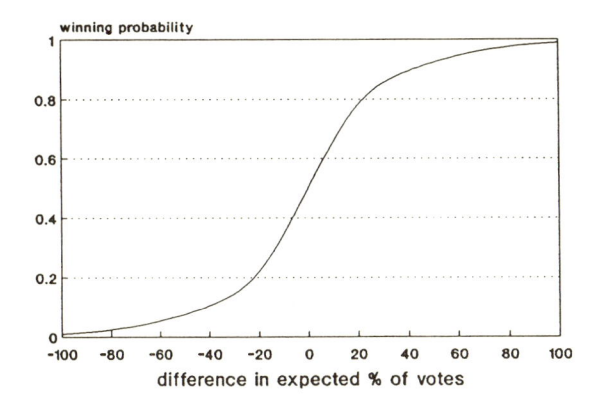

Figure 1. Winning probability and difference in expected percent of votes.

A typical example of the function π is a cumulative distribution function, as illustrated in Figure 1. An important feature of the function is that the impact of a change of D on π is largest when D is close to zero, that is, when π is close to 0.5.

A group contributes to the campaign of a party in order to enable the party to run a good campaign and increase its election chances. This is reflected in the crucial assumption that D is a function of both the platforms of the parties and their campaign spending, $D = D(x_1, x_2, y_1, y_2)$. The function D—or the composite function $\pi(D)$—can be referred to as a *vote function*. It is assumed that there are positive but decreasing voting returns to campaign spending:[9]

$$D_1^y := \partial D/\partial y_1 > 0 \quad D_2^y := \partial D/\partial y_2 < 0,$$
$$D_{11}^y := \partial D_1^y/\partial y_1 < 0 \quad D_{22}^y := \partial D_2^y/\partial y_2 > 0.$$

Finally, expected utility V of L is given by:
$$V = \pi v(x_1) + (1-\pi)v(x_2) - y_1 - y_2.$$

A first result that follows from this model is called the 'specialization theorem,' which says that an interest group will never contribute to the campaigns of both parties. To see this, note that from

---

[9] In most models the positive relationship between campagin spending and the expected percentage of votes is *assumed*. Austen-Smith (1987) is an exception. In his model the relationship is *derived* from the assumption that campaign spending enables a party to clarify its policy position to the risk-averse and incompletely informed, voters. His study tries to open up the 'black box of voting' that characterizes many other models.

$$\pi' > 0, \ D_1^y > 0, D_2^y < 0,$$

and
$$\frac{dV}{dy_j} = \pi' D_j^y [v(x_1) - v(x_2)] - 1,$$

it follows that $dV/dy_1 < 0$ for all y_1 when $x_1 < x_2$ and that $dV/dy_2 < 0$ for all y_2 when $x_1 > x_2$. Hence, an interest group never contributes to the party that it likes least. In the sequel it is assumed that party G_1 is the one with the most favorable policy position for the interest group, $x_1 > x_2$, and, for simplicity, the utility function is normalized such that $v(x_2) = 0$. The first-order condition for the optimal donation y_1 to G_1 then is

$$\pi' D_1^y v(x_1) = 1,$$

assuming that the second-order condition is satisfied, that is,

$$\pi' D_{11}^y + \pi'' (D_1^y)^2 < 0.$$

Given these assumptions, a second result is that the optimal contribution y_1 is increasing in $x_1, dy_1/dx_1 > 0$, and that we have $y_1(= y_2) = 0$ if $x_1 = x_2$. This follows from the first- and second-order conditions (when D_{11}^{yx} is not too negative). Hence, a group's contribution to a party is increasing in the attractiveness of a party's platform (relative to the platform of the other party). A third result is that the optimal contribution is increasing in π'. From the shape of the function $\pi(D)$ it follows that π' attains its maximum when $D = 0$. Therefore, this result is usually interpreted as saying that interest groups contribute more to the campaign of their favored party or candidate if the election is expected to be 'close,' (*e.g.*, Mueller, 1989, p. 209).

Finally, the behavior of party G_1 is considered. With respect to the platform x_1 it is assumed that $D_1^x := \partial D/\partial x_1 < 0$ (for $x_1 > x_2$). The idea behind this assumption is that the voters punish a party if it provides special benefits to an interest group. As a consequence, a party has to weigh the direct effect of its platform on the expected vote against the indirect impact of its platform, which runs via the campaign contributions (*cf.* Denzau and Munger 1986).[10] Assuming that G_1 attempts to maximize π, the first-order condition for an interior optimum of x_1 is: $\pi'[D_1^x + D_1^y(dy_1/dx_1)] = 0$. Phrased in these general terms, however, it is hard to derive additional propositions concerning the problems that are at issue here.

In summary, the two main competing hypotheses that can be derived from the models of the first and second type, respectively, are that an interest group mainly donates to likely winners and that contributions are particularly

---

[10] In models with two parties and two lobbies it is usually assumed that the parties play Nash amongst each other, but act as Stackelberg leaders relative to the campaign donors. Hence, a party takes the platform of the other party as given but takes account of the direct impact of its platform on the expected vote and the indirect impact via the contributions of the lobbies. See Edelman (1992) for a model with similar results, but where the donors act as Stackelberg leaders relative to the parties.

given to the favored candidates, especially in close contests. Welch (1980) mainly finds support for the former proposition, whereas, for instance, Kau, et al. (1982), Poole and Romer (1985) and Schlozman and Tierney (1986) find support for both relationships. Therefore, Mueller (1989, p. 213) concludes that lobbies contribute to campaigns of parties and candidates both to elicit a favorable policy from the elected party *and*—simultaneously or at other instances—to affect the election outcome.

The following can be concluded with respect to the problems central to this survey—the determination and explanation of the level and kind of activities of interest groups and the influence of each upon government policy. The first type of models—assuming that interest groups donate in order to affect the candidates' policy positions—are essentially similar to the type of models employing an influence function (Section 16.2). Some interesting results can be derived concerning the *level* of resources spent—in particular that contributions are increasing in a candidate's electoral prospects—, but a major drawback is that it is assumed that, but not explained why, a party's policy position changes in response to campaign contributions.

The second model type assumes that interest groups aim to increase the election chances of favored candidates; hence both interest groups and parties are players in the game. In this sense, these models give a rational foundation for both the demand and the supply side of the policy process. Furthermore, the level of campaign contributions was seen to be increasing in the platform difference between the candidates and the expected closeness of the election. These features are considered interesting assets of the models. There is, however, one major shortcoming, namely, that interest groups take the policy position of the candidates as given. Interest groups take actions to influence the behavior of *voters*—and thereby the (re)election chances of candidates—but not the behavior of *candidates*. Although affecting voting behavior is, of course, a means to influence government policy, it can be argued that the activities alluded to in phrases like 'exerting influence on government' in particular refer to situations in which the aim is to affect the behavior of those presently in power. Those situations, however, are not covered by these models.

16.4 Models with a Composite Utility Function

The models to be discussed in this section exhibit some cooperative features, contrary to the models presented in the previous sections. This cooperative element shows up in the distinctive characteristic of these models, namely that government policy is in accordance with the maximization of a weighted representation of the utilities of different (interest) groups. This feature is best illustrated as follows. There are N groups in society, with $v^i(x)$ the utility function of group L^i. Furthermore, let λ^i denote the 'power weight' of group $L^i (i = 1, \ldots, N)$. Below, it will be seen how these weights are determined by the political process. The behavioral assumptions underlying the models imply that the value of x can be determined by the maximization of a *composite utility function*:[11]

$$x = arg\ max \sum_{i=1}^{N} \lambda^i v^i(x). \qquad (1)$$

The most important differences among models of this class concern the behavioral assumptions that lead to equation (1), and the determination of the power weights λ^i. Three types of models can be distinguished in this respect: models that explicitly use a *cooperative solution concept* (Aumann and Kurz 1977, Zusman 1976), models that use the *interest function approach*, developed by van Winden (1983), and finally models that hypothesize *probabilistic voting* (Coughlin, et al., 1990 and Lindbeck and Weibull 1987).

Both Aumann and Kurz (1977) and Zusman (1976) use (a version of) the so-called Harsanyi-Shapley-Nash value for nontransferable utility games. For the details of this cooperative solution concept the reader is referred to Harsanyi (1977, Ch. 12) or Shapley (1988).[12] An attractive feature of this concept is that the power weights λ^i for each player are determined endogenously. Loosely speaking, the λ^i solve out two conditions: (a) a player receives the sum of his or her expected marginal contributions to any possible coalition of players that can be formed, and (b) the game between a particular coalition C and the coalition of all players outside this coalition $(N \backslash C)$, is determined by the 'Nash bargaining solution.'[13] Underlying this solution are 'maximal threats,' which the coalitions commit themselves to should bargaining break down. A typical feature of cooperative solution concepts, however, is that bargaining (between the coalitions) never breaks down, because all players anticipate on the commitment to carry out threats; Pareto inefficient outcomes are, thus, avoided.

In Aumann and Kurz's (1977) theoretical model of redistribution it is assumed that the income distribution $(x = x^1, \ldots, x^N)$ is determined by a majority voting rule. The players in the game are all (N) individuals in society, having utility functions $v^i(x^i)$ for income, and a fixed pre-tax income or endowment, denoted by y^i. The feasibility constraint implies that total after-tax income $(\sum_{i=1}^{N} x^i)$ equals total pre-tax income $(\sum_{i=1}^{N} y^i)$. Groups enter the picture because individuals can form a majority coalition, C, and then redistribute all income from the individuals outside the coalition $N \backslash C$ to the

---

[11] Hence, these models are in a formal sense essentially equivalent to models that hypothesize a benevolent government. This suggests an interesting link between the 'positive' (political economic, public choice) approach and the more traditional 'normative' (social welfare maximization) approach in public economics.

[12] It must be noted that Harsanyi's and Shapley's versions differ, but the ideas underlying the solution are similar (*cf.* Owen 1982, Ch. 13). The crucial point is that the λ_i make the utilities of the players (locally) transferable, after which the Shapley value for transferable utility games is applicable. Here no full justice can be done to the formidable (technical) details of the models of Aumann and Kurz (1977) and Zusman (1976); only some main features are discussed.

[13] Binmore and Dasgupta (1987) and Binmore, et al. (1987) show that it is possible to derive the 'Nash bargaining solution' from an underlying non-cooperative bargaining game.

members of coalition C. The crucial point is that in this game between C and $N\backslash C$ the latter group can threaten to destroy its own pre-tax income $\sum_{i \in N\backslash C} y^i$, leaving nothing to be redistributed to C. The outcome of this game is determined by the Nash bargaining solution. Proceeding in this way for all possible coalitions, an individual's 'power' (Shapley value) can be derived from the (expected) contribution to all possible coalitions. Aumann and Kurz show that an individual's power over the *resulting* income distribution equals $\lambda^i = 1/v^{i\prime\prime}(x^i)$; that is, an individual's power equals the reciprocal of his or her *ex post* marginal utility. Furthermore, the model implies that the tax t^i an individual has to pay is $t^i = v^i(x^i)/v^{i\prime\prime}(x^i) - c$, where the first term on the right-hand side of this equation is a measure of risk aversion, called 'fear of ruin,' and c is a positive constant (a tax credit). The more fearful a player, the larger the tax (s)he pays. As noted above, the assumption that commitments are possible implies that the threat—to destroy one's endowments—is never carried out. Furthermore, no coalitions ('interest groups') actually form. Thus, one could say that x results from pressure activities that could, but do not actually arise.[14]

In Zusman (1976) government policy x refers to the regulated consumer and producer prices in a regulated market. There are two interest groups: the consumers L^1, with $v^1(x)$ denoting consumer surplus, and the producers L^2, with $v^2(x)$ denoting producer surplus. The government G is the third player and its objective $u(x)$ is to minimize subsidy costs. Zusman assumes that the two groups employ threats and promises to influence the government. To that purpose he introduces 'strength functions' $s^i(y^i)$, where y^i denotes the amount of resources spent by $L^i(i = 1,2)$. Zusman shows that the cooperative solution of this game is equivalent to the maximization of $u(x) + \lambda^1 v^1(x) + \lambda^2 v^2(x)$, where λ^i is equal to the 'marginal strength' ds^i/dy^i when L^i uses an optimal amount of resources y^i. A problem with this model is the specification of the strength functions s^i, as it is unclear what kind of activities would be involved to announce or carry out threats and promises. A similar problem was met with the employment of influence functions (Section 16.2).

The *interest function approach* is employed in, for instance, Borooah and van der Ploeg (1983), Drissen and van Winden (1991, 1992), Przeworski and Wallerstein (1988), Renaud and van Winden (1988), van Velthoven (1989), and van Winden (1983). Although the details of the models differ somewhat, the principal ideas are as follows. There are three basic groups or classes in society: public sector workers (politicians and bureaucrats), capitalists, and private sector workers, having utility or interest functions $u(x,y), v^1(x,y)$ and $v^2(x,y)$, respectively (in some models also the 'dependents', that is, the unemployed, disabled and retired, are included as a separate group). The value of x is determined by the public sector workers and $y = (y^1, y^2)$ are the actions taken by groups L^1 and L^2, the capitalists and private sector workers, respectively. Groups 1 and 2 play a non-cooperative game. Each group L^i maximizes its utility function $v^i(x,y)$, taking the actions of the government

---

[14] See Gardner (1981) and Petrakis (1990) for the introduction of a government as a player in the game and Peck (1986) for an incorporation of incentive effects of taxation.

(x) and the other group (y^j) as given. This determines the best reply functions of the two groups: $y^1 = \sigma^1(x, y^2)$ and $y^2 = \sigma^2(x, y^1)$. The Nash equilibrium of this game, determines the actions of the two groups as a function of the government's action: $y = (y^1, y^2) = y(x)$. The crucial assumption is that the public sector workers (group G), when deciding upon the value of x, take account—to a greater or lesser extent—of the interests (v^1 and v^2) of the other groups because of pressure (and voting) by these groups. Hence, x is assumed to be in accordance with the maximization of the composite utility (complex interest) function: $u(x, y) + \lambda^1 v^1(x, y) + \lambda^2 v^2(x, y)$. Now, two variants can be distinguished: (1) G does not take account of the impact of x on $y = (y^1, y^2)$, that is, it plays Nash against the private sector, and (2) G does take account of the reactions [$y = y(x)$] of the groups to x, that is, it acts as a Stackelberg leader relative to the private sector. In either case, the decision variables (x, y) can be derived as a function of the 'power weights' λ^i, which are assumed to be built up by pressure.

In principle it is possible, as in Zusman (1976), to estimate the power coefficients λ^i from observed data on government policy (x). In turn, these power weights could then be regressed on group characteristics and activities to provide insight into the factors that determine the influence of groups on government policy.[15] A major problem with such an analysis is that in the composite utility function of equation (1) the parameters of the utility functions of the groups interact with the power coefficients. As a consequence, it is difficult to disentangle (identify) in the estimates the effects which are due to preferences and those which are due to power. For instance, large government spending could be due to little power within groups L^1 and L^2 as well as to a high utility derived from such expenditures by L^1 and L^2. As a first attempt the numerical strengths of the groups could be taken as an explanatory variable for the λ^i. Such an exercise allows for an interesting (dynamic) interaction between political and economic factors. The power weights determine government policy, whereas government policy in its turn co-determines economic development, in particular the levels of employment in the private and public sector, which again co-determine the relative power of the different groups. Some empirical support for the hypotheses derived from such a theoretical exercise is reported in van Velthoven and van Winden (1985, 1986). Nevertheless, this approach still shows some important lacunae, as, so far, it offers only empirical, but no rigorous behavioral-theoretic, support for the use of numerical strength as proxy for the power of a group (see below, however).

Interest groups are introduced in a *probabilistic voting model* by Coughlin, *et al.* (1990) and Lindbeck and Weibull (1987). It is assumed that an incumbent government or party G has to choose its policy or platform x in a forthcoming election. There are N groups in society and group L^i has n^i members ($i = 1, \ldots, N$). Each individual member j of group L^i has the same utility function $v^i(x)$ over G's policy, but in addition a personal utility 'bias' b_{ij} in favor of ($b_{ij} > 0$), or against ($b_{ij} < 0$), G's position. It is assumed

---

[15] See Svenjar (1986) for an interesting estimation along these lines of a cooperative game model of union-firm bargaining.

that b_{ij} is a random variable with uniform distribution over the interval (l^i, r^i). Normalizing the utility obtained from the challenging party to zero, it is assumed that voter ij will vote for G if and only if $v^i(x) + b_{ij} > 0$. Assuming that $l^i < v^i(x) < r^i$, the following result applies. If G chooses its platform so as to maximize its expected margin of victory then it will set x in accordance with equation (1), with $\lambda^i = n^i/(r^i - l^i)$.

Apart from voting there is no strategic behavior of interest groups in the model. Individual voters are assumed to vote for the party they prefer, but it is not necessarily the case that all members of the same group vote for the same party. Groups enter the picture only in that they determine a systematic part of a voter's preferences, and are as such a focus for parties in determining their platforms. Nevertheless, it is a remarkable result that the assumption that the government cares only about re-election can lead to behavior that is formally similar to a behavioral rule that would apply to a benevolent government caring about the (weighted) welfare of its citizens.[16] A further interesting result is that the extent to which the interests $v^i(x)$ of a particular group L^i are taken account of by G are positively related to the size of the group— thereby providing some theoretical underpinning for the use of size as a proxy for power (see above) — and inversely related to the degree to which there is uncertainty about the preferences of the members of L^i. The representative interests of large homogeneous groups are best represented in the government's policy position.

Finally, the models in this section will be evaluated with respect to the central problems mentioned in the introduction. First, it is concluded that the incorporation of interest group *activities* is not fully satisfactory. The models following the interest function approach do not incorporate any kind of activities, whereas the probabilistic voting models focus solely on voting. The cooperative model of Zusman assumes that the interest groups have the possibility to threaten and reward the government. To do this they have to spend resources, but what activities are involved to establish these sanctions remains unspecified. Only Aumann and Kurz are explicit about the kind of activities which may be involved. They assume that (coalitions of) individuals can threaten to destroy their endowments. The credibility of these threats, however, depends crucially upon the assumption—which is a sort of *deus ex machina*—that binding commitments can be made. This assumption, which is typical to cooperative solution concepts, implies that threats never are (never need to be) carried out.

Regarding the explanation of the impact of interest groups on government policy, it is noted that the cooperative models do *explain why* these interest groups have influence on government behavior. Groups can use threats and they are assumed to commit themselves to carry out these threats in case of a disagreement. This commitment possibility makes the government susceptible to the threats. Also the probabilistic voting models explain why the preferences of groups count in the political process. A government's concern

---

[16] Baldwin (1987) arrives at a similar result for a model with vote maximization and campaign contributions.

to be reelected makes it dependent on the vote potential of interest groups. Moreover, the models quite precisely *determine how* the influence of an interest group on government behavior works out. The government is induced to take account of the interests of the different groups when determining its action. Furthermore, some indicators for the extent to which the interests of a group count were derived. A group's threat potential, and the size and the homogeneity of its membership were seen to be relevant in this respect.

16.5 Games with Asymmetric Information

The models discussed so far show two major shortcomings. First, the very activities involved in influencing government policies are largely implicit. Typically, the spending of resources is the only activity—apart from voting—that is focussed upon. The reason why precisely such spending changes political behavior, such as voting in case of campaign contributions, is not clarified. Second, the policies of political decisionmakers are either taken as given for the interest groups, through the assumption of Stackelberg leadership for the former, or simply assumed to depend on the resources spent by such groups. The former assumption is typical for campaign contribution models, and the latter for influence function models. Certainly, these assumptions have been helpful in gaining knowledge regarding the determinants of interest group activity and the extent to which the interests of such groups will be taken into account by political decisionmakers. What is missing, however, is a model that (a) endogenizes the behavior of political decisionmakers as well as that of interest groups, (b) allows for influence attempts by interest groups, and (c) makes explicit the activities involved. With an influence attempt we mean any action by an agent L intended to change the behavior of a governmental agent G, relative to what this behavior would be, had agent L not acted or acted differently. We believe that influence attempts in this sense are more characteristic for what in common parlance is meant by lobbying, political pressure or the influence of interest groups. Moreover, they are not restricted to elections, which form only one—periodic and formally regulated—channel of political influence.

It can be argued that influence attempts typically involve the intended (costly) transmission of information by L to G on potential sanctions (see Potters, 1992, for a more rigorous definition). This implies that attention should be focussed on situations in which G has incomplete information. A distinction can further be made between situations where the sanction involves an action (reward or punishment) by L, and situations where it involves an action by another agent (including 'nature'; think, for example, of environmental groups). In the former case we will speak of *pressure*, and in the latter case of *lobbying*. In this section models will be discussed that have recently been developed to analyze these situations.

16.5.1 A Basic Model of Lobbying

From a positive-theoretic point of view, the amount of lobbying that is empirically observed is not unproblematic. Assuming that interest groups behave in a self-interested manner, why should policymakers believe their messages? On the other hand, if policymakers cannot simply be assumed to believe such messages, why would interest groups take on the—often substantial—cost or trouble of lobbying? This raises the following questions: (1) is there a scope and rationale for lobbying in a world of self-interested agents with rational expectations?; (2) if such a base exists, when is lobbying more or less likely to occur?; and (3) when is the policymaker's response likely to be advantageous to the interest group?

The following game-model (Ainsworth 1993; Potters and van Winden 1992a) illustrates that these questions can be addressed in a fundamental way by incorporating all of the necessary ingredients for strategic lobbying in a simple setting. There are two players, a policymaker G and an interest group L. G has to select one of two actions, x_1 or x_2. The payoffs (utilities) the players derive from G's action depend on the 'state of the world', that can be either of two types, denoted by t_1 and t_2. Which type prevails is private information to L. The state of the world refers to the reactions to G's action (sanctions) by agents other than L. Before G selects its action, L can send a message m from a set of feasible messages M. Sending a message bears a fixed cost c to L, whereas not sending a message—denoted by n—is costless. G cannot check the accuracy of a message. G's prior belief $p\,(1-p)$ that the state of the world is t_2 (t_1), as well as any other element of the game (except for L's private information on the state of the world), is common knowledge. The (normalized) payoffs over action-state pairs are:

	t_1	t_2
x_1	$a_1, 0$	$0, 0$
x_2	$0, b_1$	a_2, b_2

where $a_i > 0, i = 1, 2$. Thus, assuming (expected) payoff maximization, a_i denotes the payoff to G of making the best choice (x_i) when the state is t_i. Furthermore, G's action x_2 gives L a (net) payoff of b_i if its private information is t_i. We will speak of 'type' L_i if the interest group's private information is t_i.

Using the concept of a sequential equilibrium, a number of interesting results can be derived for this 'signaling game.' First of all, it is noted that three basic situations or incentive structures can be distinguished for this game, dependent on b_i: (1) $b_1 < 0 < b_2$, (2) $b_2 < 0 < b_1$, and (3) $b_i > 0$ (or, equivalently, $b_i < 0$). In the first case there is *no* conflict of interest between G and L, because both G and L prefer x_i if the state of the world is t_i. As interests are completely congruent, the interest group never has an incentive to dissemble, and the policymaker has no reason to mistrust a message; consequently, there is no problem for transmission of private information from L to

G in this case.[17] In the second case, there is a *full* conflict of interest between G and L, as G always prefers to play the action that is different from the action preferred by L. Hence, L always has an incentive to dissemble (misinform G), and, due to the rational expectations character of the equilibrium concept, there is no scope for information transfer; consequently, no message will be sent in this case. In the third case ($b_1, b_2 > 0$, or similarly, $b_1, b_2 < 0$) there is a *partial* conflict of interest. Whereas L_2 would like to report truthfully on its private information, since its interests coincide with G's, L_1 has an incentive to dissemble. The problem of the scope of information transfer and the rationale for sending costly messages is most pertinent, here ($b_1, b_2 > 0$).

A first result in this case shows that nothing changes in terms of equilibrium outcomes when it is assumed that the message space M contains only one element, m say. The intuition is that once L has decided to send a message it bears the fixed cost c independent of the content of the message, which is essentially 'cheap talk' then. It is only the fact that a costly message is received (or not) that can reveal information to G. Another result says that no information transfer can occur if the interest group's preferences carry information in the 'wrong direction,' which is the case if $b_1 > b_2 > 0$. Then, L_1 has a larger stake in persuading G that the state of the world is t_2 rather than L_2. Knowing this, G is inclined to interpret a message as coming from L_1 rather than L_2, which is, of course, disadvantageous to L. Consequently, no message is sent and G will behave according to its prior beliefs.

Hence, a necessary condition for informative messages is that $b_1 < b_2$. It requires that there is sufficient congruence of interests, in the sense that L's stake in persuading G is larger when its private information is such that it justifies persuasion from G's point of view. Obviously, another necessary condition is that lobbying costs are not prohibitive (that is, at least $b_2 > c$). Now, let σ_i denote L_i's strategy, that is, the probability that L sends a message (m) when its private information is t_i, and let $\rho(\cdot)$ denote G's strategy, that is, the probability that G selects x_2 after a message, $\rho(m)$, or no message, $\rho(n)$. Then, the following equilibrium is obtained if $p < a := a_1/(a_1 + a_2)$, that is, if G would select x_1 (which is unfavorable to L) on the basis of its prior belief p:

(a) if $c < b_1 < b_2$, then
$$\sigma_1 = \alpha := p(1-a)/(1-p)a, \ \sigma_2 = 1, \ \rho(n) = 0, \ \rho(m) = c/b_1;$$

(b) if $b_1 < c < b_2$, then
$$\sigma_1 = 0, \ \sigma_2 = 1, \ \rho(n) = 0, \ \rho(m) = 1.$$

If lobbying costs are prohibitive for type L_1 (regime b) then only L_2 sends a message, which is conclusive evidence that the state is t_2. If costs are not prohibitive (regime a) then L_2 always sends a message and L_1 plays a mixed strategy. The intuition is that G will select x_2 only if its belief in

---

[17] Compare in this regard the seminal Crawford and Sobel (1982) model, where costless information transfer (cheap talk) is possible only if the interests of the players are sufficiently alike.

the state t_2 increases, which requires that a message is more likely to come from L_2 than from L_1. Therefore, L_1 must play a mixed strategy. Although informative, a message still leaves G in doubt about the state of the world as both σ_1 and σ_2 are positive. This uncertainty—more specifically, the fact that G's Bayesian updated probability belief equals a—induces G to play a mixed strategy, which in turn justifies L_1's mixed strategy. No message, however, is conclusive evidence that the state is t_1, in which case G chooses x_1, as G would have chosen according to its prior belief p ('silence is consent,' one could say).

Coming back to the first question raised in the beginning of this section, these results show that there is a scope for information transfer through lobbying and a rationale for costly lobbying, if the interests of L carry information in the 'right direction' ($b_1 < b_2$) and lobbying costs are not prohibitive ($c < b_2$).

As regards the second question—the expected occurrence of lobbying $[(1-p)\sigma_1 + p\sigma_2]$—the quite intuitive result is obtained that lobbying is more likely to occur with lower costs and/or a higher potential benefit or stake (through a switch from regime b to regime a). Moreover, the expected occurrence is increasing in p, which implies that lobbying is more likely if G is already more inclined to select the action x_2 (preferred by the interest group) on the basis of its prior beliefs.

Finally, regarding the response to lobbying $[\rho(m)]$ the results show that this is increasing in c and decreasing in b_1. Thus, G 'discounts' L's message depending on the stake L_1 has to dissemble, relative to the cost of lobbying. If messages become costless (the 'cheap talk' case), $\rho(m) = 0$ and G acts according to its prior beliefs; there is no scope for information transfer and political influence in that case.

So far it has been assumed that the prior beliefs of G ($p < a$) are such that it would pick the action (x_1) that is unfavorable to the interest group. In the reverse case ($p > a$) it turns out that there are multiple equilibria. No lobbying is always an equilibrium in this case, as one would expect. However, there also exists an equilibrium where both types of L lobby (if costs are not prohibitive, of course), although the response of G is the same (x_2) as in the equilibrium with no lobbying. This shows that lobbying can be a pure social waste. On the other hand, the equilibrium of regime b when $p < a$ shows that there are cases where policymakers as well as interest groups can benefit from the possibility of lobbying.

16.5.2 Extensions and Further Issues

The above lobbying model illustrates that, in case of conflicting interests with policymakers, types of interest groups should somehow be able to distinguish themselves from one another in order to influence policies through information transfer. As shown, fixed positive lobbying costs give such an opportunity. From this perspective it should not be surprising that the scope for information transfer and the response to lobbying increases if there is no restriction on the cost of a message, that is, in case of *endogenous cost*. Suppose that y denotes the (observable) cost that L chooses to invest in the message (with $y = 0$

meaning that L does not send a message). As shown in Potters and van Winden (1992a) this leads to a full revelation of information ('separating') equilibrium for the above lobbying model. Type L_2 invests just enough ($y = b_1$) to make it unprofitable for L_1—who wants to misinform G—to send a message. Consequently, in equilibrium G selects x_2 if and only if a message is received.

Apart from endogenous costs there are other situations that facilitate the transfer of information. A number of recent studies have shown the importance in this respect of the possibility that messages can be screened, multiple interest groups or policymakers (receivers) are present, or that reputations can be built up through repeated play. Another possibility that has been pointed at is that interest groups may be able to distinguish themselves through sanctions (pressure) instead of messages (lobbying).

In case of *screening of messages* it is assumed that there is some mechanism or institution that enables the policymaker to discriminate, to some extent, between true and false messages. To illustrate, consider again the above lobbying model but suppose there is an intermediary agent (a bureaucratic agency, a congressional committee, or a private consultant) that first evaluates lobby reports (messages). Let π_i denote the exogenous and commonly known probability that the agent comes up with a positive recommendation effectively saying that the state is t_2 (which is favorable to the interest group L) when actually the state is t_1, and assume that $0 \leq \pi_1 < \pi_2 \leq 1$; note that π_2/π_1 in fact measures the (perceived) reliability of the agent. As shown in Potters and van Winden (1992a), the scope for information transfer and the impact of messages on the policymaker's (G's) action increases in this case. Even costless messages ($c = 0$) can now induce G to select x_2 if there is sufficient confidence in the agent (more specifically, if $\pi_2/\pi_1 \geq 1/\alpha$, with α defined as before). Similarly, in Milgrom's (1981) 'persuasion game' and in Milgrom and Roberts' (1986) model of 'competition among interested parties' costless messages are informative due to the assumption that lying is impossible ($\pi_1 = 0$), and in Kambhu's (1988) model of a regulated firm costless messages by the firm can be informative due to the assumption that true reports will not be found false (*cf.* $\pi_2 = 1$) and false reports are detected with positive probability ($\pi_1 < 1$).

Instead of relying on an intermediary agent, the screening may be more direct, as through monitoring or auditing, as in Austen-Smith and Wright (1992). In this model an interest group L again prefers one of two possible actions by a legislator G. Although this preferred action gives a fixed payoff which is independent of the state of the world (*cf.* $b_1 = b_2$), L can, nevertheless, send informative messages because lying is expected to be costly. The reason is that in equilibrium there is a probability that G will check L's message and, if caught dissembling, a (given) penalty has to be paid by L. This model also shows that the legislator may want to rely on the lobbying process instead of firsthand data acquisition, even when the cost involved in such acquisition is lower than the cost of monitoring the lobbyist. A weakness of this model is the implicit assumption that G can commit itself to impose a penalty on L in case the latter is checked and found to be dissembling.

In fact Austen-Smith and Wright's model deals with two interest groups with opposed interests, and it shows that the presence of such *multiple groups* may increase the scope for information transfer. The reason is that the group for which the legislator's (G's) prior belief is favorable will also lobby if the probability that the other group will successfully mislead the legislator is sufficiently high. In that case the private information of the groups is fully revealed in equilibrium, as the legislator's threat to check for sure is credible, because of the opposed interests of the groups (implying that one of them is lying for sure if they send the same message).[18]

In Potters (1992) the increased scope for information transfer is shown by incorporating two groups, with opposite interests concerning G's actions, in the basic lobby model discussed above. Even if lobbying costs are not prohibitive for either group, full revelation of information is possible in this case, because the group with 'bad' information can be deterred from sending a (false) message by the lobbying of the group with 'good' information. It is an equilibrium for both groups to separate then, thereby in a sense providing an 'oversupply' of information (as one group separating would be sufficient).

Multiple agents also play a role in the political participation games studied by Ainsworth and Sened (1993) and Lohmann (1993). In these models the agents, holding private information that is relevant for a policymaker, may have incentives to take a costly political action to signal their information to this policymaker who conditions her decision on the number of individuals engaged in political participation. Lohmann, *inter alia*, shows that there can be an oversupply of costly (uninformative) action. Ainsworth and Sened introduce a lobbyist who is known to be fully informed and, upon entry, provides an informative signal to the agents to participate and to the policymaker to choose a particular action. They, *inter alia*, show the importance of a sufficiently high entry cost for the lobbyist.

In the 'one-shot' games discussed so far there is no endogenous penalty on lying (false messages). One way such a penalty could come about is through a loss of credibility or reputation. Perhaps the most natural way to allow for this is to model the interaction as a *repeated game*. Sobel (1985) analyzes a finitely repeated signalling game that is relevant in this respect. In this model a receiver (G) is uncertain regarding the preferences of a sender (L), which is, with a commonly known probability, either a 'friend' (identical preferences as G) or an 'enemy' (completely opposite preferences). In each period of the game the players are confronted with one of two possible states of the world (with a commonly known probability), about which only L is informed. L

---

[18] In this model the groups can acquire (complete) information on the state of the world against a cost that is also known to G. Moreover, it is assumed that G can observe the information acquisition by a group (but not the content of the information), in which case G knows that the group is informed. In Austen-Smith (1994) it is assumed that neither the cost nor the acquisition of information by the sender (L) is observable by the receiver (G). However, (only) an informed L can prove that she is informed if she wishes to do so. By allowing in this way that informed types who acquired unfavorable information pool with the uninformed, it turns out that the scope for information transfer increases compared with the case that L is known to be informed.

then sends a costless message concerning the state of the world to G, who then selects an action that is payoff-relevant to both players, after which the true state is revealed. The principal equilibrium of this game shows that L typically sends truthful information for the first several periods, increasing its reputation of being a friend when there is a positive probability that an enemy would have lied. Eventually, however, an enemy will mislead G, in which case L loses its reputation and the opportunity to deceive G in the future.

Repeated play also provides an opportunity to an interest group to influence the decision of a policymaker through sanctions—*pressure*—instead of messages (lobbying). In a one-shot game, an announcement of a punishment or a reward by L (L_1) is not credible, as is easily seen by applying a backwards-induction argument. However, in case of repetition and asymmetric information, L may be motivated to enhance its reputation for being a type (L_2) prefers to carry out sanctions. This is shown in Potters and van Winden's (1990) pressure model, which is an adaptation of Kreps and Wilson's (1982) reputation model. The anticipation of L's willingness to build a reputation through sanctions may induce G to 'concede' and take the action which is preferred by L. Furthermore, in order to elicit concession, the interest group needs less initial credibility (a lower prior belief of being L_2) the larger the number of repetitions of the game. Interestingly, after a sanction the probability that G concedes L is increasing in the cost of a sanction to L_1, and decreasing in the benefit to L_1 of having G concede. These results correspond to those obtained for the basic lobby model.

Earlier it was discussed that the presence of multiple interest groups (senders) may increase the scope for information transfer. It turns out that this scope, and thereby the possibility to influence the decision of policymakers, may also increase if there are *multiple receivers*. This is shown in Farrell and Gibbons' (1985) model with two 'audiences' (see also Austen-Smith 1993). An informed sender can send a costless message—in private or in public—to two interested but uninformed receivers, who then take actions which affect the payoff of the sender as well as the receiver. It is studied how the incentives for information transfer to one receiver are affected by the presence of the other. One of the interesting outcomes is that there may be a separating equilibrium in public, but no separating equilibrium in private. For instance, if the sender's preferences over the receivers' actions are independent of its true type (as in the basic lobby model), we know that cheap talk in relation to each of the receivers separately (that is, in private) cannot be informative. However, Farrell and Gibbons demonstrate that if these preferences go in opposite directions, so that the sender would be tempted to lie in opposite directions in private, its message may be credible when it is communicated to both audiences in public.

16.6 Conclusion

In this survey we discussed four modelling approaches to study the influence of interest groups. The first approach, using an 'influence function', focuses on the strategic interaction between interest groups in influencing government policies; policymakers or voters are not involved as players. The second approach, concentrating on campaign contributions and using a 'vote function', adds political candidates as players (typically as Stackelberg leaders); interest groups now take policies as given, but influence the election outcome through their contributions, exploiting the vote function. The third approach, employing a 'composite utility function', stands out because of its cooperative features; it turned out, however, that these functions can be supported by non-cooperative (electoral competition and campaign contributions) models. The fourth approach, finally, focuses on the opportunities for interest groups to influence policymakers through strategic information transfer.

In our view, the most important achievement of the models developed so far has been to incorporate interest group activity into the formal positive analysis of government behavior. Notwithstanding the fact that they can be easily criticized regarding their neglect of certain strategic or institutional aspects, at least to some extent these models meet the generally felt need to allow for the political influence of interest groups. By investigating the opportunities for such influence outside the election context—in particular, through strategic information transmission—they help to redress the imbalance in public choice theory, which almost exclusively focused on the electoral nexus between policymakers and agents in the private sector. Importantly also, the research covered in this survey has produced many results concerning the determinants and impact of interest group activity that can be translated into testable hypotheses.

This brings us to one of the topics that was not addressed in this paper, which concerns the empirical support for the models discussed. The need here for brevity is not the only limitation; rigorous applications and tests (except perhaps for the case of campaign contributions in the U.S.) are also lacking in the literature. Although 'stylized facts' based on empirical studies and statements are often referred to (see, *e.g.,* Morton and Cameron 1992, Mueller 1989 and Potters 1992), the character of the evidence put forward is typically piecemeal and casuistic. No doubt, this is to a significant extent due to the nature of the subject investigated. It seems quite obvious that adequate field data concerning the dynamics and impact of lobbying and pressure will be hard evidence to come by. Although our improved theoretical understanding of the mechanisms involved may further the acquisition of better data sets, we expect that laboratory experiments—which facilitate the investigation of particular aspects in a controlled environment—will become an important additional tool for empirical investigation in this area (for a first attempt concerning the basic lobby model, see Potters and van Winden, 1992b).

Another topic that was hardly addressed regards the welfare aspects of interest group behavior. This issue is particularly focussed on in the many rent-seeking models that have been developed lately, where interest groups compete for a monopoly rent provided by the government. However, the main research interest here is in the extent to which these rents are dissipated in the competition process, and not the way they are established or influenced through interest group activity. Principal-agent models of asymmetric information form another line of research in this area. This literature is typically concerned with the normative (mechanism design) problem of the determination of optimal incentive schemes for agents, given the objectives and observations of the principal (the policymaker).[19] By assuming that the principal can commit her or himself to a message-response profile a specific—in particular a more efficient—equilibrium can be selected. Incidentally, also in these models it is found that the influence of an interest group depends on its stake, the costs of exerting influence, and the type of its interests (which have to go in the 'right' direction), as was established for the basic lobby model (see, *e.g.*, Laffont and Tirole 1991).

These models and the models using a 'compromise utility function', discussed in Section 16.4, point at an interesting and important area for future research, which consists of exploring the correspondence between the maximization of a social welfare function (with political weights attached to the utility of social groups) and the outcome of political economic processes with endogenous incentives, that is, without exogenously given commitment possibilities. This correspondence has already been shown for some electoral competition models (Baldwin 1987, Coughlin, *et al.* 1990), but as yet this is not the case for models focussing on interest group activity outside the election context.[20]

Apart from this, an important future research task consists of extending and linking up the simple and isolated models that have been developed so far (*cf.* Kolman 1992). And, finally, we emphasize the need for more, and, particularly, more appropriate, empirical studies. In our view, laboratory experiments may be very helpful here, not only because of the aforementioned difficulties in getting adequate field data, but also to check the soundness or the predictive value of the rationality assumptions of the present models. In this regard, such experiments would seem to be an excellent tool for the development and testing of 'bounded rationality' models.

References

Ainsworth, S. 1993. "Regulating Lobbyists and Interest Group Influence," *Journal of Politics* 55: 41-56.

Ainsworth, S. and I. Sened. 1993. "The Role of Lobbyists: Entrepreneurs with Two Audiences," *American Journal of Political Science* 37: 834-866.

Appelbaum, E. and E. Katz. 1987. "Seeking Rents by Setting Rents: The Political Economy of Rent-seeking," *Economic Journal* 97: 685-699.

Aranson, P., and M. Hinich. 1979. "Some Aspects of the Political Economy of Election Campaign Contribution Laws," *Public Choice* 34: 435-461.

Aumann, R. and M. Kurz. 1977. "Power and Taxes," *Econometrica* 45: 1137-1161.

---

[19] See, e.g., Baron (1989), Baron and Myerson (1982), Laffont and Tirole (1991), and the critique in Milgrom and Roberts (1986).

[20] Suggestive in this respect is the pressure model of Potters and van Winden (1990), where the impact of pressure is that it causes a temporarily inefficient outcome, forestalling a redistribution of the payoffs to the disadvantage of the agent exerting pressure. This suggests that as long as the influence (power) structure is not contested a social welfare function might do.

Austen-Smith, D. 1987. "Interest Groups, Campaign Contributions and Probabilistic Voting," *Public Choice* 54: 123-139.

Austen-Smith, D. 1993. "Information and Influence: Lobbying for Agendas and Votes," *American Journal of Political Science* 37: 799-833.

Austen-Smith, D. 1994. "Strategic Transmission of Costly Information," *Econometrica* 62: 955-963.

Austen-Smith, D. and J. Wright. 1992. "Competitive Lobbying for a Legislators' Vote," *Social Choice and Welfare* 9: 229-257.

Baldwin, R. 1987. "Politically Realistic Objective Functions and Trade Policy," *Economics Letters* 24: 287-290.

Baron, D. 1989. "Service-induced Campaign Contributions and the Electoral Equilibrium," *Quarterly Journal of Economics* 104: 45-72.

Baron, D. and R. Myerson. 1982. "Regulating a Monopolist with Unknown Costs," *Econometrica* 50: 911-930.

Becker, G. 1983. "A Theory of Competition among Pressure Groups for Political Influence," *Quarterly Journal of Economics* 98: 371-400.

Becker, G. 1985. "Public Policies, Pressure Groups, and Dead Weight Costs," *Journal of Public Economics* 28: 329-347.

Binmore, K. and P. Dasgupta, eds. 1987. *The Economics of Bargaining.* Oxford: Basil Blackwell.

Binmore, K., A. Rubinstein, and A. Wolinsky. 1986. "The Nash Bargaining Solution in Economic Modelling," *Rand Journal of Economics* 17: 176-188.

Borooah, V. and F. van der Ploeg. 1983. *Political Aspects of the Economy.* Cambridge: Cambridge University Press.

Brock, W. and S. Magee. 1980. "Tariff Formation in a Democracy," in *Current Issues in Commercial Policy and Diplomacy*, J. Black and B. Hindley, eds. London: Macmillan.

Cairns, R. 1989. "Dynamic Rent-seeking," *Journal of Public Economics* 39: 315-334.

Coggins, J., T. Graham-Tomasi, and T. Roe. 1991. "Existence of Equilibrium in a Lobbying Economy," *International Economic Review* 32: 533-550.

Congleton, R. 1983. "Committees and Rent-seeking Effort," *Journal of Public Economics* 41: 441-448.

Coughlin, P., D. Mueller, and P. Murrell. 1990. "Electoral Politics, Interest Groups, and the Size of Government," *Economic Inquiry* 29: 682-705.

Crawford, V. and J. Sobel. 1982. "Strategic Information Transmission," *Econometrica* 50: 1431-1451.

Delorme, C. and A. Snow. 1990. "On the Limits to Rent-seeking Waste," *Public Choice* 67: 129-154.

Denzau, A. and M. Munger. 1986. "Legislators and Interest Groups: How Unorganized Interests Get Represented," *American Political Science Review* 80: 89-106.

Drissen, E. and F. van Winden. 1991. "Social Security in a General Equilibrium Model with Endogenous Government Behavior," *Journal of Population Economics* 4: 89-110.

Drissen, E. and F. van Winden. 1992. "A General Equilibrium Model with Endogenous Government Behavior," in *Political Economy; Institutions, Competition, and Representation*, W. Barnett, M. Hinich, and N. Schofield, eds. Cambridge: Cambridge University Press.

Edelman, S. 1992. "Two Politicians, A PAC, and How They Interact: Two Extensive Form Games," *Economics and Politics* 4: 289-305.

Elster, J. 1986. "Further Thoughts on Marxism, Functionalism, and Game Theory," in *Analytical Marxism*, J. Roemer, ed. Cambridge: Cambridge University Press.

Feenstra, R. and J. Bhagwati. 1982. "Tariff-seeking and the Efficient Tariff," in *Import Competition and Response*, J. Bhagwati, ed. Chicago: University of Chicago Press.

Farrell, J. and R. Gibbons. 1985. "Cheap Talk with Two Audiences," *American Economic Review* 79: 1214-1223.

Findlay, R. and S. Wellisz. 1983. "Some Aspects of the Political Economy of Trade Restrictions," *Kyklos* 36: 469-481.

Fisher, R. 1992. "Endogenous Probability of Protection and Firm Behavior," *Journal of International Economics* 32: 149-163.

Gardner, R. 1981. "Wealth and Power in a Collegial Polity," *Journal of Economic Theory* 25: 353-366.

Harsanyi, J. 1977. *Rational Behavior and Bargaining in Games and Social Situations*. Cambridge: Cambridge University Press.

Hillman, A. and E. Katz. 1984. "Risk-averse Rent-seekers and the Social Cost of Monopoly Power," *Economic Journal* 94: 104-110.

Hillman, A. and E. Katz. 1987. "Hierarchical Structure and the Social Costs of Bribes and Transfers," *Journal of Public Economics* 34: 129-142.

Hillman, A. and H. Ursprung. 1988. "Domestic Politics, Foreign Interests, and International Trade Policy," *American Economic Review* 78: 729-745.

Johansen, L. 1979. "The Bargaining Society and the Inefficiency of Bargaining," *Kyklos* 32: 497-522.

Kambhu, J. 1988. "Unilateral Disclosure of Information by a Regulated Firm," *Journal of Economic Behavior and Organization* 10: 57-82.

Kau, J., D. Keenan, and P. Rubin. 1982. "A General Equilibrium Model of Congressional Voting," *Quarterly Journal of Economics* 97: 271-293.

Kau, J. and P. Rubin. 1979. "Public Interest Lobbies: Membership and Influence," *Public Choice* 34: 45-54.

Kolman, K. 1992. "What Do We Know?: Review of Rational Choice Models of Interest Groups," Typescript: Northwestern University.

Kreps, D. and R. Wilson. 1982b. "Reputation and Imperfect Information," *Journal of Economic Theory* 267: 253-279.

Laffont, J. and J. Tirole. 1991. "The Politics of Government Decisionmaking: A Theory of Regulatory Capture," *Quarterly Journal of Economics* 106: 1089-1127.

Levy, D. 1989. "Equilibrium Employment of Inputs by a Rent-seeking Firm," *Public Choice* 60: 177-184.

Lindbeck, A. and J. Weibull. 1987. "Balanced Budget Redistribution as the Outcome of Political Competition," *Public Choice* 52: 273-297.
Lohmann, S. 1993. "A Welfare Analysis of Political Action," in *Political Economy: Institutions, Competition, and Representation, op. cit.*
Magee, S. and W. Brock. 1983. "A Model of Politics, Tariffs, and Rent-seeking in General Equilibrium," in *Human Resources, Employment and Development*, Vol. 3, B. Weisbrod and H. Hughes, eds. New York: St. Martin's Press.
Michaels, R. 1989. "Conjectural Variations and the Nature of Equilibrium in Rent-seeking Models," *Public Choice* 60: 31-39.
Milgrom, P. 1981. "Good News and Bad News: Representation Theorems and Applications," *Bell Journal of Economics* 12: 380-391.
Milgrom, P. and J. Roberts. 1986. "Relying on the Information of Interested Parties," *Rand Journal of Economics* 17: 18-32.
Mitchell, W. and M. Munger. 1991. "Economic Models of Interest Groups: An Introductory Survey," *American Journal of Political Science* 35: 512-546.
Mitra, P. 1989. "Tax-price Reform with Directly Unproductive Profit-seeking (DUP) Activities," *Economics and Politics* 1: 207-224.
Morton, R. and C. Cameron. 1992. "Elections and the Theory of Campaign Contributions: A Survey and Critical Analysis," *Economics and Politics* 4: 79-108.
Mueller, D. and P. Murrel. 1986. "Interest Groups and the Size of Government," *Public Choice* 48: 125-145.
Mueller, D. 1989. *Public Choice II.* Cambridge: Cambridge University Press.
Owen, G. 1982. *Game Theory*, 2nd edition. Orlando: Academic Press.
Peck, R. 1986. "Power and Linear Income Taxes: An Example," *Econometrica* 54: 87-94.
Petrakis, E. 1990. "Voting for Taxes: Introduction of Government," Typescript: UCLA.
Pincus, J. 1975. "Pressure Groups and the Pattern of Tariffs," *Journal of Political Economy* 83: 757-778.
Plotnick, R. 1986. "An Interest Group Model of Direct Income Redistribution," *Review of Economics and Statistics* 68: 594-602.
Poole, K. and T. Romer. 1985. "Patterns of Political Action Committee Contributions to the 1980 Campaigns for the United States House of Representatives," *Public Choice* 47: 63-112.
Potters, J. 1992. *Lobbying and Pressure: Theory and Experiments.* Typescript: University of Amsterdam.
Potters, J. and F. van Winden. 1990. "Modelling Political Pressure as Transmission of Information," *European Journal of Political Economy* 6: 61-88.
Potters, J. and F. van Winden. 1992a. "Lobbying and Asymmetric Information," *Public Choice* 74: 269-292.
Potters, J. and F. van Winden. 1992b. "An Experimental Study of Lobbying." Typescript: University of Amsterdam.
Przeworski, A. and M. Wallerstein. 1988. "Structural Dependence of the State on Capital," *American Political Science Review* 82: 11-29.
Renaud, P. and F. van Winden. 1988. "Fiscal Behaviour and the Growth of

Government in the Netherlands," in *Explaining the Growth of Government*, J. Lybeck and M. Henrekson, eds. Amsterdam: North Holland.

Rodrik, D. 1986. "Tariffs, Subsidies and Welfare with Endogenous Policy," *Journal of International Economics* 21: 285-299.

Rogerson, W. 1982. "The Social Costs of Monopoly and Regulation: A Game-Theoretic Analysis," *Bell Journal of Economics and Management Science* 13: 391-401.

Salamon, L. and J. Siegfried. 1977. "Economic Power and Political Influence: The Impact of Industry Structure on Public Policy," *American Political Science Review* 71: 1026-1043.

Schlozman, K. and J. Tierney. 1986. *Organized Interests in American Democracy.* New York: Harper and Row.

Shapley, L. 1988. "Utility Comparison and the Theory of Games," in *The Shapley Value*, A. Roth, ed. Cambridge: Cambridge University Press. Originally published in *La Decision*, 1969.

Sobel, J. 1985. "A Theory of Credibility," *Review of Economic Studies* 52: 557-573.

Svenjar, J. 1986. "Bargaining Theory, Fear for Disagreement, and Wage Settlements: Theory and Evidence for the U.S. Industry," *Econometrica* 54: 1055-1078.

Tollison, R. 1982. "Rent-seeking: A Survey," *Kyklos* 35: 575-602.

Tullock, G. 1980. "Efficient Rent-seeking," in *Towards a Theory of the Rent-seeking Society*, J. Buchanan, R. Tollison, and G. Tullock, eds. College Station: Texas A and M University Press.

Tullock, G. 1989. *The Economics of Special Privilege and Rent-seeking.* Boston: Kluwer.

Ursprung, H. 1990. "Public Goods, Rent Dissipation, and Candidate Competition," *Economics and Politics* 2: 115-132.

van Velthoven, B. 1989. *The Endogenization of Government Behaviour in Macroeconomic Models.* Berlin: Springer-Verlag.

van Velthoven, B. and F. van Winden. 1985. "Towards a Politico-Economic Theory of Social Security," *European Economic Review* 27: 263-289.

van Velthoven, B. and F. van Winden. 1986. "Social Classes and State Behaviour," *Journal of Institutional and Theoretical Economics* 142: 542-570.

van Winden, F. 1983. *On the Interaction between State and Private Sector.* Amsterdam: North Holland.

van Winden, F. 1988. "The Economic Theory of Political Decision-making," in *Public Choice*, van den Broeck, ed. Boston: Kluwer.

Welch, W. 1980. "The Allocation of Political Monies: Economic Interest Groups," *Public Choice* 35: 97-120.

Wellisz, S. and J. Wilson. 1986. "Lobbying and Tariff Formation: A Dead Weight Loss Consideration," *Journal of International Economics* 20: 367-375.

Wilson, J. 1990. "Are Efficiency Improvements in Government Transfer Policies Self-defeating in Political Equilibrium?" *Economics and Politics* 2: 241-258.

Wong, K. Y. 1989. "Optimal Threat of Trade Restriction and *quid pro quo* Foreign Investment," *Economics and Politics* 1: 277-300.

Zusman, P. 1976. "The Incorporation and Measurement of Social Power in Economic Models," *International Economic Review* 17: 447-462.

17. Partisan Electoral Cycles and Monetary Policy Games

Rebecca B. Morton[1]

17.1 Introduction

A current trend in the literature of macroeconomic theory is to incorporate an explicitly modeled political sector in order to positively explain policies and outcomes. In particular, the influence of majority rule elections on macroeconomic conditions and the possibility of politically induced business or budget cycles are examined. Elections and macroeconomic policies have been modeled in one of two ways:[2] either as a relationship that is (1) opportunistic: incumbents create cycles in order to increase the probability of reelection; or (2) partisan: candidates have policy preferences and voters are unable to anticipate fully the policy of the candidate to be elected.[3] The seminal work on the partisan model is contained in Hibbs (1977, 1987) and the papers of Alesina, with and without various coauthors.[4] Hibbs' early work, termed 'Partisan Theory' (*PT*) assumed a long run trade-off between unemployment and inflation, *i.e.*, a stable Phillips curve. The new approach used by Alesina, *et al.* assumes instead (like macroeconomic thought after the rational expectations revolution) that agents form expectations rationally and that the long run rate of growth of output is unaffected by inflation.

Electorally induced policy cycles raise concerns about the discretion permitted elected officials in implementing macroeconomic policies, and so about the design implicit in democratic governments. If elections lead to an increased variability in business cycles that is not fully understood or eventually wanted

---

[1] Thanks are due to Betty Daniel, Tom Husted, Larry Kenny, Bob Reed, John van Huyck, Franz van Winden, and Chris Waller for many helpful discussions of the issues presented in this chapter.

[2] The literature on the interaction between politics and macroeconomics is larger than the specific papers reviewed in this paper. The interested reader should also consult van Winden (1983) and van Winden, Schram, and Groot (1987) for a complex model in which the economy and political sector are modeled in detail with agents who assume distinct roles in the economy. Schneider and Frey (1988) and Frey (1978, 1983) also develop a detailed model with partisan politics affecting economic outcomes. See Renaud and van Winden (1987) for an empirical test of the Frey and Schneider model on the Netherlands. See also the work of Borooah and van der Ploeg (1983).

[3] Examples of the opportunistic approach can be found in Nordhaus (1975), Persson and Tabellini (1990), Rogoff (1990), and Rogoff and Sibert (1988). In Boylan, Ledyard, and McKelvey (1991) political business cycles are shown to be possible in a neoclassical growth model when candidates commit to given policies for multiple periods.

[4] Alesina (1987, 1988a, 1988b, 1989), Alesina, Cohen, and Roubini (1991), Alesina, Londregan, and Rosenthal (1991), Alesina and Rosenthal (1989), Alesina and Roubini (1990), and Alesina and Sachs (1988). Havrilesky (1987) and Hess (1991) also present partisan political business cycle models.

by voters, then perhaps political institutions should be altered. The likelihood, the severity, and the cause of electorally induced cycles may indicate whether change is needed. Because of the limited degrees of freedom in the data, however, clear empirical evidence of partisan cycles has not been found. Since presidential elections take place only every four years, testing the model on the U.S. economy requires analysts to look at long time spans during which fiscal policies and monetary control systems change significantly. For example, Alesina, Londregan, and Rosenthal (1991) use data from 1915 to 1988. Or cross-sectional tests of Rational Partisan Theory (RPT) require the use of data from countries with vastly different political institutional structures. The debate over the role of elections in macro-economic policy outcomes, then, has depended substantially upon the strength of the theoretical foundations used in the models. Hence, models of politically induced business cycles need to be carefully examined for the reasonableness of the microfoundations of the assumptions and for consistency in the analysis of human behavior.

Building a model that combines a political and economic sector in the context of rational choice is complicated. It requires incorporating two literatures with disparate aims and focuses: macroeconomic theory and formal political modeling. Unfortunately, RPT fails to provide a satisfactory combination. In this paper shortcomings, including: (1) the applicability of the macroeconomic model (Section 17.2), (2) the reasonableness of assuming partisan differences (Section 17.3), and (3) the relevance of the assumptions about the electoral game (Section 17.4) are analyzed. In Section 17.5 the analysis is summarized and its implications for the utility of RPT results as the basis for designing political institutions are discussed.

17.1.1 The Macroeconomic Foundations of Rational Partisan Theory

The Macroeconomic Model. The RPT model is based upon Fischer (1977) and assumes that labor contracts are made for one period in advance, with the goal of setting the rate of growth in the nominal wage such that the real wage is kept constant (or growing at a rate equal to an exogenously given rate of productivity growth):

$$w_t = \pi_t^e \tag{1}$$

where w_t is the rate of growth in the nominal wage in period t and π_t^e is the expected rate of inflation in period t, given information available at period $t-1$. Assuming no physical capital, the rate of growth of output in the economy at period t, y_t, is then a function of the "natural" rate of growth of output y^n, and unexpected inflation, : $\pi_t - \pi_t^e$:

$$y_t = y^n + \gamma(\pi_t - \pi_t^e) \tag{2}$$

where y^n is nonnegative and γ is a positive constant. In Alesina, Londregan, and Rosenthal (1991), some persistence is allowed in the growth of output.

Monetary business cycles can occur in the fixed nominal wage contract model when unexpected monetary shocks cause unexpected inflation and deflation. In the cycle, as unexpected inflation (deflation) occurs, real wages fall (rise), increasing (decreasing) employment and output growth. However, the assumption in the model is that the rate of growth of output is not affected by changes in inflation in the long run, or that output will increase (decrease) only temporarily, returning to the long run rate of growth.

The fixed nominal wage contract story of business cycles has been criticized on several different grounds. Barro (1977) noted that the labor contracts are incompletely specified, since the quantity of labor supplied is not discussed. Obvious mutual advantages to trade are overlooked in these contracts as a consequence. Moreover, it is not clear why contracts are stated in nominal rather than real terms. Unfortunately these issues remain unresolved; Hall and Lazear (1984) and Azariadis and Stiglitz (1991) have considered incompleteness of the contracts, while only un-formalized "stories" exist concerning the non-indexation of contracts.[5] Whatever the reason for the fixed nominal contracts it cannot be minimization of the variance in the real wage, since indexation would be more effective than even optimal discretionary monetary policy in an unindexed world, as pointed out by Fischer (1977).

While the microfoundations of the wage contracts are uncertain, the defense offered by Fischer (1986) for assuming their existence in a macroeconomic model is somewhat persuasive: "This characterization is based on a reading of actual labor contracts, which do specify wage rates, typically with an overtime schedule, but do not specify the amounts of labor to be supplied. The labor contracts are extremely detailed, and it is simply not plausible that there is an implicit contract that determines the labor input in each state of nature. It is a fact that the firm determines the input of labor."

Can the Reasons for Existence of the Contracts be Ignored in RPT? The nominal wage contracting story results in partisan political business cycles in the following manner: Nominal wages are fixed prior to elections. Voters make systematic errors in the expected inflation rate, since, in *RPT* the inflation preferences of parties are fixed and divergent and the outcome of elections is uncertain. The electoral game assumed between parties is "one-shot" and hence, since re-election is not a consideration, parties always enact their ideal points. Given party preference differences then, under the liberal party (in the U.S. the Democrats), the inflation rate will be higher than under the conservative (Republican) party.

The errors of the voters are such that when the Democrats win, inflation is greater than expected and when the Republicans win, inflation is less than expected. Note that even if the Democrats succeed themselves in office, inflation will still be greater than expected. When Democrats (Republicans) win, unexpected inflation (deflation) occurs and output grows at a higher (lower) rate, returning to the long run rate of growth after nominal wage contracts are adjusted. If Republicans win, output grows at a rate below the natural rate

---

[5] See Fischer (1986) for a discussion.

and a recession results, while if Democrats win a boom is caused. The model predicts that the recession or boom will be short-lived, however, with output adjusting in the second period. In two papers by Alesina,[6] the relationship between a popularly elected president and an independently elected legislative branch that faces reelection more often than the president is incorporated in *RPT*. In these papers, voters use the legislative branch to "balance out" or "moderate" unexpected presidential election results.

However, using Fischer's macroeconomic model in *RPT* leaves unanswered a major theoretical question: why don't rational workers (or firms) demand contingent contracts to avoid unexpected inflation or deflation? When this issue is raised, Alesina, *et al.* generally observe that neither do contingent contracts occur in reality (presumably because they are too costly), nor is it the purpose of the model to explain this empirical regularity.[7] This is basically the same defense used by Fischer in his work. The issue cannot be so easily dismissed in *RPT*, however, and suggests a deeper problem with applying the (1977) Fischer model to endogenous government decision making.

Fischer (1977) considers two types of contracting models: (1) fixed nominal wage contracts set for one period only; and (2) overlapping fixed nominal wage contracts set for two periods each. In each model, output and the money supply in period t are subject to disturbances, μ_t and ν_t, respectively. Each disturbance is first-order autoregressive and affected linearly by mutually and serially uncorrelated stochastic terms with zero expected values and finite variances, ε_t and η_t, respectively.

In the first model (assumed in the applications of *RPT*), Fischer demonstrates the standard result of Lucas (1972) and Sargent and Wallace (1975): With rational expectations, if the money supply rule is known to economic agents (in *RPT*, nominal labor contracts are made for only one period at a time), then both economic agents and the monetary authority have the same information, and monetary policy can be effective only by doing the unexpected. Essentially, with a known money supply rule, and assuming money is neutral, output in period t will be a function of the period's current shocks.

The primary contribution of Fischer's paper is his second model in which workers sign nominal wage contracts for two periods at a time in an overlapping system. For a given period t, "...half the firms are operating in the first year of a labor contract drawn up at the end of $(t-1)$ and the other half in the second year of a contract drawn up at the end of $(t-2)$. There is only a single price of output." Fischer shows that in this context, a *known* money supply rule can have real effects on output in period t because the monetary authority is able to react to the shocks which occur in period $(t-1)$. Nominal wage contracts drawn up at the end of period $(t-2)$ will not be able to account for both the shock and the monetary adjustment. As Fischer notes: "...between the time the two-year contract is drawn up and the last year of operation of that contract, there is time for the monetary authority to react to new information about recent economic disturbances. Given the negotiated second-

---

[6] See Alesina, Londregan, and Rosenthal (1991) and Alesina and Rosenthal (1989).
[7] See for example Alesina 1989, p. 92 and Alesina 1988a, pp. 60-61.

period nominal wage, the way the monetary authority reacts to disturbances will affect the real wage for the second period of the contract and thus output."

In the Fischer models the concern is whether monetary policy can be used to *stabilize* the economy. His argument is that if nominal wage contracts exist for a long enough time, then unexpected price shocks to the economy can be destabilizing and monetary policy can be used, once the nature of the shock is revealed, to counteract price changes. In the Fischer model: (1) economic agents are not able to sign contingent contracts to prevent destabilizing price shocks because the shocks are neither predictable nor systematic; and (2) economic agents have no desire to sign electorally contingent contracts because the government uses policy to minimize business cycles, stabilize output. In fact, Fischer explicitly pointed out in his article that: "...the stabilization is achieved by affecting the real wage of those in the second year of labor contracts and thus should not be expected to be available to attain arbitrary levels of output—the use of too active a policy would lead to a change in the structure of contracts." In conclusion Fischer argued further against the likelihood of successful *manipulative* monetary policy: "An attempt by the monetary authority to exploit the existing structure of contracts to produce behavior far different from that envisaged when contracts were signed would likely lead to the reopening of the contracts and, if the new behavior of the monetary authority were persisted in, a new structure of contracts."

Monetary policy in Fischer is postulated as "helping" the nominal wage contracts work as designed, not as systematically manipulating workers and firms from their preferred equilibrium, as in *RPT*. In Fischer, rational economic agents accept non-electorally contingent nominal wage contracts, while in *RPT* they may not. Explaining the existence of rational non-electorally contingent contracts is crucial to justifying "Rational Partisan Theory". The reason why the "contracts exist defense" is acceptable in Fischer and unacceptable in *RPT* is that the two models differ in purpose. Fischer's work is "normative"; he is concerned with whether monetary policy can effectively reduce business cycles in a nominal wage contract world. The reasons for the existence of such contracts are unimportant to the questions he raises. In contrast, *RPT* is "positive" and seeks to explain partisan political business cycles as a phenomenon of rational behavior over many years. Arguing that electorally contingent contracts include aspects of reality outside the scope of models of political business cycles ignores the full implications of the rationality assumption in *RPT*.

An obvious explanation for non-electorally contingent nominal wage contracts missing in Alesina, *et al.*, is available. If the partisan cycles induced are preferred for some reason by workers and firm owners, non-electorally contingent nominal wage contracts make sense. Unlike the standard assumption, workers and firms may not be trying simply to minimize the variance in the real wage. Normally, and according to the hypothesis of Hibbs (1977, 1987), we think of Democrats representing workers, who supposedly benefit from high output growth and high inflation (under such conditions the relative share of income of lower classes is thought to increase) and Republicans as representing firm owners, who are postulated to prefer the opposite (when the relative share of income of higher classes is believed to increase). If non-electorally contingent nominal wage contracts were to work, one would anticipate the expected benefits to Democratic supporters from an economic boom to be at least as great as the expected costs of a Republican caused recession; the converse assumption is made for Republican supporters.

What sort of redistribution occurs in the monetarily induced business cycle of *RPT*? It is fairly obvious that in the partisan caused boom, real wages fall. Although employment rises temporarily, it is not clear that any significant rise in the relative share of income received by labor occurs. The direction of change will depend upon the elasticity of labor demand, the more inelastic the demand for labor is, the less likely an increase in their share of income will result. (Recall that workers are "off" the labor supply curve when unexpected inflation or deflation occurs.) In a recession, general real wages rise, implying higher costs of labor for firm owners. Employment should decline, but it is questionable that the decrease in employment falls enough for firm owners to benefit from a recession. *RPT*, then, does not appear to explain the redistribution observed in business cycles. In fact, empirical studies of general real wages suggest that they are slightly pro-cyclical, rising (falling) a little in booms (recessions).[8] In conclusion, the monetary cycles induced by partisan political activity in *RPT* requires non-rational behavior on the part of the economic agents and cannot predict actual general real wage movements in business cycles.

It is possible to create a rational partisan theory that has non-electorally induced cycles, *i.e.*, *reactive*, partisan cycles, that simulate the way in which governments react to unexpected shocks. In Husted, Morton, and Waller (1992) a variant of *RPT*, a *Two-Sector Rational Partisan Theory* (*2SRPT*) is presented in which the parties are assumed to differ in their *responses* to unanticipated shocks, causing partisan cycles in macroeconomic policy. The two sectors of *2SRPT* are either classical or non-classical. In the classical sector real wages are fully flexible and the labor market always clears; in the non-classical sector fixed nominal wage contracts are made instead, as is assumed in *RPT*. An unanticipated shock is expected to cause greater variation in output in the non-classical sector than in the classical sector. Thus, the party representing the non-classical sector will prefer a more active *responsive*, macroeconomic policy than the party representing the classical sector, even assuming that preferences over the preferred level of variation in output is identical across sectors. In the spirit of Fischer's second model, partisan cycles are not electorally induced; rather differences are assumed to result from partisan reactions to unexpected shocks. Moreover, *2SRPT* fits the empirical evidence on real wage movements during cycles better than *RPT*; that is, in contrast to the general real wage movements discussed above, real wages in the unionized sector are countercyclical.[9]

---

[8] See for example Keane, Moffit, and Runkle (1988).
[9] See Raisian (1979) and (1983).

17.2 Party Preferences

The Macroeconomic Inflation/Output Loss Function. RPT adapts an often used macroeconomic unemployment and inflation cost function for policymakers to a two party case (Barro and Gordon 1983). Party j wishes to minimize a macroeconomic "loss" function, $L^j = L^j(\pi, y)$. The loss function is assumed to take the following particular form:

$$L^j = \frac{1}{2} \sum_{\text{all } t} \beta^t \left[(\pi_t - \pi^j)^2 + b^j (y_t - y^j)^2 \right]. \tag{3}$$

β^t is the discount factor for period t which does not vary across parties, π^j is party j's ideal inflation rate, b^j is the weight party j places on output deviations, and y^j is the ideal rate of growth of output for party j. Note that equation (3) could be rewritten purely in terms of inflation differences:

$$L^{j'} = \frac{1}{2} \sum_{\text{all } t} \beta^t \left[(\pi_t - \pi^j)^2 + b^{j'} (\pi_t - \pi^j - y^{j'})^2 \right] \tag{3'}$$

where $b^{j'} = b^j \gamma^2$ and $\gamma^{j'} = (\frac{1}{\gamma})[y^j - y^n]$.

Sometimes the function given in (3) or (3') is multiplied by a negative sign in front, and maximized.

In *RPT* the assumption is made that for the two parties, $j = D, R$, at least one of the inequalities listed below will hold strictly, such that the two parties have distinct preferences.

$$\pi^D \geq \pi^R \geq 0 \tag{4a}$$

$$b^D \geq b^R \geq 0 \tag{4b}$$

$$y^D \geq y^R \geq y^n \tag{4c}$$

is the utility or objective function that party j wishes to maximize (Alesina and Roubini 1990). Note that Alesina, *et al.*, use different variations of the function and various combinations of the strict inequalities in $(4a, b, c)$. Alesina and Rosenthal (1989) use (4a) only; and Alesina and Sachs (1988) use only (4b). In Alesina (1987) and Alesina, Londregan, and Rosenthal (1991) the sign on the second term is reversed and y^j is assumed equal to zero, as in (3'') below:

$$L^j = \left(\frac{1}{2}\right) \sum_{\text{all } t} \beta^t [(\pi_t - \pi^j)^2 - b^j y_t]. \tag{3''}$$

In the standard macroeconomic use of a function like (3), (3'), or (3'') all government policymakers are identical, that is, $y^D = y^R \geq y^n$, and $\pi^D = \pi^R \geq 0$. This type of function has been used by a number of researchers to analyze a game between economic agents and the policymakers in which the public desires to minimize being "fooled",[10] *i.e.* to minimize $(\pi_t - \pi_t^e)^2$.

In the monetary policy game, policymakers cannot commit to a given monetary policy rule, and there is an incentive to engage in surprise inflation or to deviate from a promised rule, since a surprise can raise the real rate of growth temporarily, and even a temporary increase will increase the utility of the policymakers. This is known as the time inconsistency problem. As a consequence, policymakers may use discretionary monetary policy even if they know that inflation is inefficiently high and that such a measure cannot change the long-run equilibrium rate of growth of real GNP.[11]

The standard rationale for the loss function without two party competition is multifold: (1) the first term reflects the desire to set an optimal rate of inflation for seigniorage; and (2) the second term reflects the fact that the natural rate of growth of output may be less than the desired government level. Alesina (1988) summarizes the various reasons that have been offered for the assumption that the government desired choice of output is greater than the natural rate: "The second term . . . can be justified by either of three non-mutually exclusive arguments. The first one is that various distortions in the labor market, such as taxation, minimum wage laws, *etc.*, generate an output growth without policy intervention...which is too low. Thus, the policymaker may want to increase growth, with a monetary shock. The second argument is that labor unions which maximize the welfare of employed union members (as opposed to social welfare) keep the real wage too high, so that the labor market clears with too much unemployment. The third argument is that the policymaker weighs heavily the welfare of the unemployed and has preferences 'inconsistent' with the market."[12] He also justifies the second (inflation) term of equation (3') as an inflation surprise that may be desired independently as a revenue raising device. "In addition, the policymaker may desire to reduce the real value of non-indexed government debt by means of unexpected inflation, particularly if it disregards the welfare of bond holders" (1988a).

In *RPT* voters are assumed to be aware of the time inconsistency problem and to anticipate that the inflation rate actually implemented will be different, for this reason, from the elected party's ideal point. Accordingly nominal wage contracts are adjusted for time inconsistencies. There are no information problems as discussed in Canzoneri (1985). Therefore, if a party is elected with certainty, there are no inflation surprises; however, inflation surprises may arise in *RPT* when partisan differences and electoral uncertainty do exist. Indeed partisan differences in preferences, as summarized in the set of inequalities $(4a, b, c)$, and electoral uncertainty and fixed nominal wage

---

[10] The possible equilibria in this game have been considered, for example in Barro and Gordon (1983), Backus and Driffill (1985), and Canzoneri (1985).

[11] See Auernheimer (1974), Barro and Gordon (1983), Calvo (1978), Canzoneri (1985), and Kydland and Prescott (1977). Calvo (1978) and Fischer (1980) demonstrate that the time inconsistency problem in monetary policy can arise if policymakers and the economic agents have the same preferences. Much of the recent literature examines the role of reputation, information, and repeated elections in mitigating the problem.

[12] Canzoneri (1985) uses the second justification and notes the existence of an argument similar to the third, while Barro and Gordon (1983a) use the first.

contracts are expected to result in partisan political business cycles. An examination of the microfoundations for the shape of the preference functions in (3), (3'), or (3") and the set of inequalities in (4a, b, c) is necessary to evaluate the reasonableness of RPT.

17.3 The Microfoundations of Party Differences in Inflation and Output Preferences

The microfoundations of each of the proffered justifications and the possibility of consistent partisan differences are analyzed below. I begin with the justification for the inflation terms in (3), (3)', and (3)" and inequality (4a) and then discuss the justifications for the output and growth rates of terms in (3), (3)', and (3)" and inequalities (4b, c).

17.3.1 The Optimal Seigniorage Argument

Inflation is a tax on holding real money balances. When the government inflates, it exchanges larger quantities of fiat money for more real resources. As with all commodity taxation, inflation is distortionary, since it reduces the demand for real money balances. Inflation also reduces the value of the real debt of the government.[13] In a second best world, in which non-distortionary taxes do not exist, an optimizing government will use expected inflation taxes in combination with other taxes to raise revenue, as discussed in Mankiw (1987). Thus, the assumption that an optimal rate of expected inflation for tax purposes may exist is reasonable.

For the inflation tax story to result in partisan political business cycles, as described in RPT, the two parties must differ in their preference for the inflation tax. Inequality (4a) implies that Democrats prefer greater rates of expected inflation for tax purposes than Republicans. Alesina, *et al.* usually justify this inequality by arguing that Democrats prefer a higher level of government spending and that the optimal tax literature implies that all tax rates should be increased as desired revenue increases, as discussed by Mankiw (1987).[14] Is this a reasonable story? What are the microfoundations?

In Mankiw (1987) it is assumed that the government is choosing a tax structure in order to minimize the present value of the social deadweight losses from taxation. Mankiw examines the optimal tax problem in the context of a *classical* model of the economy, in which monetary policy is purely neutral. He argues that the model could be interpreted "...as applying in the longer run in which the economy maintains output and employment at the natural rate." Formally, the government minimizes the following expression, subject to the budget constraint of raising a given level of revenue:

---

[13] See Grossman and van Huyck (1986) for an analysis of the revenue raising properties of inflation.

[14] See for example Alesina, 1988a, p. 21 and Alesina and Rosenthal, 1989, p. 377.

$$E_t \int_0^\infty e^{-\beta s} \left[f(\tau) + h(\pi) \right] Y_t ds \tag{5}$$

where $f(\tau)Y_t$ is the deadweight social loss induced by the tax on output, and $f(\tau)$ is assumed increasing in the tax rate, t, at an increasing rate. "$h(\pi)$" is the deadweight social cost of inflation; $h(\pi)$ is assumed to be increasing in inflation at an increasing rate. Y_t is the level of output in period t.[15] Analysis of the first order conditions demonstrates that the government will choose a mix of fiscal and monetary policy such that the marginal social cost of raising revenue through direct taxation is equated with the marginal social cost of raising revenue through seigniorage. That is:

$$h'(\pi_t) = f'(\tau_t).^{16} \tag{6}$$

Mankiw also notes that this result implies that an increase in the total level of government spending will increase the use of both tax instruments. This is the microfoundation of the RPT assumption that Democratic preference for higher government spending implies that Democrats prefer higher expected inflation rates.

How applicable is the Mankiw model to the analysis of partisan differences over expected inflation? In the Mankiw model, as in most of macroeconomic analysis, a representative individual, and a government that maximizes the welfare of this individual, are assumed implicitly. Presumably, the level of government spending is also chosen to maximize the representative individual's welfare. RPT assumes that heterogeneous preferences will be reflected in differences over the level of government spending and ignores redistributional partisan disputes.

The majority of current federal government expenditure in the United States is redistributive in nature.[17] Moreover, most of the rise in government expenditures in the post World War II era has been in redistributive expenditures. It is well known that the increase has been significant and has taken place during both Democratic and Republican administrations. The assumption in RPT that the partisan difference between Democrats and Republicans is a debate over the level of government spending appears to miss the real issue. That is, there are more significant partisan differences in the degree and direction of redistribution engaged in by the federal government. Havrilesky (1988) has made a similar point: "...pre-election promises and voter expectations regarding the unemployment and inflation goals of either party

---

[15] The reader is referred to Mankiw (1987) for more detail on the model. In the model the level of output is exogenous, the standard equation is used to describe the demand for money, and the government is allowed to issue debt.

[16] This formulation assumes that real balances do not adjust to the level of inflation. Mankiw shows that allowance for such an adjustment does not change the main conclusions.

[17] According to the Gwartney and Stroup (1990): Approximately 32% of the federal budget in 1988 was for cash income maintenance, 11.3% for helping people buy essentials, and 13.4% net interest, all of which can easily be classified as redistributive. It is more than likely many of the other expenditures could also be so considered.

are usually similar, but their redistributive programs differ immensely, at least in the United States. In contrast, pre-election promises, *e.g.*, Social Security, Medicare, agricultural subsidies, various tax preferences, *etc.*, are the meat of practically every presidential election campaign." Quinn and Shapiro (1991) present empirical evidence on partisan differences over redistribution via the tax system. They find that Republicans and Democrats do significantly disagree over the distribution of the tax burden, with Democrats increasing the tax burden on firms and their owners and Republicans engaging in the opposite behavior. It is generally accepted that Democrats prefer greater degrees of progressive redistribution, redistribution from the rich to the poor and middle class, than Republicans, and, as Havrilesky argues, the disagreement over redistributive issues fuels much of the debate over the level of government spending.

If Democrats prefer higher degrees of progressive redistribution, then it is not clear they will prefer a higher rate of expected inflation as a tax than Republicans. Inflation is, after all, generally believed to be a regressive tax; or it is well known that the income elasticity of money demand is less than 1 (Kenny 1991). If the income tax is non-indexed, then inflation also causes "bracket creep" which is more likely to affect those with lower incomes than higher ones, since the wealthy are often already in the highest brackets. Even the effect of inflation on non-indexed government bonds is at best likely to be borne primarily by the middle class; the wealthy have greater abilities to invest in real wealth or indexed debt. Many have noted that inflation can "tax" parts of the economy that might be able to avoid other forms of taxation; that is, economic agents engaged in explicit criminal activity or those who under-report their true income by requiring cash payments. Nevertheless, it could be argued that economic agents in the underground economy are more likely to be skewed toward the lower end of the income distribution. Thus, it appears likely that expected inflation is a regressive tax and that certainly, other taxes, such as the income tax, can be made more progressive than expected inflation.[18] The government objective function in (5) then is not applicable to distributional issues. When distributional issues are of concern, minimization of the simple sum of deadweight losses from taxation does not capture the partisan tax structure preference problem.

There are several ways we could modify the objective function in (5) to take account of redistributional issues. One simple way is to assume that the tax on output is progressive, while the tax on inflation is regressive. Total net progressive redistribution from taxation, $R(\tau, \pi)$, is determined as follows:

$$R(\tau, \pi) = [R^\tau(\tau) - R^\pi(\pi)] Y_t. \tag{7}$$

$R^\tau(\tau) U_t$ is the net income redistributed to the poor and middle class from the output tax; $R^\tau(\tau) Y_t$ is increasing in t at an increasing rate. $R^\pi(\pi) Y_t$ is the

---

[18] The empirical evidence on the distributional consequences of long term inflation suggests that there is some slight but insignificant evidence that inflation redistributes income from the rich to the poor. See Blinder and Esaki (1978), Hibbs (1987), and Peretz (1983). Blinder and Esaki (1978) note: "...the effects of inflation on the income distribution simply are much less important than those of unemployment."

net income redistributed to the rich from inflation; $R^\pi(\pi)$ is increasing in π at an increasing rate. Assume also that for each tax, the rate of increase in redistribution is always less than the rate of increase in deadweight losses such that the difference between the two is increasing. That is,

$$h'(\pi_t) > R^{\pi'}(\pi_t),\ f'(\tau_t) > R^{\pi'}(\tau_t),\ h''(\pi_\tau) > R^{\pi'}(\pi_t),$$

and
$$f''(\tau_t) > R^{\tau''}(\tau_t), \forall\, t.$$

If we assume that redistribution and deadweight losses from taxation enter into party preferences linearly and are equally weighted, then party D will wish to choose an output tax and inflation tax combination that minimizes the sum of deadweight losses and redistribution to the rich and the objective function for party D will be given by:

$$E_t \int_0^\infty e^{-\beta s}[f(\tau) + h(\pi) - [R^\tau(\tau) - R^\pi(\pi)]]Y_t ds. \qquad (8)$$

Now party D's optimal mix of fiscal and monetary policy must meet the following criteria:

$$h'(\pi_t) + R^{\pi'}(\pi_t) = f'(\tau_t) - R^{\tau'}(\tau_t). \qquad (9)$$

Clearly, in such a framework, the marginal social costs of the two taxes will not be equated if the taxes differ in redistributional considerations. As might be expected, the tax rate on output will be higher and the inflation rate will be lower than the optimal rates derived earlier for any level of government spending.

In contrast, we assume that party R wishes to choose an output tax and inflation tax combination that minimizes the sum of deadweight losses and redistribution to the poor and middle class; R's objective function is as follows:

$$E_t \int_0^\infty e^{\beta s}[f(\tau) + h(\pi) + R^\tau(\tau) - R^\pi(\pi)]Y_t ds. \qquad (10)$$

And the combination of fiscal and monetary policy chosen by party R will meet the criteria below:

$$h'(\pi_t) - R^{\pi'}(\pi_t) = f'(\tau_t) + R^{\tau'}(\tau_t). \qquad (11)$$

Party R, then, will prefer a rate of inflation higher and an output tax lower than the optimal rates without redistributional concerns for any given level of government spending. If government spending is held constant, and inflation is more regressive than the output tax, then party R prefers higher inflation rates than party D.

Suppose party D prefers a higher level of government spending? Minimization of deadweight and redistributional losses will, in this simple framework, result in an increase in both tax rates as the desired level of government spending is increased. By assumption an increase in the output tax rate will increase the RHS of equation (9), so an increase in the inflation rate, which will by assumption increase the LHS of equation (9), will be necessary. But it is not evident that Party D will necessarily prefer a higher inflation rate than party R. The closer the two parties agree about the level of government spending, the more likely it is that party D will prefer lower inflation rates. The parties would have to differ drastically over the level of government spending for party D to actually prefer a higher inflation rate. Casual empirical evidence suggests that large partisan differences in the level of government spending do not exist in the U.S. Hence, the assumption that differences in the level of government spending will imply that Democrats prefer a higher level of expected inflation than Republicans for tax purposes ignores the regressive nature of the inflation tax and the well known partisan differences between Democrats and Republicans over redistribution through the tax system. When such factors are incorporated, Democrats may actually prefer lower expected inflation rates for tax purposes than Republicans.

17.3.2 The Barro-Gordon Argument

Taxes, Unemployment Compensation, and Minimum Wage Laws Cause Too Low Output Growth. Under the Barro-Gordon scenario, the assumption is made that if income taxes and unemployment compensation were equal to zero and there were no minimum wage laws, then the natural rate of growth of output, y^n, would be equal to some y^*. Thus, when fiscal distortions exist, $y^n < y^*$, and the desired rate of unemployment, U^*, will equal kU^n, $k < 1$. Barro and Gordon (1983) point out: "Governmental decisions on taxes and transfers will generally influence the value of k. However, given that some government expenditures are to be carried out, it will generally be infeasible to select a fiscal policy that avoids all distortions and yields $k = 1$. We assume that the government's optimization on the fiscal side—which we do not analyze explicitly—results in a value of k that satisfies $0 < k < 1$. The choice of monetary policy is then carried out conditional on this value of k."

In a partisan model, will the desired level of output vary with the party in power (as represented by inequality 4c) and/or the preferences for growth vary with the party in power (as represented by inequality 4b)? The answer to this question requires at the minimum heterogeneous preferences for growth. Here traditional macroeconomic theory with representative consumers gives little guidance. In Barro-Gordon, since all economic agents are identical, no redistribution occurs in the business cycles that may result. Note that no business cycles actually occur since the rational representative agent realizes the time inconsistency problem faced by his or her elected representative. Output growth is "good" for everyone without disagreement, so the unsuccessful attempt to "fool" is what any representative consumer would want, given that no system of constraint on the discretion of policymakers exists.

Partisan differences in ideal output growth rates imply that output growth is not always preferred. For some agents in the economy temporary output surges are not desired as much. In RPT the assumption is generally made that for all j, $y^j > y^n$. It is important to note that it is implicitly assumed in *RPT* that y^n is unaffected by the party in power. This is implied in equation (2). What is necessary for y^n to be independent of party? In the Barro-Gordon assumption, y^n is less than desired because of fiscal policies. Therefore, it seems that a constant y^n across parties implies that there is fiscal policy agreement on income taxes, unemployment insurance, and the minimum wage that does not change with the party in power. Such postulated agreement is, of course, completely unrealistic. As noted in Subsection 17.3.1 Democrats and Republicans differ strongly over redistribution, and the tax rate combination approved by each party is unlikely to be the same.

An alternative assumption that could justify a constant natural rate of growth of output across parties is that while parties may advocate different tax structures, somehow the overall deadweight loss is unaffected. This is questionable if parties disagree over the level of government spending, an assumption made in *RPT* to justify inequality (4a), and if taxes differ in their effects on real variables and redistribution. Equation (2) implies then that either the fiscal policy structure is independent of party changes or that any partisan fiscal policy structure changes, including different levels of government spending, do not affect the deadweight losses from taxation.[19]

Given that the overall deadweight loss from taxation is unaffected by partisan differences, why then will parties differ in their preferences for additional growth? Since all are aware that any increase in growth will be temporary, a business cycle effect, then differences in preferences for growth in strict inequalities (4b, c) must reflect differences in preferences for the business cycle. Party D must prefer more of a "boom" than party R. As discussed above in the analysis of the application of the Fischer model to *RPT* in general, it is questionable that the Democratic party, which is typically assumed to represent workers, would prefer a monetary induced boom, as occurs in *RPT*, or that the Republican party, which is typically assumed to represent firm owners, would prefer less output growth than Democrats. In the monetary induced boom, workers move *off* their supply curve and supply more labor than they find optimal at the real wage, while firms are still *on* their demand curve for labor. Why would workers have a greater preference than firms for what is, from the workers' perspective, a non-optimal move? No explanation is offered in *RPT*, with or without microfoundations.

17.3.3 The Canzoneri Argument

Labor Unions Keep Real Wages Too High Resulting in Too Low Growth. In Canzoneri (1985) the justification for $k < 1$ (in Barro-Gordon notation) is that labor is supplied only by union members, but that the policymaker wishes to maximize a social utility function that gives weight to the welfare of

---

[19] In contrast, Havrilesky's (1987) partisan political business cycle model assumes that when a party is in power it taxes only the members of the other party. The party in power engages in monetary surprises to increase tax revenue by increasing output. The "surprise" has less deadweight loss attached since it is assumed to be unanticipated. Havrilesky's model ignores the likelihood that in a repeated game such monetary surprises may become anticipated by both parties and voters.

all workers, including the unemployed. In this case, the assumption that y^n is unaffected by the party in office is more reasonable. That is, it is straightforward to show that a "profit maximizing" union supplying labor to perfectly competitive purchasers (firms) will choose a labor supply such that less labor is supplied than without the union. And the existence of such a union could, perhaps, be assumed to be independent of the party in power.

In the single party story, the government desires a greater output level than the level that results endogenously, because it cares about both the unemployed and employed. The implied assumption is that unemployed workers do not receive their proportionate share of union "profits" and desire an output level greater than the union recommends. "The labor supply curve includes only union members, and wage setters' behavior systematically excludes other workers. By contrast, the social utility function includes all workers."[20] Presumably, then either the functional form of the second terms of (3) or (3″) can be postulated to represent the government's preference for higher than normally achieved real growth.

What about the partisan differences assumed in $(4b, c)$ in the labor union story? One possibility does suggest itself as an explanation of worker support of a boom: If the unionized workers perceive that it is desirable to distribute "profits" to the unemployed to maintain union control over the labor market and are prohibited from distributing the optimal amount, then a boom may be useful as a mechanism for providing these benefits.[21] Assume for example that Democrats represent all workers, who are organized in a labor union and who choose a nominal wage to maximize the expected net returns to labor, given the expected price level. Postulate further that the union is unable to fully distribute its profits among those members employed and unemployed. Then the union cartel is "unstable". Unemployed workers would prefer an increase in employment at a lower real wage. Union workers may be willing to suffer the temporary decrease in net return in order to maintain the union's support from all workers.

Can this story also explain Republican preference for a lower rate of growth? If firm owners wish to break union monopolization and are represented by Republicans, then they would be against the use of a boom to help unions with the distributional problem. They may prefer growth to some extent because of the increase in profits that might result, yet not as much as the workers. While the union distributional story may be appealing, it is basically *ad hoc* and its power to explain Democratic and Republican preferences crucially depends on large union control over nominal wage contracts and unspecified costs that prevent redistribution from employed workers to the unemployed. Such a story, or any like it, is not discussed in *RPT*.

17.3.4 The Biased Policymaker Story

The Natural Rate of Growth of Output is Misperceived or The Policymaker

---

[20] Canzoneri (1985, p. 1580).
[21] This was suggested by Bob Reed.

Does Not Represent the Representative Agent. The misperceiving policymaker story has the least justification. According to the hypothesis, as stated by Canzoneri, y^n is equal to the ideal level, but policymakers irrationally either underestimate the natural rate of unemployment or overestimate the evils of inflation. Applied to the partisan model, the irrationality explanation is such that Democrats always err in the first direction and Republicans in the second. Since the story assumes at the outset irrational behavior it cannot be reasonably used in a theory with the word "rational" as part of its title. The second version, which Alesina seems to refer to in the quote above, is the story of the biased policymaker, who assigns weights to members of the economy disproportionate to their weight in the economy's social welfare function. Therefore, Democrats prefer higher rates of output growth because they assign greater weight to the unemployed than Republicans. This rationale clearly cannot stand on its own. It is well known that Democrats and other leftist parties usually receive strong support from organized labor. The rationale needs further justification, perhaps along the lines outlined in Subsection 17.2.3 above, to explain party differences. Hence it cannot serve as an independent explanation of the preference differences.

The Surprise Inflation Tax Story and the Objective Function (3'). Suppose we assume that parties do not differ in their preferences for output growth, or believe that an increase in output growth is desirable. Even in this case inflationary "surprises" may be plausible as a method of increasing government revenue. An inflation "surprise" is a "better" tax than expected inflation, just as any "surprise" tax on economic activity is "better" than an anticipated tax. That is, surprise taxes allow government to raise revenue without distorting current, pre-surprise initiated economic actions. By using surprise inflation the government can increase revenue without influencing the current demand for real money balances. Moreover, the government can reduce the real value of its outstanding non-indexed debt through "surprise" inflation. Thus the government can tax without reducing output. Surprise inflation, then, may be desirable regardless of output effects. The functional form used in (3') best captures this story.

For the surprise inflation tax story to result in partisan political business cycles as described in *RPT*, it is required that the two parties differ in their preference for the surprise inflation tax. Inequality (4c) implies that Democrats prefer greater inflation tax surprises than Republicans and inequality (4b) implies that Democrats have a greater preference for inflation tax surprises than Republicans. Alesina, *et al.* usually justify these inequalities by the same argument used to justify (4a): Democrats prefer a higher level of government spending, and optimal tax literature implies that all tax rates should be increased as desired revenue increases. Yet, as argued above there is evidence to suggest that inflation is a regressive tax. Hence, Democrats may be less likely to prefer higher inflation rates for tax purposes than Republicans, if a less regressive tax is available.

As noted, any "surprise" tax can raise revenue without affecting economic activity. Thus, if Democrats have some other tax that can be used as a "surprise," and it is less regressive than inflation, one would expect that Democrats would use the alternative less regressive surprise tax rather than inflation. Conversely for Republicans. Therefore, for the surprise inflation tax story to justify assumptions (4b,c), then Democrats must prefer a significantly larger level of government spending than Republicans or the Democrats prefer only a little more government spending and no other less regressive tax can be used as a surprise by the government. Otherwise, one would expect that Republicans would engage in more surprise inflation for tax purposes than Democrats.

17.4 The Electoral Game in *RPT*

Party Myopia. In most versions of the *RPT* model it is assumed that parties behave as if the electoral game is one shot, not repeated. There are good reasons for this assumption; in particular, a repeated game of the complexity analyzed in the full *RPT* model discussed above is difficult to solve. Therefore, the assumption is made "...that the policymakers' horizon coincides with their term of office; thus the infinite horizon game is divided into a series of two period games" (Alesina 1988a). Since elections take place every other period, the assumption essentially is that at each election a new set of two parties with fixed preferences compete over the outcome. Even in Alesina, Londregan, and Rosenthal (1991) and Alesina and Rosenthal (1990), in which Congressional elections take place every period, the game is seen as "ending" with the end of the President's term after the second period.

The one shot nature of the game is crucial to the explanation of partisan induced business cycles in *RPT*. Because the game ends with the second period, the optimal policy for the party in power is to choose the party's ideal time consistent inflation rate. This rate is greater than π^j for party j for the reasons discussed in the literature on monetary policy games. Thus, parties do not converge; the expected positions of the two parties are distinct. If the two parties converged in positions, then no cycles would result in *RPT*.

Clearly the one shot game is unrealistic, particularly for analyzing political economic behavior over a period of many years. Moreover, versions of the *RPT* model that do allow for repeated interaction find that convergence of policy positions and smoothing of any partisan caused cycles is likely. For example in Alesina (1988b) such interaction is examined. He shows that repeated interaction of political parties can diminish the amplitude of policy oscillations. In Alesina (1987) it is argued that reputational mechanisms can be used by parties to reduce fluctuations. And in Alesina and Spear (1988) the authors show that if a party is modelled as a sequence of overlapping generations of politicians with finite lives with a transfer scheme in which the future generation of policymakers compensates the current generation of policymakers for not diverging from the optimal long term policy positions, convergence is probable. Thus, the one shot nature of the *RPT* game overstates the likelihood of partisan induced business cycles.

The *RPT* model also postulates that no third parties emerge and that the preferences of the parties are constant over time. While perhaps empirically relevant for the United States, clearly an advantage exists for a third party, particularly a party that is not constrained by policy preferences. An accepted rational choice explanation for the persistent divergence of party positions in the U.S. and the stability of the two party system is still unavailable. Although it is less than completely satisfactory, the "this is part of reality" defense of this assumption in *RPT* is hard to criticize. Yet it is a crucial assumption for *RPT*. Without divergent policy preferences, no partisan political business cycle will result. As a consequence, if we are to continue to model the electoral competition as a game between parties with fixed and divergent platforms, some rational explanation needs to be developed as a microfoundation for this assumption. This, I believe, is the next step in such research.[22]

Voter Uncertainty. In most versions of the *RPT* model, voters are not explicitly modeled; parties simply maximize a probability of winning function that depends on the positions of the parties such that no party wins the election with complete certainty. (See for example, Alesina 1987, 1988a and Alesina and Sachs 1988). In Alesina, Londregan, and Rosenthal (1991) and Alesina and Rosenthal (1989) voters are included in the model. As noted earlier, partisan political business cycles do not result in *RPT* unless there is electoral uncertainty. Therefore, if the model includes fully informed and rational voters, then there will be no uncertainty in the electoral outcome unless the party positions are *a priori* distributed such that the two parties offer equivalent utility to the median voter. At this point, then, the assumption of full information used throughout *RPT* must be dropped. *RPT* does assume that there exist random influences on voter preferences that cannot be predicted by either the parties or the voters do exist. It is particularly necessary that the position of the median voter is uncertain. The nature of random effects is not fully explored; however, it is suggested in Alesina (1988b) and Alesina and Sachs (1988) that abstentions (discussed in Ledyard, 1984) may explain these deviations.

Clearly the degree of uncertainty assumed is extremely limited. The theoretical research on signalling in electoral games suggests that voters would still be able to rationally estimate true candidate positions[23] if more uncertainty were allowed, *e.g.*, voters uncertain about candidate preferences, *etc*. Therefore, the only possible rational sources of uncertainty are fluctuations in voter preferences and/or unpredictable effects from the costs of voting. There is little empirical information that voter preferences change drastically over time. The magnitude of the uncertainty created by turnout is often not large. In fact, many researchers might argue that only a few presidential elections have had truly uncertain outcomes, even months before the election, as postulated in *RPT*. Hence it is doubtful that the electoral uncertainty assumed in *RPT* is large enough to affect inflation signficantly.

---

[22] Kenny and Morton (1991) develop a model in which two probability maximizing parties compete for campaign contributions in order to provide voters with information. As a consequence they diverge in the policy services offered to contributors.

[23] See Banks (1990).

17.5 Conclusion

RPT is an ambitious attempt to develop a combined political economic model. The analysis of this paper has shown that *RPT* suffers from a number of problems. In particular *RPT* fails in the following areas:

1. The macroeconomic model is inappropriate:

    (a) business cycles occur because non-electorally contingent nominal wage contracts are signed and workers move "off" their labor supply curve, which is suboptimal for the economic agents;

    (b) the predicted real wage movement in the cycle is not empirically justified.

2. The assumed partisan differences over inflation and output are unreasonable:

    (a) Democrats are unlikely to prefer a higher expected inflation rate, or inflation surprises, for tax purposes than Republicans because the inflation tax is generally regressive; and

    (b) the justifications for differences in preferences for monetarily induced booms are without microfoundations and often conflicting with the economic effects in the macroeconomic model.

3. The assumptions about the electoral game are not justified:

    (a) the electoral game is assumed often to be one shot, ignoring the likelihood of convergence over time;

    (b) a rational explanation of party preference divergence is not offered; explicitly, the possible emergence of third parties is ignored; and finally,

    (c) changes in voter preferences over time and unpredictable cost effects on turnout are assumed to exist; the assumed sources of randomness in voter preferences, are not likely to be significant enough to cause much variation in inflation.

As noted in the introduction the possibility of the existence of partisan political business cycles may influence the debate over the appropriateness of various political institutions in controlling economic variables. As Alesina points out (1988): "This line of research also has important normative implications. Models which explicitly address the relationship between alternative institutional settings and the economy can determine the optimal institutional arrangements, given that 'benevolent dictators' do not exist. For instance, this literature provides a conceptual framework to ask the question of who should control the Central Bank, and it sheds some new light on the old question of 'rules versus discretion.'" In Alesina (1989), the argument is made that the theory might be used to suggest that legislative control over the Central Bank is preferable to executive control.

It is important to carefully examine the theoretical underpinnings of *RPT* before using its results to alter political institutions, especially since the limited degrees of freedom in the relevant data make definitive conclusions from empirical analysis difficult. If the monetarily induced partisan cycles are neither based on the actors' rational behavior nor consistent with simple facts about business cycles and partisan preferences, then policy implications that develop from *RPT* should be viewed with skepticism. *RPT*, as currently formulated, is too imperfect a theory to use as a justification for major political institutional changes.

References

Alesina, A. 1987. "Macroeconomic Policy in a Two-Party System as a Repeated Game," *Quarterly Journal of Economics* 102: 651-678.

Alesina, A. 1988a. "Macroeconomics and Politics," in *NBER Macroeconomic Annual 1988.* Cambridge, Mass.: MIT.

Alesina, A. 1988b. "Credibility and Policy Convergence in a Two-Party System with Rational Voters," *American Economic Review* 78: 796-805.

Alesina, A., G. D. Cohen, and N. Roubini. 1991. "Macroeconomic Policy and Elections in OECD Democracies," NBER Working Paper No. 3830.

Alesina, A., J. Londregan, and H. Rosenthal. 1991. "National Elections and the Economy: Evidence from the 20th Century U.S.," presented at the Seventh International Symposium in Economic Theory and Econometrics at Washington University in St. Louis.

Alesina, A. and H. Rosenthal. 1989. "Partisan Cycles in Congressional Elections and the Microeconomy," *American Political Science Review* 83: 373-398.

Alesina, A. and N. Roubini. 1990. "Political Cycles in OECD Economies." NBER Working Paper No. 3478.

Alesina, A. and J. D. Sachs. 1987. "Political Parties and the Business Cycle in the United States, 1948-1984," *Journal of Money, Credit, and Banking* 20: 63-82.

Auernheimer, L. 1974. "The Honest Government Guide to the Revenue from the Creation of Money," *Journal of Political Economy* 82: 598-606.

Azariadis, C., and J. E. Stiglitz. 1991. "Implicit Contracts and Fixed-Price Equilibria," in *New Keynesian Economics,* Vol. 2, N. Mankiw and D. Romer, eds. Cambridge, Mass.: MIT Readings in Economics.

Backus, D. and J. Driffill. 1985. "Inflation and Reputation," *American Economic Review* 75: 530-538.

Banks, J. 1990. "A Model of Electoral Competition with Incomplete Information," *Journal of Economic Theory* 50: 309-325.

Barro, R. J. 1977. "Long-Term Contracting, Sticky Prices, and Monetary Policy," *Journal of Monetary Economics* 3: 305-316.

Barro, R. J. and D. P. Gordon. 1983. "A Positive Theory of Monetary Policy in a Natural Rate Model," *Journal of Political Economy* 91: 589-610.

Borooah, V. K. and F. van der Ploeg. 1983. *Political Aspects of the Economy.* Cambridge: Cambridge University Press.

Boylan, R., J. Ledyard, and R. D. McKelvey. 1990. "Political Competition in a Model of Economic Growth: Some Theoretical Results." Typescript: California Institute of Technology.

Calvo, G. A. 1978. "On the Time Consistency of Optimal Policy in a Monetary Economy," *Econometrica* 46: 1411-1428.

Canzoneri, M. B. 1985. "Monetary Policy Games and the Role of Private Information," *American Economic Review* 75: 1056-1071.

Fischer, S. 1977. "Long Term Contracts, Rational Expectations, and the Optimal Money Supply Rule," *Journal of Political Economy* 85: 191-206.

Fischer, S. 1986. *Indexing, Inflation, and Economic Policy.* Cambridge: MIT Press.

Frey, B. S. 1978. *Modern Political Economy.* New York: Wiley.

Frey, B. S. 1983. *Democratic Economic Policy: A Theoretical Introduction.* New York: St. Martin's Press.

Grossman, H. I. and J. van Huyck. 1986. "Seignorage, Inflation, and Reputation," *Journal of Monetary Economics* 15: 21-32.

Gwartney, J. D. and R. L. Stroup. 1990. *Economics: Public and Private Choice.* Fifth Edition. San Diego: Harcourt, Brace, Jovanovich.

Hall, R. E. and E. P. Lazear. 1984. "The Excess Sensitivity of Layoffs and Quits to Demand," *Journal of Labor Economics* 2: 233-257.

Havrilesky, T. 1987. "A Partisanship Theory of Fiscal and Monetary Regimes," *Journal of Money, Credit and Banking* 19: 308-25.

Harvrilesky, T. 1988. "Two Monetary and Fiscal Policy Myths, in *Political Business Cycles: The Political Economy of Money, Inflation, and Unemployment*, T. D. Willett, ed. Durham, N.C.: Duke University Press.

Hess, G. D. 1991. "Voting and the Intertemporal Selection of Tax Rates in a Macro-Economy," *Economics and Politics.* 3: 41-62.

Hibbs, D. A. 1977. "Political Parties and Macroeconomic Policy," *American Political Science Review* 71: 1467-87.

Hibbs, D. A. 1987. *The American Political Economy: Macroeconomics and Electoral Politics.* Cambridge: Harvard University Press.

Husted, T., R. Morton, and C. Waller. 1992. "Political Business Cycles in State Economies." Typescript: Texas A and M University.

Keane, M., R. Moffit, and D. Runkle. 1988. "Real Wages over the Business Cycle: Estimating the Impact of Heterogeneity with Micro Data," *Journal of Political Economy* 96: 1232-66.

Kenny, L. 1991. "Cross Country Estimates of the Demand for Money and its Components," *Economic Inquiry* 29: 696-705.

Kenny, L. and R. B. Morton. 1991. "Special Interests, Parties, and Platform Divergence." Typescript: Texas A and M University.

Kydland, F. and E. Prescott. 1977. "Rules Rather than Discretion: The Inconsistency of Optimal Plans," *Journal of Political Economy* 85: 4730-4791.

Ledyard, J. "The Pure Theory of Large Two-Candidate Elections," *Public Choice* 48: 7-41.

Lucas, R. E. 1972. "Expectations and the Neutrality of Money," *Journal of Economic Theory* 4: 103-124.

Mankiw, N. G. 1987. "The Optimal Collection of Seigniorage: Theory and Evidence," *Journal of Monetary Economics* 20: 327-341.
Nordhaus, W. D. 1975. "The Political Business Cycle," *Review of Economic Studies* 42: 169-90.
Peretz, P. 1983. *The Political Economy of Inflation in the United States*. Chicago: University of Chicago Press.
Persson, T. and G. Tabellini. 1990. *Macroeconomic Policy, Credibility and Politics*. Chur: Harwood Academic Publishers.
Quinn, D. P. and R. Y. Shapiro. 1991. "Business Political Power: The Case of Taxation," *American Political Science Review* 85: 851-874.
Raisian, J. 1979. "Cyclic Patterns in Weeks and Wages," *Economic Inquiry* 17: 475-495.
Raisian, J. 1983. "Contracts, Job Experience and Cyclical Labor Market Adjustments," *Journal of Labor Economics* 1: 2: 152-170.
Renaud, P. S. A. and F. van Winden. 1987. "On the Importance of Elections and Ideology for Government Policy in a Multi-Party System," in *The Logic of Multiparty Sytems*, M. J. Holler, ed. Dordrecht: Martinus Nijhoff.
Rogoff, K. and A. Sibert. 1988. "Elections and Macroeconomic Policy Cycles," *Review of Economic Studies* 55: 1-16.
Schneider, F. and B. S. Frey. 1988. "Politico-Economic Models of Macroeconomic Policy," in *Political Business Cycle*, Thomas D. Willett, ed. Durham, N.C.: Duke University Press.
van Winden, F. 1983. *On the Interaction Between State and Private Sectors*. Amsterdam: North-Holland.
van Winden, F., A. Schram, and F. Groot. 1987. "The Interaction Between Economics and Politics: Modelling Cycles," *European Journal of Political Research* 15: 185-202.

18. Hypothesis Testing and Collective Decision-Making

Krishna K. Ladha[1]

18.1 Introduction

There are four main steps to hypothesis testing. First, the feasible states of the world are mapped onto a pair of hypotheses on the premise that one hypothesis is true (better) and the other false (worse). Second, a critical region, depending on the costs of Type I and II errors, is specified. Third, a sample statistic is obtained from a random sample. Finally, by rule, the null hypothesis is rejected if and only if the sample statistic falls in the critical region. The procedure is such that the probability of a correct decision is well-defined.

Hypothesis testing, however, requires individual, not collective, decision; indeed collective decision is not an option. Hence, lacking a consensus, competing hypotheses often coexist as they do in macroeconomics, medicine and physics; even in mathematics unproven conjectures, which are either true or false, abound.

Lacking a consensus, majority-rule voting provides a procedure to choose between a pair of hypotheses. The Condorcet jury theorem is the main result about the quality of such a collective decision.

The Condorcet Jury Theorem: Let it be the case that every individual votes for the better of two hypotheses with probability π, and let $\xi(n)$ be the corresponding probability for a majority from n individuals. If $\pi > .5$ and the votes are statistically *independent*, then $\xi(n) > \pi$ and $\xi(n)$ approaches 1 as the number of voters approaches infinity.

Thus, a majority of voters is better informed than any one voter, implying that majority-rule voting aggregates decentralized information. For example, if $\pi = .6$, then $\xi(9) = .727$, and $\xi(100) = .98$. Each additional voter contributes new information about the true hypothesis, and in the limit majority-rule voting attains the true hypothesis.

The Condorcet Jury theorem has been viewed as a result about choosing between two alternatives. Surprisingly, these alternatives have never been interpreted as hypotheses subject to statistical testing. Doing so provides a firm foundation for the jury theorem; in particular, it removes the vagueness about the meaning of the probability of choosing the better alternative.

---
[1] I wish to thank Norman Schofield for his critical comments and helpful suggestions on this chapter. The work here is based on research supported by NSF Grant SES-92-10800.

To recap, hypothesis testing and the jury theorem provide two approaches to choosing the better of two hypotheses under uncertainty. Each approach has its strength and limitation. Hypothesis testing is unambiguous about the probability of a correct decision, but it disallows collective judgment. By contrast, the jury theorem is vague about the probability of a correct decision, but it allows collective judgement.

In this chapter, I seek to link hypothesis testing with the jury theorem by combining the strengths of the two approaches. However, I concentrate on independent voting with only a brief consideration of dependent voting. Chapter 19 of this volume explores the substantive consequences of the jury theorem for dependent votes.

18.2 The Probability of Being Correct

Consider the null hypothesis H_0 and the alternate hypothesis H_1, which are mutually exclusive and collectively exhaustive. An error occurs when the true hypothesis is rejected (Table 1):

Table 1.
Type I and II Errors

	H_0 is true	H_1 is true
Accept H_0	Correct decision	Type II error
Accept H_1	Type I error	Correct decision

Thus, if the null hypothesis, that the prisoner is innocent, is true, then a conviction would lead to a Type I error. If the alternate hypothesis, that the prisoner is guilty, is true, then an acquittal would lead to a Type II error. Apparently, a Type I error is more serious than a Type II error. In scientific studies, however, one type of error may be as serious as the other.

A decision entails two error probabilities:

$$\alpha = \Pi(\text{Type I error}) = \Pi(\text{Reject } H_0 \mid H_0), \text{ and}$$
$$\beta = \Pi(\text{Type II error}) = \Pi(\text{Reject } H_1 \mid H_1),$$

where Π stands for the probability operator. Thus, if the true hypothesis is H_0, the probability that a decision is correct is $1 - \alpha$; if the true hypothesis is H_1, the probability that a decision is correct is $1 - \beta$. This chapter presents the jury theorem in terms of α and β.

18.3 Notation

Consider the null and alternative hypotheses about a population with an unknown mean but known variance:

$$H_0 : \mu = \mu_0, \text{ and } H_1 : \mu = \mu_1, \text{ where } \mu_1 > \mu_0.$$

Let there be n jurors indexed by i. Let

1. S_i = the mean of a random sample obtained by juror i. It is a random variable before the sample is drawn.

2. s_i = a realization of S_i.

Each juror:

1. selects a critical value k_i (see Figure 1) with a view to the losses associated with Type I and II errors;

2. draws a random sample and computes the sample mean s_i;

3. accepts H_1 if $s_i > k_i$; accepts H_0 if $s_i \leq k_i$.

Thus, before a sample is drawn, juror i knows $\Pi_i(S_i > k_i \mid H_j)$, $j = 1, 2$, because she is assumed to know the distribution of the sample mean S_i given H_j. After a sample is drawn, the juror learns the realization s_i of S_i, and makes a decision as per (3). (See Winkler and Hays 1975.) Once made, the decision is either right or wrong, with probability 1. Hence, *all probabilities pertain to the phase during which the sample information is unknown.*

For $i = 1, \ldots, n$, let

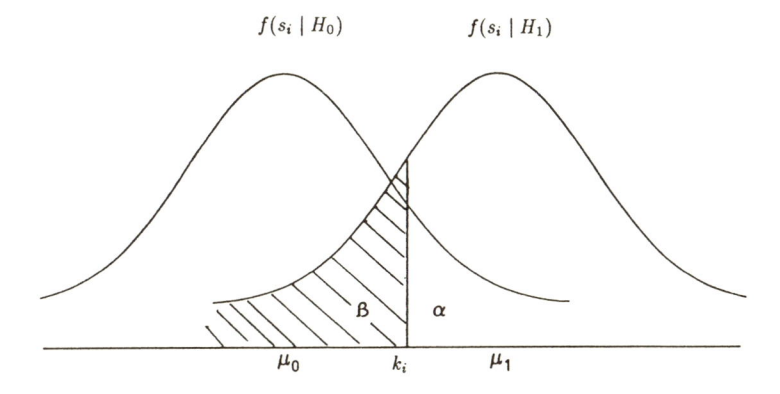

$$\chi_i \begin{array}{l} = 1 \text{ if individual } i \text{ accepts } H_1 \text{ (rejects } H_0), \\ = 0 \text{ if individual } i \text{ accepts } H_0 \text{ (rejects } H_1). \end{array}$$

Figure 1. Sampling distributions of S under H_0 and H_1.

The potential error probabilities (see Figure 1) are specified:

$$\alpha_i = \Pi(i \text{ commits a Type I error}) = \Pi(i \text{ votes for } H_1 \mid H_0)$$
$$= \Pi(S_i > k_i \mid H_0) = \Pi(\chi_i = 1 \mid H_0);$$
$$\alpha_{maj} = \Pi(\text{a majority commits Type I error}) = \Pi(\text{majority for } H_1 \mid H_0)$$
$$= \Pi(\sum \chi_i > \tfrac{n}{2} \mid H_0);$$
$$\beta_i = \Pi(i \text{ commits a Type II error}) = \Pi(i \text{ votes for } H_0 \mid H_1)$$
$$= \Pi(S_i \leq k_i \mid H_1) = \Pi(\chi_i = 0 \mid H_1);$$
$$\beta_{maj} = \Pi(\text{a majority commits Type II error}) = \Pi(\text{majority for } H_0 \mid H_1)$$
$$= \Pi(\sum \chi_i < \tfrac{n}{2} \mid H_1).$$

18.4 Information Aggregation by Majority-Rule Voting

If the true hypothesis were known, all individuals would vote for it. Individuals differ however in (1) their samples of the distribution; and so (2) in their assignments of critical values. Different critical regions reflect different evaluations of Type I and II errors.

18.4.1 Identical Critical Regions

First suppose that all individuals employ the same critical region: thus, $k_i = k$ for all i. The case of different $\{k_i\}$ is discussed in section 18.4.2. Consider three situations:

(a) A sample is drawn, and it is publicly observed;

(b) Each individual draws a random sample, and the sample information remains private;

(c) Each individual possesses some public and some private infomation.

Case (a). We have $k_i = k$ and $S_i = S$ for all i. All individuals vote identically, or their votes are perfectly positively correlated. Hence,

$$\Pi(\text{a majority votes for } H_j \mid H_j) = \Pi(\text{any } i \text{ votes for } H_j \mid H_j), j = 1, 2.$$

There is no gain from having more than one person.

Case (b). We have $k_i = k$ for all i. Each individual draws a random sample leading to s_i, which remains i's private information. Because the samples are independent, the $\{S_i\}$, and hence the votes $\{\chi_i\}$, are statistically independent. For example, $\Pi(\chi_i = 1, \chi_j = 1 \mid k) =$

$$\Pi(S_i > k, S_j > k \mid k) = \Pi(S_i > k \mid k)\Pi(S_j > k \mid k) = \Pi(\chi_i = 1)\Pi(\chi_j = 1)$$

where the penultimate equality follows from the independence of S_i and S_j.

If the individual samples are not only independent but also of the same size, then the $\{S_i\}$ would be independent and identically distributed. Therefore, for all i,

$$\alpha = \alpha_i = \Pi(\chi_i = 1 \mid H_0) = \Pi(S_i > k \mid H_0), \text{ and}$$
$$\beta = \beta_i = \Pi(\chi_i = 0 \mid H_1) = \Pi(S_i \leq k \mid H_1).$$

The Jury Theorem in Terms of Type I and II Errors. Let it be the case that every individual commits a Type I error with probability α, and a Type II error with probability β. If $\alpha < .5$ and $\beta < .5$, and the votes are independent, then $\alpha_{maj} < \alpha$ and $\beta_{maj} < \beta$. Moreover, both α_{maj} and β_{maj} approach 0 as n approaches infinity.

Proof. See Appendix.[2]

Of course, it could be the case that while $\alpha < .5$, $\beta > .5$. Table 2 summarizes the results for four sets of values of α and β.

Table 2. Condorcet's Jury Theorem
In Terms of the Error Probabilities

	$\beta < .5$	$\beta > .5$
$\alpha < .5$ As $n \to \infty$	$\alpha_{maj} < \alpha$, $\beta_{maj} < \beta$ $\alpha_{maj} \to 0$, $\beta_{maj} \to 0$	$\alpha_{maj} < \alpha$, $\beta_{maj} > \beta$ $\alpha_{maj} \to 0$, $\beta_{maj} \to 1$
$\alpha > .5$ As $n \to \infty$	$\alpha_{maj} > \alpha$, $\beta_{maj} < \beta$ $\alpha_{maj} \to 1$, $\beta_{maj} \to 0$	$\alpha_{maj} > \alpha$, $\beta_{maj} > \beta$ $\alpha_{maj} \to 1$, $\beta_{maj} \to 0$ or $\alpha_{maj} \to 0$, $\beta_{maj} \to 1$.

Consider the case $\alpha < .5, \beta < .5$ in Table 2. The top line states that if $\forall i$:

1. $\alpha = \Pi(\chi_i = 1 \mid H_0) < .5$, then $\alpha_{maj} < \alpha$. Thus, a majority of the group would commit a Type I error with a probability lower than that of an individual.

2. $\beta = \Pi(\chi = 0 \mid H_1) < .5$, then $\beta_{maj} < \beta$. Thus, a majority of the group would commit a Type II error with a probability lower than that of an individual.

The second line states that as n approaches infinity, the probability that a majority commits an error of either Type I or Type II approaches zero.

Consider the case of $\alpha < .5; \beta > .5$. What is different is that while
$\alpha_{maj} = \Pi(\text{majority commits Type I error})$ approaches 0,
$\beta_{maj} = \Pi(\text{majority commits Type II error})$ approaches 1. To understand this, suppose that in order to run a very low risk of Type I error, the critical

---
[2] To prove the theorem for n even, a tie breaking assumption is needed: Should a tie occur, a fair coin is tossed allowing each hypothesis to be chosen with proability 0.5.

value k is set higher than μ_1 of the alternate hypothesis, so that $\beta_i = \Pi(\text{Accept } H_0 \mid H_1) > .5$ for all i, hence $\beta > .5$. (See for example Figure 2.)

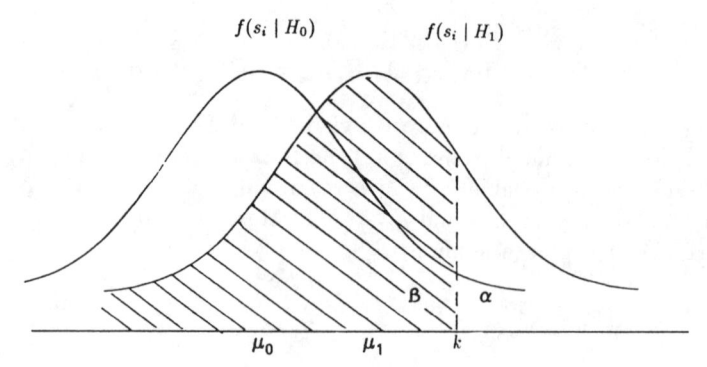

Figure 2. Sampling Distributions of S under H_0 and H_1.

As the number of voters in the group increases, the information becomes increasingly refined, and by the strong law of large numbers, the sample mean approaches in probability[3] the true population mean, μ. Since $\mu_0 < \mu_1 < k$, this implies that the probability that any realization s, of S, exceeds k must approach zero as n approaches infinity. Thus the hypothesis H_0 is accepted with near certainty. Consequently, the probability of a Type II error approaches 1 (that is, $\beta_{maj} \to 1$) and that of Type I error approaches zero (that is, $\alpha_{maj} \to 0$).

For sufficiently large samples, moving k to the right of μ_1 reduces α by a small amount, but increases β greatly. For most practical problems, when the sample is sufficiently large, it would be imprudent to set k to the right of μ_1. When $\mu_0 < k < \mu_1$, the case $\alpha < .5, \beta < .5$, is the relevant one, and the Jury Theorem as stated above, applies.

Finally, for some skewed, possibly bizarre, distribution both α and β could exceed .05. In the limit, however, both α_{maj} and β_{maj} cannot approach 1; one must approach 0 and the other 1.

Case (c). We have $k_i = k$ for all i. Each individual possesses some public and some private information. Thus, the random variables $\{S_i\}$ are no longer independent, so the votes $\{\chi_i\}$ are statistically dependent. Obviously, the dependency arises from common information. We might suspect that the greater the common information, the greater the dependency among voters.

Suppose that the votes are exchangeable, so that $\alpha = \alpha_i, \beta = \beta_i$ for all i, and the pairwise correlation coefficients $\rho(\chi_i, \chi_j) = \rho$, for all $i \neq j$. Let $\alpha < .5$ and $\beta < .5$. Then, under rather general conditions: $\alpha_{maj} < \alpha$ and $\beta_{maj} < \beta$, though for $\rho > 0, \alpha_{maj}$ and β_{maj} do not approach zero as n becomes large.

---

[3] In other words, for any $\epsilon > 0$ and any probability level, π, there is a sample size n such that the probability $\Pi(\mu - \epsilon < s_n < \mu + \epsilon)$ exceeds π, where s_n is the realization of S from the sample.

The result for exchangeable votes is a direct consequence of Ladha (1993). When the votes are arbitrarily correlated, a version of the results of Ladha (1992), adapted to this case, would apply.

18.4.2 Different Critical Regions

Now assume α_i
$$\begin{aligned} &= \Pi(\chi_i = 1 \mid H_0) &= \Pi(S_i > k \mid H_0) \\ &= \Pi(\mu_0 + \epsilon_i > k) &= \Pi(\epsilon_i > k - \mu_0). \end{aligned}$$

Thus, given the distribution of $\{\epsilon_i\}$, what is relevant in the specification of α is the difference $k - \mu_0$. If $\{\epsilon_i\}$ are independent, the votes are independent; if not, the votes are dependent. The jury theorem for independent and dependent votes discussed in Section 18.4.1 assumes the value of k is the same for all voters. Now, suppose that different individuals use different critical regions.

Consider the simplest case first: $K_i = k + \delta_i$ where $\{\delta_i\}$ are random variables. Then,

$$\alpha_i \begin{aligned} &= \Pi(\chi_i = 1 \mid H_0) &= \Pi(S_i > K_i \mid H_0) \\ &= \Pi(\mu_0 + \epsilon_i > k + \delta_i) &= \Pi(\epsilon_i - \delta_i > k - \mu_0). \end{aligned}$$

Once again, given the distribution of $(\epsilon_i - \delta_i)$, what is relevant in the specification of α is the difference $k - \mu_0$. If the $(\epsilon_i - \delta_i)$'s are independent, the votes are independent; if not, the votes are dependent. What is different now is the additional source of correlation: the critical region.

The dependence of K_i and K_j, or equivalently of δ_i and δ_j, could arise from a lack of knowledge of the similarity in the training and experiences of the jurors. For example, if I know that two jurors strongly consider a Type I error (caused by, say, the approval of an unsafe drug) to be more serious than a Type II error, but I do not know the intensity of this belief, then by knowing the decision of one juror, I learn something about the decision of the second juror. The votes of the two jurors are, therefore, dependent. If the votes are dependent due to similar or dissimilar critical regions of the jurors, then the Condorcet Jury Theorem for dependent votes applies (see Ladha 1992, 1993).

The above discussion considered only α, the probability of a Type I error. A similar analysis can be made for β, the probability of a Type II error.

18.5 Conclusion

This chapter has attempted to connect hypothesis testing with the jury theorem. The connection is essential because, when the information possessed by different people cannot be directly pooled, the approach of hypothesis testing is less useful. In such situations the jury theorem provides a more useful vehicle to aggregate information through majority-rule voting. The jury theorem extends the ideas of hypothesis testing to the case of collective judgment. Hypothesis testing, in turn, provides a precise meaning of "the probability of the correctness of a voter's opinion" (Black 1958, p. 163).

References

Black, D. 1958. *The Theory of Committees and Elections.* Cambridge: Cambridge University Press.

Ladha, K. K. 1992. "Condorcet's Jury Theorem, Free Speech and Correlated Votes," *American Journal of Political Science* 36: 617-634.

Ladha, K. K. 1993. "Condorcet's Jury Theorem in Light of De Finetti's Theorem: Majority-Rule Voting with Correlated Votes," *Social Choice and Welfare* 10: 69-85.

Winkler, R. L. and W. L. Hays. 1975. *Statistics.* New York: Holt, Rinehart and Winston.

Appendix

Proof of the Jury Theorem in Terms of α and β. We only need to prove that $\alpha_{maj} < \alpha$ and $\alpha_{maj} \to 0$ as $n \to \infty$; the identical proof involving β_{maj} and β is omitted. Recall, $\alpha = \Pi(\text{Reject } H_0 \mid H_0) = \Pi(\chi_i = 1 \mid H_0)$ and $\alpha_{maj} = \Pi(\text{a majority rejects } H_0 \mid H_0)$. Let $\chi = \sum_{i=1}^{n} \chi_i$. Use E for the expectation operator. We consider two cases.

Case (i) Let n be odd and the majority, $m = \frac{n+1}{2}$. Then, $\alpha_{maj} < \alpha$, if the following inequality holds:

$$\alpha_{maj} = \sum_{k=m}^{n} \Pi(\chi = k \mid H_0) < \tfrac{1}{n} n\alpha = \tfrac{1}{n} E(\chi \mid H_0) = \tfrac{1}{n} \sum_{k=0}^{n} k\Pi(\chi = k).$$

Suppressing the conditioning on H_0 and rearranging terms gives:

$$\sum_{k=m}^{n} (n-k)\Pi(\chi = k) < \sum_{k=0}^{m-1} k\Pi(\chi = k). \quad (*)$$

On the left-hand side, let $j = n - k$, so $j = 0$ when $k = n$ and $j = m - 1$ when $k = m$. Then we require: $\sum_{j=0}^{m-1} j\Pi(\chi = n - j) < \sum_{j=0}^{m-1} j\Pi(\chi = j)$.

Thus, $\alpha_{maj} < \alpha$ if for each $j = 0, \ldots, m - 1$, $\Pi(\chi = n - j) < \Pi(\chi = j)$.

Now $\Pi(\chi = j) = \binom{n}{j} \alpha^j (1-\alpha)^{n-j} = \binom{n}{n-j} \alpha^j (1-\alpha)^{n-j}$.

Thus the required inequality is $\alpha^{n-j}(1-\alpha)^j < \alpha^j(1-\alpha)^{n-j}$, or $\alpha^{n-2j} < (1-\alpha)^{n-2j}$, i.e., if $\alpha < .5$, which is assumed. Note $n - 2j > 0$ for all admissible values of j. Thus $\alpha_{maj} < \alpha$ when n is odd.

Case (ii) For n even, and $m = \frac{n}{2}$, instead of $(*)$, we require (because of the tie-breaking assumption) that

$$\sum_{k=m+1}^{n} (n-k)\Pi(\chi = k) + [\tfrac{n}{2} - m]\Pi(\chi = m) < \sum_{k=0}^{m-1} k\Pi(\chi = k).$$

This can be shown precisely as above.

When H_0 is true and $n \to \infty$, the fraction of voters rejecting H_0 approaches $E(\chi/n \mid H_0) = \alpha < .5$. Thus, in the limit more than half the voters choose correctly. Hence the probability a majority errs (α_{maj}) approaches zero.

19. Political Discourse, Factions, and the General Will: Correlated Voting and Condorcet's Jury Theorem

Krishna K. Ladha and Gary Miller [1]

19.1 Introduction

Can a group of people, operating under majority rule procedures, make better judgments than any one of the individuals comprising the group? Rousseau's notion of the "general will" seemed to suggest a positive answer to this question, at the same time that it generated criticism as an overly romantic or even mystical construct. However, in an insightful paper, Grofman and Feld (1988) argue that Rousseau's notion of the general will is supported by Condorcet's jury theorem.

Condorcet considers group choice situations in which only one of two alternatives is correct for the group. His theorem shows that, if each individual in a group has a probability of being correct that is greater than .5, then the probability that the majority of the group is correct will be larger yet; further, the majority will approach perfect accuracy in judgment as the size of the group increases. Grofman and Feld argue that this result supports Rousseau's faith in the "general will". The previous chapter in this volume by Ladha provides a short proof of the theorem in the case that voters' choices are independent, and connects the theorem to hypothesis testing.

While at first blush Condorcet's result seems to support Rousseau, a closer reading of Rousseau raises several points of controversy. The limitations on Condorcet's jury theorem are so restrictive that they seem to apply neither to Rousseau's argument nor to the real world of politics. In particular, Condorcet's jury theorem requires independent voters. But in the real world of politics, individuals may be presumed to debate issues in attempts to convince each other of their points of view. Furthermore, people who become convinced of a common point of view may coalesce into factions, and rely on each other for support and reinforcement. This kind of political intercourse, which we would regard as normal and healthy, would likely lead to inter-dependent voting. But without the assumption of independence, Condorcet has nothing to

---
[1] The work in this chapter is based on research supported by NSF Grant SES-92-10800. This chapter was written before Chapter 18 of this volume.

say about whether groups are more likely to be correct than their constituent members. The presence of political dialogue and political factions seems to render Condorcet's jury theorem irrelevant to our assessment of Rousseau and to majority rule judgments (Black 1958). Rawls (1971) puts the problem succinctly: because in the normal course of politics "votes of different persons are not independent," then "the simpler sorts of probabilistic reasons (including the Condorcet jury theorem) do not apply" (p. 358). In the presence of correlated voting, Condorcet's jury theorem has nothing to say about group judgments and the "general will."

Or even worse, a sterile, noninteractive political process may appear necessary to satisfy the assumption of voter independence, and thus, preserve the virtue of majority rule judgments (Estlund 1989; Waldron 1989). Hence, a major concern is whether the jury theorem would seem to indicate a conflict between the requirements of effective majority rule (*i.e.*, voter independence) and the desiderata of a libertarian state (*i.e.*, open discourse and voluntaristic associations).

For this reason, it is essential to find out whether majority rule judgmental synergies of the sort proven to exist in the presence of independent voting also exist in the presence of correlated voting. If so, then accurate majority rule judgments do not forbid political debate and factions.

The purpose of this paper is to show that a generalization of the jury theorem, due to Ladha (1992), requires much less stringent conditions under which majority rule voting can improve on individual judgment. In the process, Ladha provides a means for understanding the role that political discourse, factions and free speech play in effective majority rule decision-making. This investigation reveals that we need neither distort Rousseau nor abandon a Condorcetian approach to Rousseau. Using Ladha's result, we show that factions do not necessarily reduce the effectiveness of majority rule voting. On the contrary, the most important and counter-intuitive discovery is that *the difference of opinion between factions makes a valuable contribution to the effectiveness of majority rule judgment.*

Thus, the new work on the Condorcet jury theorem does not impose a sterile scenario of atomistic voters casting ballots in isolation from each other. Rather, it encourages a vision in which the "general will" emerges from a vigorous political discourse between voters of similar and opposing viewpoints.

19.2 Rousseau's General Will and Condorcet's Jury Theorem

Coleman and Ferejohn (1986) provide what they call the "epistemic interpretation of voting" as a defense against Riker's criticism of populist democracy. Voting in the normal social choice interpretation expresses preferences and the logical problems to which Riker alludes characterize difficulties in coherently aggregating these preferences. Coleman and Ferejohn suggest that a defense of populism may view voting (at least on occasion) "as consisting in *judgments*—which can be either true or false—rather than in expressions of *preferences*—which are neither" (1986: 16). As they point out, "the desirability of a voting rule will then depend on its reliability—the extent to which the collective judgments it generates converge with what is in fact the correct judgment" (1986: 16-17).

In their epistemic interpretation, Coleman and Ferejohn naturally refer frequently to Rousseau and his notion of the general will. According to Rousseau, the purpose of the general will is the good of all. The general will is general by virtue of the common interest by which the people are united. By definition, then, the general will is the correct course of action for a people, a course which each citizen may fail to ascertain. Acting together, however, the people can discover the general will.

Grofman and Feld make the link between Rousseau and Condorcet through this possibility of synergistic discovery—the ability of the group to make judgments that are beyond the abilities of any single member. They refer to a result which would seem to be central to the epistemic interpretation of voting, although Coleman and Ferejohn do not refer to it at all. Condorcet assumed that there was some binary decision facing a group of people, all of whom had a shared interest in discerning the correct alternative. He also assumed that every individual had a probability $\pi > .5$ of being correct. (Note that for a binary decision, a person could be correct half of the time simply by flipping a coin; thus, assuming a 50% "floor" for individual expertise is not an unreasonable starting point for analysis of binary decisions.)

Condorcet's jury theorem proves that a majority of such a group will be correct more frequently than π. For example, assume that $\pi = .6$ for each of three voters. Assuming independence, all three will be simultaneously correct 21.6% of the time, and two out of three will be correct another 43.2% of the time. Altogether then, a majority of the three voters will be correct 64.8% of the time. By simply operating under a majority rule mechanism, the group can achieve an improvement of 4.8% in their judgmental reliability.[2]

Furthermore, this judgment reliability increases with group size. In Condorcet's words:

> ... if the probable truth of [the choice] of each voter is greater than $\frac{1}{2}$, that is to say if it is more probable than not that he will decide in conformity with the truth, the more the number of voters increases, the greater the probability of the truth of the decision. The limit of this probability will be certainty (Condorcet [1785] 1976: 48-49).

This startling degree of certainty would seem to be the kind of "evidence" about majority rule "reliability" that Coleman and Ferejohn claim would be necessary for an epistemic defense of populist democracy. Further, Grofman and Feld argue that "the Condorcet jury theorem accurately captures the basic ideas underlying Rousseau's notion of the general will." They focus

---

[2] For research related to the jury theorem, but assuming independence, see Schofield (1972), Grofman, Owen and Feld (1983), Young (1986), and Miller (1986).

on several isomorphisms: that both Condorcet and Rousseau were concerned with situations in which individuals shared a need to find a common good; that each individual was not always accurate in his judgment; and that the vote of the people is a better indicator of the public good than the beliefs of any one individual. They offer a compelling argument that Condorcet provides a mathematical formalism supporting an "understanding of democracy as a means to collective ends."

19.3 On Public Deliberation

Yet a number of troubling issues arise from this argument, most of them hinging on Condorcet's technical assumption of independence among the voters. Independence assumes that if one voter (Anne) has a $(\pi) = .6$, then she has the same probability of being correct whether or not any other voter is correct. If Anne is either more or less likely to be correct when any other voter votes correctly, then the assumption of independence is not met, and Condorcet, narrowly interpreted, has nothing to say about whether or not majority rule will effect an improvement in judgmental decision-making.

While the Condorcet jury theorem makes no direct statements about the effect of interdependent voting, interdependence can be destructive of synergistic group judgment (Nitzan and Paroush 1984). This analysis drives Grofman and Feld (1988, 1989) to remark on the pitfalls of political factions and to question the effects of group deliberation. If Anne always consults with Betty, and votes the same way that Betty does, then Anne's vote does not help to make the group more efficacious. A three-person group including Anne and Betty is effectively a two-person group, and majority voting is no more accurate than relying on one or the other of the two independent decision-makers. Thus, the conclusion can easily be reached that Anne should be prohibited from any discussion with Betty, and forced to use her best judgment completely on her own.

Two political philosophers have demonstrated the troubling problems that this independence assumption raises with regard to the applicability of Condorcet to Rousseau. (Waldron 1989: 1325) observes, "[I]f the Condorcetian approach precludes discussion, it is entirely at odds with the spirit of the participatory tradition in which Rousseau's political theory is usually located." Waldron is particularly disturbed by the implication that public deliberation may be detrimental.

> [I]f one source of average incompetence is unfamiliarity with the range and complexity of a problem, bringing citizens together in an assembly where they can be exposed in a discussion to a range of perspectives other than their own may make it more likely that reason rather than prejudice will prevail as they address the problems of a large society (Waldron 1989: 1327).

This insight, which most people of a democratic persuasion would endorse, seems very difficult to reconcile with the assumption of independence and with the analysis of the jury theorem. Thus Condorcet's insight seems to political scientists to be an arcane irrelevancy to the real world of political decision-making, or a disturbing invitation to limit the kind of debate that is essential to a free society.

19.4 On Political Factions

The assumption of independence becomes especially problematic when one considers political factions. We presume that the members of factions have an especially high degree of correlation in voting. This presumably reduces the benefits of majority rule voting. As Estlund notes, "If individuals vote in blocks, the effective number of voters is reduced from the number of individuals to the number of blocks, and this reduces the competence of the group, other things being equal" (1989: 1318). Does this mean that an effective search for the general will must prohibit the voluntaristic clustering of like-minded individuals?

Grofman and Feld point out that Rousseau is not friendly toward factions; at one point, Rousseau seems to echo clearly a Condorcetian concern with correlated voting in factions:

> If, when the people, being furnished with adequate information, held its deliberations, the citizens had no communication one with another, the grand total of the small differences would always give the general will, and the decision would always be good. But when factions arise, and partial associations are formed at the expense of the great association, the will of each of these associations becomes general in relation to its members, while it remains particular in relation to the State: it may then be said that there are no longer as many votes as there are men, but only as many as there are associations. The differences become less numerous and give a less general result (Rousseau [1762] 1952: 396).

What then is to be done about factions? As Madison reminds us, it is possible to control factions "by destroying the liberty which is essential to its existence." However, this remedy "is worse than the disease. Liberty is to faction what air is to fire, an aliment without which it instantly expires. But it could not be less folly to abolish liberty, which is essential to political life, because it nourishes faction, than it would be to wish to annihilate air" ([1787] 1937: 55).

Rousseau himself is unclear about what to do about factions. He would rather they did not exist: "It is therefore essential, if the general will is to be able to express itself, that there should be no partial society within the State, and that each citizen should think only his own thoughts: which was indeed the sublime and unique system established by the great Lycurgus" ([1762] 1952: 396). He follows this with an apparently favorable footnote to Machiavelli, saying that "sects and parties" are harmful, and that the founder of a Republic ought to prevent enmities "from growing into sects." This gives support to an interpretation of Rousseau which emphasizes the potential for totalitarian collectivism in Rousseau.

Yet Rousseau suggests that, "If there are partial societies [factions], it is best to have as many as possible and to prevent them from being unequal" ([1785] 1952: 396). This ambiguity is reflected in the small literature on the Condorcet paradox: is the suppression of faction necessary in order to experience the judgmental synergies of majority rule? Or can factions be numerous and small enough to have only a minor impact on the results of the jury theorem?

Estlund suggests that factions might actually be helpful if majority rule is used within factions. Grofman and Feld (1989) counter with results showing that there is inevitably a reduction in overall competence by embedding majority rule within groups. However, their analysis of sub-groups within groups maintains the assumption of independence among voters, and therefore seems notably inappropriate for the analysis of factions, where presumably there would be strong positive correlations among members of a faction, and low or negative correlations between members of different factions. The question is then still open: how do we characterize the effect of correlated groups of voters on the efficacy of majority rule? And if public deliberation and political factions have deleterious effects on group judgment and must be "controlled," then are the requirements of effective majority rule inconsistent with normal democratic views of civil liberties?

19.5   On the Scope of Political Participation

A related concern regarding the implications of the jury theorem for democracy has to do with the desirable scope of participation. Condorcet himself believed that only a limited number of people in any society would have sufficient competence to participate in democratic decisionmaking. "A very numerous assembly cannot be composed of very enlightened men." In a large assembly, therefore, "there will be a great number of questions upon which the probability of the truth of the vote of each voter will be below $\frac{1}{2}$" (Condorcet [1785] 1976: 49). As Condorcet pointed out, in such a case, the accuracy of majority rule tends toward zero, rather than one, as group size increases. This seems necessarily to support a narrow scope for majoritarian politics.

Condorcet's views on this point have been shared by many in politics who have supported restrictions on the suffrage in American history. Francis Parkman set the tone for many of the Progressive era suffrage restrictions by blaming the "diseases of the body politic" on "indiscriminate suffrage," which had given equal votes to members of an "ignorant proletariat" (Schiesl 1977). Southerners in the U.S. used similar claims regarding the dangers of allowing the illiterate to vote as rationales for the disenfranchisement of blacks by means of the poll tax and other registration requirements (Kousser 1974); and similar arguments were maintained throughout the controversy over the Voting Rights Act of 1965.

In sum, the view of democracy that seems to follow from the Condorcet jury theorem is disturbing indeed. In order to keep voting independent, free speech may need to be limited and factions may need to be controlled. In order to keep individual proficiency levels up, participation may be limited to an "informed" elite. Is it really necessary to conduct political decision-making in a sterile environment, limited in discourse and in scope of participation?

The primary contribution of this paper is to demonstrate that, with the correct understanding of the effect of correlated voting on group judgments, it is possible to reconcile a libertarian public deliberation, vigorous political factions, and widespread political participation with effective majority rule.

19.6 The Generalization of Condorcet's Jury Theorem

This section offers a sufficient condition for Condorcet's result to hold when the votes are correlated in any manner whatsoever; for a more complete development, see Ladha (1992). By allowing interdependence among voters, this generalization, unlike the original jury theorem, provides insight into the value of political deliberation, political factions, and Rousseau's general will.

Suppose a group of individuals faces a binary choice such that one alternative is Pareto superior to the other; if everyone had perfect information, the vote for the superior alternative would be unanimous. Let $\chi_i = 1$ if member i votes for the Pareto superior alternative, and $\chi_i = 0$ otherwise. We will let $\pi_i = Pr(\chi_i = 1)$; π_i is thus the probability that individual i votes for the superior alternative. We let $q_i = 1 - \pi_i$.

Unlike Condorcet, we want to allow for the possibility of interdependent voting. We define r_{ij} to be the probability that both individuals i and j simultaneously vote for the Pareto superior alternative:

$$r_{ij} = Pr(\chi_i = 1; \chi_j = 1).$$

With independent voting, r_{ij} must equal $\pi_i \pi_j$—but we specifically allow r_{ij} to be different from the product $\pi_i \pi_j$; note that $r_{ii} = \pi_i$. Define the following averages:

$$\overline{\chi} = \frac{\sum_i^n \chi_i}{n}; \; \overline{\pi} = \frac{\sum_i^n \pi_i}{n}; \; \overline{q} = \frac{\sum_i^n q_i}{n} = 1 - \overline{\pi}; \; \overline{r} = \frac{\sum_i^n \sum_{j \neq i}^n r_{ij}}{n(n-1)},$$

where $\overline{r}$, the average $\{r_{ij}\}$, is a measure of the degree of inter-dependent voting.

Let σ_i^2 be the variance of χ_i. Because χ_i is a dichotomous random variable, it follows that $\sigma_i^2 = \pi_i q_i$. Let σ^2 be the variance of $\overline{\chi}$. Then (Billingsley 1986: 77):

$$\sigma^2 = \frac{\overline{\pi}}{n} + \frac{n-1}{n}\overline{r} - \overline{\pi}^2. \tag{1}$$

We are now in a position to state a sufficient condition for majority rule judgmental superiority, *even without independent voting*. The condition restricts the average level of inter-dependent voting $\bar{r}$.

Theorem 1: Let $\xi(n)$ be the probability that a majority of n individuals selects the superior of two alternatives and π_i be the probability that individual i selects the superior alternative. Let $\bar{\pi} > 0.5$ be the average $\{\pi_i\}$. Then, by Cantelli's inequality:

$$\xi(n) > \frac{\delta^2}{\sigma^2 + \delta^2}, \qquad (2)$$

where $\delta = 0.5 - \bar{\pi}$ and σ is as defined above. Moreover

$$\xi(n) > \bar{\pi} \text{ if } \bar{r} < \bar{\pi} - \frac{n}{n-1}\frac{(\bar{\pi}-0.25)\bar{q}}{\bar{\pi}} \equiv r^*(n,\bar{\pi}), \qquad (3)$$

where $\bar{r}$ and $\bar{q}$ are as defined above.

Proof. See Appendix I.

Condition (2) guarantees that the judgmental competence of majority rule will be greater than a ratio given by the variance of $\bar{\chi}$ and $\delta = .5 - \bar{\pi}$. Using this fact, condition (3) states that if $\bar{r}$ were less than $r^*(n,\bar{\pi})$, then Condorcet's result would hold. If the average correlation is low enough, then majority rule will result in better decisions than the average voter could make.

For a three-voter example, consider a situation in which the respective levels of "expertise" among the three voters are $\pi_1 = .48$, $\pi_2 = .65$, and $\pi_3 = .88$. The average level of expertise of the three voters is .67. Then by equation (3), the critical value for $\bar{r}$ is $r^*(3, 0.67) = .3597$. As long as the average degree of interdependence is less than that, then majority rule will result in the selection of the correct outcome more than 67% of the time.

Notice that this condition allows *some* voters to be highly inter-dependent, as long as the average level of interdependence is low enough. For instance, suppose $r_{23} = .575$, indicating that the two of them form a faction which votes together with greater frequency than independence would allow (if voters 2 and 3 were independent, then r_{23} would be equal to $(.65) \times (.88) = .572$). As long as $r_{12} + r_{13} < .5041$, then $\bar{r}$ would be less than .3597, which is the critical level of dependence.

Thus, majority rule accuracy would exceed that of the average voter (.67) even in the presence of one relatively uninformed voter ($\pi_1 = .48 < .5$) and even in the presence of one interdependent faction comprising voters 2 and 3. The Condorcet result is not as sensitive as one might think to variations in expertise and to inter-dependent voting.

Note that Theorem 1 holds whatever may be the distribution of $\bar{\chi} = \sum_{i=1}^{n}\frac{x_i}{n}$. Results stronger than Theorem 1 are obtainable by requiring $\bar{\chi}$ to follow specific distributions; see Ladha (1993, 1995).

19.7 The Special Case of Equal Expertise

The connection between the inter-dependence terms r_{ij} and correlation coefficients means that the condition for majority rule judgmental superiority can be stated in terms of the correlation coefficient. Let ρ_{ij} be the coefficient of correlation between χ_i and χ_j. By definition, $\rho_{ij} = \frac{(r_{ij} - \pi_i \pi_j)}{\sigma_i \sigma_j}$ for $i \neq j; \rho_{ii} = 1$. The average of the coefficients of correlation is given by $\bar{\rho} = \sum_i^n \sum_{j \neq i}^n \frac{\rho_{ij}}{n(n-1)}$.

Because of this, requiring $\bar{r}$ to be small is akin to requiring the average correlation coefficient to be small. To see this, note $r_{ij} = \rho_{ij}\sigma_i\sigma_j + \pi_i\pi_j$. Thus, given $\{\pi_i\}$, and hence $\{\sigma_i\}$, lower $\{r_{ij}\}$ correspond to lower $\{\rho_{ij}\}$.

Further insight can be developed by considering the special case in which all individuals have equal levels of expertise, so that $\pi_i = \pi$ for all i. Then it must be the case that $\sigma_i^2 = \pi q; r_{ij} = \rho_{ij}\pi q + \pi^2$; and $\bar{r} = \bar{\rho}\pi q + \pi^2$. Substitute $\bar{r}$ in (3) to obtain:

$$\xi(n) > \pi \text{ if } \bar{\rho} < 1 - \frac{n}{n-1} \frac{\pi - 0.25}{\pi^2} \equiv \rho^*(n, \pi). \qquad (4)$$

Condition (4) states that if the votes are not "highly" correlated, then Condorcet's theorem is still valid. For instance, suppose $n = 37$ and $\pi = .6$. Then the majority of the assembly will select the superior alternative with a probability greater than .6 as long as $\bar{\rho}$ is less than $\rho^*(37, 0.6) = 0.0008$.[3]

Once again, (4) constrains the mean, $\bar{\rho}$, not individual ρ_{ij}. Thus, some votes may be highly correlated so long as the average correlation is below the threshold defined by $\rho^*(n, \pi)$. In contrast, for independence, it is necessary, but not sufficient, that $\rho_{ij} = 0$ for all $i, j, i \neq j$.

Table 1. The Upper Bound on the
Average Correlation by Cantelli's Inequality

n	$\pi = .51$	$\pi = .6$	$\pi = .75$	$\pi = .9$
3	- 0.499	- 0.458	- 0.333	- 0.204
5	- 0.250	-0.215	- 0.111	- 0.003
9	- 0.125	- 0.094	0.000	0.097
25	-0.041	-0.013	0.074	0.164
100	-0.010	0.018	0.102	0.189
435	-0.002	0.026	0.109	0.196
10000	0.000	0.028	0.111	0.197

Note. Suppose each of the n individuals votes for the superior alternative with $\pi > 0.5$. Then, a majority of them would do so with probability $> \pi$ if the average of the coefficients of correlation is less than the cell entry for (n, π).

---

[3] In particular, if the votes were uncorrelated, there would exist an integer K for each π such that $\xi(n) > \pi$ for groups of size $n > K$.

Table 1 presents values of $\rho^*(n, \pi)$ for selected values of n and π. As the table indicates, with small numbers of voters and relatively low values of π, strong differences of perspective (as manifested in negative average correlations between voters) are required to guarantee that majority rule is more accurate than a randomly chosen voter. As individual $\pi_i's$ increase, and as the number of voters increases, the average correlation coefficient can become higher, while preserving the effectiveness of majority rule judgments.

19.8 Political Participation: The Effect of Increasing Numbers of Interdependent Voters

The original Condorcet theorem not only stated that majority rule was superior to the individual voter, but that reliability of majority rule approached perfection as the size of the electorate increased. Does that result persist in the presence of interdependent voting? The following corollary establishes that conditions much weaker than independence will guarantee the same result.

Corollary: Suppose the average probability $\bar{\pi}$ of choosing the superior alternative is such that $\bar{\pi} > 0.5 + \epsilon$ where ϵ is an arbitrarily small positive number. Let $\bar{r}$ be the average of the joint probabilities r_{ij}. If $\bar{r} \to \bar{\pi}^2$ as $n \to \infty$, then $\xi(n) \to 1$.

Proof. See Appendix I.

When votes are independent and $\pi > 0.5$, we know from the Jury Theorem that as $n \to \infty$, $\xi(n) \to 1$. The Corollary states that the result holds under much weaker conditions. To interpret $\bar{r} \to \bar{\pi}^2$, let $\pi_i = \pi$ for all i. Then, $\bar{r} = \bar{\rho}\pi q + \pi^2 \to \pi^2$ if $\bar{\rho} \to 0$. Thus, as $n \to \infty, \xi(n) \to 1$ if $\bar{\rho} \to 0$. That is, as the average correlation tends to zero, group judgment can approach perfection. Again, *individual* coefficients of correlation may be quite high or low without changing this result.

The Corollary has very important implications for the scope of democratic participation. Unlike the original Condorcet jury theorem, it discourages elitist visions of limited participation. The Corollary establishes that the majority rule tends toward infallibility with greater participation as long as the *average* level of expertise is greater than .5, and the *average* correlation approaches zero. This means that everyone who has an expertise greater than .5 is contributing toward the average expertise constraint. Arguments that limit political participation to those few with levels of expertise in the very high range (for example, $\pi_i > .8$) are inappropriate if they would greatly reduce the beneficial effects of increasing numbers. To the extent that such "experts" might have more homogeneous points of view, limiting political participation to them might endanger the low average correlation which is also necessary for this result.

Indeed, the Corollary does not preclude relatively "uninformed" voters ($\pi_i < .5$) from enhancing the accuracy of majority rule, as long as their numbers do not lower the average probability below .5. A stronger case that recognizes the contribution of "uninformed" voters is offered below.

19.9 How Can "Uninformed" Voters Contribute?

We begin with an example that makes an important substantive contribution to understanding majority rule judgments.

EXAMPLE. For a group of three voters, let voters 1 and 2 be "informed" in the sense that $\pi_1 = \pi_2 = 0.8 > 0.5$. Suppose that the informed voters vote correctly together 60% of the time; thus, $r_{12} = 0.6$. Let voter 3 be "uninformed" in the sense that $\pi_3 = 0.4 < 0.5$. Suppose further $r_{13} = 0.2 < \pi_1\pi_3 = 0.32$, and $r_{23} = 0.2 < \pi_2\pi_3 = 0.32$. Thus voter 3 votes with the two informed voters *less* often than if he were independent of them. That is, the action of voter 3 is negatively correlated with the actions of voters 1 and 2. Thus, voter 3 is not only uninformed, he tends to do the opposite of what the two informed voters do. Would it be better to disenfranchise this uninformed, contrary voter?

Without the uninformed voter, either informed voter is correct 80% of the time, and they are both right 60% of the time. We would do better to allow either informed voter to be a dictator than to require them to agree.

However, by allowing the uninformed voter to vote, and using majority rule, the situation is much improved. To see this, note that $\bar{\pi} = \frac{2}{3} > 0.5, \bar{r} = \frac{1}{3}$. By (1), $\sigma^2 = 0$; hence, $\frac{\delta^2}{(\delta^2+\sigma^2)} = 1$. Observe that, since $\sigma^2 = 0$, there will be *exactly* two votes for the truth on every occasion. Since two comprise a majority, it is evident that $\xi(n) = 1$, as demonstrated formally by (2).

The example reveals much about the desirable scope of political participation and furnishes a deeper insight into democracy. It seems patently obvious that more uninformed voters can only harm the political process—obvious, but wrong. In the example, the uninformed voter adds to the strength of the voting process by contributing a different point of view. By themselves, the two informed individuals attain the superior alternative with a probability no greater than 0.8. But with the uninformed voter, they attain the superior alternative with probability 1.0 using majority rule. The uninformed voter, far from diluting the expertise of the two informed voters, allows them to achieve perfect reliability by means of majority rule.

The remarkable contribution of the uninformed is not too difficult to decipher: it lies in his negative correlations with the other voters. The negative correlations are valuable because they tend to reduce the variance of the sum of the votes which, in turn, helps increase the probability of attaining the superior alternative. Appendix II illustrates the counter-intuitive result that an uninformed voter could enhance group effectiveness.

This does not mean that we should entrust the collective decision to the uninformed voter. In fact we should not, just the way we refrain from investing all resources in one security with a relatively low return. Yet, we may want the uninformed voter to participate in the decisionmaking process, just the way we include the security, with a low return, in our portfolio. The contribution of the uninformed voter to the society is akin to that of the security to the portfolio: Both reduce the variance of the underlying random variable. The low-yield security is valuable because it reduces the portfolio variance or risk; the uninformed voter is valuable when he reduces the variance of the sum of the votes, and thereby, increases the value of $\xi(n)$, the probability that a majority of voters selects the superior alternative.

As an illustration, imagine that there are three geologists trained under three different systems for identifying oil reserves, who rely on different characteristics of land formation to make their predictions. Two of the systems are notably more accurate than the third; nevertheless, the landform characteristics utilized by the third geologist (and ignored by the first two) have some predictive ability. When the two more reliable geologists agree, they are very likely to be correct. In those rarer situations in which the two more successful geologists disagree, then the information supplied by the third geologist is better not ignored. Rather than flipping a coin in those situations in which the two successful geologists disagree, it is better to go with the majority that includes the less successful geologist.

While counter-intuitive, the importance of (negatively correlated) uninformed voters is similar to the argument made by Calvert (1985) about the "value of biased information." Calvert argues that a decision-maker may prefer to have a biased adviser on her staff, on the grounds that on those rare occasions when the biased adviser councils contrary to his bias, that is a strong signal. Similarly, on those occasions in which two Senators who normally disagree find themselves on the same side of an issue, that is a strong signal (even if one Senator has less of a reputation for wisdom than the other).

Note that under the assumption of independence, $\xi(n) = 1$ only if the group is infinitely large; with correlated voting, it is possible to achieve the same degree of democratic perfection with a small number of voters.

As long as the *average* probability of choosing the superior alternative is greater than .5, then the greatest danger to majority rule judgments comes from prohibiting freedom of expression rather than from permitting a minority of uninformed persons to participate politically. Freedom of speech emerges from this analysis of correlated voting as essential, because it protects the eccentric points of view that are negatively correlated with orthodox opinion.

Franklin Roosevelt evidently had a strong intuitive understanding of the role of negative correlations in effective group judgment. When questioned about some of the unorthodox ideas that were being floated around his administration, Roosevelt responded "You sometimes find something pretty good in the lunatic fringe." After all, he said, America had been remade by "a whole lot of things which in my boyhood were considered lunatic fringe" (Schlesinger 1965, 526-27). Freedom of speech is, from this perspective, a vital institutional protection for those persons who interpret the world in a different way and are thus likely to vote in a way that is negatively correlated with some number of other voters in society.

19.10 Negative Correlation and Factions

The example of the previous section is designed to provide an extreme result such that the different perspective of voter three allows majority rule to achieve perfect reliability. While extreme, the result is a general one: the more negatively correlated are the voters' choices, the greater is the reliability of majority rule (Ladha 1992).

The contribution of different perspectives to majority rule judgment is the means by which we can reconcile effective majority rule with group deliberation. While Grofman and Feld believed that the independence assumption of the original Condorcet theorem required "each voter [be] polled about his or her independently reached choice, without group deliberation," we can now see that group deliberation is acceptable as long as it includes those with different (negatively correlated) points of view.

Thus, while the individuals within a faction may have positively correlated votes, the importance of factions is that correlations across factions are likely to be negative; indeed, the term "faction" seems to imply a difference of opinion between factions just as much as it implies homogeneity within. Webster's dictionary defines faction as a group "that is often contentious." Contentiousness across factions allows for a low average correlation.

For example, imagine a five-voter electorate with two factions: one faction of three voters and one faction of two. Imagine the average probability π is equal to .6. The correlation between two members of the same faction we will assume to be high—for example .75. If the existence of factions merely implied agreement within groups, then effective majority rule would be unlikely.

However, the existence of two factions must imply a low level of correlation between two voters of different factions—otherwise, the factions would be in agreement and they could not be properly regarded as factions. Furthermore, there are more cross-faction correlations (six) than there are within-faction correlations (four). The *average* correlation may then be quite low for this majority rule electorate, despite the high positive correlations within factions.

With $\pi = .6$ and $n = 5$, the critical value for $r^* = .308$. With the intrafactional correlations equal to .75, this critical value will be reached as long as the *cross-factional* correlations are less than or equal to .013. This means that majority rule will result in a success rate of greater than 60% *despite* the fact that the three-person faction tends to see things similarly.

The importance of this example is that it demonstrates the compatibility of correlated voting and factions with effective majority rule judgments. While positive correlations would seem to be typical within factions, low or negative correlations across factions would seem to be just as inevitable.

19.11   Rousseau on Factions

Does this analysis allow us to say anything more about the role of factions in politics? In particular, can we defend Rousseau's claim that if factions are to exist, "it is best to have as many as possible and to prevent them from being unequal" (Rousseau [1762] 1952: 396)?

Let us assume that the correlations among voters in each faction is high and positive. Let us further assume that the defining characteristic of a faction is the disagreements its members have with other factions. Assume that the inter-faction correlations are *all constant and low*, and the intra-faction correlations are *all constant and high*. Clearly, the average correlation will be lowest when the difference between the number of intergroup and intragroup correlations is as large as possible. What would minimize the average correlation? That is, what would maximize group effectiveness? We propose the following result:

Theorem 2.: For a given number of factions, group effectiveness is maximized when the factions are of equal size.

To prove Theorem 2 (see Appendix I), it is required to show that the difference between the number of interfaction and intrafaction correlations is maximized when the factions are of equal size.

Furthermore, the number of inter-faction correlations will naturally increase as the number of factions increases, holding the population constant. Thus, for a given population and degree of individual expertise, Rousseau's speculation about factional structure is exactly supported by the analysis of group judgments with correlated voting. As long as intra-factional correlations are higher than inter-factional correlations, the average correlation could be expected to be lower than the critical value for effective group judgments with many equally sized factions.

The revised version of the jury theorem therefore leads us with a much more positive view of factions, in which the factional conflict is not an evil to be controlled, but the means by which groups synergistically make progress toward truth. As John Stuart Mill wrote:

> Truth, in the great practical concerns of life, is so much a question of the reconciling and combining of opposites, that very few have minds sufficiently capacious and impartial to make the adjustment with an approach to correctness, and it has to be made by the rough process of a struggle between the combatants fighting under hostile banners (Mill [1859] 1952: 289).

This contention was irrelevant to the original version of the Condorcet jury theorem; the analysis of correlated judgments embraces Mills' view as a necessary condition for the democratic synergies postulated by Rousseau.

19.12 Conclusion

The original interpretation of the Condorcet jury theorem left analysts wondering if perhaps political discourse and factions limited the efficacy of majority rule. This would have been an uncomfortable conclusion to reach, as it would have implied that different democratic values would be in opposition. The generalized Condorcet jury theorem shows that group judgments are not so fragile that they require an antiseptic environment—without discourse, or factions—in order to be effective in the search for the general will. Discourse is not detrimental as long as it allows all points of view to be heard. Factions, indeed, are to be encouraged because they harbor and protect the uncorrelated (or negatively correlated) points of view that drive effective majority processes.

This result greatly strengthens the case for the epistemic interpretation of voting of Coleman and Ferejohn (1986). It also increases the possibility of reconciling civil libertarianism and majority rule democracy. If effective majority rule decision-making required the regulation of discourses and factions, then that would raise the specter of a majority rule process that infringed on civil liberties. But through the lens of the generalized Condorcet jury theorem, the requirements of effective majority rule decision-making are thoroughly civil libertarian: the most effective decisions are made when all points of view are protected by freedom of speech and encouraged to engage in a free-wheeling political discourse. Minority points of view are valuable, even when held by the uninformed, because they add to the number of factions and because they introduce the highly valued negative correlations with the rest of the electorate. Factions are to be encouraged, as long as they harbor people who have quite different points of view. Political discourse and the presence of multiple, competing factions are thus the ingredients for an effective majoritarian search for the general will.

Appendix I

Proof of Theorem 1.[4] Let $\delta = 0.5 - \overline{\pi}$; thus, $\delta \in (-0.5, 0)$. By Cantelli's inequality: $\xi(n) = Pr(\overline{X} > 0.5) = Pr(\overline{X} - \overline{\pi} > \delta) \geq \frac{\delta^2}{\delta^2 + \sigma^2}$.

Hence, $\xi(n) > \overline{\pi}$ if $\frac{\delta^2}{\delta^2 + \sigma^2} > \overline{\pi}$,

i.e., if $\overline{\pi}\sigma^2 < (1 - \overline{\pi})(\overline{\pi}^2 - \overline{\pi} + 0.25)$,

i.e., if $\overline{\pi}\left[\frac{\overline{\pi}}{n} + \frac{n-1}{n}\overline{r} - \overline{\pi}^2\right] < (1 - \overline{\pi})(\overline{\pi}^2 - \overline{\pi} + 0.25)$, by (1).

Collecting terms gives (3).

Proof of the Corollary. If $\overline{r} \to \overline{\pi}^2$ as $n \to \infty$ then by (1), $\sigma^2 = \frac{(\overline{\pi} - \overline{r})}{n} + \overline{r} - \overline{\pi}^2 \to 0$; and by (2), $\xi(n) \to 1$.

---

[4] The proof of Theorem 1 and that of the Corollary appear in Ladha (1992). Being brief, they are reproduced here for the reader's convenience.

Proof of Theorem 2. Suppose there are $m = nk$ members who constitute k factions of size $n_1, \ldots, n_k$ possibly of unequal size. Let M_{intra} and M_{inter} be the number of intragroup and intergroup coefficients of correlation, respectively. Then:

$$M_{intra} = \sum_{i=1}^{k} n_i(n_i - 1) = \sum_{i=1}^{k} n_i^2 - m;$$

$$M_{inter} = \sum_{i=1}^{k} \sum_{j=1; j \neq i}^{k} n_i n_j = \sum_{i=1}^{k} n_i \sum_{j=1}^{k} n_j - \sum_{i=1}^{k} n_i^2 = m^2 - \sum_{i=1}^{k} n_i^2.$$

We wish to show that $M_{inter} - M_{intra} = m^2 - 2\sum_{i=1}^{k} n_i^2 + m$ is maximized when $n_i = n \ \forall \ i$, that is, $m^2 - 2kn^2 + m \geq m^2 - 2\sum_{i=1}^{k} n_i^2 + m$, or equivalently, when $kn^2 \leq \sum_{i=1}^{k} n_i^2$ holds.

By the Cauchy-Schwarz inequality, $\left(\sum_{i=1}^{k} n_i\right)^2 \leq k \sum_{i=1}^{k} n_i^2$.

Hence, it suffices to show that $kn^2 \leq \frac{1}{k}\left(\sum_{i=1}^{k} n_i\right)^2$.

However, $m = nk = \sum_{i=1}^{k} n_i$, so the inequality is satisfied.

Appendix II

This Appendix illustrates the result that under majority-rule voting, an uninformed voter ($\pi_3 = .4$) *could* enhance the effectiveness of two informed voters ($\pi_1 = .8 = \pi_2$). Let Π denote the probability operator. Now

$$\begin{aligned}
\xi(3) &= \Pi(\chi_1 + \chi_2 + \chi_3 \geq 2). \text{ Let} \\
\Pi(x_1, x_2, x_3) &= \Pi(\chi_1 = x_1, \chi_2 = x_2, \chi_3 = x_3). \text{ Moreover} \\
r_{ij} &= \Pi(\chi_i = 1, \chi_j = 1), \text{ given } i \neq j. \text{ We have} \\
\xi(3) &= \Pi(1,1,0) + \Pi(1,0,1) + \Pi(0,1,1) + \Pi(1,1,1) \\
&= \Pi(1,1,0) + \Pi(1,1,1) + \Pi(1,0,1) + \Pi(1,1,1) + \\
&\quad \Pi(0,1,1) + \Pi(1,1,1) - 2\Pi(1,1,1) \\
&= r_{12} + r_{13} + r_{23} - 2\Pi(1,1,1).
\end{aligned}$$

If the χ_i's were independent, the probabilities would be as in Table 2 with $\xi(3) = 0.768$.

Table 2. Probabilities for Independent Votes.

	$\Pi(1,1,0) = .384$	
$\Pi(1,0,1) = .064$	$\Pi(1,1,1) = .256$	$\Pi(0,1,1) = .064$
$\Pi(1,0,0) = .096$	$\Pi(0,0,1) = .016$	$\Pi(0,1,0) = .096$
	$\Pi(0,0,0) = .024$	

From Table 2, $r_{12} = .384 + .256 = .64, r_{13} = .064 + .256 = .32 = r_{23}$, and $\xi(3) = .768$.

In the example of the text, however, $r_{12} = 0.6, r_{13} = 0.2$, and $r_{23} = 0.2$, which implies that the probabilities are as in Table 3.

Table 3. Probabilities for Negatively Correlated Votes.

	$\Pi(1,1,0) = 0.6$	
$\Pi(1,0,1) = 0.2$	$\Pi(1,1,1) = 0.0$	$\Pi(0,1,1) = 0.2$
$\Pi(1,0,0) = 0.0$	$\Pi(0,0,1) = 0.0$	$\Pi(0,1,0) = 0.0$
	$\Pi(0,0,0) = 0.0$	

As observed in the example, the distribution of $\overline{\chi}$ has all its mass on $\frac{2}{3}$, so $\xi(3) = 1$.

Note that it is rather simple to construct examples where the probability that the majority is correct is between 0.768 (independent voting) and 1. An intermediate stage between Tables 2 and 3 is shown in Table 4, where the votes are uncorrelated.

Table 4. Probabilities for Uncorrelated Votes.

	$\Pi(1,1,0) = 0.40$	
$\Pi(1,0,1) = 0.08$	$\Pi(1,1,1) = 0.24$	$\Pi(0,1,1) = 0.08$
$\Pi(1,0,0) = 0.08$	$\Pi(0,0,1) = 0.00$	$\Pi(0,1,0) = 0.08$
	$\Pi(0,0,0) = 0.04$	

Here $r_{12} = .64; r_{13} = .32$. As before, $\pi_1 = .8 = \pi_2$ and $\pi_3 = .4$. $\text{Cov}(\chi_1, \chi_2) = E(\chi_1\chi_2) - E(\chi_1)E(\chi_2) = .64 - .64 = 0$. Likewise, $\text{Cov}(\chi_1, \chi_3) = 0$, and $\text{Cov}(\chi_2, \chi_3) = 0$. Clearly $\xi(3) = .8$.

References

Billingsley, P. 1986. *Probability and Measure.* New York: Wiley.

Black, D. 1958. *The Theory of Committees and Elections.* Cambridge: Cambridge University Press.

Calvert, R. 1985. "The Value of Biased Information: A Rational Choice Model of Political Advice," *Journal of Politics* 47: 530-555.

Coleman, J. and J. Ferejohn. 1986. "Democracy and Social Choice," *Ethics* 97: 26-38.

Condorcet, Marquis de. [1785] 1976. *Essay on the Application of Mathematics to the Theory of Decision-making.* Reprinted in *Condorcet: Selected Writings,* K. M. Baker, ed. Indianapolis: Bobbs-Merrill.

Estlund, D. 1989. "Democratic Theory and the Public Interest: Condorcet and Rousseau Revisited," *American Political Science Review* 83: 1317-1322.

Grofman, B., and S. L. Feld. 1988. "Rousseau's General Will: A Condorcetian Perspective," *American Political Science Review* 82: 567-576.

Grofman, B. and S. L. Feld. 1989. "Rejoinder to Estlund and Waldron," *American Political Science Review* 83: 1328-1335.

Grofman, B., G. Owen, and S. L. Feld. 1983. "Thirteen Theorems in Search of the Truth," *Theory and Decision* 15: 261-278.

Grofman, B., G. Owen and S. L. Feld. 1984. "Group Size and the Performance of a Composite Group Majority: Statistical Truths and Empirical Results," *Organizational Behavior and Human Performance* 33: 350-359.

Kousser, M. 1974. *The Shaping of Southern Politics: Suffrage Restriction and the Establishment of the One-Party South.* New Haven: Yale University Press.

Ladha, K. K. 1992. "Condorcet's Jury Theorem, Free Speech and Correlated Votes," *American Journal of Political Science* 36: 617-634.

Ladha, K. K. 1993. "Condorcet's Jury Theorem in Light of De Finetti's Theorem: Majority-Rule Voting with Correlated Votes," *Social Choice and Welfare* 10: 69-85.

Ladha, K. K. 1995. "Information Pooling through Majority Rule Voting: Condorcet's Jury Theorem with Correlated Votes," *Journal of Economic Behavior and Organization* 26: 353-372.

Madison, J. [1787] 1937. *The Federalist: No. 10.* New York: The Modern Library.

Mill, J. S. [1859] 1952. *On Liberty.* Reprinted in *Great Books of the Western World*, Vol. 43. R. Hutchins, ed. Chicago: Encyclopedia Brittanica.

Miller, N. R. 1986. "Information, Electorates, and Democracy: Some Extensions and Interpretations of the Condorcet Jury Theorem," in *Information Pooling and Group Decision Making.*

Nitzan, S. and J. Paroush. 1984. "The Significance of Independent Decisions in Uncertain Dichotomous Choice Situations," *Theory and Decision* 17: 47-60.

Rao, C. R. 1973. *Linear Statistical Inference and its Applications.* New York: John Wiley.

Rawls, J. 1971. *A Theory of Justice.* Oxford: Oxford University Press.

Riker, W. 1982. *Liberalism against Populism: A Confrontation between the Theory of Democracy and the Theory of Social Choice.* San Francisco: W. H. Freeman.

Rousseau, J-J. [1762] 1952. *The Social Contract: Or Principles of Political Right.* Reprinted in *Great Books of the Western World*, Vol. 38. R. Hutchins, ed. Chicago: Encyclopedia Brittanica.

Schiesl, M. J. 1977. *The Politics of Efficiency: Municipal Administration and Reform in America.* Berkeley: University of California Press.

Schlesinger, A. M., Jr. 1965. *The Coming of the New Deal.* Boston: Houghton Mifflin.

Schofield, N. 1972. "Is Majority Rule Special?" In *Probability Models of Collective Decision Making*, R. Niemi and H. Weisberg, eds. Columbus: Merrill.

Waldron, J. 1989. "Democratic Theory and the Public Interest: Condorcet and Rousseau Revisited," *American Political Science Review* 83: 1322-1328.

Young, H. P. 1986. "Optimal Ranking and Choice from Pairwise Comparisons," in *Information Pooling and Group Decision Making, op cit.*

Name Index

Abreu, D. 76-77;

Ainsworth, S. 355, 358;

Aizerman, M. A. 80;

Aldrich, J. 120, 146;

Alesina, A. 363-364, 370, 382;

Allum, P. A. 326, 331;

Alt, J. E. 315, 319, 333;

Andrae, C. 122, 147;

Appelbaum, E. 341, 358;

Aranson, P. 19, 342, 358;

Arrow, K. 1, 3, 8-9, 19, 25-26, 31, 63, 66, 69, 77;

Auernheimer, L. 382;

Aumann, R. J. 2, 19, 266, 277, 291, 346-347, 349, 358;

Austen-Smith, D. 13, 19, 114, 118, 134, 137, 139-142, 146-147, 266, 277, 291, 342-343, 346-347, 354-356, 358-359;

Axelrod, R. 128, 147, 265, 267, 276-277, 292, 317, 331;

Azariadis, C. 365, 382;

Backus, D. 382;

Badinter, E. 4, 20;

Badinter, R. 4, 20;

Baigent, N. 84, 87-88, 91;

Bailyn, B. 7, 20;

Balboni, E. 331;

Baldassare, A. 327, 331;

Baldwin, R. 349, 358-359;

Balinski, M. 125, 134, 147;

Banks, J. 6, 13, 19-20, 113, 125-126, 128-130, 142, 145-147, 382;

Barberà, S. 28, 59;

Barnes, S. 321, 331;

Baron, D. 358-359;

Barrera, P. 329, 332;

Barro, R. J. 365, 370, 382;

Becker, G. 338-340, 359;

Bergstrom, T. 2, 20;

Berl, J. E., 160, 177;

Bhagwati, J. 338, 360;

Billingsley, P. 409;

Binmore, K. 346, 359;

Black, D. 1, 3-5, 20, 25-26, 40, 59, 113, 147, 391- 392, 409;

Blackorby, C. 29, 59;

Blau, J. A. 25-26, 28-29, 59;

Boland, P. J. 3, 20;

Borda, J. C. 95, 110;

Border, K. 27, 51, 54, 56-57, 59;

Bordes, G., 14, 20, 27, 46, 52, 54, 57, 59;

Borooah, V. 347, 359, 363, 382;

Borre, O. 274, 279, 292;

Bossert, W. 59;

Boylan, R., 383;

Brams, S. 87, 91, 144-145, 147;

Brock, W. 342, 359-360;

Brown, D. 9, 20;

Browne, E. 265, 277, 324, 332;

Budge, I. 266, 268, 272, 277-278, 327, 332;

Burns, N. E. 315, 319, 333;

Caciagli, M. 321, 332;

Cairns, R. 338, 359;

Calise, M. 332;

Calvert, R. 409;

Calvo, G. A. 370, 383;

Cameron, C. 337, 357, 361;

Campbell, D. E. 34, 57, 59, 69-72, 74-75, 77;

Canzoneri, M. B. 370, 383;

Carreras, F. 261;

Cazzola, F. 321, 332;

Chichilnisky, G. 5-6, 20;

Coggins, J. 359;

Cohen, G. D. 363, 382;
Coleman, J. 409;
Condorcet, M. J. A. N., Marquis de 1, 3-4, 20, 95, 110, 409;
Congleton, R. 338, 359;
Converse, P. E. 272-273, 278, 292;
Coughlin, P. 20, 183, 346, 348, 359;
Cox, G. 10, 20, 114, 131-134, 147, 184, 226, 236;
Crawford, V. 352, 359;
Damgaard, E. 276, 278;
Dasgupta, P. 346, 359;
De Grazia, A. 98, 104, 110;
Debreu, G. 1, 19;
Delorme, C. 339, 359;
Denzau, A. 183, 344, 359;
De Swaan, A. 265, 267-268, 276, 278, 292;
Della Sala, V. 329, 332;
DiPalma, G. 326, 332;
DiScala, S. M. 329, 332;
Dodd, L. 265, 278, 327, 332;
Dogan, M. 326, 332;
Donaldson, D. 29, 56, 59, 63, 77;
Downs, A. 12, 20, 113, 124-126, 136, 147;
Dreijmanis, J. 265, 277;
Driffill, J. 382;
Drissen, E. 347, 359-360;
Easton, S. T. 319, 334;
Eavey, C. L. 14, 20, 161-164, 173-176, 178, 342, 344, 360;
Edelman, G. S. 342, 344, 360;
Elster, J. 337, 360;
Enelow, J. M. 6, 20, 59, 113, 146-147, 183;
Estlund, D. 409;
Fan, K. 2, 20;
Farlie, D. 268, 277;

Farneti, P. 321, 332;
Farrell, J. 356, 360;
Feenstra, R. 338, 360;
Feld, S. L. 3, 21, 143, 148, 159, 178, 280, 292, 334, 409-410;
Felker, L. 278;
Ferejohn, J. 409;
Findlay, R. 338, 360;
Fiorina, M. 13-14, 20, 156-164, 177-178;
Fischer, S. 365, 383;
Fishburn, P. 59, 87, 91;
Fisher, R. 338, 360;
Flanagan, S. C. 268, 278;
Franklin, M. N. 265-266, 278, 324, 332;
Frey, B. S. 363, 383-384;
Gaertner, W. 26-27, 60;
Gale, D. 2, 20;
Galli, G. 321, 323, 332;
Gamson, W. A. 265, 278;
Gardner, R. 347, 360;
Geanakopolis J. 2, 21;
Gibbard, A. 66, 70, 77;
Gibbons, R. 356, 360;
Gilligan, T. 146-147;
Glazer, A. 176-177;
Golan, E. 292;
Goodstein, E. 155, 160, 164, 177, 179;
Gordon, D. P. 370, 382;
Graham-Tomasi, T. 359;
Greenberg, J. 115, 118, 120-123, 126, 140, 145, 147;
Groennings, S. 272, 278;
Grofman, B. 3, 21, 159, 176-178, 265-268, 270-272, 274-275, 278-280, 292, 334, 409-410;
Groot, F. 363, 384;
Grossman, H. I. 383;

Guarnieri, C. 332;
Guha, A. S. 66, 70, 77;
Gwartney, J. D. 383;
Hall, R. E. 365, 383;
Hammond, T. H. 8, 21, 149, 178-179;
Harsanyi, J. 346, 360;
Hart, S. 261-262;
Havrilesky, T. 363, 383;
Hayes, W. L. 387, 392;
Hellman, S. 326, 332;
Hearl, D. 266, 272, 278, 332;
Herman, V. 278, 332;
Hess, G. D. 363, 383;
Hewitt, R. 3, 7, 21;
Hibbs, D. A. 363, 383;
Hillman, A. 339, 360;
Hinckley, B. 265, 278;
Hinich, M. 6, 19-20, 59, 113, 134, 137, 146-147, 183-184, 358;
Hoffman, E. 13, 21, 159-164, 178;
Husted, T., 383;
Ianada, K. I. 60;
Isaac, M. 151-152, 155, 178;
Jefferson, T. 7;
Johanson, L. 337, 360;
Kalai, E. 26-27, 31, 33-34, 36-38, 43, 54, 60;
Kambhu, J. 354, 360;
Kannai, Y. 57-59;
Katz, E. 339, 341, 358, 360;
Katz, R. S. 332;
Kau, J., 337, 345, 360;
Keane, M., 383;
Keenan, D. 337, 345, 360;
Kelly, J. S. 72, 76-77;
Keman, H. 327, 332;
Kenny, L. 383;
Kim, K. H. 26, 60;

King, G. 315, 319, 333;
Kirman, A. 9, 21;
Koehler, D. 265, 279;
Kolman, K. 337, 360;
Kousser, M. 410;
Kramer, G. 4, 21, 183, 226, 236;
Krehbiel, K. 146-147;
Kreps, D. 356, 360;
Kurz, M. 261-262, 346-347, 349, 358;
Kydland, F. 383;
Ladha, K. K. 391-392, 410;
Laffont, J. 358, 360;
Laing, J. D. 158-159, 171-172, 175-176, 178;
LaPalombara, J. 333;
Laver, M. 143, 236, 265-266, 279-280, 315, 319-320, 324, 333-334;
Lazear, E. P. 365, 383;
Le Breton, M. 10, 14, 20-21, 27, 38, 40, 46, 52, 54, 57, 59-60, 63, 77;
Ledyard, J. 134, 137, 147, 383;
Leiserson, M. 265, 279;
Leonardi, R. 323, 333;
Levy, D. 338, 360;
Lewis-Beck, M. S. 333;
Lijphart, A. 266, 279, 333;
Lindbeck, A. 346, 348, 361;
Lohmann, S. 355, 361;
Londregan, J. 363-364, 382;
Lucas, R. E. 383;
Luebbert, G. M. 265-267, 279;
Mackie, T. T. 265-266, 278, 332;
Madison, J. 7-9, 410;
Magee, S. 342, 359-360;
Mankiew, N. G. 384;
Mannheimer, R. 321, 323, 328, 332-333;
Manzella, A. 333;
Marradi, A. 276, 279, 324, 333;

Mas-Collel, A. 2, 20, 66, 70, 77;

Maschler, M. 266, 277, 291;

Maskin, E. 26-27, 54, 60, 76-78;

Mastropaolo, A. 321, 333;

Matsushima, H. 76, 78;

May, K. 89, 91;

Mayston, D. J. 60;

McKelvey, R. D. 2, 6, 13-14, 16, 21, 127, 147, 149, 153, 156, 160, 165-167, 169-173, 175-178, 183-184, 226-227, 230, 236, 266, 279, 292, 315, 317, 333, 383;

McKenzie, L. 1, 21;

McLean, I. 3, 7, 11, 21;

Mershon, C. 317, 319-320, 330-331, 333;

Michaels, R. 338, 361;

Michener, H. A. 150, 179;

Milgrom, P. 354, 361;

Mill, J. S. 122, 148, 410;

Miller, G. J. 8, 21, 149, 152, 155, 156, 160-161, 167- 169, 178-179;

Miller, N. R. 176, 179, 184, 410;

Mitchell, W. 337, 361;

Mitra, P. 338, 361;

Moffit, R. 383;

Mokken, R. 267, 278;

Moore, J. 76, 78;

Morgan, M. J. 265, 267, 275-276, 279;

Morgenstern, O. 38, 61, 201-205;

Morton, R. 337, 357, 361, 383;

Moulin, H. 13, 21, 80, 91, 118, 148;

Mueller, D. 337, 344-346, 348, 357, 359, 361;

Muller, E. 26-27, 31, 33-34, 36-38, 43, 54, 59-60;

Munger, M. 337, 344, 359, 361;

Murrel, P. 337, 346, 348, 359, 361;

Myerson, R. 358-359;

Nachbar, J. 3, 21;

Nagahisa, R. I. 57, 59, 74, 76-78;

Nakamura, K. 10, 21;

Nash J. F. 2, 21;

Nitzan, S. 38, 410;

Nixon, D., 21;

Nocifero, N. 326, 329, 333;

Nordhaus, W. D. 384;

North, D. 333;

Noviello, N. 176-177;

Nyarko, Y. 3, 21;

Olmsted, S. 158-159, 171-172, 175-176, 178;

Olomoki, D. 21;

Oppenheimer, J. 167-169, 179;

Ordeshook, P. C. 22, 39, 127, 134, 137, 147, 149, 153- 155, 156, 160, 164-167, 169-173, 175-177, 178-179, 184, 266, 279, 292;

Owen, G. 176-177, 251, 261-262, 266, 279, 346, 361, 410;

Page T. 2, 21;

Paine, T. 7;

Palfrey, T. 6, 21, 76, 78, 115, 145, 148;

Parisi, A. 321, 334;

Parks, R. 183;

Paroush, J. 410;

Pasquino, G. 321, 334;

Peck, R. 347, 361;

Peleg, B. 28, 59, 292;

Peretz, P. 384;

Persson, T. 384;

Petracca, O. M. 334;

Petrakis, E. 347, 361;

Pincus, J. 337, 361;

Plotnik, R. 337, 361;

Plott, C. 4, 11, 13-14, 20-22, 75, 78, 80, 91, 151- 152, 155-164, 177-179, 183;

Polemarchakis, H. 2, 21;

Pollio Salimbeni, A. 334;
Poole, K. 345, 361;
Potter, K. 150, 179;
Potters, J. 350, 354-357, 361;
Powell, G. B., Jr. 334;
Prandi, A. 321, 323, 332;
Prescott, E. 383;
Przeworski, A. 347, 361;
Pustetto, M. B. 334;
Quinn, D. P. 384;
Rae, D. 4, 19, 22;
Raisian, J. 384;
Randall, W. S. 7, 13, 22;
Rao, C. R. 410;
Rapoport, A. 266-267, 279, 292;
Rawls, J. 410;
Redekop, J. 57, 59;
Renaud, P. 337, 347, 361, 363, 384;
Repullo, R. L. 76, 78;
Rhodes, M. 321, 334;
Riker, W. 22, 95, 110, 114, 117, 128, 142, 148, 265, 279, 292, 334, 410;
Ritz, Z. 26, 60;
Roberts, J. 354, 361;
Robertson, D. 13, 22, 134, 136-137, 148, 266, 272, 278, 332;
Rodrik, D. 338, 341, 362;
Roe, T. 359;
Roemer, J. E. 59;
Rogerson, W. 338, 362;
Rogoff, K. 384;
Rohde, D. W. 265, 279;
Romer, T. 345, 361;
Rosenthal, H. 267, 279, 363-364, 382;
Roubini, N. 363, 382;
Roush, F. W. 26, 60;
Rousseau, J-J. 3-4, 393-399, 406-407, 410;

Rubin, P. 337, 345, 360;
Rubinstein, A. 10, 22, 144, 148, 359;
Runkle, D. 383;
Rusk, J. G. 274, 279, 292;
Saari, D. 6, 22, 94, 97-100, 110; 94, 101-102, 104- 105, 108-110;
Sachs, J. D. 363, 370, 382;
Saijo, T. 76, 78;
Sakurai, M. 150, 179;
Salamon, L. 337, 362;
Salant, S. W. 155, 160, 164, 177, 179;
Salles, M. 14, 20;
Sani, G. 321, 323, 328, 333;
Satterthwaite, M. 27, 31, 33-34, 36-38, 43, 54, 60;
Savage, L. 2, 22;
Schelling, T. C. 160, 178;
Schiesl, M. J. 410;
Schlozman, K. 345, 362;
Schneider, F. 363, 384;
Schofield, N. 4-6, 10, 13-14, 21-22, 127, 143, 148- 150, 178-179, 183, 221, 225-226, 230, 236, 266-267, 279-280, 292, 315, 317, 319-320, 324, 330, 333-334, 410;
Schram, A. 363, 384;
Schwarz, T. 184;
Sen, A. K. 67, 78; 80, 91;
Sen, Aruvna 76-77;
Sened, I. 21, 355, 358;
Shapiro, R. Y. 384;
Shapley, L. S. 251, 253-254, 256-259, 262-263, 346, 362;
Shepsle, K. 118, 120-123, 126, 140, 143, 145, 147-149, 179, 184, 292;
Shubik, M. 251, 262;
Sibert, A. 384;
Siegfried, J. 337, 362;
Slater, M. 321, 333;
Smith, Adam 1, 22;

Smith, V. 150, 179;
Snow, A. 339, 359;
Sobel, J. 352, 355, 359, 362;
Sonderman, D. 9, 21;
Sonnenschein, H. 2, 22, 66, 70, 77;
Spotts, F. 327, 334;
Srivistava, S. 76, 78;
Stiglitz, J. E. 365, 382;
Straffin, P. 144-145, 147, 265-267, 270, 280, 292;
Strnad, J. 10, 22, 76, 78;
Strom, G. S. 334;
Strom, K. 315, 317, 319, 321, 323, 327, 334;
Stroup, R. L. 383;
Sugden, R. 114, 121-124, 131, 148;
Suzumura 80, 91;
Svenjar, J. 348, 362;
Tabellini, G. 384;
Tarrow, S. 334;
Taylor, M. 19, 22, 265, 280;
Tierney, J. 345, 362;
Tirole, J. 358, 360;
Tollison, R. 337, 362;
Tovey, C. 176, 179;
Trannoy, A. 27, 40, 60;
Tsebelis, G. 334;
Tullock, G. 338-339, 362;
Ursprung, H. 119, 148, 342, 360, 362;
Valdini, S. 326, 329, 333;
Valen, H. 272-273, 278, 292;
van Huyck, J. 383;
van der Ploeg, F. 347, 359, 363, 382;
van Velthoven, B. 347-348, 362;
van Winden, F. 337, 346-348, 350, 354, 356-357, 359- 363, 384;
Venditti, R. 334;
von Neumann, J. 38, 61, 201-205;

Waldron, J. 410;
Walker, M. 9, 22;
Waller, C. 383;
Wallerstein, M. 347, 361;
Warwick, P. 319, 334;
Weber, S. 115, 118, 120-123, 126, 147;
Weg, E. 266-267, 279, 292;
Weibull, J. 346, 348, 361;
Weingast, B. R. 168, 179, 184;
Welch, W. 342, 345, 362;
Wellisz, S. 338, 360, 362;
Wertman, D. 333-334;
Weymark, J. A. 29, 56, 59, 63, 77;
Wieser, T. 327, 334;
Wilson, J. 338, 342, 362;
Wilson, R. B. 66, 69, 78, 356, 360;
Winer, M. 127, 147, 160, 169-172, 177-179, 266, 273- 275, 279-280, 292;
Winkler, R. L. 387, 392;
Winter, E. 262;
Wright, J. 354-355, 359;
Wolinsky, A. 359;
Wong, K. Y. 338, 362;
Xu, Y. 87-88, 91;
Young, H. P. 99, 110, 125, 134, 147, 410;
Yuen, K. 150, 179;
Zuckerman, A. 321, 334;
Zusman, P. 345-349, 362;

Subject Index

acyclic 9, 11, 76, 79-80, 84, 86, 186, 189; triple acyclic 80-81, 84;

agendas 97, 141;

altruism 170;

anonymity condition 87-90;

anonymous legislative voting rule 116-117, 136;

approval voting 87, 89-90, 133;

arbitrage 5;

Arrovian Research Program 2;

asymmetric substitution of alternatives 84, 86, 88;

Aumann Research Program 2;

backward induction 300-301, 306, 308, 311-314;

bargaining counter-proposals, by individuals 242-245, by groups 243-244;

bargaining sets of coalition members 123, 135, 142-143, 196, 221, 266, 284-285;

binary voting decisions 95, 97, 105-106, 108-109;

binomial theorem 3;

biostochastic matrix 42;

bliss (ideal) points 4, 6, 39-41, 117-119, 123, 130, 132, 156-160, 169, 172-173, 189, 193, lattice of 295-297, 301, 305, median voter 130, 137, satiation 39;

Borda count 11, 12, 97-98, 103-105, 174;

Borda voting system 93, 97-99, 100-109; Condorcet rankings of 97-99, 101, 105-107, 109-110;

bounding coalitions 196;

budget constraint 39;

C^0 topology 187-190;

C^1 topology 183, 188-189, 221, 226-227;

cabinet appointments 126, 240, 295, 397, 299-305, 299-305, 308-314;

cabinet resignations 297, 299;

campaign contributions 342-345;

candidate platforms 114, 118-121, 123-125, 127-128, 130-131, 133-136, 141-143, 145-146, 348, slates of 123-124;

canonical voting models 113, 142, 146;

caretaker governments 126, 295;

Cartesian product space 10, 26, 28-29, 45-56, 65, 69-70, 183, 191, 296;

centroid 157, 159, 161, 163;

chaos 6, 7, 12-13, 97, 150;

checks and balances 8;

city block preferences 160;

civil liberties 394, 398, 402, 404;

coalition formation 142-144, 170, 175, 241, 245, 295-296, 299, 301;

Cobb-Douglas spaces 11, 68-74, 86;

collegium 9-10, 86;

common knowledge 200-205;

compact 2, 4, 9, 12, 56-57, 189, 191, 206;

competitive solution, experimental observations of 167, 170-172;

complete information 119, 146, 153-155, 158-162, 166;

Condorcet cycles 4, 6, 10-11;

Condorcet Jury Theorem 385-386, 391, 393-399, 402, 406-407;

Condorcet Research Program 4, 6;

Condorcet winner 97-98, 105-110, 151, 156; Condorcet loser 98, 107-110;

conflict of interest 352;

Congressional committees 150, 159, 171;

connected preference domains 11, 26, 30-32, 39, 42-43, 48-51, 64, 69-70;

connected preferences 128, 265, 267-268, 270-271, 275-277, 281, 283, 287-291;

continuity 2, 11, 25-28, 34, 37, 46, 48, 54, 57, 63- 64, 68, 71-72, 222;

continuous paths 192-193;

convergent preferences 73, 184, 189, 192, 203, 208;

convexity 4, 10, 34-36, 46, 48, 56, 116, 134-136, 146, 148, 187, 190-191, 204;

core 4, 12-13, 149-155, 158, 160-164, 172, 176, 184, 186, 189-192, 194-195, 222, 225, 266, 317, 319;

core parties 194-198, 200, 321, 330;

correlation coefficient 398-409, 393, 395, 403, 408;

corruption 241;

credible commitment 204, 206, 296, 299, 303-304, 306-307;

cyclic preferences 110, 186-187, 189-196, 222, 298, 304;

decisive sets 9, 67-68, 185-190, 222;

delegitimization of cabinet, opposition 319, 323, 328;

deterministic voting assumption 202, 204;

dictatorial rule 9-11, 26-28, 31-34, 42-43, 46, 54, 58, 64-66, 68, 78, 86;

dictatorship theorems 69-76;

dimensionality constraints 186, 188-189, 196-201, 206, 222, 225;

direct democracy 142, 184, 192;

direction gradients 188, 191, 221-223;

discrete alternatives 151, 153, 155, 165, 174;

dominant party 107, 196, 239, 299, 301, 304, 306- 310;

dominant preference relation 153, 155, 160-164, 166;

Downsian voting model 132, 136-140, 183-184, 203-205;

economic growth rates 368, 370-371, 375-376;

efficient election rule 116-117, 136;

election outcomes, Euskarian parliament 252; Italy 319-321;

election paradox 99-100;

electoral risk 201-203, 250, multi-party models of 204-205;

electoral uncertainty 204;

envious preferences 152;

Euclidean spatial mappings 34, 39, 115, 118, 125, 132, 185, 230-231, 293, metrics 34, 188-189, 193, 268-269, 301;

exchange economy 5, 57;

exchange voters 321, 327;

executive appointments, transferable benefits of 245;

executive decree 327, 329;

executive veto 150;

experimental payoff structures 156, 158- 159, 161-162, 166-168, 172-173, 175

experimental settings: competitive solution 170; core design 156, 158-160, 180; skew star design 171, 174-177, 181; standard house design 169, 174-177, 181;

factions 8, 239-241, 246, 393-394, 396-401, 405-408;

fair outcomes 153-156, 158-159, 161-164, 168, 170- 175;

Fan equilibrium condition 2-5;

first-past-the post elections 135, 295;

fixed number election rule 120, 122, 132, 140, 145;

fixed standard election rule 115, 118, 120-127, 130, 135, 138, 143;

fixed term governments 300, 303-304;

floor motions 157,
two-party committee model of 184;

free preference domains 30, 37, 42, 55;

free triples 11, 30, 32-34, 36, 38-41, 46-47, 50, 54, 57, 66-71, 73-74;

generic voting paradox 183, 186-189;

government duration 315, 320, 331

government opposition 317, 319, 323, 326;

half-space 225;

Hausdorff topology 183, 187-189;

heart 184, 189-235;

Helly's Theorem 5;

hyperplanes 37;

hypersaturing preference domains 10-11, 53-58;

hypothesis testing 385-391;

incentive compatibility 71, 74-76, 144, 205-206;

income, redistributive and taxable 346-349;

incumbent government 295, 297, 299, 301-305;

inflation 370-376, 381;

independence of irrelevant alternatives 9, 12, 63, 67-70, 85-86; binary 25, 29, 31-33, 37, 43-44, 51-52, 54, 56;

independent candidates 139, 239;

indifferent preference 9, 64-66, 70;

induced value theory 150;

information, incomplete 119, 153-155, imperfect 146;

inter-factional interdependence 393, 396, 399-401, 408;

inter-personal comparisons 164;

intersection properties: α contraction (Chernoff) 80-83; β expansion 81-83; γ expansion 79, 83;

intra-factional interdependence 397-398, 406, 408;

kernel 244-245;

law of large numbers 390;

legislative elections 113-114, 130, 133, multi-district 141;

legislative representation 131, 135-136, 138, 140-143;

legislatures, Downsian spatial models of 115, 119, 121-122, 124-126, 135, 137, 141-143, 145;

lower hemi-continuity 11, 184, 189-191;

majoritarian 225-226, 230-321, 234;

majority coalition governments 126, 135, 194, 276-277, 296-297, 302-306, 346;]

majority rule voting 392-395, 398, 402, 404, 407;

market surplus 347-350;

median hyperplanes 225-226;

median lines 176, 234, 297;

median position 13, 130, 137, 140, 193, 198, dimension-by-dimension 297-299, 301, 303-304;

median rule 115; binary voting decisions 104, 109;

messages, candidates 204-205, lobbyists 351- 356; repeated rounds of 354, 356;

minimal winning majority coalitions 162-164, 174- 175, 194, 196-199, 253-254, 256, 258, 265, 269, 272-274, 276-277, 284-285, 330;

minimum integer weights 155, 160-161, 195, 198, 253, 293, 403, 409;

ministerial assignments 296-297, 303, 305, 319, 320, 324-325, 328-329, transferable benefits of 241, 243;

minority governments 194-195, 197-200, 246, 297, 299, 303;

mixed strategies 126, 202, 205;

monotonicity 10-11, 25, 34-38, 46, 49, 54-55, 57, 222, 255;

multi-candidate electoral districts 113, 131, 134, 136, 141, double-member 131, single-party 239, two-party 134, 136;

Nakamura number 185-189, 196, 222;

Nash equilibrium 13, 124, 129, 142, 144, 184, 202, 205, 339-340;

Nash Research Program 2, 13;

neutrality condition 87-89;

nominal wage rates 364-365;

non-collegial 9, 10, 66, 255;

non-dictatorial 29, 64, 25-29, 31-35, 37, 43-44, 51- 52, 56-57, 73, 76, 85-86;

non-imposition condition 11, 63, 65, 69-71, 73, 76; strict 64-65, 67-70;

non-linear dynamics 97;

non-negative consumption 27, 34, 39, 53, 42, 70;

non-trivial pairs 30, 32, 39-44, 46-48, 50-52, 54- 56;

office-seeking assumption 137, 183, 203;

oligarchy 9, 11, 64, 70, 78, theorems 70-71, 73, 75-76;

opinion voters 321, 323, 327;

pareto improving 186, 189, 195, 227-228, 230, 232, pareto set 184, 195; unanimity condition 9, 11, 70, 76, 85-86, weak 25, 29, 31-34, 43-44, 46, 51-52, 54, 56-57, 90;

partisan preferences, macroeconomic assumptions of 363-364, 370-376, 378-382;

party constitution 135;

party extremists 139-140;

party leaders 240;

path independence 80-82;

perquisites, policy allocations of 13, 126, 185, 202-203, 206-209, 211;

Pigou-Dalton condition 42;

pivotal strategy sets 129-130, coalitions 165-166, 174-175, 320-321, 324-325;

Plott independence condition 11, 75-76;

plurality rankings 93-95, 97, 100-101, 104, 106-107, 109

policy declaration 126, 134-139, 143, 198-199, 201, 203-204, 206;

policy-seeking 114, 118-119, 127, 134, 204-205, 265, 282, 296;

policy space, one-dimensional 13, 26, 195, 198, 200, 189- 190, 271, 289-290; two-dimensional 34, 38, 42, 46, 157, 176, 193, 195, 197-200, 251, 254, 258, 261, 276, 321; three-dimensional 194-195, 197;

political dialogue 394, 398-399, 407;

political economy 183-187;

political equilibrium, joint best response correspondence 202, 204, 207, 209-211, multiparty model of 207;

political interest groups 337-356;

portfolio distribution 126-127, 129-130,

portfolio jurisdictions 296-297, 299, committee 149;

positional voting methods 93, 95-97, 106;

positive consumption 27, 34, 37, 53, 56;

preference cones 221;

prime minister 320, 330;

prisoners' dilemma 141, 144;

private information 352, 389-390; cardinal values, experimental rankings of 151, 153, 155, 166;

proportional representation 120-121, 124, 126, 246;

protocoalition formation 266-270, 274, 276, 290, sequential models of 256, 258, 261, 268-270, 274, 276, 284-290, 293;

public alternatives 8-9, 42, 45, 183;

public information 388-390; ordinal rankings 151, 153-155, 157-162, 166;

pure strategies 7, 12, 201-202, 204-205, 207, 209, 211;

quasi-concave preferences 114, 138, 191, 202, 226;

quasi-transitive preference 64-65, 68, 72, 76, 79, 84;

quota rules 119, 253;

random population samples 167, 386, 389-392;

rational voting assumption 118, 122 124-125, 129, 132, 134, 136, 142;

Robert's Rules of Order 157-164;

runoff elections 97;

saturating preference domains 10-11, 32-33, 38-39, 42-43, 46, 48-49, 51, 55-56;

Schur convexity 42;

seat shares 115, 117, 126, 129, 131, 135, 142-143, 184-185, 193, 204, 241, 243-244, 265, 268-269, 288, 282, 289, 291-292, 296 300, 315, 317, 321, 323, 326, 328, 330;

secret ballot 319-320, 326, 329-330;

separability of utility 122;

sequential voting 153, 158, 171-172, 226;

Shapley-Shubik index 251, 253, 256-259, 263;

simple majority rule 122, 124-125, 151-152, 158-160, 166, 246;

simple plurality rule, multi-candidate elections 134;

simultaneous voting 153, 399;

sincere preference 12, 113, 119,121-123, 125, 129, 132-135, 145;

single non-transferable voting 239;

single-party governments 194-195, 197-200, 240, 296-297, 299, 303, 318- 319, 321, 330;

single-peaked preference 4, 12, 26;

size, increasing returns of 341, 338-344, equivalent units 389, 406, 408;

smooth utilities 183, 188-189, 221, 226-227;

social welfare function 25, 27-28, 31-33, 43-44, 51-52, 54, 56, 73, 76;

spherical indifference curves 190;

structure-induced equilibria 143-144, 146;

subcultural voters 321, 323, 327;

subgame perfect equilibria 300-303, 306;

supersaturating preference domains 46-54;

support coalitions 165, 169, 266-267, 273, 276;

surplus majority coalition 196, 199-200, 244, 329;

symmetric substitution of alternatives 83-84, 86, 88;

tax rates 373;

ties 98, 107, 201, 203;
tie-breaking rule 38, 98, 107, 389, 391;

tight coalitions 283;

transferable value bargaining sets 241-245;

transitive preference 8, 9, 43, 55-56, 63-65, 67-69, 79-81, 85-86,

trivial alternative subsets 30, 43-44, 46, 54-55, 143-144;

truthful revelation 352-353;

two-stage elections 119, 124, 142, multi-stage, 119, 126, 145;

uncovered set 150, 155, 176, 189-192, 195, 201-202, 222, 225, 227;

undersecretary assignments, Italian government 320, 325-326, 328;

unemployment rate 363, 372-373, 376;

uniform domains 44;

universal preferences 11;

utility maximizing 347-348, 350;

vertex sets 191;

vote of investiture 297, 300-303, 307, 319, 327-328, 330;

voter profile of election rankings 67-69, 71-72, 93-99, 102, 108, 165, 167, universal set of 12, 97-100, 102-104;

voter rankings, 11, 25, 76;

voting, binary 395, 399-400, 499;

voting rule 222;

voting systems, vectors of voter rankings in 11, 25, 76, system profiles of 96-101, properties 95-99, 105, 107, relationships between 95, 97-101, 105-110;

wall-to-wall coalitions 240;

weak symmetric substitution 83-84, 88;

weak transitivity 36, 90;

weakly dominant preference sets 114, 118, 136;

weighted voting rule 93-94, 101-109, 241, 243-244, 348-349;

Whitney topology 183, 188-189, 221, 226-227;

winner-take-all elections 145;

yolk 176, 195.